T0158134

FAITH and FREEDOM
Gandhi in History

FAITH and FREEDOM
Gandhi in History

Mushirul Hasan

Published by

NIYOGI BOOKS

D-78, Okhla Industrial Area, Phase-I
New Delhi-110 020, INDIA
Tel: 91-11-26816301, 49327000
Fax: 91-11-26810483, 26813830
Email: niyogibooks@gmail.com
Website: www.niyogibooksindia.com

Text©: Mushirul Hasan

Editors: Nandita Jaishankar/Shaurya Shaukat Sircar/Niyogi Books
Cover Design: Arati Devasher
Layout: Nabanita Das/Niyogi Books

ISBN: 978-93-81523-31-5

Year of Publication: 2013

Printed at: Niyogi Offset Pvt. Ltd., New Delhi, India

In acknowledgement of Chris Bayly's warm
friendship and profound scholarship

CONTENTS

I

Section I

Introduction

Hun garmi-i nishat-i tasavvur se naghma sanj
Main andalib-i gulshan-i na afridah hun
From the heat of the joy of imagination I keep singing
I am the nightingale of the garden that awaits us.

-Ghalib[1]

Since 1921 I have worked in such close association with the Congress leaders that I can hardly describe any episode in my later life without referring to my relations with them. For though Lokamanya, Shraddhanandji, Deshbandhu, Hakim Sahib and Lalaji are no more with us to-day, we have the good luck to have a host of other veteran Congress leaders still living and working in our midst. The history of the Congress is still being made. And my principal experiments with Truth during the past seven years have all been made through the Congress. A reference to my relations with the leaders would therefore be unavoidable, if I set about to describe my experiments further. And this I may not do, at any rate for the present, if only from a sense of propriety. Lastly, my conclusions from my current experiment can hardly as yet be regarded as decisive. It therefore seems to me to be my plain duty to close this narrative here. In fact, my pen instinctively refuses to proceed further.

-C. F. Andrews (ed.), *Mahatma Gandhi: His Own Story*, p. 332.

Thomas Jefferson's legacy is intact in Charlottesville, Virginia. Charles de Gaulle is a towering personality in France. In June 2011, the Macedonians placed a statue of Alexander the Great on a high pedestal in their capital, Skopje, to buttress the nation against the trauma of free market, political strife and independence.[2] While Greece accuses Macedonia of stealing its history and national symbols,

---

1   Syed Akbar Hyder, 'Ghalib and His Interlocutors', in Manu Bhagavan (ed.), *Heterotopias: Nationalism and the Possibility of History in South Asia* (Delhi, 2010), p. 90.

2   *International Herald Tribune*, 24 June 2011.

Mustafa Kemal Ataturk remains, notwithstanding the change in regime in the summer of 2011, Turkey's icon. Ayatollah Khomeini is venerated as the Imam in the Islamic Republic of Iran; his status unassailable. The mausoleums of Mohammad Iqbal, the Urdu poet, and Mohammad Ali Jinnah, Pakistan's Qaid-i Azam, are pilgrimage sites in Lahore (Punjab) and Karachi (Sind) respectively. In 1948, Horace Alexander of the Society of Friends (the Quakers) attempted in vain to persuade the Nobel Prize Committee to award the Peace Prize posthumously to Mohandas Karamchand Gandhi. When he concluded his lecture in Oslo, a profound silence was followed by thunderous applause.[3]

Khwaja Hasan Nizami (1878-1955) of Delhi lived in an atmosphere of intense other-worldliness in the company of other Sufis. In close proximity were the shrines of Nizamuddin Auliya, the Chishti saint, Amir Khusro, his disciple and poet, and Ziauddin Barani, the historian of the early Turks. The Khwaja engaged in polemical debates with some of his contemporaries.[4] Gandhi's asceticism and emphasis on the spiritual resonates with him, 'who likens him to a sort of modern day Kabir marked by a fundamental ambivalence with regards to his Muslimness and Hinduness'. He appropriated Gandhi's thought in his witty fictional travelogue set in the year 2050. At the end of the journey, beginning 1 January, he discovers Gandhi's humanism: 'I saw Gandhi's followers throughout the world; specifically in America.'[5] If this travel narrative were true, one would have to agree that Gandhi's influence is now so universal that his fame will continue for centuries. 'During the last days,' he continued, 'our Mohandas Gandhi has conquered Europe and America with his spiritualism even though the British have put him in jail near Poona, his spiritual ideas have caught the imagination

---

3   Geoffrey Carnall, *Gandhi's Interpreter: A Life of Horace Alexander* (Edinburgh, 2010), p. 218.

4   'Guests are Pests', in Ralph Russell (ed.), *Hidden in the Lute: An Anthology of Two Centuries of Urdu Literature* (Delhi, 1995), pp. 117-24.

5   'Hasan Nizami's Journey around the World in the Year 2050', trans. from the Urdu and introduced by Zain Shirazi, in Shobna Nijhawan (ed.), *Nationalism in the Vernacular: Hindi, Urdu, and the Literature of Indian Freedom* (Delhi, 2010), pp. 481 onwards.

of (the people) in the West, specially the democratic-loving people of Great Britain.'[6]

It used to be said in Oxford in 1925 that the mere mention of the word *India* emptied the city's smallest lecture-hall. Gandhi changed all of that. 'Like a colossus he [Gandhi] stands astride half a century of India's history, a colossus not of the body but of the mind and spirit,' Jawaharlal Nehru, free India's first prime minister, declared on 2 February 1948 while announcing the assassination of the 'Father of the Nation'. One assumed that such a person would remain constant and there would be, in line with other countries, a persistent interest in keeping alive his inheritance. In spite of this, as will be clear by now, the twenty-first century takes what it wants from Gandhi and neglects what it thinks it doesn't need. One must, therefore, rid oneself of the illusion that his ideas ring truer with each passing day or that he lives amongst us as a force. At most places his faded portraits are callously hung, making it all the more difficult to connect a bygone time with our present which is flitting away from us. They gather dust with every passing year. The Gandhian institutions have produced little of enduring value or quality.

In Gujarat, the province of Gandhi's birth, some persons experienced another form of the grim reality when watching the film *Hey Ram*. The cinema hall erupted into wild applause at the very moment when Nathuram Godse, a Hindu militant belonging to the Rashtriya Swayamsewak Sangh (RSS), was depicted pumping bullets into Gandhi.[7] Once upon a time, garish portraits of Gandhi hung on mud walls alongside pictures of Hindu deities like Lord Krishna.[8] When, on the other hand, Martin Luther King Jr. asked Jawaharlal if his young countrymen were inclined to preserve his memory, the prime minister (1947-64) responded that he didn't think so. In 1959, one of Gandhi's biographers ruled out his revival.[9] That very year, a leading but controversial public intellectual bemoaned his calculated defilement:

---

6   Hasan Nizami, *Gandhi-Nama* (Delhi, 1922), p. 47. On Nizami, see Khwaja Hasan Sani Nizami, *Khwaja Hasan Nizami* (Delhi, 1987).

7   *Outlook* (Delhi), 2 May 2011, p. 67.

8   George E. Jones, *Tumult in India* (New York, 1948), p. 71.

9   Geoffrey Ashe, *Gandhi* (New York, 1968), pp. 386, 387.

'Gandhism in politics and in practice came to stand for very little other than a congealed mass of atavistic aspirations and prejudices.'[10] As for Gujarat, it disowned Gandhi long ago. 'One is not surprised,' writes Ashis Nandy, 'that the Sabarmati Ashram, instead of becoming the city's major sanctuary, closed its gates [during the communal riots] to protect its properties.'[11]

Is this because fellow-Indians tend to forget their benefactors, or is it because Gandhi upheld principles that no longer find resonance with the times?[12] The fact is that, apart from the National Rural Employment Guarantee Act (NREGA), his name scarcely figures in nation-building schemes; it is exploited to merely legitimise public activism, as in the case of Anna Hazare and his companions. Gandhi's village-based projects remain undervalued, while the burgeoning modernising elites subject the incongruities in his imaginings to critical scrutiny.

Generations that pay no attention to the inner significances of human history do violence to history.[13] The novelist V.S. Naipaul, deeply imbued with Orientalist arrogance, is scornful of Gandhi and Hind Swaraj.[14] There is so little truth in his point of view as he is less than objective in his pose or posture. He pretends to take at face value Gandhi's statements, but ends up denying the obvious. He ventures to create an image, albeit a false one, by losing sight of the difference between progress and regression, and calls upon the reader to separate what is really valid from that which is false or unproved by empirical data.

---

10   Nirad C. Chaudhuri, *Thy Hand Great Anarch! India 1921-1952* (Delhi, 1987), p. 876; *The Autobiography of an Unknown Indian* (Hyderabad, 1994), pp. 517-18.

11   Ashis Nandy, 'Obituary of a Culture', and Bhikhu Parekh, 'Making Sense of Gujarat', *Seminar* (Delhi), May 2002, p. 513.

12   Mohammad Mujeeb, *Islamic Influences on Indian Society* (Meerut, 1965), p. 184. Gopalkrishna Gandhi argues to the contrary in Suparna Gooptu (ed.), *On Gandhi* (Calcutta, 2012), pp. 37-40.

13   F.M. Powicke, *Modern Historians and the Study of History* (Watford, 1955), p. 192.

14   A tract Gandhi wrote for his friend Dr Pranjivan Mehta on his return journey from London to South Africa in ten days between 13 and 22 Nov. 1909. On Pranjivan Mehta, see *The Collected Works of Mahatma Gandhi* (*CWMG*) (1 Dec.1939-15 Apr. 1940), p. 238.

Impregnated with a diffused radicalism, Marxist historians see the bankruptcy of Gandhi's tactics and strategy at the Round Table Conference when he compromised with the princes and the landlords, the bulwark of the Raj. K.M. Ashraf, who aligned himself with the Congress before joining the communist movement, felt disillusioned after the visit of Stafford Cripps, the Labour Party statesman, in December 1939. He saw nothing but bourgeoisie manoeuvres, pressure politics and the fear of the masses coming up.[15]

Gandhi's thinking on economic and social matters did little to cheer up fellow-Marxists. M.N. Roy, who dismissed his political ethics, pictured the toothless little gentlemen sitting placidly at his spinning wheel betraying the cause of labour. Acharya Narendra Deva, the Uttar Pradesh (UP) leader, spoke of his and his party's persistent neglect of the poor.[16] The reality is that Gandhi had made much interest in the cause of labour, and poured out his grief to Gangabehn, a widow he met at the Broach Educational Conference in 1917.[17] Once, quite a number of Gujaratis had spinning wheels in their homes. Umar Sobhani, a mill owner, not only gave Gandhi the benefit of his own knowledge and experience, but also put him in touch with the other mill owners.[18]

After Independence, the Communist Party of India (CPI) described the transfer of power as surrender to imperialism, and Gandhi as a tool in its hands. There is no novelty in this argument. Besides, the Marxian views were, mostly, not so much the result of any inductive or factual study as of a speculative and dogmatic deduction.

Gandhi's self-styled followers responded unpersuasively to such criticism.[19] If they gave an impetus for a few fruitful studies, they also

---

15   Horst Krüger (ed.), *Kunwar Mohammad Ashraf: An Indian Scholar and Revolutionary, 1903-62* (Delhi, 1969), p. 413.

16   Hari Deo Sharma (ed.), *Selected Works of Acharya Narendra Deva*, vol. 1 (Delhi, 1998), p. 45.

17   J.P. Haithcox, *Communism and Nationalism in India: M.N. Roy and Comintern Policy, 1920-1939* (Princeton, N.J., 1971), p. 256.

18   C.F. Andrews (ed.), *Mahatma Gandhi: His Own Story* (London, 1930), p. 326.

19   C. Rajagopalachari, in Ved Mehta, *Mahatma Gandhi and His Apostles* (New York, 1976), p. 49.

generated an enormous bulk of hagiographic literature. They were 'ineffectual pacifists or non-resisters of the Tolstoyan variety' or just members of a narrow sect out of touch with life and reality.[20] Nirmal Kumar Bose, the social anthropologist, had this to say:

> Those who claim to follow you cannot very often fail to act unitedly among themselves, quite apart from acting jointly with men of other faiths. Some of them even appear to have become very individualistic, lost in their social-mindedness and seem to be satisfied with a set of rituals representing the 'cult' into which non-violence has degenerated with them.[21]

Many 'Gandhians' have yet to purge their mentor of the supernatural, romantic, and exaggerated versions of events they have assiduously cultivated around themselves and others. At the present moment, their theories are outdistanced and repudiated in their specific traits. 'We ourselves have become old and stiff—and resistant to change,' said one of them icily after Gandhi's assassination.[22]

Men of strong minds and conviction possess vast abilities to grasp, arrange, and appropriate to themselves the big, heavy, solid responsibility of achieving social cohesion. Gandhi looked upon his people as a loose constellation of classes, communities and religious groups, and because he had no illusions about the nature of polity, he united it in a way that it had never been united before.[23] In those days, Muslim politicians were Gandhi's right hand and at his left, they were his eyes and ears. This, to the point, is what Gandhi tried doing: to build an edifice which, in the view of other people, and ultimately his own, symbolised cultural and social fusion. With his strong sense of ethics and morality, he made it abundantly clear that, 'as a Hindu I cannot be indifferent to their

---

20   Jawaharlal Nehru, *An Autobiography* (London, 1936), p. 548.

21   Bose to Gandhi, 3 Jan.1947, Nirmal Kumar Bose papers (269 C), National Archives of India (NAI).

22   Gopalkrishna Gandhi (ed.), *Gandhi is Gone. Who will Guide us now?* (Delhi, 2007), p. 43.

23   Ravinder Kumar (ed.), *Essays on Gandhian Politics: The Rowlatt Satyagraha of 1919* (Oxford, 1971), p. 12.

[Muslim] cause [of Khilafat]'. He wrote to the British viceroy that 'their sorrows must be our sorrows', and continued in the same vein:

> In the most scrupulous regard for the rights of these States and for the Muslim sentiment as to the places of worship and in your just and timely treatment of the Indian claim to Home Rule, lies the safety of the Empire. I write this, because I love the English Nation, and I wish to evoke in every Indian the loyalty of the Englishman.

From the time Gandhi became a votary of pan-Islamism,[24] he tried to soothe ruffled feathers within his party. But his critics repeatedly lampooned him for aligning with a religious class who offered a simplified version of Indian Muslims' many identities. He constructed, in his imaginings, a homogenised Muslim entity. After the Khilafat crumbled, the pan-Islamists added their names to the growing list of Gandhi-baiters. In addition, the Muslim League suspected everything he did to portray him as enemy No. 1.[25] Gandhi admitted, rather painfully: 'During the Khilafat the Muslims accepted me as their true friend. I have now come to be regarded as so evil and detestable.'[26]

Moving to another theme, one has assumed all along that Gandhi wanted the Dalits to fight for their rights and secure a more profound understanding of and harmony with the world. Increasingly, all the same, their national consciousness is attributed to their own continuing struggle against social, political, cultural, and economic inequalities.[27] If anything, Gandhi idealised the caste system, called the Dalits 'Harijans' to

---

24 Unlike pan-Africanism, which is a fairly precise geopolitical concept in political analysis, pan-Islamism was more in the nature of a mystique, which directs its appeal to the faithful on the basis of the concept of *umma*, a unified and undifferentiated community of believers.

25 J.B. Kripalani, *Gandhi: His Life and Thought* (Delhi, 1970), p. 391.

26 D.G. Tendulkar, *Mahatma: Life of Mohandas Karamchand Gandhi* (New Delhi: Publications Division, Govt. of India), vol. 6, p. 193.

27 Badri Narayan, *Woman Heroes and Dalit Assertion in North India: Culture, Identity and Politics* (Delhi, 2006), p. 96; V. Geetha, 'Periyar, Women and an Ethic of Citizenship', in Mary John (ed.), *Women's Studies in India* (Delhi, 2008), p. 145.

keep them within the Hindu fold,[28] and, apart from preaching intangible reforms, he operated only to the point where egalitarianism ran the risk of challenging social unity in which practice was hierarchical.[29] 'What can Gandhism offer to the untouchables?', asked M.N. Roy. 'To the untouchables, Hinduism is a veritable chamber of horrors.' He mentioned the Vedas, Smritis and Shastras and the iron law of caste as 'instruments which have 'mutiliated, blasted and blighted the life of the untouchables.'[30]

In his stand against separate electorates he brought advantages to the upper castes but damaged Dalit interests.[31] One must not be surprised, therefore, that Mayawati, leader of the Bahujan Samaj Party and formerly chief minister of UP, fired her salvo in 1997, the fiftieth year of Independence, and, again, on 29 June 2009. She identified, for political reasons, what is separate, without mentioning what is identical in the Gandhian discourse.

Public opinion itself is a kind of weathercock which is turned by any change in the wind, but is it fair to deduce that interest in knowing Gandhi has steadily diminished? Whether we investigate the subjective no less than the objective, it is right to ask why the statues of B.R. Ambedkar alone and not all that many of Gandhi dot UP's landscape? The truth seems to lie somewhere between those who believe in Gandhi's omnipotence, which he himself so consistently repudiated, and his appropriation by the elites and the under-classes.

Women were, in fact, the ideal satyagrahis, the natural subject in Gandhi's narrative. They weren't to be bound by domesticity, but neither were they to discard their duties. In effect, they were to assume responsibility for the nation, as they did for the home and family.

---

28   Baren Ray (ed.), *Gandhi's Campaign Against Untouchability, 1933-34: An Account from the Raj's Secret Official Records* (Delhi, 1996); G. A. Biradar, *Mahatma Gandhi's Campaign Against Untouchability in Karnataka* (Mysore, 2011); Rammanohar Lohia, *Guilty Men of India's Partition* (Delhi, 2000), p. 75.

29   Christophe Jaffrelot, *India's Silent Revolution: The Rise of the Low Castes in North India* (Delhi, 2003), p. 18.

30   B.R. Ambedkar, *What Congress and Gandhi Have Done to the Untouchables* (Bombay, 1945), pp. 307-8.

31   V. Geetha, 'Periyar, Women and an Ethic of Citizenship', in Mary John (ed.), op. cit., p. 135.

Sarojini Naidu for example, became more and more involved in the freedom struggle, and, as a woman of special talent, she became the prized trophy of the Congress. Gandhi called her Bharat Kokila—India's Nightingale. She projected the 'modern' face of Indian womanhood—confident, assertive and politically motivated. In an otherwise all-male delegation, she visited Punjab in March 1923 to study the deterioration in the communal situation. She was depressed with the escalation of communal violence and the growing frictions in the Congress over the establishment of the Swaraj Party, but she was not the one to dampen her spirits. 'Let us go on churning the ocean till we do evolve some supreme gift of Harmony', she wrote to Nehru from the Taj Mahal Hotel, her favourite haunt in Bombay. For M.C. Chagla, the lawyer, the hotel was 'a sort of Mecca' to which he returned. Here, he'd also meet Ruttie, who was estranged from her husband, Jinnah. There were innumerable days and evenings spent in her room—always the same—talking to her. He was 'enchanted by her grace, her beauty, and the uninhibited way in which she conducted herself.'[32]

Soundaram and her husband, Ramachandran, a sociologist, were a charming couple, and a kind who did extraordinary things without much fuss or self-advertisement. Their marriage was revolutionary: a widow remarriage between an Iyengar's daughter and the son of a Dalit. What is more, they received very little help from anyone else except Gandhi. With his encouragement, they went on to do good work in rural Tamil Nadu.[33] But for their close association with him and the ashram we would otherwise have known next to nothing about their insecurities, achievements, and failures.

In spite of that, the very varied feminist groups take to task Gandhi for using traditional Hindu models of feminity for appeals to women to play a public and private role distinct from that of men and not in competition with them. They also express disapproval of his spurning modern forms of birth control.[34]

32　Jawaharlal Nehru (ed.), *A Bunch of Old Letters: Being mostly written to Jawaharlal Nehru and some written by him* (Delhi, 1988), p. 25; M.C. Chagla, *Roses in December* (Delhi, 1973), p. 89.

33　Jean Lyon, *Just Half a World Away: My Search for the New India* (London, 1955).

34　Judith M. Brown, *Gandhi: Prisoner of Hope* (Cambridge, 1991), p. 391.

In theory, the national movement paid adequate attention to women's rights, and declared clearly, in the Karachi resolutions (1931) and elsewhere, that there should be no disqualification on the ground of sex in exercise of any public function. Yet, in July 1936, women complained against the Congress' indifference towards them. Only a few of them crossed the gender gap.

I appraise the times in which Gandhi grew up, and ask: How did he move millions with so little effort, including Orissa's caste-ridden village womenfolk, who placed jewellery at his feet for Dalit emancipation? Without closing our eyes to them, we weigh their worth and value them. How did their spirit soar, how did new paths appear, and how on those paths did they march hand in hand?[35]

There are, moreover, numerous general issues that remain unanswered despite the vast volume of literature on Gandhi. They are: How did Gandhi make an entire generation virtually his own? Why did he succeed in most cases and contingencies but not when it came to engaging with 'Muslim nationalism'? Is it not ironical that the messenger of non-violence lived through a violent event: the subcontinent's Partition?[36] Or, that he approved of India's action in sending troops to Kashmir to repel the tribal invaders?[37] How had this new situation arisen?

Memory generates the chain of tradition which passes an occurrence from generation to generation. While accepting with equanimity a re-evaluation of the past and progress into the future, we reap the knowledge to engage with the future from the wisdom, sagacity, and follies of the 'unthinkable multitude' and their leaders. As one proceeds, I hope readers will understand me as my works are, in all probability,

---

35   6 Oct. 1939, S. Gopal (ed.), *Selected Works of Jawaharlal Nehru* (*SWJN*) (Delhi: Jawaharlal Nehru Memorial Fund), vol. 10, p. 588.

36   Mushirul Hasan, *Legacy of a Divided Nation: India's Muslims since Independence* (London, 1997); *Moderate or Militant: Images of India's Muslims* (Delhi, 2008), and the three anthologies: *India's Partition: Process, Strategy and Mobilization* (Delhi, 1993); *India Partitioned: The Other Face of Freedom*, in 2 vols. (Delhi, 1995); and *Inventing Boundaries: Gender, Politics and the Partition of India* (Delhi, 2000).

37   D.N. Panigrahi, *Jammu and Kashmir: The Cold War and the West* (Delhi, 2009), p. 73.

familiar to them. They will, nonetheless, want me to defend my writing yet another book on Gandhi.

Comrade-in-Arms

Obviously, the keystone in the architectural plan for leaders was political management, each with his *Weltanschauung*. All the same, inter-party tensions flared out into the open and led to the mushroom growth of other fronts. Gandhi felt chastened by the fragile nature of the coalition that he had assiduously tried to build, and unsettled by the widening arenas of challenge. Once he lay down the law, as it were, that, 'the love of my conception, if it is as soft as a rose petal, can also be harder than flint.'[38] Still, his desire to forge friendships intensified after every disappointment; every loss opened up newer opportunities to strike alliances. He wanted to gain as many co-workers as he could by whom he could swear. He told Mahadev Desai, whom he recruited in his inner circle, how he had enlisted them in South Africa, determined to make something of them. Such bluntness of personal approach and such free admission of self-interest were, of course, 'objectified' by the offer of participation in a universal appeal.[39]

While he had a good cause and lent every ounce of his physical and mental capacity to the fight,[40] Gandhi used to say that his so-called greatness depended on the incessant toil and drudgery of select, devoted, and pure workers, men as well as women. Think of the Gandhi men in South Africa, the El-Dorado of European rulers. They were mostly of profound discernment and judgement of character.

Henry S.L. Polak, a key figure in the 100 acre Phoenix Settlement on Tolstoyan principles, gave Ruskin's *Unto This Last* to Gandhi, a book which 'marked a turning point' in his life. He told Polak plainly: 'You are

---

38   *Harijan*, 9 Jan. 1940, *CWMG* (1 Dec. 1939-15 Apr. 1940), p. 94.

39   Erik H. Erikson, *Gandhi's Truth: On the Origins of Militant Nonviolence* (New York, 1969), p. 312.

40   'In finding his feet there, he formed the persona he would inhabit in India in the final thirty-three years of his life, when he set an example that colonized peoples across the globe, including South Africans, would find inspiring.' Joseph Lelyveld, *Great Soul: Mahatma Gandhi and His Struggle with India* (New York, 2011), p. 7.

mine and the responsibility to provide for you and your children is mine, not yours.'[41] John Dube and Gandhi were neighbours in Inanda, and each influenced the other, for both men established, at about the same time, two monuments to human development within a stone's throw of each other, the Ohlange Institute and the Phoenix Settlement, situated about 14 miles from Durban, in the midst, at the time, of the sugar-cultivated lands of Natal's north coast. Gandhi appreciated the point of view of Rev. J.J. Doke and his potentialities, and complimented C.F. Andrews, the Carlisle-born Anglican missionary, with the remark: 'If I were to compete with him as to which of us had the greatest influence with these people in South Africa, I am not sure that he wouldn't floor me.'[42] About to board ship on the dock in Cape Town on 18 July 1914, Gandhi placed his hand on Polak's shoulder and said: 'I carry away with me not my blood brother, but my European brother. Is that not sufficient earnest of what South Africa has given me, and is it possible for me to forget South Africa for a single moment?'[43] Finally, a man of unblemished reputation, in his generation and for a considerable time afterwards, Maganlal Desai was, by all accounts, worthy of Gandhi's trust.[44]

A wealthy architect and an erstwhile German Jew, Hermann Kallenbach had bought Tolstoy Farm at Lawley in Johannesburg, worked splendidly during the Newcastle strike, and, when the time came, cheerfully went to jail. It is doubtful if they were as congenial to him as they seemed, but he nonetheless devoted his thought and energy wholeheartedly to his duties. Kallenbach deserved, according to Gandhi, the professional rewards 'not because you are a clever[er] architect than others but because you are truer'.[45] There was always between them a bond of reciprocal admiration which soon deepened into affection and love.

---

41 Erikson, *Gandhi's Truth*, p. 312. Polak came to India in 1909 to press for abolishing the system of indentured labour emigration to Natal.

42 Daniel O'Connor, *A Clear Star: C.F. Andrews and India 1904-1914* (Delhi, 2005), p. 190.

43 Ibid., p. 132.

44 A grandson of an uncle of Gandhi, he died on 23 April 1928 in Patna.

45 Gandhi to Kallenbach, 24 Sept. 1909; 26 (month not legible) 1913; 3 Jan. 1909, 21 Sept. 1909, 28 Sept. 1909, Gandhi-Kallenbach papers, NAI.

Gandhi placed Kallenbach's portrait on the mantlepiece opposite his bed in Phoenix. 'How completely,' he wrote, 'you have taken possession of my body.' 'This,' he continued with exaggerated politeness, 'is slavery with a vengeance.' Indeed, he fulfilled a role that his father should have filled had he survived. This is observable from Gandhi's undated letter, the 'Upper House', to Kallenbach, the 'Lower House'. In it, Gandhi mourned his brother's death, but the shock did not make him fearful of death.[46] Softening, his heart yearned often to write long letters to Kallenbach, who had a close and searching mind, but he denied himself the pleasure.[47] Nonetheless, Gandhi's letters to him speak of purpose and achievement and excite interest because they reveal unexpected light and shadows. Their tone indicates the vivid impression that he made on Gandhi's mind and influence on his thinking.

In sum, affinity of interests and aspirations united these individuals. No wonder then that Gandhi spoke, in one of his farewell speeches at Durban on 8 July 1914, of the happiest and most lasting friendships with both Europeans and Indians. Gopal Krishna Gokhale, a moderate in the rough-and-tumble arena of public life, used to say that Gandhi 'can mould heroes out of common clay.'

My intention in this book is to link his moments of greatness with his dependence on all his co-workers who facilitated his task in South Africa (where the Satyagraha began in September 1906 and closed in June 1914), and made it easier for him to physically and spiritually relocate in India.[48] The personages, although they make themselves out to be prominent, are really of my choice. After all we must each serve according to our lights, not borrowed.[49] Without recording Gandhi's closeness to or acquaintances with innumerable men and women, I attempt to deepen and enrich the shadows of

---

46 N.d., Steve Linde papers, courtesy, Ornit Shani.

47 Gandhi to Kallenbach, 23 Jan. 1909, Gandhi papers.

48 Thomas Weber, 'Gandhi Moves: Intentional Communities and Friendship', in Debjani Ganguli and John Docker (eds), *Rethinking Gandhi and Nonviolent Relationality: Global Perspectives* (Delhi, 2009), p. 123.

49 18 Nov. 1929, Uma Iyengar and Lalitha Zackariah (eds), *Together They Fought: Gandhi-Nehru Correspondence 1921-1948* (Delhi, 2011), p. 101.

their pictures insofar as they affected and shaped Gandhi's politics. This might stimulate and encourage us, as students and teachers, to explore the political heritage bequeathed by the struggle for the indentured in South Africa.

It was different back home. Gandhi's circle of friends included G.D. Birla, an 'extension of Gandhi's conscience'; Vallabhbhai Patel, labelled as a Gandhi-ite (as distinct from a 'Gandhian') Gujarati; C.Rajagopalachari, the 'Conscience-keeper'; Motilal Nehru, who confessed that he loved the old man but never understood him; C.R. Das, who died, in the height of his powers and reputation, and died more than twenty years too soon; and Jayaprakash Narayan (JP), the exemplar, at least in Bihar, for the pre-1947 generation of the necessary marriage of 'Marxism of the mind' and 'liberalism of the heart'. The little courtesies and attentions Gandhi bestowed on these men and on many others remained a grateful remembrance. They happened to be posted at the point of cross-section or the focus of the intellectual and political currents of society.

'Here it was that national and family history met,' writes Nayantara Sahgal, novelist and daughter of Vijaya Lakshmi Pandit, with reference to the role of the Nehrus in the freedom struggle.[50] With very few exceptions, the Nehrus represented the triumphant, rationalist, humanist 'Enlightenment' of the eighteenth century. Whenever they spoke the secular language, their eyes sparkled with fervour. Whatever their private religious beliefs, they spurned irrational behaviour and institutions, and, whether within the home or outside in the wider fields of life, demonstrated an excellence and appealing quality of outlook. Motilal inspired his son to introduce freshness and vitality into his thinking. Like the bourgeois liberals, they believed that the human social order and individual man could be perfected by applying reason, and were destined to be so perfected.

Friends recalled the years when Motilal was at the height of his powers and fame. In many places there were those who thought of him with respect and gratitude, of the criticism that chastised them, and the

---

50　　Nayantara Sahgal, *Jawaharlal Nehru: Civilizing a Savage World* (Delhi, 2010), p. 2.

wisdom that steadied them. Among those who didn't know him, he acquired an almost legendary quality.

Ties with Bapu brought 'an irreplaceable solace' to the Nehrus.[51] Motilal, Jawaharlal, his sisters and cousins have recorded their appreciation of the man and his mission. Indira Nehru, still young, regarded him more as a family elder to whom she went with difficulties and problems.[52] Occasionally, Gandhi lapsed into sloppy sentimentality, as the touch of elegance and depth of his bond with them grew.

Friendships inspired by shared ideals and endeavours survived. This is illustrated by the public lives of Motilal and C.R. Das, Calcutta's renowned barrister. The two, dissimilar as they were in some ways, combined effectively, each in some measure competing for the other's deficiencies. Each had authorised the other to use his name for any statement or declaration, even without reference or consultation,[53] preserved undefiled their personal integrity, and avoided imposing their will arbitrarily upon the other. Although represented as a gambler for glittering stakes,[54] Das gave up his princely lifestyle during Non-Cooperation. He felt his limbs fettered and body bound with heavy iron chains. This was the agony of servitude. With all of India being one great prison, it did not matter whether he lived or died.

Gandhi hardly ever swerved throughout the exercise of his great task from the path he followed from South Africa: promoting inter-faith dialogue and understanding. However, some in public life sought abrupt changes, which were too vigorous and at times misdirected. For nearly a decade, the Ali brothers (Mohamed and Shaukat), for example, kept the Aligarh College simmering and exploding with angry broils, punctuated by rival pamphlets, which they enjoyed as a fish takes to water. They threw themselves heart and soul into various enterprises

---

51   Ibid., p. 4.

52   Inder Malhotra, *Indira Gandhi: A Personal and Political Biography* (London, 1989), p. 35.

53   Nehru, *An Autobiography*, p. 105. A profile of Das in M.R. Jayakar, *The Story of My Life*, vol. 1, 1873-1922 (Bombay, 1958), pp. 344-47.

54   For a refutation of this view, see Rajat Kanta Ray, *Social Conflict and Political Unrest in Bengal, 1875-1927* (New Delhi, 1984), p. 347.

after the Turko-Italian War and the revocation of Bengal's partition in 1911, and quite often, if not always, honoured the wrong things and prized the wrong values. In consequence, their old traditions of friendships with Gandhi ceased to hold mythical status. Their alliance had been critically important during the Khilafat euphoria, but once they broke free over the Nehru Committee Report of August 1928, Gandhi, of all persons, felt sorry that 'life in future would be the less full, the less rich for want of such friends as you and I have been'.[55] I have tried to situate Gandhi's relationship with the Ali brothers, and show up the fault lines that inevitably appear at the end of the Khilafat and Non-Cooperation campaigns.

Gandhi had ties, sometimes very close ones, with Muslim scholars, in the main of a traditional variety. Their letters illustrate how personal regard enlivened the discussion of minute points of scholarship. For example, the youthful ardour and zest of the Mecca-born Maulana Abul Kalam Azad, clear of head and sound of heart, enabled Gandhi to appreciate the ethical and moral base of his outlook and orientation. Through him, he constructed an entirety of the universe throbbing with life. His friendly features, his beard, his *sherwani* and *topi*, give a pleasant idea of him in the portrait now hanging in the Maulana Azad Library at the Aligarh Muslim University. After years as education minister, he died, leaving a composite reputation as a journalist, preacher, theologian and statesman, which has now receded into the dimmer past as happens to the fame of all save the very great.

So far, in historical scholarship, Azad and the Ali brothers have played the role of an incidental appendix which is mechanically attached to their valuable interpretation of Gandhi. This approach can aid little in analysing Gandhi's rather complex and fluid relationship with the Congress Muslims, a relatively unknown species, and the reasons why they so very vigorously contested the League's claim to construct an all-embracing conception of 'Pakistan'. 'Is it not wonderful,' Sarojini Naidu, an intelligent, bright, and witty woman, asked a friend, 'how in the very midst of our own troubles we can find the leisure and the inclination instinctively to think of other people's

---

55   Mushirul Hasan (ed.), *Muslims and the Congress: Select Correspondence of Dr. M.A. Ansari, 1912-1935* (Delhi, 1985), p. 66.

concerns?'[56] Mukhtar Ahmad Ansari and his senior, Hakim Ajmal Khan, were two such individuals. Ansari, who had moved from Mori Gate in the old city to Daryaganj in 1925, lived more than anyone in the 1920s to give a much needed sense of the value of Swaraj. Joseph Conrad (1857-1924)—born and bred in Poland—wrote in his preface to A Personal Record (1912): 'Those who read me, know my conviction that the world, the temporal world, rests on a few very simple ideas; so simple that they may be as old as the hills. It rests notably, among others, on the idea of Fidelity.' This governing idea of fidelity, of faith-keeping between man and man, was the mainspring of Ansari's life. Beneath his seriousness he was ardent and affectionate. Sarojini Naidu and others thought, that he was sincere, kind, warm-hearted, and quite innocent of guile.

Take a few paces from the Jamia Millia Islamia Higher Secondary School in New Delhi and you come across an impressive grave. This is the last resting place of Ansari, Gandhi's 'Infallible Guide' on Hindu-Muslim matters. A man who struggled so hard and who did more than any other to express a 'nationalistic' voice; Gandhi mourned his death on 10 May 1936. The social anthropologist Satish Saberwal sagely proclaimed: 'We need to face up the past in full measure, reckoning the costs, historically, of choices made—paths taken and those not taken—and think of the options for the future.'[57] Have we learnt enough to do this now, and will the future give us the opportunity to put this knowledge into practice?

Every historian of the nationalist movement tends to get lost in detail. In this book, despite everything, I've left aside questions of facts,

---

56   Sarojini Naidu to Syed Mahmud, 30 May 1917, in V.N. Datta and B.E.
      Cleghorn (eds), A Nationalist Muslim and Indian Politics: Being the Selected
      Correspondence of the late Dr. Syed Mahmud (Delhi, 1974), p. 29. 'Sita was
      a leader in the new social world. She won people with her charm, intrigued
      them with her calculated attack on conventions, titillated them with her
      cynical coquetry, and impressed them with her hospitality and her wealth.
      She had become a patroness of the arts, a benefactress of impecunious
      writers and artists, [and] a collector of ancient works of art and young
      lovers.' Attia Hosain, Sunlight on a Broken Column (Delhi, 2009), p. 175. I
      assume she is describing Sarojini Naidu.

57   Satish Saberwal, Spirals of Contention: Why India was Partitioned in 1947
      (Delhi, 2008), p. 177.

and merely offered little more than a resumé of Non-Cooperation (1920), Civil Disobedience (1930-31), and Quit India (1942). I have left out many topics, and not discussed many arguments threadbare. As Gandhi reiterated, let each one of us select our task, adhere to it, and stick to it through thick and thin. Let us, moreover, not think of the vastness and pick up that portion which we can handle best.

This book offers a grand account of India's modern history through themes, significant people and events that are not tied to a chronological narrative framework. I've neither been precise about either the chronological or the geographical boundaries nor covered personal details. One expects interested readers to look into the most recent biography by Joseph Lelyveld, a former editor of the New York Times. Although acclaimed in some circles, Rajmohan Gandhi, the Mahatma's grandson and a prolific writer, thinks that the book seemed designed 'to put Gandhi down to ground level, slight his role, and diminish his compelling figure'.[58]

Scholarship on Gandhi and his era, in all its variety and vigour, flows on ceaselessly, but the writings, as is to be expected, can hardly be brought within the terms of a single description. Those in search of a first-hand or day-to-day accounts access Mahadev Desai, Gandhi's secretary for 25 years, till the very end of his life (16 August 1942); Rajendra Prasad, the first president of the Republic; Pyarelal, Gandhi's associate and secretary; D.G. Tendulkar, Gandhi's biographer; Narayan Desai, son of Mahadev Desai; and Indulal Yagnik. The great human books some of them wrote clear the air and we need more of them.

Clearly I make no extravagant claims on behalf of professional historians like Jacques Pouchepadass, Ravinder Kumar, David Hardiman, and Dennis Dalton, except that they have made Gandhi real and intelligible. We must also constantly bear in mind the writings of Judith M. Brown, Rajmohan Gandhi, Raghavan Iyer, B.R. Nanda, Bhikhu Parekh, Thomas Weber, and Claude Markovits. They have woven the exploits of the Mahatma into the texture of our history, and attempted to write a composite narrative weaving in the different strands of Gandhi's life. We read their synthesis of history with pleasure and profit.

---

58   Rajmohan Gandhi, 'Looking for the Dust', EPW, 3 Dec. 2011, p. 33.

I hope my sources reflect the debt I owe to them and other scholars. At the same I cannot help pointing out that they have not always treated Gandhi's intimate understanding and interpretation of Islam and the Muslim communities in South Asia clearly and intelligently.

Someone once reaffirmed that errors can scarcely be avoided in an enterprise whose purpose is to offer a kind of bird's-eye view of a particularly luxuriant forest; so luxuriant that one may not be able to see the wood for the trees. 'To work thou hast the right, never to the fruit thereof' is one of the golden precepts of the *Bhagavadgita* 'which sets forth in precise and penetrating words the essential principles of a spiritual religion which aren't contingent on ill-founded facts, unscientific dogmas or arbitrary fancies'.[59] I revert to Gandhi for answers and explanations because, 'like the Ghost in Hamlet, he won't be laid to rest until we either accept him or turn your nose up at him—and do so honestly, without prevarication, without hedging our bets'.[60] Moreover, as H.S.L. Polak said in his appraisal of Gandhi, 'he will teach both the precept and by example. But he will go his own way untrammeled by precedent, carefully analyzing the criticism to which he is bound to be subjected, holding himself answerable, however, to his own conscience alone. For he is of the prophets, and not merely of the secondary interpreters of life.'

---

59   S. Radhakrishnan, *The Bhagavadgita* (London, 1943), p. 14. A British Theosophist friend in South Africa gave him Annie Besant's translation of the *Gita*. He read it immediately.

60   T.K. Mahadevan, *Gandhi My Refrain: Controversial Essays: 1950-1972* (Bombay, 1973), p. 206.

Gandhi's photograph taken in London, 1906.

1
The Tyranny of the Past

What do you mean? 'Progress', 'Association' –
Listen to me, I'll tell you how it's done.
'He owns the buffalo who wields the cudgel.'
Ti-tum ti-tum ti-tum ti-tum.

-Akbar Ilahabadi, 1846-1921.

'With flaming eyes her grandfather would then demand of them: 'Could we
have watched, with any equanimity, the English *firangis* walking through
our marble palaces where flowed the *Nahr-i-Bihisht*, the Stream of Paradise,
keeping the halls cool and fresh? Could we have tolerated a stranger delivering
judgement under our scales of justice etched so beautifully on the arch of
Diwan-e-Aam, where the Emperor Shah Jehan first held public audience?
And what about Amir Khusraw's immortal proclamation engraved on the
archway of the Hall of Private Audience—*If there be a Paradise on Earth, it
is this, it is this, it is this!* Could we have stood aside and watched Paradise
turn to infernal hell? No, no! Our eyes had to turn away from these scenes
of humiliation.' He would then recount how after long years of dangerous
wandering they had ultimately come to Hyderabad and found shelter there.
Even though the Nizam had declared himself an ally of the British, at least
here, there was still some vestige of Muslim culture left.

-Zeenuth Futehally, *Zohra* (Delhi, 2004), p. 9.

N o one can conceive Gandhi's role in the public domain without
coming to terms with his friends, admirers, and allies. Indeed, it
seems worthwhile bringing them at once in touch with him. This will
require me to devote a couple of chapters to exploring the different
stages of their intellectual development in the light of the cumulative
effect of colonialism. In Gandhi's case, Lelyveld discusses his great South
African experience but takes no notice of the grim and grey features of
British rule that figure so prominently in Gandhi's reconstruction of
the colonial past. Over and over again in his story, the pangs of hunger
and thirst are stressed, so regularly, that their removal became Gandhi's
agenda and the agenda of every political group.

As is evident Indians would have, given a choice, chosen to bear the ills they knew rather than cope with those whose ways weren't their own, whose principles and motives were generally beyond their comprehension, and whose laws and regulations they cared little for. The sum of events through which Gandhi had lived since childhood enabled him to uncover an incoherent and contradictory relationship between the coloniser and the colonised. Like many others before and after him, its liquidation wasn't other than a prelude to complete liberation, to self-recovery.[1] His first thought was, therefore, to drive the East India Company (EIC), known as *jan kampani* and thence by corruption as John Company, bag and baggage, out of India.[2] His boast had an emphasis, a particularity showing a backbone of solid meaning within the mystery or vagueness of expression.

Robert Clive blazed the trail of an imperial destiny and, tormented by the flames of ambition, bludgeoned his opponents into submission. The siege and capture of Arcot fort in September 1751, well before the decisive battle at Plassey, sealed the fate of Dupleix, French governor of Chandernagore and then governor-general (1741-54). Gandhi followed the fortunes of other company servants too, 'Birds of Prey and Passage' (Edmund Burke): walking through vaults piled with gold and jewels before returning to their own country as millionaires, a goal on which their eyes were constantly focused. He remembered those who amassed fortunes with 'the meanness of a peddler and the profligacy of pirates'.[3] For example, Lawrence Dundas, one of the foremost eighteenth-century contractors, acquired a vast estate, together with personal and landed assets.[4] Others, of course, lost out

---

1   Albert Memmi, *The Colonizer and the Colonized* (Boston, 1957), p. 151.

2   3 Mar. 1918, Mahadev Desai and Narhari D. Parikh (eds), *Day-to-Day with Gandhi: Secretary's Diary* (Varanasi, 1968), vol. 1, p. 56.

3   India Office Records (IOR). L/PJ/12/411. A favourite after dinner toast was to turn the traditional lament "'Alas and alack a day" into "A lass and a lakh a day!"—an aspiration natural to men who saw a lakh, or 100,000, rupees as a proper object of ambition and a *bibi*, or Indian mistress, as a fitting companion'. Emily Eden, *Up the Country: Letters from India* (London, 1983).

4   G.E. Bannerman, 'The "Nabob of the North": Sir Lawrence Dundas as government contractor', *Historical Research*, vol. 83, no. 219, Feb. 2010, p. 102.

to their rivals in their bid to add to their riches. Richard Bourchier, Bombay's governor for nine years, died insolvent; John Spencer, Clive's rival, died bankrupt after holding lucrative posts in Bombay; and Governor Charles Crommelin accepted a subordinate office in Goa after four decades of service.[5]

When Wellesley, the governor-general, marched triumphantly into Delhi and took Shah Alam, the Mughal emperor, hostage in the spring of 1804, the British cast their eyes on an extensive territory to be administered by a public-private partnership of the company and the state.[6] Their greed extended to other parts of Asia and to Africa. Here too young Britons followed the fortunes of raiders and soldiers. They had their ups and downs, but in 1877 England annexed the Transvaal, a region which became Gandhi's battleground, and created the conditions for the Boer War. 'Sooner or later,' Winston Churchill, then only twenty-one, asserted: 'in a righteous cause or a picked quarrel, with the approval of Empire, for the sake of our honour, for the sake of the race, we must fight the Boers.'[7]

The colonial enterprise sought to transform Indians by their progressive approximation to the ideals of Western civilisation. Joseph Chamberlain justified: 'We develop new territory as Trustees for Civilisation, for the Commerce of the World.' This is 'psychic disempowerment'. He and others claimed to have brought light to Africa, the Dark Continent, by transforming the so-called natives into progressive citizens ready to take their place in the modern world.[8] In India, they set in place fundamental categories of analysis, constructed a comparative philology, and established enduring structures of Hindu and Muslim laws. With the conquest and the consequent creation of the scientific apparatus of the Victorian era, they welded their scattered insights together into an ideology that sought at once to explain India's

---

5   James Douglas, *Round about Bombay* (Bombay, 1886), p. 16.

6   H.V. Bowen, Margarette Lincoln, and Nigel Rigby (eds), *The Worlds of the East India Company* (Suffolk, 2002), p. 221.

7   Randolph S. Churchill, *Winston S. Churchill: Youth 1874-1900* (Cambridge, 1966), p. 435.

8   Caroline Elkins, *Imperial Reckoning: The Untold Story of Britain's Gulag in Kenya* (New York, 2005), pp. 4-5.

enduring difference and its relationship to Europe.[9] The Orientalists agreed with Thomas Babington Macaulay that a single shelf of a good European library was worth the whole native literature of India and Arabia. They endorsed the view that Arabic and Sanskrit poetry wasn't comparable to the European languages and their creative writings. Romesh Chunder Dutt, a civil servant, gave the British a dressing-down for the 'exile mentality' of the ruling race. He remarked:

> ... unlike the Mahomedan settlers in India, he [the Englishman] does not mingle with the people, does not familiarize himself with their language ... even during his tenure of office and power in this country, he still turns towards England as his home, feels like an exile, and looks forward to the quiet retirement of an English home as the reward of a life of cares and troubles An exile's sympathies with the native population can hardly be strong.[10]

The Christian missions legitimised British imperialism, knowing full well that their future depended on the stability of British rule. John Wilson, a Bombay-based missionary writing in 1829, investigated religious tenets and observances to unfold 'the truths of divine revelation',[11] and speculated on a never-ending secular and spiritual conflict between the East and the West. Missionaries like him tended to be blinkered and justified their crude concepts of medieval polemic with a view to bringing the Christian West to the East, the land of idolatry par excellence. As in Africa, they played around with the idea of trusteeship: a moral compulsion and commitment to make amends for the 'backward heathens'. In other words, whereas Buddhism and Hinduism are religions of resigned acceptance or of despair, Christianity

---

9   T.R. Metcalf, *Ideologies of the Raj*, III. 4 (Cambridge, 1998), p. 15; Bernard S. Cohn, *Colonialism and its Forms of Knowledge: The British in India* (Princeton, N.J., 1996); N.B. Dirks (ed.), *Colonialism and Culture* (Michigan: Ann Arbor, 1992); and his *Castes of Mind: Colonialism and the Making of Modern India* (Delhi, 2002).

10   Meenakshi Mukherjee, *An Indian For All Seasons: The Many Lives of R.C. Dutt* (Delhi, 2009), p. 41.

11   John Wilson, *The Parsi Religion* (Bombay, 1843), p. 26.

came to India in an era of new activity and hopefulness, and as a fully equipped religion of effort and hope.[12]

The doctrine of racial superiority increasingly overshadowed the colonial imagination. The Ilbert Bill (introduced by the Legal Member, Courtenay Ilbert), drew upon a theory of 'difference', whose origins could be traced back to the codes of Hindu and of Muslim general law under Warren Hastings.[13] With the Raj perceived as the physical expression of a superior race, the embodiment of a saga of sacrifice, devotion, and perseverance for promoting civilisation in an alien and savage land,[14] racism became more explicit and aggressive in bolstering a conquering, civilising, and technologically advanced Anglo-Saxon nation.[15] The apologists of the Raj juxtaposed an exaggerated notion of the British body as Anglo-Saxon against that of a variety of Indian bodies all trapped by their biological inheritance in an inferior position on the scale of humankind.[16] Railway carriages, station retiring rooms, clubs, and park benches reserved 'For Europeans Only' testified to a sense of *herrenvolk* and master race.[17] Above all, the hill stations marked out and defined the boundaries that sustained the British characteristics as agents of the superior culture. Here they nurtured

---

12 W.W. Hunter, *The India of the Queen and Other Essays* (London, 1903), pp. 221-2; Gerald Studdert-Kennedy, *Providence and the Raj: Imperial Mission and Missionary Imperialism* (New Delhi, 1988), on 'constitutional engineering, institutional ideology, social theory, literature and higher education, perception and misconceptions of Gandhian nationalism'.

13 Metcalf, *Ideologies of the Raj*, p. 206. For the Ilbert Bill, see Edwin Hirschmann, *White Mutiny: The Ilbert Bill Crisis in India and the Genesis of the Indian National Congress* (Delhi, 1980).

14 Suhash Chakravarty, *The Raj Syndrome: A Study in Imperial Perceptions* (London, 1980), p. 27.

15 Sudipta Sen, *Distant Sovereignty: National Imperialism and the Origins of British India* (London, 2002), p. 148.

16 E.M. Collingham, *Imperial Bodies: The Physical Experience of the Raj, c. 1800-1947* (London, 2001), p. 198. David Arnold takes the body as a point of contest between the rulers and ruled, and brings the historical contests to life through accounts of responses to smallpox, cholera, and plague, and the British attempts to contain and control them. *Colonizing the Body: State Medicine and Epidemic Disease in Nineteenth-Century India* (California, 1993).

17 Sahgal, *Civilizing a Savage World*, p. 2.

closed communities of their own kind in a setting of their own design. Here they built political headquarters and military cantonments;[18] centres of power from whence they issued and executed orders with an Olympian air of omnipotence. Flora Annie Steel (1847-1929) unveiled India as grotesque and gruesome, thus making Anglo-Indian seclusion defensible, and fabricates preposterous theses on Indian propensities and purports to explain political disorder.[19]

Once, Charles Turner, chief justice, hosted Justice Syed Mahmood, son of Syed Ahmad, at the Madras Club. He should have known that natives weren't allowed; both had to leave.[20] P.D. Martyn, who served in Jalpaiguri in Bengal, couldn't remember any non-official Indian (Hindu or Muslim) being entertained socially in his bungalow, let alone the club.[21] Racism, thus, established a fundamental discrimination between colonisers and colonised, a sine qua non of colonial life, and laid the foundation for the immutability of this life.[22] Actually, the colonised afforded material for satire and contempt for the 'natives'. Walter Scott neatly articulated the prevailing racial sentiment in *St. Ronan's Well* through the speech of Captain MacTurk: 'Py cot! and I can tell you, sir! … Cot tamn! —Compare my own self with a parcel of black heathen bodies and natives that never were in the inner side of a kirk whilst they lived, but go about worshipping stocks and stones, … like beasts, as they are!'[23]

Two anecdotes about Malcolm Hailey, governor of Punjab and UP, are worth mentioning. As Delhi's chief commissioner, he let another man do his own job with the following instruction to a district magistrate: 'You'll have a trying day tomorrow. You'll probably have a riot. But I've discussed all your arrangements and I approve of them.

---

18   Benita Parry, *Delusions and Discoveries: India in the British Imagination, 1880-1930* (London, rpt, 1998), p. 120.

19   Ibid., p. 125.

20   Henry J.S. Cotton, *New India or India in Transition* (London, 1907), p. 50.

21   IOR. MSS EUR F 376/1, Memoirs of P.D. Martyn, p. 3.

22   Memmi, *The Colonizer and the Colonized*, p. 77.

23   Cotton, *New India*, p. 46; John Strachey, *The End of Empire* (New York, 1964), p. 55.

One embarrassment at least you shall be spared. I'm going fishing.' The same Hailey, serving as Punjab's governor, went for an after dinner walk with his dog in the pouring rain. He saw a procession pass, shouting slogans and, wondering how the police dealt with such events, joined it. Next day, he sent for a copy of the police report and read with delight that a disreputable European had joined the procession with a dog.[24]

The novelist D.D. Arnold depicted India's European as a whole more reminiscent of England's past, when an entrenched aristocracy lived degenerate lives filled with gambling, boozing, and whoring.[25] Quite a few, intoxicated by power and wealth, emulated the Mughal nobility, continuing their orgies until the brilliant sun shone into their rooms, whereupon they'd stagger to their palanquins. Bengal's gentlemen and ladies lived both splendidly and pleasantly. They spent the forenoon dedicated to business and after dinner to rest, and in the evening to recreation in chaises or palanquins in the fields, or to gardens, or by water in their budge roes. When close to a river, they had time for fishing or fowling or both.[26]

Recently, Elizabeth Kolsky introduces us to the empire's most closely guarded secrets: white violence. Drawing attention to the crimes committed by a mostly forgotten cast of European characters—planters, paupers, soldiers, and seamen—she demonstrates violent behavior to be an endemic rather than an ephemeral part of colonial rule.[27] British laws enabled and protected certain kinds of violence, largely by placing

---

24 Dennis Kincaid, *British Social Life in India, 1608-1937* (London, 1938).

25 Steven Patterson, *The Cult of Imperial Honor in British India* (London, 2009), p. 2.

26 Kincaid, op. cit., p. 101; R.V. Vernède (ed.), *British Life in India: An Anthology of Humorous and Other Writings perpetrated by the British in India, 1750-1947 with some latitude for works completed after Independence* (Delhi, 1995); Eden, *Up the Country;* Teresa Hubel, *Whose India?: The Independence Struggle in British and Indian Fiction and History* (Leicester, 1996); P.J. Marshall, 'British Society in India under the East India Company', *Modern Asian Studies* (*MAS*), 31, 1, 1997, pp. 89-108, for 'a distinctive British presence in India.'

27 Elizabeth Kolsky, *Colonial Justice in British India: White Violence and the Rule of Law* (Cambridge, 2011), p. 2.

British Indian subjects above the law. Racial fighting was also condoned by the law that institutionalised legal inequality.

So far everything is quite simple and direct, except that, by the time Warren Hastings departed in 1785, the Company creamed off the resources through high land revenue, an exorbitantly costly administration, and remittances home; in fact, the fruits of the pillage were the initial capital for Britain's industrial revolution, moved the masses of the long-dormant peasant populations to cities and industrial centres, and offered unheard of opportunities to accumulate wealth and acquire social status and prestige.

As for Europe, the revolution multiplied the number of Europeans both in absolute terms as well as in relation to the size of the non-European population, provided them with more overpowering weapons and efficient techniques to master nature's adverse forces, and created the opening to subjugate non-industrial economies through the guiding principle of free trade and the subtle mechanism of dual economics. As Adam Smith saw it, in ancient times the opulent and civilised had a rough time defending themselves against the poor and barbarous nations; in modern times, the poor and the barbarous defended themselves against the opulent and civilised.

Gandhi deprecated industrialism, and stood up against a regime that engendered exploitation, injustice, and social inequities. He felt wretched at the distressingly uniform condition of the villages. Born in debt, cultivators lived in debt and died in debt. Forty million people passed through life with only one meal a day,[28] each in a huddle of mean houses, tiled or thatched, built of mud or dry stone, and containing only one or two rooms.[29]

One-third of Bengal's population perished in 1770; the famine swept like a besom of death, leaving in its wake black shadows of plague and pestilence. The government contributed substantially to its devastation, having left large regions prey to economic stagnation, even social

---

28   E.P. Thompson, *Enlist India for Freedom!* (London, 1942), p. 89.

29   Sir Edward Blunt, *Social Service in India: An Introduction to some social and economic problems of the Indian people*, pp. 78-79.

disintegration.[30] People died as they were poor and not because the rains failed them. W.S. Blunt, who visited India during Lytton's viceroyalty, caught more than a glimpse of the skeletal figures of the starving ryots.[31] Allan Octavian Hume, who served in Etawah, wrote 'The Old Man's Hope' to draw attention to the people's toil, hunger, sickness, suffering, and sorrow. His prayer was, 'God save the people.'[32] In early December 1928, Horace Alexander felt 'ashamed', 'disgusted', and 'sick', by Orissa's impoverishment.[33] With changes in economy adding to the growing pains of the poor after the First World War,[34] Edward Thompson, the son of a Wesleyan missionary and a political liberal, quipped, 'We give ourselves more bouquets than we deserve.' Even though some writers attempted to fend off such views with a variety of arguments, Stafford Cripps, on a mission to resolve the crisis over the transfer of power, spoke of the infinite sadness of the people's grinding poverty.[35] That was gloomy enough.

While degradation consumed some observers, most enjoyed lavish parties, *shikar*, polo, and long stays in the cooler climes. And the Great Durbar of 1877? A gaudy, ill-timed, and expensive grand extravaganza to please the sovereign. Winston Churchill, who came to India planning a lifelong career in the cavalry, reported in 1897 that polo playing, pig sticking, horse racing, and shooting big game played a constant part in the affairs of the army. Curzon built a sprawling Government House, as vulgar a display of wealth and power, modelled

---

30   William Digby, *Prosperous British India: A Revelation from Official Records* (New Delhi, 1969, rpt). For example, John Bright: 'if a country be found possessing a most fertile soil and capable of bearing every variety of production, yet notwithstanding, the people are in a state of extreme destitution and suffering, the chances are there is some fundamental error in the government of that country.'

31   W.S. Blunt, *India Under Ripon: A Private Diary* (London, 1909), pp. 6-7.

32   William Wedderburn, *Allan Octavian Hume: Father of the Indian National Congress, 1829-1912* (London, 1913), p. 61.

33   Carnall, *Gandhi's Interpreter*, p. 76.

34   H.N. Brailsford, *Rebel India* (London, 1931), p. 34. Tagore described it as 'an eminently honest book which can only be written by a type of Englishman with whom we are least familiar in India'. Sisir Kumar Das (ed.), *The English Writings of Rabindranath Tagore* (New Delhi, 1996), pp. 882-83.

35   Peter Clarke, *The Cripps Version: The Life of Sir Stafford Cripps 1889-1952* (London, 2002), p. 136.

on the family seat at Kedleston in Derbyshire. The first view of Calcutta from Garden Reach was its long rows of shipping, the lines of stately white houses, and the beautiful villas with their luxuriant gardens.[36]

Of all his contemporaries, Munshi Sajjad Husain, editor of *Avadh Punch* (Lucknow), dared to take on the imperious protocols of a culture frozen in Victorian values, contrasting the imperial pomp and pageantry with the plight of the masses afflicted by the severe famines (1899-1900). He indicted the courtly regimes and the Delhi Coronation of King Edward VII on 1 January 1903, which far surpassed Lytton's splendour and magnificence.[37] The Delhi Durbar of 1911-12 was, similarly, nothing more than 'the sham life of an Empire'. Those were dark days of shame, concerned quite specifically with the fostering of an illusion. 'The jaded King of England was trotted out to Delhi … to impress the grandeur of the 'Empire' on the minds of the assembled hosts of Hindustan.'[38] It evoked a muted response from Akbar Ilahabadi, once a government employee.

Railways were rapidly built not for the forces of production but to facilitate the export trade, fulfill military needs, and connect the subcontinent by a thousand threads of steel to the capitalist market.[39] In the process, railways destroyed indigenous handicrafts industries. Part of the reason was the internal tariff duties imposed against the Indian goods, as also the discriminatory prices paid to the weavers. In Africa, the British spoke of a 'Dual Mandate' through which both parties were to gain from infrastructure, education, and production. In spite of everything, building the railways, as in Africa (the Uganda Railway completed in December 1901), took an enormous toll on capital and manpower. Britain imported over 30,000 'coolies' from India, nearly a third of whom were killed or maimed by the punishing work, disease, and frequent attacks by lions.

---

36   John Beames, *Memoirs of a Bengal Civilian* (London, 1961), p. 78.

37   Mushirul Hasan, *Wit and Humour in Colonial North India* (Delhi, 2007).

38   O'Connor, *A Clear Star*, p. 81.

39   Amiya Kumar Bagchi, *The Political Economy of Underdevelopment* (Cambridge, 1982), pp. 85-87; and Dharma Kumar and Meghnad Desai (eds), *The Cambridge Economic History of India*: vol. 2, c. 1757-c. 1970, for the impact of railways and irrigation works. In 1867, there were only 3000 miles of railway; by 1910 there were over 32,000 miles.

Networks of railways (telegraphs and telephones) symbolised slavery rather than freedom.[40] Thus, the British subverted the Mughal Empire's survival to a new use without resurrecting anything resembling the old empire. The empire had its own inequities, but these were altogether different in form and content. Earlier despotisms were tempered by a political culture that insisted on the rulers offering service and great expenditure in return for high revenue. The *angrezi sarkar* acknowledged few such restraints. Its legitimacy was as much a moral as an economic one.[41]

Dadabhai Naoroji and Romesh Chunder Dutt, whose lives overlapped with many public figures of their time, wrote on the continuing impoverishment and exhaustion, and a ruinously heavy tribute. In fact, 'no civil servant of Dutt's generation was so agitated by the conditions of the Bengal peasants, whose improvement became his lifelong crusade.' The economic issues on which he confronted the rulers relentlessly—unfair taxation, neglect of irrigation, destruction of a thriving handloom industry, draining the country's wealth to fight wars on other soils, etc, were the results of his grass-roots experience as an administrator.[42] When Gandhi read Dutt's *Economic History of India*, he wept. He responded to that particular strand of his closely knit narrative which describes the decline of Indian handloom through unfair competition with machine-made cloth imported from Manchester.[43]

The Dutt-Naoroji combine calculated the drain in 1882 amounting to Rs 1,355 million (at 1946-47 prices), over 4 per cent of the national income that year. Later, they and others established that India paid approximately

---

40   Furthermore, the principle of domination was the conception of the revenues as gross profits, and the drain of wealth through public and private channels, encouragement of the production of raw materials for which demand increased steadily in the industrial establishments, and the transfer of profits back home right from the outset without any significant investment in all-round local development.

41   C.A. Bayly, in Sugata Bose (ed.), *South Asia and World Capitalism*, p. 11; Meghnad Desai, *The Rediscovery of India* (Delhi, 2009), p. 49; Roderick Matthews, *The Flaws in the Jewel: Challenging the Myths of British India* (Delhi, 2010), pp. 267-9.

42   Mukherjee, *An Indian For All Seasons*, pp. xix, 307.

43   Ibid., p. 194.

40 million pounds (equivalent to a normal year's revenue) to meet the cost of the 1857 revolt. Public debt, which had arisen from nearly 34 million pounds in 1857 to 97 million pounds in 1862,[44] increased further owing to the redemption of the EIC's stock in 1874, by wars in Afghanistan and Burma, and by the famines of 1874-77 and 1896-1900.

The defence expenditure rarely fell. Contemporary cartoons therefore depict military expenditure as a monster in military uniform. He rides on two human figures, one the 'Income Tax' and the other the 'Salt Tax', and mercilessly employs the whip.[45] Public intellectuals, thus, criticised military expenditure and the associated public debt, the stagnation and depression in the world economy.

Bharatendu Harishchandra was disconcerted by the flow of wealth to a foreign land and the aggrandisement of the rulers at the expense of the exchequer. His reactions set the pattern for the outlook of his fellow Hindi litterateurs, who chided the government for the high prices, famine, disease, and heavy taxation. What distinguished them from one another was the proportion in which loyalty to and indictment of British rule coexisted in each one of them.[46]

From all this, Gandhi deduced that industrialism and competition ensured the loss or erosion of traditional markets. He used to say that the villages producing handicrafts lost their traditional markets in neighbouring agricultural villages, forcing craftsmen to abandon their looms and spinning wheels and return to the soil for their livelihood. He didn't pay much attention to the internal tariff duties against local goods and the discriminatory prices paid to the weavers, but exposed the malaise that led to 'ravaged villages' (*ujre gaon*). With the rural hinterland living in the shadow of collapse, their plight was precipitated. Akbar Ilahabadi, drawing on the narrative of loss, lamented: 'If you should pass that way you'll see my ravaged village/A Tommies' barracks

---

44   John McGuire, 'The World Economy, the Colonial State, and the Establishment of the Indian National Congress', in Mike Shepperdson and Colin Simmons (eds), *The Indian National Congress and the Political Economy of India, 1885-1985* (Aldershot, n.d.), p. 48.

45   9 Apr. 1891, *Selections*, p. 273.

46   Sudhir Chandra (ed.), *Social Transformation and Creative Imagination* (Delhi, 1984), pp. 153, 155.

standing by a ruined mosque.' In general, the white man's cultural and political ascendancy occupied his mind.[47] He attacked the Christian religion, which he equated with the West, and set Western morality in contrast to the traditional Indian mores.

Exploitation and servitude went hand-in-hand. Poverty wasn't due to the poor person's natural inferiority or the inscrutable laws of God, but because others picked their pockets. Through this process nearly a million people died of starvation and consequent disease in Orissa in 1865. Excessive rents, land taxes, and the usury affected Awadh, an area of 37,169 sq. m., and a population of nearly 12.5 million. An *Avadh Punch* cartoon depicts a 'native' lady holding John Bull, a symbol of enslavement, by the arm and pointing out to him half-starved men, women, and children. They stand behind her appealing for relief.[48] Here and elsewhere, famine in the form of a demon or vampire attacked starving men, women and children seated on the ground in grief and sorrow. Badri Narayan 'Premghan', the Hindi poet, captured the mood in the 1890s:

> Run, O run, there is a terrible famine,
> Black clouds of ruin gather over India;
> Trade and commerce are at a standstill;
> Enterprise and industry are all gone.

The overwhelming sentiment is the sense of separation from one's own world and of being thrown into a social system in total disarray. The same sense of alienation afflicted those who were a witness to India becoming a barrack on the Oriental seas from which Britain could draw any number of troops without paying for them. Not only did the taxpayer bear their cost, but something akin to half the army was billeted upon him. Hence the revenues and manpower provided the rod of the empire, the shield of defence, and the sword for further advance from Zanzibar and Basra eastwards to the Yellow Sea. In addition, the Indian bastion protected Australia and New Zealand too.

---

47   Sadiq-ur-Rahman Kidwai, 'Poet who Laughed in Pain: Akbar Ilahabadi', in Mushirul Hasan (ed.), *Islam in South Asia: The Realm of the Secular*, vol. 4 (Delhi, 2009), p. 336.

48   25 June 1891, *Selections*, p. 443.

Lord Wellesley used to say that he'd stalk about like a royal tiger without even a friendly jackal to soothe the severity of his thoughts. The Indian Civil Service (ICS) formed the apex of the system. Martin (b. 1905), a Cornishman, recalled its dominant, not to say unique, position. With the old Hailesbury tone pervading, he and his ilk insisted on all the external gestures of deference and respect from the 'natives', who had a leaning towards sycophancy, resulting from generations of subjection and foreign rule.[49]

In December 1927, there was not a single official of consequence, whether in Writers' Building or Government House. Ministers were the only exceptions.[50] A decade later, only one Indian held a cut above post in Writers' Building. Just prior to Independence, P.D. Martyn, a district officer serving in Bengal for seventeen years, recounted: 'We, the British, had served our time. For me that was symbolised one day towards the end when, at a meeting of Secretaries in Writers' Building, there were only two Europeans present, the rest being Indians'.[51] The wheel had turned full circle.

A District—more resembling a French *department* than an English shire—varied in size and population (from 1 to 3 million people, and an area of from a 1000 to 5000 sq. m.).It was presided over by the district officer, the hand and eye of the Government. As an indispensable cog in the colonial machine, his writ ran from the central secretariat at the top to the officer at the base.[52] As Rudyard Kipling put it, the district officer assumed the White man's burden. The simple folk feared rather than loved him, and bore his cruelty, including whipping as a judicial punishment. Henry Cotton was addicted to it, although he came to simply loathe this form of punishment after a while.[53]

Alfred Lyall, lieutenant-governor of the North West Provinces (1882-87), compared the district officer's powers to those of an intendant of a

---

49   Henry Cotton, *Indian & Home Memories* (London, 1911), p. 66.

50   IOR. MSS EUR F 376/1.Memoirs of P.D. Martyn.

51   Memoirs, 20 Sept. 1977, IOR. P.D. Martyn Papers, Centre for South Asian Studies (CSAS), Cambridge.

52   Chakravarty, *The Raj Syndrome*, pp. 132-34.

53   Cotton, op. cit., p. 80.

province under Louis XIV: both shared similar executive, magisterial, and financial responsibilities in their respective domains. They could become much more senior officials but never greater potentates.[54] In a very real sense, they were thought of as having a direct line back to the palace. The *patwari,* something between a bailiff and an estate agent, was more often than not an extortionate despot.[55] Equally so was the moneylender; the proverb goes, that 'the bania goes in like a needle and comes out like a sword'. In his own district, a little community of doctors, engineers, inspectors of schools, and assistant magistrates, looked up to him as to a magnate;[56] The Raj is the lord of the *bhog* [revenue]; We are the lords of the *bhoom* [land]. The district savoured and defended their privileges with harshness, and whenever colonialism was imperilled, they defended it.

Painting an unflattering picture of the district officer's temper and manners in general, *Avadh Punch* looked up to them matter-of-factly as negligent, selfish, and corrupt. As miniature despots, they lacked imagination, insight, and sympathy. What is more, they were brusque in manner.[57] E.M. Forster's district officer in *A Passage to India* is pompous and absurd and wants 'to flog every native in sight'.

A Call to Conscience

A victim's conquest is complete when he hugs the chains that bind him and begins to imitate the manners and customs of his captor. With this remark, Gandhi recounted his household turning upside down when the senior Gandhi attended the Durbar during a governor's visit. Someone whose general footwear was soft leather slippers, he had to wear stockings or boots: 'if I was a painter I could paint my father's disgust and torture on his face as he was putting his legs into his stockings and feet into ill-fitting and uncomfortable boots.'[58]

---

54   David Gilmour, *The Ruling Caste: Imperial Lives in the Victorian Raj* (New York, 2005), p. 103.

55   R.E. Vernède, *An Ignorant in India* (London, 1911), p. 195.

56   George R. Aberigh-Mackay, *Twenty-One Days in India, or, the Tour of Sir Ali Baba, K.C.B.; and the Teapot Series* (London, 1910), p. 67.

57   Metcalf, *Ideologies of the Raj*, p. 25; Mackay, quoted in Vernède (ed.), *British Life in India*, pp. 12-16, on the Collector.

58   *Harijan,* 3 Feb. 1940, *CWMG* (1 Dec. 1939-15 Apr. 1940), p. 152.

Eventually, he viewed the colonial situation as the collective political and cultural oppression that increased the people's under-development.[59] He contested the foundation of British rule, and despised especially the racial and cultural ideas through which colonialism was rationalised. *Hind Swaraj* is a fascinating glimpse of precisely what constituted, to his sensibility, the general historical on the hidden mechanism of oppression and the evil effect it exerted on the colonised. It opened up the Indian mind to certain dimensions of the colonial/Western world.

Gandhi saw the urban bourgeoisie managing, almost intuitively, to conceptualise and contextualise the cost of colonial rule, and some turning inwards to discover the malaise in manners and morals, social mores, and cultural practices. He knew of the self-introspection, the prolonged and deep intellectual debates in Maharashtra and Bengal and the strife between Eastern orthodoxy and Western culture.[60] He was, moreover, informed of the more vociferous elements that held the West guilty of shallowness and materialism. Someone once voiced his consciousness in this fashion: 'Ride the waves of the sea, climb to the summits of the mountains, steal the stars from the sky, and with both hands grasp the storm, the meteor, and the thunder-flash'.

On the threshold of Bengal's renaissance stood Raja Rammohun Roy, a catalyst for diffusing intellectual enlightenment. The Brahmo Sabha (later Samaj), his brainchild, sought a return to the monotheistic purity of the Upanishads. Dwarkanath Tagore, his successor, found a corrective in the earliest principal beliefs of Hinduism. This, combined with other factors, gave rise to 'the hymnology of the new patriotism'. Tagore, the author of *Sonar Bangla*, sung in September 1905 by himself, contributed immensely to this hymnology.

The more they tighten their hands, the more will our bands snap:
The more their eyes redden, the more will our eyes open.[61]

---

59   Ibid., p. 151.

60   Surendranath Banerjea, *A Nation in Making: Being the Reminiscences of Fifty Years of Public Life* (Calcutta, 1925, rpt, 1963), p. 2.

61   Bipin Chandra Pal, *Swadeshi and Swaraj (The Rise of New Patriotism)* (Calcutta, 1954), p. 101.

The reformists and their opponents had already drawn the battle lines in Maharashtra. While Gokhale championed compulsory education and, in 1905, founded the Servants of India Society to harness the evolution of a common nationality based upon common traditions, common hopes, and common aspirations, B.G. Tilak, ten years older, unfurled the banner of orthodoxy in the teeth of European influences. He revived the Shivaji and Ganapati festivals in 1893, opposed the Age of Consent Bill, which sought to fix twelve years as the minimum age of marriage, and denounced the measures to curb the bubonic plague in 1897. His was a voice of a resurgent Hindu nation. The political mobilisation, which included the revival of the Shivaji and Ganapati cults, gave him greater public approval among non-Muslims than Gokhale.

In Punjab, the Arya Samaj engaged at once in a fundamental religious and national revival. The persistent cry of its founder, Dayanand Saraswati, was 'Back to the Vedas'. His following didn't come from Gujarat, a state to which he belonged, but from the land of the five rivers. Here, in this Muslim-majority province where Islam had spread with the aid of the Chishti and Suhrawardy saints but which also had a substantial Sikh population, the Arya Samajists were incandescent with the ardour of their faith and the vastness of their transcendental experience. Their reformism was premised on strong grounds, but they expended their energies on a thorough denunciation of Islam, and undermined Punjab's strong and long-standing composite traditions. In this way, they turned the gains of the past few centuries into tangible losses.

Signs of change were visible in Bengal, a province in which the Muslim majority, principally rural-based, had suffered adversely from the time Warren Hastings and Cornwallis had introduced judicial and educational reforms without taking cognizance of their adverse impact on the urban-based Muslim service classes. The winds of reform impacted the local and migrant Muslim communities in Calcutta.

Muslims turned brusquely away, at least until the 1880s, from Syed Ahmad Khan's passion for Western education. They did not nevertheless deter him and his associates from bringing the daring and energetic together on a political, social, or educational platform. They were, to a great extent, the most suitable under the existing circumstances. Owing to their persistence, the dream of a Muslim institution in Aligarh and elsewhere came true. The 'Aligarh movement' was, in this manner, the result of a great many trials and errors, and the experience of a great many individuals during several generations.

Delhi's traditionalists, who followed the eighteenth-century scholar Shah Waliullah and had once decried the Western-oriented curriculum at the Dilli Kalij (Delhi College), recognised, howsoever grudgingly, Syed Ahmad's institution as a visible symbol of colonial modernity. Slowly but inevitably, the Western and the traditional systems of education spread among the *ashraf*, high born, and the *ajlaf*, the low born. They differed not in that one group did something while another didn't, but only in the forms of doing it.

Above and beyond the specific communitarian orientations, reformers forged contacts with and discovered points of convergence with the quasi-political bodies in their locality or the province. The most celebrated among these, which began to receive nationwide attention were: the British Indian Association (BIA), which came into being in 1851 at Calcutta[62]; the Madras merchants opened a local branch in February 1852 to be replaced six months later by the Madras Native Association; and the Indian Association was formed in July 1876. The Madras Mahajana Sabha campaigned for temple reforms and against zamindari litigation, income tax, the increase in excise duties, and land revenue resettlement policies. Lytton fuelled the growing social and political disgruntlement with the Vernacular Press Act, 'that wretched piece of legislation'. It was repealed in 1880. The Arms Act, another bombshell for the educated in the Presidencies, introduced the licensing of firearms while exempting Europeans from it.[63]

---

62   S.R. Mehrotra, *The Emergence of the Indian National Congress* (Delhi, 1971), p. 358. Briton Martin Jr., *New India, 1885: British Official Policy and the Emergence of the Indian National Congress* (Bombay, 1970).

63   Ripon, who assumed charge as viceroy on 8 June 1880, had them in mind when he tendered the following advice: 'Unless we are prepared to afford to these men legitimate openings for their aspirations and ambitions, we had better at once abolish our Universities and close our Colleges, for they will only serve to turn out year by year in ever-increasing numbers of men who must inevitably become the most dangerous and influential enemies of our rule.' Anil Seal, *The Emergence of Indian Nationalism: Competition and Collaboration in the Later Nineteenth Century* (Cambridge, 1971), p. 148.

Ripon's policy, which had been bolstered by Gladstone's government in Whitehall, failed over the Ilbert Bill in early February 1883.[64] The unreasonable clamour and rancour of opponents was spread by the European community, the civil servants, and Calcutta's European capitalists, who were afraid of any diminution in the power and prestige of their local agents.[65] A cartoon in *Punch*, caricatures the viceroy riding an elephant as its mahout, with a number of Europeans leaning out of the *howdah* to attack him: it was entitled 'The Anglo-Indian Mutiny'.[66] Ripon was, along these lines, harassed and hampered to an inconceivable degree by his fellow-countrymen's bigotry and racism.[67] Before leaving India in December 1884, he bowed before the storm without being able to buy peace between the 'whites and blacks', who split into two hostile and vociferating camps.

Of all the persons, A.O. Hume, the civil servant and later 'father of the Congress', summed up the prevailing mood.[68] Born to Joseph Hume, a radical British MP during the second half of the nineteenth century, Hume cut short his career in the ICS to bridge, in response to the 'blundering' government machine, the gulf separating the rulers from their *raiyyat* (subjects). He believed in governance with the consent of the governed and consultation with Indian officials and local leaders.[69] Likewise, with political activism springing into life and the excitement over the resurgence of a new nation growing, Bipin Chandra Pal, the

---

64   It enabled Indian judges to try European British subjects on criminal charges.

65   *Aftab-i Punjab* (Lahore), 22 June 1883, *Desh Upkarak* (Lahore), 23 June 1883; *Selections*, Punjab, p. 541.

66   Kincaid, op. cit., p. 127. Dennis Kincaid (1905-40) joined the ICS in 1928 and was Bombay's assistant collector.

67   Cotton, *Indian & Home Memories*, p. 180.

68   'The prevailing idea is this, if with such a viceroy things are to be thus, what hope is there for the future? We have never had a viceroy more honestly and earnestly desirous of doing us justice and yet he appears as absolutely impotent to correct crying and wicked evils as a man like Lord Lytton ... The Government seems to be a great, cruel, blundering machine, running on by its own weight ... even the driver being incapable of directing its course.'

69   Introduction, S.R. Mehrotra and Edward C. Moulton (eds), *Selected Writings of Allan Octavian Hume: District Administration in North India, Rebellion and Reform, vol. 1, (1829-1867)* (Delhi, 2004), p. vii.

storm petrel of Bengal, explained the prevalence of 'new patriotism'.[70] A Bombay newspaper commented in 1884: 'When the light of truth dawns upon the minds it cannot but expel those stagnant notions of honour and decency which spring and are reared up in the darkness of ignorance.'[71]

'New India' was unveiled in Bombay in December 1885. The Indian National Congress, the party of the present and future, came into being through an alchemy of lawyers, journalists, artists, teachers, and caste and community institutions coming together in the right combination at the right time. Even some rajas and *taluqdars* came on board; so much so that the great tent in which they met glowed with the varied colours of the turbans they wore. Hume got the alchemy going to ensure an open, flexible, and resilient Congress; in other words, a body capable of seeing through hard and comfortable times. The event was historic, unique, momentous, colourful, national, and thoroughly representative.[72]

Adam Smith had however stated in *The Wealth of Nations* that Britain couldn't voluntarily abandon all authority over her colonies, and leave them to elect their own magistrates or to enact their own laws. 'No nation,' he made clear, 'ever voluntarily gave up the dominion of any province, soever troublesome how it might be to govern it, and soever small how the revenue which it afforded might be in proportion to the expense which it occasioned.'[73] By this logic, the Congress demands infringed the sacred rights of their British 'guardians'. Dufferin, the viceroy (1884-88), stubbornly belittled its leaders, and chided their 'foul torrent abuse' of his administration.[74] He missed the significance of the coming together of many segments of the populace, and the growing sense of patriotism which became increasingly intertwined with nationalist pride.

---

70   Pal, *Swadeshi and Swaraj*, p. 190.

71   *Native Opinion*, 6 Apr. 1884, Bombay, Native Newspaper Reports (NNR).

72   Martin Jr., *New India*, 1885, p. 292.

73   David Sidorsky (ed.), *The Liberal Tradition in European Thought* (New York, 1970), p. 313.

74   Cotton, *New India*, p. 9.

Imagine Dufferin sleeping in bed and dreaming of fairies throwing flowers on him.[75] Elsewhere, a character from the *Punch*, London, tells him that the outside and inside of a man should be the same.[76] In *Charpuz* (Moradabad), the viceroy is shown preparing for his departure. The letterpress bears a Persian verse meaning: 'Thy arrival is the cause of our ruin, and thy departure is a matter of joy for us.'[77] In *Parsi Punch* (21 November 1885), Ripon is like a cup of sweet milk, whereas Dufferin is a tamarind.[78]

Let the Trumpet Sound

'The new wine was fermenting in the old bottles, and at any moment the bottles might burst and the wines be spilled,' wrote William Wedderburn, admonishing the government that the path of safety lay in trusting and associating the people in managing their affairs.[79]

It was Monday 28 December 1885. Never before had so many venerable gentlemen walked through the gates of Gokul Dass Tejpal Sanskrit College! Never before had so many walked so purposefully, as if they were on the verge of creating history! Dadabhai Naoroji, son of a Parsi priest and the first Indian professor of mathematics at Elphinstone Institution (later, College), goaded colleagues to burn the midnight oil and asked for a committee to investigate the working of the administration and demand simultaneous examinations for the ICS. He had posed the following question at a meeting of the East India Association in May of 1867: 'Why should not 200 million of your fellow subjects who contribute so largely to your wealth and prosperity, and who form an integral part of the British empire, have a few representatives in the Imperial Parliament to give their voice in Imperial questions?' He had an innate sense of his audience. He was part preacher, part rabble-rouser, styling himself as an underdog vying with the establishment to attract attention.

---

75   5 Apr. 1888, *Selections*, Punjab, p. 443.

76   13 Sept. 1883, ibid., p. 443.

77   28 July 1887, ibid., p. 498.

78   Bombay, Native Newspaper Reports (NNR), p. 717.

79   Wedderburn, *Allan Octavian Hume*, p. 2.

Pherozeshah Mehta was, noticeably, in full flow; Surendranath Banerjea, a lifelong educationist and publicist, Lal Mohun Ghose, a brilliant orator whose eloquence excited the admiration of John Bright, and Anand Kumar Bose walked up and down acquainting fellow delegates with the inequities enshrined in the Vernacular Press Act (1878); Ananda Charlu of Madras Mahajana Sabha and Subramania Iyer, editor of *The Hindu* (1878-98), were drawn into the net; W.C. Bonnerjee, with his white hair and flowing beard, paid serious attention to their conversations and, when the time came to deliver the presidential address, he contradicted those who called the newly-born Congress 'a nest of conspirators and disloyalists'. A decade later, he contested Barrow-in-Furness as a Liberal Party candidate.

Hume, who had brought them all here, opened the first session by calling for 'Three times three for Her Majesty the Queen Empress, God bless her!' A very storehouse of Indian knowledge given his vast administrative experience, his words were wise. The audience loved to listen to his conversations with the officials, and they cheered him for seeing the big picture without pandering shamelessly to the xenophobic fears about caste and community domination. Revolt and rebellion were far removed from their minds. 'What is it for which we are now met?' Naoroji asked in 1886. 'Is this Congress a nursery for sedition and rebellion against the British government [cries of 'No! No!'], or it another stone in the foundation of the stability of that Government [Cries of 'Yes! Yes!'] ... Let us speak out like men and proclaim that we are loyal to the backbone.'[80] Hume proclaimed loyalty and engaged with Gokhale in creating a political personality within the imperial matrix. Both were sublimated in the image of a functionally organic society and in the larger interest of retaining the British connection.

Notwithstanding their very different backgrounds, Hume, Naoroji, and Gokhale defined nationalism as an inclusive concept that transcended horizontal ties of class, caste, region, and religion. They extricated themselves from debates over reforms, judging it a losing stand in a highly religious and caste-stratified social order. Their

---

80   R.P. Masani, *Dadabhai Naoroji: The Grand Old Man of India* (London, 1939), p. 253.

speeches were short on religious matters; their goal was to fuse on to one national whole all the different elements that made up India. The people needed greater self-belief to overcome the burden of colonialism and to take pride in their achievements and build on them.[81]

There were other voices too; their nationalism was a parallel growth to a similar movement in Europe arising from similar circumstances, that is, resistance to foreign rule. With Giuseppe Mazzini, the Genoa-born architect of the Italian unification and the Irish patriots as models, Surendranath Banerjea coupled nationalism with the notion that fidelity to the populace preceded loyalty to the sovereign.[82] Lala Lajpat Rai considered himself to be Mazzini's and Garibaldi's disciple. In others we see a tenuous fusion of interests in public employment, moving in opposition to bureaucratic changes, with independently generated organisations expressing wider cultural changes. More generally, these trends drew upon, as the Cambridge historian C.A. Bayly points out, and recast some patterns of social relations that had come into existence before British rule was established in the subcontinent.[83]

Naoroji chaired the second Congress at the close of 1886. 'Never, I suppose, was a more interesting and picturesque assemblage collected there, from all parts of India, from Lahore and Sind to Travancore', reported the civil servant Henry Cotton.[84] He attended the Congress along with another official, Charles Elliott, then president of a committee to inquire into public expenditure. It was in the light of this experience that Cotton wrote to Ripon on the representative element in the Legislative Council, but nothing much happened until Gladstone's powerful intervention in 1892 (Lansdowne was viceroy from December 1888-1893) made a small advance in introducing a representative element into the Councils.

---

81   Edward C. Moulton, 'The Early Congress and the British Radical Connection', in D.A. Low (ed.), *The Indian National Congress: Centenary Hindsights* (Delhi, 1988), p. 29.

82   Banerjea, *A Nation in Making*, pp. 38, 40.

83   C.A. Bayly, *Origins of Nationality in South Asia: Patriotism and Ethical Government in the Making of Modern India*, in *The C.A. Bayly Omnibus* (Delhi, 2009), p. 1.

84   Cotton, *Indian & Home Memories*, p. 199.

The 1887 Congress illustrates the intricate relationship between different groups.[85] Each of the activists belonged to a tiny and disparate Western-educated elite from Madras city. The other great faction belonged to the commercial powers, the mercantile elite, wealthy landowners, and the Shankaracharya of Kumbakonam and the Pandarasanidhi of Dharmapuram. The 'communal' split had yet to occur in the late-1880s. Among the sixty-seven Muslims who attended the Congress were the prominent Persian Badsha family of Madras city and the Maracair Muslims of Nagapattinam. Tyabji, the chairperson, urged influential Muslims, notably Syed Ahmad and Ameer Ali, to back the Congress. They didn't, although the ebullient scenes worked across, at least for the time being, long-standing divides. On the contrary, the opinion gained ground in official circles, to which the English staff of Muhammedan Anglo-Oriental (M.A.O.) College lent credence, that it was time to use the iron fist in the velvet glove, to put down the Congress.

The Madras Congress provides a political map of the presidency in which were drawn both the boundaries of local political constituencies and the threads connecting them.[86] As virtually every indigenous power felt the government's prodding, so virtually every major interest rallied around the Congress to secure a larger share in administration; reform of the legislative councils; appointment of Indians to the secretary of state's council and the executive councils; separation of the judicial function from the executive; reduction of the tax burden and military expenditure; diminution of peasant debt; promotion of primary education, and conveniences for industrial and technical instruction. With all its nebulous aims and conflicting visions, the Congress moved along nicely, trying to reconcile long-standing disputes and evolving its own distinct discourse.[87]

Allahabad means 'City of God'. This is a holy city, where the confluence of the Ganga and the Yamuna takes place. Pilgrims to this sacred city come

---

85   D.A. Washbrook, *The Emergence of Provincial Politics: The Madras Presidency 1870-1920* (Cambridge, 1976), for the Congress session at Madras in 1887.

86   Ibid.

87   C.A. Bayly, *The Local Roots of Indian Politics: Allahabad, 1880-1920*, in *The C.A. Bayly Omnibus*, p. 156.

from everywhere, especially during the great Kumbh Mela, held every 12 years. Every year smaller pilgrims attend the Magh Mela. They plod patiently along in the heat and dust, but are supported and sustained by an unwavering faith and belief. They are serenely content at the prospect of being cleansed from every vestige of sin by those holy waters.

Mark Twain described Allahabad—the British section—in the following words:

> It is a town of wide avenues and noble distances, and is comely and alluring, and full of suggestions of comfort and leisure, and of the serenity which a good conscience buttressed by a sufficient bank account gives. The bungalows (dwellings) stand well back in the seclusion and privacy of large enclosed compounds (private grounds, as we should say) and in the shade and shelter of trees. Even the photographer and the prosperous merchant ply their industries in the elegant reserve of big compounds, and the citizens drive in thereupon their business occasions. And not in cabs—no; in the Indian cities cabs are for the drifting stranger; all the white citizens have private carriages; and each carriage has a flock of white-turbaned footmen and drivers all over it.

Allahabad, now the capital of the North-Western Provinces and Awadh, was already in the throes of much activity. Benaras was, by contrast, 'a sleepy hollow having nothing but the 'Leader' to cater to their patriotism'.[88] The People's Association's early initiatives and the Kayastha Clubs Association in Allahabad became the hunting ground for rabble-rousers. Consequently, the 1888 Congress session struck the right note.[89] That year, Rajendra Prasad's brother returned from the holy city to Chapra, Bihar, carrying swadeshi cloth and the seeds of the Swadeshi idea.

Another Congress session in Allahabad took place in 1892, where Tej Bahadur Sapru, a Kashmiri Pandit, was swept off his feet by

---

88   Motilal to C. Vijayaraghavachariar, 18 Dec. 1918, Ravinder Kumar and Hari Dev Sharma (eds), *Selected Works of Motilal Nehru* (*SWMN*), vol. 1, p. 184.

89   Bayly, *The Local Roots of Indian Politics*, p. 140.

Surendranath Banerjea's eloquence.[90] Just as the epic heroism, unity, and patriotism of the Russo-Japanese war of 1904-05 inspired Gandhi in South Africa,[91] Tilak and Gokhale, the two contemporary politicians, utilised this event, in conjunction with the Russian revolution of 1905, to stimulate nationalism at Allahabad in 1907. Students from the Muir Central College unhitched the horses from the carriage and drew it through streets jammed with cheering people.[92] Such enthusiasm matched the mood of rejoicing in a sense of liberation from the past, and taking great delight in Japan's victory and the affront to the West.

Curzon, the conservative viceroy (1859-1925), was arrogant and populist to detractors and charismatic and visionary to supporters. In 1900, he believed that the Congress was tottering to its fall, and his great ambition was to assist it to a peaceful demise. His disdain for the *bhadralok,* whose material interests were tied to the land east of Calcutta, was evident in the decision to divide 80 million Bengalis into two realms and create a new province, with a predominantly Muslim population as a counterpoise to the Hindus. This ill-advised strategy, despite everything, set a match to the tinderbox of revolutionary passions. The curtain of the past was dropping on old Calcutta in 1906. The labours of the publicists were already bearing fruit. The masses, whose economic plight pushed them inevitably towards the anti-government movement, backed swadeshi, boycott, and national education. The 'middle-classes', of course, responded energetically to the growing solidarity and self-consciousness. All in all, Curzon's decision illustrated the worst features of bureaucratic rule: '... its arrogant pretensions to superior wisdom, and its reckless disregard of public opinion.'

Almost the entire Bengali *bhadralok* rose like a man to protest.[93] Tagore, 'the great sentinel', spoke of a unity of consciousness, based on kinship and the blood bonds of the people,[94] while Pal announced the

90   S.K. Bose, *Tej Bahadur Sapru* (Delhi, 1978), p. 5.

91   *Indian Opinion*, 10 June 1903, *CWMG*, vol. 4, p. 467.

92   Krishna Nehru Hutheesing, *We Nehrus* (Bombay, 1967), p. 37.

93   *SWMN*, vol. 1, p. 91.

94   Rabindranath Tagore, My *Life in My Words*. Selected and edited by Uma Das Gupta (Delhi, 2006), p. 33.

birth of 'a most inspiring hymnology of the new cult of patriotism'.[95] While the poor stirred, demanding bread, jobs, and an end to rural indebtedness, the political classes broadened their social base. The song *Bande Mataram* became the common form of salutation, and thousands took the swadeshi vow at the Kali temple. With his image sullied, Curzon left India unwept, unhonoured, and unsung. He left behind a divided legacy in the form of Bengal's partition. Its revocation in December 1911 worsened Hindu-Muslim relations in Bengal.

The political turmoil following the Swadeshi movement continued until the closure of the War when prices soared and unemployment deepened the people's anxieties. The government, instead of embarking on a policy of political and economic liberalisation, resorted to repression. These developments drew into active public life a number of high-minded men and women whose temperaments and orientations would probably have kept them remote from politics in quieter times. In 1915, the 'extremists' found a benevolent autocracy to be infinitely worse than an openly oppressive and malevolent one.[96] They didn't differ that greatly from the 'moderates', except in their social conservatism, religiosity, and regional chauvinism. On the other hand, the extremists' style of politics loaded the scales heavily in their favour in two regions, Maharashtra and Bengal, with their pockets of revolutionary terrorism, with the Surat split in December 1907.[97]

The Servants of India Society and the Home Rule League, which owed its existence to Annie Besant who had set foot on Indian soil on 16 November 1893, had little awareness of the real life and problems of the people in the rural and urban areas and couldn't, therefore, sustain the interest of all those who were in search of something new or incredible; something that would mobilise not one or two groups and communities, but bring the entire nation to its feet marching towards *purna swaraj*.

The moderate-extremist gap widened. The founding fathers, impregnated with the concepts and values of political liberalism to

---

95   *New India*, 19 Jan. 1903; Pal, *Swadeshi and Swaraj*, p. 97.

96   Ibid., 19 Mar. 1901; ibid., p. 29.

97   S.R. Mehrotra, 'The Early Congress' in B.R. Nanda (ed.), *Essays in Modern Indian History* (New Delhi, 1980), p. 59.

such a degree, were slowly becoming isolated from the populace in their modes of living, their thought, and their language.[98] Bengal's senior Congressman Bhupendranath Basu bemoaned in 1914 that the Congress was turning into a decadent party. Decadent it wasn't, but divided it was.

Andrews, who had come to Delhi in 1904 as an Anglican priest and lecturer at St. Stephen's College, saw the writing on the wall. 'I have a great happiness and blessing in store for me—to see Mohandas Gandhi,' he wrote on 12 December 1913. 'No life lived in our day,' he continued, 'could be more moving than this. My journey will be a pilgrimage to touch his feet.'[99] As a matter of interest, nine 'prominent Indians' invited Gandhi to the 1911 Congress session. Having accepted the honour, he demanded a free hand.[100]

In the meantime, Gandhi's Phoenix family, headed by Maganlal, reached Santiniketan; W.W. Pearson had already been there since the previous year. They stayed near Tagore's house at Dehali. Gandhi came on 17 February 1915, but couldn't meet Tagore. He returned on 6 March, when the two finally met along with Kakasaheb Kalekar, a wandering sadhu. Both shared a passion for freedom and spoke the language of universalism, humanism, and pluralism. I will not wish to write more, but I will close this chapter by recalling to your minds the early meeting of two great Indians of our time. Kalekar describes their meeting:

> We went into the drawing-room with Bapu. Ravi-babu rose from the sofa on which he had been sitting. His tall, stately figure, his silvery hair, his long beard, his impressive *choga* [gown]—all this went to make a magnificent picture. And there, in almost comical contrast, stood Gandhiji, in his skimpy *dhoti*, his simple *kurta*, and his Kashmiri cap [*dupalli*]. It was like a lion confronting a mouse!

---

98   Tilak was condemned to deportation on 24 June 1908 and released in July 1914, Gokhale's death on 19 February 1915 left the Congress in the doldrums.

99   Hugh Tinker, *The Ordeal of Love: C.F. Andrews and India* (Delhi, 1979), p. 79.

100   Gandhi to Kallenbach, 30 Sept. 1911, Gandhi-Kallenbach papers.

[Great Indian Poetess, Mrs. Sarojini Naidu, noticing Gandhi's protruding ears, used to call him 'Mickey Mouse'!][101]

Inevitably and eagerly, Gandhi did his bit in the Home Rule Movement of which he can hardly have been aware when it began; he respected the Theosophists as a whole, and their political activities in particular. His principal interest lay in gathering insights into the thought processes of the upper stratum of the Congress leadership. The Lucknow meeting in 1916 offered him the opportunity to do so. This was evidently a golden opportunity; for the young lawyer, and that too, a not so successful one, to aspire to play a part in public affairs.

---

101   Madho Prasad, *A Gandhian Patriarch: A political and spiritual biography of Kaka Kalekar* (Delhi, 1965), p. 149.

2
'Green Fields and Pastures New'

'Towards the small hours of the morning I woke up somewhat earlier than usual, I was still in that twilight condition between sleep and consciousness when suddenly the idea broke upon me—it was as if in a dream. Early in the morning I related the whole story to Rajagopalachari.

The idea came to me last night in a dream, I said, that we should call upon the country to observe a general hartal. Satyagraha is a process of self-purification, and ours is a sacred fight, and it seems to me to be in the fitness of things that it should be commenced with an act of self-purification. Let all the people of India therefore suspend their business on that day, and observe the day as one of fasting and prayer.'

-M.K. Gandhi, in C.F. Andrews (ed.),
Mahatma Gandhi: His Own Story, p. 299.

'There are few towns in India of which the first appearance charms the stranger more than Lucknow,' observed the French traveller Louis-Théophile Marie Rousselet (1845-1929).[1] In size it was the largest city in the British Empire, with the exception of the three presidency towns of Calcutta, Bombay, and Madras. Lucknow was a great centre of landed power. In 1900, the *taluqdars* numbered well over 250, controlled two-thirds of the territory in Awadh, and realised one-sixth of the province's total revenue. According to a description, 'one could barely recognise the nawabs after dusk, in their white *angarkha*, tight pyjamas, and fine white caps, with their mouth full of betel nut and their dress wafting a bewitching odour of oriental perfume as they walked towards the Chowk, where most of them had dancing girls in their pay ... feudalism in all its charms and evils reigned supreme ...'[2] The result was for everyone to see; Awadh's social disorganisation led to intellectual decay rather than intellectual blossoming.

---

1   Louis Rousselet, *India and its Native Princes: Travels in Central India and in the presidencies of Bombay and Bengal* (London, 1882), p. 549.

2   Choudhry Khaliquzzaman, *Pathway to Pakistan* (Lahore, 1961), p. 5.

28 December 1916 was a perfect north Indian winter day, the sky stretching blue and cloudless to the horizon, the air bitterly cool. From Qaiser Bagh, built in 1848-50 at a cost of Rs 10,000,000 and now the home of the British India Association, a long view from the Congress *pandal* extended, broken here and there by neem trees and mango groves. Much bonhomie prevailed. People exchanged notes on how Warren Hastings robbed the begums of Awadh of their assets. They wondered, furthermore, how the Awadh nawabs built such splendid structures at such high cost. In this context, someone mentioned Claude Martin, the architect of La Martiniere and other structures. He had arrived at the Awadh court in 1780. The tour de force of the Congress delegates concluded with the 1857 Revolt, Nawab Wajid Ali Shah's removal, Begum Hazrat Mahal's woes, and Lucknow's destruction by the British troops. They symbolised, in the words of the novelist-historian Abdul Halim Sharar, 'The Last Phase of an Oriental Culture'.

That evening, when history was being told through the art of *qissa-goi*, a practice that virtually died with the nawabs, nearly all the great and distinguished in politics were dutifully present. For the young Swarup Rani Nehru, it was thrilling to see them all.[3] She felt good from the time Jawaharlal presented her, for *bhaiya dooj* (brother's day), a gold pin with the letters HR set in emeralds and rubies representing the Home Rule colours.

With Tilak's homecoming after nine years, the Congress bustled with energy. The 'moderate' and the 'extremist' leaders had a star value. Besides, they found common cause to settle their differences and forged an alliance with the 'Young Party' Muslims.[4] With overall goodwill prevailing, the 'elegant and arrogant' barrister, M.A. Jinnah, sported 'a fine rapier of fine toledo steel in a velvet scabbard with a hilt made

---

3   Vijaya Lakshmi Pandit, *The Scope of Happiness: A Personal Memoir* (New Delhi, 1979), p. 62.

4   In UP, Sapru, Jagat Narain Mulla, and Motilal supported, between July and December 1915, the UP Municipalities Bill and conceded the principle of separate representation to Muslims. Francis Robinson, *Separatism Among Indian Muslims: The Politics of the United Provinces' Muslims, 1860-1923* (Cambridge, 1974), pp. 247-51.

of carved cold jade'.[5] Gokhale had told Sarojini Naidu before his death that Jinnah 'has true stuff in him, and that freedom from all sectarian prejudice which will make him the best ambassador of Hindu-Muslim unity.'[6] At the 1915 Congress session, she recited, in Jinnah's honour, her poem 'Awake'. In December 1916, when the Congress-League Pact was signed, she described him as the ambassador of Hindu-Muslim unity. She believed that his searching and quintessentially 'secular' mind led him to cooperate with the Congress at that juncture. This is what she thought of him:

> Never was there a nature whose outer qualities provided so complete an antithesis of its inner work. Tall and stately, but thin to the point of emaciation, languid and luxurious of habit, Mohammad Ali Jinnah's attenuated form is the deceptive sheath of a spirit of exceptional vitality and endurance. Somewhat formal and fastidious, and a little aloof and imperious of manner, the calm hauteur of his accustomed reserve but marks—for those who know him a native and eager humanity, an intuition quick and tender as a woman's, a humour gay and winning as a child's. Pre-eminently rational and practical, discreet and dispassionate in his estimate and acceptance of life, the obvious sanity and serenity of his worldly wisdom effectually disguise a shy and splendid idealism which is the very essence of the man.[7]

Sarjoini Naidu and Annie Besant attracted a great deal of attention. The latter is described as 'a leader in the new social world. She won people with her charm, intrigued them with her calculated attack on conventions, titillated them with her cynical coquetry and impressed them with her hospitality and her wealth. She had become a patroness of the arts, a benefactress of impecunious writers and artists, [and] a collector of

---

5   Makarand Paranjape (ed.), *Sarojini Naidu: Selected Letters, 1890s to 1940s* (Delhi, 1996), p. 122.

6   Stanley Wolpert, *Jinnah of Pakistan* (Delhi, 1984), p. 35.

7   Kanji Dwarkadas, *India's Fight for Freedom, 1913-1937: An Eyewitness Story* (Bombay, 1965), pp. 63-64.

ancient works of art and young lovers.'[8] The 'Golden Threshold', her home in Hyderabad, hosted poets, writers, and painters. Her brother Harindranath was a poet and an irrepressible singer and *bon viveur*. Visitors were attracted to the house no less by her own talents than by the reputation of other family members. Padmaja Naidu, her daughter, was endowed in large measure with all the charm and characteristics of her accomplished mother.

As a cloud of parrots burst from a nearby tree and momentarily turned the air into a whorl of glittering green, an 'incongruous figure in his large Kathiawar turban and swathed in shawls against the north Indian winter'[9] crouched over a brazier of charcoal to warm his hands and shins. He was of medium size, slender built, and above a rather heavy lipped mouth he had a small dark moustache. His hair wasn't as closely cropped as it was subsequently, but he had a shaven look. His eyes were always his most remarkable feature, commented Millie Graham Polak, a young copy editor on the *The Critic* who first saw him in South Africa in 1905, 'and were in reality the lamps of his soul; one could read so much from them.'[10]

As the typical ascetic of the East,[11] Gandhi kept a low profile.[12] Rather than participating in the daily dealings or the tedious procedures, he took stock of the existential realities,[13] defended the custom against inter-caste dining, and spoke on South Africa. Even so, his speech failed 'to throw light on the mettle of the man.'[14] It is not known for certain whether or not he endorsed separate electorates and weightages, but Tilak did so under pressure of the non-Brahman protest in the

8   Hosain, *Sunlight on a Broken Column*, p. 175.

9   Vijaya Lakshmi Pandit, *The Scope of Happiness*, p. 64.

10   Millie Graham Polak, *Mr. Gandhi: The Man* (London, 1931), p. 18.

11   Preface to 'Mahatma Gandhi in the Transvaal', by A.R. Chamney (1999), p. 3. IOR. A. R. Chamney papers.

12   Lionel Curtis was the Round Table group founder and leader. He was present at the Lucknow Congress. For profile, Arnold J. Toynbee, *Acquaintances* (Oxford, 1967), pp. 128-48.

13   Rajendra Prasad, *Autobiography* (Bombay, 1957), p. 81.

14   Kripalani, *Gandhi: His Life and Thought*, p. 58.

Deccan.[15] In the subjects committee and open sessions. Gandhi listened to the negotiations without participating in them.[16] The pact started the nationalists on the slippery slope towards the recognition of the Congress of Hindu-Muslim separation.[17]

The Nehrus had taken a break in Kashmir, their ancestral home. They came to Lucknow with great expectations, but the twenty-seven year old Jawaharlal, who returned home in the autumn of 1912 from Cambridge, found Gandhi to be a distant, and apolitical person. His language seemed incomprehensible.[18] Swarup Kumari Nehru, his younger sister, saw him from a distance; she became acquainted with him four years later at Anand Bhawan (Home of Joy) in Allahabad.[19] By this time, Gandhi held the world in thrall. Those familiar with him saw something 'intangible' in his spirit and his amazing knack of reaching the hearts of people.[20] B.K. Nehru, son of Brijlal and Rameshwari Nehru who edited a Hindi women's magazine *Stri Darpan*, was born in a room at the extreme north-west corner of Anand Bhawan. Bijju, as the family referred to him, recalled Gandhi's presence in Qaiser Bagh. It is agreeable to the reader that so many different accounts of Gandhi are in substantial harmony which is not usually the case.

Braj Kishore Prasad, a lawyer, and Raj Kumar Shukla, Champaran's well-to-do middle-class peasant and moneylender, met with Gandhi and pleaded with him to travel to Champaran to see for himself the plight of the riots caused by the indigo farmers. Gandhi agreed. His mission was to make peace with honour.[21] With rumours afloat of his

---

15   Bhupendra Yadav, 'Tilak: Communalist or Political Pragmatist', in Biswamoy Pati (ed.), *Bal Gangadhar Tilak: Popular Readings* (Delhi, 2010), p. 56.

16   I. K. Yagnik, *Gandhi As I Knew Him* (Lucknow, 1943), p. 19.

17   B.K. Nehru, *Nice Guys Finish Second* (Delhi, 1997), p. 23.

18   Nehru, *An Autobiography*, p. 35.

19   Anne Guthrie, *Madame Ambassador: The Life of Vijaya Lakshmi Pandit* (New York, 1962), pp. 15-17, 25-6.

20   Nehru, *An Autobiography*, p. 72; Vera Brittain, *Envoy Extraordinary: A Study of Vijaya Lakshmi Pandit and her contribution to Modern India* (London, 1943), p. 43.

21   Gandhi to Morshead, Commissioner, 13 Apr. 1917, in B.B. Misra (ed.), *Select Documents on Mahatma Gandhi's Movement in Champaran 1917-18* (Bihar, 1963), p. 59.

coming on 4 March 1916,[22] the indigo planters and the district officials panicked. On 10 April 1917, Gandhi travelled to Patna, met Mazharul Haque, a fellow student of his in London, and left for Champaran the following morning. In Muzaffarpur, his next halt, he encountered Acharya J.B. Kripalani, then a college teacher. Rajendra Prasad, another fresh acquaintance, didn't take to Gandhi at first, but vouched for his approach within weeks.

The dominant impulse under British rule was that of fear: a pervasive, oppressive, strangling fear; fear of the army and the police; fear of the official class; fear of laws meant to suppress and of prison; fear of the landlord's agent; fear of the moneylender; fear of unemployment and starvation, which were always on the threshold. Gandhi raised his quiet and determined voice against this all-pervading fear.[23] At the dawn of history he had learnt from Janaka and Yajnavalkya that the leader's function was to make their people fearless. This lesson would have been at the back of his mind. By submitting to the penalty of disobedience, he reiterated his conviction in Fearlessness (*abhaya*) and Truth, and action allied to them.[24]

As in 1894 in Durban, in 1903 in Johannesburg, and in 1913 in Newcastle, he saw an opportunity to fight fear and helplessness. 'For me', he stated, 'the road to salvation lies through incessant toil in the services of my country and of humanity.'[25]

The insights from these years were the best and speediest road to fame. As for the audience, they understood the relative unity, force, and objectiveness of his thinking and speech and responded well to his transforming the Congress, a pressure group of the classes, to a mass movement. In Bihar, he tasted success when the government abandoned the proceedings taken against him.

---

22   4 Mar. 1916, ibid., p.51.

23   Jawaharlal Nehru, *The Discovery of India* (Delhi, 1985), p. 358.

24   It is in this light that one interprets his letter to Motihari's sub-divisional magistrate on 18 April 1917. Andrews (ed.). *Mahatma Gandhi: His Own Story*, p. 338.

25   Rajmohan Gandhi, *Mohandas: A True Story of a Man, his People and an Empire* (Delhi, 2006), p. 203; Andrews, op. cit., p. 338.

As Gandhi moved about in the villages, asking the poor and the landless to voice their grievances,[26] his admirers spoke of his deeds in songs, stories, and pamphlets.[27] Rajendra Prasad, Mazharul Haque and Syed Hasan Imam, the lawyer, became his trusted allies in Bihar;[28] Birla and Bajaj hauled his cart through the streets of Calcutta's Bara Bazaar and shouted '*Karamvir* Gandhi *ki jai*'. His lifestyle impressed Birla.[29] The 'warmth of militant fire' had been kindled in Gandhi, when Indulal Yagnik hosted Gandhi in Godhra (Gujarat) in January 1917.[30] He recognised him and the Congress to be inseparable in the rough and tumble of unparalleled activism. His enthusiasm couldn't stand on its own without being juxtaposed against the nationwide caravan with the Congress as its centrepiece.

The Whiteheads—Right Reverend Henry and his wife Isabel—were Gandhi's admirers from the time the Bishop of Madras served as the president of the South African League. When he arrived on 13 February 1916 by slow train, third class, they were immediately struck by 'a delightful person, very simple in his life and very warm hearted and affectionate and most responsive to the appeals of poverty and suffering'. Two days later, they introduced their guest to friends in Madras, and acted as the conduit between him and the many Westerners who favoured the aspirations of the Congress.[31]

C. Rajagopalachari (CR) believed, when comparing Gandhi with Tilak: 'Here are two men who … may well be literally worshipped as a real embodiment of the Spirit of Bharata Varsha, whose words and acts have passed through the Sacrificial Fire, in whom love of country

---

26   W.H. Lewis to W.B. Heycock, 29 Apr. 1917, Appendix D to Proceeding No. 323 of Home Pol., A, July 1917, Nos. 314-40, p. 102; 28 Apr. 1917, *Selected Documents on Mahatma Gandhi's Movement in Champaran*, p. 96.

27   Jacques Pouchepadass, *Champaran and Gandhi: Planters, Peasants and Gandhian Politics* (Delhi, 1999), p. 232.

28   Prasad, *Autobiography*, p. 86; K.K. Datta, *History of the Freedom Movement in Bihar*, vol. 1 (Patna, 1957), p. 279.

29   Medha M. Kudaisya, *The Life and Times of G.D.Birla* (Delhi, 2003), p. 39.

30   Yagnik, *Gandhi As I Knew Him*, p. 22.

31   Susan Billington Harper, *In the Shadow of the Mahatma: Bishop V.S. Azariah and the Travails of Christianity in British India* (Michigan, 2000).

and political thought burn with the fire and the light of true religion.'[32] Jawaharlal wrote of the 'thrill' of listening to his quiet and low voice that was somewhat different from the others, and yet there seemed to be steel hidden away somewhere in it. Courteous and appealing, every word of his carried meaning and earnestness. The path of Self-purification was hard and steep, and to attain 'perfect purity', a man or woman had to rise above the opposing currents of love and hatred, attachment and repulsion, and to become absolutely passion-free in thought, speech and action.[33]

From Porbandar to Durban

The Indian states differed greatly in size, population, and importance. Hyderabad, a historic city, was as large as Italy. 'What a magnificent scene', wrote a French traveller in 1937, as he witnessed the minarets soar the sky and the white houses and terraces tinted with the ever changing hues of the sunset. 'One minute they were rose, then they became mauve, afterwards, a red-orange halo enriched the entire city. Some minutes later, the traveller was among the crowd: noise, music, fez, an odour of musk, camels with their proud heads held high ... Thousands of lights twinkle out.'[34] At the other end of the scale were minute holdings in Kathiawar of a few acres only. It abounded in tiny states largely due to Jonathan Duncan's benevolence. The governor of Bombay (1795-1811) recognised people as 'Princes': it all depended on how they paid their dues to the Paramount power.

Mohandas, born on 2 October 1869, spent his childhood in a surrounding with all the infinite variety and charm of the expanse of ocean around it. His father, Karamchand Gandhi, following in the footsteps of his forefathers, served as Porbandar's dewan for twenty-five years, as also of Rajkot and other states in Kathiawar. Putlibai, his wife, ran a comfortable and well-managed home and exercised a dominant influence on her son. He received a 'Messianic turn' from her temperament.[35] He was never

---

32   Kumar (ed.), *Essays on Gandhian Politics*, p. 67.

33   Jawaharlal Nehru, *Glimpses of World History* (Allahabad, 1939), p. 713; Andrews (ed.), *Mahatma Gandhi: His Own Story*, p. 334.

34   Louis Revel, *The Fragrance of India: Landmarks for the world of tomorrow* (Bombay, 1946), p. 189.

35   Chandulal Bhagubhai Dalal, *Harilal Gandhi: A Life* (Delhi, 2007), p. xxv.

fond of gloom, but had sufficient sunshine during his younger days. He had shown himself wild, dissipated, and addicted to low pleasures, but he cast them aside among the forgotten and forgiven frailties of youth, and seldom thought of them again, except in his *My Experiments with Truth*, an autobiography written in the midst of struggle rather than in retirement. He had a personal attachment to and pleasant memories of the time he spent at home.

The boy completed schooling at Rajkot in 1887. Next year, he married Kasturba, also thirteen; it had an invigorating and eventually beneficial effect on them. They were together for the first five years and were evidently happy. All the circumstances of their situation seemed to draw them together; they were like two grown up children who go hand in hand, pressing closely to each other. The young bride maintained her poised dignity and gave birth to a son in 1888, called Harilal. In this way, she continued the illustrious breed as a matter of duty and conscience. On September 4, Mohandas travelled to London to study law. Full of misgivings and awe, Kasturba may have held Mohan's hand in her own trembling one and broken into a little nervous, hysterical laugh, more touching than any tears could be.

Gandhi sailed for England, a voyage Rajmohan Gandhi, his biographer, describes elegantly. In London, he suffered deeply from solitude and time and again nearly lost his bearings. His mother's love haunted him: 'at night the tears would stream down my cheeks, and home memories of all sorts made sleep out of the question'. Eventually however he showed grit and determination. He didn't, it is true, attain nearly the full measure of what might have been his faculties, but recovered them sufficiently to prepare for the life of a lawyer. Articled to a solicitor, he would every now and again put on his best clothes and go to a dance hall in the evening. A picture of him in his black suit and bowler hat would make him laugh in later years as he enjoyed the contrast to his by then world-famous position. He grasped the *English spirit* or the *English genius*, the largeness of vision in British institutions, the emotion, pathos, humour, and depth in English prose and poetry, the freshness of scientific discoveries, and religious tolerance. Even so, the aggressive codes of modern day living irritated him and self-doubt tormented him. Industry showed up badly beside agricultural life. In most other cases and contingencies, he was repelled by lust and brigandage, reckless fantasies, and the cult of materialism with all its cruel and intermittently dreadful costs. Rather than the delight in living or the display of love and high spiritual aspiration, he felt awkward with Victorian moral values without being in any sense a moral rebel. Instead, he drew on his inherited core of religious and intellectual ethics to concretise his thinking on appropriate conduct.

'If we have faith enough,' Gandhi stated on 3 November 1917, 'we can wield that force over the whole world. Religion having lost its hold on us, we are without an anchor to keep us firm amidst the storm of modern civilisation, and are therefore being tossed to and fro.'[36] As he gained more than a nodding familiarity with the *Gita*, which he read during 1888-9 and later recognised as his *kamadhenu*, his guide, on hundreds of moments of doubt and difficulty, he felt enormously exhilarated by supplication, worship, and prayer. This prayer ground was the only place where he'd make political points; and bring 'revolution' into the content of prayers.[37] The *Gita*, after all, helps even those 'who wander in the region of the many and variable',[38] and gives utterance to the aspirations of pilgrims and all those seeking to tread the inner way to the city of God. Indeed, the *Gita* represents not only Hinduism alone but religion as such, in its universality, without limit of time and space.[39]

Stray ideas seized Gandhi once he dug in his heels and fought the bouts of homesickness. In spite of that, his immediate thought, for which he had made personal sacrifices and for which his parents had borne the burden of separation, was to earn the law degree. As it transpired, he was called to the Bar from the Inner Temple on 10 June 1891. At this juncture his thoughts would have been all wrapped up in the pleasure and prosperity and ambition of a life at home.

Back home, his soul in entirety was burning with enthusiasm, but success in his profession didn't knock at his door. He may have given

---

36   M.K. Gandhi, *Speeches and Writings*, with an introduction by C.F. Andrews (Madras, n.d.), p. 348.

37   Gandhi (ed.), *Gandhi is Gone*, p. 92.

38   Radhakrishnan, *The Bhagavadgita*, p. 11.

39   Ibid., p. 12.

it a miss given his restless disposition, a natural or inbuilt reticence, and rugged honesty;[40] the pompous atmosphere of Bombay High Court and the elaborate ceremonials designed to strike Indians with awe and reverence. His heart sank and his head reeled when it came to cross-examining the plaintiff's witnesses.[41] He begged to be relieved of his case and left the Court 'in shame and anguish, vowing not to appear again until he had learned to master himself and could use his brain and body as the instruments of his will'.[42]

Gandhi, of course, gave a different twist to his temperament. Shyness was his shield and buckler; it helped in his discernment.[43] Jinnah, also a Gujarati, whose home and family gave him an exceptionally close and sheltered background, set about acquiring fame and fortune with astonishing speed. Admitted to the Bar in 1905, five years after Gandhi, he learnt his politics at Naoroji's feet. Gandhi, too, learnt a great deal from this Parsi wizard,[44] but the contrast in their style and disposition became apparent in next to no time.

Making the Indian Self

As far back as November 1860, the first Indian labourers were shipped to South Africa from Calcutta and Madras. Three decades later, Natal alone had 41,142 Indians. Leavened by a sprinkling of Muslim merchants of higher standing, they were mostly of humble Hindu origin. In 1893, one such merchant, Abu Bakr Amod Jhaveri, invited Gandhi to Natal to represent him in a business dispute with his brother. He confronted the white colonists over the Muslims wearing headgear, a day after landing in South Africa on 22 May 1893. He protested. He proved his mettle. Thereafter, he wrestled with intricate legal cases, and, in the process, added to his readings

---

40   C.F. Andrews, *Mahatma Gandhi's Ideas: Including Selections from his Writings* (London, 1929), p. viii.

41   M.R. Jayakar, *The Story of My Life* (Bombay, 1959), vol. 2 for professional life in the Bombay High Court, pp. 52-56.

42   H.S.L. and M.G. Polak, 'Mohandas Karamchand Gandhi', in L.F. Rushbrook Williams (ed.), *Great Men of India* (Colombo, n.d.), p. 320.

43   Ibid., p. 62.

44   Wolpert, *Jinnah of Pakistan*, p. 17; 3 Nov. 1917, *CWMG* (Aug. 1919-Jan. 1920), pp. 124-25.

of law books to further his self-education. He upset the status quo. His critics speedily called him 'An Unwelcome Visitor', a pariah, and the Law Society swifty opposed his application for Supreme Court membership on the ground that a colonial person could not be admitted to practise.

Gandhi longed to express himself and he did so remarkably well: his new-found friendships, some of which endured for decades, gave him an opportunity to do so. Soon, his reputation soared with the repeal of an old Republican law of 1885 setting out how the Asiatics in the Transvaal area, the most industrialised and wealthy land on the African continent, lived and conducted business within certain areas. His mental and moral courage, which he displayed consistently, raised him far above the common standard of achievement in leading his fellow men.[45]

Gandhi's ejection from a first-class compartment traumatised him.[46] In spite of that, he dealt with his personal ordeal at Pietermaritzburg not merely by drafting petitions and representations, the standard practice of the 'moderate' Congress leaders in India, but by exposing racism and the incredibly mind-blowing laws. Taking a long-term view and bearing in mind his matchless probity and innocence, he almost perfected the art of revealing the wrongdoings of the white ruling class. The buoyant optimism of his speeches and writings contain little other than revealing a mind in revolt. This didn't mean that an unfocused despair didn't grow within him. What had he in common with the white people? Would they laugh if he described his encounter at the Grand National Hotel in Johannesburg? Would they laugh at a policeman's threatening posture in front of President Paul Kruger's house in Pretoria? No, they wouldn't. Only a few would smile politely, and then bow their heads, acknowledging his difference from them.

Notwithstanding the inner turmoil, Gandhi's conversion to 'passive resistance' strengthened the self in him and established the symbolic

---

45   Lt.-Colonel The Hon. C.B. Birdwood, *A Continent Experiments* (London, 1945), p. 47.

46   'If it wasn't character forming, it must have been character arousing to be ejected,' writes Lelyveld in *Great Soul*.

basis for future actions. One of the earliest mention of *Satyagraha* goes like this: 'Call this force *daya-bal* [love-force], call it *atmabal* [soul force] or call it Satyagraha.'[47] Satyagraha seemed like 'an infallible panacea'. Without leading to chaos or confusion, it had suited 'the nursery of the most ancient religions and had very little to learn from modern civilisation—a civilisation based on aggression of the blackest type, largely a negation of the Divine in man, and which is rushing headlong to its own ruin'. The idea came from a Gujarati poem which Gandhi learnt at school as a child. Quite probably, it also came from the passages from the Sermon on the Mount.[48] In next to no time, Gandhi became an exemplar of self-reliance, assuring the sober, industrious, and honest South African Indians of an upward climb. His image of himself is the popular conception of the self-created man whose own will, so he believed, would determine his destiny.

Gandhi resisted racism. He set up the Natal Indian Congress on 22 August 1895, a smart move to lend coherence to disparate groups pulling one another in different directions. He quickened their conscience too. He was, throughout, a self-propelled whirlwind, in constant motion from meeting to meeting, rally to rally, riding up and down the railway where he encountered his first fateful venture just two years earlier.[49] He recalled the horrors perpetrated on the Zulus during the Zulu Rebellion, the lacerated backs of those who had received stripes and were brought to the ambulance corps which he headed because no white nurse was prepared to look after them. His strictures were all perfectly justified.

In Natal, Gandhi was denied entry to the church where Andrews had been invited to preach. He stated candidly to Rev. S.S. Tema from Johannesburg that Christianity, as was known and practised during his days, couldn't bring salvation to his people.[50] The church seemed

---

47   Ajay Skaria, 'The Strange Violence of Satyagraha: Gandhi, *Ithihaas*, and History', in Bhagavan (ed.), *Heterotopias*, p. 177.

48   Gandhi would repeat: 'Resist not him that is evil: but whosoever smiteth thee on thy right cheek, turn to him the other also,' and 'Love your enemies and pray for those who persecute you that you may be sons of your Father who is in heaven.'

49   Lelyveld, *Great Soul*, p. 113.

50   *Harijan*, 18 Feb. 1939, *CWMG* (Oct. 15, 1938-Feb. 28, 1939), p. 273.

unbearably cold, promising nothing but sin and repentance. Christianity, with its present unholy alliance with the white race, was unable to cope with the evil of racism.[51]

In a racially-segregated social order, all dignity of life was lost. In a polity where dissent invariably led to the ignominy of arrest, imprisonment, and deportation, the authorities adopted the same methods to counter Gandhi. For his part, he emerged not only smiling, often before the expiry of the sentence imposed, but learnt with good effect the ways and means of rescuing the indentured from an eternity of suffering. He had learnt to free himself from the sentimentality that had so often overwhelmed him in London, and the melodramatic tendencies which he so vividly narrated in his autobiography. So much so, that life ceased to be a dim prelude to the promise of immortality but the fulfilment of a promise to God to strive for self-realisation by 'a humble aspirant for perfection'. The blackness he had known and could depict from experience and the ideal he had already discovered, both co-existed in his creative mind; both propelled him to accomplish his announced goal.

A.R. Chamney arrived in Dublin as an immigration officer shortly after 1902. He 'found a much younger man than his fame had led him to picture him'. Dressed in neat European clothes, he spoke quickly rather than fluently, quoting from Charles Dickens, the Sermon on the Mount, and Tolstoy, whose works he had read in 1908-9 and 'enjoyed thoroughly': 'they have a ring of truth about them which other works seem to me to lack'.[52] With his rare gift of making a good impression at a first meeting, he discussed 'with frankness and without any sign of the astuteness characteristic of his official or political utterances'.[53] Chamney, and others like him, had unconsciously flattered themselves with the idea that there would be a gleam or halo of some kind about his persona, which would ensure an acceptance of his sterling gentility, or, at least, a tacit recognition of it.

---

51   Tinker, *The Ordeal of Love*, p. 88.

52   Gandhi to Kallenbach, 3 Jan. 1909, Gandhi-Kallenbach papers.

53   A.R. Chamney, 'Mahatma Gandhi in the Transvaal' (TS), CSAS, Cambridge, p. 9.

'Art is inspiration,' commented William Blake; so is politics. All said and done, while others did certain things painfully and imperfectly, Gandhi had an inborn aptitude and propensity to do them comparatively easily. While most stood apart and coldly exposed others without desiring to help them, Gandhi, watchful and wary, brought out the inner truth of his character by exposing oppression and exploitation. 'Unadulterated' passive resistance is what he believed in to overcome the suffering in the Transvaal. He had faith enough in suffering to know that it would speak for itself.[54] Later, when he was asked if one should not press one's pursuit of truth upon the world, Gandhi, looking down as the questioner tensely waited, replied that truth couldn't be so circumscribed and its expression 'has in it the seeds of propagation, even as the sun cannot hide its light'.[55] There wasn't an ounce of pride or hypocrisy in him; all that he did – his writings allude to this – arose from an intuitive love for human beings. In 1913, the viceroy himself expressed 'the sympathy of India, deep and burning ... and of all lovers of India for their compatriots in South Africa in their resistance to invidious and unjust laws'.

'Where is Mr. Gandhi?' Andrews asked on the Durban quay where Polak and Kallenbach greeted him in early January 1914. Polak turned to a slight ascetic figure, dressed in a white *dhoti* and *kurta* of such coarse material as an indentured labourer might wear. Andrews bent down swiftly and touched his feet.[56] Gandhi made known in a low tone, 'Pray do not do that, it is a humiliation to me'.[57]

When did people first call Gandhi 'Mahatma'? In South Africa, it happened by 1908, fifteen years after his arrival. In India, Jawaharlal stumbled upon him first in 1916; he was Mahatma then. Sarojini Naidu met him a year earlier; he was already a Mahatma.[58] It was a perfect end to a perfect stay. Naoroji's granddaughter applauded:

---

54   Gandhi to Kallenbach, 17 July 1909, Gandhi-Kallenbach papers.

55   Tendulkar, *Mahatma*, vol. 4, p. 13.

56   Benarsidas Chaturvedi and Marjorie Sykes, *Charles Freer Andrews: A Narrative* (London, 1949), p. 94.

57   Tinker, *The Ordeal of Love*, p. 84.

58   Padmini Sengupta, *Sarojini Naidu: A Biography* (Bombay, 1966), p. 86.

I met the South African Mr. Gandhi last summer. I found him an extremely interesting and sincere man. He simply worships you. I had a very long talk with him about the organisation of the agitation in South Africa and all he said about it was that they had your example before them and they were following it with perfect faith.

Naoroji felt happy that his granddaughter had met 'Mr. Gandhi, a very good man', who had been 'fighting a great patriotic battle'.[59]

Hind Swaraj: A Testament of Hope

If the intellectual is the critical conscience of the general public in each of its historical epochs, his role is to question and to deal critically with contemporary society and culture. We see Gandhi doing just that in *Hind Swaraj*, written in Gujarati and serialised in the Gujarati edition of *Indian Opinion*, the weekly newspaper. The tract, reflecting the best of Gandhi's thinking in the form developed in South Africa, conceptualises some of the central problems and concerns of a world in violent flux, of apartheid, of colonialism, of monarchies, and despotism. Its ideas could have been derived from Plato's concept of an ideal state and from the impulse to react against the moral and spiritual decay of the nation state, although *Hind Swaraj* distils the author's experience up to then and his plans for the future. As a confession of faith and a justification of passive resistance, it conjures up clear, transparent, and intense pictures, excels in delineating human character, and reveals the exalted consciousness of self, which develops into a penetrating and complex psychological reflection, and finally, becomes a philosophy. Here the inner vision is fully realised. Long years after the publication of *Hind Swaraj*, Gandhi recalled:

I am enunciating no new ideas here. They are to be found in *Indian Home Rule* (*Hind Swaraj*) which was written in 1908 when the technique of Satyagraha was still in the process of formation. The *charkha* had become part of this mission of love. As I was picturing

---

59   Gandhi papers, NAI; and for Gokhale, see Gandhi, *Speeches and Writings*, p. xv.

life based on non-violence, I saw that it must be reduced to the simplest terms consistent with high thinking.[60]

In 1910, a cartoon in *New Age*, an English journal, represented the epitome of the hypocrisy of the Industrial era that had grown as terrible as a wolf through its hunger for wealth and pursuit of worldly pleasures.[61] Just a couple of years earlier, *Hind Swaraj* depicted the ills of the Industrial Age, asserted innovative principles, spelt out facets of Thoreau's asceticism, and defined the outline of a possibly, 'gigantic transformation'. At least, it offers to a new *Yuga* dharma for a sustainable moral civilisation. Like Lord Krishna, who motivated Arjuna to perform the inherent duty (*swadharma*), Gandhi, through the dialogic mode, sought liberation from the lure of the modern materialistic world, and inspired people to adhere to true swaraj.[62] He modified some statements and underplayed others without toning down his disparaging remarks on Western civilisation. He essentialised the West without diluting his intense judgment.

In British India, the poor toiled under a huge machine that exploited and crushed them: the machine of the new imperialism. As Western Europe advanced, the land of Buddha and Asoka grew steadily more poverty-stricken. Behind the jewel on the crown was a tale of squalor, hunger, filth, disease, and beggary.[63] Grinding poverty became the basic reality in the myriad mud villages and in the dark hovels and alleys

---

60   *Harijan*, 13 Jan. 1940, *CWMG* (1 Dec. 1939-15 Apr. 1940), p. 94.

61   Ramashray Roy, *Gandhi and Ambedkar: A Study in Contrast* (Delhi, 2006), p. 126.

62   Anthony J. Parel (ed.), *Gandhi: 'Hind Swaraj' and Other Writings* (Delhi, 1997); M.P. Mathai and John Moolakkattu (eds), *Exploring Hind Swaraj* (Delhi, 2009), p. 6.

63   Charles Allen (ed.), *Plain Tales from the Raj* (London, 1975), p. 246. A great poet of an earlier day wrote about another land that suffered colonial rule bemoaning: 'She stood before her traitors bound and bare,/ Clothed with her wounds and with her naked shame/ As with a weed of fiery tears and flame,/ Their mother-land, their common weal and care,/ And they turned from her and denied, and sware/ They did not know this woman nor her name./ And they took truce with tyrants and grew tame,/ And gathered up cast crowns and creeds to wear,/ And rags and shards regilded. Then she took/ In her bruised hands their broken pledge, and eyed/ These men so late and so loud upon her side/ With one inevitable and tearless look,/ That they might see her face whom they forsook;/ And they beheld what they had left, and died.'

of the towns, driving a growing number of people every year into the legion of beggars.[64] Gandhi, who severely berated the British connection, attributed their ruin to virtually direct plunder, thinly disguised as commerce. India spun and wove in her millions of cottages, but the incredibly heartless and inhuman processes ruined the weavers. As for the narrative of loss and salvage, which is one of the major themes in *Hind Swaraj*, Gandhi reclaimed spinning to reinvigorate rural life. Spinning and the *charkha* became the essence of India's iconography.[65] He decided to chant the *khadi mantra* as long as there was life in him, believing it would bring deliverance.[66] He hoped that the weaving looms would serve to feed millions of starving poor and also be a nucleus for Congress activism in villages. He therefore wanted the people to be supplied with cotton on credit as well as spinning wheels and carding apparatus, wishing too that their wages be credited to their account. All of India had to accept the spinning wheel as a daily sacrament, and the use of homespun cloth as a privilege and a duty.[67] Acharya Kripalani, having dismissed spinning, took it up when 'that old man made a connection between spinning wheel and revolution'.[68]

At the beginning of the Second World War, Gandhi may well have inspired Josh Malihabadi, the Urdu poet, to write 'An Address to the Sons of the East India Company', a popular poem that became so popular that students and others formed processions and went round singing it from street to street, with the demonstrators being trailed everywhere by the police. Josh captures, in this enchanting poem, some of the ugly features of British rule:

Do you recall the story of your limitless oppression?
Do you recall the Company's age of crime?

---

64   M.K. Gandhi, *An Autobiography or the Story of My Experiments with Truth*, trans. from the original in Gujarati by Mahadev Desai (Ahmedabad, 1927), p. 434.

65   Rebecca M. Brown, *Gandhi's Spinning Wheel and the Making of India* (London, 2010), pp. 8-9.

66   *CWMG* (1 Dec. 1939-15 Apr. 1940), p. 64.

67   Andrews, *Mahatma Gandhi's Ideas*, p. 370.

68   Gandhi (ed.), *Gandhi is Gone.*, p. 92.

When in caravan upon caravan the wealth of India
Was circulating unprotected, you went round looting it.
You went round cutting off the weavers' thumbs
You filled their weaving pits with their lifeless corpses.
Death overtook the handicrafts of India.
What death was that?—The death brought by your hand.[69]

Hind Swaraj has both popular and quasi-scholarly dimensions. Jawaharlal described it as completely unreal, though, to be sure, the contents helped to shape the mood through the nature of the subject and the drive behind Gandhi's impulse to reflect on the blending of politics, ethics, and morality. Today, its contents are read and interpreted differently,[70] but the consensus is that *Hind Swaraj* disentangles the needless controversies of contemporary life. Not content with a diagnosis of gloom and leaving it at that, it holds out a promise and a cure to stimulate change. At this level of thought, Gandhi's solutions were neither transient nor territorially bound. They were universally relevant. Gandhi himself contended that his experiences since 1908-9 lent credence to them and confirmed the truth of his beliefs.

As for Gandhi's assertions or intellectual apprehensions on the goals and objectives of an industrial civilisation, they require extensive research for them to be either proved or disproved. Their beauty however lies in looking at life through the eyes of childhood with all its power of illusion and hope. The contrasting images are, similarly, interesting: the image of innocent joy and love and the disenchantment brought by experience. The *Gita* conditioned his reflexes so completely that he found no joy in transgressing its prescribed boundaries, whereas the Christian and Islamic texts extended and enriched his understanding. He realised both and lived them passionately and fervently.

The first volume of *The Story of My Experiments with Truth* appeared in 1927, and the second two years later. It was probably inspired by Tolstoy's

---

69   Translated from Urdu and introduced by Christopher Shackle, Nijhawan
       (ed.), *Nationalism in the Vernacular*, p. 199.

70   Partha Chatterjee, *Nationalist Thought and the Colonial World: A Derivative
       Discourse* (Delhi, 1986), pp. 85-87.

work *My Confession*, about which Gandhi wrote: 'No writings have so deeply touched Mr. Kallenbach as yours, and, as a spur to further effort in living up to the ideals held before the world by you, he has taken the liberty, after consultation with me, of naming his farm after you.' Gandhi sent Tolstoy the relevant issues of *Indian Opinion*.[71] Like *Hind Swaraj*, *The Story of My Experiments with Truth* captured the anger and indignation over the appointment of an all-white Statutory Commission on 8 November 1927. The Congress in Madras voted to boycott it, proclaimed Independence as its goal, and decided to draft a constitution. The Liberal Federation, the Muslim League, and the Hindu Mahasabha on 12 February 1928 joined this enterprise. Motilal and Jawaharlal were there, as were Jinnah, Ansari, Sapru, the UP politician Rafi Ahmed Kidwai, Lajpat Rai, M.M. Malaviya, Bombay lawyer and legislator M.R. Jayakar, and most other politicians of consequence. Ansari, the Congress President at Madras, had intervened on innumerable occasions on such matters. Encouraged, his optimistic, liberal, and rationalist nature asserted itself.

The Story ... expresses Gandhi's innermost feelings and impassionate detachment. The site of the self becomes a site of relentless self-examination and rigorous trial of oneself against certain timeless values. Gandhi believed in a core private self that was 'incommunicable', and hence couldn't be narrated. His account, in this way, becomes a transcendental narrative where the act of writing helps the narrator to cross the limitation of the self itself.[72] Such is the underlying moral basis of exalted commitments that a moving sincerity emanates from the book. Besides lyrically revealing the uniqueness of individual destiny and correcting the value of emotion for its own sake and as an end in itself, boundaries of disputes are, quite often, overwhelmed by a moral and political point of view. To those who read the book, Gandhi's story guided all those who had been waiting in a stage of transitional indecision.

A rather flattering comment came from Mrs H.R. Scott, a missionary in Surat. She found the *The Story* ... written in Gandhi's clear and

---

71   Gandhi to Tolstoy, 15 Aug. 1910, Steve Linde papers.

72   E.V. Ramakrishnan, *Locating Indian Literature: Texts, Traditions, Translations* (Delhi, 2011), p. 65.

fascinating style, and was certain of its wide circulation. Moreover, 'it will certainly help the cause of social reform, encourage liberty and independent thinking ...'[73]

In sum, the autobiography and *The Story* ..., besides having a great stimulative influence among sections of the intelligentsia, pointed to Gandhi's deep and continual preoccupation with ethical standards, and a conception of society rooted in principles which, for all their individuality of emphasis, are characteristic of the pattern of, broadly speaking, Indian thought. The books have stood the test of time also because they give flesh and blood to 'the greatest struggle of modern times' in the Transvaal. Writing to Tolstoy from Westminster Palace Hotel on 4 Victoria Street in London, he couldn't accept distress and trauma as the *natural* arrangement. He continued: 'I am not aware of a struggle in which the participators aren't to derive any personal advantage at the end of it, and in which 50 per cent of the persons affected have undergone great suffering and trial for the sake of a principle.'[74]

On Louis Napoleon's coup d'état in 1851, Karl Marx had commented that 'men make their own history, but they do not make it just as they please; they do not make it under circumstances chosen by themselves, but under circumstances directly encountered, given and transmitted from the past ...' In South Africa, Gandhi subordinated all other goals and made a determined bid to change the status quo. Taking off the turban he customarily wore in the Supreme Court, he announced, 'I should not exhaust my skill as a fighter'. 'Remembering—which is also recreating—the various pasts and histories that may appear to constitute a nation ... requires a new perception of the politics of the present, if those pasts are to be remembered for the good of all the nations ... including those whose string was indeed broken.'[75]

Besides Henry David Thoreau, Ruskin's *Unto This Last* transformed Gandhi overnight from a lawyer and city dweller into a rustic living

---

73   To Director of Public Instruction, 13 March 1928, IOR, Hugh Robert Scott papers (C 487).

74   Gandhi to Tolstoy, 10 Nov. 1909, Steve Linde papers. Dennis Walder, *Postcolonial Nostalgias: Writing, Representation, and Memory* (London, 2011), p. 71.

75   Walder, op. cit., p. 71.

far away from Durban on a farm. Tolstoy furnished a reasoned basis for non-violence and ideas of the basic moral value of physical labour and of natural diet. Kallenbach introduced elements of the *kibbutz* movement, and Kropotkin, the idea of a country of village communes. Oscar Wilde extolled Kropotkin's life as 'one of the most perfect lives' in his own experience. With these complex, diversified and shifting conceptions around him, Gandhi's inner process of self-realisation took place. With this came the desire to create a world in which the values centring on the individual would gain precedence over, and even be in conflict with, the collective. In this context, Gandhi trod a middle path, free alike from the outstanding merits and the disturbing faults of more spectacular Indian revolutionaries. He disagreed with Madame Bhikaji Cama's rhetoric of armed rebellion, although he went into virtual raptures over her 'patriotic fervour' and published some of her writings in *Indian Opinion* just before Cama famously unfurled the first Indian tricolour in the German town of Stuttgart.[76]

Priests and scholars gave Gandhi inkling into a hitherto little known area of discussion: comparative religions. Christian influences kept alive in him the religious sense. Theosophists drew him into their fold. He later devoted himself entirely to an almost random reading towards which his political commitments and his moral rigour directed his attention. He assiduously read Max Müller on the Vedas, biographies of the Prophet of Islam, works on Buddhism, and a book on Zoroastrianism. He read Edwin Arnold's verse translation, *The Song Celestial*, and his epic poem *Light of Asia*, on the Buddha. Besides opening up to him the new frontiers of knowledge, these readings encouraged him to put into practice whatever appealed to him. One of them was to amalgamate ideas of quite different religions and cultural praxis. Thus, every now and again he'd refer to the Truth in Buddhist and Brahmanical texts, or give examples of Christian forbearance and forgiveness. He'd periodically proclaim that Rama was the same everywhere, whether called Allah, Khuda, Rahim, Razzaq (bread giver), or any other name that comes

---

76   Dinyar Patel, 'Like the Countless Leaves of One Tree', 'Gandhi and the Parsis', the 'Prince of Wales Riots', and the 'Rights of Minorities' (unpublished paper).

from the heart of a faithful devotee. This is what Kabir and Guru Nanak had taught. By and large, the 'Christ of the Sabarmati' (a reference to M.K. Gandhi by Sarojini Naidu) spoke the sterner truth, but neither as apocalyptically as Swami Vivekananda, nor seductively, as Tagore.

The harmony of temperament and life were, from the outset, united in a fusion with political creed and approach. True, Gandhi neither defined nor elucidated the meanings of certain terms in a standardised fashion. When asked to precisely define swaraj, he refused to settle for a single word or a set of words. Instead, he laboriously traced its roots through a rare and felicitous harmony to the deep felt longing for self-rule. In common parlance, Independence could mean the licence to do as one wished and be construed negatively, but Gandhi considered swaraj to be a sacred word, a Vedic word, which meant, sufficiently comprehensively, self-restraint, self-control, and self-discipline. Moreover, *his* swaraj was the poor man's swaraj. This was to stress his empathy with the poor and resistance to servitude and tyranny. He expected a true satyagrahi to do the same, that is, to create a moral universe where truth, uprightness, justice, fair dealing, and open-mindedness would prevail.

If passive resistance was the divine force, Satyagraha was the master key to the innumerable hardships in individual and collective life. In this way, Gandhi made evident the consistency of his thought and deed. When he referred to Satyagraha in Bagasra (in Kathiawar), the secretary of the Bombay government objected. 'Is this not a threat?' he asked. Gandhi replied that he had merely placed before the people remedies for legitimate grievances: 'The struggle is important and it must be prolonged and why not? The more prolonged it is, the greater the opportunity for the people to educate themselves in a most practical and effective manner.'[77] As a non-violent weapon and a sovereign remedy, Satyagraha was, for him personally, a conspicuous milestone, a biographical episode of considerable significance, and his model or prototype for effective political action.[78]

By the time Gandhi left Cape Town on 18 July 1914, he had good reasons to treasure Satyagraha, though he didn't trade on it. Modest

---

77   Ibid., 9 Feb. 1909.

78   Lelyveld, *Great Soul*, p. 105.

and self-effacing, he reversed the fortunes of the indentured. Once, every Indian was called a 'coolie'; now that name was erased as a prefix. India had been elevated by a man and a method.[79] With his fledgling experiments in the crucible of South Africa, he would return time and time again to weaken the moral and ideological foundations of a cruel, almost barbaric regime. From South Africa, 'the cradle of Satyagraha', Sarojini Naidu applauded in early 1924: 'I cannot sleep in South Africa and it's all your fault. You haunt the land and its soil is impregnated with the memory of your wonderful struggle, sacrifice and triumph.'[80]

Bearing the Cross

The 'meek but oh! How mighty Mahatma!' A beam of light pierced the darkness and a whirlwind to upset many things. Gandhi spoke the language of the millions, drawing incessant attention to their plight. Typically, behind the language of peace that he spoke, was the quivering shadow of action and a determination not to submit to a wrong.[81] These were largely Jawaharlal's words; his most familiar lines make their impact anew at every encounter. Although the words remain the same, their effect is infinitely variable.

Miss Madeline Slade (later given the name Mirabehn by Gandhi), the thirty-three-year-old daughter of an English admiral, was perhaps Gandhi's closest woman companion. Almost immediately after coming to India, she realised his extraordinary hold. Besides the pressing, surging crowds that thronged the platform at every station, the air throbbed with the cry 'Mahatma Gandhi ki Jai' (Victory to Mahatma Gandhi):

> The faces did not reflect the excitement of people out to catch a glimpse of a celebrity, but the eager, thirsting look of devotees seeking to set eyes on some holy person, a savior on whom they had pinned all their hopes with a faith which they would not have

---

79   E. Stanley Jones, *Mahatma Gandhi: An Interpretation* (London, 1948), p. 189.

80   Sarojini Naidu to Gandhi, 29 Feb. 1924, in Paranjape (ed.), *Sarojini Naidu: Selected Letters*, p. 172.

81   Nehru, *The Discovery of India*, p. 358; Nehru, *Glimpses of World History*, p. 713.

been able to explain or express in so many words, but which drew them irresistibly. At the smaller stations, where the peasantry from the surrounding countryside gathered, this was most striking. Their eyes had an inspired glow about them as the peasants pressed toward the carriage window with folded hands and no thought in the world but to obtain the *darshan* (sight) of him they were seeking. I watched in wonderment, and was deeply moved. Then I looked at Bapu to see the reaction. There he sat perfectly quiet and still, with hands folded in acknowledgment of the salutations, and with a stern look upon his face. This impressed me still more—the throbbing, surging mass of humanity on one side, and the still, small stern figure on the other.[82]

A born artist knows how bad his first work is and is willing to learn from others and, in pursuit of adequate expression, he or she takes infinite pains. Gandhi followed Gokhale's advice to travel in order to appraise the India he imagined. An intense *sadhana* ensued. While census enumerators, ethnographers, authors of gazetteers, and settlement reports remained hopelessly unaware of the soul of the multitude, Gandhi found it hidden in village hamlets and urban ghettos. He hit upon much more than that. To him, society presented itself as a brute struggle for existence at its meanest. All he saw was rapacity, poverty, cruelty, and degradation in conjunction with caste oppression, untouchability, and superstitions. He saw the scars on the rural hinterland, its inhabitants clamouring for an end to poverty, destitution, and exploitation, and to live another life to taste what they believed was their due in this world. Administrators and their apologists were themselves not tired of pointing with pride to what they claimed to have done and were doing for them, but Gandhi claimed to know another side which couldn't fail to prove a disillusionment to all who learn the truth about a system of progressive exploitation, together with a ruinously expensive military dispensation. The troops weren't stationed as philanthropists, nor was there any altruism in their continuing presence.[83]

---

82   Mirabehn, *The Spirit's Pilgrimage* (London, 1960), p. 73.

83   Pyarelal, *Mahatma Gandhi: The Last Phase* (Ahmedabad, 1956), vol. 1, bk 2, pp. 5, 6.

In point of fact, Gandhi embodied India's wounded pride. On its table of wrongs and injustices, subjection and exploitation were written. Shortcomings, inaction, incompetence and internal disarray were rampant. The wrongs and shortcomings were, in Gandhi's mind, dependent upon each other. He felt that unless India changed from within, it couldn't demand better from external sources. That is why he didn't expend his energy on bitterness or on self-deprecation, which he regarded as forms of negative revolt. He told the viceroy: 'In my opinion the ordinary method of agitation by way of petition, deputations and the like is no remedy to moving to repentance a government so hopelessly indifferent to the welfare of its charge as the government has proved to be.'[84]

In the harsh face of the land in Champaran, the land of King Janaka, who combined the virtues of a King and a Saint, and in the proud spirits of its peasantry, Gandhi found a congenial home, and for decades he not only held them in thrall, but gave to the region an idea that stirred their imagination and a cause that counted its adherents in hundreds and thousands. He listened to various individuals who laid bare the truth and then fought back doggedly. In actual fact, these were the early signs of a rebel, dramatised by the considerable crowds congregating at the district court to demonstrate solidarity. They thronged around Gandhi-baba in all the villages he visited, and flocked to his lodgings in Motihari and in Bettiah,[85] recognising in his frail persona the peculiar sweetness in smile, depth, and manliness, and a rugged harmony in the tones of his voice. His clear and limpid voice purred its way into their hearts, evoking an emotional response, and gave each one a sense of communion with him.[86] Millie Graham Polak, who bumped into Gandhi in 1905, was struck by his 'soft, rather musical, and almost boyishly fresh voice'.[87] It hadn't changed. Shortly after reaching Bettiah, the sub-divisional commissioner reported:

84   Gandhi to S.R. Hignell, 2 Aug. 1920, Home Pol. (Dep.), Aug. 1920, file no. 38, NAI. Halide Edip, *Inside India*, introd. and ed. Mushirul Hasan (Delhi, 2000), p. 171.

85   Pouchepadass, *Champaran and Gandhi*, pp. 216, 217.

86   Nehru, *An Autobiography*, p. 129.

87   Millie Graham Polak, *Mr. Gandhi: The Man*, p. 18.

We may look upon Mr. Gandhi as an idealist, a fanatic or a revolutionary according to our particular opinions. But to the raiyats, he is their liberator, and they credit him with extraordinary powers. He moves about in the villages, asking them to lay their grievances before him, and he is daily transfiguring the imagination of masses of ignorant men with visions of an early millennium.[88]

What did he achieve? The exploitation of landlords continued and there was no end to the tenants and farmers groaning under their tyranny. Some of Gandhi's own projects were far from complete.[89] At the same time, Champaran heralded the conjunction of the middle-class nationalist intelligentsia in search of a mass following with the dominant peasantry, whose economic rise since the 1860s and ascendancy over the countryside was about to find expression in the realm of modern style institutional politics.[90] Attentive to the anti-colonial awakening in certain pockets, Gandhi connected Satyagraha with the refusal to pay taxes and transformed, with astuteness and agility, anger into passive resistance. In this way, his few months' work had broad ramifications on peasant mobilisation in terms of injecting fresh energy into the rural poor.[91] Suddenly, the lesson indelibly imprinted on their minds was that their salvation depended upon themselves and their capacity to suffer and sacrifice.[92] Suddenly, peasants in Kheda, an agricultural district in Gujarat, acted freely and fearlessly.[93] Finally, a movement so widely reported, and which frightened the government so much, for however brief a spell, influenced the commission to offer some relief to the *ryots*. Gandhi's measured intervention in parts of Awadh also boosted the morale of the downtrodden *kisans* who were never short of suffering owing to high prices and shortage of supplies.[94]

---

88   Pouchepadass, op. cit., pp. 217-18.

89   Prasad, *Autobiography*, pp. 104-5; Gandhi, *My Experiments with Truth*, p. 426.

90   Pouchepadass, op. cit., p. 233.

91   Datta, *History of the Freedom Movement in Bihar*, vol. 1, p. 276.

92   Yagnik, *Gandhi As I Knew Him*, p. 47.

93   7 Mar. 1918, Desai, *Day-to-Day with Gandhi*, vol. 1, p. 59.

94   Uma Iyengar (ed.), *The Oxford India Nehru* (New Delhi, 2007), p. 80.

The Kisan Sabhas brought alive UP's lazy rural hinterland, while young idealists like Jawaharlal were thrown into contact with a pauperised and degraded peasantry. It was the zest of a man in the thick of a fray that carried forward the torch he bore to enable India to live in light and freedom. Besides the 'emotional exaltation, wrapped up in the action', he trudged many a mile across fields to discover an entire countryside ablaze with excitement. One village communicated with another and the second with the third, and so on. Sometimes an entire village emptied out, and right across the fields men and women and children marched towards the meeting place. Otherwise, more swiftly still, the cry of 'Sita Ram … Sita Ra-a-a-m' would rend the air, and echo afar and be echoed back from other villages, and then people would come streaming out or even running as fast as they were able to. Men and women marched towards the realisation of a dream they had long nurtured: *azadi* or *swatantrata*.

The unemployed were the worst off, while the demobilised soldiers disturbed the countryside's placidity. At the end of the day, the war-weary population had little prospect of peace and betterment. Filled with despair, they stretched out their friendly arms to Gandhi. With his success in building a movement brick by brick, he overnight became the catalyst for expressing their despondency. Suddenly, Shahzada Ghulam Ali echoed the bubbling madness, reckless youth, raw emotion, and naked challenge that fired the youth in Amritsar, the site of the sacred Golden Temple. He realised that Gandhi (Banaji) lit up his life with hope and fulfilment.[95] Elsewhere, like a tidal wave, news of Rama of Ayodhya descending from the heavens swept across the land. As a god in the vast Hindu pantheon, people pinned their hopes on the coming of a new age of hope and freedom. Crowds overflowed on to the railway tracks wherever Gandhi's special train passed, and through some magical grapevine, word of his approach reached remote villages for hundreds of miles, no matter how secretly his travel was planned.[96]

---

95   Saadat Hasan Manto, *Black Margins*, (ed.) Muhammad Umar Memon (Delhi, 2001), p. 109.

96   Jones, *Tumult in India*, p. 70.

In Gorakhpur's backward and poverty-stricken district, thousands came 'like sheep, inspired by blind faith', and 'with devotion in their hearts and returned with feelings and ideas'. Guru-Gandhi's name spread to all four corners of the district.[97] When it came to arresting him, officials apprehended that Gandhi was 'a semi-divine person and one against whom we should not take action except in direct extremity'.[98]

Politics without partners was a lost game and therefore Gandhi began assembling a well-knit team. This venture, the success of which could hardly be presumed, took him to varied destinations. He moved slowly to test the waters, well aware that the bond of expediency between the high-ranking and the powerless had a degrading element in it.[99] After all, moderation sprang from 'the colourless principle of expediency'.[100] His moderation paid off. In Punjab, the people used 'Mahatma Gandhi *ki jai*' as their battle cry; they considered him to be the leader of the popular cause against the government.[101] Responding to their enthusiasm, Gandhi hammered the rank and file into some form of cooperation. He did this with surprising speed. In line with these developments, he made the Congress amend its constitution to bring it in line with the changing public mood and to open up the party to the public. The Congress in December 1920 ensured permanence, continuity, party discipline and a chain of command from the top downwards. The All India Congress Committee (AICC) headed the machine; it wasn't, unlike the League, marked out by birth or wealth. A few bigwigs close to Gandhi dominated the Congress Working Committee (CWC).

Gandhi sounded a note of optimism, but felt hemmed in on all sides. 'Distress pleads before me from all sides,' he moaned in April 1918, 'but

---

97 Shahid Amin, 'Gandhi as Mahatma: Gorakhpur District, Eastern UP, 1921-22', *Subaltern Studies III*, (ed.) Ranajit Guha (New Delhi, 1984); Chandan Mitra, 'Images of the Congress: U.P. and Bihar in the Late Thirties and Early Forties', in Low (ed.), *The Indian National Congress*, pp. 158-59.

98 Note by W.H. Vincent, Home Pol. (A) Dec. 1920, nos. 210-16 & K.-W, NAI.

99 Ibid.

100 Tagore, *My Life in My Words*, p. 359.

101 Note by H.D. Craik, 14 Aug. 1919, Home Pol. (A) Dec.1920, nos. 210-16 & K.-W, NAI.

I daren't refuse help where I know the remedy.'[102] In the final analysis, he shaped the country for his causes. Visible in the intelligentsia was a new resurgence sparked and driven by Woodrow Wilson's Fourteen Points, Lenin's denunciation of imperialism, and the example of the Russian revolutionaries in declaring the people's right to secede from the Czarist Empire. Some other ingredients were nonetheless necessary to complete the pudding.

In England, Gandhi would have seen a striking comment in volume 19 of the *History of Indian Mutiny* by John Kaye and Colonel Malleson: 'If there be fuel prepared, it is hard to tell whence the spark shall come that shall set it on fire. The matter of sedition is of two kinds, much poverty and much discontent.'[103] Now, Gandhi maintained his influence partly because of the recurrent economic distress and partly because of the government's habitual attempts to rob people of their freedom. In the circumstances, he employed a quest for truth; a quest for the new, a struggle for change, and a 'matchless force' to arouse the national conscience. He met with a fair measure of success. A new generation began to make sense of 'conscience' and 'resistance' as a moral force in relation to foreign rule.[104] Gandhi influenced them by word and deed. His values became all-pervading. Those who came to his meetings from village, town or city, rich or poor, imbibed his manners, ideals, and modes of thought, which they transmitted wherever they subsequently went.

The British lion uncurled its big claws; repression was unleashed. James Morris, the novelist, described the Jallianwala Bagh massacre as 'one of those markers in time ... by which imperial patterns can best be traced. It was recognised even then as the worst of all stains on the imperial record.'[105] Tagore renounced his knighthood.[106] Still, the terrible event didn't prick the conscience of Britain's high-souled liberal public opinion. An eloquent lady, writing in *The Statesman*, Calcutta, urged all right-minded people to

---

102 To Esther, n.d., Desai (ed.), *Day-to-Day with Gandhi*, vol. 1, p. 78.

103 Ashe, *Gandhi*, p. 47. Frederich Pinentt gave Gandhi the volume to read.

104 Manto, *Black Margins*, p. 110.

105 B.D. Garga, *From Raj to Swaraj: The Non-fiction Film in India* (Delhi, 2007), p. 28.

106 To Chelmsford, 31 May 1919, Fakrul Alam & Radha Chakravarty (eds), *The Essential Tagore* (Visva Bharati, 2011), pp. 99-100.

contribute to the 'Dyer Fund'.[107] Gandhi had already passed through the fire of persecution and the smoke of the colour bar, and now:

> Each insult is a nail driven into his soul, each sinking into him and wounding his instinctive vanity, jarring his moral courage and awakening it into compassion for his fellow man—the outcaste and untouchable coolie of the white man's land.[108]

As one who occupied a high moral ground, Gandhi couldn't acquiesce in or submit to force and vengeance. At that juncture, he pressed his dharma vis-à-vis the 'satanic' government. The man who recruited Indians to fight for Britain returned, with scornful composure, the medals he had received for his war effort. He demanded what George Orwell called 'a sort of non-violent warfare'. His stirring words instilled the people with excitement. There wasn't anything except his personality, intense enough in its own quality, to retain a magnetic hold over their minds in the awakening to their new acquisition of explosive freedom.[109]

Words and Vision

The seventeenth-century political theorist Benedict Spinoza suggested that it is far from possible to impose uniformity of speech, for the more rulers strive to curtail freedom of speech, the more obstinately people resist them. Human nature is such that laws directed against opinions affect the 'generous minded' rather than the wicked, and they are adapted less to coerce criminals than to irritate the upright.[110] The war, in which many of the moderates took part under the illusion that it would lead to their kind of millennium, pointing out that within the Jekyll of the reforms lurked the old Hyde of repression.[111]

---

107   Edward Thompson, *The Other Side of the Medal* (London, 1925) p. 13.

108   J.F.C. Fuller, *India in Revolt* (London, 1931), p. 152.

109   Andrews, *Mahatma Gandhi's Ideas*, p. 256.

110   Sidorsky (ed.), *The Liberal Tradition in European Thought*, pp. 35-36.

111   Chelmsford's government failed to respond to the revolutionary fervour or deal swiftly and effectively with extensive confusion and disgruntlement. It follows, plainly, that the Rowlatt Committee report was deeply offensive.

Moving from strength to strength, Gandhi brought together the threads of unrest and wove them into a pressure group. Thus, shutters were down on 6 April 1919 as Hindus and Muslims, for their own specific and generalised complaints, responded to *hartal*, an idea designed to improve the social tone and morale of the aggrieved and discontented. Added to this was fasting, which, he was to say later, 'isolates the forces of evil'. His fast in Kheda had proved to be a dialogic exercise; a moral one aimed at the employers and the mill hands of Ahmedabad to awaken them and the moneyed classes to their *dharma*.[112]

Gandhi reminded the future generations that, 'we who witnessed the innocent dying did not ungratefully refuse to cherish their memory'.[113] 'We shall be judged not by our words, but solely by our deeds,' he once decreed.[114] A heightened political atmosphere stimulated the urban middle-classes to rethink their traditional subservience. They were on the threshold of something splendid and final. In a wild moment, Saadat Hasan Manto's classmate took off his silk jacket and threw it into the huge bonfire the boys had lit in front of the town hall and the police headquarters.[115] Manto was an upcoming Urdu writer. In Allahabad, politics spilled over into the city. At one rural polling station, the voters stayed away. Cloth merchants pledged themselves not to import or purchase cloth. This sort of fervour testifies to an awareness of the 'extraordinary stiffening-up' of demoralised, backward, and broken-up people taking part in disciplined,

112   Ganguli and Docker (eds), *Rethinking Gandhi*, p. 99.

113   12 May 1920, Raghavan Iyer (ed.), *The Essential Writings of Mahatma Gandhi* (Delhi, 1996), p. 47.

114   Speech at Madras, 18 Mar. 1919, Gandhi, *Speeches and Writings*, p. 426.

115   Born into a Kashmiri family of Amritsar, this enfant terrible of Urdu literature wandered from place to place, as many creative writers did during those days, before returning to Bombay in 1943 to work with a group of friends at the famous Bombay Talkies. Manto wrote: 'It happened in 1919. The whole of Punjab was up in arms against the British. Sir Michael Dwyer had banned Gandhiji's entry into the province under the Defence of India rules. He had been stopped at Palwal, taken into custody and sent to Bombay. I believe [that] if the British hadn't made this blunder, the Jallianwala Bagh incident couldn't have added a bloody page to the black history of their rule in India.' Saadat Hasan Manto, *Naked Voices: Stories and Sketches*, trans. from the Urdu by Rakhshanda Jalil (Roli Books, 2008), p. 142.

joint action.[116] Those were brave days, and their memory endured and became a cherished possession. They transformed Congress into a mass party, and its followers animated by democratic ideals and contempt for innate privilege. Nayantara Sahgal writes about them:

> When the speaker was Mamu, the speech would start on a reflective note but soon flash fire, sending a thrill through its audience. If Gandhiji was the leader of the struggle, Mamu personified its romance, its spirit of high adventure, its appeal to the patriotic young. In Allahabad the student body had a special claim on him. Living as he did just down the road from the university.[117]

Patience yields results, just as fortune favours the brave. Gokhale and Naoroji had passed away after doing their best to stir the conscience of the rulers; Tilak and Surendranath Banerjea were out of contention in the race for leadership;[118] Annie Besant became the target of japes and jeers;[119] the Liberals virtually disappeared from the face of the earth; Jinnah, with all his deadly earnestness at this time, operated on the fringes. As luck would have it, the Congress received the mixed blessings of an individual who was made of the stuff of which heroes are made. Not only was he different from the rest but he also brought a sense of difference with his views on politics, morality, and justice. Above all, he overcame the inertia wrought in the popular conscience, bridged the difference between ideals and realities, and contested the assumptions of those who had so far projected themselves as infallible.

---

116   Nehru, *An Autobiography*, p. 76.

117   Sahgal, *Civilizing a Savage World*, p. 76.

118   Stanley A. Wolpert, *Tilak and Gokhale: Revolution and Reform in the Making of Modern India* (California, 1962), p. 270.

119   Annie Besant, an Irishwoman, founded Central Hindu College, subsequently the nucleus of the Banaras Hindu University, and in 1914 converted the *Madras Standard* into *New India*. The weekly *Commonweal* and religious journals turned her into the most formidable press baron in Madras. The Home Rule League, which she founded, gave the British reason to see the organisation as a potential menace to their continued existence. It had so aroused feelings against the government that the Madras governor interned its founder in mid-1917.

Plato tells us that, 'Poetry comes nearer to vital truth than history'. Allahabad is a holy city, where the confluence of the Ganga and the Yamuna takes place. Pilgrims to this sacred city come from everywhere, especially during the great Kumbh Mela, held every twelve years. Every year smaller pilgrims attend the Magh Mela. They plod patiently along in the heat and dust, but are supported and sustained by an unwavering faith and belief. They are serenely content at the prospect of being cleansed from every vestige of sin by those holy waters. In a lyrical outburst, Akbar Ilahabadi, a government servant who lived in Allahabad, shows that man is predestined to nothing that wise choices cannot abrogate. His *Gandhi-Nama*, which remained unpublished until his death on 9 September 1921,[120] reveals his admiration for Gandhi. It must be read as well as heard before its meaning can be grasped, because its poet won appreciation and celebrity for his agile wit, impudent humour, purposive mind, and skills in composing verses that are built around images.

The fact that he is more in sympathy with Gandhi than critics have admitted is reflected in his highly-praised verses, which aren't wholly satirical. He was empathetic to the great moments of history; to the great resistance Gandhi launched. As we read *Gandhi-Nama*, we see images correspond to something that is credible or intelligible.

Times change, new movements, a new world succeeds the old.
The tale of kings has ended; Gandhi's tale is being told.
In the age of Gandhi there is no need for foresight;
He who walks in a dust storm shuts his eyes.
The torch of the East was running the risk of being extinguished by
        the storm of the West,
We are assured of light because of Gandhi.
The Shaikh is welcome to think of Constantinople and Persia;
I would prefer to say: Victory to Gandhi.[121]

---

120   With 271 verses, it was published in Allahabad, in 1948, by his son Syed Mohammed Muslim Rizvi.

121   Muhammad Sadiq, *Twentieth Century Urdu Literature* (Karachi, 1983), pp. 34-35. See also, Ghulam Husain Zulfiqar, *Mohandas Karamchand Gandhi: Lisaul Asr ki Nazar Me* (Lahore, 1994).

There are, in addition, numerous verses such as the ones quoted below which offer an appraisal of Gandhi's skills and virtues.

گر و کوئی نہ رہا ان مہاتما کے سوا

سب ان کے چیلے ہیں آل فاطمہ کے سوا

No mentor is left, except this Mahatma
Everyone is now his disciple, except the family of Fatima.

تم نے د با د با کر اس ملک کو گھلا یا

مرزا پچک رہے ہیں گاندھی نے منہ پھلا یا

You have impoverished and depleted this country,
Mirza feels irked, and Gandhi too is angry.

لشکرِ گاندھی کو ہتھیاروں کی حاجت کچھ نہیں

ہاں مگر بے انتہا صبر و قناعت چا ہئے

The army of Gandhi does not need any weapons,
Yes, they do need limitless contentment and patience.

نہ مولانا میں لغزش ہے نہ سازش کی ہے گاندھی نے

چلا یا ایک رخ ان کو فقط مغرب کی آندھی نے

Neither the Moulana has any weakness, nor has Gandhi conspired,
Their moving in the same direction is compelled by the Western storm.

Equally, Gandhi's choice of word and image inspired other creative writers; the rhythm of restrained emotions, self-abnegation, moral fervour, and concern for the downtrodden. Maulana Ahsan Mirza collected their compositions between 1917 and 1918 and published them from Lucknow in 1921 as *Jazbat-i Qaumi wa Mahatma Gandhi*. He saw Gandhi as a vigorous man desiring change, and acknowledged his idealism. Gandhi disapproved of the commendations he heard of himself. Even so, to put it in the words of Emerson, 'praise is looked, homage tendered, love flows from mute nature, from the mountains and the lights of the firmament'.[122]

---

122   R. E. Spiller (ed.), *Selected Essays, Lectures, and Poems of Ralph Waldo Emerson* (New York, 1965), p. 223.

Initially, Gandhi didn't seize upon the means to achieve the ends: that lofty sight where Truth reveals its true meaning and Reality appears in its true colours. The success of the Rowlatt Satyagraha made it apparent that he was, after all, predestined to become the promoter of change and progress. His forays took many forms, but lest we forget, he not only pleaded guilty before Justice Broomfield in 1922, but explained that, if and when freed, he'd do the same again and 'play with fire'. Essentially, he neither accepted the burden nor the tyranny of the past. He feared that otherwise his soul would be shackled, his free will be robbed, and, eventually his dignity as a human being lost. His unruffled acceptance of arrest (nine months in confinement on this occasion) raised the estimation of 'Mickey Mouse', as Sarojini Naidu, a poet bubbling with wit, humour and charm, laughingly called him.

If one proceeds from this picture, we perceive forthwith the sharp distinction between the goal of constitutional advance and Satyagraha, an instrument not only to voice unfairness but also to bring about social betterment and profound social change. Eventually, the man who had abandoned the black tailcoat and striped trousers smashed the factions to become, beyond doubt, the trendsetter. He had no arms or ammunition to fight; he didn't believe in their use. In the years to come, he didn't back the revolutionaries, not even Sardar Bhagat Singh and his two associates, because he loathed and deplored violence. Methods or means mattered as much as the attainment of high goals. 'By making a dharma of violence,' Gandhi broadcast promptly, 'we shall be reaping the fruit of our own actions.'[123] Every revolution was first a thought in one man's mind, and when the same thought occurs to another man, it is the key to that era.[124]

A different kind of revolution—slow but steady—was being staged in a different arena, the ashrams of Gandhi. Groups of exalted men and women flung themselves into his welcoming arms, embracing celibacy, asceticism, or observing rituals with passionate abandon. The Sabarmati ashram itself was an unselfish brotherhood with no caste, community, or gender frontiers except the frontier imposed by the responsibility to maintain a high standard of duty and devotion.

---

123 *Navajivan*, 29 Mar. 1931, *CWMG* (Dec. 1930-Apr. 1931), p. 360.
124 Spiller (ed.), *Selected Essays*, p. 222.

3
On the Banks of the Sabarmati: The Din-i Ilahi

اس وقت شیخ جی کو گا ندھی سے میل سوجھا

صاحب نے روک چاہی ان کو بھی کھیل سوجھا

دونوں نے آخر اپنی اپنی نکا س دیکھی

اسکیم ان کو سوجھی، اوران کو جیل سوجھا

The Sheikh has now decided, to patch up with Gandhi.
The British wanted to stop it, but then they too were amused;
At last both of them sought their own exit.
One, in scheming, and the other, in prison.

-Akbar Ilahabadi

گورنمنٹیوں میں بڑی عقل ہے

مگر ان میں ایکا نہیں ہے نہ جوش

جو گا ندھی کے پیرو وہ اکثر اجڈ

مگر اک امنگ ان میں ہے اوراک جوش

The supporters of the British Government are intelligent,
But they lack unity and fervor;
Those who support Gandhi are largely rustic,
But they have a zeal and vigour.

-Akbar Ilahabadi

The real and unavoidable factors in life and history have been beliefs. Hymns, ritual texts, and philosophical treatises embodied the religion that developed around 2000 BCE until roughly 500 BCE;

they have composed the essential part of human mental baggage. In other words, without organised religion at the dawn of civilisation in the Indo-Gangetic belt, consolidation—occasionally identified as one of Hindu fusion or orthodox blending—occurred between the time of the late Vedic Upanishads and the Gupta kings (c. 320-540 BCE). These facts are scarcely news. It is known too, that the word Hinduism, derived from the river Indus, goes back to the time when invaders reached the river Indus, or Ind, and called the inhabitants 'Hindi', and covers not a single doctrine but legends and myths, and the various cultural agencies: belief, religion, law, and the like. Worship ranges from idol worship to meditation in search of union with the supernatural source of all creation. As Gandhi put it, self-abnegation was one of the most remarkable characteristics of the Hindu religion, and unlike other world religions, it didn't derive its name from any prophet or teacher, although it counted some of the greatest within its fold.[1] Hinduism gave the freest scope to imagination, speculation, and reason.

Gandhi defended, controversially, inborn differences between individuals and groups, and the widely varying levels of material wealth, status, and religious purity they produced.[2] Today, the caste system, for long conceived as a ritual-status system, has imploded. In contrast to the *sectarian* view that views caste as an insolable religious community distinguished from others by idiosyncratic doctrine, ritual, or culture,[3] many castes have, as it happens, severed their relationship with the system of ritual obligations and rights that once governed their economic and social existence and lent them a distinctiveness in terms of status in the ritual hierarchy.[4] In line with the *organic* view, the standing of a caste is determined by the share of mundane accomplishments and resources and not by Hindu ritual

---

1   *Indian Opinion*, 5 Mar. 1905, *CWMG*, vol. 4, p. 370.

2   At one time, in each linguistic region about 200 caste groups were further subdivided into about 2000 smaller units, each of which were endogamous and constituted the areas of social life for the individual.

3   Marc Galanter, *Law and Society in Modern India* (Delhi, 1994, 2nd imp.), p. 142.

4   D.L. Sheth, 'Caste and the Secularisation Process in India', in Peter R. De Souza (ed.), *Contemporary India: Transitions* (Delhi, 2000), p. 247.

standards.[5] In addition, caste in urban areas is dissimilar from that in rural areas, with mobility creating a breach between caste and traditional occupation.[6]

Gandhi's views on the caste system account for only a fraction of what he wrote about, the rest being open and political. He sought inspiration from, and gathered together, multiple sources into a single whole and created a synthesis. For him validation of ideas was above all else, both the end point and beginning of his quest for harmony. His target was to compare the various religions, discover the truth underlying in them, and demonstrate how they were only among so many roads leading to the realisation of God, and how they ought not to dub any of them false.[7]

Gandhi articulated the *truth* of his time and place by extolling religion and exhorting the application of the ideas of the *Gita* in daily life. 'For me', he said not once but repeatedly, 'the *Gita* and Tulsidas suffice', and advised people to read the *Gita* 'over and over again'. Given his faith and beliefs, he regarded himself as an instrument to save Hinduism, a religion he loved, cherished, and practised. 'Most religious men I have met are politicians in disguise; I, however, who wear the guise of a politician, am at heart a religious man.'[8] Whether it was with prolonged silence or prolonged activism, he strove after perfection, i.e. self-realisation. Weaknesses and imperfections didn't lower this ideal but reinforced his determination to nurture the national and democratic thought. We see this in evidence during the second Civil Disobedience Movement from 1930 to 1932.

With religion as the source of existence and the means towards attaining a good life, dharma and politics (*rajaprakarna*) were intertwined rather than isolated into as many units.[9] So also was the indissoluble link between politics and religion. Politics bereft of religion

---

5   Galanter, op. cit., p. 143.

6   A.M. Shah, in M.N. Srinivas (ed.), *Caste: Its Twentieth Century Avatar* (Delhi, 1997).

7   *Indian Opinion*, 15 Apr. 1905, *CWMG*, vol. 4, p. 405.

8   Gandhi, *Speeches and Writings*, p. xxiv.

9   Gandhi, *My Experiments with Truth*, pp. 370-1.

kills the soul.[10] Therefore, Gandhi aspired to infuse, with spiritualism as the bedrock, the social order with a pioneering spirit. This was achievable in India where the amalgam of different traditions was sufficiently adequate to withstand the assault of other cultures. When he embarked on a fast unto death on 20 September 1932, 'as a man of religion', Andrews understood the reason behind it.

Gandhi rescued the new asceticism of simplicity out of the old ideal of total renunciation which could be practised only by the few.[11] He resisted ease and sloth and settled for a life of asceticism, though not as an acetic. In 1909, he abhorred the first class life and the pampering that went on board the ship.[12] Fasting, celibacy, bodily discipline, and penance, which were cultural components, became the *essentials* for realising the truth and buttressing the search for 'external guides of conduct'. He began, single-handed, to revive the *charkha* as well. In 1921, khadi became one of the principal items of the Congress' constructive programme and occupied the centre of its flag. The spinning wheel served as a road map for survival and individuals, rich and poor. 'Kill khadi and you must kill the villages and with them non-violence', Gandhi wrote.[13] The *charkha*, the 'golden bridge', united him with the poor.[14] Above all, a simple and austere life inspired the combined feeling of reverence and awe, though the world didn't know, so said Sarojini Naidu jokingly, what it cost to keep Gandhi in poverty. Mohamed Ali, editor of *Comrade*, referred to his simple attire and to his walking barefoot to mourn Gokhale's death. 'The thorns that prick the bare feet of Mr. Gandhi', Mohamed Ali said, 'are the thorns that should pierce through the hearts of all Indians.'[15]

10   *Young India*, 3 Apr. 1924, *in* Iyer (ed.), *The Essential Writings of Mahatma Gandhi*, p. 33; Andrews (ed.), *Mahatma Gandhi: His Own Story*, p. 338.

11   J.C. Winslow and V. Elwin, *Gandhi: The Dawn of Indian Freedom* (New York, 1931), p. 49.

12   Gandhi to Kallenbach, 3 July 1909, Gandhi-Kallenbach papers.

13   Tendulkar, *Mahatma*, vol. 3, p. 272.

14   *Harijan*, 29 Nov. 1938, *CWMG*, p. 60.

15   B.R. Nanda, *Gandhi: Pan-Islamism, Imperialism and Nationalism in India* (Bombay, 1989), pp. 198-99.

'Your world is the world of fish and fowl. My world is the cry at dawn.'

-Mohammad Iqbal

Gandhi spoke freely, in short incisive sentences. He listened as easily and naturally as he spoke, and conversation with him tended to take the form of question and answer and the interchange of opinions rather than of rapid give and take. The principal parameters of his thinking process are well established. Enough is understood now about them to examine their links with other aspects of the 'experiments'. We shall see how the same maxim that one cannot create something from nothing applies to Gandhi too. We shall also attempt to validate his claim about their utility in preserving the social and intellectual basis of creativity, and his blending of religious symbols with progress that made his approach pivotal as a springboard to reach out to, and for serious enquiry into, the mass response to mediation, out-of-the-box thinking, and the like.

Let's begin with Gandhi turning into a brahmachari in 1900; by the time the second call from South Africa came, he had no carnal appetite. Six years later, he took a vow of celibacy at Phoenix Farm, situated about 14 miles from Durban in the midst of a sugar-growing region. The vow wasn't only a means of recognising the value of God's beatific vision, but also the penance voluntarily imposed for proving untrue to his father ('The shame of carnal desire even at the critical hour of my father's death...') during the last moments of his life.[16] It was also intended to reduce to their basic components problems that resisted solution in terms of existing paradigms. In his letters to J.C. Kumarappa and others, he underlined the fact that a vow 'means unflinching determination, and helps us against temptations ... Taking vows is not a sign of weakness but of strength ...' Later in life, he felt he wasn't yet out of the woods and had to reiterate:

I am the same celibate as I was in 1906 when I vowed to abstain from sexual intimacy ... At present I'm a better celibate than I

16   Nirmal Kumar Bose, *My Days with Gandhi* (Calcutta, 1974), p. 16.

was in 1901 [when the idea took possession of him in a nebulous form]. My experiment has made me a confirmed *brahamchari*, the objective for which I have striven all these many years.[17]

Andrews disagreed: Only a man who 'takes with him no empty, attenuated, emasculated life-experience can live, truly, the life of the sanyasi.'

Gandhi regarded marriage as a hindrance to public and humanitarian work and, at the same time, reassured himself that a Hindu wife held obedience to her husband as the highest religion. He doesn't tell us what Ba, as she was known by her near and dear, thought of his unilateral decision,[18] imagining her to be meek and submissive. Although she had refused to clean chamber pots in Durban and expressed displeasure at being transplanted from the town to more primitive conditions at Phoenix Settlement, her feelings weren't taken into account, not even her fear of snakes and lizards. Likewise, whether she understood the implications of her husband's spiritual and ethical beliefs is only a matter of conjecture; in all likelihood, she didn't. Even if she did, the chances are that Gandhi would have carried out penance unmindful of what his immediate family thought, to salvage humanity and rescue Hinduism from perdition. Sarojini Naidu described Kasturba, in 1914, as 'a kindly gentle lady, with the indomitable spirit of the martyr.'[19]

Turning to habits of life, Gandhi gave the peasants lessons in courage so that they could eradicate injustice or traditional wrongs and unmask falsehood. He lay emphasis on unity for this lofty task. Even so, he instinctively avoided seeking uniformity in any dimension. For example, he didn't insist that his followers don the same kinds of clothes or follow his dietary habits. He simply expected them to moderate their requirements and attend the weaker party. Beyond this, he expected the *Gita*, with its dynamic worldview to guide India, as it had done through much of its history. The critical issue is whether the political classes could accept these views or the persona of an

---

17   Gandhi to Birla, 9 Apr. 1945, G.D. Birla (ed.), *Bapu: A Unique Association* (Delhi, 1977), vol. 4, p. 376.

18   Gandhi, *My Experiments with Truth*, p. 185.

19   Sengupta, *Sarojini Naidu*, p. 90.

individual in a set up where the balance has generally been skewed against innovators.

Clothes could make the man if the man made his clothes a sign of his internal condition, observed Jean-Jacques Rousseau. The French philosopher advised Polish patriots to revive traditional Polish peasant costumes to throw off Poland's enslavement to French culture. A Pole who tried keeping up with Paris fashions only proclaimed his abasement, his lack of self-reliance, his shame in his own condition, the fate of being a Pole.

The clothes Gandhi wore reflect the various phases in his encounters in South Africa, London, and finally, India. Whether or not they reflected his mind set is unclear, but they did carry a message. Those in South Africa noticed his black professional turban, an easy lounge suit, a stiff collar and tie, with shoes and socks for outdoor wear. He returned to the lounge suit but no longer starched collars for ordinary wear.[20] In London, he appeared as a pre-War English gentleman: a silk hat, well cut morning coat, smart shoes and socks. In India, he wore a dhoti, a loose coat reaching to his knees, a shoulder scarf, and a Kathiawar turban, all made of rough mill cloth, and sandals. On his feet, when walking in the street, he had a clumsy variety of sandals on; otherwise, his feet were bare. In May 1921, when he called on Reading, the viceroy, he wore a white dhoti and cap woven on a spinning wheel, which he put in plain words in *Hind Swaraj* as the panacea for the growing pauperism in India. In Munshi Premchand's novel, *Chaugan-i Hasti*, published in 1925, he is symbolically represented in the figure of Surdas, the great Hindi poet, with his emaciated body, his protruding ribs, and his firm yet humble expression, insistent on his truth.[21] In 1931, when Irwin summoned him for talks, Winston Churchill dreaded 'a seditious middle temple lawyer' striding half naked up the steps of the Viceroy's Lodge. Indifferent to the absence of tolerance in the stuffy world of Churchillian correctness, Gandhi spun his daily quota of yarn at 1.30 a.m., went to bed at 3.00 a.m., and was up for prayers an hour later.

---

20   This description is based on Polak, *Mr. Gandhi: The Man*, p. 175.

21   Alok Rai, 'Introduction', in Premchand, *Ranghbhumi: The Arena of Life*, trans. Christopher King (Oxford, 2010), p. ix.

A scene flashed before Irene Bose, a British lady full of admiration for Gandhi's simple ways: Gandhi seated upon a table in front of a packed auditorium, bare to the waist, a shawl besides him should he feel cold. In his tiny ashram room, he sat upon a mat on the mud floor, his sole possession a back rest, a shelf of books, several changes of clothing, his bedding, and a cushion or two. He started speaking, poked fun, and chuckled over an insurmountable impasse with the Muslim League.

Again a change of scene as Irene and her husband, Vivian Bose who died at the age of eighty-two, went for an evening stroll. As the stars came out, one of the men lit a lantern and walked ahead. They followed, his cotton dhoti caught up above his bare knees, shawl thrown over his shoulders, and a staff to help him along. In the glow of the lantern they saw him, at that moment India's poor man. Irene Bose found 'no red carpets or decorated arches, only the empty fields and sandal shod feet leading in the gleam of a lamp. Which was power?'[22]

The last scene in my narrative is from the verge of the wasteland that encircled Delhi. Set against a background of barren boulders and dusty earth stood Bhangi Colony, the venue of the CWC meeting on 4 June 1947. Alan Campbell-Johnson, the viceroy's aide, contrasted the pomp and circumstance between the Vatican and Bhangi Colony, the Mahatma and the wizard from Wales; 'the points of religious and political comparison', he noted, 'are perhaps the deeper reality'.[23]

Taking a Vow

Vows constitute a 'bulwark of strength' and a part of the cult of purity, love, and self-suffering. Before sailing for London, Gandhi had vowed before a Jain monk that he'd not touch wine, women, and meat, and that he'd remain the same decent, honest, and studious Hindu. His mother blessed him. From now on, through making and holding onto vows, the son trained himself to become someone who could trust

---

22   Irene Bose papers, box 2, p. 209. Centre for South Asian Studies, Cambridge.

23   30 July 1947, Alan Campbell-Johnson, *Mission with Mountbatten* (London, 1951), p. 147.

himself and who could be trusted by others.[24] Fidelity to them held all the observances together and in turn bound him to them. The urge to self-purify was so great that he would on and off expect others to follow suit.[25]

Kaka Kalelkar, in charge of the education portfolio in the ashram, believed that vows 'bind the future of changing circumstances and situation and circumscribe the freedom of the will'.[26] The swadeshi vow symbolised the use of a moral weapon from the private to the public.[27] By extending it to the public domain, Gandhi sought to promote a collective commitment to a public good. In this case, a *full* vow is what he had in mind in relation to clothing, be it made of cotton, silk, or wool, to breathe new life into the almost lost art of hand-weaving, and to save crores annually spent abroad for imported cloth. In this, as in other matters of faith, he laid bare not only the *Gita*'s lofty ideals, but also beliefs and actions.[28] The quintessence of Hindu philosophy was action without expectation of fruit (*anasakti yoga*). With knowledge, devotion and *bhakti*, says the *Gita*, 'do your allotted work but renounce its fruit—be detached and work—have no desire for reward and work'.[29] The sacred text served as 'an infallible guide of conduct', and a 'dictionary of daily reference'.[30]

As for diet, Gandhi vowed to eat only one meal a day until the iniquitous tax was repealed. A.R. Chamney, who lunched with him in Johannesburg, noticed:

---

24   Sissela Bok, quoted in D. Dalton, *Mahatma Gandhi: Nonviolent Power in Action* (New York, 1993), p. 200.

25   To Meera, 31 Jan. 1927, p. 24.

26   Madho Prasad, *A Gandhian Patriarch: A Political and Spiritual Biography of Kaka Kalelkar*, p. 169.

27   'With God as my witness, I solemnly declare that from today I shall confine, myself, for my personal requirements, to the use of cloth, manufactured in India from Indian cotton, silk and wool; and I shall altogether abstain from using foreign cloth, and I shall destroy all [such] cloth in my possession.'

28   Edip, *Inside India*, p. 171.

29   M.K. Gandhi, *The Gospel of Selfless Action: or The Gita according to Gandhi*, trans. Mahadev Desai (Ahmedabad, 2007, rpt), p. 131.

30   Ibid., p. 134.

As a strict Hindoo, abstinence from fermented liquor of any kind was essential. He paid the very strictest attention to his bodily health and ate sparingly but of the most nutritious products that his vegetarian ménage could supply, and in the event of illness relied on his own curative 'simples' of which he had a wide knowledge. During the whole course of our acquaintance Mr. Ghandi, at intermittent periods sometimes far apart, practiced fasts of varying duration and was sometimes none the better for them. He didn't always accept defeat with a good grace but I never knew him lose his temper.[31]

Gandhi stated that man was born to live on fruits and herbs that the earth grows, and so he retained his faith in the value of uncooked food. He enjoyed grapes and mangoes. Apples he tried, but his teeth couldn't work through them unless they were stewed. With his blood pressure fluctuating, for which he once rested and recuperated in Nandi Hills near Bangalore, he added juice of fresh neem leaves to his milk.[32] He gave his word in 1912 not to drink milk or milk products, partly because he found the methods of milking cows and buffaloes to be cruel. Having vowed not to consume more than five things in all during the entire day, he lived on goat's milk (though he gave up a goat milk diet at the doctor's advice), bread, and raisins instead of fruit and nuts. He told Kallenbach in August 1928 that his life was simpler than ever. He didn't abjure salt because one ingested inorganic salt from water and inhaled it from the sea air.[33] He added juices of citrus fruit to make water drinkable during his imprisonment at Aga Khan Palace.

There were times when Gandhi could be self-indulgent. When staying for a while at 88 Knightsbridge in London during the Second

---

31   'Mahatma Gandhi in the Transvaal', by A.R. Chamney, p. 17.

32   He referred to curbing his 'animal passion': 'I can no longer claim that immunity. I can only say in all humility that though I am conscious of that passion, I can keep it under subjection and appear before the world a respectable human being from whose lust no woman need fear. But it costs me all my strength to keep the brute in me under disciplined subjection and control.' To Gregg 26 Apr. 1927, E.S. Reddy, *Mahatma Gandhi: Letters to Americans* (Mumbai, 1998), p. 60.

33   Desai (ed.), *Day-to-Day with Gandhi*, vol. 2, p. 189.

Round Table Conference, he partook of all but five of a box of dates, a finger-bowl full of sliced tomatoes, rusks soaked in milk, grapes, celery, and honey or *gur*. Mirabehn watched him finish his meal as if to satisfy herself of her master's normal appetite. She dressed in brown *khaddar* and wore heavy coarse sandals.[34]

بھائی گاندھی کی روش میں بہت امید نہیں
ہے وہ دلچسپ مگر وسعتِ تقلید نہیں

There is not much hope from brother Gandhi's agitation,
Interesting it is, but lacks the expanse of following.

Besides, the sentiments of the poet Akbar Ilahabadi some of Gandhi's other associates, such as Andrews, disputed his reasoning on celibacy and on the ashram codes.[35] Motilal doubted the logic behind fasting.[36] In 1931, his son wondered: 'If Bapu died! What would India be like then? And how would her politics run? There seemed to be a dreary and dismal future ahead, and despair seized my heart when I thought of it.' Then, a few paragraphs later: 'what a magician ... how well he knew how to pull the strings that move people's hearts.'[37]

Gandhi's decision to fast from 8 May 1933 upset Tagore.[38] He sent a brief message from Darjeeling: 'May your penance bring you close to the bosom of the Eternal away from the burdensome pressure of life's malignant facts thus freshening your spirit to fight them with vigorous detachment!'[39] Azad conveyed his ambivalence without interfering in Gandhi's decision.[40]

Gandhi was, of course, mindful of what they and others thought, but a serene and radiant expression left Mahadev Desai to sing his favourite

---

34   Benthall papers.

35   Tinker, *The Ordeal of Love*, p. 112.

36   Motilal to Purshotamdas Thakurdas, 8 Oct. 1924, *SWMN*, vol. 4, p. 78.

37   Nehru, *An Autobiography*, p. 370.

38   Tendulkar, *Mahatma*, vol. 3, p. 201.

39   22 May 1933, Gandhi, S.N. papers (21331).

40   Gandhi to Azad, 9 May 1933, Gandhi, S.N. papers (21250).

bhajan in a trembling voice.[41] In August 1933, he used gestures for speech, punctuated less and less frequently by his animated smile. The magic worked on the audience.

Sulh-i Kul

The *Gita* recommended fasting or *tapas* (austerity) for the *karmayogi*. Fasting for light and penance, Gandhi explained, could be observed commonly in Christianity and Islam, while Hinduism is replete with instances of fasting for purification. It's a privilege and a duty. Along with his ceaseless effort to attain self-purification, Gandhi heard clearly the still small voice within and penance in obedience to it. He observed silence and prayed whenever he wanted to rid himself of impurities.[42]

Fasting in South Africa had fostered a splendid *espirit de corps*,[43] but Gandhi's first public fast took place between 15 and 18 March 1918, when he refused to touch food unless the strikers in the Ahmedabad mills rallied and continued the strike till they reached a settlement or left the mills altogether. Three days later, he secured what he wanted—a just settlement. While the fast raised his relationship with the people to a mythical level, it aroused veneration everywhere else.[44]

As a personal penance for the riots in Bombay on 17 November 1921, Gandhi reiterated his statement on non-violence as a cardinal moral principle, and proclaimed by the beat of the drum that the sword should not be drawn but sheathed. Thus when the people of Kohat, a 40-mile drive from Peshawar, resorted to large-scale rioting, Gandhi embarked on a fast at the Ali brothers' house. It was in Kucha-i Chelan in Old Delhi.[45] While politicians wrung their hands and racked their brains

---

41   This was on 8 May 1933. Gandhi to Padmaja Naidu, 8 May 1933, in Paranjape (ed.), *Sarojini Naidu: Selected Letters*, p. 286.

42   *Harijan*, 10 Dec. 1938, p. 172; To Amrit Kaur, 30 Nov. 1938, *CWMG* (Oct. 15, 1938-Feb. 28, 1939) p. 172.

43   Gandhi, *My Experiments with Truth*, p. 331; Rajmohan Gandhi, *Mohandas*, pp. 183-84.

44   Rajmohan Gandhi, op. cit., p. 21.Tridip Suhrud, 'Emptied of All But Love: Gandhi's First Public Fast', in Ganguli and Docker (eds), *Rethinking Gandhi*, p. 98.

45   Rajmohan Gandhi, op. cit., p. 294.

without offering either diagnosis or remedy, most people's attention was focused on this house for 21 days. 'My penance is the prayer of a bleeding heart' or 'the penance of Hindus and Mussalmans is not fasting but retracing their steps.' 'The fast,' wrote Fischer dramatically, 'was an adventure in goodness. The stake was one man's life. The prize was a nation's freedom.'[46] At Mohamed Ali's house, Gandhi secured freedom and a freshness of outlook, which generated sublimity and solemnity. Mirabehn prayed silently.[47]

To make the event worth its while, Mohamed Ali presented Gandhi, on 8 October 1924, a cow he had purchased from a butcher.[48] Two Muslim physicians stood in constant attendance. On the twentieth day, following 'days of grace, privilege, and peace,' friends prayed. On the twenty-first day, Gandhi asked Andrews, the *jagatmitra* (friend of all the world), to sing his favourite Christian hymn. He was at home with the best things. At the final service a hymn and an excerpt from the Upanishads were read out in the presence of Imam Sahib, Gandhi's co-prisoner in South Africa. Ansari, with his gracious and courteous bearing, offered Gandhi orange juice.

In 1925, Gandhi put his name down for another round of cleansing not to punish two boys guilty of sexual misconduct, but to restore the moral regime without any external intervention, animate the spiritual impulses of the ashram inmates, and to get them to perform certain positive acts for everyone's benefit. In this and other contexts, his pungent, direct, critical yet humane reflections are similar to John Stuart Mill's theory in his most famous essay, *On Liberty*. They differed insofar as Gandhi underscored individual penance, while Mill relied upon the instruments of state, such as the court of law, to ensure justice.

Seven years elapsed before Gandhi made the call to fast on 20 September 1932 against the provision of separate electorates for Dalits in

---

46   Louis Fischer, *The Life of Mahatma Gandhi* (New York, 1983 edn), p. 223.

47   Mirabehn, *The Spirit's Pilgrimage*, p. 63.

48   This carried more than symbolic significance for a man who had joined several *ulama*, including Abdul Bari and Hasan Nizami, to urge their Muslim brethren to refrain from cow-sacrifice during Id.

the Communal Award.[49] Jayakar, who had negotiated with the viceroy on the eve of the Gandhi-Irwin Pact, had not much faith in miracles worked by emotion: it would be wisdom, he proclaimed, 'to harness the present emotion to remove the barriers which have so far kept apart the depressed classes who form our kith and kin in Hinduism.'[50] CR, on the other hand, found a parallel for the nation's anguish in Athens twenty-three centuries earlier when the friends of Socrates surrounded him in prison and importuned him to escape from death.[51] Tagore, his mind filled with ever-increasing awe, rushed to see Gandhi, who lay on a *charpai* under a mango tree with Kasturba altering the position of his pillow and rubbing his forehead with olive oil. Besides, no one can forget Ambedkar, who fought every inch for Dalit rights. His first words were, 'Mahatmaji, you have been very unfair to us'. 'It is always my lot to appear to be unfair,' answered Gandhi. On Amritlal V. Thakkar or Thakkar Bapa's rejoinder to Ambedkar, Gandhi countered: 'But who can wake up a person pretending to sleep?'[52] Victory, for which the sixty-three-year-old prisoner paid a price, veered into sight. This restored Gandhi, who spoke increasingly of prayer for purification and for greater vigilance and watchfulness in connection with Dalit causes. Ambedkar told him, 'if you devoted yourself entirely to the welfare of the Depressed Classes, you would become our hero.'[53]

Recreate in your mind the scene on Tuesday 20 September 1932 at Yervada Jail, with Gandhi lying on a *charpai* surrounded by over 100 persons, including Sarojini Naidu, Vasanti Devi, Swarup Rani Nehru, Urmila Devi, Ambalal Sarabhai and his family, Patel and Mahadev Desai. Someone had sprinkled the yard with water. Someone offered Gandhi his usual meal of milk and fruit in the morning. Someone recited the *Gita* from half past six to eight, followed by a dose of lemon juice and honey with hot water. Meanwhile, the fateful hour approached for singing a song sent to Gandhi by Raihanaben, Abbas Tyabji's eldest

49   On 17 Aug. 1932, Ramsay MacDonald announced the Communal Award.

50   Speech on 7 Oct. 1932, Jayakar papers (355/1932).

51   Pyarelal, *The Epic Fast* (Ahmedabad, 1932), p. vii.

52   Gandhi to Thakkar, 2 Nov. 1938, *CWMG*, (Oct. 15, 1938-28 Jan. 1939), p. 87.

53   Rajmohan Gandhi, *Mohandas*, p. 374.

daughter.[54] 'A shadow is darkening today over India like a shadow cast by an eclipsed sun.' This was Tagore's voice.[55] Pyarelal captured the significance of the dramatic hour.[56]

With the completion of the 11 days of anguish on 26 September,[57] Gandhi's fast had been cushioned and curtained, soothed, solaced, served by a thousand modern conveniences and contrivances apart from the unflagging care and devotion without which he may not have survived the first fortnight of his ordeal. According to Sarojini Naidu, 'he has undoubtedly some inner well-spring of sustenance but as undoubtedly he is dependent on and demanding the material adventurous aids as well.'[58]

Tagore led the prayer by singing 'When the heart is hard and parched up, come with your shower of mercy'. This was followed by a recitation of Sanskrit verses and then was sung, all joining in, Gandhi's favourite 'Vaishnava janato'. Kasturba offered orange juice. Bapu and Gurudev embraced each other. Mahadev Desai brought in a picture of Andrews, then in London. With Bapu's face turned towards Mahadev, his eyes were wet with tears of joy. A jubilant Pyarelal noted: 'it was a day of jubilation and union of hearts in common thanksgiving to the Almighty God in that little world in Yervada prison; the milk of human kindness asserted itself and for once the woodenness of jail discipline was forgotten.'[59] The celebrations continued the next day; according to the Indian calendar, it was Gandhi's 64th birthday.

On the night of 28-29 April 1933, 'some voice—within or without— told Gandhi that he should fast. Jawaharlal demurred. He attached urgency to coordinating the anti-colonial struggle rather than dissipating the nation's energies. 'Life and death matter little,' he wrote in an emotional tone, 'or should matter little. The only thing that matters is the cause that

---

54   'O Traveller, arise, it is dawn; where is the night that thou still sleepest?'

55   Tendulkar, *Mahatma*, vol. 3, p. 168.

56   Ibid.

57   Pyarelal, *The Epic Fast*, p. vii.

58   Sarojini Naidu to Padmaja and Leilamani Naidu, 25 May 1933, in Paranjape (ed.), *Sarojini Naidu: Selected Letters*, p. 191.

59   Pyarelal, *The Epic Fast*, p. 80. Gandhi was in Yervada Central Prison from 5 May 1930 to 26 Jan. 1931. He was released along with Jawaharlal and Sarojini Naidu.

one works for, and if I could be sure that the best service to it is to die for it, then death would be simpler.'[60] Gandhi paid no attention to this veiled plea to abandon his plan and began his fast at Lady Thackeray's residence in Poona on 8 May 1933.[61] Earlier, he took pains to convince Andrews that fasting had a definite place in Hinduism, and properly so. It was a privilege that came only to a few, and it came in obedience to a call from above. On the morning of 28 May, before beginning his weekly silence, at half past eleven, he exchanged the following with Mahadev Desai:

'Better fix up the plan for tomorrow. Dr. Ansari will read something from the Koran; we might have a Christian hymn, and then our song of the true Vaishnava.'

'We have fixed it all up,' replied Mahadev. 'We shall begin the prayers at half past eleven and finish everything by twelve when you will break your fast.'

'No,' said Gandhi, 'the prayers cannot begin at that hour and I cannot break the fast until after thanksgiving.'

Kasturba put in: 'That will delay the breaking of the fast.'

'No,' repeated Gandhi, 'nothing until after the prayers which should begin at 12, when the vow was taken.' Mahadev was summoned again in the evening to receive instructions: 'You had suggested *Ishopanishad* for tomorrow. No, I think the verse in our hymn-book containing the words *Siddho tha Buddho thava* should be sung. Then the poet's song should be sung, either by his secretary or by you.'

On 29 May, Gandhi expected a Harijan student with an orange but he didn't turn up, feeling he was too humble to be admitted to the function. By twelve noon, prayers were over. Before sipping the orange juice, Gandhi dictated to Mahadev Desai a brief note to be read out to the assembled:

Within a minute or two I am going to break the fast. In His name and with faith in Him was it taken, in His name it terminates.

---

60   Gandhi S.N. Series (21181).

61   For Gandhi's fasts in India, 1915-48, Peter Gonsalves, *Clothing for Liberation: A Communication Analysis of Gandhi's Swadeshi Revolution* (Delhi, 2010), see app., pp. 137-38.

My faith is not less today. You will not expect me to make a speech on this occasion. It is an occasion for taking the name and singing the glory of God. But I may not forget the doctors and friends who have poured their affection on me during these days of privilege and grace. I am glad that Harijans are here with us today. I do not know exactly what work God expects from me now. But whatever it may be, I know that He will give me strength for it.'[62]

Were fasts a form of moral coercion as against rational persuasion, or political blackmail? 'Yes, the same kind of coercion which Jesus exercises upon you from the cross,' Gandhi responded.[63] Personal affliction enabled him to test his own prowess,[64] facilitate his transition from tumult into peace, and secure peace and joy.

Sarojini Naidu correctly apprehended a preparation for another fast.[65] 'My impotence has been gnawing at me of late,' he clarified. 'It will go immediately once the fast is undertaken … The final conclusion has flashed upon me and it makes me happy. No man, if he is pure, has anything more precious to give than his life.'[66]

Often, he brought into play faith, soul, and God to emphasise the moral dimensions of fasting. Thus, he convinced the political classes in Calcutta that disunity would increase hate, conflicts, and aggression. Often, his fast isolated the forces of evil so that the nation was infected with his know-how and made it fast/pray with intelligence, honesty, and intensity.[67] Indeed, the strength of the dramatic became all the more apparent when he raised the 1942 struggle from a physical to a moral

---

62   Tendulkar, *Mahatma*, vol. 3, p. 207.

63   Jones, *Mahatma Gandhi*, p. 143.

64   Brown, *Gandhi: Prisoner of Hope*, p. 200.

65   Sarojini Naidu to Padmaja and Leilamani, 25 May 1933, in Paranjape (ed.), *Sarojini Naidu: Selected Letters*, p. 290.

66   Pyarelal, *Mahatma Gandhi: The Last Phase*, vol. 2, p. 702.

67   Gandhi to Mazharul Haque, 20 Mar. 1920, Shivaji Rao Ayde, *Message of Ashiana* (Calcutta, 1962), p. 70.

and spiritual level through his penance,[68] or when he persuaded rioters to give their word that henceforth they would do as they were told.

Which politician enjoyed the luxury of people taking out processions to beg forgiveness?[69] It happened in Calcutta, and it happened owing to Gandhi's intervention.

'In the evening of my life,' Gandhi stated after the Delhi fast on 13 January 1948, 'I shall jump like a child to feel that the dream has been fulfilled.' This was his last fast directed 'to the conscience of all', in India and Pakistan. The dream worked. When Gandhi began his fast, Delhi was tense. But, on the fifth day, 18 January, the day Bapu broke his fast, 'the black clouds of trouble had cleared, sunlight glinted through, Light now shimmered in hearts that had once been tarnished.'[70] Thousands pledged to look after each other. Delhi's government employees, including policemen, resolved to strive for peace.[71]

These trends gave the secular nationalists the much-needed moral strength to renew their fight for the composite and tolerant society that so many had dreamt of; perhaps, Gandhi's mere presence [in Delhi] stunned the government and an army of stupefied Congress workers into action.[72] 'It engraved,' wrote Louis Fischer, 'an image of goodness on India's brain.'[73]

---

68   B.N. Pande (ed.), *A Centenary History of the Indian National Congress, 1935-1947* (Delhi, n.d.), vol. 3, p. 588.

69   Linlithgow to Hallet, n.d. Mushirul Hasan (ed.), *Towards Freedom*, (hereafter *TF*), 1939 (pt 2), p. 705.

70   Anis Kidwai, *In Freedom's Shade* trans. Ayesha Kidwai (Delhi, 2011), p. 31.

71   Abul Kalam Azad, *India Wins Freedom* (rev. edn Delhi, 1988), p. 220. Azad describes the scene: 'We all assembled in his room the next day at ten o'clock. Jawaharlal was already there...Gandhiji made a sign to indicate that those who wanted to repeat their pledge to him should do so. About 25 leaders of Delhi, including all schools of political thought among Hindus and Sikhs came up one by one and vowed that they would faithfully carry out the conditions laid down by Gandhi. He then made a sign and the men and women of his circle started to sing Ramdhun. His granddaughter brought a glass of orange juice and he made a sign that she should hand the glass to me. I held his glass to his lips and Gandhiji broke his fast.'

72   Gyanendra Pandey, *Remembering Partition: Violence, Nationalism and History in India* (New York, 2001), p. 141.

73   Fischer, *The Life of Mahatma Gandhi*, p. 494.

The purists were unhappy with the lights and sound around a solemn and poignant occasion. Gandhi was equally uncomfortable: when CR referred to the possibility of a fast to intensify the anti-untouchability crusade, Gandhi cautioned him: 'such exploitation robs a spiritual act of all its value'.[74] What sort of information did he want readers to access to establish the rightness of his cause? A smattering of everything? On 10 August 1942, the war cabinet learnt of Gandhi's fast.[75] The customary drill got underway. The viceroy set out procedures concerning visitors, doctors, medical bulletins on 29 December 1944. Doctors recorded Gandhi's daily weight, his intake and output of fluid, together with an account of the blood and urine. Officials read out health reports at street corners with breathless interest. Messages, entreaties, and appeals poured in from all sides. The official view was:

> Varied and lofty are the motives ascribed to Gandhi in thus endangering his life by voluntarily depriving himself of the means of sustaining it; but it is at least open to question whether it wasn't more than happy coincidence that turned these sacrifices so substantially to his political advantage.[76]

Sapru's view corresponded more or less with Jawaharlal's appreciation of Gandhi's fast. When news of his impending fast reached this Allahabad lawyer, he wrote in early November 1944:

> I am very anxious that you should on no account undertake a fast. I know how deeply spiritual you are and I also know that in your case the call of religion means much more than in the case of 99 out of a hundred. You will pardon me if I take a matter-of-fact and practical view of the thing. I am definitely certain that although it may bring solace to your heart and you may feel that you have done the penance for what you consider to

---

74   Tendulkar, *Mahatma*, vol. 3, p. 197.

75   IOR. L/PJ/8/600.

76   Ibid.

be the evils of the present day, your fast will not melt the heart of your opponents. On the contrary I feel some of them may be uncharitable enough to attribute to you unworthy motives. Never before in our history was it more necessary than now that you should live to guide the people of this country on the true path of nationalism.[77]

Ibadat Khana

A gong sounded. Gandhi descended the steps of the porch and sat at the centre of the opening. Scribbling secretaries gathered papers scattered about the floor. One of them was Mahadev Desai. Some young men popped in and applied mud-poultices on Gandhi's abdomen. Children moved and whispered, mothers leant over to silence them. A mother fed her baby at her breast. One heard the cluck, cluck of the tiny throat as it swallowed. Others pushed their babies towards Gandhi's feet. Young brides sought blessings, the sick his healing touch. A great many peasants stuck out their fingers when Gandhi turned to them smilingly. Dhoti-clad politicians squatted on the floor, often uneasily.

Wrapped in that white mantle, his shoulders two edges, his face immobile, Gandhi looked like Gautam Buddha.[78] The old pundit opposite tuned his sitar. The atmosphere took hold of the crowd.

Tolstoy Farm was situated in the loneliness of the veldt, 5000 ft or more above sea level.[79] Here the settlers adhered to the simple life close to nature and, in the communality of living and in the warmth of shared living, they found the touchstone of human progress. Each project stemmed from a practical problem, from a social task requiring immediate solution. Gandhi was called upon to solve the problems of 133 men, 66 women, and 78 children. Each one of them looked for

---

77   Sapru to Gandhi, 4 Nov. 1944, Rima Hooja (ed.), *Crusader for Self-Rule: Tej Bahadur Sapru & the Indian National Movement* (Delhi, 1999), p. 413.

78   Chandrashanker Shukla (ed.), *Reminiscences of Gandhiji by forty-eight contributors* (Bombay, 1951), pp. 87-91; Ian Stephens, *Monsoon Morning* (London, 1966), p. 94.

79   Mark Thompson, *Gandhi and his Ashrams* (Bombay, 1993), pp. 37-90.

something different and permanent, persisting through the chaos or unhappiness in their lives. They belonged to different backgrounds and nationalities and walked into a new and different world.[80]

Gandhi wanted to set up Sabarmati ashram at a place where he could revive the cottage industry with the help of Ambalal Sarabhai, Kasturbhai Lalbhai, Jamnalal Bajaj, and Ahmedabad's expanding resources from textile manufacturing.[81] Bajaj, a cotton merchant banker from Central Provinces (CP & Berar), was 'a sturdy figure of six feet, a pleasant dark face, friendly eyes, and the whitest of teeth which constantly flash, for he is a jolly good fellow'.[82] Many were struck with the conversion of 'an astute, shrewd, calculating merchant prince into a close adherent.[83]

The ashram was Gandhi's *Ibadat Khana* (House of Worship) or a *khanqah* (Sufi hospice); a place for cleansing the impurities of the mind; its inmates followed a dharma or *deen*.[84] *Satyagraha* began with discarding mill-woven cloth, settling for a few handlooms, adopting Gandhi's dietary habits, and praying for redemption, reminiscent of mystics. Even in the best of times, the scenes couldn't be re-enacted without Gandhi, the presiding deity.

The crowd was of mixed faith; the individuality of each stood out but when the pandit sang, the audience was one. They had no differences, not even to the eye. '*Raghuvar Tumko meri laj …*' sang the pandit. The music of the sitar strings trailed on, and the entire crowd, the whole place, dissolved in it. The moon emerged from behind the clouds. Some Jamia teachers, in their tightly buttoned coats and white Gandhi-caps, were sharply outlined; the others in their loose clothing vaguely so.

Halide Edip, the Turkish author who lived through some dizzying changes in her generation, had heard nothing like it. Beethoven, at times, reached a height where one is no longer harassed by emotion,

---

80   'My heart sank when I saw the place. Everything was so utterly drab and so unpleasant to the eye.' This was Vijaya Lakshmi's first response to an austere lifestyle.

81   Andrews (ed.), *Mahatma Gandhi: His Own Story*, p. 245.

82   Edip, *Inside India*, p. 189.

83   Jayakar, *The Story of My Life*, vol. 2, p. 375.

84   To a gentleman in Ranchi, n.d., Desai (ed.), *Day-to-Day with Gandhi*, vol. 2, p. 21.

but aware only of a serene intellectuality. The tune she heard not only lacked the disturbance of emotion, but freed one from one's body. One rose above one's bodily existence without being overwhelmed by a sweeping mystical rapture. One was released from all worry, and from the consciousness of the accumulated trash of the past. The words were from *Al-Fatiha*. In the absence of an *alim*, Kanu read the Quran in the special guttural, singsong way. A 'Hindu friend' reproached Gandhi: 'you have now given the *kalima* a place in the ashram. What further remains to be done to kill your Hinduism'. To this acidic remark, Gandhi sharply retorted: 'I am confident that my Hinduism and that of the other ashram Hindus has grown thereby.'

Music is in the highest degree a universal language, which is related in reality to the universality of concepts, much as they are related to particular things.[85] Friedrich Nietzsche's definition fits in squarely with its soothing and elevating effect on ashram life. With Kakasaheb's help, Pandit N.M. Khare compiled an anthology of hymns 'full of fragrance and reality'. Manu sang them during the early morning prayer 'when the world is still in bed, only a few early birds are shaking sleep from their wings, only a few fishing boats ripple the dreaming water'.[86] Gandhi joined the chorus from within his curtained bed. On another occasion, sitting cross-legged with head bowed and a loudspeaker marked 'Chicago Radio Company' placed near him, women recited, first in a wandering key, from the *Gita*, and, later, the exuberant and rhythmic *Ram nam*. To this, the audience kept time by clapping their hands at an ever-increasing tempo. Once, not long before his assassination, Gandhi heard Manu and Abha, his grand-nieces sing a *bhajan*. They were out of tune, for which Gandhi gently reprimanded them.

In front of Halide Edip was the façade of the house overlooking a vast field where, in the distance, fires were lit and figures in white moved about. The fires were yet only wreaths of smoke lazily curling upwards. Before the house into which all the rooms of the first floor opened was

---

85   Friedrich Nietzsche, *The Birth of Tragedy and the Case of Wagner*, trans. with commentary by Walter Kaufman (New York, 1967), p. 101.

86   Sarojini Naidu to 'My darling child', in Paranjape (ed.), *Sarojini Naidu: Selected Letters*, p. 183.

a spacious porch. Gandhi's room was large with a concrete floor. Papers and books were scattered on the mat. Gandhi's eyes were 'always his most remarkable feature and were in reality the lamps of his soul'. They could read so much from them.[87] They were deep-set and clear, and slightly drawn towards the narrow temples, in a somewhat Mongolian fashion. The eye-folds were however not tautly drawn towards the raised delicate eyebrows. As the face bent forward, there appeared a baldish dome where a Hindu lock appeared, a tiny curl, on top of it.

The door opened continually. Men wearing different clothes entered, fell on their faces at the fringe of the mat, and then sat with their hands folded on their knees before submerging themselves in Gandhi's personality. They sat in rows to consult him on personal and professional matters. Mothers led their children by the hand or carried them in their arms. In next to no time, a crowd in the form of a great horseshoe gathered. At the open end of the horseshoe, a volunteer placed a few carpets. No more gold in the sky, but the dusk was velvety. The fires, which had been smoking, were now flames licking the dusk, while tiny groups of people appeared as white smudges against them.

A gong sounded. Gandhi came down. The crowd rose with a rustle, women dragged their chattering babies, and men adjusted their clothing. All hurried towards the steps of the porch. Children moved and whispered. There was something contagious in their happiness; more than their elders they seemed to have a greater awareness of the activity around them. The women sought Gandhi's blessings, or perhaps beseeched him to heal their sick ones. 'Now, now, now …', he'd say to them, 'you don't mean that …' He scolded them for their incurable idolatry.

Scene two of this fascinating and rather poignant description is from Wardha. It is four o'clock. Darkness was thinning away, and stars were pale. The silence grew deeper; the ghosts of the days gone by stalked stealthily among the trees. As darkness receded, devotees squatted on the floor with their hands on their knees and their heads piously bent. A low table with three legs had a *diya* on it.

---

87   Polak, *Mr. Gandhi: The Man*, p. 18.

Mirabehn absorbed the unique multicultural atmosphere to become the educator of the inmates. Habituated to her companionship, Gandhi grew youthful while she sat right behind him. 'Here is the only countenance that reflects the liquid flame; the rest are dim outlines.'[88]

Someone sang a Sanskrit invocation; other voices joining in the collective chanting conveying the impression of a subterranean, even sepulchral hum. The music had an enrapturing and enervating effect. The mother's influence perpetually returned to Gandhi's mind and conscience, lending fragrance and sweetness to the text. Nothing in the world could compare with them in beauty and truth and sweetness. At the end of the collective hum, the assembly repeated the eleven vows,[89] which contained both the essence of Gandhi's teachings as well as the secret longings of inarticulate human beings. They were renewed every morning. Gandhi persisted that they be fulfilled both in letter and spirit.A chord in Halide Edip's heart was touched.[90]

At eight o'clock the men walked through the arched gate for sanitation and scavenging, carrying shovels and spades on their shoulders or a bucket in their hands. Two hours later, they and others had their first meal of rice, vegetables, and fruit. Gandhi's afternoon walk followed, after which he'd spin, talk, and welcome guests. Once, Shriman Narayan heard Louis Fischer, Gandhi's future biographer, say that he had travelled from Wardha railway station in a rickety *tonga* in sweltering heat.[91] At five, Gandhi settled for the day's second and last meal. *Shanti, Shanti, Shanti!* The invocation for peace echoed against the walls. Two hours later, he walked up for the evening prayers. Purple and crimson shadows settled on the sombre green foliage. Mirabehn's flute produced, as the three stars in the flushed and gilded firmament

---

88   Edip, *Inside India*, p. 185.

89   They were: (1) Non-violence, (2) Truth, (3) Non-stealing, (4) Celibacy, (5) Non-possession, (6) Bread-labour, (7) Control of palate, (8) Fearlessness, (9) Equal respect for all religions, (10) Swadeshi, (11) Eradication of untouchability. C.F. Andrews, *Mahatma Gandhi: His Life and Ideas* (Bombay, rpt, 2005), p. 28. On this point, *see also* Sheila McDonough, *Gandhi's Responses to Islam* (Delhi, 1994), p. 7; Gandhi, *My Experiments with Truth*, p. 455.

90   Edip, *Inside India*.

91   Shriman Narayan, *Memoirs: Window on Gandhi and Nehru* (Bombay, 1971), p. 9.

above glittered, pastoral and poignant notes which fell one by one into the hushed and flushed night.

Mirabehn decorated Gandhi's room, to which he retired after a hectic day: *Oum*, a palm tree, a peacock, and the *charkha* symbolised God, nature, living beings, and human activity. The room had the following inscription on the wall: 'When you are in the right you can afford to keep your temper, and when you are not in the wrong, you can not afford to lose it.' Kasturba's room was next to Gandhi's. Mahadev Desai stayed in one of the two rooms in front; the other served as a museum of handicrafts and as a guest room. The boys' and women's hostel was about two miles away.

Another day began: The same spectacle of a people labouring, enjoying themselves, and growing in strength together. All over again, Gandhi's warmth and smile transformed the exacting, monastic, puritanical atmosphere. He shared aspects of his spiritual life with the audience in a low voice.[92] Jayakar returned from the ashram convinced of his earnestness and faith. His fervour, sacrifice, and asceticism touched him.[93]

Jean-Jacques Rousseau's society needed a new civic religion for a true community spirit to be active. Gandhi justified ashram life on similar lines without ruling out individual failings. He did, aside from that, seek answers to the reasons why some inmates gradually forsake *ahimsa*?[94] Why did they not purge luxury and self-indulgence? Why did caste prejudices persist? Why did the furore over a *shed* (Dalit) family joining the ashram take place?[95] All manner of uncertainties assailed the minds when Chhaganlal Gandhi faced charges of embezzlement. Pressures and expectations produced persons who would ordinarily be regarded as 'cranks', or when the inmates encountered opposition from the very people who benefited from spinning, road construction, house building, or sanitation work. When that happened, the wall dividing Gandhi from the inmates became higher and thicker. In

---

92   John Haynes Holmes, *My Gandhi* (London, 1954), p. 45.

93   Jayakar, *The Story of My Life*, vol. 2, p. 24.

94   Thompson, *Gandhi and his Ashrams*, p. 203.

95   B.R. Nanda, *In Gandhi's Footsteps: The Life and Times of Jamnalal Bajaj* (New York, 1990), p. 31.

1939, he described Sabarmati ashram as 'an asylum for the insane, the infirm, the abnormal and the like'; the bickering among the inmates made him consider its closure.[96] But he postponed the decision towards the end of 1944 owing to the rioting in Bihar. In August 1945, he considered shifting to Sevagram or Wardha, but decided against it on 20 November 1946. A sad end to an innovative enterprise!

To sum up, Gandhi rarely looked at the individual simply qua the individual. Almost invariably he saw him or her as functioning within a series of concentrically larger social units. He therefore envisaged the ashram as a collectivity, with the goal to give people better access to a different way of life and a venue to share values. However, Nirmal Kumar Bose found his approach flawed for two reasons. First, the people's apprenticeship had been insufficient, and yet they were expected to work with courage, persistence, and confidence. Second, it was wrong for Gandhi to expect them to practise virtues even when they were not capable of this. This imposed strain on them, as indeed it did in the case of several men and women Bose knew.[97] Gandhi's response was that diversity provided the necessary condition to think and act differently.

The political and religious requisites for preserving diversity in every nook and corner lay in preserving the sanctity of two major symbols: the cow and the Khilafat. In fact, just when Sabarmati ashram was beginning to promote creative impulses, Gandhi was drawn to the Khilafat, probably one of the most controversial aspects of his public life. In South Africa he'd been aware of its emotive value and identified himself with it; now, he demonstrated the consistency of the elaborate but mostly Hinduised ashram codes with his endorsement of a Muslim religious subject. Realistically speaking, he had access to no 'out of the ordinary' paradigms, and the availability of any other option led him to reiterate his allegiance to *dharma*, 'a very catholic, all-embracing creed', and, at the same time, uphold his stand on the Khilafat. He was transported to the seventh heaven; in that endeavour, he enhanced his strength to save Hinduism from harm. He concluded with a cautionary note: 'The danger that hovers over Hinduism from the brute-force of

---

96   Brown, *Gandhi: Prisoner of Hope*, p. 286.
97   Bose to Gandhi, 3 Jan. 1947. N.K. Bose papers (269 C).

European powers is quite as great as that over Islam. Only it is Islam that bears the brunt of the attack today, while Hinduism's turn may come tomorrow.'[98] 'With heat, hammer and chisel,' writes Rajmohan Gandhi, and through 'self-denials, fasts, suppression and sublimations—he had moulded himself to be loyal to every Indian but not confined to any section of India, to any single caste, community or region.'[99]

---

98   Desai (ed.), *Day-to-Day with Gandhi*, vol. 1, p. 236.

99   Rajmohan Gandhi, *The Good Boatman: Portrait of Gandhi* (Delhi, 1995), p. 110-11.

4
The Journey to Swaraj:
Paths Taken and Not Taken

Awwal-i shab wo bazm ki raunaq, Shama bhi thi Parwana bhi...

What it (*Pax Britannica*) successfully does is to ensure the protection, by means of extraordinary military and other dispositions of the Europeans who are exploiting the country. *Pax Britannica*, therefore, in so far as it is common to the whole of the country, is not a blessing calculated to advance the nation either economically or politically. It has emasculated the people and reduced them to a state of helplessness. My suggestion, therefore, is that common birth, common distress, common manners and common bondage are each in itself and all collectively a real cohesive force, not *Pax Britannica*. Consciousness of distress and consciousness of bondage are unifying the people in a manner in which they have never before been unified. And when these become a thing of the past as they are bound to, common birth will prove a force that will make the nation irresistible.

-M.K. Gandhi, *The Way to Communal Harmony*, pp. 14-15.

Commentators have pointed out that the Khilafat issue transcended religious and sectarian particularism and provided a broader basis for political activism. On these lines, they connect the pan-Islamic surge with the furore over a regressive piece of legislation which, in turn, widened the gulf between the colonised and their rulers. This general thesis obviously contains an important element of truth, and there are indeed striking parallels with the messianic movements in some parts of Black Africa.[1]

Another striking feature of the Khilafat campaign was the presence of a large number of leaders, whose experience in public affairs was brief. This was particularly so with the ulama who were, in fact, not what they symbolised. Some were estimable but not necessarily learned.

---

[1]   John Middleton (ed.), *Black Africa: Its People and their Cultures Today* (London, 1970), p. 226.

Some were theologians; others were school or college teachers or prayer leaders in mosques. The sympathy they evoked was largely localised. It does not seem unreasonable to claim that they were a problem, and it may well have enlarged their disagreements with Gandhi. The rabble-rousers, in particular, caused incalculable damage to their alliance.

'Khilafat Day' on 17 October 1919, a day of protest, brought Gandhi face to face with a demand he couldn't let pass. He predicated his initiatives on the conviction that cross-community linkages would broaden understanding of, and tolerance for, conflicting religious and cultural components. There were of course some drawbacks to this arrangement, especially becaue it rested on the assumption that the political climate was stable and the strategies to deal with it were variable. Nonetheless, Gandhi assumed that the Khilafatists burned with a common desire, a *resentment* of British rule. Exalting self-sacrifice for lofty principles as a unique virtue, he explained on 3 May 1920:

> If I kept aloof from the Khilafat question, I would consider myself as having lost all my worth. That work is my dharma *par excellence*. It is through the Khilafat that I am doing the triple duty of showing to the world what *ahimsa* really means, of uniting Hindus and Muslims and of coming in contact with one and all. And if the non-cooperation movement goes on all right, a tremendous brute-force will have to yield to an apparently simple and negligible power. Khilafat is the great churning process of the ocean that India is.[2]

Gandhi blamed the government for breaking the Khilafat pledges, and announced his resolve to stand by the Muslims in their hour of trial. His tone sounded gentle and soothing, yet it contained the bitterness of sarcasm. With his faith in *Pax Britannica* undermined by the Turkish Peace Terms and the Hunter Report, he linked rightness, whether for oneself or for the greater good, with ethics and morality. He believed that a movement claiming cultured men and women as willing and unenthusiastic sufferers had to be fostered and not crushed. This meant eschewing any form of condition for his support: 'Light brings

---

2   Desai (ed.), *Day-to-Day with Gandhi*, vol. 2, p. 154.

light not darkness, and nobility done with a noble purpose will be twice rewarded.'[3]

If Satyagraha was a moral revolution, then civil resistance was its integral component. This is where Gandhi differed with Tilak. His rejoinder to Tilak's interpretation of the *Gita* affirmed that the law wasn't to return evil for evil but good for evil. He turned to soul force and renunciation rather than advocate, as Tilak or the revolutionaries did, physical force and counteraction. Lastly, he used 'politics' to incorporate strong elements of ethics and morality. Tilak, on the other hand, considered politics to be a sport for worldly people and not for saints and sadhus. This is also the point of difference between Gandhi and Tagore. While the poet-philosopher wondered about the world around him from the point of view of an intellectual humanist, Gandhi undertook to cleanse society and dismantle the colonial edifice step by step. The heart of many educated Indians was still with Tagore who, while as much a patriot as Gandhi, had a greater sense of *joie de vivre* and freedom of the spirit.[4]

True, Gandhi engaged in debate, argument, disagreement, compromise, and cooperation, but his interventions were largely over and above the routine political engagements. Along these lines, he could be hard and unbending, because his self-belief was too strong to be rationally explained. He connected a purely political decision—to embark on a fast against the breach of covenant in the princely state of Rajkot—with God. Inner promptings motivated his 'inexplicable actions', because he had no other resource as a satyagrahi.[5]

On 9 September 1920, people largely jealous of his meteoric rise and the loss of face, girded their loins to oust the upstart at the Calcutta session of the Congress. It however took Gandhi barely 20 or 25 minutes

---

3   *Young India*, 22 Dec. 1920, *CWMG* (Nov. 1920-1 Apr. 1921), p. 105.

4   S. Gopal, *Radhakrishnan: A Biography* (Delhi, 1989), p. 68.

5   *Harijan*, 11 Mar. 1939, M.K. Gandhi, *The Indian states problem* (Ahmedabad, 1911), p. 205. Elsewhere, he noted: 'He who has urged me to undertake the fast, will give me strength to go through it, and if it is His will that I should still live for a while on this earth to carry on the self-chosen mission of humanity, no fast, however prolonged, will dissolve the body.' Gandhi, *The Indian states problem*, p. 207.

to prove, as if any proof was necessary, that he was no upstart.[6] Gandhi won over Lajpat Rai, who touted himself as a figure of cross-party unity, converted Motilal who had the intellectual depth for his policy swings to carry conviction, brushed aside Jinnah's pompous legalities, countered Pal's casuistic arguments, and closed his eyes to Annie Besant's exuberance. As Jayakar put it: 'His whirlwind campaign none could withstand, while weaker men stumbled and tottered, he took himself from one conquest to another and his increasing boldness in proclaiming his doctrines staggered not a few.'[7] Out of discomfiture for their former fervour, opponents cleared their throats and spoke no word more about Non-Cooperation, pretending that nothing had really happened.

The fuss attending Non-Cooperation served to make the Congress the tail of the Khilafat lion,[8] but obscured what would later prove to be far more momentous developments. The Ali brothers, who wore loose long robes and red Turkish caps, swung the pendulum to carry the Non-Cooperation resolution. The death of Abdul Bari's daughters prevented him from attending the special Congress, but he ensured a large Muslim presence in Calcutta.[9]

Following this decisive victory, Gandhi spent some time in Visva Bharati's idyllic surroundings before boarding the train to Aligarh, where he addressed the students at Syed Ahmad's Muslim University.[10] He spoke haltingly in Hindustani, without being heard amidst the din at the Union Hall. The audience had decidedly made up its mind against Non-Cooperation. In jeering tones, they advised Gandhi to 'convert' those at Banaras Hindu University before preaching to others. He retorted that the weeds needed to be rooted out to sow a good crop. He envisaged a larger, nobler, and purer Aligarh.

---

6   Yagnik, *Gandhi As I Knew Him*, p. 154.

7   Jayakar, *The Story of My Life*, vol. 2, p. 375.

8   M. Naeem Qureshi, *Pan-Islam in British Indian Politics: A Study of the Khilafat Movement 1918-1924* (Leiden, 1999), p. 243.

9   Francis Robinson, *The 'Ulama of Farangi Mahall and Islamic Culture in South Asia* (Delhi, 2001), p. 156, and in *Separatism Among Indian Muslims*, pp. 304-25.

10   For a detailed account of his activities, of Azad and the Ali brothers, see Home Pol. (A) Dec. 1920, nos. 210-16 & K.-W, NAI.

Gandhi conveyed his magnanimity to young men and women. He had a kind, somewhat whimsical manner, and was blessed with a great capacity for affection. No wonder some of the students who were to join the freedom struggle as activists felt that he and Tagore were the two guiding stars who inspired the new spirit within them, and that, unlike the haughty, moralistic, and patronising traditional gentry, the Mahatma spoke every word from the depth of his heart and meant everything he uttered. No wonder, some Aligarh students nursed the desire to create an alternate stream of consciousness. They founded the Jamia Millia Islamia. A decade of their activism manifested itself spectacularly in the awareness that they had to take matters into their own hands. Gandhi provided the inspiration.

Outside Aligarh, Gandhi inaugurated National College and Gujarat National University on 15 November. Professor Gidwani, having left St. Stephen's College, joined National College, which began with 300 students. Similarly, a National College got going in Patna on 5 January 1921. These many-sided activities vindicated Gandhi's ideas on voluntary initiatives to be carried out by citizens whose traditions had inclined them to practice a high degree of cooperation as protection against an external enemy. It was however different with the overall Non-Cooperation agenda, which could scarcely capture party policy outright.

In the Christmas week of 1920, a team of workers boarded a railway special, travelling from Ahmedabad to Nagpur, with others joining at different stations up to Surat and Bardoli. 'We were fed and feasted during our journey as never before—and never since,' a delegate recalled. At the Congress site were simple huts with shaky *charpais* for nearly 15,000 delegates.[11] In one of them, Gandhi gathered his ammunition. His opponents were expected to storm Nagpur, the venue of the Congress in December 1920.[12] As in Calcutta a few months back, tension mounted in the open session. Gossip mongers spread

---

11   Yagnik, *Gandhi As I Knew Him*, p. 168.

12   D.E.U. Baker, *Changing Political Leadership in an Indian Province: The Central Provinces and Berar 1919-1939* (New Delhi, 1979), pp. 72-73, for the Nagpur Congress.

rumours and reporters filed unsubstantiated reports. Ultimately, the imposing phalanx of veteran warriors gave in after the smoke of battle cleared. C. Vijayaraghavachariar, up to then lukewarm towards Non-Cooperation, cooperated; Lajpat Rai, the 'Lion of Punjab', roared in Calcutta but was silenced in Nagpur; G.S. Khaparde, a Tilak loyalist, buckled under pressure; and C.R. Das softened his stand. By this time, polling in the elections had taken place and the boycott of legislatures, to which he was largely opposed, had ceased to be a live issue. Under the circumstances, Das wanted to orchestrate an anti-British campaign which would be more obstructive than Gandhi's Non-Cooperation.[13] Endowed with great abilities and force of character, he gave away his large fortune principally for girls' education.

At Nagpur, the Congress forsook the time-honoured procedure of begging for something and instead took to the path of defiance.[14] What A.O. Hume had envisaged in 1885 had at last come true. The delegates asked themselves and each other, 'who is this man that speaketh with a tone of authority and whence doth he come?'[15] Who was this man who intoxicated them, carried them off their feet, almost hypnotised them, and moved them and others by his gospel of non-violent Non-Cooperation?[16] Whatever cynical motives some of his contemporaries attributed to Gandhi, the people venerated him as a saint and quite a few as an incarnation of the divine. Their path seemed to lie clear in front and they marched ahead, buoyed by the zest of others, and in turn helping to swell the tide.[17] Gandhi himself disclaimed the role of a saint. He wanted the word to be ruled out of present life. It was too sacred a word to be lightly applied to anyone, much less to one, like himself, who claims only to be a humble searcher of the truth. He made clear to Kallenbach in South Africa: 'I know that in many things there is

---

13   Ray, *Social Conflict and Political Unrest in Bengal*, p. 262.

14   Walter Hauser, 'Swami Sahajanand and the Politics of Social Reform, 1907-1950', *Indian Historical Review*, vol. 18, nos. 1-2, (July 1991 and Jan. 1992), p. 72.

15   B. Pattabhi Sitaramayya, *The History of the Indian National Congress 1885-1935* (Madras, 1935), vol. 1, p. 348.

16   Nehru, *Glimpses of World History*, p. 716; Yagnik, *Gandhi As I Knew Him*, p. 174.

17   Nehru, *An Autobiography*, p. 69.

room for improvement. Only I cannot see it. I do need a friendly critic.'
Elsewhere, he stated:

> 'Acharya Kripalani is quite correct in saying that there is no such
> thing as Gandhism. Insistence on truth is an eternal principle.
> While contemplating on it the jewel of non-violence was discovered
> and as a result of the experiments in non-violence emerged the
> programme of 1920. Trying to attain independence without it is as
> pounding chaff.'[18]

Popular preachers, drawn from the same social stratum as their simple
audience, presented the word 'Khilafat' less as a pan-Islamic wrong and
more as a new and completely different social order, the millenarianism
of Islam's egalitarianism, and the alleviation of all distress. In effect, they
conjured up a picture of a better world under Gandhi's direction. They
spread the news that one little tiny man like him, frail in body and all
alone, brought to his knees the great Burra Lat Sahib.[19] They spread
stories of his miraculous powers; like the one where the doors just flew
open at the time of his imprisonment in Surat. Certainly, the Muslims
in Dumri exhorted the gathering to go to jail, as did the Ali brothers for
two years apiece. The man who sang the song slipped away thereafter,
but the crowd marched to the *thana* to the cry of '*Gandhi Zindabad*'.
That day, the people's movement in Dumri and their fascination with
the Mahatma were compounded.[20] Without giving a firm answer on the
gains and losses of such occurrences, what deserves explicit recognition
here is their convergence.

Besides the mighty wave of hero worship, the view gained credence
that Gandhi could compel even the heavens above to shower the manna
of freedom upon them. It was reinforced by his routinely visiting a place,
large or small, lecturing in *maidans*, and moving on after establishing

---

18   Gandhi to Kallenbach, Gandhi-Kallenbach papers. 'A Foreword', *CWMG*
      (1 Aug. 1937-31 Mar 1938), p. 308.

19   Ray, *Social Conflict and Political Unrest in Bengal*, p. 251.

20   Shahid Amin, *Event, Metaphor, Memory: Chauri Chaura 1922-1992* (New
      Delhi, 1995), p. 171.

public contact. In this way, he entered 'the humblest hut.'[21] As in Bihar, people lined up at the rail stations to shower their love in the form of flowers and money (and innumerable garlands of thick misshapen yarn). A Gandhi puja took place at Ghazipur in eastern UP. 'It is good to be alive these days,' Andrews declared, echoing Wordsworth in the French Revolution. 'The whole of India is aflame.'[22]

Both in religion and politics, the source of every action is some individual person. As I see it, and as women from the middle classes too saw it, Gandhi inspired them to straddle the domestic and the public domain with ease. Thus the mother of the Ali brothers, the wife of Maulana Hasrat Mohani,[23] Begum Ansari, Attia Fyzee and many other ladies jumped into the fray during the Khilafat movement. Many more responded in 1920-21. Avantikabai Gokhale and Kamaladevi Chattopadhyay, who was called in her days in Britain 'the uncrowned Queen of India', were among the first women satyagrahis a decade later. She was 'the natural feminine who could effortlessly match the masculine power with a smile, humour and laughter', writes Kapila Vatsayan, Kamaladevi's protégé.[24]

Sarojini Naidu headed the Rashtriya Stree Sabha, an independent women's organisation with Goshiben Naoroji and Avantikabai Gokhale. Potentially a poet of major rank, she was deflected from the highway of poetry by her engagement in politics. She had a strong urge to express her moods through her writings, and to register the events she witnessed in a way that reflected her thinking and her views of them. That Tyabji women were also sympathetic to Gandhi's cause, then and later, may be

---

21 Edip, *Inside India*, p. 167. Mushir Hosain Kidwai, a *taluqdar* of Gadia in Barabanki district, added elsewhere: 'No longer does a European dare to throw out unceremoniously the luggage of an Indian from a railway carriage and quietly occupy his seat. No longer does an English grocer's son or grandson, when out in India, treat a respectable Indian with contempt.' Kidwai, *Swaraj and How to obtain it* (Lucknow, 1924), p. 38.

22 Andrews to Tagore, 15 Oct. 1920; Ray, *Social Conflict and Political Unrest in Bengal*, p. 251; Tinker, *The Ordeal of Love*, p. 171.

23 Atiq Siddiqi (ed.), *Begum Hasrat Mohani aur unke khatut* (Delhi, 1981).

24 Kapila Vatsyayan, 'Education through the Arts: Values and Skills' (First Kamaladevi Chattopadhyay Memorial Lecture), Centre for Cultural Resources and Training, 29 May 2009.

seen in their attending and speaking at nationalist meetings, staying at his ashrams, and courting arrest for civil disobedience acts.[25]

Women went as far as worshipping Gandhi and putting their babies on his lap.[26] They came in thousands, often removing their age-old veils to see him, and showered their copper, silver, gold ornaments and jewels at his feet. In Panipat, Hakiman, called Hakko, calmly took off her earrings, necklace, bangles, and wristbands for the swaraj fund. In Patna, Begum Mazharul Haque gave away her four choicest bangles made up of pearls and rubies. Gandhi thanked God that He had brought him in touch with the Tyabji family.[27] In Awadh, the gentry cast off their silks and muslins of foreign manufacture. Khadija *phupi* (aunt), who was associated with Shah Abdul Haq's much venerated shrine in Rudauli (Barabanki district), donned *khaddar*.[28] Nazar Sajjad Hyder, wife of the Urdu journalist-scholar Sajjad Hyder Yildirim, gave up purdah in 1920 and wore printed khadi saris. In the novel *Jaanbaaz*, the heroine sets fire to the English thread she used for crocheting her laces. With Kamla, a friend, she set up a small 'factory' to weave towels. Her fiancé Qamar, a superintendent of police, joined the non-cooperators.[29] Hakiman smiled when Gandhi called them 'weapons in our battle for freedom'. She gave away her entire life's savings, and the hopes of her children's future for the nation. Consider too the mood of the time, captured by the novelist Attia Hosain:

---

25   Siobhan Lambert-Hurley, *Atiya's Journeys: A Muslim Woman from Colonial Bombay to Edwardian Britain* (Delhi, 2010), p. 40.

26   Judith M. Brown, *Gandhi's Rise to Power: Indian Politics 1915-1922* (Cambridge, 1972), p. 347.

27   4 Dec. 1920, *CWMG* (Nov. 1920-Apr. 1921), p. 70.

28   Hameeda Salim, *Shorish-i Dauran: Yaden* (New Delhi, 1995), p. 34. Gandhi stated the following at Tinnevelly on 23 Sept 1921: 'Hakim Ajmal Khan, in his old age, Dr. Ansari, Maulana Abdul Bari, and many other distinguished Mussulman countrymen of ours and Pandit Motilal Nehru, in his old age, having been born with a silver spoon in his mouth, and C.R. Das enjoying a practice that was second to none in all India, were not joking when they adopted khaddar. Their wives are not joking when they adopted heavy khaddar just as heavy as you see myself, Maulana Saheb and Dr. Rajan wearing and spinning from day to day as a sacrament.'

29   Qurratulain Hyder, *The Sound of Falling Leaves* (Delhi, 1994), p. ix.

Sita and I had watched from the balcony of the house and a hot sickness burned inside us, a fear and an anger; and we had vowed when we were old enough to fight for our country's freedom as the Satyagrahis did, to lie on the spit-stained pavements in front of treacherous shops that sold foreign cloth, to march in peaceful protest, to defy the might of the arrogant whites. From that day we had stopped singing the alien National Anthem at school concerts, and we used to leave the cinema when its first chords were struck. We had felt we were part of a great movement, and the taunts of Anglo-Indian girls at school had lost their power.[30]

In November 1921, the Congress party's ship rode on the crest of a wave of exuberant and uncontrolled excitement during the visit of Edward, Prince of Wales, and later King Emperor Edward VIII. It was a prodigious flop. The bureaucracy's decision to invite him was ill-timed, while the repression by Reading's government, in the aftermath of bloodshed in Bombay, deepened anti-colonial feelings. 'Such a beautiful edifice built on the bedrock of unstinted sacrifice and patient suffering,' observed the *Young Patriot* from Nagpur, 'is likely to last as long as the Sun and the Moon continue to shine in the heavens. It is not too much to thank the viceroy for affording rare opportunities for Indians to build their temple of liberty....'

At the close of 1921, Gandhi was riding high. The Congress took place at Ahmedabad. To mark the spirit of the time the great tent was made up of native spun cloth; delegates squatted on the ground. They had mostly discarded European dress. Noel Carrington, a 'boxwallah' had this to say in his memoir:

The hold he (Gandhi) established over the masses was a phenomenon hitherto unknown to Anglo-India where it was an established myth that nationalism was more or less confined to the middle classes.[31]

---

30   K.A. Abbas, 'The Mahatma and the Older Weaver Woman', Mushirul Hasan (ed.), *Islam in South Asia: Negotiating Diversities*, vol. 5 (Delhi, 2010), p. 48; Hosain, *Sunlight on a Broken Column*, p. 91.

31   'Ebb and Tide of the Raj', IOR, Noel Carrington papers (C 392).

The Passionate Liberator

BEHIND THE FAÇADE OF THE DESTRUCTION OF THIS FOSSILIZED MAN
THE WORK OF CREATING A NEW MAN IS IN PROGRESS.

This kind of emotional intensity received greater press coverage than ever before, and attracted younger, tougher adherents who were more ready and more able to boycott schools, colleges, law courts, and risk being imprisoned. Shabbir Hasan Khan, popularly known as Josh Malihabadi, enunciated a theory of revolution for national regeneration.

Jayaprakash Narayan, born in a tiny Bihar village, was among the thousands 'swept away and momentarily lifted up to the skies'. He wore khadi and learnt to spin on the *charkha*. His wife Prabhavati, daughter of a famous Patna barrister Braj Kishore, was initiated into the faith of fundamental simplicity and stability at the ashram. She considered it a pious duty to shake off the lust imprisoned in a mortal body and became a *brahmacharya*. Gandhi humorously dubbed her as his hostage from the socialist movement.[32]

On 2 November 1927, Gandhi visited Jamia. He did not enter a *biradari* torn by rival fanaticisms. Jamia's prevalent tone, both before and after moving to its new site in Okhla in south Delhi, was moderation in politics, interest in language and literature, and earnest but philosophical religion. Thus, Gandhi came across boys spinning the *takli*. He looked closely at everything, seemed pleased, and suggested enrolling non-Muslim students if they desired learning about Islam. Shafiqur Rahman Kidwai, a teacher at Jamia, a sister university of Bihar and Kashi Vidyapeeth, wore *khaddar* and the Gandhi cap. The soul of Jamia spoke through him. Zakir Husain, co-author of the Wardha scheme in 1937, Mohammad Mujeeb and Abid Husain were the other Jamia figures. Besides their liberal-orientation, they were indefatigable in work. About Zakir Husain, Gandhi had many kind words to say. As for Jamia's chancellor, he put out mischievously: 'Dr. Ansari is concerned primarily with rejuvenation and offering one the chance of becoming thirty again and having a harem.'[33] Genial and kindly, colleagues relied

---

32   Allan and Wendy Scarfe, *J.P.: His Biography* (Delhi, 1977), p. 67.

33   20 July 1947, Campbell-Johnson, *Mission with Mountbatten*, p. 146.

on his earnestness, shrewdness, common sense, and instinct. As for Gandhi's sparkling humour, which he sometimes concealed, it brought relief in those trying days when Jamia was yet to get off the ground. He recalled the memorable day, 11 October 1920, when he persuaded Mohamed Ali and his friends to start Jamia:

> Even after seven years, I don't feel the least sorry for that nor do I think that I committed a blunder in that. I believe that those who gave up their studies at the Government institutions did a great service to the country. I am sure that when the history of that period in India will be written the historian will no doubt have to write that those who boycotted Government institutions did great good to themselves and to their country ... I am glad to find here some of the traces of those proud days, and I am very happy that you are trying your utmost to keep the flag flying. Your number is small, but the world never overflowed with good and true men. I ask you not to worry yourselves about the smallness of the number, but to remember that however few you may be the freedom of the country depends on you ... I do not mind the unsatisfactory state of your finances. In fact I am glad that we should be living from hand to mouth, so that we may all the better cherish our Maker and fear Him.

Turning the Tide

Politicians do not think in a void, and their politics is often influenced by social background, experience, and reflections on the records of previous politicians. That is why men of contrasting training and temperament give different answers and adduce facts of their common observation to defend themselves. In CP, the Brahman-dominated intelligentsia, mostly followers of Tilak, preferred responsive cooperation. Jayakar and N.C. Kelkar brought out the essential incompatibility between the Maratha mind as moulded by Tilak and Gandhi's teachings, and attacked his 'blind chelas'.[34] Spiritualism may succeed in attaining moksha but

---

34   Milton Israel, *Communications and Power: Propaganda and the press in the Indian nationalist struggle, 1920-1947* (Cambridge, 1994), pp. 232, 233.

not swaraj.[35] So that the non-violent doctrine resulted in indifference, despondency, inaction, and political imbecility. We pursue this debate elsewhere; here, we concentrate on, first of all, the perception of the Khilafat friends, who had a blunt realism that the outcome of their joint endeavours will induce the government to reconsider its stand on Turkey. Later, we discuss how the same persons refused to follow the counsel of the 'man of practical wisom'.

To begin with, the Khilafat party was energetic, replete with practical capability, and strong in spontaneous impulse, but some of its stalwarts were less capable of the kind of tenacity necessary to hold their gains. Non-Cooperation wasn't a movement to be worked either in fits and starts or by instalment. Confusion prevailed over the meanings they and others attached to swaraj, Satyagraha, and *tark-i mavalat*; equally, some people doubted the wisdom of wooing the Muslim orthodox elements. They asked whether Gandhi had acted responsibly and wisely by passing on their Khilafat mantle to them without adequate foresight and whether the long-term results justified his actions. Indulal Yagnik, sub-editor of *Navajivan*, resigned in June 1920 as Gandhi, 'firmly clung to the ark of Muslim opinion, which was thoroughly sectarian and superstitious from our point of view'. According to him: 'Veritable floodgates of the old-world superstitions and crazy sentiments were let loose on the people … with a view to rush them headlong into a new programme which was to be implicitly followed in the light of religious belief and emotional enthusiasm to the exclusion of the cold light of reason and arguments of 'political expediency'.[36]

The ulama weren't the most informed. Grudgingly, they turned to the Westernised Muslims whom they always distrusted. They didn't however find any convergence of ideas with regard to both the kind of conceptual problems they faced, and their consequences. They were doubtless inspired by patriotic sentiments but their loud,

---

35   Report on Indian Papers, CP and Berar, 27 Oct. 1921. *Bharat Dharma*, Note on the Press, UP, 5 Dec. 1925.

36   Yagnik, *Gandhi As I Knew Him*, pp. 135, 117; Sarat Chandra Chattopadhyay's 'The Current Hindu-Muslim problem' in Joya Chatterjee, *Bengal Divided: Hindu communalism and partition, 1932-1947* (Cambridge, 1994), pp. 269-70.

adventurous, and pseudo-heroic cheap demagogy was unworthy. Looked at the other way, being different entailed feelings of alienation that only a strong sense of personal and group characteristics could overcome, but they set aside dominant views and followed their own hunches, however much they conflicted with Gandhi's opinions. Slowly, they plunged further and further into the dark corners of their mosques or seminaries, and, little by little, expressed their rage and frustration.

During the Rowlatt Satyagraha, Hindu, Muslim, and Sikh blood had 'mingled' at Jallianwala Bagh and became *one* in death. On almost every front, India's heart throbbed with a new hope and new faith. On 11 May 1921, Gandhi recorded an increase in Muslim membership of the Congress. In 1922, Ajmal Khan and Ansari stated that, 'our Hindu brothers ... are our brothers in all truth, for the Holy Qur'an teaches that the friends of the faith are our brothers'; hence 'let us remain faithful in thought, word and deed, faithful to our cause, to our country, and to the leader we have chosen—Mahatma Gandhi.'[37] Almost suddenly, however, this kind of enthusiasm more or less ran out of steam and triggered a reaction that led, in the worst-case scenario, to inter-community strife. It was an ugly turn to an otherwise happy situation.

The targets the AICC set at Bezwada in the last week of March 1921 weren't achieved.[38] The rural upliftment schemes fell by the wayside. Instructions on proper *khaddar*-wear were ignored. Barely 50 were dressed in hand-spun *khaddar* from top to toe in Allahabad and Benaras. Others did so for outer covering, all the rest being attired in foreign cloth. Gandhi ruefully catalogued hundreds who went to jail knowing nothing about the pledge. They wore the 'foreign' attire in goal.[39] He felt frustrated by the 'impious' impulses to alter his model. 'Patient suffering may secure Heaven but never swaraj,' a newspaper

---

37   Mushirul Hasan, *A Nationalist Conscience: M.A. Ansari, the Congress and the Raj* (Delhi, 1989), p. 93.

38   Raising a crore of rupees for the Swaraj Fund, enrolment of one crore members for the Congress, and the operation of 20 lakhs of spinning wheels. These targets weren't achieved.

39   Amin, *Event, Metaphor, Memory*, p. 186.

commented.[40] The promised Golden Age for which Hakoo lived and Josh Malihabadi dreamt appeared little more than a fantasy.

The number of students at the Jamia Millia Islamia declined and their discipline grew lax, partly because the standard of ability and conscientiousness among the teachers was lowered. Mohamed Ali was rewarded with the principalship, a post of increasing difficulty for which he was by nature unfit. He proved to be fussy and tactless, unable to deal with the young men or old. Jamia's well wishers knew that their institution had been going downhill, and to restore its discipline and learning they looked around for a strong administrator. Such a man they rightly saw in Zakir Husain, the Munich-educated economist. He never wrote any works of pure learning but possessed varied skills. Through the political controversies in the 1930s and 40s he observed prudence and care which helped raise his prestige.

With pan-Islamism becoming increasingly inimical to political democracy, Gandhi was unable to curb the exuberance of its vocal proponents. He tried slowing them down, but without uncovering new relationships and inventing new paths. He encountered multiple sets of groups; his exchanges over conversions during the Moplah riots on 19 August 1921 illustrated that the pan-Islamists were still bound in a thousand chains. The other group from Deoband and Nadwat al-ulama was still busy using the vocabulary of political Islam to dignify their activism and image as custodians of social order.

Gandhi saw his own flock drifting from the right path, and yet he stuck to his ideals.[41] The entire enterprise made sense only in terms of moral convictions; he, therefore, had to get back to the moorings. If Non-Cooperation had to be suspended, he would have had to lead not a non-violent but a violent struggle. He did not know how to disentangle himself from a sticky situation until the Chauri Chaura incident took place. Yet, his critics thought differently, as Indulal Yagnik indicated:

---

40   *The Prajapaksha* (Akola), 27 Nov. 1921, Report on Indian Newspapers, CP and Berar.

41   'It is undoubtedly true that non-violence is spreading like the scent of the otto of roses throughout the length and breadth of the land, but the foetid smell of violence is still powerful, and it would be unwise to ignore or underrate it.' Gandhi to Jawaharlal, 19 Feb. 1922, in Nehru (ed.), *A Bunch of Old Letters*, p. 24.

To the common untutored mind of the masses, as well as the practical intelligence of the political classes, the incident of Chauri Chaura appeared as a dark, but comparatively insignificant speck on the white sky of India, and all the vast torrents of spiritual sophistry and political casuistry with which Gandhi sought to justify his decision only succeeded in evoking further criticisms, almost amounting to recriminations.[42]

By suspending Civil Disobedience, Gandhi dropped a bombshell on the Ali brothers and the Muslim religious class. They felt betrayed. They knew not what to do. Instead of remaining true to their anti-colonial ideologies, which was their great strength and to which Gandhi granted much ammunition, they wanted to bask under the sunshine of the Montagu-Chelmsford Reforms and gain concessions for the religious establishment. Other than that, they turned to *tabligh* and *tanzim*, an inherently divisive preoccupation, and avoided the route of education and social reforms. The Deobandi ulama took to debating theological issues with the Arya Samaj and the Barelwis, and the Shias. They took a narrow-minded view in engaging with the Shias. They nursed each others bigotry with *tabarra* (Shia cursing the first three Khulafa) and *madhe-sahaba* (In praise of the Khalifa).

It was not at all prudent to open up so many different fronts at a time when self-interest and internal bickering had fouled the political climate. Neither the Sunni nor the Shia scholars built a bridge between opposing parties in religion, and give scholars something better to think about than the barren polemics of sectarian hatred.

We can gauge the magnitude of the problem by reverting to the earlier description of Gandhi's penchant to tap the sources of Muslim creativity through the Khilafat issue. For the time being, he worked the magic but eventually his approach led him and others to a dead end. Borrowing and adaptation was an effective strategy in the light of post-war economic distress, but not when the society's ability to re-invent itself had been sapped. Therefore, Hindu-Muslim disputes took hold of the public in north India and became reinforced elsewhere. While

---

42   Yagnik, *Gandhi As I Knew Him*, p. 287.

Gandhi earned the credit for forging a united front on the strength of the Khilafat, it cost him, and the Congress in lost potential.

In the Lonely Desert

Dasht-i Tanhai Me

Prison is a place where 'each day is like a year, a year whose days are long,' wrote Oscar Wilde. 'How should prison life and fare be a privation to me, since they couldn't possibly be simpler than the life and the food I am accustomed to?' Gandhi remarked on 10 March 1922. Prison was hardly a place to live in even for a short while, much less for long years, although Gandhi learnt about the quickly changing situation whose fate he tried to influence. He kept up his links with friends and co-workers and informed them of his health, diet, spinning routine, and reading habits. Bhulabhai Desai provided Gandhi with a direct link to Syed Abdullah Brelvi of the *Bombay Chronicle*, and he learnt Urdu with the outside help of Zohra Ansari and Rehana Tyabji. He read Shibli Nomani's biography of the Prophet while in jail.[43]

Gandhi's influence was sufficiently strong for a recognised trend to flourish in the form of the Swaraj Party, founded by Motilal and Das. While the swarajists moved in the direction of responsivist cooperation, the erstwhile nationalists despaired and the younger men advanced their interests regardless of the means. Locked in intense rivalries, their intrigues replaced ideals.[44] Members of the Assembly and the Councils stealthily attended official functions, while the feeling between the European and Indian leaders in some places was transformed into one of mutual esteem and respect.[45] The pull of acquisitive habits was too strong for the bond of ideas; the Non-Cooperation idea did not survive for long.

The poison of communalism spread far and deep, and many a Congressmen was communalist beneath a cloak.[46] As a student at

---

43   A former professor of Arabic at M.A.O. College, Aligarh, and co-founded Nadwat al-ulama, the theological seminary at Lucknow. He published extensively on Islam and on Persian Literature.

44   Nehru, *An Autobiography*, p. 98.

45   Banerjea, *A Nation in Making*, p. 311.

46   To Jawaharlal, 1 Dec. 1928, Sharma (ed.), *Selected Works of Acharya Narendra Deva*, vol. 1, p. 1; Nehru, *An Autobiography*, pp. 139-40.

Cambridge, Jawaharlal had taken exception to Lajpat Rai's unkind attributions to Muslims in a lecture.[47] Later, Lajpat Rai and Madan Mohan Malaviya wore secularism with conscious pride more as a jewel rather than practice it as an article of faith.[48] Together, they thwarted endeavours to keep the Swaraj Party firm against the communal blitzkrieg, and, in the build up to the provincial and central assembly elections in 1925-6, they accused Motilal of eating beef and stigmatised the Congress as a prostitute of 'Muslim India'.[49] As *Assad*, a Urdu newspaper, pointed out, 'the only difference (if there be any) between a Hindu nationalist and a Hindu communalist is that while the former wants to render the Muslims insensible [*sic*] by administering sugar-coated pills, the latter wants to bring them to their knees by manly vigour and force of arms.'[50]

Meanwhile the silver lining were the peasant and workers' movements and their coalescing with other forms of protests. Persons wondered what it might mean to live under a socialist government. With the Communist Party in place, terms like 'class war', 'dictatorship of the proletariat', and 'dialectical materialism' became part of the nationalist/revolutionary vocabulary. Those were truly exciting times in which to live. They stimulated debates on the everyday life of the common individuals and on colonial rule itself. A decade later, the Karachi Congress adopted an important resolution on fundamental rights and an economic programme. This was a radical blueprint in the light of the controversies engendered by Jawaharlal and Bose on the *purna swaraj* resolution.

Pockets of anti-colonial resistance were not new; they had existed outside India during the First World War, notably the Silk Letter Conspiracy, and continued intermittently in the form of a Turkish-

---

47   Nehru, *An Autobiography*, p. 158.

48   Nehru, *Glimpses of World History*, p. 720; Kamaladevi Chattopadhyay, *Inner Recesses, Outer Spaces: Memoirs* (New Delhi, 1986), p. 207.

49   Motilal to Jawaharlal, 2 Dec. 1926 in Nehru (ed.), *A Bunch of Old Letters*, pp. 51-52; Gyanendra Pandey, *The Ascendancy of the Congress in Uttar Pradesh: Class, Community and Nation in Northern India, 1920-1940* (Delhi, 2002), pp. 99-101.

50   4 May 1935, United Provinces Native Newspaper Reports (UPNNR).

German plot to overthrow the British. In Maharashtra, Savarkar was arrested for seditious libel in 1908 and remained in Jail until 1921. Madanlal Dhingra of the India House Group shot and killed Curzon Wyllie, political aide-de-camp to John Morley, Secretary of State for India. In 1910, A. Kanhere, a Chitpavan Brahmin like the Chapekar brothers, shot Nasik's district magistrate. In Bengal, terrorist activities were responsible for killing 82 and wounding 121 persons between 1906 and 1917. Early in 1908 the bomb outrage at Muzaffarpur, followed by the Maniktala conspiracy, occured. Aurobindo Ghose was deeply involved in revolutionary activities. Swami Vivekananda's younger brother, Bhupendranath Datta, was his principal associate in the revolutionary conspiracy of the Jugantar group. The Sedition Committee Report (1918) provides many other details.

In 1926, Jawaharlal met Raja Mahendra Pratap, one of the architects of the Silk Letter Conspiracy, in Switzerland and described him as: 'a delightful optimist, living completely in the air and refusing to have anything to do with realities' and 'a character out of medieval romance, a Don Quixote who had strayed into the twentieth century'. Besides two other early revolutionaries, Maulvis Obaidullah Sindhi, a Sikh convert to Islam, and Barkatullah, other Indians were floating about the face of Europe, speaking a revolutionary language. Earlier, Sindhi had wanted to unite the oppressed nations of Asia against England.[51] The Naujawan Bharat Sabha and Hindustan Republic Association carried forward the revolutionary spirit. Sardar Bhagat Singh, Sukhdev, and Rajguru paid a price for their bravery; they were hanged. Jatin Das fasted for 61 days before his death. The Congress protested in March 1931, but *ahimsa* came in the way of Gandhi upholding their cause. Some of his colleagues hoped that he would secure clemency for Bhagat Singh and his comrades when he met Irwin on March 9, 1931, but that was not to be. The viceroy argued that it would be improper to postpone Bhagat Singh's execution, scheduled for March 24, on political grounds. The Naujawan Sabha criticised Motilal Nehru's refusal to allow a motion of sympathy for Bhagat Singh and B. Dutt, at the July meeting of the All India Congress Committee, because that would contravene Congress' non-violent creed. The Bhagat Singh

---

51   IOR. L/PJ/12/241.

worship, Gandhi wrote in *Harijan* on July 30, 1931, had done incalculable harm to the country. He didn't even approve of the Karachi resolution urging the government to commute the death sentence.

Such a scene appears promising from a distance, but the other side of the picture reveals the dark shades and fatigue afflicting the masses. As Manto put it: 'it was as if they were runners in a marathon who had been told by the organisers to stop running, return to the starting point, and begin again.'[52] The tents disappeared from Jallianwala Bagh, only a few pegs in the ground scattered here and there as reminders of a time gone by. *Inquilab Zindabad* lost its previous resonance.[53] Already, stories of Shraddhanand's speech at Delhi's Jama Masjid; Motilal and Ajmal Khan praying together at the Golden Temple, the holy shrine of the Sikhs; Hindus and Muslims offering *namaz* at Calcutta's Nakhoda mosque had faded from people's memory. Inevitable or not, newspapers reported violent outbursts every single day. Should Muslims sacrifice a calf at Baqr Id, or should they cut the branches of a sacred pipal tree; should a Hindu place a dead pig in a mosque, or blow a conch shell at the time of prayer? With riots spiralling across the country, each incident in one city caused resounding repercussions in others. Intolerance increased and passion and prejudice displaced sanity and reason. The result was that, in the course of time, one had a choice, at every railway station, of 'Hindu water', and 'Islami water', 'Hindu tea' and 'Islami tea'. No one had a satisfactory answer to Ghaffar Khan's question: Why does a Hindu or a Muslim object to drinking clean water from each other's vessels?[54]If drinking water from the same glass or vessel was a caste taboo, why was it not observed before with such tenacity? After all, members of different religious communities had been drinking water from the same source at railway stations.

What raised Motilal many notches in public estimation was the calmness with which he took the affair. Quite early in public life, he had dreaded the rupture between the leaders filtering down to the lower

---

52   Saadat Hasan Manto, *Mottled Dawn: Fifty Sketches and Stories of Partition* (New Delhi, 1997), p. 71.

53   Manto, *Black Margins*, p. 131; Manto, *Bitter Fruit*, p. 174.

54   D.G. Tendulkar, *Abdul Ghaffar Khan: faith is a battle* (Bombay, 1967), p. 174.

classes. That is when he feared that nation-building would become a thing of the past and the beginning of broken heads at unseemly quarrels. Now, his critics faulted him for not accepting the so-called historic chasm. Aware that the masses had been good friends and neighbours, he couldn't understand how and why such elements aroused hatred to such a pitch; so much so that he even considered retiring from public life. Indeed, this experience of religious symbols being manipulated for political ends led him and Sapru to establish the Indian National Union to foster a national consciousness in order to relegate religious and communal conflicts to a subordinate plane. However, his initiative couldn't clear the debris of Hindu-Muslim ill-will.

The Unity Conference on 26 September 1924 attempted to get to the root of the problem, but failed, as was widely predicted, to cure the basic malady. Extremists, who flexed their muscles and demanded that everyone else submit to their views, came in the way of a compromise. Motilal suspected that they were most insistent on his chairing the meeting so that he would fail and they'd have a fling at him.[55] Although the next conference the following year moved beyond the propagandistic mudslinging and the previous barren exercises, the Congress faced a new problem: how to resist the mounting Mahasabha pressure? It could not. Every time the Mahasabha contrived to shirk the immediate issue and defer decision on some flimsy pretext or the other. Here, it might have been thought, was the end of the matter. When politicians from different parties met again towards the end of February and 1 March, they went through the motions of trying.

Tagore condemned 'Dharma moha ... delusion disguised as faith', and called for 'the light of knowledge in this benighted land.'[56] Gandhi, who had himself withdrawn from the hurly burly of active politics and had, at the beginning of 1926, imposed upon himself a year of silence, advised Motilal to let the evil forces of communalism play themselves out and, in the meantime, to wait, watch, and pray. He admitted his own imperfection as an instrument for restoring peace. Having approached

---

55   Motilal to Purshotamdas Thakurdas, 8 Oct. 1924, *SWMN*, vol. 2, p. 77.

56   Sabyasachi Bhattacharya, *Rabindranath Tagore: An Interpretation* (Delhi, 2011), p. 137.

the communal issue from the standpoint of the early attainment of swaraj only, he resigned himself to His grace because the vision of swaraj dimmed in the dust of internal strife. He seemed satisfied with outward unity on some working formula, but his elevated precepts weren't, as a rule, effective. He therefore hardly ever bolstered carefully calibrated policies or prepared a blueprint for an action plan to counter conflict-ridden leanings and inclinations. His maxims were doubtless admirable, but their appeal increasingly diminished as caste and community conflicts intensified by the day. The simple diet of patriotism or nationalism wasn't sufficiently adequate for power-hungry politicians. 'Who can drive away the bee perched on honey? Who can arrest the momentum of the moth circling around the candlestick?'[57]

The conventional wisdom was that the communal deadlock had to be resolved not by sheltering behind empty phrases and sentiments, but by exploring new ways and means of expression, conducting a continuing and fruitful exchange of ideas with the political classes, and penetrating their minds and hearts. It didn't help to spurn one's adversary on the ground that he or she was intransigent or a member of the old school, but to share their concerns, anxieties, and aspirations. Undoubtedly, the want of clear ideals and objectives aided the growth of communalism.[58]

The government remitted Gandhi's sentence in February 1924. Gandhi introduced, at the Belgaum Congress, certain amendments in the Constitution: every Congress member had to spin or get spun by others the prescribed quality of yarn.[59] The Nehrus didn't agree to membership being limited to those who gave a certain amount of self-spun yarn instead of the four annas,[60] while sceptics questioned the daily task of spinning for the overall spread of the ashram system.[61] And because Khadi symbolised what Gandhi aspired to achieve—the

---

57   Gandhi to Birla, 9 Apr. 1925, in G.D. Birla (ed.), *In the Shadow of the Mahatma: A Personal Memoir* (Bombay, 1968), p. 10.

58   Nehru, *An Autobiography*, p. 137.

59   Datta, *History of the Freedom Movement in Bihar*, vol. 1.

60   Ibid., p. 128.

61   Thompson, *Gandhi and his Ashrams*, p. 152.

very overthrow of a satanic civilisation—it presented the British with the challenge of a reinvented and proud society. In the tones of reason, justice, and morality, Gandhi also led a crusade alongside untouchability, alcohol, and narcotics.

A rolling stone gathers no moss. A decade separated the first from the second resistance campaign, but Gandhi operated, notwithstanding the changing global and domestic contexts, from a position of strength at the beginning of the 1930s. True, Hindu-Muslim unity ebbed; the riots in Bombay on 3 February 1929 severely undermined unity efforts. As the first one petered out, Gandhi picked up the pieces to create a fresh plan reflecting not the romance but the more serious aspects of anti-colonialism. The feelings against the Raj were as strong as ever, and his own support base embraced even those who had hitherto been outside the frame of institutional politics. Earlier, Satyagraha had been his principal weapon; now, the Dandi March became yet another commanding and emotive symbol in his armoury. Jawaharlal stated: 'Many pictures rise in my mind of this man [Gandhi], whose eyes were often full of laughter and yet were pools of infinite sadness. But the picture that is dominant and most significant is as I saw him marching, staff in hand, to Dandi on the Salt March in 1930. Here was the pilgrim on his quest of Truth, quiet, peaceful, determined and fearless, who would continue that quest and pilgrimage, regardless of consequences.'[62] In this way, the two apparently separate pathways led to the same destination. That is my *raison d'être* for re-evaluating them.

The Gathering Storm

A British astrologer prophesied in 1931 that, after 13 February, Civil Disobedience would unleash a terrible war between the government and the public. It would result in scores of deaths. He also prophesied that socialism would gain in strength from March to June with women in the lead. Some would be hanged and others transported for life; the government would declare martial law. From June 21 to July 21, it would seek, in vain, a compromise with the leaders. The Mahatma would then

---

62   Mushirul Hasan (ed.), *Nehru's India: Select Speeches* (Delhi, 2007), p. 275.

produce a miracle and place a movement on a new path forcing the authorities to buckle down. In June, July, or September, a new world would suddenly come to the fore. In 1935, everything would happen in accordance with India's wishes and, in 1940, it would achieve liberation. If, however, the rulers refused to tone up their administration, they and the Anglo-Saxon empire and race would face extinction.[63]

We shall examine this prophecy, but there is no denying that a leader doesn't create a mass upsurge out of nothing, as if by a stroke of the magician's wand.[64] He can merely take advantage of the conditions themselves when they arise; he can prepare for them but not create them. Gandhi did this, as he built change into his model.

A great general strike of the Bombay textile workers occurred in 1928, from which grew the Girni-Kamgar Union. In July–August-September 1929, the wave of strikes spread. Steel, mill, and railway workers were on a warpath. Parallel with outbursts of unorganised anger, the Communist Party's revolutionary slogans filled the air. Back in India from the US towards the end of November 1929, Jayaprakash Narayan felt that India was on the verge of a great leap forward to liberty. At Lahore, it seemed as if a new world had come into being.[65] For Swami Sahajanand, the *kisan* leader from Bihar, Gandhi's every word was like a thunderbolt against the government. It seemed as if Shiva, the God of Destruction, was raging and that in a little while the great deluge would follow.[66] In the North-West Frontier Province hundreds of Pathan tribesmen danced wildly by night on the banks of the Ravi. Moved by the ecstasy of glorious ideals, 'Independence Day' celebrations kindled their spirit. In Bengal, Nirad Chaudhuri, sounding much less cynical at this juncture, veered round to a passionate approval of Gandhi's methods and became 'an almost idolatrous worshipper of his personality'.[67]

---

63   *Hind Rajasthan*, reproduced from the *Aikya* (of Satara). The United Provinces of Agra and Oudh (UPNNR), 6 Feb. 1932.

64   Nehru, *An Autobiography*, p. 119.

65   Allan and Wendy Scarfe, *J.P.: His Biography*, p. 71.

66   Hauser, 'Swami Sahajanand and the Politics of Social Reform, 1907-1950', p. 72, and his 'Changing Images of Caste and Politics', *Seminar* 450, Feb. 1997.

67   Chaudhuri, *The Autobiography of an Unknown Indian*, p. 476.

The Bardoli Satyagraha was a curtain-raiser. Without itemising its operation, it would suffice to say that 40 or 50 villages faced risks and hardships. Women refused to pay taxes till they received the go ahead from Patel. Their men explained that, at the prevailing prices as owner-cultivators, they earned less than a day labourer's wage. At the end of the conversation, they paid with the aim of winning swaraj. One of them, wearing a khadi shirt, sang, 'Ishwar and Allah are thy names/Do thou, O Lord, grant right understanding to all men'.[68]

While Gandhi regarded the no-tax drive a victory for Truth and non-violence,[69] Satyagraha symbolised the triumph of moral right over arbitrary power. An idea prevailed; the spirit of religious and social purification prevailed; truth prevailed. What's more, the non-violence creed revealed the possibilities of a new type of warfare to the millions.[70] On 2 March 1930, Gandhi embarked upon Civil Disobedience. Ten days later, he called the Salt Tax the most inhuman poll tax the ingenuity of man could devise: a tax not on a superfluous item (such as tea) or an object of privilege (such as land) but on a primary need; a commodity equivalent to air and water which belonged to all and which everyone had a natural right to consume. The government steals and then exploits; the poor had to rise to recover what belonged to them. He fought to get freedom for them.

Frail, gap-toothed, and sparkling with energy, Gandhi left Sabarmati ashram on 14 March at 6.30 a.m. with 78 followers. Along the three miles of road to Ahmedabad, at least 100,000 saw him go towards Dandi, a small, desolate village on the coast in Surat district, a distance of about 150 miles. Gandhi felt privileged to ride the whirlwind and direct the storm. 'The whirlwind that we hope will soon descend on our country,' Jawaharlal hinted, 'will either clear this country of slavery and cowardice and usher in a better day or will blow away many of us to the nothingness from where we came.'[71] His march awakened the villages to a sense of power, set

68   H.N. Brailsford, *Rebel India*, p. 34.

69   Dalton, *Mahatma Gandhi*, p. 95.

70   Winslow and Elwin, *The Dawn of Indian Freedom*, p. 144.

71   To Ansari, 5 Apr. 1930, Zakir Husain papers, Jamia Millia Islamia, New Delhi.

nationalism on a new course, and converted the volunteers into activists.[72] A spectacular show produced spectacular results. Today, Nandlal Bose's iconic drawings have entered the iconographic repertoire and can be found on posters, advertisements, in film promotional materials, and in sculpted form.[73] Shyam Benegal's film on Gandhi's early years, as indeed Richard Attenborough's epic movie, have profoundly impacted their viewers.

The nation was astir. On 13 April, about a 100,000 persons on the Chowpati sands saw an effigy of the Salt Tax being flung into the sea. Rajagopalachari's salt march was staged from Trichinopoly to Vedaranniyam on the Tanjore coast; in mid-April, T. Prakasam and K. Nageswara took charge in Madras; Satyagraha struck a chord in Travancore, a princely state, and in Alleppey. People refrained from drinking alcohol, burnt foreign cloth, established courts, and refused to pay taxes. Women volunteers picketed liquor shops in Jabalpur. Bombay's piece-goods dealers refused to indent any foreign cloth for a year. Delhi's automobile dealers boycotted rubber products and accessories of British firms. In Agra and Rae Bareli, the *kisan* movements gathered momentum in spite of the 'hesitant approach of Congress' and the holding-up operation of the big landlords. When Bengal heard that Gujarat was refusing taxes, it followed suit.

Civil disobedience encompassed a number of daring acts, including the Chittagong Armoury Raid on 17-18 April 1930 and the three young men's assault on Writers' Building. On 23 April, troops fired twice on an unarmed demonstration of workers and peasants in Peshawar, killing between 200-300, and wounding many more. At Sholapur, scores of textile workers were killed. People sensed the surge towards life. In Allahabad, Gandhi's magical touch created a new India: 'the past has made life worth living and our prosaic existence has developed something of epic greatness in it.'[74] Jawaharlal was set free in October

---

72   Horace Alexander, *Gandhi Through Western Eyes* (Philadelphia, 1984), p. 62; Yagnik, *Gandhi As I Knew Him*, p. 499; Brailsford, *Rebel India*, p. 35; Dalton, *Mahatma Gandhi*, p. 101; Thomas Weber, *On the Salt March: The Historiography of Gandhi's March to Dandi* (Delhi, 1997), p. 481.

73   Rebecca M. Brown, *Gandhi's Spinning Wheel and the Making of India*, p. 113.

74   To Gandhi, 28 July 1930, Iyengar and Zackariah (eds), *Together They Fought*, p.124

for eight days in the course of which he started a district-wide no-land-tax drive. A Congress committee confirmed exorbitant land revenue, rural indebtedness, excessive interest rates, a steep rise in prices, and the absence of suitable remissions. 'These crores of agonised souls are fast being driven to a line beyond which even they will refuse to be driven,' warned the *Leader* of Allahabad.[75] While Sangamlal in *Lagān Rōkne kā Ailān* (Declaration for Withholding the Rent) outlined their plight, officials closed their eyes to their complaints.[76] This lent momentum to the no-rent campaign, and led to 12,536 convictions until November 1932.[77]

Rural unrest expressed itself in the response to Gandhi's call in 1930. 'The fight in India,' a jubilant JP noted, 'is going on with unabated vigour.'[78] Consequently, the boycott of foreign goods and the no-rent campaign got underway. Thus the three office bearers of the local Congress committee in Sultanpur instructed volunteers not to allow the sale of even an inch of foreign cloth.[79] The government, in fact, banned public meetings and the carrying of the Congress flag.[80] Ram Lal Misra of Sultanpur, 'the most rabid [sic] non-cooperator of the place' lost his moveable property because he couldn't pay the fine.[81] Pandit Sarag Prasad faced conviction for leading the no-rent campaign.[82] Sangamlal, a pleader, and Bajrang Bali and Ram Bali were convicted for distributing Congress literature in Sultanpur. Six others paid the price for holding aloft the Congress flag.[83] Pandit Bishambar Dayal did something silly; he pulled the chain of a running train to distribute pamphlets in Hindi, Urdu, and English. Sampurnanand,

---

75   2 Sept.1931, UPNNR.

76   Ibid., for the week ending 31 Jan. 1931.

77   FR (UP), Nov. 1932, Home Pol., file no. 18/14, 1932.

78   JP to Mukherjee, 2 June 1930, Bimal Prasad (ed.), *Jayaprakash Narayan: Selected Works*, vol. 1 (1929-1935) (Delhi, 2000), p. 49.

79   Box no. 4, file no. 20, 1932, Uttar Pradesh State Archives (UPSA).

80   Box no. 4, file no. 114, 1932, UPSA.

81   Collectorate records (CR), box no. 4, file no. 34, 1932, UPSA.

82   Box no. 3, file no. 3, 1932, UPSA.

83   Box no. 4, file no. 39, 1932, UPSA.

acting-president of the Hind Provincial Congress Committee, wrote one of the pamphlets.[84]

Sangamlal announced that Sultanpur's Congress Committee would refuse to pay the rent and launch Satyagraha.[85] Earlier, he had urged the peasants to be steadfast. He assured them of ultimate victory.[86]

1. Observe peace and non-violence: A peasant brandishing a cane/club is the greatest enemy of the fellow peasants. Suffer coercion without retaliation.

2. Every peasant is a Satyagraha volunteer: All those who do not pay the rent must consider themselves as such. Every village must have a Congress worker; another person should replace him if he is arrested or incapacitated.

3. Boycott of confiscated land/goods: No one should till the land that is confiscated due to non-payment of rent; no one should purchase any confiscated/auctioned goods; the porters should boycott the hauling of such goods.

4. Reporting arrests: All arrests/coercion must be reported to the divisional/*tahsil* or district Congress office.

5. Support to the family: The village should support the family of a man arrested and sent to jail, if he has no other relative.

6. Stop signing official papers: Refuse putting your signature on any document presented by the *Patwari*, *Tehsildar* or any other government servant or the landlord. Refrain from giving false evidence at their instigation; and boycott meetings convened by the government or the landlord.

---

84   Box no. 5, file no. 51, file no. 268, file no. 296, and file no. 302, 1932, UPSA.

85   *Lagān Rōkne kā Ailān* [Declaration for Withholding the Rent] by Sangamlal, Satyagraha Committee, District Congress Committee, Sultanpur 6 Dec. 1931. Printer: Pt. Rambharos Malaviya, Abhudaya Press, Prayag; Publisher: District Congress Committee, Sultanpur, F.no. 360, 1 Sept. 1932, UPSA.

86   *Lagānbadī ke Bāre Mein Kāngres kā Ādesh* (Directive of the Congress regarding the Stoppage of Rent) by Sangamlal, Satyagraha Committee, District Congress Committee, Sultanpur, 6 Dec. 1931. Printer: Pt. Rambharos Malaviya, Abhyudaya Press, Prayag; Publisher: District Congress Committee, Sultanpur, 2 folios. CR. Sultanpur. F.no. 360, 1 Sept. 1932, UPSA.

7. Supremacy of the Panchayat: All disputes pertaining to the village should be solved by the village Panchayat and everyone should obey its instructions. A Panchayat should be constituted. It will have the authority to boycott anyone who tills the land that is confiscated due to non-payment of rent or purchases any confiscated/auctioned goods.

8. Service class to help the peasants: Villagers or town dwellers who aren't farmers should help their peasant brothers in this movement.

9. Unified stand: Do not go if summoned by representative of the government or the landlord; if any peasant is beaten up or coerced, all others should stay together, for unified support in the face of coercion imbues steadfastness.

10. Insurmountable rent: The peasants cannot possibly pay the full rent, even if they sell their belongings; therefore, they should not have any attachment for household wares.

Another speaker urged the residents of Sultanpur, where the government promulgated Section 144 and jailed 150 people, to join the Gandhi army to secure freedom.[87] He emphasised its non-violent character.[88]He hoped that the high rent levied (at the rate of one-sixth of the produce) would be halved with the establishment of swaraj; *nazrana* and *begar* would stop; the atrocities of the *taluqdars* and the police would end. If a drop in crop production or drop in income happens due to a fall in food grain prices, the swaraj government will also provide sufficient rebates in the halved rent.

Protests and processions were rampant in Hardoi district. Vidya Dhar carried a tri colour flag and organised the boycott of foreign cloth.[89] Bachan Lal and Karan Singh faced conviction for the same reason in Railwayganj, while Bhabuti Singh of the Hardoi Congress Committee

---

87 *Karāchī Kāngres kā Faislā: Jab Swarāj hōgā tab Lagān sadā ke liye Ādhā hō jāyegā* [Decision of the Karachi Congress: With the establishment of Swaraj, the rent will be perpetually halved], by Provincial Congress Committee, n.d, np, 1 folio, F.no. 180/1932.

88 *Sultānpur Zilā Rājnaitik Kānfrence ke Sabhāpatī Kā Bhāshaṇ* [presidential address of the Sultanpur District Political Conference] by Badridutt Shukla, n.d, np, 2 folios. F. no. 70/1932.

89 CR, Hardoi, box no. 4, F. no. 142, 1932, UPSA.

and the Bilgram *tahsil* committee, courted imprisonment.[90] More people followed suit after the district magistrate enforced Section 144 in anticipation of Gandhi's arrest. To begin with, the officials didn't want Gandhi to be a martyr or to incite the young extremists waiting for an excuse to strike.[91] However, after Gandhi's arrest on 25 January, a couple of hundred protesters defied orders and shouted *Gandhiji ki jai*, 'Freedom or death.'[92] Repression angered more and more people in Hardoi and Sultanpur. Mill hands to a man stopped, workshops were shut down, and students cut telephone lines. Officials faced boycott in some villages.

Although scores of ulama courted imprisonment, they were principally concerned with the fate of Kashmiri Muslims, for which Husain Ahmad Madani, principal of Darul-ulum in Deoband, and Maulana Ahmad Said, the vocal Jamiyat leader, were arrested.[93] In Delhi, activists were out of sight.[94] In UP, they stated that they wouldn't imitate the throw of a gambler. The administration backed them in order to weaken the radicals in the Congress.[95] According to Edward Thompson, 'the rank and file of our Europeans in Calcutta are squealing in the opposite direction—put down all this nonsense with a firm hand, clap everyone in jail, go back to the Middle Ages, and sequestrate the Congress Funds.'[96]

The Elusive Gandhi

Gandhi's release had been as unexpected as his arrest: in this and other incidents, the muddle of his arrest, release, and re-arrest

---

90   Ibid., F. nos. 159 and 92, 1932.

91   To Mum and Daddy, 6 Apr. 1930, box 1, H.A.N. Barlow papers.

92   Ibid., F. no. 3, 1932.

93   FR (Delhi), 15 Apr. 1932, Home Pol., F. no. 18/7, 32.

94   Home Pol. F. no. 18/8; F. no. 18/9, 1932, NAI.

95   A.P. Hume to G.K. Darling, 4 May 1932, A.P. Hume papers, Centre for South Asian Studies, Cambridge; Qureshi, *Pan-Islam in British Indian Politics*, p. 410; Pandey, *The Ascendancy of the Congress in Uttar Pradesh*, pp. 106-7; J.M. Brown, *Gandhi and Civil Disobedience: The Mahatma in Indian Politics 1928-34* (Cambridge, 1977), pp. 124, 148-9, 291.

96   Edward Thompson, *A Farewell to India* (London, 1931, 2nd imp.), p. 277, Jawaharlal Nehru to Gandhi, 28 July 1930, *CWMG* (July-Dec. 1930), p. 468.

exemplified the incongruity and the helplessness of the British rulers. Officials were, nonetheless, determined to return him to prison if he took the 'wrong turning'.[97] The Karachi Congress gave Gandhi the go-ahead signal to join the Second Round Table Conference between 14 September and 1 December 1931;[98] earlier, he had refused without 'a change of heart' to attend the first. He himself had no clue what he was going to do at the conference. For nearly three decades London hadn't known what it wanted, except to 'divide and rule'. Personally, he was prepared to go far along the road of concession to meet Muslim claims and establish the common front which he so greatly desired, but he carried with him no blueprint to harmonise the contesting claims or to mediate, as a senior statesman. He was, *The Times* remarked on 29 September 1931, the delegate of the Congress party but not its plenipotentiary.

Scattered information suggests that people heard different stories and, accordingly, echoed their dream. In a Punjab village, the local schoolmaster subscribed to a periodical and became aware of 'leaders' going to London to ask for more power (*hakumat*). Some others informed Malcolm Darling, who spent most of his 36 years' service in Punjab: 'We have heard that the Hindus want the land and become King.' Another person pronounced: 'we know his name [Gandhi], but we have no certain knowledge of what he teaches: we have not seen him'. 'If he is a saint,' a sceptic spoke, 'let him put right our water-logging and our prices'.[99]

The princely states fuelled the speculation that Ramsay MacDonald had put up an impressive show only to expose the hollowness of the Congress claims to represent all of India. They were not prepared to enter a federation. Indeed, they were not—in 1930 or 1940—ready to brace themselves to endure the climate of representative government. Even so, Lucknow's *Hamdam* and Bijnor's *Medina* hoped that Gandhi

---

97   To Mum & Daddy, 22 Feb. 1931, box 1, Barlow papers.

98   This followed protracted negotiation with Irwin until 4 Mar. 1931. Gandhi had his way at Karachi on 29 March despite murmurs in certain quarters.

99   Malcolm Darling, *Wisdom and Waste in the Punjab village* (Oxford, 1934), p. 29.

would end the Hindu-Muslim deadlock but were disappointed by his defeatist outlook. 'O Torn from within, how we can obtain swaraj,' he said; and 'when Hindus and Muslims fight on political issues I feel I am a sinner because I am responsible for the awakening. You want to send a man who will approach the question with faith and hope. I am losing faith.'

In lieu of a posh locality, Gandhi lived in the depressed area of East End. His delegation hardly knew what was he going to say, or, for that matter, did he really know himself? Miss Lester and Mirabehn, both jealous of each other, monitored his crowded itinerary in such a way that he was left with very little time to explain the Congress plan.[100] At any rate, he didn't expect much from the scheduled meetings as the authorities had shelved the crucial subjects, such as responsibility and safeguards, and planned most things in the wrong order. His speeches were rambling, twisted, and teasingly ambiguous.[101] He waited for his inner voice to guide him.[102] If the Indian delegates knew what measure of responsibility was to be at the centre, they would have settled the minorities question among themselves.[103] This was too optimistic a view. And the *Avadh Punch* maintained in its usual humorous style that delegates preferred pelf to patriotism and speechifying to action.[104]

Gandhi didn't exert himself sufficiently to keep alive his own principles. His failure was more than political; it was spiritual.[105] He denied the charge, adding that the real lovers of unity should sit still and simply pray, 'showing in their individual action what a living unity of hearts can mean'. He enquired: 'Do you not meet in your practice with boils which grow worse with teasing? I find communal discord in such

---

100   James D. Hunt, *Gandhi in London* (Delhi, 1978), pp. 202-3.

101   Edward Thompson, *A Letter from India* (London, n.d.), p. 37.

102   Benthall to P.H. Brown, 1 Sept. 1931, Benthall papers.

103   Memorandum of Conversation with G.D. Birla, 4 Oct. 1931, Benthall papers.

104   31 Jan. 1931, UPNNR.

105   Thompson, *A Letter From India*, p. 37.

a boil. The more you tease it the worse it becomes.'[106] I see a serious flaw in this line of reasoning. At a time when serious and contentious issues were under discussion, the people and public intellectuals expected a pro-active policy and not discreet silence. They sought long-term results rather than short-term solutions. Inordinate delays complicated the problems at hand, as illustrated by the impasse over the provision of separate electorates for the Dalits in the communal award.

During the Second Round Table Conference, Ruth Benthall had the following conversation with Gandhi:

'Mr Gandhi, what do you do with your spare time in London?'

'You see, Mrs Benthall, with all this Round Table Conference work and many engagements, I have no spare time.'

'But, Mr Gandhi, you ought to take some relaxation for the good of your health. Do you never go to the cinema?'

'No, Mrs Benthall, I am too busy.'

'But you ought to relax. Haven't you seen Charlie Chaplin's latest film?'

'Who is Charlie Chaplin?'

'Oh, you must know who he is – one of the most famous men in the world.'

'No, Mrs Benthall, you see I live like a toad in a well immersed in my own affairs.'[107]

Shortly, Gandhi was bound for home; a warm welcome awaited him.[108] Sure enough, he would have liked to read about Charlie Chaplin but

---

106   Gandhi to Ansari, 18 Mar. 1934, Mushirul Hasan (ed.), *Muslims and the Congress: Select Correspondence of Dr. M.A. Ansari, 1912-1935* (Delhi, 1985), pp. 106-7.

107   Diary, p. 111, Benthall papers.

108   Wrote *Sandesh*: 'The man before whose feet the irresponsible imperialistic powers tremble, at the sight of whom diabolical autocracy full of brutality shudders and the most callous brute force bends its head, whose penance and renunciation are more formidable than the thunderbolt of Indra, who is king, who is the slave of the poor, that greatest man of the world will place his feet on the soil of India.' Report on Native Newspapers, CP, 1932.

the government sent him back to prison. H.A.N. Barlow, posted in Lucknow, reported: 'Gandhi has been arrested, and we are at war with the Congress again. But I am afraid we are in for a troublesome year. One does not realise the blessings of peace until one has lost it'.[109]

---

109   3 Jan. 1931, Barlow papers.

5
'We Want You off Our Back'

The sound of voices came in chanting unison, the shouted call and the full-
throated chorus:

Inquilab....................Zindabad! Long Live Revolution!

Inquilab....................Zindabad! Long Live Revolution!

British Raj....................Murdabad! Death to British Imperialism.

British Raj....................Murdabad! Death to British Imperialism.

Azadi ki....................Jai! Hail Freedom!

Azadi ki....................Jai! Hail Freedom!

Then the road was alive with defiant, determined young people. The sound
of their marching feet and angry voices was a surging sea, a roaring tempest.
In the forefront was a group of girls. Was Nita among them? They marched
across our range of vision and out of it and their voices faded behind them.

-Attia Hosain, *Sunlight on a Broken Column*, p. 162.

It was a matter of no little pride for the Congress that it accomplished
a great deal of success in certain directions. In 1930, it took the
UP *kisans* under its protection; the result was remissions in rent and
water-rates amounting to nearly a 100 crores. In 1932, Gandhi forced
the government to immediately address the issue of Dalit upliftment.
Two years later, he undertook to develop rural industries to awaken
the slumbering soul of the villages; the government provided a crore of
rupees.[1] However, Verrier Elwin, who met him three times in Bombay,
was struck by his 'ecstasy of renunciation'. He noticed the strains upon
him too great to bear and the opinion in Bombay 'gloomy', but he
expressed the hope 'that light will come'.

The start of 1934 found Gandhi emotionally bedeviled. Released
prematurely from gaol at Kirkee, he toured India in order to collect
money for the Bihar Earthquake Relief Fund. With earthquakes
taking a heavy toll of human lives, he thought it to be a divine chastisement

---

1   To M.R. Jayakar, 11 Nov. 1933, Jayakar papers.

for the sin of untouchability. Tagore ridiculed his logic, but Gandhi didn't entertain questions about the rationality of divine action. Once again the two differed in their outlook, one eschewing, so others believed, the path of rationality, and the other adhering to scientific humanism.

Gandhi agreed not to take part in agitation, but his abstention did not mean that he had ceased to be a Congressman, or that he would hide his colours. It meant that he'd not offer civil resistance himself, nor incite others to do so.[2] At this juncture, politics was neither his business nor his job. While his own conduct reveals him to be a strategist, a tactician, and an excellent manager of men and women, the shift in his preoccupations indicate his sense of the political. His goal was to hasten the downfall of untouchability, to bring about a union of hearts between Hindus and Muslims, enforce total prohibition, promote spinning, self-help, self-sufficiency, and plan for the upliftment of seven lakh villages. He let Mirabehn know that 'the wheel and thinking about it make the time fly'.[3]

Halide Edip spent three days in Wardha. She sat down with Kasturba, before a large plate of wheat to clean to enter, into the spirit of the movement. Gandhi chaired her lecture at Jamia on a cold and windy night in February. As she spoke, eyes from the packed audience were riveted on his fragile figure sitting on a cushion surrounded by charcoal braziers. The atmosphere was suffused by a mixture of profound affection and mystic fervour. The speaker herself thought of Gandhi's greatness throughout the meeting.[4]

The provisions of the Act of 1935 raised hopes in different circles. Even with a limited franchise, millions were prepared to vote. Even without adult suffrage, self-government appeared to be real. Gandhi, of course, mediated between the rival Congress factions, who were polarised, on whether or not to contest elections (under the Act of 1935), and accept office. Earlier, the Swaraj Party, and now, in 1934, he blessed

---

2   Gandhi to L.N. Brown, 4 Mar. 1934, IOR, L.N. Brown papers (D 537).

3   Rahul Ramagundam, *Gandhi's Khadi: A History of Contention and Conciliation* (Hyderabad, 2008), p. 133.

4   Halide Edip, *East Faces West: Impressions of a Turkish Writer in India*, (ed.) Mushirul Hasan (Delhi, 2009).

office acceptance to keep at bay a bloody revolution.[5] He explained: 'My participation in Congress affairs is confined to rendering service on the issues involved in office acceptance and on the policies to be pursued in the prosecution of the march to the goal of complete independence.'[6]

Nothing much moved without Gandhi's blessing or approval; an otherwise democratic body, the Congress was tied to his apron string. Even after the ministries were sworn in, he pulled the strings from Segaon. 'These offices have to be held lightly, not tightly. They are or should be crowns of thorns, never of renown,' he wrote.[7] Whenever any minister ignored his directives, he would not let him get off the hook.[8] He flattered himself with the belief, which he shared with Tagore, that the ministries would show the way out to the hungering world and support struggling causes and oppressed nationalities. He attached, moreover, the utmost value to hand-spun khadi, Hindu-Muslim unity, rural education, and decentralisation of production and distribution.

The experiment on which the Congress ministers embarked had no historical precedent, and therefore it was all the more necessary for them to navigate between the demands of political incumbency and the poor people's aspirations. In this respect, they managed to curtail the economic and political power of the zamindars in some states, offered concessions to the workers, and enhanced expenditure on rural development and cottage industries.[9] The North West Frontier Province (NWFP) government scrapped the *lambardari* system, and the Agricultural Debtors' Relief Act limited the rate of interest realised by moneylenders and cancelled interest due to creditors. The UP Tenancy Bill, the CP and Berar Relief of Indebtedness Act, and the CP Revision of Tenancy (Amendment) Act

---

5   Mushirul Hasan, *M.A. Ansari: Gandhi's Infallible Guide*, pp. 243-46.

6   Birla (ed.), *Bapu: A Unique Association*, vol.1, p. 25.

7   Tendulkar, *Mahatma*, vol. 4, p. 185.

8   The Congress contested 1,161 of the 1,585 seats and won 716. With 30 million voters, only a tenth of the population, it won a clear majority in 6 of the 11 provinces and emerged as the largest single party in three others. Success was written all over UP, Bihar, Orissa, CP, Bombay, Madras, Assam, and the NWFP.

9   Claude Markovits, *Indian Business and Nationalist Politics 1931-1939: The Indigenous Capitalist Class and the Rise of the Congress Party* (Cambridge, 1985), p. 159.

altered, even if slightly, the fragile balance of power in the countryside.[10] In Orissa, tenants received relief from debt,[11] giving the peasant a start towards security such as he had not had before. Edward Thompson discovered the new spirit in the UP villages and the first experimental assault on India's age-old evils.[12] L. Brander lived in Lucknow. He thought, 'here at last you had politicians taking power and at last the administration doing their proper work, and not having to attempt work they couldn't do.[13] G.A. Haig, posted in Moradabad, thought well of Govind Ballabh Pant, the Premier, and Lal Bahadur Shastri, men with a standing and ability to hold ministerial positions in any other province.[14] Pant added a note of optimism in describing UP:

> The dull placid apathy prevailing in the country seems to be gradually giving place to new pulsations of thought and life, and there is a certain amount of desirable and healthy activity in both urban and rural areas. People are waking up all over and issues are being clarified.[15]

The NWFP ministry passed a significant law on women's inheritance under which the daughter inherited a share equivalent to half that of her brother.[16] The Bombay government enacted the Harijan Temple Worship (Removal of Disabilities) Act as well as the Removal of Civil Disabilities Act, Madras. For those whose lives were woven around worship and pilgrimage, temple entry was the acid test for eradicating untouchability. Three provinces had Dalit ministers, of which Assam

---

10   Although they by and large protected the vested interests had watered down certain laws applicable to the rural hinterland,

11   Satyamurti to Gandhi, 15 June 1939, K.V. Ramanathan (ed.), *The Satyamurti Letters: The Indian Freedom Struggle Through the Eyes of a Parliamentarian* (Delhi, 2008), vol. 2, p. 237.

12   Thompson, *Enlist India for Freedom!*, p. 87.

13   Oral Archives, p. 45, IOR, L. Brander papers (F-4111).

14   IOR, G.A. Haig papers (F 180/75).

15   Pant to Jawaharlal, 30 May 1938, B.R. Nanda (ed.), *Selected Works of Govind Ballabh Pant* (Delhi, 1997), vol. 8, p. 297.

16   Mukulika Banerjee, *The Pathan Unarmed: Opposition & Memory in the North West Frontier* (Oxford, 2000), p. 168.

had two, Bihar and Madras one each. While UP had two Harijan parliamentary secretaries, Bihar, and Madras had one each.

Tolstoy had suggested that revolutionaries in authority periodically behave worse than those they replace because they come fresh to it. In certain respects, the ministers, instead of engaging with poverty and underdevelopment,[17] hankered after small, matter-of-fact benefits. What is more, they ignored civil liberties. Even though Gandhi secured the release of nearly 2000 political prisoners, they received retributive and not reformative punishment. With Harry Haig, UP's lieutenant governor, not yielding to G.B. Pant's demand on the release of political prisoners, Gandhi intervened to resolve the ministerial crisis.[18]

Gandhi expected honest, selfless, industrious ministers solicitous of the welfare of the starving millions. One of his homely precepts was that they should avoid rushing in and making a foolish display of power and authority. Many of the legislators however proved themselves bankrupt with their stock-in-trade, that is, their avowed non-violent weapon.[19] They fell into a rut.[20] An indignant Congressman accused them of forsaking Gandhi's ideals and his disregarding opinion that a just administration implied an era of truth or swaraj, *dharmaraj, Ramarajya* or people's raj (democracy). [21] The result: 'we are skating on dangerously thin ice'. Likewise, Gandhi lampooned, unreservedly, the legislators for wire-pulling and manoeuvring.

The *Leader* of Allahabad felt that the ministers had bungled outright in dealing with the communal malaise; the prescription they consistently followed was to ignore or shelve the problem and leave it to the discretion of the steel-framed services to handle the local situation

---

17   Jawaharlal to Pant, 1 Oct. 1938, Nanda (ed.), *Selected Works of Govind Ballabh Pant*, vol. 8, p. 461.

18   Pant to Haig, 24 Feb. 1938, ibid., pp. 268-69.

19   *Harijan*, 10 Dec. 1938, CWMG (Oct. 15, 1938-Feb. 28, 1939), p. 170.

20   Marguerite Rose Dove, *Forfeited Future: The Conflict over Congress Ministries in British India, 1933-1937* (Delhi, 1987), pp. 437-48.

21   V. Sadananda to *Nirmal Kumar Bose, 3 July 1940, Nirmal Kumar Bose* papers, group 13, sr. nos. 1 – 76; *Harijan*, 3 Feb. 1940, CWMG, vol. 71, p. 158.

as best as they could.[22] The excessive use of force during the communal riots in Allahabad (in March 1938) hurt Gandhi, and he pronounced the Congress ill-suited to substitute the British authority.[23] Robbed of sleep, he was overtaken by 'the inner despondency'.[24] He feared that the people would defy the Congress directives, if illegalities and irregularities went unreported and unchecked.[25]

Jawaharlal speculated about how the ordinary folk would react to red-liveried *chaprasis* hovering about them and the enervating aroma of power surrounding them, and the convict of yesterday becoming a minister. [26] 'We are sinking to the level of ordinary politicians who have no principles to stand by and whose work is governed by a day-to-day opportunism,' he informed Gandhi.[27] He found their private lives to be 'lamentably prosaic, barren and stupidly sordid'.[28]

In Bihar, the ministry dithered over the thorny question of *bakasht* land; the Bihar Restoration of Bakasht Lands and Reduction of Arrears of Rent Act, 1938, didn't add up to very much. The gulf between the Congress and the *kisan* movement made certain Congress committees demand a ban on the movement of Swami Sahajanand Saraswati. In fact, the Bihar Pradesh Congress Committee (B.P.C.C.) directed Congressmen not to participate in the Kisan Sabha rallies. In Saran district, Rahul Sankrityayan, a Hindi writer and Buddhist scholar, faced conviction for the Amwari Satyagraha and denied the status of a political prisoner. Patel, hero of the Bardoli Satyagraha, banned the *kisan* rally and *kisan* conference in Vithalnagar. In spite of that, 2000

22   *Leader*, 21 Nov. 1939, Hasan (ed.), *TF*, 1939 (pt 1), p. 220.

23   For statement of Pant in the UP Assembly on 22 March 1938, see Nanda (ed.), *Selected Works of Govind Ballabh Pant*, vol. 8, pp, 104-06.

24   To Jawaharlal, 30 Apr. 1938, in Nehru (ed.), *A Bunch of Old Letters*, p. 277.

25   *Harijan*, 19 Nov. 1938, *CWMG* (Oct. 15, 1938-Feb. 28, 1939), p. 125; Tendulkar, *Mahatma*, vol. 4, p. 307; Gandhi to Birla, 26 Aug. 1938, in Birla (ed.), *Bapu: A Unique Association*, vol. 3, p. 187.

26   Jawaharlal Nehru, *The Unity of India: Collected Writings, 1937-1940* (London, 1928, 3rd imp., 1948), pp. 62-63.

27   To Gandhi, 28 Apr. 1938, in Nehru (ed.), *A Bunch of Old Letters*, p. 277.

28   G.B. Pant to Jawaharlal, 23 Mar. 1938, p. 278, Nanda (ed.), *Selected Works of Govind Ballabh Pant*, vol. 8, p. 278.

peasants marched past the national flag with their own national and red flags, and 10,000 gathered for meetings. Then, the ministry suppressed the strike over the Industrial Disputes Bill on 7 December 1938.

JP had moved out of the communist camp to establish the Congress Socialist Party in May 1934. He found the Congress converted into a handmaid of vested interests. 'We are faced today,' he warned sagely, 'with the real danger, of Indian industry being made a synonym for Indian nationalism.'[29] 'A vulgarisation of Gandhism,' he protested, 'makes this transition easy and gives this new Congress the requisite demagogic armour.'[30] He condemned the ministries for binding the workers' organisations and delivering them to the employers, and pointed his finger at their astuteness and the large element of artificiality and expediency in their behaviour. His verdict: 'no Congressman can be proud of the record of two years of the Congress ministry.'[31] Other young socialists, who had spread their gospel in many directions and influenced a considerable fraction of the socialist movement, sensed the drift towards constitutionalism and accommodation. The Berlin-educated Ram Manohar Lohia was one of them. He was articulate and incisive but provincial in his outlook.

Fierce and sustained criticism came from the Muslim League as well. According to the *Hindustan Times*, 'the game of bullying has been started in right earnest against Mahatma Gandhi, the Congress, and the leaders.'[32] The League did not expect the Congress, which had failed to satisfy its own constituency, to treat the religious minorities fairly.[33] In this way, the imagination of its leaders magnified atrocities.[34] The fact is that, by and large, the spoils of office flowed along party lines. The Muslims may not have gained much, but they were not victims of overt discrimination.[35] In

---

29   Allan and Scarfe, *J.P.: His Biography*, p. 107.

30   JP to Jawaharlal, 23 Nov. 1938, Bimal Prasad (ed.), *Jayaprakash Narayan: Selected Works*, vol. 2 (1936-1939) (New Delhi, 2001), p. 230.

31   *Congress Socialist*, 18 June 1838, ibid., pp. 181-82.

32   6 Jan. 1939, ibid., p.1742.

33   26 Jan. 1939, Hasan (ed.), *TF*, 1939 (pt 2), pp. 1750-53.

34   R.J. Moore, *Churchill, Cripps, and India, 1939-1945* (Oxford, 1979), p. 2.

35   F.V. Wylie to Linlithgow, 18 Apr. 1939, IOR, L/PJ/8/688.

fact, the rural development scheme in UP benefited some of them; equally, those who qualified in the competitive services occupied 39.6 per cent of the posts in the provincial executive service, 25 per cent in the judicial service, and 24.4 per cent in the agricultural service. In Bihar, Muslims received their fair share of appointments.[36] Similarly, they received certain major concessions from the CR ministry in Madras. The viceroy concluded:

> As you know I never took those complaints too seriously, and I should be surprised if they do not prove to be either psychological in character or the type of quite minor oppression, insolence, injustice,which in a country so immense as this, so densely populated ... is bound to happen once the impression gets abroad in a major province that there is a 'Hindu Raj' or a 'Muslim Raj' as the case may be in the government of that province.[37]

Probably, some in the Congress were drunk with victory, hence, a little flattery here and conciliation there should have got the path opened, which might otherwise be blocked, and made the Muslims feel that in pushing them onward they were doing credit to themselves.

Ministries in Command: Basic Education[38]

What is the educational system but a gigantic farce: a body without a soul, a show without substance! Gandhi described it as stagnating and largely attuned to the needs and self-image of a relatively small, restricted elite. His own priority was to popularise *Nai Talim* (new or basic education) as an innovative and change-oriented structure. More exactly, he wanted to instil in students the spirit of freedom, pride, independence, courage, and sincerity in order to raise nations from the depths of degeneration and shake off the semblance of servitude, exalt cooperation above competition, service above exploitation, and non-

---

36   6 Feb. 1939, *TF*, 1939 (pt 2), pp.1754-55.

37   Linlithgow to Amery, 8 Jan. 1942, IOR, L/PJ/8/686.

38   While I have made substantial additions and revisions, this section draws on Mushirul Hasan and Rakhshanda Jalil, *Partners in Freedom: Jamia Millia Islamia* (Delhi, 2006), pp. 104-9.

violence above violence. The teacher, like the artist, the philosopher, and the man of letters, can only perform her work adequately if she feels herself to be an individual directed by an inner creative impulse, not dominated and fettered by an outside authority.

Gandhi wanted to make education self-supporting by centreing it on a craft: or rather, the craft of spinning, the 'pivot and centre of education', and encourage teaching on the spinning wheel or spindle rather than learning by rote. Certain of the utility of universal hand-spinning and the universal manufacture and use of hand-spun cloth, he believed that hand-woven cloth would be a substantial, if not absolute, proof of genuine unity and non-violence. To recognise a living kinship with the dumb masses, he upheld the dignity of working with one's hands and discarded the distinction between intellectual and manual labour.

At Gandhi's behest, a committee at Wardha drew up a scheme of primary education to shape the *new* qualities, both intellectual and political, among the school personnel. Its report recommended community engagements for enabling children to carry the outlook and bearing acquired in the school environment into the wider world.[39] Its central idea was, indeed, to harmonise with the best trends of progressive educational thought. Zakir Husain, its chairman, valued not merely training village children in handicrafts but making them a medium of teaching language, history, geography, mathematics, science, and other subjects.[40]

---

39 K. G. Saiyidain explains their central idea: 'That work, done with integrity and intelligence, is ultimately the only proper medium through which human beings can be rightly educated and that schools must become active centres of doing and learning by doing, both organized in integral relationship with each other. This appreciation of the intrinsic relationship between doing, learning, and living is no accidental 'off-shoot', which his philosophy of life has put forth; it springs from the deepest sources of his thought.'

40 Other members of the committee were Aryanayakam, Vinoba Bhave, Kakasaheb Kalelkar, Kishorilal Mashruwala, president of Gandhi Seva Sangh, J.C. Kumarappa, secretary of All India Village Industries Association, Shrikrishnadas Jaju, president of the Maharashtra Branch of the All India Spinners' Association, K.T. Shah, Shrimati Ashadevi, a Gandhian educational worker, and Saiyidain, then director of Education in Kashmir, presented such a scheme in early Dec. 1937 and by Mar. 1938 it had prepared a syllabus. This came to be known as the Wardha Scheme.

Tilak Maharashtra Vidyapith near Poona, and the Basic School and Basic Training School at Sevagram implemented the Wardha Scheme. In 1921, Tagore added a university to his school. Apart from learning domestic science and handicrafts, the boys developed a spirit of social service at an agricultural research station with schools of spinning and tanning for those living in the surrounding villages. In Bombay, B.G. Kher, the chief minister, evinced keen interest in *Nai Talim*. Avinashilingam Chettiar conducted basic education in Madras. In Jamia, the 'project method' was designed to promote individual initiative, spontaneity, group cooperation, and integrated physical and mental development processes. As a matter of fact, *Hamdard-i Jamia* boasted the success of the 'Bank Project', the 'Dehat [Village] Project', and the 'Subzi Mandi Project' on fruits and vegetables. Students learnt swimming, spinning, weaving, carpentry, and drawing to produce toys and painted nature, men, and the old tales. G. Ramachandran and Devdas Gandhi, their teachers, instilled in them the feeling that the *khaddar* they wore was a debt that could only be paid off in full by spinning cotton. Jamia resounded to the tik-tik of the *takli*. Wheels turned with gusto, spinners spun swiftly, and boys took to making their own cloth.

Manual work was the best way of training and equipping students to deal with various contingencies. A sound educational principle for them! Moreover, learning Hindustani quickened their mind and spirit. St. Paul had put the case well: 'If I pray in an unknown tongue, my spirit prayeth, but my understanding is unfruitful.' The issues seemed plain enough: craft-centred basic education had a natural discipline of its own, which was usually self-imposed.[41] Gandhi was fortunate insofar as he had a following amongst that small and select group of educationists who sought to transform the educational structure and remonstrated against its academic and bookish stress. His concept of 'Activity School' germinated in Jamia's nursery. This was the precious gift Zakir Husain brought from George Kerschensteiner, a German who conceived of 'Education through Activity'.

---

41   As Zakir Husain said: 'If all the products of craft work from the Basic
      schools in India were eventually to be drowned in the ocean, I would still
      insist that every single article should be prepared with the utmost efficiency
      and intellectual and practical integrity of which an individual is capable.'

Education and Faith had all along been the twin engines to propel the Jamia fraternity (*biradari*). The founders expected to colour *deen* (faith) with the many-splendoured hues of *ilm* (knowledge) and vice versa. To achieve this, Faith had to be viewed not in a narrow, bigoted sense but by creating an ambience for its true understanding, of real belief in its truest, widest, highest sense. W. C. Smith, who visited Jamia in the mid-1930s, observed with the perspicacity of an outsider how Jamia had refurbished its methodology, and put in practice an education that borrowed from the discoveries of the modern West and, at the same time, also those that were relevant to India.

Students studied, ate, and lived together. Under their green *chogha*, they wore white *khaddar* pyjamas, the dhoti, and even the occasional *shalwar*. They shunned mill-made cloth, be it for attire or upholstery, and placed *khaddar* sheets over rough cotton *durries* or straw mats on the floor. A dream of better times caused them to leave their homes in far-off lands to live a spartan life. Thus, dozens of Hindu students from Assam, Bengal, and Punjab flocked to Jamia for precisely the sort of heady brew that men of learning such as Marmaduke William Pickthall, a British convert to Islam, had to offer. P.S. Gupta and Surya Kant Shastri taught science and Sanskrit, respectively, and D.P. Singal the *Gita* and economics. The best loved of them all, A.J. Kellat, came from Kerala to serve Jamia.

The new educational scheme had to live or die by its own merits or want of them. Its cardinal points were well understood, but their application ran into rough weather. Gandhi failed to persuade the elites to accept his scheme and also could not work out the problem of the role played by teachers in its implementation. Second, the Congress itself did not regard the conception of *Nai Talim* as a viable substitute to the existing system of school education.[42] Third, students from intellectually impoverished backgrounds failed to secure jobs in factories and mills after obtaining their degrees. A difference emerged between the mental qualities or mind characteristics of run-of-the-mill students and the more-endowed ones. Finally, the League attacked the Vidya Mandir Scheme in CP as a diabolical plot to 'de-Islamise the Muslim nation'.

---

42   Henry Fagg, *A Study of Gandhi's Basic Education* (Delhi, 3rd imp., 2008), pp. 62-63.

Basic education stood condemned not only as an attack on Muslim culture but on all ideas of decency.

Little by little, Jamia came to be identified with Gandhi's unholy project. The League publicists abused its teachers and ridiculed their Gandhi cap. Zakir Husain had to change his cap; Jinnah described him as a 'Quisling' and 'utterly and entirely unacceptable'. His contempt for the rationalists, which is what Ansari, Azad, and Zakir Husain were, made him one of the harshest critics of the public intellectuals.

In the next section I move from the macro to the micro, to consider the effects of other ministerial policies.

The Spinning Brigade

It is possible and, for the sake of clarity, absolutely essential to distinguish between the high-level concepts that were bandied around and the harsh realities of power politics. The question before all was: Will political independence help to diminish poverty as well as the numerous ills that flow from it? John Locke had stated that the end of government was 'the public good'; others described it as 'the greatest happiness of the greatest number....'. Gandhi, who hardly ever denied harmony between policies and implementation, had no expectations of apocalyptic success. He did however consistently and ceaselessly hanker after the interests of the underprivileged in the absence of their 'natural defenders'. With his faith in James Mill's idea of 'protection', he expected the government to minimize their pain and suffering. *Ramarajya* meant good government, an attainable goal. Similarly, he came close to endorsing John Stuart Mill's thesis that the best form of government is that which provides the greatest amount of good to the people at large, immediate and prospective. However, unlike Mill, he wasn't prepared to passively yield to the desires and the law as the will of the superiors. He therefore defied the salt laws without devoting much time to elucidating intricate legal problems.

What, then, had to be done? We seem to have come full circle. An endeavour to achieve clarity and exactness is evident by the choice of well-demarcated and concrete subjects, as also by the assertion that politics had to remain in touch with real life and its exigencies. Jails had to be turned into educational reformatories and workshops. Khadi had to be purchased as an act of swadeshi; Gandhi spoke of a connection between swaraj and khadi, which provided dignified labour to the millions. Also, salt had to be free for the poor. However, the success of large-scale and long-range aims depended upon the ministers, although their phrases and slogans became dangerous companions without being allied to well-considered objectives.[43]

Before long, the ministries, having clutched at straws in the hope that somehow they'd play a longer innings, were quickly pushed off their pedestals. The Kisan Sabhas spearheaded Satyagraha in some Bihar districts. The problem didn't stop there. In November 1934, the Progressive Writers' Movement took shape, though the germ from which it sprang is to be found in 1932 when Syed Sajjad Zaheer, back in India from his studies in London, and some other like-minded writers, produced a collection of stories called *Angare*.[44] Sajjad Zaheer, son of the well-known lawyer-politician Syed Wazir Hasan; Rashid Jahan, a woman who was sensitive to opinion and eager for appreciation; Ahmed Ali, the author of the novel *Twilight in Delhi* (1940); and Mahmuduzzafar, the contributors to this collection, brought light and hope to the dark areas of prejudice, ignorance, rigid partitions, or fetters. In general, they reflected more and more against division through sex, and opened the doors wider and wider to their participation in the democratisation process. In the process, they antagonised Lucknow's organised conservative establishment. The storm over *Angare* broke out; the UP government banned it on 15 March 1933. But in Aligarh, Ismat Chughtai, then a student at the Girls' College, turned the tables on Shahid Ahrawi, a cleric. His funeral procession was taken around the hostel.[45]

---

43   Hauser, 'Swami Sahajanand and the Politics of Social Reform, 1907-1950', pp. 59-75.

44   Ali Ahmad Kazmi, *Sajjad Zaheer: Ek Tarikh ek Tehrik* (Allahabad, 2006); Ralph Russell, *Pursuit of Urdu Literature: A Select History* (Delhi, 1992); Rajwanti Mann, *Social Radicalism in Urdu Literature: A Study of Gender Issues and Problems, 1930-1960* (Delhi, 2011); Zahida Zaidi, *Glimpses of Urdu Literature: Select Writings* (Delhi, 2010). Basudev Chatterjee (ed.), *TF, 1938* (pt 1), pp. 898-911.

45   Ismat Chughtai, *A Life in Words: Memoirs*, trans. from Urdu by M. Asaduddin (Delhi, 2012), p. 154.

Progressive writers presented, in general, a creatively emancipatory rendition of the past: a mutually illuminating vision that is both the product of and an aid to shaping a cosmopolitan ethos or ethics.[46] They exposed social abuses and pretences, voiced human sufferings, weighed everything anew, and discarded conventions. They saw poverty and exploitation and they saw, too, a way of organising society on Marxian lines. Often they fused romance and sentimentality with rebellion and revolution.

With the strain of industrial capitalism acting as a powerful stimulus for the overthrow of the colonial system, they brimmed with radical ideas, debated such daring questions as atheism and pure theoretical communism in terms of the Hegelian dialect, and reiterated what Marx had written: 'Capital is dead labour, that, vampire-like, only lives by sucking living labour' and that capital came into the world 'dripping from head to foot, from every pore, with blood and dirt'. At one meeting, 'Bimaar' was read out, followed by a recitation on the misdeeds of zamindars, and a drama depicting the drawbacks of the existing system of society, and a story on the poverty of the village.[47] The widespread appeal of Marxism was due to the vigour with which the analysis is argued, the assurance of certainty and of ultimate success, eventually translating into a communist society in which injustice and oppression are to cease.

Mulk Raj Anand, who ran the Indian Progressive Writers' Association (with Pramode Ranjan Sengupta) after Sajjad Zaheer's departure, published *Untouchable* and *The Coolie* with the Communist form of Wishart-Lawrence, an amalgamation of Wishart & Co. and Martin Lawrence & Co.

In the villages, the bards came into their own, expressing their grief and sorrows, their amours and joy of life in forms that were rooted in the rural areas. It was reported: 'After Buddha Baba, a number of young poets came and sang their songs to the accompaniment of the harmonium and the drum. Their poems were all revolutionary, calling

---

46   Syed Akbar Hyder, 'Ghalib and His Interlocutors', in Bhagavan (ed.), *Heterotopias*, p. 109.

47   IOR. L/PJ/12/499.

upon the peasants to give up all thought of fate and to live a life of action. A Village Poets' Conference was held on 14-15 May 1938.[48]

Trade union unrest had spread rapidly in the early 1930s and continued until the end of the decade. A major strike erupted in the Ahmedabad textile mills following police-worker collision in Bombay, Sholapur, and Nagpur. Rallies, demonstrations, and strikes took place in the Digboi oilfields and Bombay Cotton Mills. In April 1933, Bombay's Police Commissioner hit back on B.T. Ranadive as a 'mischief-maker: he is a communist pure and simple; his policy is to incite the workers against the police and against government.'[49] In UP, a major strike occurred in Kanpur in 1938. In Bihar, conflict erupted at the Dalmia and Tata factories, and in Bombay, the first sit-in-strike in a textile mills took place in April 1939. A general strike took place in March 1940, despite the revolutionary movement ordinance, which had come into effect a year earlier.

Songs on Gandhi, swaraj and *inquilab* filled the air. Poets extolled him, his voluntary incarceration, and Civil Disobedience.[50] Satyamurti sounded an optimistic note in an otherwise dismal projection of national and global affairs: 'if we play our cards well, bring about reasonable Hindu-Muslim unity by tackling the problem, province by province, and Joint Electorates of separate electorates and completely ignore Jinnah and his crowd, ...there is no power on earth which can stand between us and our freedom.'[51]

The Left in 1939 attracted the working class into mainstream politics. The May Day Manifesto sought to harness optimism and hope in towns

---

48   Chatterjee (ed.), *TF*, 1938 (pt 1), pp. 912-25.

49   IOR. L/PJ/8/584.

50   They tried to capture a Bhojpuri wife's plea to her husband not to go away to
       a distant place in search of work.
       Now my beloved I will spin the charkha, please do not leave me
       Bring me a charkha so that I may spin
       That is how swaraj will come
       The country's prestige depends on the charkha
       That is Gandhi's message
       Beloved please do not leave me ...
       Chandan Mitra, 'Images of the Congress: U.P. and Bihar in the Late Thirties
       and early Forties', in Low (ed.), *The Indian National Congress*, p. 159.

51   Satyamurti to Asaf Ali, 26 Sept. 1939, Ramanathan (ed.), *The Satyamurti
       Letters*, vol. 2, p. 261.

and rural areas.[52] There was however widespread disappointment with the new managerial and manipulative class guiding the liberation struggle.[53] M.N. Roy asked if the Congress would permit its liquidation and engage itself in reformist politics, and whether Gandhi would sacrifice freedom for the cult of non-violence. Should Gandhi's personal prestige be allowed to stand in the way of rank and file action?[54] In the midst of a mass of platitudes and hopeless self-contradictions, Roy wrote from prison, Gandhism harps on one constant note—a conception of morality based upon dogmatic faith.[55]

All in all, the Left attracted to its ranks the finest examples of crusading spirits, although they couldn't be assimilated into Gandhi's standard of truth and morality. Satyamurti put his finger squarely on the problem: 'Even today the Congress is filled with both right and left wings ... India cannot and will not accept that Socialism with its main three doctrines, viz., the abolition of all private property, the creation and the perpetuation of class warfare and the dictatorship of the proletariat.'[56] This was the 'spectre of communism' haunting Europe too: fear of the proletariat affected not merely Congress stalwarts but civil servants, the priestly classes, and professional men alike.

The storm in the teacup threatened to assume larger proportions. The *kisans* and workers demanded not merely bread and employment, but *azadi*. The intelligentsia, on the other hand, spoke of putting India

---

52   Some semblance of unity between the two groups persisted until JP's
      declaration, in Dec. 1939, that the Communist Party was the CSP's
      sworn enemy.

53   The left parties in 1939 were: The Revolutionary Socialist Party, the
      Forward Bloc of Subhas Chandra Bose, and Roy's Radical Democratic
      Party. They were loosely linked with the All-India Trade Union Congress,
      the All-India Kisan Sabha, the All-India Students' Federation, a nursery of
      new ideas inaugurated by Jawaharlal in 1936, the Anushilan Samiti
      and Jugantar groups of Bengal revolutionaries, and the Hindustan
      Republic Association.

54   Sibnarayan Ray (ed.), *Selected Works of M.N. Roy, 1932-1936*, vol. 4 (Delhi,
      2000, paperback), p. 166.

55   M.N. Roy, *India's Message* (Calcutta, 1950), pp. 209-11, 217.

56   Satyamurti to Gandhi, 31 Aug. 1939, Ramanathan (ed.), *The Satyamurti
      Letters*, vol. 2, pp. 257-58.

on the map of the great world powers,[57] and of aligning it on the side of Poland's allies to ensure Hitler's defeat.

In January 1939, Gandhi comforted Manilal and Sushila Gandhi: 'what does it matter if I or anybody at Akola dies when you are not here?'[58] He seemed anxious and impatient, probably preparing himself for the fight at the forthcoming Tripuri Congress. The battle lines were drawn after Pattabhai Sitaramayya, the veteran Andhra leader and Gandhi's nominee for Congress presidentship, lost to Bose by a majority of 203 votes. Bose's victory may not have meant much to those for whom the national movement was pure sacrifice and dedication, but Gandhi's description of Bose's victory as his own defeat deepened factionalism. No two men could be more unlike in social affiliation, upbringing, character, temperament, opinions, and behaviour. Besides, they stood for wholly different forms of the nationalist movement, and the great paradox was that Bose stood for a form that was already obsolescent, whereas Gandhi, nearly 30 years his senior, led the form that represented the present and the future.[59] While Bose sympathised with the fascist conceptions of the state, Gandhi found his strategy unsuited to a country engaged in a non-violent struggle in the midst of a world war.

What was invisible and hidden from scrutiny at the time was that, rather than resolving the confusion over the boundaries of words, Gandhi and Bose refused to retrace their steps. As far as party affairs were concerned, Gandhi had to be a step or two ahead of his colleagues in order to be in full control of party affairs. The Congress policies were, in the main, of his shaping and he jealously guarded them, and ultimately decided who to entrust or deny authority and responsibility. On the other hand, the Bengal tiger, who had himself to blame for his numerous indiscretions, resigned on 29 April 1939. It seemed 'as if the Boses had neither the boldness to defy Gandhi and try to assert

---

57   Asaf Ali to Satyamurti, 22 Sept. 1939, Ramanathan (ed.), *The Satyamurti Letters*, vol. 2, p. 260.

58   To Manilal & Sushila Gandhi, 25 Jan. 1939, *CWMG* (Oct. 15, 1938-Feb 28, 1939), p. 329.

59   Chaudhuri, *Thy Hand Great Anarch!*, pp. 502, 503.

their power ... nor the manliness to accept defeat without rancour'.[60] Angry Bengali's could do nothing except to regret the unhappy and anxious circumstances which led to the withdrawal of Bose from the mainstream of political life. As time went on, both the spirit of reaction and revolutionary discontent became more intense, and those who tried to follow a middle course were placed between two fires. The fact is that most Bengali politicians paid no more than lip-service to Gandhi's leadership. Already, his settlement of the internal succession dispute following C.R. Das' death had alienated them.[61] On that occasion too, Bose was left out in the cold.

Today, after so many decades, this outrage unites the otherwise fragmented political classes in Bengal. Bose, with his pro-fascist inclinations, is a hero of the left front, the Congress, and the newly-elected party, the Trinamool Congress. Ultimately, the baton was passed on to the CWC to carry out Gandhi's programme.[62]

Retreat and Resignation

The declaration of war on 4 September 1939 constituted the most important historical, cultural and psychological watershed in the British Empire. Gandhi and CR were prepared to support the British, along with Rajendra Prasad, Acharya Kripalani, and Shankar Rao Deo. Jawaharlal, on the other hand, wanted a declaration of war aims; only a free India would, he said, join against the unwanted fascist aggression. Azad, the Congress president-elect, agreed. Their views prevailed. Edward Thompson put it succinctly: 'The Indian had this added misery, of knowing that his own country was throughout a tool and puppet—that she could do nothing except utter protests which no one heard, and that when the crush came she would be dragged along the line with it.'[63]

'Time passes,' Jawaharlal wrote on 19 October 1939, 'and the world changes and the national demand of yesterday is already history. It may

---

60   Ibid., p. 517.

61   Chatterjee, *Bengal Divided*, pp. 43-44.

62   Jawaharlal to Gandhi, 20 Apr. 1939, Iyengar and Zackariah (eds), *Together They Fought*, p. 366.

63   Thompson, *Enlist India for Freedom!*, p. 27.

not be adequate enough for tomorrow.'[64] 'The Congress had already warned that its leader might declare Civil Disobedience.[65] The author of non-violence felt bound to fight when he felt the urge from within. He delayed without abandoning the fight.

In May 1940, a member of the House of Commons asked: 'India? India! But what's wrong about India? There's no reason to think about India!' Two years later, he had to eat his words; India came alive with Gandhi's call to 'Quit India'. Wars are not fought on battlegrounds but in a space smaller than the head of a needle.[66] With a virtual golden trophy in hand, Gandhi declared, 'there is no turning back'. 'Our case is invulnerable. There is no giving in. Only I must be allowed to go my way in demonstrating the power of non-violence when it is unadulterated.'[67] At the same time, he could ill-afford to remain supine in the face of the greatest world conflagration known to history. Familiar with the petty arguments and controversies abroad, he went ahead with one more battle, the last.

In Gandhi's scheme of things, the fear of violence was either imagined or sedulously aroused in the people's mind. A typical example are these lines from a novel: 'O, the threat "Quit India, Quit India." Rev. Bannerjee got up angrily and began pacing the room. 'Stupid fools! Asses! If the English leave, we will return to the barbaric dark ages of tyranny and corruption!'[68] A narrow sectarian or communitarian horizon bounded the universe of those who were either hesitant to join the Quit India campaign or were sceptical of its outcome.

The two-word resolution of 9 August 'cut clean the Gordian knot of British-Indian politics of legal phrasemongering.'[69] Acharya Vinoba Bhave was the first Satyagrahi. Jawaharlal, who dreaded much more than Gandhi, the success of Nazism and Fascism, was arrested on 31 October at Chheoki Junction, near Allahabad. Surely, he was wrong

---

64   *SWJN*, vol. 10, p. 203.

65   Nehru, *The Unity of India*, p. 122.

66   Ben Okri, *The Famished Road* (New York, 1991), p. 498.

67   Gandhi to Jawaharlal, 24 Oct. 1940, Nehru (ed.), *A Bunch of Old Letters*, p. 457.

68   Qurratulain Hyder, *Fireflies in the Mist: A Novel* (Delhi, 1994), p. 164.

69   Pande (ed.), *A Centenary History of the Indian National Congress*, vol. 3, p. 461.

in having imprisoned such a powerful friend and ally. They faced the consequences like anybody—several terms of imprisonment. 'Remember', Sarojini Naidu told daughter Leilamani from Yervada on 5 March 1933, 'the darkenss holds the light within'.

We return to a mood of expectation awaiting the political classes, except the Communist Party which called for a 'People's War' as against the path of 'national suicide', i.e., the Quit India movement. Many saw Gandhism as the prelude to a *Ramarajya*, in which all wrongs would be righted. Hundreds and thousands flocked to hear him speak. Industrial strikes and peasant riots succeeded. Although Gandhi had asked students to eschew Satyagraha, over 1,500 raised red flags in Lucknow University against the curtailment of civil and academic rights.[70] Youth enthusiasm spurred them. Some of them belonged to a literary club in Firangi Mahal, Lucknow. They spent innumerable evenings sitting, talking, and smoking together at Hazratgunj's Coffee House. Ali Sardar Jafri, a leading Urdu poet from the Balrampur state, was one of them. However, K.M. Ashraf, whose modesty and simplicity of life were equalled only by his scholarship, decried that Gandhi reluctantly built a mass movement at a time when national and international conditions were so ripe.[71]

One could write much more about the *andolan* (movement) than we have space set out here; except that there was little reason to assume that any political movement would automatically result in violent outbreaks or necessarily lead to the break down of law and order. Even though daily lists came out of processions, attacks on trains, pillar boxes, and telegraph lines, sabotage of the railways, and firings to disperse mobs in outlying areas, these events symbolised different things in many different places at different times.[72] Suffice it to say that the police firing added to the rising tension in the early months. This was so at the Gwalia Tank Maidan in Bombay on 9 August 1942. With 8 deaths and 169 injuries, Gandhi wrote to Linlithgow on 14 August 1942:

---

70   K.N. Panikkar (ed.), *TF*, 1940 (pt 2) (Delhi, 2011), p. 960.

71   Ibid., p. 1006.

72   Jim Masselos, *The City in Action: Bombay Struggles for Power* (Delhi, 2007), p. 275.

If notwithstanding the common cause, the Government's answer
to the Congress demand is hasty repression, they will not wonder
if I draw the inference that it was not so much the Allied cause
that weighed with the British Government, as the unexpressed
determination to cling to the possession of India as an indispensable
part of the imperial policy.

The kisan sabhas, the trade unions, and the intelligentsia were the
greatest force in stimulating anti-colonial sentiments. Disturbances in
UP and Bihar were spread; in Punjab, they were localised owing to the
weak opposition to the war effort and the relatively weak position of
the Congress. In Bombay, the movement was linear, diachronic, and
temporal. It was also fresh, creative, and innovative. 'A new nationalist
event was being created, a new text in the battle against the Raj,' writes
the historian Jim Masselos.[73] Gandhi's call and prompt incarceration
touched off a sharp reaction in Poona, Sholapur, Nasik, Ahmednagar,
Satara, Chimur (Chanda District), and Ashti (Wardha district). From
9 August to the end of 1942, 60,229 persons were arrested. Midnapur,
Bengal's south-western district, revolted.[74] Peasant movements, with their
own peculiar semi-religious fervour, also evolved in other districts.

Students, freed from material temptations, which seem the
necessary leap of faith for Gandhi's stewardship, closed down
colleges for extended periods, assumed a key liaison role between the
underground leaders and the movement, published 'illegal' newspapers,
and operated a clandestine radio station.[75] About 15,000 of them were
involved in the day-to-day organisational work or in sabotage. Thus,
Patna Medical College students picketed two cinema houses and shops.
Their counterparts in Darbhanga formed themselves into a procession
in Madhubani division.[76] Revolutionary groups, such as the Siaram

---

73   Ibid., p. 243.

74   Sanjiv P. Desai (ed.), *Calendar of the 'Quit India' Movement in the Bombay
      Presidency* (Bombay, 1985). Bidyut Chakrabarty, *Local Politics and Indian
      Nationalism, Midnapur, 1919-1944* (Delhi, 1997), ch 3.

75   Philip G. Altbach, in *Daedalus*, Winter 1968, p. 259.

76   For statistical information, IOR, L/PJ/8/630.

Dal, came to the fore in Bhagalpur. On their 'spirit of defiance and demonstration', the *Congress Bulletin* stated:

> It is probably not an exaggeration to say that fewer than 10 per cent were helpful or sympathetic to the government at that time, and that probably 90 per cent of the literate population was with the Congress. The party was more or less 100 per cent in the insurrection, although one or two raised ineffective cries against the excesses committed. The Congress Socialist Party was entirely in it .... Many *kisan* leaders were in it and no *kisans* opposed it. A prominent *kisan* leader, Pandit Jamuna Karjee, instigated the attack on Pusa, though he did eventually call it off, whether in order to save himself from punishment, or as a result of his secret employment by a wealthy European planter of the neighbourhood, is not known. The attitude of the Muslim League before the decision of the All India Committee on 16 August has been construed as armed neutrality; prior to this date a few Muslims backed the authorities.[77]

The All-India Spinners' Association and the All-India Village Industries, which Gandhi headed, played a major role in 1942. The former, with its 600 production centres, employed over 3,000 workers in 1940; the number of spinners and weavers was about 2.5 lakhs and of other artisans over 4,000. Also, owing to the involvement of 'Big Business', R.D. Tata, Ardeshir Dalal, Kasturbhai Lalbhai, Lala Shri Ram, and G.D. Birla embarked on a scheme of 'benevolent capitalism' working through a National government with full freedom in economic matters.[78]

The wonder is that British rule lasted as long as it did.[79] With the sound of revolution reverberating, Ian Stephens, who joined *The*

---

77   Transcripts of reports of D.M. Darbhanga to Chief Secretary of Bihar and Commissioner of Tirhut Division, IOR. R.N. Lines papers, MSS Eur. F. 346/2.

78   IOR. L/PJ/8/618A.

79   Trevor Royle, *The Last Days of the Raj* (London, 1997), p. 260.

Statesman as editor on 21 August 1942, found the British hold to be 'shaky'.[80] Tossed on the waves of the storm, like a ship in peril on the sea, most Indians pulled together like sailors pulling at one rope. *Insaf*, an Urdu newspaper, summed up in a verse: 'On this side there is reliance on fate, on that side there is reliance on force; God save the country, the blows are equally matched.'[81] When a questioner asked Gandhi to distinguish between his policy and that of Nero, fiddling while Rome burned, he reacted loudly: 'Instead of fiddling in Sevagram you may expect to find me perishing in the flames of my own starting if I cannot regulate or restrain them.'[82]

Nationalism however works both ways: while some dreamt of freedom for all, others were adamant that *azadi* should be secured only for the Muslim nation. Even though Gandhi tried to reduce problems to the basic, if any, components, his systems and approaches could have worked earlier but not when conflicting goals came in his way. As one who travelled with bewildering frequency across the subcontinent, he sampled the prevalence of what would be described in present-day terminology as 'fundamentalism' and an outlook characterised by continuing sectarianism. Yet, Truth and non-violence remained his sheet-anchor. They sustained him. He hoped that light will shine through the surrounding darkness.[83]

The Writing on the Wall

'Doomsday in miniature on the Frontier: Martyrdom of four hundred sons of Islam. Arrest of thirty thousand lovers of Liberty!' This is how an Urdu newspaper announced the sacrifices made in 1932.[84] Without a doubt, Gandhi depended heavily upon his very substantial following from the Khudai Khidmatgars, Jamiyat al-ulama, All India Momin

---

80   Stephens, *Monsoon Morning*, p. 5.

81   Note on the Press, United Provinces of Agra and Oudh, for the week ending 16 Jan. 1932.

82   The name of Seagon, near Wardha, was changed to Sevagram in 1940 to avoid its mix up with Shegaon, a station on the main line about 132 m. west of Wardha.

83   To Agatha Harrison, 29 Dec. 1943, IOR, R/3/1/309.

84   Note on the Press, United Provinces of Agra and Oudh, 16 Jan. 1932.

Conference, and the Ahrars, who spearheaded the revolt against the oppressive Dogra regime in the Kashmir valley. Sceptics apart, a strong body of opinion had endorsed the 1929 Independence Resolution.[85] *Medina*, a newspaper from Bijnor (UP), expected the Muslims, for whom complete Independence was the goal, to strengthen the Congress.[86] It added: 'The demand for the settlement of rights is quite proper in its own place ... but we cannot hold its fulfilment as the preliminary condition of Muslims' participation in the movement for freedom.'[87] Ghaffar Khan, a lifelong critic of the separatist paradigm, challenged the mechanistic world view of focusing on religious solidarity. His own sagacity was never at fault, his reliability was taken for granted, and his loyalty was unfailing.

The old actors were however deserting Gandhi. What were muted voices during 1930-2, that is, *La-tufsidwa-fil-arz* (Do not go around spreading disturbances in the country), arrayed against the 'Quit India' call in 1942.[88] Jinnah's enthusiastic reception in Calcutta amazed Ian Stephens: 'this seemed something altogether new; the League had hitherto been little more than a debating club for middle-aged gentry.'[89]

This being so, the masses marched with Jinnah; there was, at any given point of time, no room, and no need, for them to be cynical or sceptical. In Bihar, the home of Mazharul Haque and Mohammad Shafi, only a few Muslims were arrested or convicted. Of the persons detained from August to October, there were only ten.[90] In Gujarat, the Muslims stayed away from anti-government demonstrations. The call to Quit India failed to stir up the Baroda Muslims.[91] In UP, Congress's

---

85   Ibid., 11 Jan. 1930.

86   Ibid., 18 Jan. 1930.

87   Ibid., 1 Feb. 1930.

88   Chakrabarty, *Local Politics and Indian Nationalism*, pp. 141-2.

89   Ibid., p. 97.

90   Datta, *History of the Freedom Movement in Bihar*, vol. 3, app. H.

91   David Hardiman, 'The Quit India Movement in Gujarat', in Gyanendra Pandey (ed.), *The Indian Nation in 1942* (Calcutta, 1988), pp. 92-93.

conciliatory gestures didn't assuage their feelings.[92] Only a few went to jail in Benaras, Azamgarh, and Ghazipur districts.

Scores of Muslims courted imprisonment in 1920-21,[93] but they drew a blank in 1942. Here and elsewhere, the landlord-League combination worked well, while some sections of the bourgeoisie, having found their deepest satisfaction in raising Jinnah's profile, challenged Gandhi's authority. Bhikampur's nawab Muzammilullah Khan refused to subscribe for his Aligarh visit or to advance a loan to the commandant of the Aligarh College Volunteer Corps.[94] Maulana Abul Hasan Ali Nadwi, whose family had spent a lifetime with the pro-Congress Jamiyat al-ulama, was reminded of the Civil Disobedience Movement when a Hindu Marwari asked what religion he professed. 'Islam,' Abul Hasan replied. 'Do you belong to Abbas Tyabji's religion?' he asked. That is when Abul Hasan realised that one's religion earns respect for sacrifices made for the nation.[95]

During the war, imperial interests coalesced more closely with the aspirations of the bourgeoisie, landed classes, and the ulama of different schools. Notwithstanding Cripps' dismissal of Jinnah's case as 'a dog-in-the-manger attitude',[96] Linlithgow, in between the appropriate platitudes, honoured his part of the bargain with Jinnah. In fact, a slight tilt towards his adversary made the Qaid conjure up the self-image of a wounded soul. Besides, nothing the Congress offered satisfied him. He asked for more than it could guarantee. That was the crux of the problem. Under the circumstances, the Congress-League divisions exacerbated.[97]

---

92   *Aligarh Mail* commented: 'It is as if the Congress spider is out of the parlour and inviting the Muslim fly to meet the former on an outwardly safe ground. We are quite sure that if the fly even approaches the spider the latter will pounce upon the former and drag it to its death-trap. Once entrapped there, the fly will be devoured' for the week ending 1 Feb. 1930.

93   Pandey (ed.), *The Indian Nation in 1942*, p. 149.

94   *Himmat* (UP), 5 Sept. 1931.

95   A.H.A. Nadwi, *Karawan-i Zindagi* (Lucknow, 1983), pp. 250-1.

96   Clarke, *The Cripps Version*, p. 141.

97   Linlithgow to Amery, 21 Jan. 1942, *TOP*, vol. 1, par. 13, p. 48.

As for the Congress, it muddled through various negotiations with misplaced hypotheses. Instead of 'softening up' for the sake of unity, it hardened its stand. And, instead of using the mass contact campaigns as a force for social unity rather than as a political lever, the right wing virtually forced Jawaharlal to abandon his initiatives. To add insult to injury, the Mahasabha and RSS fouled the political climate with their virulent anti-Muslim and anti-Gandhi campaigns. They looked at the contemporary debates all around with a Hindutva perspective—narrow and without energy and clarity.

It is in this light that the resignation of the ministries was, from hindsight, an ill-advised decision. Apart from buttressing the League claims, it put on hold some pro-poor schemes. T.A.K. Sherwani once suggested that the Congress should aim at grabbing power. Success lay with those in authority, because that's when the masses were spurred into action against the bureaucracy.[98] Subhas Bose had cautioned: 'It is one thing to take a plunge and enter a swimming bout, it is quite a different thing to be pushed into the water from behind when the sight of it gives you cold hands and feet'.[99]

The Congress didn't bring itself round to recognising political diversity. This was, if truth be told, its handicap. Aware of this, Satyamurti, the party's chief flag-carrier in Madras after Rajaji's resignation,[100] suggested a Gandhi-Jinnah conclave on the eve of the Quit India call. He did so on the strength of the argument that the Congress had ultimately to depend upon Muslims agreeing to live in peace with their Hindu counterparts.[101]

Weighed down by the implications of the Bombay resolution about which he drew up a strongly worded letter to Azad,[102] Gandhi realised that Jinnah had etched the writ of Pakistan deep upon the

---

98   To Ansari, 2 Dec. 1934, Hasan (ed.), *Muslims and the Congress*, pp. 202-3.

99   Mushirul Hasan (ed.), *TF*, 1939 (pt 1), p. 231.

100   The venerable Rajaji was ousted from the Congress and the Madras legislative assembly after Gandhi put down his formula: he proposed acceptance of the Partition demand if the League insisted upon it.

101   Satyamurti to Gandhi, 22 Apr. 1942, Ramanathan (ed.), *The Satyamurti Letters*, vol. 2, pp. 353-54.

102   Gandhi to Azad, 10 Dec. 1941, ibid., pp. 332-33.

Muslim consciousness. Moreover, he was not to yield an inch without inviting the wrath of the constituency he had so assiduously created and cultivated.[103] In the end, he became a victim of his own miscalculation.

This is not true of the Nehrus. They thought and acted differently, mostly with exemplary grace and dignity. In all the political events during the twentieth century, however faint they might appear now, they are always present. How and why? This is the theme pursued in the following chapter.

---

103   Gandhi to Satyamurti, 17 Apr. 1942, ibid., p. 353.

Section II

Gandhi and Nehru leaving Segaon to attend the Working
Committee meeting at Wardha, September 1939

6
We the Nehrus

The Nehrus had, and still have, an aura of saintliness because they gave up
their wealth and great position, and an easy life, for the sake of India.
To Indians this is a holy thing to do, following the tradition of Buddha
himself. My brother, and my father, too, did not rise step by step to the
position of leaders of the people, but sprang into it the moment they made
the renunciation.

-Krishna Hutheesing, *We Nehrus*, p. 229.

That humble and lonely figure, standing erect, on the firm footholds of
faith unshakable and strength unconquerable, continues to send out to his
countrymen his message of sacrifice and suffering for the Motherland.

-Motilal Nehru

A French traveller boarded a train from Kanpur which followed the
right bank of the Ganges until it reached Calcutta, that is a distance
of about 628 miles. The train covered the distance between Kanpur and
Allahabad in six hours, passing through the Lower Doab, 'one of the
finest and richest districts in India.'

Situated at the point of junction of the Ganges and the Yamuna,
Prayag or Ilahabad was an administrative division under Akbar, the
Mughal emperor, before the high court was established in March 1866
and the provincial government two years later. Its changing profile drew
Kashmiri Pandits, *prabasi* Bengalis, the Kayasths, the Muslim elites, and
the local or émigré Brahmins to the city, as is reflected in the increase
in population from 72,093 in 1863 to 143,693 in 1872. Allahabad, the
capital of the North-West Provinces since 1858, earned fame for its high
court and legal luminaries. Local Brahmans, originally from Gujarat,
and Vaisyas arrived, followed by the Kashmiris. The Nagar Brahmans
were, in fact, their principal competitors in the high court. Along
with the *ashraf* Muslims, such as Syed Mahmood, son of Syed Ahmad
Khan, they belonged to the Persian- and Urdu-speaking service elites.
Ajudhia Nath Kunzru, who moved from Agra to Allahabad, derived his

substantial income principally from lucrative zamindari litigation.[1] He was the Congress' leading protagonist, and the one to inspire another Kashmiri Pandit, Tej Bahadur Sapru, to attend its session in 1892. In 1917, he and Motilal joined the Home Rule Movement.

Muslims comprised 3.4 per cent of the entire population in 1911. Most lived in little clusters, including the depressed areas of Daryabad, a poor and crowded locality. This was the home of the *wasikadars*,[2] the pensioners of Mughal times. They were kept in good humour by the local government. Lawyers and teachers, many of whom were from the mofussil towns, lived in relatively better localities. Rousselet wasn't concerned with them but with the city's changing landscape. He prophesied, in the 1870s, that 'soon [Allahabad] will no longer be so lavish of its space, air, and verdure'. With urban decay setting in owing to the steady migration from the rural hinterland, the long tree-lined avenues, well laid out public gardens, and large houses standing amidst lush green lawns disappeared.

Once, the town was divided into the English and the Indian quarters, only a few Indians lived in Civil Lines, as the English sector was called. Ward I and II of the municipality included the new Civil Lines, the cantonment, and the residential areas of Katra and Cannington. Marie Rousselet described the cantonment:

The cantonments of Allahabad are in fact a town in every sense of the word, for they contain at the present day the largest assemblage of Europeans out of the three presidential cities. Certainly the houses separated from each other by such extensive gardens, the streets lined with trees and broad as highroads, and the squares as large as esplanades, give to this English town more of the aspect of the suburbs of some great capital than of a town.[3]

---

1   Henny Sender, *The Kashmiri Pandits: A Study of Cultural Choice in North India* (Delhi, 1998), p. 243.

2   Malcolm Speirs, *The Wasikadars of Awadh: A History of certain Nineteenth Century Families of Lucknow* (Delhi, 2008).

3   Rousselet, *India and its Native Princes*, p. 555. And a recent collection of essays in A.K. Mehrotra (ed.), *The Last Bungalow: Writings on Allahabad* (Delhi, 2007).

The British elite lived in an ordered environment, in spacious houses enclosed by large gardens adjoining wide, straight roads.[4] They had their Allahabad Club, their newspaper (*Pioneer*) and their shopping centre which sold British goods, particularly apparel. Men of wealth and power drove out in smart carriages to take in the air and listen to music at a beautiful park named after Prince Khusrau, and Company Bagh, so called after the East India Company. The Company Bagh benches were marked 'For Europeans Only'. The few Indians who went in wouldn't risk insult and so walked around the garden or sat on the grass. Solicitously, they prompted each other to give news of the absentees, if any.

On a normal day half a dozen horses galloped in a pack. Nearby, cricket was played. Wives of officials, or the 'Europeans', drove to the site in their carriages to listen to the military band every Saturday. They were always eager for someone to talk about. Everyone gossiped about everyone else, with great delight and sweet viciousness.

Allahabad offered, unlike Lucknow, its jealous partner, a wide variety of opportunities to the service and professional people.[5] Kunzru, whose secular outlook evidently went beyond the merely rhetorical, was one of them. The other was Sapru, who moved from Moradabad to Allahabad in 1898 to join the High Court Bar. Remarked Edward Thompson: 'If you are going to start talking about Moslem culture, where are your finest examples? In picking the best that All India could afford you would have to include both the Maulana [Abul Kalam Azad], who presides over the National Congress, and Sir Tej Bahadur Sapru, who is a Hindu by birth.' 'Why,' asked Thompson, 'should the Moslem League veto till the crack of doom any implementation of the now old pledge of Dominion Status?'[6]

4　　'It is a matter of wonderment that when the plague is working havoc in our rural quarters, cantonments, as a rule, remain free. Reasons for such immunity are obvious. In the cantonments the atmosphere is pure, houses detached, roads are wide and clean, the sanitary habits of the residents are exceptionally sound, whereas ours are as unhygienic as they well could be. Out closets are pestilentially dirty. Ninety per cent of our population go barefoot, people spit anywhere, perform natural functions anywhere and are obliged to walk along roads and path thus dirtied. It is no wonder that the plague has found a home in our midst.' M.K. Gandhi, *Select Speeches*, pp. 352-53.

5　　Bayly, *The Local Roots of Indian Politics*, pp. 57-61.

6　　Thompson, *Enlist India for Freedom!*, p. 55.

Sapru's outlook was strongly ecumenical. Religious or political fundamentalism had no place in his world made up of law, literature, and politics. His drawing room, with its parallelograms of light, was full of Urdu and Persian books. He read, recited, and reproduced the verses of Mir Taqi Mir, Ghalib, Shaikh Saadi, and Hafiz Shirazi. There were many such in that era, though the anti-Urdu crusade was already well underway in Allahabad. Sapru, who knew Persian and Urdu, was a vocal protagonist for Hindustani. 'Why should people assume,' he once wrote, 'merely because I know Persian that I am antipathetic to my Hindu heritage. I have really been proud of it.'[7] Besides, his equanimity was bottomless, as was his lack of ambition. He assumed that everyone else was like him. He resembled the Nehrus in his pride, quickness of temper, and in an urbanity deriving as much from an Indo-Persian background as from a punctilious adherence to the forms of late-Victorian politesse.[8]

Pandit Motilal Nehru was his close friend. The family has a photograph of a Saraswat Brahman, in his formal cutaway coat of English broadcloth and grey striped trousers, with a stiff shirt, high collar, and satin tie. Motilal's rather full face had a handle bar moustache, which he shaved off. This photograph was taken in 1899. Artists portrayed him as a vigorous man with the clear cut and domineering mask of a Roman senator, his bearing irresistibly youthful to the very end. He lived on Elgin Road until 1900. Thereafter, he moved to a forty-two room house on Church Road in Civil Lines and decorated it with expensive European artefacts. Already an adult, he married the fourteen-year-old Swarup Rani Thussu, a shy and beautiful Kashmiri girl—'a little ivory figurine, with big almond-shaped hazel eyes, exquisite hands and feet and bright chestnut hair falling in thick waves far below her waist.'[9] She'd often hear the tinkle of ice cubes as her husband sat next to a low wooden lamp holding a gin and tonic in his hand. During the 40 years preceding March 1921, Motilal had rarely missed a drink for 11 months

---

7   Bose, *Tej Bahadur Sapru*, p. 191.

8   Ibid., p. 134.

9   Vijaya Lakshmi, *The Scope of Happiness*, p. 38; Nehru, *An Autobiography*, p. 7; Krishna Nehru Hutheesing, *With No Regrets* (London, 1944), p. 122.

in the year. He abstained for a month simply to avoid getting enslaved to the habit.[10] 'I know you will feel polluted if you eat at my table,' he told one of his uncles, 'but it won't hurt you to drink a whisky and soda with me.'[11] He drank wine publicly, and in the course of an after dinner speech he preached that, 'water has been called pure, but wine is made after being distilled thrice. It is, therefore, purer than water.'[12]

Their son wandered off the portico on to the gravel path behind the roses. In his younger days, a melancholy hovered about him, even as he did his best, usually with success, to cope with life in Anand Bhawan. His was a pampered childhood given his father's indulgence and mother's care and affection. In England, he showed signs of the effects which a distinctly exceptional education produced, though there were no hints yet of greatness in the spheres in which he would excel: leadership and statesmanship. He had adapted to the conventions of Harrow, the famous British public school he joined in the Christmas term of 1905 at the age of 16. He liked Byron's poetry much better than he should, because he was at Harrow, where after the first bleakness which Jawaharlal experienced at a public school, he was happy.[13] Lord Zetland, Samuel Hoare, Winston Churchill and L.S. Amery, all closely connected with India, were fellow-Harrovians.

In Trinity College, Cambridge, Jawaharlal found a stimulus to the busy exercise of a very independent mind. In his letters, he seemed intimately acquainted with its history and developed a punctilious regard for its traditions. He took a keen interest in India, Russia, and Ireland. To a cousin, he wrote saying simply, 'Three cheers for Togo', a reference to the annihilation of Russia's European Baltic battle fleet at the battle of Tsushima on 27 May 1905. In June 1912, he was called to the Bar. In autumn he returned home after seven years. Still young enough to be filled with high hopes of the promise thus held out, he left England in great expectation of a career very different from the reality his family members were destined to witness.

---

10   To Gandhi, 10 July 1924, *SWMN*, vol. 4, p. 47.

11   Hutheesing, *We Nehrus*, p. 21.

12   Motilal to Gandhi, 10 July 1924, *SWMN*, vol. 4, p. 47.

13   Thompson, *Enlist India For Freedom!*, p. 29.

It is undeniably true that Jawaharlal questioned conventional wisdom and home-grown truths, but there wasn't anything iconoclastic about his radicalism. In the Congress they twitted him about his 'Anglo-Saxon' ways. He told K.N. Knox, Allahabad's district magistrate, on 17 May 1922: 'I looked upon the world almost from an Englishman's stand point. And so I returned [from England] to India as much prejudiced in favour of England and the English as it was possible for an Indian to be.'[14] Once, when Edward Thompson entered the CWC room, CR responded to his greeting with an outstretched hand, and apologised. 'It is his Anglo-Saxonism' (with a wave towards Jawaharlal) 'that gets us into these bad ways.' 'Talk that over with Jawaharlal,' said Gandhi to the same person, 'he thinks like your people.'[15]

The contrast with Cambridge's cloistered world couldn't have been starker. For a while Jawaharlal found the 'utter insipidity of life' disconcerting, but quickly discovered fun and excitement around him. After the stuffiness of Trinity College, talking to friends, visitors, and relatives was like a breath of fresh air. He was closest to Vijaya Lakshmi, 11 years younger, with whom he spent much time reading and reciting poetry. He was also fond of Krishna Hutheesing (b. 1907). All in all, these three looked out over the world from lofty isolation and saw new faces amidst all the hustle and bustle.

Munshi Mubarak Ali managed the household, and Asghar Ali, the butler, took care of their needs. Each one of them also had an English governess. The child widow Bibi Ama, Swarup Rani's sister, ran the household chores. There was desperation in many of her actions, or something unnamed that made her keep a close vigil on what went on in the household. When Jawaharlal got married, the gentle Kamala Nehru suffered at her hands. The Nehrus were wary of her petty intrigues, but maintained a dignified silence.

Houses have the corporate soul of their inhabitants. Daryaganj is Delhi's original cantonment. After 1803, a native regiment of the Delhi garrison was stationed here, after which it was shifted to the Ridge area. The British Daryaganj Cantonment was one of the earliest

---

14   Statement at Trial, *Leader*, 19 May 1922, *SWJN*, vol. 1, p. 253.

15   Thompson, *Enlist India for Freedom!*, p. 29.

establishments in Old Delhi. East of Daryaganj was the Yamuna River. Nearby lived Dr Mukhtar Ahmad Ansari, who had moved from Mori Gate in the old city to this area in 1925. He lived more than anyone in the 1920s to give a much-needed sense of the value of swaraj. Joseph Conrad (1857-1924)—born and bred in Poland—wrote in his preface to A Personal Record (1912): 'Those who read me, know my conviction that the world, the temporal world, rests on a few very simple ideas; so simple that they may be as old as the hills. It rests notably, among others, on the idea of Fidelity.' This governing idea of fidelity, of faith-keeping between man and man, was the mainspring of Ansari's life. Beneath his seriousness he was ardent and affectionate. Others thought that he was sincere, kind, warm-hearted, and quite innocent of guile.

Once, Darus-Salam (Abode of Islam) used to be a landmark, not far from Jama Masjid, the great mosque built by Shahjahan. Ansari hosted Indians and guests from Britain, Turkey and Egypt. Halide Edip, whom he first met as the leader of the Indian Medical Mission to Constaintinople in 1912, stayed here for two months in 1935. She dug deep into Delhi's intellectual history, with a deep understanding of the circumstances in which changes occurred from time to time, describing Darus-Salam as 'an historical place where the ancient, the medieval, and the modern came together: the ideas and aspirations of divergent personalities meet, coalesce, and the personalities disperse to set in motion new trends elsewhere. In the free India of the future, that house will be one of the principal landmarks in its making'. Her very personal narrative is closely woven into the fabric of the family history of the Ansaris.[16] Dr Ansari himself had done much to maintain the right atmosphere.

In Lucknow, 'Ashiana' was one of the city's signposts which Halide Edip so vividly described; in Allahabad, 19 Albert Road, the home of Tej Bahadur Sapru, was a familiar sight. So was the 'Golden Threshold' in Hyderabad, a spacious bungalow with a walled-in compound. It had a lovely garden with fully grown trees. Wherever Sarojini Naidu was, that was her kingdom. She loved a beautifully appointed home, rich food, beautiful clothes and jewels, and a house filled with people

---

16   Edip, *Inside India*, p. 15.

involved with stirring events. It was an authentic 'salon' like those of Mme de Staël and Europe's other famous intellectual hostesses. Margaret Cousins commented that one can 'speculate romantically about her last incarnation, and dream of her as the bright and shining star of some brilliant French salon at the height of France's glory.'[17] On 11 May 1925, Jawaharlal listened to the sun-birds and honeybirds making music in the garden among the flaming Gul Mohurs and Scarlet Roses.[18] Here, the host would sit cross-legged on a divan and talk with a brilliance that would remind one of her visitors of 'Lady Oxford at her best, in the old Bedford Square days, when yellow tulips were two shillings a dozen and sherry was just drink, and not an Event.'[19] In less happier times, Sarojini Naidu bore the hardships during the Home Rule Movement and Rowlatt Satyagraha with much stoicism and humour. Once seen, she couldn't be forgotten because of her verbal ingenuity and the gift of electrifying audiences by her powerful oratory skills. Her exuberance was such that she'd put all her strength into whatever she said. Her technique, combined with her poetic nature, made her performance remarkable. She didn't prepare speeches. To speak was as easy for her as it was for a fish to swim.

In Allahabad, near Bharadwaj Ashram (in ancient days the site of a university), is a place where once Rama and Bharat met after Lord Rama returned from exile. Here stands the Anand Bhawan, 'a family residence of this type is like the ancestral house of a clan in the highlands of Scotland' (C.F. Andrews). When Jawaharlal was 10 years old, his father purchased it. It had a huge garden and big verandas all around, a summer house and a tennis court. Inside the summer house Shiva's image was mounted high on large stones, which were placed one on top of the other to make it look like a miniature mountain. From Shiva's head a tiny stream trickled down into the pool at the foot of it.[20] Anand Bhawan bustled with activity. Guests associated the sound

---

17   Quoted in V.S. Naravane, *Sarojini Naidu: An Introduction to her life, Work and Poetry* (New Delhi, 1996), p. 143.

18   Nehru (ed.), *A Bunch of Old Letters*, p. 42.

19   Beverley Nichols, *Verdict on India* (London, 1944), p. 150.

20   Hutheesing, *With No Regrets*, p. 7.

of laughter with the house.[21] But it was far more than just a structure of brick and concrete; more than a private possession. It was intimately associated with the freedom struggle. Great events occurred within its walls; great decisions were taken. From the verandas one could view a great expanse of garden redolent with gladioli, daffodils, sweet peas, chrysanthemums, delphiniums, and roses. One could see hundreds of birds flitting about, adding their melodious songs and bright colour to its beauty. Trees were life-giving and offered a refuge; the young in the family loved climbing and hiding there, in a little nook.

Motilal wanted them and his friends to share the good life with him. M.R.A. Baig, a Sandhurst-educated future diplomat, found his second Indian home after England at Anand Bhawan. Similarly, Choudhry Khaliquzzaman, Manzar Ali Sokhta, Wahid Yah Khan, T.A.K. Sherwani, Shuaib Qureshi, son-in-law of Mohamed Ali, and A.M. Khwaja did not find their host lonely, or bored, or despondent; instead, he was jovial, easy going, and generous. The effect of one of his anecdotes was to make them reflect on humankind and its failings. Sarojini Naidu admired the Nehrus.

In short, Sarojini Naidu found a haven in the home of kind and congenial friends like Motilal Nehru. An outspoken opponent of religious rituals and superstitions, he didn't harp on trifles and eschewed religious controversies. Sarojini Naidu shared his modern sensibilities and his spacious and unprejudiced outlook on the past and present. Indeed, they combined to add a cosmopolitan element to the Congress activities. They were both faithful to their wider political interests and were moved and uplifted by M.K. Gandhi's rise to power. Even if some differences cropped up and a shift in political outlook took place, their vigour was unabated to the end. What is more, both strove for dignity in public life.

Motilal's social life included a fine group of interesting personalities living nearby and a constant stream of others attached to the high court, the university, and, above all, the great confluence of the sacred rivers. The western wing was the site of lavish entertainment: the guest list included everyone who was anyone in Allahabad: politicians, journalists, poets, and British administrators. Harcourt Butler, Lieutenant-

---

21   Vijaya Lakshmi, *The Scope of Happiness* pp. 42-43.

Governor of UP, was also a close friend of the Raja of Mahmudabad, a man of piety who served many good causes and patronised several young and intelligent persons. Often, he and Motilal met at the Raja's home in Qaiser Bagh, Lucknow, and enjoyed life as it came their way. As knives and forks appeared on the dining table in Anand Bhawan, social conversation would veer mostly around Shakespeare and nineteenth-century Romantic poets. Those guests who were in a pensive mood would spend the late evenings gazing at the stars. On other occasions, Urdu poets would entertain them with their *ghazals*. Musicians, many of whom belonged to the Awadh *qasba*s sang the *ghazals* of Mir, Ghalib, Momin Khan 'Momin', and Zauq. Come Muharram and they, regardless of their religion, would put away their musical instruments in memory of the martyrdom of Imam Husain, the grandson of the Prophet of Islam. These clear expressions of tolerance and respect for religious practices survived well until the 1930s,[22] when Shia-Sunni animus and Hindu-Muslim conflicts, with their attendant bloodshed, began to polarize Awadh's composite milieu.

With the *angrezi* or Anglo-Indian culture fast expanding, playing games or watching sporting events were the pastimes of rich Indians. Small and large cricket fields dotted Allahabad's landscape. Often, friends dropped by to enjoy the spacious garden in Anand Bhawan, sit around the tiered fountain at the centre of the courtyard, or take a dip in the indoor swimming pool in a great, cavernous, damp smelling room. At one end of the pool there was large carved-stone crow's head from whose mouth fresh water poured to fill it. Sapru couldn't swim and would not therefore move from the first step in 15 inches of water.

There wasn't anything bohemian about Motilal's lifestyle. Stories of linen being washed in Paris and his Sauterne from France were apocryphal, but not the tale of his acquiring a set of Bohemian glass, the kind just purchased by King Edward VII. 'Who in Allahabad is going to appreciate these,' wondered Swarup Rani, by now accustomed to her husband's princely habits, 'and why should we be like King Edward?' Gandhi pictured her to personify dignified bravery and sacrifice.

---

22   Madhu Trivedi, *The Making of the Awadh Culture* (Delhi, 2010), and her *The Emergence of the Hindustani Tradition* (Delhi, 2012).

The family tree of some neighbours was bare, as well as rootless, but the place of the Nehrus was firmly assumed in the upper echelons of society. Their lives combined the benefits of privilege with the satisfaction on the side of freedom: freedom from caste and religious conventions with the confidence and assurance of being a part of a long and proud tradition. Motilal, in particular, stood out in every society. Whichever place he sat at a table became the head of the table. Occasionally the young Jawaharlal would peep at the guests from behind a curtain. If he was caught he would be dragged out and made to sit on his father's knee. Occasionally, he and the servants faced his uncontrollable temper. When that happened, he would rush to mother Swarup Rani, who lived and retained her orthodox ways. Once, when Motilal beat him up for stealing a fountain pen, he did that, and for several days creams and ointments were applied to his aching and quivering body. When the unsuspecting Jawahar saw his father drink claret or a deep red wine for the first time, he hurried to tell her, 'Father's drinking blood'.

When it came to Motilal's turn to give an account of friends, it was impossible not to be influenced by the lasting friendships; many played a significant part in his professional and political life. Friends loved him for his searching, lucid, and incisive mind. They were captivated by his aristocratic manner, his humour tempered with good taste in poetry, and his sophistication, which under no circumstances degenerated into 'showing off'. They however also judged him to be too worldly, domineering, acerbic, wilful: flaws of character which, in their minds, were redeemed by his gracious and courteous bearing and the humility that endeared him to those who knew him well.

At the Political Crossroads

When Motilal stumbled across the political field, in the grip of illogical certainties, he had no idea of what he was about politically, where he was going, what his plan was. He was in this state exchanging letters with his son in England.

Meanwhile, Annie Besant, the Theosophist leader, who, at one time, attracted and repelled many, roused public consciousness to the same anomalies that had struck Gandhi after his return from South Africa. Despite the fact that Motilal risked employing Ferdinand T. Brooks as his son's tutor, the politics of the tutors was much too heady a drug for him. His apprehensions came true when Annie Besant initiated Jawaharlal into the Theosophist Society; fortunately for him, the boy outgrew the cloudy mysticism and turned to the anti-colonial currents worldwide. Then someone broke the stillness of Anand Bhawan in 1919. By this time, there was, besides the fun and frolic, an understanding of what freedom could mean, and what sacrifices would be involved in the years to come. Normally, Motilal would take control of a situation like this, but on this occasion he paced the hallway before he saw Swarup Rani approach within earshot and look on with an impenetrable gaze. Everything converged. Jawaharlal hovered on the peripheries. One evening the host told Gandhi in his low and soft voice:

> You have taken my son, but I have a great law practice in the British courts. If you will permit me to continue it, I will pour great sums of the money I make into your movement. Your cause will profit far more than if I give it up to follow you.

'No,' the esteemed guest exclaimed with an indulgent smile and with his head held high. 'No! I don't want money. I want you—and every member of your family.' According to Gandhi, Motilalji was the first to join the Movement (Non-Cooperation). Andrews still remembers the sweet discussion that he had with him on the resolution.[23]

Suddenly, Anand Bhawan turned noisy and alive. One of the great thrills of Nayantara Sahgal's childhood was the sight of thousands coming to see the house and get a glimpse of Mamu (Jawaharlal). Even so, it wasn't easy adjusting to the changing times or making sense of anti-government chanting and public processions.[24] Gandhi tried to impose order on the Nehrus. But Swarup Rani couldn't cope with the 'political realities'; she only learnt to serve her husband, a role she played without much song and dance. Motilal saw no wisdom in taking

---

23   Hutheesing, *We Nehrus*, p. 34; Andrews (ed.), *Mahatma Gandhi: His Own Story*, p. 330.

24   Nayantara Sahgal, 'Life with Uncle', in Rafiq Zakaria (ed.), *A Study of Nehru* (Delhi, 1959), p. 139.

on the government and getting locked up in jail. He believed that the road to freedom was strewn with difficulties, and that its eventual attainment depended upon learning the art of self-government step by step. He pinned faith in English institutions, and having established warm contact with several Liberal leaders during his visits to England in 1899, 1900, 1905, and 1909, he found them to be committed to some form of Indian representation in legislative bodies.

Motilal's one desire, which he shared with Swarup Rani, was to somehow insulate their Cambridge-educated son from the hurly burly of politics.[25] Once or twice he slept on the floor to try to experience one of the minor discomforts that his rebellious son would have to undergo when the time came for him to go to jail. Even after the acceptance of arrest, prosecution, and prison, he painfully recorded his only son boarding a third-class railway compartment: 'this is a time when he should be enjoying himself, but he has given up everything and has become a *sadhu*'. The son, in turn, was unable to sleep at the thought of going against his father, wandering alone through the grounds in misery. He wondered if he was repaying in any way the love and care that had been lavished upon him from the day of his birth.[26]

Motilal wasn't a radical, and yet nowhere did he suggest that Gandhi cease his efforts on behalf of fellow Indians. Arguing that change, in and for itself, wasn't necessarily good, and that progress must be built on the pyramid of the past, he was bold enough to stand up to Gandhi. He hoped Jawahar would, in next to no time, realise that Gandhi's preachings were destructive to law, but the son wasn't convinced. Even at Harrow, his father's 'immoderately moderate' tone made him feel uncomfortable,[27] and his contention that, 'it is not in the [John Bull's] nature to mean ill'.[28] He had a soft corner for the Sinn Fein in Ireland who, he thought, resembled the Indian extremists,[29] and, back home, questioned the self-image of

25   Vijaya Lakshmi, *The Scope of Happiness*, pp. 69-70.

26   Hutheesing, *We Nehrus*, p. 41. Jawaharlal to Mahadev Desai, August 1923, *SWJN*, vol. 1, p. 364.

27   To Father, 20 Dec. 1907, ibid., pp. 39-40.

28   Ibid., 19 Apr. 1907, ibid., p. 23.

29   Ibid., 7 Nov. 1907, ibid., p. 37.

those as the 'natural leaders'. He hoped that a 'little stirring up' would help those whose voice was little more than a whisper in the newspapers.[30] Clearly, Jawaharlal had already chosen the ground from which he would not move during his ever-widening survey of history and politics. This became more and more apparent when Gandhi's words winged their way to the innermost recesses of his mind and heart.[31]

Meanwhile, bitter exchanges between father and son ensued. Desertion rocked Motilal's well-ordered private world, and his veneration for the rule of law handed down through the centuries by the Roman and British jurists. The political stir came closer to his genteel world and he knew not what to do except to wish for stability and progress in a world cut adrift from what he considered to be its liberal moorings. At times Jawaharlal's sharp comments irked him.[32] He'd tell him so. He was too self-willed and proud a man to ingratiate himself to senior government officials, and wasn't the kind to hanker after honours.

Roughly speaking, up to that time Gandhi and Motilal had contrasting estimates of political realities. The former interconnected the Jallianwala Bagh cataclysm, the Punjab wrongs, and the Khilafat episode; the latter was unprepared to be swept off his feet by the tide of passion. He acquiesced in Satyagraha without endorsing the wording of the pledge. Nonetheless, Jallianwala Bagh made the Nehrus realise, after all, that the real Britain wasn't all rational, all harmonious, orderly, and tolerant. Motilal, in particular, tried to mould his children, down to the very last bourgeois detail, but felt uncomfortable with the spinning wheel, non-violence, and Gandhi's politico-religious philosophy. Accordingly, he didn't want Gandhi to convert the Congress, with which he had by now begun to deal with, into a spinners' association. His doubts extended also to Non-Cooperation; like Jinnah, he was aware of the many things nearer home than the Khilafat question.[33] Also, like Jinnah, he expected

---

30   Ibid., 7 Nov. 1907, ibid., p. 37. Ibid., 2 Jan. 1908, ibid., p. 41.

31   Nehru, *An Autobiography*, p. 83.

32   On 30 June 1908, he ventured to tell his father: 'The government must be feeling very pleased with you at your attitude. I wonder if the insulting offer of a Rai Bahadurship, or something equivalent, would make you less of a Moderate than you are.'

33   Brown, *Gandhi's Rise to Power*, p. 198.

Gandhi's projects to bring about civil strife. He wasn't prepared to accept them simply because they came from him.[34] Later, when Gandhi wanted to know about his drinking habits, Motilal's characteristic response was:

> As I have made clear to you from time to time, my agreement with you on several items of your programme is not based on the identical grounds upon which you rely and, if I have come to the same conclusions as you have, it is on purely political or economic and sometimes also moral grounds, having no reference whatever to the religious beliefs of any section of the Congress.[35]

Gandhi smiled. On 28-30 November 1920, he stormed Allahabad with his speeches at two public meetings, a women's gathering, and a student's assembly at Anand Bhawan. He did not support the council entry programme but allowed Motilal sufficient leeway to make 'a brave show of *khaddar* in the citadel of the bureaucracy' and to plant the National flag in the heart of the Council Chamber.[36] When it came to honouring him, Gandhi made the 'boisterous old fellow' lead the Congress in 1928. In this way, he firmed up a relationship with an almost iconic figure among the Kashmiri Pandits.

During the All Parties Conference in early 1928, Gandhi discussed, from the Nandi Hills, his dietary habits and spinning, and, incidentally, produced nuggets such as 'typewriter is a cover for indifference and laziness'. Still, he evinced interest in the Nehru Report, named after its chairperson. Motilal worked with him to promote dominion status, which he endorsed, and examined the impartial weighing of arguments and counter-arguments on Hindu-Muslim representation. He was sufficiently shrewd not to pick up the gauntlet when Muslim groups approached him. Instead, he was forever at the beck and call of the Committee.[37] After a brief hiatus, its work was over.

---

34   Motilal to Jawaharlal, 27 Feb. 1920, *SWMN*, vol. 2, p. 101.

35   Motilal to Gandhi, 10 July 1924, ibid., vol. 4, p. 47.

36   18 Apr. 1924, K.M. Panikkar & A. Pershad (eds), *The Voice of Freedom: Selected Speeches of Motilal Nehru* (Delhi, 1961), p. 518.

37   *Young India*, 16 Aug. 1928; *Pioneer*, 9 Sept. 1928; *SWMN*, vol. 5, pp. 220, 242.

Motilal expounded his views with his usual energy, raising interesting points and subjecting many neglected facts to penetrating analysis. Without him, Gandhi stated, there would have been no Committee, no unanimity, and no report. Motilal's stature, in fact, lent the Nehru Report a touch of the incredible being made credible. 'I have decided to see you to my utmost,' he wrote to Gandhi, who wrote back, 'Most willingly I place myself at your disposal.'[38]

The Patriarch

The Nehrus wrote their own histories, the only family to do so with such consistency, and did this rather well. Their original name was 'Kaula', a word used in medieval Kashmiri texts for a devotee of Shakti, the goddess of power and energy. Their ancestors had undertaken, in search of greener pastures, the long trek from Bij Bihara, a small village in the Kashmir valley, to the Gangetic plain. Pandit Raj Kaula received a favourable opportunity from Farukhsiyar, the Mughal emperor (1714-19). A Persian and Sanskrit scholar, he moved to Shahjahanabad in 1716 and, like all worldly men, settled along one of Delhi's canals (*nehr* in Farsi) and took Nehr-Kaul as his surname. The family prospered. Pandit Lakshmi Narayan, Motilal's grandfather, served the East India Company, a comfortable position for any new aspirant to the judicial service. Government employment is the prize to which all qualified Indians aspired, and Narayan was delighted to have it. There, indeed, he was ushered into a new life, and gained many experiences, good and bad. In 1857, in a little painting, his son Pandit Gangadhar (Motilal's father), a police officer, wears the Mughal court attire and holds a curved sword in his hand. Mother Indrani, known as Jiyo Maji, learnt and quoted from the Persian poets.

The Nehrus are Kashmiri Pandits. Being Kashmiris they had a common bond with, say the Saprus, who had migrated to Delhi towards the end of the eighteenth century. Pandit Radha Kishan, the grandfather of the Liberal politician Sapru, taught Mathematics at Delhi College before joining the government. The Nehrus were concentrated in Lahore, Lucknow, and Allahabad where the Ganga meets the Jamuna and the fabled subterranean stream Saraswati; family histories celebrate ancestry

---

38   Jayakar papers (441).

and their virtuous deeds. Into this family came Bishen Narayan Dar, who travelled overseas. For that, he had to eat cow dung as repentance. They say marriages are made in heaven. They were also contracted within the caste. So it was that some marriages, as of Krishna Nehru (later Hutheesing, for example, to a non-Brahman), upset her mother. 'The Kashmiri community,' an indignant Jawaharlal told Gandhi, 'disgusts me; it is the very epitome of the petty bourgeois vice which I detest.'[39] This apart, the Nehrus married outside their fold; B.K. Nehru, a cousin of Jawaharlal, married a Hungarian. The family valued and appreciated the good things of life, set great store by education and took pride in their love of literature, art, and music. They also drew comfort from their own code of manners and sense of fun.

Swarup Kumari Nehru, known as Nan to her immediate family and friends (later Vijaya Lakshmi Pandit) boasted. 'We were Kashmiris whereas everyone else was "they".'[40] When asked if the Nehrus had been a trifle arrogant, B.K. Nehru retorted: 'But of course. And why the hell shouldn't we be?'[41]

'Not true,' thought Jawaharlal. 'I am called a Kashmiri in the sense that ten generations ago my people came down from Kashmir to India. This is not the bond I have in mind when I think of Kashmir, but other bonds which have tied us....'[42] The fact is that his kinsmen saw one another as one family living together. In spite of all his western ideas, Motilal firmly believed in families being closely knit together and 'so with our first, second or even farther removed cousins we looked upon one another as brothers and sisters.'[43]

39   To Gandhi, 25 July 1933, Iyengar and Zackariah (eds), *Together They Fought*, p. 185

40   Born and bred in Allahabad, she married Ranjit Sitaram Pandit in 1921, and entered local politics in the same city. This *biradari* (solidarity) is illustrated by Jawaharlal's birth to Swarup Rani, a Kashmiri Pandit from Lahore, on 14 Nov. 1889, a century after the storming of the Bastille, and his marriage to Kamala Kaul on 8 Feb. 1916.

41   B.K. Nehru, *Nice Guys Finish Second*, pp. 18-19.

42   Robert Hardy Andrews, *A Lamp for India: The Story of Madame Pandit* (London, 1967), pp. 244-5.

43   Krishna Hutheesing, 'My Brother—Then and Now', Zakaria (ed.), *A Study of Nehru*, p. 131.

It is one thing to be aware in day-to-day life of public duties and to possess a strong sense that one's duty to oneself entailed duty to others, but Motilal's haughtiness came with a combination of family ancestry and worldly gains. In consequence, the family bonding running in his blood caused him to take charge of his not so well-to-do relatives. When Shri Dhar, a nephew of his and son of Bansi Dhar, joined the Civil Service in 1912, Motilal said, 'Why, we should conquer the world with these and their descendants who I am sure will go on adding fresh lustre to the family name as the years go by.'[44] His son, Jawaharlal, shared his father's trait. His affection spread to uncles, aunts, numerous cousins, and other family members.

The Ganga-Jumni *Ways of Living*

Being a father gave Motilal's life a new meaning. Not surprisingly, Jawaharlal became the centre of his hopes and feelings. He arranged everything for him so that he could grow up to be his pride.[45] As in other matters, his instincts were based on the confidence that everything was achievable for an aristocratic family like his, and that he had played his part in preparing his son for a role in running the world. Once, after returning from Europe, he claimed to have sown the seed of his future greatness.[46] He bequeathed to his children this fusion of professional commitment and family pride.

---

44   'My fondest hope of seeing the Nehru name universally loved and respected is now being gradually realized. What single family in India can boast of such a galaxy of intellect among its scions as the Nehru family. B. Nehru M.A. (Oxon) of the Inner Temple Esq, Dr. K. Nehru M.B., Ch.B., B.Sc (Edin), J. Nehru M.A. (Cantab) of the Inner Temple Esq. And last comes the great scholar and scientist Dr. S.S. Nehru.' To Bansi Dhar Nehru, 9 Oct. 1912, *SWMN.*, vol. 1, p. 175.

45   Like a true patriarch, he wrote on 20 Oct. 1905: 'You must bear in mind that in you we are leaving the dearest treasure we have in this world, and perhaps in other worlds to come.... It is not a question of providing for you, as I can do that perhaps in one single year's income. It is a question of making a real man of you which you are bound to be. It would be extremely selfish—I should say sinful—to keep you with us and leave you a fortune in gold with little or no education. I think I can without vanity say that I am the founder of the fortunes of the Nehru family. I look upon you, my dear son, as the man who will build upon the foundations I have laid and have the satisfaction of seeing a noble structure of renown rearing up its head to the skies.' To Jawaharlal, 20 Oct. 1905, ibid., p. 175.

46   To Bansi Dhar Nehru, 9 Oct. 1912, *SWMN*, vol. 1, p. 175.

Motilal took young lawyers and journalists under his wing and placed his knowledge and experience at their disposal. He encouraged man or woman, old or young, cultivated or callow, and recognised good everywhere, however unexpected its source might be. He dispensed patronage with dignity. Blessed with a large capacity for affection, generous and indulgent, he had a kind, somewhat whimsical, manner.

White collar employment depended upon learning English. In this respect, the Pandits were equal to the Kayasths but more consistent than the Muslims. What made Western learning useful and productive were the rewards brought by litigation over land and debt. To cope with this demand, the district courts and the high courts required lawyers who could interpret religious as well as secular laws. Hence a law degree offered the route to fame and fortune. UP had four advocates and thirty *vakils* up to 1870; during 1891-1900, they were up by 100 and 235, respectively. Kunzru, who consolidated his position by gradual but incessant effort, reaped the benefits from the lucrative land cases that came from Allahabad's rural areas and southern Awadh. In 1910-14, Kailash Nath Katju, a lawyer in Kanpur, earned Rs 4000-5000 a month. He exuded confidence with his newly-acquired platform of representing public opinion.[47] The earnings further bolstered his position.

In one big case, Motilal earned a fee of around Rs 200,000. By 1905, at 35, his earnings had increased fourfold from Rs 2000 a month. Begums and ranis would come to Anand Bhawan in a curtained car or horse carriage, enter Motilal's study, and sit behind the screen in purdah. Despite their generally secluded life, which was reinforced by the *zenana* (women) and the *mardana* (men) portions of a *haveli* or palace, some women were dogged in pursuing complicated cases of divorce, marriage, succession, and inheritance. When dragged to the courts by litigation, they felt that they were entering upon a struggle with their enemies, that all things were fair in war, and that it was necessary to circumvent the enemy if it meant spending large sums of money. It was simple enough: Motilal wanted money, worked for it, and

---

47   The Kashmir Pandits proved their mettle in the civil service too; two of
      Motilal's nephews entered the ICS.

got it. He had plenty, not by seeking favours, but through diligence and intellect. People took him to be a magician.

Finer sensibilities came with cultural syncretism. It can be said of the Kashmiri Pandits generally that they navigated the crosscurrents of history deftly chiefly due to their ability to culturally adapt to their situations. Motilal was a good example of that adaption. His pluralism wouldn't let him indulge in, for example, *prayaschit* (purification ceremony). 'No,' he confirmed after returning from his first ever visit to Europe in 1899, 'not even if I die for it.'[48] Gandhi, by contrast, justified his own conduct on excommunication: 'Had I agitated for being admitted to the caste … I should on arrival from England, have found myself in a whirlpool of agitation, and perhaps party to dissimilation.' Nor did Motilal abandon his entire *Weltanschauung*. When he heard of his excommunication from his caste, his crusading fervour came to him naturally: 'I will ruthlessly and mercilessly lay bare the tattered fabric of its [caste] existence and tear it into the minutest possible shreds'. True, religious zealots were knocking at every door to challenge the pluralist inheritance, but Motilal didn't want their narrow-mindedness to influence his kith and kin or filter down to the masses.[49] Prayag had a shared value for the Hindus, but its salience, as in the case of the *qasba* sites of Awadh, lay in its composite history.

Motilal did not believe in saints and godmen. He did not read religious texts. Instead, he read Hafiz of Shiraz, Shaikh Saadi, Mir, and Mirza Ghalib, the Delhi poets of the land where his ancestors had established themselves as the *shurafa* (respectable gentlemen). His spirit survived, buoyed with an optimism that owed nothing to hope of a next world, or *moksha*, unqualified by the wrath to come. Intuitive scepticism had shown itself early and he adopted a utilitarian approach towards religion and religious matters. His travels to Europe and his studying European writers brought with them a whiff of the unorthodox. He found in them an exhilarating confirmation of his inner beliefs. Science and the secularisation of Europe hardened his sceptical dissent, and he saw religion less as a substitute to the glamour and attraction of a modern life. 'Pilgrimages,' he'd say, 'should lead to

---

48   Motilal to Pirthinath Chak, 22 Dec. 1909, *SWMN*, vol. 1, p. 53.

49   To Jawaharlal, 25 Mar. 1909, *SWJN*, vol. 1, p. 141.

the West—to Europe, to America, in search of the key to progress so that we can open the door to a fuller, richer life for ourselves.'

Outside Allahabad, Brij Narain 'Chakbast' (1882), another Kashmiri Pandit who studied in Lucknow's Canning College, exemplified this composite character of Awadh society. He was a poet-editor.[50]

Voyage to an Unknown Future

Jawaharlal grew up with the mixture of what is every now and then called Muslim culture in language, in ways of life, food, and the like. He didn't believe in religious solidarity, because the ties that bound the people were common economic interests and a common national interest. The real conflict had nothing to do with religion, though religion often masked the issue, but was essential between those who stood for a socially revolutionary policy and those preserving the relics of a feudal regime.[51] In this and many other ways, Jawaharlal eradicated some of the ambiguity and fuzziness in nationalist thinking about the corporate personality of the Muslims.

Others in the family also upheld the values associated with religious pluralism. B.K. Nehru's mother learnt Persian, to the extent of reading Saadi's *Gulistan* and *Bostan* from a *maulvi* and Hindi from a Pandit.[52] Jawaharlal's niece, Nayantara Sahgal, saw it all: a tradition of serene and symmetrical architecture, an elegant school of dance, Hindi and Urdu prose and poetry, and excellent cuisine. Cultural identification affected political outlook, and vice versa. Krishna Nehru Hutheesing's indoctrination as a child was going to the nearby Anglican Church of the Holy Trinity with a Miss Hoper on Sundays.

In 1874, Viceroy Northbrook laid the foundation of Muir Central College to the north of Alfred Park beyond Thornhill Road. William Emerson designed it, together with the Cathedral and other buildings in Allahabad. In 1887, Alfred Lyall, the lieutenant-governor, inaugurated the Allahabad University. Motilal's earliest impressions were received at the feet of the Muslim teachers at this college that unfolded a vigorous

---

50   Saraswat Saran Kaif, *Chakbast* (Delhi, 1986).

51   *SWJN*, vols. 2, and 8, 3, pp. 121, 133, 203.

52   B.K. Nehru, *Nice Guys Finish Second*, p. 12.

life, cheerful, optimistic, and earnest. More accurately, he learnt history, culture, and contemporary politics from Augustus Harrison and W.H. Wright. They introduced him to a society whose core philosophy he admired. Besides, he shared, noticeably, the college's enlightened regime with Mukhtar Ahmad Ansari, later his physician and Congress president in 1927. Trained in Edinburgh, Ansari counted Motilal among the influences in his public career. Both were faithful to their wide intellectual interests.

By the 1890s, the Congress had many new groups coming close to it. Of the 43 delegates to the first Provincial Conference in Allahabad in 1907, 8 were Kashmiri Pandits.[53] Until then, Motilal had no overpowering impulse to follow suit. In 1904 and 1905 he attended the Congress, but two years later he didn't sympathise with its modus operandi and turned his back on them when some delegates threatened to shoot him down at the United Provinces' Conference which he chaired at the age of 46. He however softened after Lajpat Rai's arrest and deportation to Mandalay and took part in organising the Congress's annual session in 1909. He attended the big event a year later too, after which he caught a chill and was laid up for several days.

Motilal despaired of forcefulness, derided the 'extremists' carrying bombs and bullets, abhorred fuss and rhetoric of the kind that came into play from the time of the Swadeshi Movement. Tilak's revolutionary speech at Muir College in late January 1907 upset him; so also the radical exuberance of Lajpat Rai and B.C. Pal. He spent sleepless nights worrying over their gathering strength vis-à-vis the Moderates.[54] In theory, the two approaches conflicted; in practice, there was not much to choose between them. Motilal was, nonetheless, in the Moderate camp. He didn't regard British rule as the fortuitous dispensation of divine providence, but he didn't doubt its good intentions either. He trod the political ladder warily. He courted the storm and braved it: 'the greater the opposition the merrier it is for me,' is how he reacted to a local newspaper which fulminated against him. In September 1918, he planned to launch a new daily newspaper.[55] He did so on 5 February 1919 with the *Independent* to 'think aloud for India.'

---

53   Sender, *The Kashmiri Pandits*, p. 261.

54   To Jawaharlal, 20 Dec. 1907, *SWJN*, vol. 1, p. 135.

55   Motilal to Bhagwan Das, 29 Sept. 1918, *SWMN*, vol. 1, p. 177.

Motilal enjoyed the bustle and excitement around him, including the strain and stress of the conferences in Allahabad. Nonetheless, he was cut off from the common man and those who agitated for a while. He feared the people's credulity and irrationalism to be the greatest threat to civilisation, and underlined thinking afresh the structure of society, new methods of education, and the role of religion. Jawaharlal, on the other hand, clearly indicated where his sympathies lay: 'Ours have been the politics of cowards and opium-eaters long enough and it is time we thought and acted like live men and women who place the honour and interests of their country above the frowns and smiles of every Tom, Dick and Harry who has I.C.S. attached to his name.'[56]

A fierce uproar raged over the Russian revolution and its explosive effects globally. Admiring Karl Marx and Lenin meant going against conventional standards of propriety: preaching class war, and discarding religion. The British believed that the landlords were the 'natural leaders'; those who exercised authority by virtue of their traditional status would also be the appropriate persons to induce the people to adopt the benefits of civilisation. Not surprisingly, the landlords and government servants shook their heads in alarm when they heard the socialist chatter. Just a mention of it sent tremors across the council chambers. The government struck terror in the hearts of the people, reminding them of the terrible upheavals that would recur if socialism wasn't immediately thwarted. The managers of the great empire, which sprawled over the largest portion of the earth's surface, made a bid to throttle their protagonists.

Motilal insisted that the masses wanted bread and not imported theories and dogmas.[57] He didn't refer to class struggle as he had no conception of a clash of interests among the various strata. When he reached Moscow on 8 November 1928 for the tenth anniversary of the Russian Revolution, he received a visa because a 'Brahmin capitalist' like him was the least likely to be Bolshevized.[58] On his own he neither sympathised with nor disparaged the Russian Revolution and the

---

56   Letter to the Editor, *Leader*, 21 June 1917, ibid., 1, p. 107.

57   Panikkar & Pershad (eds), *The Voice of Freedom*, p. 69.

58   Note by M. Seton, 17 Oct. 1937, IOR.L/PJ/12/313.

USSR.[59] George Lansbury, Labour MP, ridiculed him as 'a bloated bourgeoisie lawyer like Sir Douglas Hogg'.[60] Watching his butler serve him a dish of eggs, a horrified visitor wondered, 'Panditji, you aren't going to eat those eggs!' 'I most certainly am,' he replied, 'and in another few minutes, I am going to eat their mother too.'

The Conscience of a Liberal

Gradually, a few clear principles of action and a combination of instinctive choices and aversions brought Motilal close to public life. Annie Besant's internment in June 1917 accelerated the process. Jallianwala Bagh left Motilal with a different, and much darker view of *Pax Britannica*. He lashed out at the authorities for behaving with a unique, one might say inspired blend of stupidity and panic,[61] and, as a member of the Congress Enquiry into the Punjab disturbances, he saw the ill-effects of martial law.[62] On 2 March 1919, he chaired the Allahabad Satyagraha Sabha meeting. At Amritsar that year, he followed the line, 'if a king tolerates one grain of oppression...', with an indictment of General Reginald Dyer: 'What words, fellow delegates, can I use to express your feelings and mine whose kith and kin were mercilessly shot down by the hundred in cold blood?' He grieved in the words of the Persian poet:

> Our country is flooded with sorrow and woe,
> O, for our land woe!
> Arise and for coffin and cerements go!
> O, for our land woe!
> With the blood of our men killed in this pursuit
> The moon shines red;
> Hill, plain, and garden blood-red glow;
> O, for our land woe![63]

---

59   IOR.L/PJ/12/292.

60   IOR.LP/J/12/13.

61   He cited the Persian verse, 'if a king tolerates one grain of oppression, his retinue will inflict a ton of misery', and reserved his harsh comments for Dyer.

62   On Motilal's Punjab visit, *SWMN*, vol. 2, p. 22.

63   Panikkar & Pershad (eds), *The Voice of Freedom*, p. 23.

Pure idealism had no place in politics, and it was a happy dream that sooner or later ended in a rude awakening. Motilal's faith in British rule rudely shaken, he decided to throw his weight behind the major nationalist initiatives. There were a wave of whispers and giggles; eyes winked and hints were dropped. Everyone began guessing who would want to go with whom. If Motilal periodically changed his public stance, it was because of his hurt and indignation, heightened by the all white Simon Commission.[64] Tensions flared up in city after city. 'The blows, which fell on me today,' Lajpat Rai stated after the injuries he suffered, 'are the last nails driven into the coffin of British Imperialism.' Lajpat Rai died after being beaten down by *lathi*-swinging police. Jawaharlal recalled: 'The raj was thought to have bared its teeth, and its actions, … evoked memories of Amritsar in 1919.'[65] The socialist Yusuf Meherally coined the 'Simon Go Back' slogan. Forced into a drum and rolled for a long distance on the road, he described it wryly as 'a moving experience.'[66]

Road to Change

Besides such and many more acts of heroism, the events of the next few months must be considered with the scepticism necessary to understand the story of the ceaseless inter- and intra-party battles with the government at the head of it all. Only a man of Motilal's stamina and dexterity could stay the course. His forbearance and vitality of mind and senses well known,[67] the wheels of chance meshed together and produced meaningful interactions with Gandhi. At the end of the day, it proved to be a meeting of an introvert with an extrovert.[68] Setting the pattern for the future, he off-loaded his practical as well as his emotional feelings in letters to his son.

---

64   As Congress president in 1928, Motilal thundered: 'To my mind, the circumstances attending it are symptomatic of a grave organic infection and not merely of the well-known functional incapacity of the Government. It shows the presence of the toxin of Dyerism in their internal economy.'

65   S. Gopal, *Jawaharlal Nehru: A Biography*, vol. 1 (Delhi, 1986), p. 119.

66   Garga, *From Raj to Swaraj*, p. 41.

67   Rajendra Prasad, *Autobiography*, p. 328.

68   Nehru, *An Autobiography*, p. 65.

Whatever the exact mixture of feelings, part approbation, part envy, even the hand of fate couldn't have held Motilal back from joining Gandhi. At 58, UP's most distinguished lawyer renounced the gains of a few decades: 'free from all earthly trammels to devote ourselves to the only earthly cure for earthly troubles—non-cooperation.'[69] He had dreaded the thought of his son languishing in prison; now, the British gave him a personal taste of prison life. Solitude and inaction ate deeply into the spirit of this active and gregarious man, yet, his isolation from 6 December 1921 to 6 June 1922 neither broke his will nor destroyed his mind. 'I am [therefore] settling down for another six weeks or so in solitary glory with my nose touching the eastern wall of the jail & back rubbing the wall,' he wrote from Naini Tal's district jail.[70] By and by, his image was of a virtuous leader who made huge sacrifices for Bharat Mata. With him the Nehrus were well on the path of glory. According to the poet Karunesh:

> Seeing the bludgeon of the wicked, harsh, and hard hearted administration, he has gone to inform the Protector of the poor. To bring peace for those mad after freedom O Karunesh, he has gone to revive the dead. He has gone to get back his sacred strength, he has gone to bring a new era to India.[71]

Motilal changed his lifestyle by taking to swadeshi ways. He wore a khadi *topi*, but, typically, he still wanted 'the brand new commode' in Sabarmati.[72] He still wanted to have his two pegs (whisky and soda) before dinner.[73]

The wife took to khadi and wore coarse saris whose weight she could hardly bear. Her daughter Swarup Kumari (Nehru) appeared dressed in

---

69   Nayantara Sahgal (ed.), *Before Freedom: Nehru's Letters to His Sister 1909-1947* (Delhi, 2000), p. 35.

70   To Jawaharlal, 24 May 1922, *SWMN*, vol. 3, p. 220.

71   Note on the Press, United Provinces of Agra and Oudh, for the week ending 14 Feb. 1931.

72   To Gandhi, 25 Nov. 1925, *SWMN*, vol. 4, p. 177.

73   Hutheesing, *We Nehrus*, p. 49.

khadi on her wedding day: 'there were universal exclamations of delight' when Motilal took his daughter's hand and placed it in Ranjit's (Ranjit Sitaram Pandit), stretched out to receive it.[74] Everyone else wore khadi, though the sartorial change wasn't the only one in Anand Bhawan. People noted the tilt in Motilal's *khaddar* cap, as it sat on his forehead, and wondered why it looked different. To this, Motilal remarked, 'you have to be born a Kashmiri to know this, a rugged Maratha like you can hardly understand this business.'[75]

If one returned to Anand Bhawan after several years, as Krishna Hutheesing did, one could feel the warmth of a brother's love and a sister's care, and to feel a carefree girl of eighteen years once again. No longer so. The cheerful and jovial chat of yesteryears vanished. Instead heavy political discussions took place, except when Motilal injected a note of light-heartedness and laughter. Krishna was delighted. Interspersed with Urdu and Persian poems, she noticed his Urdu speech to be soft and beautiful. Sarojini Naidu, who found a haven in Anand Bhawan, charmed everyone with her own wit. She shared Motilal's modern sensibilities and his spacious and unprejudiced outlook on the past and present. Indeed, they combined to add a cosmopolitan element to the Congress' activities. Faithful to their wider political interests, they were both moved and uplifted by Gandhi's rise to power. What is more, both strove for dignity in public life. M.R.A. Baig's abiding impression of the patriarch of the Nehru household is of 'an imperious Roman Senator in a snow-white toga presiding like a patriarch at a table ...'. His impact on a future diplomat, 'remains the greatest of the great.'[76]

Similarly, Sarojini Naidu and Jawaharlal were free from the entanglements of prejudice and convention. This trait in their worldview lingered long in the thoughts of friends and companions. When they came to political affairs, they were on each other's side—Jawaharlal led and Sarojini followed. Her almost wayward impatience sometimes amused him, but her intellectual serenity in a crisis impressed him. She,

---

74   Guthrie, *Madame Ambassador*, pp. 54-5.

75   Jayakar, *The Story of My Life*, vol. 2, p. 350.

76   M.R.A. Baig, *In Different Saddles* (Delhi, 1967), p. 66.

in turn, had faith in his 'incorruptible sincerity and passion for liberty.'[77] Once, she reminded him that 'liberty is the ultimate crown of all your sacrifice', and assured him that 'you will not walk alone.'[78] On his fiftieth birthday, she expected him to transmute sorrow, suffering, sacrifice, anguish and strife 'into the very substance of ecstasy and victory—and freedom.' She described him as 'a man of destiny born to be alone in the midst of crowds, deeply loved and but little understood. ...'[79]

Other visitors to Anand Bhawan talked politics, perhaps to plan the next move against the government. On her own, Krishna Hutheesing endorsed Gandhi's creed 'not for the moment only, but for our entire lives.'[80] How well she remembered her first sari made of khadi, 'a coarse, shapeless thing that felt like sackcloth.'[81] While Motilal and Jawaharlal languished in Lucknow's district jail, she, Swarup Rani, and Kamala travelled third class to Sabarmati. She sneered at Gandhi's prayer meetings until her new life began watching the saintly figure metamorphose into an astute politician without losing his integrity.[82]

Indira Gandhi, only three in 1920, climbed up to the terrace and set alight her doll. She used to round up the family retainers and exhort them to strive for freedom. Many years later, she acknowledged her debt to Gandhi: 'He forms part of my earliest memories, and as a very small child.'[83]

Once the pride of the household, the Spode china and Venetian glass, the stock of choice wines, and the prized horses and dogs, all disappeared; the stables closed. In the good old days, two kitchen establishments, one English and the other Indian, accompanied Motilal to the hills. Now the brass cooker alone replaced the two kitchens along with a solitary servant. Hunting gave place to long walks and the rifles

---

77   Sarojini Naidu to Jawaharlal, 29 Sept. 1929, Nehru (ed.), *A Bunch of Old Letters*, p. 75.

78   Ibid.,13 Nov. 1937, p. 255.

79   Ibid., Diwali 1939, p. 407.

80   Hutheesing, *With No Regrets*, p. 13; Sahgal, *Civilizing a Savage World*, pp. 2-3.

81   Hutheesing, *We Nehrus*, p. 49.

82   Ibid., p. 57.

83   Trevor Drieberg, *Indira Gandhi: A profile in courage* (New Delhi, 1972), p. 6.

and guns to books, magazines, and newspapers.[84] Holidays to Mussoorie and Kashmir became a thing of the past. To understand how Motilal, with an epicure's enjoyment of life, could quietly give up the luxury in which he indulged and, with it, a lifelong appreciation of the British, is to understand a fraction of the mind of a nation bewitched by Gandhi.[85] Jawaharlal explained:

> His reason, his strong sense of self-respect, and his pride, all led him step by step to throw in his lot wholeheartedly with the new movement. The accumulated anger with which a series of events, culminating in the Punjab tragedy and its aftermath, filled him; the sense of utter wrong doing and injustice, the bitterness of national humiliation, had to find some way out. But he was not to be swept away by a wave of enthusiasm. It was only when his reason, backed by the trained mind of a lawyer, had weighed all the pros and cons, that he took the final decision and joined Gandhiji in his campaign.[86]

The doubts that assailed Motilal travelled with him to Calcutta in September 1920. This was the venue of a special Congress session. Political pundits expected him to vote against Non-Cooperation. He however based his judgement on another calculation—the UP Congress victory in the elections. He therefore changed his mind, resigned from the provincial council, and refused re-election. Gandhi's overpowering presence was also a reason, and a strong one, for the volte-face. Motilal desperately needed some direction for his enormous energy, and he found it in him. Next, he had in mind his son, who acknowledged Gandhi as his mentor. Lastly, Kanji Dwarkadas, Annie Besant's ardent follower, provides the following version in *India's Fight for Freedom*:

> Motilal Nehru, who had come to meet Jinnah at the Howrah station told him in my presence that Gandhiji wanted to pass a Non-Cooperation resolution and that this would mean boycott of the

---

84   Motilal to Gandhi, n.d., *SWMN*, vol. 2, p. 208.

85   Nayantara Sahgal, *Prison and Chocolate Cake* (London, 1954).

86   Nehru, *An Autobiography*, p. 65.

legislatures and he [Motilal] suggested to Jinnah that all of them together, i.e., Jinnah, Malaviya, C.R. Das, Lajpat Rai, Motilal Nehru, Mrs. Besant and others should combine to defeat the resolution. When the resolution was passed ten or twelve days later, Motilal, influenced by his son Jawaharlal, voted in favour of the resolution along with Gandhi. When the actual voting by poll was decided upon, it was felt that resolution would be defeated, but next day when the poll took place, Umar Sobani and Shankerlal managed to add over a hundred delegates from the streets and got them to vote for the resolution.

Motilal supported what he assumed to be right, unperturbed by the protestations of friends who opposed the permeation of politics by religion. He gave up a flourishing practice without the slightest thought of costs. In truth, when the lid he had put on his ideas came flying off, it fundamentally affected both his personality and point of reference in life. He obeyed the clarion call to direct the Satyagraha: No sane person, he acknowledged, would plunge the country into Non-Cooperation if he can help it, but if it cannot be helped; no price was too high to pay for freedom. On 6 December 1921, he was arrested along with his son, tried by K.N. Knox, and sent to Allahabad's district jail. 'I may land in your jail some day; will you give me champagne?' he had asked his friend Harcourt Butler.

The Nehru Report had complicated the task of reconciling the contending claims of parties and groups, and here Motilal believed that the communal issue had to be dealt with differently. Ansari, quite as sincerely, pleaded for postponing Civil Disobedience, which Gandhi announced in 1930, on the grounds that, unlike the position in 1920, Hindu-Muslim unity was still a distant dream.[87] He felt that Gandhi's ways had already proved ineffective when conditions for joint action were ideal, and reiterated his faith in mutual adjustments through dialogue.[88] Motilal, by contrast, insisted that, 'I have definitely come to hold the opinion that *no amount of formulae based upon mutual concessions which those making them have no right to make will bring us any nearer*

---

87   Ansari to Gandhi, 13 Feb. 1930, Hasan (ed.), *Muslims and the Congress*, pp. 99-100.

88   Motilal to Ansari, 17 Feb. 1930, ibid., pp. 103-4.

Hindu-Muslim unity than we are at present [emphasis added].[89] Motilal took credit for realising what it meant to throw in his lot with Gandhi. He wrote: 'Nothing but a deep conviction that the time for the greatest effort and the greatest sacrifice has come would have induced me to expose myself at my age and with my physical disabilities and with my family obligations to the tremendous risks I am incurring.'[90]

At Lahore, on the last day of the year, the sixty-year-old Motilal passed the gavel to his son. As an act of faith and sacrifice, he gifted Anand Bhawan to the Congress in April 1930 and moved across the road to a smaller house. The family's record of sacrifices for the nation became more and more impressive over time. Kamala had a brave heart and stoically underwent incarceration from 1 to 26 January 1931, making up for inexperience with her fire and energy, and within a few months became Allahabad's pride. Prabhavati, JP's wife, energetically looked after the wounded who were tended secretly at night by the Anand Bhawan doctors. The intelligence department charged that the Nehrus had instigated the riotous disorder in April 1932.[91] Finally, when Swarup Rani picketed foreign cloth shops, the police beat her up with canes; the son had nightmares thinking of his frail old mother bleeding. This incident inspired *Daily Pratap* to remark:

Each and every one of us fully remembers that day when Pandit Jawaharlal Nehru's revered old mother smilingly received the lathi on her breast and we have also seen with our own eyes that thousands of breasts were bare to receive that lathi. This is the same place where a number of men similarly received bullets, sacrificed themselves for their motherland and separated us from them for good. The same life is still found in our Prayag.[92]

As is clear by now, after the first arrest of father and son, many more family members went to gaol. For this, Sarojini Naidu held them in

---

89   Ibid., pp. 178-80.
90   Ibid.
91   FR (UP), Apr. 1932, Home Pol., F.no. 18/7, 1932.
92   21 Dec. 1935, UPNNR.

high esteem. 'Across the landscape of this moving family history,' she wrote, 'fall the brighter lights and the half lights, the dimmer and the deeper shadows inseparable from human destiny.'[93] Motilal was 'Papaji'; Kamala Nehru, 'Mammaji'; and Krishna Nehru, 'Betti'. When Vijaya married Ranjit Sitaram Pandit, the *Bulbul-e-Hind* had this to say to her: 'You are bringing as your share in that comradeship some wonderful personal gifts, enhanced by all the richness and nobility of tradition that belong to your family, as the integral part of the existing traditions, ideals and achievements which are an example and an inspiration to the nation.'[94]

Many people around Indira Nehru aided her to form ideas about the world. Reading *Joan of Arc* by night, she lectured the household servants by day and, in between, founded *Vanar Sena* (Monkey Army) to carry messages in and out of detention. Once, Jawaharlal asserted, 'well now that you have read it [the *Purna Swaraj* resolution], you too are committed to it.'[95] She nodded in approval. She felt part of the excitement, joined Gandhi's fast against the Poona Pact, and shared prison life (she was arrested on 11 September 1942) with her husband, Feroze Gandhi,[96] aunt Vijaya Lakshmi Pandit, and cousin Chandralekha Pandit, seven years younger. Freedom was, by contrast, 'like coming out of a dark passage', and she felt, 'dazzled with the rush of life, the many hues and textures, the scale of sounds and the range of ideas.'[97] Edward Thompson flattered Jawaharlal with the remark, 'you Nehrus have been very lucky in many ways, and lucky most of all in your charming and splendid women.'[98]

The death of an infant boy had led Motilal to write on 4 December 1905:

---

93 Sarojini Naidu to Jawaharlal, Diwali 1939, Jawaharlal (ed.), *A Bunch of Old Letters*, p. 407.

94 Ibid., p. 104.

95 Inder Malhotra, *Indira Gandhi: A Personal and Political Biography*, p. 40.

96 They were married on 26 Mar. 1942.

97 Drieberg, *Indira Gandhi*, p. 26. She was released from jail unconditionally on 13 May 1943.

98 To Jawaharlal, 24 Nov. 1936, Nehru (ed.), *A Bunch of Old Letters*, p. 205.

Unmixed and uninterrupted happiness is not given to the spirit which inhabits mortal clay and the true lesson of life lies in making proper use of one's misfortunes. Let us take them as warnings to help to chasten our lower nature and attune the higher self to the 'still small voice within' which is seldom heeded except on occasions like this.

Here was a man of fearless, pungent, and clear-cut speech. Without being timid or cautious, he had faith in the ultimate triumph of good over evil.[99] He did not deprive himself of the little spark of reason that had fallen to his lot. 'For that little spark I shall,' he told his son, 'if need be, fight you and him and the rest of the world to the death'.[100] He didn't need to. The founder patriarch of the Nehru-Gandhi family didn't live long enough. The strain of work took its toll. Ansari, the family doctor, advised rest; instead, he engaged with the CWC meetings, discussing the proposals of the British Prime Minister, Ramsay MacDonald. He loved life and had sailed through it with ease. But his numerous ailments ultimately caught up with him. Suddenly, one day, Motilal had to be taken to Lucknow.[101] Even with a swollen face, he joked, 'Look at my face. I am going to take part in a beauty competition'. He died on 6 February 1931. The stars were out and shining brightly when the Nehrus returned, lonely and desolate, from his last journey to the Ganga. Free from the entanglements of prejudice and convention, his memory lingered long in the thoughts of his family, friends and companions. It was often unobtrusive, but it was always to relied upon.

Even if biographies end with the subject's death, Motilal's story had no such natural termination. Had he lived until the stroke of midnight on 15 August 1947, he would have viewed a spectacular occasion: his son unfurling the tri coloured flag. Another Kashmiri Pandit saw it all: 'I must be prepared for the end soon. I must bless my stars that I have

99   Motilal to Horace Alexander, 5 Oct. 1930; Kumar and Sharma (eds), *SWMN*, vol. 7, p. 262.

100   Motilal to Gandhi, 2 Sept. 1924, *SWMN*, vol. 4, p. 73.

101   Gandhi accompanied him on 4 February 1931, the day the police raided the office of *Young India* and confiscated the cyclostyling machine.

seen the freedom of India with you at the helm.' 'Of yourself I have a composite picture in my mind—of Mazinni and Cavour,' wrote Sapru. He blessed the first prime minister with the words: '*Tum salamat raho hazaar baras/Har baras ke hon din pachaas hazaar.*'[102]

Just then, a handful of Gandhians at Sevagram discussed the country's future, their eyes riveted on Jawaharlal, 'so handsome, a confluence of truthfulness and realism'. They found many qualities in him. They concluded that he 'is not one thing on the outside and another inside. Beautiful as the form is, the spirit is pleasing in equal measure.'[103]

'*May you long remain the Jawahar, the Jewel of India*' [Gandhi]

Gandhi had enemies or ruffled the feelings of the susceptible, but he made it his business to relate, as closely as he could, his work to guide his followers. I have already discussed a strange combination—a meeting of an introvert with an extrovert—and their close friendship. In this section, I will examine how Gandhi, the saint, the stoic, the man of religion, related to a much younger person who wasn't given to enjoying the pleasures of life like his father but whose worldview was markedly different from his.

Jawaharlal held clear and definite views about many matters. As an outspoken opponent of religious rituals and superstitions, he didn't harp on trifles and eschewed religious controversies. He supported the Khilafat cause at the Bundelkhand Conference in 1922, but felt uncomfortable with the admixture of religion and politics. On the question of end and means, to which Gandhi attached such great importance, he placed the final emphasis on the end and goal in view. On non-violence, he feared that it had become an inflexible dogma as well as a sheet-anchor for vested interests, to maintain the status quo. He neither wanted to be a cloak for cowardice and inaction nor the defender of the status quo.

Such doubts remained with Jawaharlal, but after years of close association he found Gandhi to be 'the quintessence of the conscious and

---

102   Quoted in Rafiq Zakaria (ed.), *A Study of Nehru*, p. 5; Bose, *Tej Bahadur Sapru*, p. 189; Sapru to Jawaharlal, 19 Sept. 1947, Hooja (ed.), *Crusader for Self-Rule*, p. 497.

103   Gandhi (ed.), *Gandhi is Gone.*, p. 98.

subconscious will of those millions, and their idealised personification'. He marvelled at his good fortune to serve him, 'a powerful current of fresh air that made us stretch ourselves and take deep breaths; like a beam of light that pierced the darkness and removed the scales from our eyes'.[104] After a brief spell of doubting, he came to terms with Non-Cooperation as well; 'it was clear that this little man of poor physique had something of steel in him; something rock-like which did not yield to physical powers'.[105] Every word from him had an intense, piercing, and convincing quality.

The years 1920-21 became synonymous with the Golden Age when prices would fall, the peasant would own land, taxes would cease, and the goal of freedom would alleviate the everyday sufferings of the peasantry. The heady wine of Non-Cooperation fired their heads. That Jawaharlal accepted the non-violent creed is manifest from the following message he sent to Allahabad's Congress workers on 8 December 1921:

> Friends,—I go to jail with the greatest pleasure, and with the fullest conviction that therein lies the achievement of our goal. Forget not that there is a complete hartal on the 12th instant, and that it is the duty of every man to enrol himself as a volunteer. The most important thing is to preserve complete peace and an atmosphere of non-violence. In your hands is the honour of Allahabad, and I hope it is quite safe therein. I trust you will always be in the firing line in the battle of Swaraj and make the name of our city immortal.[106]

As the turbulent years passed, Jawaharlal questioned the overbearing presence of the mullahs, the suspension of Civil Disobedience, and the wilting away of Non-Cooperation. He wondered why Gandhi allowed the hopes of millions to crash to the ground, and why the 'suspects' of Non-Cooperation basked in the sunshine of official favours. He slammed all those who were hand-in-glove with the government to work the Act

---

104   Nehru, *The Discovery of India*, p. 358.

105   Nehru, *An Autobiography*, p. 129.

106   Ibid., pp. 84-5.

of 1919 and the Knights or C.I.Es and Rai Bahadurs for kowtowing before and worshipping at the feet of their masters from across the seas. As he sat idly watching the sun set on the distant horizon, he sensed the common ground between him and Bapu narrowing.

Nonetheless, he tried to ensure that the Congress factions didn't work against the established authority or engage in cloak-and-dagger work of outright subversion.[107] In a year of strife, dispute, and mutual recrimination, he maintained his hold over the party as its general secretary until 1925, and then again in 1927, the year he returned to India and reached Madras in time for the Congress session in December. According to a British intelligence officer in 1928:

> Jawaharlal Nehru is an energetic and capable leader, whose influence among subversive elements in this country has rapidly increased. His association with professional agitation in Europe, and the persistent propaganda conducted by him on behalf of the League against Imperialism, render him potentially dangerous. Though still a young man, he has already an unenviable record in Indian revolutionary affairs, and there is at present no reason to believe that his political conduct will be any the less disreputable.[108]

In December 1927, tempers frayed between those who made dominion status the pivot of the settlement and those who screamed for complete Independence. Gandhi suspected Bose, whom he regarded as his bête noire, to be conspiring against him, the CWC, and Jawaharlal and encouraging 'mischief makers' and 'hooligans'.[109] The fact is that Jawaharlal reinforced the antagonisms created by the Western political

---

107   Between Jawaharlal's first and second imprisonment, frequent controversies erupted. With the 'No-Changers' turning down the vigorous plea for council entry, the Swaraj party, formed on 1 Jan. 1923, finally turned the tide in its favour in Sept. 1923, when the Congress allowed them to breach the bureaucratic citadel from inside and outside the legislative councils. The period of Jawaharlal's imprisonment was from 6 Dec. 1921 to 3 Mar. 1922; the second lasted from 11 May 1922 to 31 Jan. 1923.

108   Note by O. Cleary, L/P &J/12/292, IOR, Bodleian Library.

109   Bapu to Jawaharlal, 4 Jan. 1928, Nehru (ed.), *A Bunch of Old Letters*, p. 59.

and cultural domination; he therefore insisted on achieving *purna swaraj* as an instrument to achieve social and economic justice for 50 lakhs of beggars dependent upon the rich and well-to-do, and five crores of agriculturists sitting idle for a portion of the year, sufficient to break the back of any country.[110]

Although a serious matter, not to be taken lightly,[111] Gandhi went along with the growing cry for complete Independence. He clarified to Jawaharlal: 'My point is not that you have not thought out any of your resolutions, much less the Independence one; but my point is that neither you nor anyone else had thought out the whole situation and considered the bearing and propriety of the resolutions.'[112]

Pushed hither and thither, Gandhi's compromise enabled the Congress to accept dominion status if the government were to extend a definite offer within a year. Without this, he left open the option of non-violent Civil Disobedience. Jawaharlal threatened to resign, but Gandhi dissuaded him from doing so. He also proceeded to establish, much to Jawaharlal's relief, the compatibility of *purna swaraj* with greater freedom.[113] From that moment, Jawaharlal had the party at his feet. His courage, earnestness, and the transparent sincerity of his life earned him this unique position. Even though some disapproved of his socialist creed, he bound the party together through the sympathetic magnetism of his nature.

As for Gandhi's 'fads and peculiarities',[114] Jawaharlal felt the difference in their respective ideals. Should anyone's prime goal be the eradication of untouchability? Should one equate spinning with virtue and prayer? In a rather long and lucid exposition, Jawaharlal disagreed with the reasoning that without khadi the people wouldn't do anything more difficult or daring. An intellectually and culturally backward village didn't necessarily embody Truth and non-violence. Narrow-minded

110   *SWJN*, vol. 3, p. 245.

111   Ibid., 17 Jan. 1928, ibid., p. 61.

112   Gandhi to Jawaharlal, 11 Jan. 1928, Iyengar and Zackariah (eds), *Together They Fought*, p. 53.

113   To Jawaharlal, 8 Nov. 1929, *CWMG* (Oct. 1929-Feb. 1930), p. 116, and 4 Nov. 1929, Nehru (ed.), *A Bunch of Old Letters*, p. 76.

114   *The Story of My Experiments with Truth* which had begun being serialised in *Young India* from the first week of December 1925.

people were much more likely to be untruthful and violent;[115] Gandhi was too good a human being to uncover their motives. In the course of yet another storm, Jawaharlal dispelled the notion that he wanted to unfurl the banner of revolt over the complete Independence resolution. 'No one has moved me and inspired me more than you [Bapu],' he proclaimed, 'even in the wider sphere am I not your child in politics, though perhaps a truant and errant child?'[116] Pyarelal referred to the 'unimpaired' mutual confidence that existed between Gandhi and his colleagues.[117]

Fair enough, but Gandhi's truce/pact with Irwin blew a fuse again. Jawaharlal wanted him to continue Civil Disobedience and not attend the Round Table Conference in the autumn of 1931. Fenner Brockway formed the following impression after meeting him:

> Jawaharlal wishes to create a movement which will have a completely new outlook, politically and socially, which will reject the religious and economic ideas which have kept India bound in superstitions and poverty, as well as the political ideas which have kept her in national bondage. He is looking for a new mind in the masses, which will discard the customs and habits associated with the castes and communities of India, and for a new movement amongst the peasants and industrial workers, which will rise up against the exploiting land system as well as the power of capitalism.[118]

Gandhi, of course, tried convincing him that nothing vital had been lost and there had been no surrender of principle. He however failed to bridge the gap between his and Jawaharlal's future vision.[119]

More generally, Jawaharlal mulled over the destructive jealousies, hatreds, and ambitions that had hitherto been concealed and unexpressed, and the mounting caste and inter-community fissures. He spoke of ideals

---

115   To Gandhi, 9 Oct. 1945, Nehru (ed.), *A Bunch of Old Letters*, p. 512.

116   Jawaharlal to Gandhi, 23 Jan. 1928, ibid., p. 379; *SWJN*, vol. 3, pp. 18-19.

117   Pyarelal, *Mahatma Gandhi*, vol. 1, p. xvi.

118   A. Fenner Brockway, *The Indian Crisis* (London, 1930), p. 114.

119   Gopal, *Jawaharlal Nehru: A Biography*, vol. 1, p. 130.

being abandoned, goals being compromised, and power being wielded by opportunists. His tale of woes extended to the CWC's backward-looking policies and ill-advised strategies. He spewed venom at the Congress, which 'from top to bottom is a caucus and opportunism triumphs'.[120]

In this difficult moral situation, Gandhi showed good judgement and admirable generosity. He advised Jawaharlal not to be unduly harsh: 'I should be myself in a wilderness without you in the Congress'.[121] Again, 'you have not lost a comrade in me. I am the same as you knew me in 1917 and after.'[122] His comments were frank but discriminating and objective. No note of personal bitterness crept into what he said. With a dead father and an ailing wife in Badenweiler, Jawaharlal needed Gandhi's comforting words. 'My mind is tired and worried,' he wrote to Gandhi on 10 September 1935. Warm, sensitive and not at all cold-blooded, as he pretended to be in public, he turned invariably to Gandhi in his hour of distress. He summed up his feelings in the following words:

For myself I delight in warfare. It makes me feel that I am alive. Events of the last four months in India have gladdened my heart and have made me prouder of Indian men, women and even children than I have ever been, but I realize that most people are not warlike and like peace and so I try hard to suppress myself and take a peaceful view. May I congratulate you on the new India you have created by your magic touch! What the future will bring I know not, but the past has made life worth living and our prosaic existence has developed something of epic greatness in it. Sitting here in Naini Jail I have pondered on the wonderful efficacy of non-violence as a weapon and have become a greater convert to it than ever before. I hope you are not dissatisfied with the response of the country to the non-violence creed. Despite occasional lapses, the country has stuck to it wonderfully, certainly far more grimly than I had expected. I am afraid I am still somewhat of a protestant regarding your eleven points. Not that I disagree with any

---

120   To Gandhi, 13 Aug. 1934, Iyengar and Zackariah (eds), *Together They Fought*, p. 225.

121   To Jawaharlal, 21 Jan. 1934, ibid. p. 219.

122   Ibid., 17 Aug. 1934, ibid., p. 229.

one of them. Indeed they are important. Yet I do not think that they take the place of independence.

In early September 1935, Gandhi asked Jawaharlal to take charge of the Congress ship the following year. Then, again, a minor crisis developed over the resignation of seven CWC members. Gandhi managed to calm things down. After a degree of admonition, he more or less repeated what he had said just a while ago about him being never 'so near [to] each other in hearts as we perhaps are today'.[123] He was happy that his protégé had come to believe in khadi's indispensability in the economy.

Clash of Ideals

How to build an independent, proud, and free nation? What are to be the foundations of the economy? How to organise production relations? How to define the relations between small-scale cottage industry (the preferred Gandhian way), and big industry? Gandhi and Jawaharlal were principally concerned to determine the correlation, if any, between economic conditions and social institutions. With numerous social forces and complex interrelations, Gandhi discovered the hazards of establishing that correlation.

As a starting point, Jawaharlal took material culture as the control of man over nature as reflected in the arts of life. This corresponds to the Marxian economic factor. His nationalism, liberalism, and socialism were all products of Europe, and he believed that if industrial modernity had to be a panacea of ills, India must free itself from the evils of capitalism, be adequately socialised, privilege science over spirituality as an essential and most revolutionary factor in modern life, and, in addition, privilege education over everything else. Accordingly, party and government had to discard the spiritual mumbo-jumbo to engage with the infinite variety of contemporary life.

With his penchant for comparisons between countries, Jawaharlal had full faith in the redemptive potential of modern industries and technological advances. Growing up with a combination of Fabian and socialist ideas, his thinking and methods were akin to what is

---

123   Ibid., 12 May 1936, p. 275.

called Western. For one, his rationale had a definite social content and implied, even if loosely, the kind of society that would synchronise with scientific and industrial advance. By 'beliefs' he understood the totality of judgments that were either beyond the competence of science or not scientifically proven. Rituals and ceremonials led many minds and caused many lives to be cluttered with the urges and irrationalities of the previous era. Personally, therefore, Jawaharlal put spiritualism out of mind; its séances and its so-called manifestations, and the legitimate and illegitimate offspring of religion.[124] Besides being one of the principal impediments to freedom, religion 'has become the old man of the sea for us and it has not only broken our backs'.[125] As he grew older he found religion and sentimentality to be 'unreliable guides'.

Of great importance here is, first, Jawaharlal's great dream to secularise the intelligentsia,[126] and second to bring about harmony drawn from the strength of the 'silent forces' working ceaselessly for a synthesis, drawing on the best, and breaking with the worst. In more general terms, he believed in diversity, and opposed the regimentation of the infinite variety after a single pattern.[127] He invoked heterodox ideas in the seventh and the fifth centuries against the caste-ridden and the highly hierarchical social structure with its in-built inequalities, and admired Gautam Buddha for founding a pan-Asian religion, repudiating the Vedas and the pre-eminence of Brahman priests, and creating the necessary condition of the mind in which the love of others ceased to conflict with

124 To Jawaharlal, 12 Jan. 1927, Nehru (ed.), *A Bunch of Old Letters*, p. 69; Jawaharlal to Syed Mahmud, 15 July 1926, Datta and Cleghorn (eds), *A Nationalist Muslim and Indian Politics*, p. 65.

125 An example of Motilal's plain speaking is the following excerpt from his presidential address at the Calcutta Congress in 1928: 'Whatever the higher conception of religion may be, it has, in our day-to-day life, come to signify bigotry and fanaticism, intolerance and narrow-mindedness, selfishness and the negation of many of the qualities which go to build a healthy society. Its chief inspiration is hatred of him who doesn't profess it, and in its holy name more crimes have been committed than for any professedly mundane object'.

126 Jawaharlal to Syed Mahmud, 15 July 1926, Datta and Cleghorn (eds), *A Nationalist Muslim and Indian Politics*, p. 61.

127 Nehru, *An Autobiography*, p. 203; *The Unity of India*, p. 15; *Glimpses of World History*, p. 253.

one's good.[128] He commended the four Noble Truths: (a) that all life is inevitably sorrowful; (b) that sorrow is due to craving; (c) that it can only be stopped by the stopping of craving; and (d) that this can only be done by a course of carefully disciplined moral conduct, culminating in the life of concentration and mediation. Buddhism appears to have influenced Jawaharlal more than any other religion. As for Jainism, Jawaharlal delineated the parameters of Jain life, which have been from early times textually defined as centring around five 'Small Vows' and parallel to the ascetic's five 'Great Vows'. He gave reasons for the survival of Jainism as a separate religion without its one-time pre-eminence whereas Buddhism struggled for existence long before the arrival of the Turks.

Mapping the metaphysical and philosophic approach to life, Jawaharlal regarded the Buddhist period to be a veritable golden age marked by a unique internationalism, tolerance, compassion, and a vigorous openness to outside influences. He interrogated the agency of the Kushan Empire, which made possible the triangular commercial and cultural contacts between India, China, and Central India, and facilitated the movement of Buddhism beyond the Pamirs and the Himalaya. In another context, he saw devotees dip into the many sacred rivers flowing from the snow white Himalayas, the 'roof of the world' covering 250,000 sq. m., and sing songs in their melodious language. Kamala Nehru's ashes were immersed in the depths of the same swift-flowing Ganga on 28 February 1936. As he stood there in homespun khadi watching the pilgrims, he wondered: 'How many of those who follow us will take that last journey in the embrace of her water! How amazingly powerful was that faith which had for thousands of years brought them to bathe in the holy river?' 'India grows upon me more and more and I am ever discovering something new in her,' he told Gandhi with whom he shared his love for Kamala.[129]

Jawaharlal was intellectually a socialist. The socialist argument consisted primarily of a demonstration that the economic system was

---

128   Escott Reid, *Radical Mandarin: The Memoirs of Escott Reid* (London, 1989), p. 290.

129   To Gandhi, 24 July 1941, Iyengar and Zackariah (eds), *Together They Fought*, p. 420.

beset by contradictions and disequilibria between production and consumption. Lenin's realism and resilience impressed him.[130] After visiting Russia in November 1927, he returned convinced that socialism would release innumerable individuals from economic and cultural bondage and, all things considered, constitute an adequate substitute for capitalism.[131] With capitalism negating justice, freedom, and democracy, the submergence of vested interests through a socialistic plan alone would improve the lot of the dumb millions. This didn't mean reducing everyone to poverty; it implied making the people at large better off.

Jawaharlal interrogated the bearing of *Hind Swaraj* on rural life only to find it unreal. Fearing the social and economic upheavals in rural society, he negotiated the 'very different ideals'.[132] He saw nothing but ugliness in poverty, which could be conquered if its victims cast off ignorance and passive resignation. 'You have stated somewhere,' he reminded Gandhi, 'that India has nothing to learn from the West and that she has reached a pinnacle of wisdom in the past. I entirely disagree with this viewpoint and I neither think that the so-called *Ramarajya* was very good in the past, nor do I want it back.'[133]

Gandhi, of course, found some of these theories to be deficient because they neither demarcated the social functions of religion nor established correlations between the beliefs and the other components of social life. Among the modern European thinkers, he was closest to D.E. Durkheim in arguing that religion served to create, expand, and enhance solidarity among its adherents, and that religious beliefs rest upon a specific experience whose demonstrative value is, in a sense, not a jot inferior to that of scientific experiments, though different from them. Truth and untruth exist; good and evil are found together. The right perception of things and the wrong also coexist, but evil is both transitory and unnecessary.

Increasingly, Gandhi attributed inequalities to industrialisation and less and less to the preponderance of the high castes and the inequities

---

130   Gopal, *Jawaharlal Nehru: A Biography*, vol. 1, pp. 108-9.

131   Presidential Address at the All-Bengal Students' Conference, 22 Sept. 1928, *SWJN*, vol. 3, p. 193.

132   To Gandhi, 9 Oct. 1945, Nehru (ed.), *A Bunch of Old Letters*, p. 513.

133   To Gandhi, 11 Jan. 1928, ibid., p. 375.

of the system they controlled.[134] More than any other contemporary politician, he presumed industrialisation to be evil; therefore it made no sense to copy the Western model or the principles and codes and rights defining the Enlightenment.[135] If, however, its use entailed progress and brought happiness, he was all for it. If not, he wanted the wild disorder of industrialism to be replaced by a clear architecture, the design of which had to be borrowed from rural life or from *Ramarajya*, meaning renunciation all along the line and self-discipline.

Gandhi went too far in the opposite direction and celebrated rural life without taking into account the reality of bonded labour, poverty, rural indebtedness, illiteracy, social backwardness, and the exploitation and degradation of the poor. Interested in the general picture, specifics didn't figure in his expositions. Alternatively, perhaps his disciples carried things to the extreme by saying that he resisted all kinds of industries which use machineries. However, M. Visvesvaraya had no reason to complain that Gandhi opposed the growth of large-scale industries.

Andrews tells us how, one evening, Gandhi asked him to read a poem that began with the words, 'Here is Thy footstool and there rest Thy feet, where live the poorest, and lowliest, and lost.' He goes on: 'It seemed to me that in the company of Mahatma Gandhi and his chosen band of followers the presence of God was almost visibly near at hand in the cool of the day there in that ashram where the poor were so loved and revered.'[136]

True, Gandhi associated with the *daridranarayana* (God in the form of the poor), the voiceless poor, and engaged with their claims for a share in the fruits of society: 'Ever since I started the khadi movement, I have been saying that I was born to serve Daridranarayana; I live for it and wish to die for it. I shall regard myself as having the satisfaction that, if I have done nothing else, I have on this account collected money for the poor.' Curiously, his solution lay in *dharma*: a nation whose life embodies

---

134   'Today,' he said, 'machinery merely helps a few to ride on the backs of millions. The impetus behind it all is not the philanthropy to save labour, but greed. It is against this constitution of things that I am fighting with all my might.'

135   Akeel Bilgrami, 'Value, Enchantment, and the Mentality of Democracy: Some Distant Perspectives from Gandhi', *EPW*, 10 Dec. 2009, p. 48.

136   Nicol Macnicol, *C.F. Andrews: Friend of India* (London, 1944), pp. 44-5.

dharma secures its good fortune and fame, and its actions are brought to fruition. In such cases, his concepts were based on nothing but absolute Truth, and religion, the most sublime of all dispositions. He linked Truth, his prayerful quest from childhood, with non-violence, equity, justice, and the realisation of his goal of a 'spiritual nation'. He searched for it ceaselessly hoping to attain spiritual deliverance in this very world.

Gandhi wanted associates to recall the face of the poorest and weakest man they had seen, and asked them if the step they contemplated would be of any use to him. He called attention to: 'We may not be deceived by the wealth to be seen in the cities of India. It doesn't come from England or America. It comes from the blood of the poorest.' Therefore, 'the test of orderliness in a country is not the number of millionaires it owns, but the absence of starvation among the masses. The hungry millions ask for one poem—invigorating food. They cannot be given it. They must earn it. And they can earn only by the sweat of their brow....' The tendency to separate economics from ethics or vice versa was wrong; economics that inculcates Mammon worship and enables the strong to amass wealth at the expense of the weak spells death. True economics implies social justice, and promotes the good of all equally, including the weakest.

Gandhi pictured a village inhabited by free men and women holding their own, who would contribute their quota of manual labour. Life would not be a pyramid with the apex sustained by the bottom. Instead, in this structure of innumerable villages would be ever-widening, never-ascending circles, until finally the whole becomes one oceanic circle whose life would be shared by all those who constitute its integral units. Economic equality would prevail. It did not mean possessing an equal amount of worldly goods, but everyone having a proper house to live in, a sufficient and balanced diet, and khadi to wear. It meant eradicating the curse of inequality through cooperative farming. Under this system, the owners would hold, till, and cultivate the land collectively, and also hold capital, tools, animals, etc. in common.

All creation is trusteeship by human beings. Trustee meant using the goods of the earth in a way pleasing to Allah. It implied non-possession (*aparigraha*) and equability (*samabhava*), and presupposed a change of heart, a change of orientation, and that those desiring salvation acting like trustees.[137] These words, along with *sarvodaya* (universal upliftment), connote the welfare of all, in contrast to Jeremy Bentham's ideal of the greatest good of the greatest number. Together with the ideal village life based on ancient models, all life had to be used to further God's will and to build His kingdom on earth. This model, having existed in ancient India, implied a peaceable social order, a classless society with opportunities for all, and achievable through democratic planning. Like Robert Owen, a Utopian socialist, Gandhi envisioned villages producing wealth within an environment manifestly superior to the turmoil of industrial life.

In Rajkot, Gandhi gave to the Girasia Mandal the same advice he had given to the princes, viz., to make themselves true servants of the people. They should hold their wealth as a trust to be used wisely in the interests of the people. They were enabled to a reasonable enrolment for themselves but only in return for service rendered. His capacity to protect them rested therefore on their willingness to adopt and live up to the ideal of trusteeship that he had placed before them.

Gandhi's ideas were based on the perfectibility of the human spirit through the cooperation of castes, classes, and religions. He wanted to build on the existing foundations and not lose sight of the grave injustice inflicted on the deprived. He recognised them as the 'conscious creators of their own history', who would accept his version of Truth to effect changes in their thinking and actions.[138] However, while making a strong case for an improved rural life, he made short work of socialism as an impediment to progress and communism as a doctrine leading to civil strife.[139]He contested the thesis that the classes and the masses were at each other's throats. Fellow-Indians were peace-loving and averse to anarchy.[140] Bolshevism can't be their choice even with the talk of revolution renting the air. 'I am not guilty,' he stated, 'of

---

137   Gandhi, *My Experiments with Truth*, p. 265.

138   'When that fitness and rarity of spirit which I long for have become perfectly natural to me; when I have become incapable of any evil; when nothing harsh or haughty occupies, be it momentarily, my thought-world; then, and not till then, my non-violence will move all the hearts of all the world.'

139   Sapru to Jayakar, 29 Sept. 1936, Jayakar papers.

140   Minoo Masani, *Bliss was it in that Dawn: A political memoir upto Independence* (Bombay, 1977), pp. 61-2.

supporting a system which involves a continuous and devastating class war or expressing approval of a system based essentially on himsa.'[141]

There was nothing new in this. In March 1919, Gandhi had pointed out that 'self-indulgence is the Bolshevik creed, self-restraint is the Satyagraha creed.'[142] Therefore, his solutions had to be *Indian* and based on the everyday life of the people. For example, every yard of foreign cloth brought into India was one piece of bread snatched out of the mouths of the starving poor. Gandhi, who regarded the spinning wheel as the answer, enjoined that no one who refused to spin should be a party member. He defended his controversial suggestion, 'I see no way except that of universalizing spinning. If you could visualize, as I can, the supreme need of the hour, which is to give India's millions a chance to earn their bread with joy and gladness, you would not object to the Spinning Franchise.'[143]

In a country where major 'schools' wrestled with each other, to influence the public discourses, Gandhi's pursuit of his goals was in alliance with the capitalists, big business, and the captains of industry to pursue some of his goals. Besides his financial dependence on them, for which Birla and Jamnalal Bajaj were two of his benefactors, Gandhi shared their passion for vegetarianism and cow protection. It was a combination of both dependence for resources and personal friendships. Sometimes personal friendships took precedence over other matters, though Jawaharlal couldn't understand why Bapu pushed only those whose merit was that they were moneyed or had succeeded in attaining a certain position in the cut-throat world.[144]

In his utopia, Gandhi didn't want power to be concentrated in the hands of the state or in those of the capitalist. At the same time, the have-nots were given the assurance that force wouldn't be used against them; instead, an atmosphere of mutual respect and trust

---

141   Gandhi to Jawaharlal, 12 May 1936, Iyengar and Zackariah (eds), *Together They Fought*, p. 275.

142   Gandhi, *Speeches and Writings*, p. 454.

143   Andrews, *Mahatma Gandhi's Ideas*, p. 240.

144   Jawaharlal to Gandhi, 25 May 1936, Iyengar and Zackariah (eds), *Together They Fought*, p. 299.

would be created.[145] He expected a voluntary abnegation of wealth from the rich, expected capitalists and the propertied classes to spend their wealth on those who helped them to accumulate their millions, and, like Talcott Parsons who underestimated the power of the business community vis-à-vis government, he viewed businessmen as custodians of economic institutions participating in attaining the central goals of society. Regardless of the costs they extracted from the community,[146] he expected them to enlist, at the very least, the cooperation of the subordinated strata. Real swaraj would be achievable not by the acquisition of authority by a few, but by everyone's capacity to resist the abuse of authority. Gandhi therefore disapproved of peasants taking to arms: 'one who seeks to destroy others invites one's own doom'. He wasn't for usurping zamindari and *taluqdari* tracts but for just regulating the relation between landlords and tenants. In fact, he avoided speaking against the semi-feudal zamindari system,[147] because he didn't want to destroy the hen that laid the golden egg. His argument was that if the landowners acted wisely, neither party was eventually likely to lose. On the other hand, their liquidation would ultimately ruin the cultivators too. He reposed faith in landowners, because they were just as good human beings, and secondly because he believed in the potency of genuine non-violence.[148] As 'patrons', he expected them to look after the peasants. He wanted the Congress to engage with them in a peace-making spirit.[149] Once earlier he had advised the UP *kisans* to report to Motilal, a person who would brook no disruption in the status quo. This couldn't have brought comfort to the *kisans*, who had raised their voices of protest during the very first moment of the new awakening.

---

145   'Jayaprakash's Picture', *Harijan*, 20 Apr. 1930, *CWMG*, vol. 71, p. 425. (1 Dec. 1939-15 April 1940)

146   Maurice Stein and Arthur Vidich (eds), *Sociology on Trial* (Englewood Cliffs, N.J., 1965), pp. 111-12.

147   Gandhi to Jawaharlal, 11 Jan. 1928, Nehru (ed.), *A Bunch of Old Letters*, p. 375; *CWMG* (Sept. 1927-Jan. 1928) app. X, vol. 36.

148   *Harijan*, 20 Apr. 1930, *CWMG* (1 Dec. 1939-15 April 1940), p. 425.

149   Rekha Trivedi (ed.), *Gandhi Speaks on Non-Cooperation in UP* (Lucknow, 1998), p. 178.

No lessons in Marxism were necessary to appreciate the dynamics of the ceaseless conflicts between the zamindars/*taluqdars* and the landless or marginal farmers. Yet, a moralistic tone, fused with a romantic construction of class relations, was Gandhi's answer to the fundamental malaise in rural society. Prem Chand, the Hindi writer, delineated the contours and contradictions of rural life most vividly. Even so, Gandhi expected the rajas, zamindars and *taluqdars* to act 'wisely'.

It was difficult to swallow the trust and confidence Gandhi reposed in the exploiting classes; if they could be as benevolent, the history of rural life would have been differently written. As with the taluqdars and zamindars, Gandhi didn't seek to coerce the landowners and princes but wanted to convert them. As with the idealisation of the *varna* system, his social model underlined the constant search for reconciliation.[150] Jawaharlal couldn't understand, however, why he virtually backed the princely states, which continued with their brazen autocracy.[151] Gandhi defended himself.[152] As always, Jawaharlal followed it up by his own spirited defence of the Congress at the All-India States' People's Conference in February 1939.

Jawaharlal turned fifty on 14 November 1939. He lived the most vivid part of his existence quite apart from the family, while the part of his life spent with friends was in jail. 'Some of us who have erred and sinned enough', he wrote to Mahadev Desai condoling him on his father's death, 'have grown hard in the ways of the world'. Bapu, then in Wardha, blessed him for his vigour, frankness, and robust humanity. We might note parenthetically at this point that he had seen a 'rebel'.

However, his affection for Gandhi became so much deeper over time that he didn't hesitate assuaging his feelings, even if it meant going along with impetuous radical instincts or naming him as his heir. Gandhi's

150   Jaffrelot, *India's Silent Revolution*, p. 31.

151   17 Oct. 1939, Gopal (ed.), *SWJN*, vol. 10, p. 503.

152   'Of course here comes in the difference of our emphasis on the method or the means which to me are just as important as the goal and in a sense more important in that we have some control over them whereas we have none over the goal if we lose control over the means.' Gandhi to Jawaharlal, 17 Aug. 1934, Nehru (ed.), *A Bunch of Old Letters*, p.124.

efforts to clear the air of suspicion and misunderstanding reflects his confidence in Jawaharlal.[153]

To sum up thus far, the polemics were clearly of two kinds: those dealing with personalities and those concerning concepts and policies. The predominance of these two sets of themes depended upon which of the many Congress factions initiated the debate. As for the litany of complaints from some Congress stalwarts who chafed under Jawaharlal's rebukes and magisterial manner, and above all his arrogation of what appeared to them his assumption of infallibility and condescension,[154] Gandhi underlined the importance of Congress unity, euphemistically described as 'national unity'.

Let us fast forward to Delhi's wintry month of January, some months after Independence. Violence stalked the land, and Gandhi, in his customary form of protest, went on fast at Birla House. Let me conclude with Anis Kidwai's eyewitness description to illustrate the depth of the Gandhi-Jawaharlal relationship:

> He [Bapu] was surrounded by people, milling around. In front of him was a glass of lemon juice and water. He had just taken a sip when Jawaharlalji arrived, and Bapu's face wreathed into a smile of such innocent delight, just like a child's upon finding a colourful toy. It was an unforgettable moment—Bapu holding the glass in his hand, his mouth open in delight on seeing this new visitor. People turned to each other and said happily, 'It would be better to leave them alone now.'[155]

Many of the approaches and interpretations exist on the themes discussed above, but in the long run there appears to be no conflict between moral

---

153   Ibid., (from Segaon), 25 Apr. 1938, 5 Oct. 1945, 4 Nov. 1939, *A Bunch of Old Letters*, pp. 213, 281, 510.

154   When the relationship between him and the CWC reached almost a breaking point in 1935-6, Gandhi reminded Jawaharlal of his irritability and impatience. 'They have chafed under your rebukes and magisterial manner,' he wrote, 'and above all your arrogation of what has appeared to them your infallibility and superior knowledge.' They grumbled that Jawaharlal didn't defend them from the socialists' ridicule and even misrepresentation. Gandhi to Jawaharlal, 15 July 1936, ibid., p. 205.

155   Kidwai, *In Freedom's Shade*, p. 31.

imperatives and practical behaviour. Jawaharlal, given his sensitive nature, was able to interpret Bapu's political message because he was a witness to his unwavering courage and the manner in which he toiled for swaraj. He submerged his personal convictions before disagreements ever approached the point of open breach. Independence could be accomplished only through coldly reasoned tolerance and unity behind the Congress.[156] He knew that his career was linked to particular intellectual paradigms that had much incentive to embrace conflicting views.

Political work and mutual attachment enabled Gandhi and Jawaharlal to survive the 'fiery ordeals'. Divergence between ethics and aspirations notwithstanding, they were one in bringing about man's highest intellectual, economic, political, and moral attainments.[157] Independence was their greatest passion in life, and they were equally united against the dragon of Western expansionism devouring weak nations. Both agreed on what constituted 'good' government and the ideal society, and offered a variety of models to choose from and allowed the free expression of alternative ideas. Even if Jawaharlal wanted a firmer line with the British, he knew the limits of the possible. Personally, though, his 'life became fuller and richer and more worthwhile.' That 'dear and precious memory' nothing could take away from him. In fact, whenever the future appeared to be dark, the vision of the past relieved the gloom and gave strength to Jawaharlal. 'I shall never forget', he wrote to Mahadev Desai sometime in August 1923, 'the advice that Bapu gave me in those far off days of the Satyagraha Sabha when the conflict in my mind was almost too great for me to bear. His healing wounds lessened my difficulties and I had some peace.'[158] With a leisured dignified tread, he walked towards the Ganga.

---

156   Robert Trumbull, *As I see India* (London, 1957), p. 118.

157   Bapu to Carl Heath, 13 Sept. 1938, *CWMG* (April 1-Oct. 14, 1938), p. 47.

158   August 1923, *SWJN*, vol. 1, p. 364.

7
On the Wings of the Mahatma

When I asked Gandhi (in April 1940) whether if the British left the Moslems wouldn't come down from the Frontier and cut all their Hindu throats, the Mahatma replied: 'And what business is it of yours if they do? You have used that excuse for a hundred years and would like to use it for another hundred years.' Gandhi added that he loved the British too much to allow them to stay as rulers in India; it was so bad for their character. 'You are the best of all Imperialists,' he said and added with a smile, 'but you are Imperialists.'

-Hicks Collection

Gandhi had agreed to South Africa's right to object to Indians on the grounds of language, standard of life, or standard of sanitation, but not race or colour. His acid test of non-violence wasn't to consider Englishmen as particularly bad or worse than other human beings but as a people capable of as high motives and actions as any other nationality. With his thought made up of faith, he didn't dislike any one or display anger and thereby lose his own inner strength or the moral force with which he'd serve humanity. Why will you not understand, he'd tell British friends, that your rule is ruining this country? It had to be destroyed even though Britain may pound Indians to powder or drown them. The choice of Reginald Reynolds, a Quaker from London, as Gandhi's messenger to the viceroy in 1930 sealed the bond between him and the British. He was not against them but against their rule. 'I seem to be born to be an instrument to compass the end of that rule.' He wrote to Franklin Roosevelt, the US president: 'Of Great Britain I need say nothing beyond mentioning that in spite of my intense dislike of British rule, I have numerous personal friends in England whom I love as dearly as my own people.'[1] He counted on their goodwill and kept watching, waiting, and praying.

---

1   Gandhi to Roosevelt, 1 July 1942, Steve Linde papers.

This said, he identified India's name abroad with sympathetic intervention for the countries under colonial domination.[2] In 1928, he wanted Lajpat Rai's writings to be published in order to illustrate the truth that the foremost nationalists of India have not been haters of the West or of England or in any other way narrow but that they have been internationalist under the guise of nationalism.[3]

Renouncing violence didn't imply apathy or helplessness in the face of wrongdoing. Accordingly, Gandhi supported the Palestinian struggle. He believed that Palestine belonged to the Arabs in the same sense that England belonged to the English or France to the French.[4] He favoured a Republican Spain during the Spanish Civil War, a battle between fascism and democracy in Europe. The gates of Madrid became the symbols of human liberty.[5] On other global issues, his conception of moral relationship stretched out to men and women in the remotest past and the most obscure corners of the globe to whom one was bound by invisible bonds and whose legitimate claims deserved a sensitive response.[6] To Franklin Roosevelt, he wrote:

> I venture to think that the Allied declaration that the Allies are fighting to make the world safe for freedom of the individual and for democracy sounds hollow so long as India and, for that matter, Africa are exploited by Great Britain, and America has the Negro problem in her own home.... If India becomes free, the rest must follow, if it does not happen simultaneously.[7]

---

2   New Scotland Yard and other intelligence agencies collected the information meticulously. IOR.L/PJ/12/293.

3   Gandhi to Andrews, 27 Oct. 1926, IOR, Andrews papers (B 264).

4   *Harijan*, 20 Nov. 1938, *CWMG*, vol.68, p. 137.

5   Jawaharlal was still full of what he had seen in Spain during the Civil War and said that he would like to see the people of Spain, Russia, China, and India united under one economic umbrella without temple, mosque, or church. When somebody suggested to him that unity was basically the consequence of people becoming different, Jawaharlal replied 'Events won't wait for you.' Hicks Collection.

6   Alexander, *Gandhi Through Western Eyes*, p. vi; Bhikhu Parekh, *Gandhi's Political Philosophy: A Critical Examination* (London, 1989), p. 197.

7   Gandhi to Roosevelt, 1 July 1942, Steve Linde papers.

Why did the intelligentsia comply with Gandhi's words? Apart from the many qualities that won him the love and gratitude, he repudiated Kipling's doctrine that 'East is East, and West is West, and ne'er the twain shall meet' in favour of Tennyson's 'Vision' which foretold the union between the two and offered ways for the East and the West to create a free, strong, moral, and peaceful East. He offered one path to salvation, not only of the East but also of the West. Tagore had expressed his disquiet: 'What irony of fate,' he wrote to Andrews, 'is this that I should be preaching cooperation of culture between East and West on this side of the sea just as the moment when the doctrine of Non-Cooperation is preached on the other side?'[8] The fact is that the 'East' and 'West', respectively, presented to Gandhi exactly what was necessary to foster rather than frustrate combined efforts to get to the bottom of the global problems of poverty, hunger, and unemployment. Halide Edip predicted: 'The key of the future will belong to that nation which knows how to blend the material and the spiritual in as near an equal a proportion as it is possible to do.'[9] After all, members of the two cultures thought and acted in creative ways, and Gandhi saw no reason why cross-cultural goodwill couldn't be revitalised and sustained, an idea close to Nelson Mandela, the greatest living legend during this millennium,[10] and Daisaku Ikeda, the Japanese pacifist for whom Gandhi's spiritual legacy is of humanity's priceless treasures.[11] Speeches and homilies on peace weren't sufficient, because the *sine qua non* for unity in its widest meaning depended on understanding secular interests.

As a person 'for all times and all places', Gandhi applied ethical standards to contemporary practice and institutions in order to explore both the sources of and alternatives to violent conduct.[12] He addressed

---

8   Tagore to Andrews, 5 Mar. 1921, Fakrul Alam and Radha Chakravarty (eds), *The Essential Tagore* (Visva Bharati, 2011), p. 103.

9   Edip, *East Faces West*, p. 219.

10   Sudarshan Kapur, *Raising Up a Prophet: The African-American Encounter with Gandhi* (Boston, 1992); Fred Dalmayar, 'Gandhi and Islam: A Heart-and-Mind Unity?' in V.R. Mehta and Thomas Pantham (eds), *Political Ideas in Modern India: Thematic Explorations* (Delhi, 2005), p. 217.

11   Daisaku Ikeda, *A New Humanism: The University Addresses of Daisaku Ikeda* (London, 2010), p. 145.

12   Ronald J. Terchek, *Gandhi Struggling for Autonomy* (New Delhi, 2000), p. 231; Parekh, *Gandhi's Political Philosophy*, p. 3.

conflicts, their causes and cures, before reaching the inescapable conclusion that non-violence was a virtue of the brave; it consisted of refraining from exercising the power to hit back. If people practised *real* non-violence and Truth, they wouldn't so often be at one another's throats.[13] Instead, he expected light to eventually shine through the surrounding darkness.[14]

Satyagraha mirrored Gandhi's hostility to the South African regime, and yet he organised the Indian Ambulance Corps during the wars against the Boers and the Zulus in 1899 and 1906 and spent over a month on the war front. In 1914-18, he threw himself into a recruiting operation on the grounds that fellow Indians should shoulder the obligations of full imperial citizenship, if they desired its privileges. In April 1918, he addressed the Delhi War Conference, following it up with a protest against the exclusion of Tilak, Annie Besant, and the Ali brothers.[15]

Hardinge decorated him. He understood him well, but the others were not prepared to admit that India was moving at whirlwind speed in a direction diametrically opposite to their own. His contacts with them suggested that, 'the chord that is once broken is not easily joined'.[16] After six interviews in Simla, Lord Reading couldn't grasp Gandhi's key concepts or their practical implications on politics. The boycott of British goods or the return of the Kaiser-i Hind medal didn't imply punishing the English.[17] But Reading thought otherwise and imprisoned him; Gandhi refused to give in bargaining over matters which he considered important.[18] He was comfortable with Irwin; their negotiations after Dandi March covered eight meetings over three weeks and ended in

---

13   When asked about democracy in the US, he replied:
      'My notion of democracy is that under it the weakest should have the same
      opportunity as the strongest. That can never happen except through non-
      violence. No country in the world today shows any but patronizing regard
      for the weak. The weakest, you say, go to the wall. Take your own case. Your
      land is owned by a few capitalist owners ... These large holdings cannot
      be sustained except by violence, veiled if not open ... Your wars will never
      ensure safety for democracy.' Dalton, *Mahatma Gandhi*, p. 197.

14   Gandhi to Agatha Harrison, 29 Dec. 1943, Steve Linde papers.

15   To Claude Hill, 26 Apr. 1918, Home Pol. (Dep.), Oct. 1918, no. 26, NAI.

16   To N.S. Hardikar, 11 Apr. 1940, *CWMG* (1 Dec. 1939-15 April 1940), p. 416.

17   Gandhi, *Speeches and Writings*, pp. 479-80.

18   N.d., Benthall papers.

the pact. Each toasted the other's health, Gandhi drinking lime juice flavoured with a pinch of illegally manufactured salt. The viceroy sipped his tea.

By October 1939, not one European member of the Viceroy's Council knew either Gandhi or Jawaharlal. This is not all. A governor left India without having met them.[19] This apart, someone in a land so bureaucratically run showed imagination. He was W.J. Benthall, who lorded over the Bengal Chamber of Commerce. During the Second Round Table Conference, he noticed that Gandhi was well disposed towards the British individually and collectively. His meetings brought back memories: of Gandhi sitting in a flat in Berkeley Square; 'an incongruous figure in a background of antique furniture and brocades'; in Birla's apartment at Grosvenor House Hotel; in Sir Cowasji Jehangir's flat in St. James' Square, and in his sister-in-law's house at the corner of Deanery Street; beside the Dorchester Hotel.[20] Many years later an ailing Gandhi sat in Calcutta's Tollygunje locality, propped up by cushions and surrounded by bottles of medicine. When Benthall entered, he rose from the floor and welcomed him smilingly. He couldn't but have a deep affection for a political opponent who could do this.[21] A senior British army officer also recounted 'a hard and clean fighter, a little man of mental and moral courage, ... a man for whom more was claimed than was his due, but who yet rose far above the common standard of achievement in leading his fellow-men.'[22]

Another picture is from the royal reception at Buckingham Palace for the delegates to the Round Table Conference. George V had initially refused to let Gandhi come to the levee wearing other than orthodox attire but eventually permitted his appearance in a dhoti. Benthall describes his conversation with him. When Gandhi's turn came, the King was seen wagging his finger at him and obviously expressing displeasure. Gandhi shifted his feet and smilingly but awkwardly answered back. More finger wagging by King George and eventually the

---

19   Thompson, *Enlist India for Freedom!*, p. 42.

20   Diary, entitled 'Gandhi', n.d., Benthall papers.

21   Diary, p. 115, ibid.

22   Birdwood, *A Continent Experiments*, p. 47.

conversation appeared to go amicably. It transpired later that the King told him: 'Tell me, Mr. Gandhi, what have I done that you should be so hostile to me nowadays? There was a time when you led an ambulance in South Africa in support of the British troops.' Gandhi's opposition wasn't to him but to his government.[23]

Yet another picture is from Wardha. Hicks, Andrews' friend, visited Delhi to promote the Cambridge University Brotherhood. He met Gandhi in Sevagram in April 1940. The hut was small and simple. There was room for a simple cot and for a few people to sit on the floor. There was a *punkha* above the cot, Gandhi now and again looped the rope around his toe in order to tug at it and operate it. A single shelf held a few books, a rack, some fountain pens, and a hook for his nickel watch. The cordial and hospitable Gandhi invited Hicks to the ashram; meals and an evening walk were thrown in for his comfort.[24]

R.H. Candy, another visitor, stated the obvious—a pleasant-mannered Gandhi showing no animus against the British.[25] Winston Churchill would have been treated similarly, but he didn't relate to Indians in a gentlemanly way. At the age of ten, his chief interest was tiger hunting;[26] otherwise, he had contempt for them. 'Nice people in India are few and far between,' he wrote to his mother during his first stint in India (September 1896-April 1897). 'They are like oases in the desert. This is an abominable country to live long in. Comfort you get—company you miss.' Minor injuries bedevilled his first few months.[27] In the years to come, he gained notoriety for his favourite epithet for Gandhi: 'fakir' and 'fanatic'. Gandhi appropriated 'Naked Fakir' as a compliment and even told Churchill that he'd love to be a naked fakir but wasn't one as yet.[28] Churchill, of course, inherited many

---

23   Diary, n.d., p. 11, Benthall papers.

24   Diary, p. 4, Hicks papers.

25   He was Surgeon-General during Gandhi's fast from 10 Feb. to 3 Mar. 1942, IOR.L/PJ/12/313.

26   Arthur Herman, *Gandhi & Churchill: The Epic Rivalry that Destroyed an Empire and Forged Our Age* (London, 2008), pp. 37-8.

27   Randolph S. Churchill, *Winston S. Churchill: Youth 1874-1900*, p. 286.

28   Fischer, *The Life of Mahatma Gandhi*, p. 441.

of the cultural and social assumptions of England's rulers and spent a lifetime recreating the sense of imperial grandeur. After the Jallianwala Bagh massacre, he foolishly insisted that Great Britain's reign in India, or anywhere else, hadn't been the outcome of physical force alone

Nothing could be further from the truth, yet Churchill convinced the hard core imperialists back home that he and his ilk were morally justified to establish the exceptional quality of Western civilisation. For him, India's loss marked and consummated the British Empire's downfall. Self-government was anathema to Churchill, who fought a rearguard action to prevent the extension of the Government of India Act of 1919. He felt that one must not delude 'a vain people with false promises'. 'The key to India is in London,' he quoted from Disraeli, 'the majesty and sovereignty, the spirit and vigour of your Parliament.' He wanted to crush Gandhi, 'a malevolent fanatic', decried the Act of 1935 as 'a monstrous monument of sham built by the pygmies', and influenced the outcome of Linlithgow's 'peace' proposal to Gandhi. Running after Gandhi and the Congress had steadily worn down every pillar of British authority.[29]

Churchill was comfortable in the xenophobic garb of class and culture; consequently, his perceptions about the non-white world were tainted with condescension. When it came to dealing with non-Westerners, his sweet tolerance turned sour. He resisted decolonisation without developing an overall conception of how the empire could adapt itself in a way that could provide conservative diehards with some comfort. He reiterated that it was better to be feared than loved. He was too haughty and self-opinionated to admit mistakes in judging the legitimacy of Indian aspirations and the charisma surrounding Gandhi. However, those who joined his funeral cortege on 30 January 1965 at Westminster Abbey would have known that the post-Second World War history wasn't on Churchill's side, and that his opinions reflected India far less than stupidly and muddle-huddled prejudice. In Gandhi's eyes, Churchill's hypocrisy was a degrading and deadly characteristic.

Antonio Gramsci, the Italian Marxist imprisoned by Mussolini between 1926 and 1937, wrote that, 'all men are intellectuals, but not all men

---

29   Moore, *Churchill, Cripps, and India*, p. 29.

have in society the function of intellectuals'. The career of several British intellectuals is exemplified in the role he ascribed to the intellectual.

While Churchill stands out as an imperialist par excellence, other Britons were connected with the production or distribution of knowledge. Ethnographers and historians unveiled and imagined India's past and present, translated ancient and medieval texts, surveyed the hitherto uncharted territories, compiled census reports and gazetteers, and produced vast amounts of literature. Fort William College, The Royal Asiatic Society of Bengal, and similar institutions lit up the dark corridors of knowledge. The scholarship they bequeathed enabled educated Indians to interpret their past. As a result, the reformers, who were emerging from the shadows, critiqued their society and its traditional modes so as to construct a new social order that harmonised with the currents of change and enlightenment. As Tagore once addressed: 'She (The East) was not ready to receive the West in all her majesty of soul. We have not seen the great in the West because we have failed to bring out the great that we have in us.'

India's lofty mountains, her mighty rivers, her historic cities, and her sacred groves enthralled quite a few British civil servants and missionaries.[30] Besides, once the Congress asked for a share in decision-making, Allan Octavian Hume and others contended that sharing power with Indians wouldn't reduce the colony, as the officialdom apprehended, 'to the deepest depth of Oriental tyranny and despotism'. William Wedderburn, founding president of the British wing of the Congress and its president in 1899, gave his body, mind, and resources to it. He wanted meetings to be held in England to describe India's woes.[31]

Among the other friends of India were: Robert Knight (1825-1890), the principal founder and the first editor of *The Times of India* (Bombay) and *The Statesman* (Calcutta); Henry Beveridge (1837-1929), a historian who served in the ICS in Bengal from 1857 until 1893; and Henry J.S.

---

30   Andrew H. L. Fraser, *Among Indian Rajahs and Ryots: A Civil Servant's Recollections & Impressions of Thirty-Seven Years of Work & Sport in the Central Provinces & Bengal* (London, 2006), p. 370.

31   Parel (ed.), *Gandhi: 'Hind Swaraj' and Other Writings*, p.15.

Cotton (1845-1915), Congress president in 1904. Knight chided those who resented Indian interest in public life, supported representative councils, and explained to Dufferin that they would be conducive to good governance.[32] These and many others knew India's sunsets, knew its seasons, and loved its rains.

Hume, Yule, Wedderburn, Col. H.S. Olcott, president of the Theosophical Society, H.P. Blavatsky, Annie Besant, and Margaret Noble (Sister Nivedita) endeared themselves to Gandhi, while Lajpat Rai praised Henry Cotton's work for Assam's tea plantation workers.[33] Even after passions were inflamed between the Punjab horrors of spring and autumn in 1919, Swami Shraddhanand exclaimed: 'How can we hate Englishmen, if we love Andrews, Wedderburn, Hume, Hardinge and others. We must conquer the English with our love.'[34]

Benarsidas Chaturvedi's article in the magazine *Hans* opens with the following remark: 'At a time when the British ruled India by various undesirable methods, when Englishmen from the viceroy down to the English sergeant were engaged in repression and when the real leaders were passing their lives in jails it would be rather inappropriate and inopportune to write anything on this subject'. Even so, Chaturvedi cites incidents from the lives of Andrews and Pearson to illustrate that they were true well wishers of India and quoted Gandhi's oft-repeated remark that Indians had no enmity with the English race although they strongly opposed its system of government.[35] Gandhi's devotion to Colonel Maddock, surgeon in the Poona hospital, the gentle nurses, and his old English visitor whose daily visit cheered him, was no less than his love for the dear friends and comrades who fought the good fight for freedom by his side.[36]

India charmed Charles Bradlaugh, a favourite with several vernacular papers because of his firm mind and character. He attended the Congress

---

32   Edwin Hirschmann, *Robert Knight: Reforming Editor in Victorian India* (Delhi, 2008), pp. 216-17

33   *Young India*, 16 Apr. 1931, CWMG (Dec. 1930-Apr. 1931), p. 398.

34   Tinker, *The Ordeal of Love*, p. 161.

35   Note on the Press, UP of Agra and Oudh, for the week ending 17 Dec. 1932.

36   Andrews (ed.), *Mahatma Gandhi: His Own Story*, p. 344.

in December 1889, ridiculed the Home government's fiscal and frontier policies in the House of Commons, and introduced a bill reforming the Indian councils. He fought from 1880 to 1886 for the right to take his seat in Parliament without swearing on the Bible at the administration of the oath. He was called in Parliament 'the Member for India'. In a cartoon, he stands next to Hume and Wedderburn with garlands of flowers around their necks. A number of Indian women throw flowers on 'The Friends of India'.[37] Bradlaugh died in 1891 and amongst those who attended his funeral at Woking, miles away from London, was the young student studying for the Bar: Mohandas Karamchand Gandhi.[38] Elsewhere, Indian ladies from different provinces stood mournfully at Bradlaugh's coffin. The mourners, kneeling down, offer a bouquet of flowers and recite an Urdu verse: 'you are gone, but to whose care have you left me?'[39] In fact, Naoroji continued to work assiduously towards reaching out to the British voter and public figures in and outside the parliament.[40] Newspapers celebrated his election in 1892 on a Liberal Party ticket.

The other well known friends saw so natural and imperceptible a change in India and entered a domain where they knew themselves to be unwelcome. They were decried by the most inveterate of Conservatives with their characteristic stubbornness, but the worldwide political climate was changing in their favour and, what's more, the anti-colonial ideology had gained ground. Fenner Brockway, a member of parliament, convened a large meeting in London on 27 October 1930.[41] The Round Table Conference in November generated interest in India's political future. Horace Alexander's Council for Indian Freedom in Birmingham supported the people's right to self-determination.

Friends of India weren't so numerous, and yet they dealt with unaccustomed things and kept up with the swiftness of the passing

---

37   *Avadh Punch*, 16 Jan. 1890. Also in Mushirul Hasan, *Wit and Humour in Colonial North India*.

38   Dwarkadas, *India's Fight for Freedom*, p. 8.

39   *Avadh Punch*, 19 Feb. 1891, Hasan, ibid, p. 58.

40   Briton Martin Jr., *New India, 1885*, ch. 9.

41   Suhash Chakravarty, *V.K. Krishna Menon and the India League, 1925-47*, vol. 2 (Delhi, 1997), pp. 17-18.

moment. Their voice was, admittedly, feeble, but they had listeners in England. Krishna Menon, whom Bertrand Russell described as 'a particularly brilliant young man', made significant inroads into this group. He was Jawaharlal's man. In the early 1930s, he campaigned for India's cause; in this, he had British allies. University professors, the most distinguished among them being Bertrand Russell and Harold Laski, took for granted that India should be free of all foreign domination. Writing to Beatrice Webb, another friend of India, Russell observed: 'People here are ignorant about India, but have strong opinions.'[42]

'India is so like a woman—she attracts and repels,' Jawaharlal told Padmaja Naidu. With this thought in mind, he sailed with Kamala, Indira, Vijaya Lakshmi, and her husband, Ranjit Sitaram Pandit for Europe on 1 March 1926.[43] His soul found its opportunity to renew its youth and glory. He nursed Kamala at a sanatorium in the hill resort of Montana, not far from Bex where Indira schooled, but took time off to visit Berlin, London, Paris, and Rome to renew his friendships and acquaintships. He met Romain Rolland, the French novelist and Gandhi's biographer, Ernst Toller, a famous German dramatist, and the 'rather fierce and terrifying' Madame Cama.

On 22 July 1931, a group of prominent British citizens formed the 'Welfare of India League'. It had the support of Edwyn Bevan and Gilbert Slater, who served for several years in India as professor of Indian Economics at the University of Madras, and Edward Thompson, Lecturer in Bengali at Oxford. They favoured the removal of existing bitterness by friendly intercourse between the literatures and literary men in England and India.[44] Apart from the somewhat floating but highly committed public intellectuals, most of whom had their eyes fixed on South Asia and for whom Gandhi, Tagore, and Jawaharlal were great draws, a small group of Britons made India their home, spent years with Gandhi (the Mahatma was too magnanimous and large hearted

---

42   Bertrand Russell, *The Autobiography of Bertrand Russell* (London, 1968), p. 257.

43   'I was going back to Europe after more than thirteen years—years of war, and revolution, and tremendous change. The old world I knew had expired in the blood and horror of the War and a new world awaited me.'

44   M.R. Jayakar papers (176).

to think in xenophobic terms), and championed far-reaching reforms in governance. British, American, European, and Japanese admirers represented the ashram's 'foreign' contingent.

In April 1940, Hicks set out on the 6 mile road to Sevagram from Wardha station. Marjorie Sykes, who had known Gandhi separately and in different circumstances over a period of three decades, visited Sevagram in 1945, 'full of new life, new experiments, and new activities'. Gandhi invited her to join the Nai Talim team and gave access to his papers for writing Andrews' biography.[45] Richard B. Gregg, an American, experienced inner peace.[46] Gandhi named him 'Govind' and his wife 'Radha'. They visited India for six weeks, shortly before the Salt Satyagraha. Nilla Cram Cook, also from the US, came to shake off fear and embrace love and goodness.

Two Japanese sadhus learnt Hindi, played the drum, and chanted mantra. Gandhi remembered the quickness, the orderliness, and utter detachment with which one of them prepared himself the day the police came (when the war with Japan broke out) to take him away.[47] Years later, he remembered the Buddhist monk at Sevagram.[48]

'Christ's Faithful Apostle': C.F. Andrews

While old acquaintances continually departed amidst the hustle and tumult, quite a few missionaries, with their 'Christian social conscience' and their spirit of service in hospitals, leper colonies, orphanages, and in schools and colleges, initiated a synthesis between the new India and the old, consecrated the imperial mission with Christian piety, and worked out the contradiction of imperialism by weaving a sense of obligation into the system.[49] J.C. Winslow's Christa Seva Sangh in Poona drew inspiration from the ashram idea, as did the thirty-three-year-old Andrews. He was

---

45 Jehangir P. Patel and Marjorie Sykes, Gandhi: His Gift of the Fight (Goa, 1986 edn), p. 138.

46 See his The Power of Non-Violence (Ahmedabad, 1938).

47 Harijan, 2 Feb. 1942, CWMG, vol. 31, p. 281; Louis Fisher (ed.), The Essential Gandhi, p. 339.

48 Speech at Prayer Meeting, 3 May 1947, CWMG (21 Feb. 1942-24 May 1947), p. 403.

49 Chakravarty, The Raj Syndrome, p. 118.

brought up in Birmingham in a family of religious preachers strictly Puritan in faith. Reading poems of Tagore from the *Gitanjali* bound him with India's life, he interpreted Christ and Christianity by his acts in such a spirit of devotion and of resolve as to give life an exceptional significance. He journeyed from colony to colony, arriving in Natal in January 1914, to become an ambassador of inter-racial friendship. Gandhi's ashram and Tagore's centre of learning brought him fulfillment during his years of alternating action and contemplation.

To tell Andrews' story is to unfold the political struggles during the last 25 years. He regarded himself, not as an isolated individual staking out a claim to interpret Hindustan, but as a modest continuation of a noble succession of missionaries whose traditions it was his duty and privilege to maintain.

From the time he arrived, the 'white caste' spirit in areas of British influence sickened him. Starting with Natal, he found a racial situation within the Church almost exactly parallel to that against which Paul had so vehemently contended.[50] How could faith in Christ be the only way to salvation with such evident truth and beauty in other religions? Were there not many parts to God as the Hindus asserted?

Andrews stepped out of his position as a foreigner to demonstrate that nationality and race were infinitely less important than truth, inner purity, kindness, brotherhood and love. He lived in the joys and sorrows of Indians, their triumphs and misfortunes, and preached the Gospel without engaging in proselytisation.[51] The spirit of Shantiniketan, 'the Abode of Peace' and a quiet haven where the vessel of his life found its anchorage, made him restful, calm, and silent. Tagore inspired him to think more and more of Jesus Christ.[52]

Andrews guided Delhi's St. Stephen's College in the years from 1904 to 1913, 'from the obscurity of a cramped, sectarian academy towards a realisation of a universalist ideal whereby it could play a significant part

---

50   Ibid., pp. 23, 24.

51   On the Gandhi-Andrews exchanges on conversion, see Sudhir Chandra, *Continuing Dilemmas: Understanding Social Consciousness* (Delhi, 2002), pp. 284-7.

52   Andrews, *Mahatma Gandhi's Ideas*, p. 343.

in educating the Indian elites during the critical years before and after independence.[53] He built up that tradition of close personal association between different communities and races; his own association with Principal S.K. Rudra became the starting point of his effort to become the living embodiment of the spirit of friendship. He joined him in protesting against the imposition of the Thirty-Nine Articles and the Athanasian Creed on the young Indian Church, placing upon its neck 'a yoke which neither our fathers nor we were able to bear.'[54] He remained on some people's horizon as someone who typified a Christ-like man.[55] Reading the 'Little Flowers of St. Francis', he'd say, 'What a strange thing this is! Why, I have been witnessing this very life of love in Gandhi himself and in many of his followers also.'[56]

Andrews and Gandhi met as brothers: it was an unbreakable bond between two seekers and servants. 'To be with him,' he goes on in *What I Owe to Christ*, 'was an inspiration that awakened all that was best in me and gave me a high courage, enkindled and enlightened by his own.' Andrews, in turn, learnt about India through Tagore, Shraddhanand, and his teaching colleagues at St. Stephen's College, particularly Susil Kumar Rudra. One important illustration of this new friendship is Abanindranath Tagore's painting, 'Troyee', depicting Gandhi and Tagore speaking to each other, with Andrews slightly in the background, the message being that he brought them together. The attempt to trace such friendships and to determine their ebb and flow unravels the complex task of writing the histories of the nationalist movement.[57]

Even before meeting Gandhi in Durban on Easter in 1914, Andrews had described him as 'a saint of action rather than of contemplation.'[58]

---

53   Tinker, *The Ordeal of Love*, p. 364. The Cambridge University Brotherhood, formed in 1877, provided the energy to the founding of St. Stephen's College on 1 Feb. 1881.

54   Macnicol, *C.F. Andrews*, pp. 18-19.

55   Chattopadhyay, *Inner Recesses, Outer Spaces*, p. 93.

56   Ibid., p. 344.

57   All quotes, unless otherwise stated, are drawn from Nicol Macnicol, op. cit., p. 16

58   Tinker, *The Ordeal of Love*, pp. 85-86. Gokhale sent Andrews to South Africa to assist the Indian community. He arrived in Natal in Jan. 1914.

Indeed, their hearts met from the first moment they saw each other, and they remained united by the strongest ties of love. Andrews saw the unfolding of the Champaran Satyagraha and the adoption of non-violence in thought, word, and deed. He saw ordinary men and women learn the ethics of Passive Resistance, and offer themselves for imprisonment joyfully.[59] He disagreed with Gandhi's recruitment campaign for the War, Non-Cooperation, and the excessive reliance on fasts, and yet a harmony of spirit brought the two closer to each other.

Gandhi appointed his son, Manilal, as Andrews' secretary, and stressed what a privilege it was to serve him.[60] Shortly after the Delhi War Conference in August 1918, he delayed replying to Andrews. When he found the time, he wrote, 'your love messages are all before me. They are like soothing balm.'[61] Once he told Mirabehn why he wasn't writing to Andrews: 'I would far rather let my silence speak to him. The pen is often a superfluity, if not hindrance, to the heart's flow.'[62]

Andrews listened to whatever Gandhi admitted as an act of penance on behalf of his people's sins and infirmities. With the exception of one night, a night of storm and thunder, Gandhi remained bright and radiant to the end when the 21 days fast in September 1924 ended. He could relax, but on his own terms, in his own way, and in his own time. When he left, after the fast, Gandhi wrote: 'I have missed you every moment today. Oh, your love!'[63]

Theirs was a friendship of equals; they were 'Mohan' and 'Charlie' to each other. All the circumstances of their situation seemed to draw them together; they were like two long lost friends who go hand in hand, pressing closely to each other through the passage of life. Once, Gandhi implored Tagore 'to lend me Mr. Andrews now and then. His guidance at times is most precious to me.' He filled the pages of *Young India* with thankful praise of him. He talked of Andrews' single minded devotion

---

59   Andrews, *Mahatma Gandhi's Ideas*, pp. 224, 254-5.

60   Tinker, *The Ordeal of Love*, p. 89.

61   Ibid., p. 141.

62   Ibid., p. 275.

63   Ibid., p. 215.

and defiance to Hicks, who visited Sevagram in April 1940.[64]Andrews had introduced this Cambridge graduate to Gandhi at the Round Table Conference. Gandhi told Agatha Harrison after Independence that the spirit of Andrews was ever with him.[65]

Charlie died with the satisfaction of having had many friends. He remarked at his deathbed: 'God has given me in life the greatest of all gifts—namely, the gift of loving friends. At this moment when I am laying my life in His hands I would like to acknowledge again, what I have acknowledged in my books; this supreme gift of friendship.'[66]

A Man of Intensity of Purpose: Verrier Elwin

As a priest, Andrews became the model for several persons connected with the Christian movement in India.[67] The best known was the Anglican priest, Verrier Elwin, son of an Anglican bishop who emerged with a new sense of personal identity and a renewed purpose. He contacted Andrews to start an ashram among the Gond tribal people of central India. At that time he was waging the same inner struggle as Andrews had done nearly 30 years earlier, to reconcile his position in the Church with a desire to identify with India.[68] Elwin, along with Algy Robertson from Cambridge and Bernard Clarke from Oxford, came on board in 1927. They had something of the flavour of the ancient hermits of the early Christian Church, images on which many non-Christians had fed so assiduously in their convent school days.[69] For this, he invited the ire of the Anglican Church. He was accused of political complicity with the Congress, and considered dangerous for 'doing the devil's work'. He declined to take an oath of allegiance to the King. When he was told that he had made great sacrifices by living in villages instead of remaining a Don at Oxford, he answered:

---

64   Hicks Collection, p. 3.

65   To Agatha Harrison, 29 Dec. 1943, IOR. R/3/1/309.

66   Tinker, *The Ordeal of Love*, p. 305.

67   Ramachandra Guha, *Savaging the Civilized: Verrier Elwin, His Tribals, and India* (Delhi, 1999), p. 26.

68   Tinker, *The Ordeal of Love*, p. 248.

69   Chattopadhyay, *Inner Recesses, Outer Spaces*, pp. 92-3.

Love had he found in huts where poor men lie;
His daily teachers were the woods and rills,
The silence that is in the starry sky,
The sleep that is among the lonely hills.[70]

Elwin first saw Gandhi at the Convocation held at National University Ahmedabad in 1928, and thought of him as 'the light of his life, his courtesy, his joy, his playfulness, his self-control, his peace, his sway over his noble splendid followers'. He found Sabarmati's simple life and pragmatic austerity captivating. He quoted Ecce Homo's saying, 'No heart is pure that is not passionate; no virtue is safe that is not enthusiastic'. Back in Poona, where a group of Christians had founded the Christa Seva Sangh, he read Gandhi's writings.[71] One of the books he co-authored illustrates the moral principles that guided Gandhi's Satyagraha at Vaikom in Travancore, in Bardoli, and in Madras. A case in point was his supreme asceticism, his clothing, and his hut at Karadi (where he was arrested in 1930), 'a symbol of the new form of government, the rule of the poor, for the poor, by the poor'. According to Elwin, Gandhi's qualities were numerous; among them were the depth of his compassion for the poor and the downtrodden, and indeed, as Andrews sermonised, 'for every slightest thing that suffered pain'. In so many ways he resembled Francis of Assisi in his love of poverty, F.D. Maurice in his social vision, Tolstoy in his sincerity, J.H. Newman in his intellectual integrity, and Romain Rolland in the generosity of his international ideal.[72] In his autobiography, he wrote:

How much we romantics have to learn! To have compassion on the rich and successful, who are often so unhappy; to love and care for the conventional and ordinary; to recognize the importance of the ugly and the dull. For me this was a hard lesson, for my poetic soul delights in the exotic and surprising, and beauty draws me with a single hair.

---

70   Tara Ali Baig, *Portraits of an Era* (Delhi, 1989), p. 51.

71   Guha, *Savaging the Civilized*; pp. 36-7.

72   Winslow and Elwin, *The Dawn of Indian Freedom*, p. 48.

Above: Gandhi with his brother, Laxmidas, 1886

Below: During the Satyagraha struggle, 1914 (left)
Gandhi and Kasturba on their return to India, January 1915 (right)

Gandhi and Kasturba with G.A. Natesan at Madras, 1915

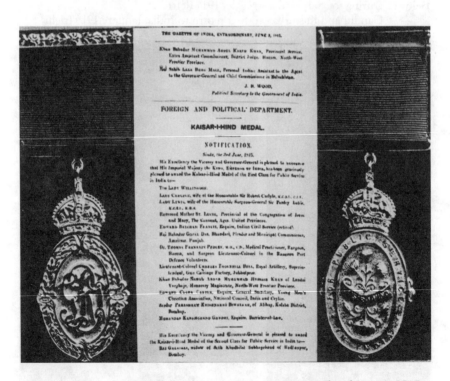

Gandhi's Kaiser-i-Hind Medal and Gazette announcement, dated June 3, 1915

Gandhi during the Kheda Satyagraha, 1918

A cartoon in response to the Chauri Chaura incident of February 1922

Gandhi on the Salt March (Dandi March) which began on 12 March, 1930

Gandhi at the open session of Karachi Congress, March 1931. With Vallabhbhai Patel, the Congress President

 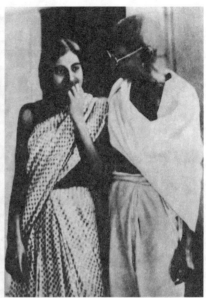

Left: Gandhi holding the steering-wheel of S.S. *Pilsna*, December 26, 1931

Right: With Indira Gandhi, c. 1933

Left: Gandhi, Nehru, and Azad checking the time, Wardha, August 1935

Right: Gandhi and Sarojini Naidu, 1938

Gandhi at the convocation of the Thackersey University for Women, Bombay, July 1, 1939

Gandhi on the way to see the Viceroy, Simla, September 5, 1939

Left: Gandhi, 1939

Right: At Vidya-Bhawan with the Prinicipal Kshitimohan Sen. Santiniketan, February 1940

With Rabindranath Tagore in Santiniketan, 1940

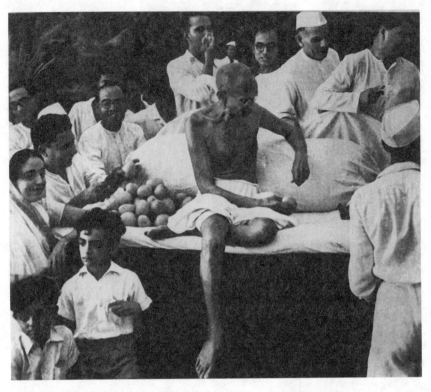

Distributing mangoes to children after the prayer, Juhu, May 1944

Samadhis of Mahadev Desai and Kasturba, Aga Khan Palace, 1944

Gandhi in a Noakhali hat,
Delhi, November 1947

Gandhi and Mirabehn (left) with Edmond Privat (right) and a delegation of the
Socialist Party at Vallorbe, in Switzerland on 6 December, 1931.

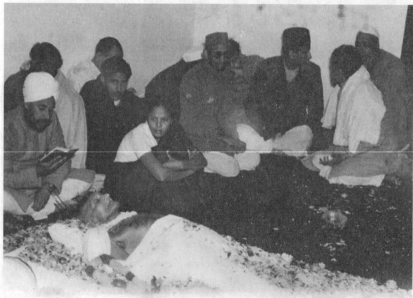

Above: Gandhi's body before the funeral procession

Facing page:
Funeral procession of Mahatma Gandhi. New Delhi, early February 1948

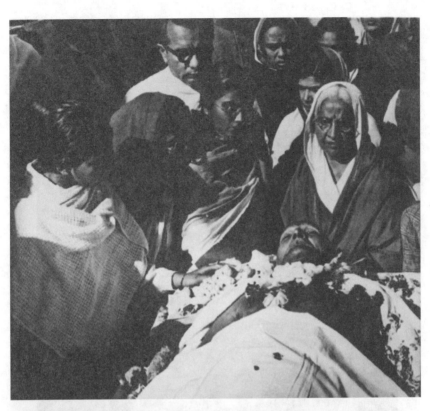

A rare studio photograph of Gandhi taken in London at the request of Lord Irwin

Gandhi and Mirabehn: Portrait of an Epic Friendship

As with Andrews and Elwin, Gandhi's great charm, his sense of humour, his recondite words, and his learned allusions charmed people across the globe. Not only did he relate quickly to dignitaries but also struck cordial relations with the old and young, men and women, especially the latter, in each case. His words and warmth inspired Miss Madeline Slade who was very proud. Setting aside all advantages of rank or status, the fair lady, having read Romain Rolland's biography of Gandhi in Paris, instinctively knew that she had to respond to the call of the man who had been at the centre of her universe for quite a while. She learnt spinning at The Kensington Weavers run by Dorothy Wilkinson, gave up alcohol, and then progressively limited her food to a purely vegetarian diet. She joined the literati, a group of individuals free from economic worries and solicitous for each other's spiritual and material improvement.[73] Her activity of body, intellect, and heart impelled her to continually perform the ordinary toils that offered themselves around her. She volunteered to live in Sindi, where she laboured every day, picking up excrement of its villages, dropped as 'night soil' along the road.[74] She undertook such tasks cheerfully, as she did everything, but with no sense of a mission to perform, and succeeded all the better for that very simplicity.

Gandhi warned that the ashram would not be a bed of roses; at the same time, he welcomed her coming with a soft, subdued, inward acquiescence. On 25 October 1925, she moved from a little village in the Rhone Valley to a mud hut in Wardha.[75] How could she? 'I hated society,' she said.

---

73 'Decades later she described vividly how Gandhi made her responsible for getting the new ashram built at Wardha, when he moved from Sabarmati. She only got the hut ready for him to move into just before the monsoon broke. As it was, she got soaked. We also talked about Sabarmati where she was with him.' Rudi von Leyden and Wilfrid Russell found her at the age of 88 'amazingly fit, physically and mentally'. She read without spectacles and had a clear and sharp mind, also a good memory. Record of a meeting with Madeline Slade at Cracking in the Vienna Woods, 7 Apr. 1981, IOR.MSS EUR C 343.

74 Lelyveld, *Great Soul*, p. 180.

75 For details, Narayan Desai, *My Life is My Message: Satyagraha (1915-1930)*, vol. 2 (Delhi, 2009), pp. 400-7; Sudhir Kakar, *Mira and the Mahatma* (Delhi, 2004).

I never accepted invitations for parties. I loved horses and dogs, and music, which I believe appealed to the spiritual side of me and the state of the world was an agony to me. There was a perpetual restlessness in me. You see, I have a gypsy ancestor, a Hungarian woman who was married to my great-great-grandfather.... She may have been the cause ....'[76]

In India, she was a bare-footed solid figure in a calico skirt and shirt, with a sleeveless hand-woven vest, which she wore in the evenings. The finely proportioned structure of her body was arresting. She had the physique and the carriage of a cowboy.[77] She was tall, big-built, and her hair fell in chestnut masses below her knees before she had them cut at Sabarmati. She wore thick homespun khadi clothes like the others.[78] She had a low and very agreeable voice, and a dark face, the effect of the Indian sun, for she must have had a fair skin once. The structure of her head was as powerful as that of her body. She had a square chin and a straight nose, Halide Edip continues:

Her large mouth remained in repose. The smile which touched it now and then was timid, hardly spoiling the repose of the features, though it leapt into her nut-brown eyes. Very brilliant those eyes, with the level thick black brows. On her shaven head she wore a calico veil, loosely framing her face. That more than anything else perhaps gave her the air of an Anatolian peasant.[79]

Romain Rolland introduced Mirabehn as someone whose 'soul is full of admirable energy and ardent devotion'. With her imaginary magnificence, she turned the ashram into a charming place with village paintings on the walls. 'I have at last come home,' she said. She had prepared herself to meet a Prophet but found an Angel in Gandhi. His admiring glance, which most other men would have cherished as a sweet recollection throughout life, was Mirabehn's great discovery. She was struck with admiration, which she didn't conceal. Never before had she

---

76   Edip, *Inside India*, p. 41.

77   Ibid., p. 40.

78   Vijaya Lakshmi, *The Scope of Happiness*, p. 67.

79   Edip, *Inside India*, p. 41.

so adequately estimated his powerful character; powerful in intellect, energy of will, and pursuit of noble ends through just means. She offered him affectionate regard because he needed so much love, and seems to have received so little. He grew youthful, while she sat by him. Almost immediately, she grew to be absolutely essential to the ashram's comfort. Whenever he had a torturing sense of the coldness and dreariness around him, her little efforts to amuse him were magnanimous. However, worst of all, the harshest stroke of fate for Gandhi to endure was Partition. The memory of it however lived beyond his life with one upon whom it was indelibly impressed. It was a great catastrophe, and Mirabehn was, admittedly, haunted by the shadows of gloomy events.

Passionate and caring, Mirabehn used the word 'Bapu' not as a term of address, but as one of endearment. She alone knew how personal and private he was, and with how much love she uttered the word.[80] She'd become physically ill at times when separated from him or when she worried about his health. This was thus 'one of the remarkable platonic associations of our age'.[81] Any imagined sensuous relationship didn't exist because, apart from everything else, Gandhi would normally have been the first to advertise, as he did in *My Experiments with Truth*, the breach of his moral conduct. There was none in this case. His sentiments for Mirabehn, without being paternal, weren't less chaste than if she had been his daughter.

A devotee of Beethoven, Mirabehn composed devotional songs, which she learnt from Ramnarayan Chaudhary. Gandhi missed her singing in Yervada prison where he had commenced a fast on 8 May 1932 against the Communal Award. More importantly, he wanted her 'to feel with me [that] the fast is a gift greater than God has ever made to me'.[82] The letters they wrote to each other tell a story of ecstasy and upheaval, danger, hope, and disappointment, all against the background of the birth of an awakened nation and resurgent nationalism. Mirabehn's letters were more mature emotionally than any written by contemporary women.

---

80   Kakar, *Mira and the Mahatma*, pp. 44, 45.

81   Fischer, *The Life of Mahatma Gandhi*, p. 440.

82   Tendulkar, *Mahatma*, vol. 3, p. 203.

Mirabehn embraced the ashram's austere regime 'with the fervour of a newly ordained Carmelite nun'.[83] Although it wasn't easy to adjust to the new ways,[84] the sense of indistinctness and unreality dimly hovered around her: the quietness of ashram atmosphere, especially the glimmering of the morning sunshine, comforted her. What impressed her most was the unity of endeavour, the hard work put in by the inmates, as if the sun was shining on them and their spiritual purposefulness. The ashram was a miniature cross-section of the everyday world, on which Bapu experimented with the loftiest and most drastic conceptions of moral, physical, and economic reforms. All who had been drawn into the great current of human life were swept along with it.

Whatever Mirabehn did, whether it was social, educational, or religious, she demonstrated the efficiency and seriousness of a practical and capable person. Even so, she avoided personal advertisement. She travelled with Gandhi, the Congress president, to Kanpur, took a vow of celibacy, and spent time at Kanya Gurukul before its head, Shraddhanand. Between severe attacks of malaria, she joined Mahadev Desai and Pyarelal in revising Gandhi's autobiography. She wanted to be among the first batch of satyagrahis during the Dandi March, but Gandhi looked right through her request, as also that of Reginald Reynolds. She sailed with Gandhi on S.S. *Rajputana* on 29 August 1931. Gandhi was to turn sixty-two on 2 October that year. She looked after the Knightsbridge house, fetched provisions from the neighbouring market, cooked the midday meal, swept the rooms and roof, and drafted notes and letters. Together, they heard the sixty-five-year-old Romain Rolland play Beethoven on their last day in Europe on 11 December. This was in Villeneuve, Switzerland. He had published Gandhi's biography in 1923. Wrote Rolland to an American friend: 'He [Gandhi] does not know Beethoven, but he knows that Beethoven has been the intermediary between Mira and me, and consequently between Mira and himself, and that, in the final count, it is to Beethoven that the gratitude of us all must go.'[85]

---

83   Kakar, *Mira and the Mahatma*, p. 32.

84   Mirabehn, *The Spirit's Pilgrimage*, pp. 70-1.

85   Tendulkar, *Mahatma*, vol. 3, p. 150.

Is she a Christian or a Hindu? Was she ever religious? Halide Edip answered:

> She must have been, but never in a denominational sense. The urge which has led her from an artificially heated drawing-room to the open spaces of India is decidedly spiritual. But it is from Mahatma Gandhi that she has imbibed the essential spirit of religion: there are no religions, there is only religion. You take the road of one of them, that which is most congenial to you, or the one in which you are brought up to believe. Hinduism regulates action, but leaves the mind free. It was so a thousand years ago when Alberuni wrote about it. It is still so. Mirabehn, whether she calls herself a Christian or not, is unconsciously fitting herself into the new mould; she is casting away all her old habits just as she has cast off her shoes— the last signs of the artificial and complicated civilization she has left behind.

Those who knew her intimately called her a Hindu of Hindus. Halide Edip was one of those. But, she added, to those who look at Hinduism as a labyrinth of castes and believe that only *birth* can make one a Hindu, she was a stranger. Her services in Gandhi's camp were of the most varied kind. The Turkish visitor saw this spiritually adopted offspring and disciple of the great Hindu leader milk the goats, clean, washes dishes, and teaches. ... She called her a great woman in those days. Further contacts of a more intimate nature convinced her of the fact.[86]

Shortly after Gandhi's address to the AICC after midnight of 8 August 1942, Gandhi was led to prison with Mirabehn, who was active in Orissa,[87] Sarojini Naidu, Mahadev Desai, and Pyarelal. In October, Mirabehn served 15 months in Lucknow jail, 'a badge of honour, and an insignia of synod.'[88] Many served Bapu, but her devotion to him was marked by a singular sense of love and dedication.[89]

---

86   Edip, *Inside India*, p. 43.

87   IOR. R.R/3/1/318.

88   Kakar, *Mira and the Mahatma*, p. 258.

89   Ibid., p. 240.

Meeting Gandhi in 1929 had an extraordinarily soothing and strengthening effect on another Briton from a political background. Fenner Brockway, Labour MP (1926-29), was born in Calcutta of missionary parents. The touch of Gandhi's hand in 1927 made him feel as if he was healed. His smiles revealed the beauty of his character. Besides the 'sweetness and simplicity of a child', his dark, luminous eyes made him appear impressive.[90] Unlike Churchill, the dogged defender of the empire, Brockway authored the Prison Enquiry Committee, and pressed for the release of political prisoners before and after the Quit India movement. He was the first in the House of Commons to move a resolution to grant independence to India, flaunted a Gandhi cap in the House of Commons, and recounted how only a man and a dog turned up to hear him speak up on independence, the dog the more attentive of the two. Gandhi visited him in hospital. As he held his hand, Brockway felt soothed and revived as though a power had passed to him.[91]

Farewell to India: E.P. Thompson

'They tell me, Mr. Thompson, that you have published a book entitled *A Farewell to India*?'
'That is so, Mahatmaji.'

'Well, it seems to me that you have been wasting your time again. How do you think that you are ever going to say farewell to India? You are India's prisoner.'[92]

Edward Thompson seemed determined to inform his audience about the dilemmas of the British-India relationship with the zeal to transform his nation's perceptions and to move their conscience. At the same time he endeavoured to persuade Indians that the British were capable to compassion, magnanimity, and penance. Unlike Edmund Chandler who had been brought up to regard nationalism as a virtue among his own

---

90   Brockway, *The Indian Crisis*, p. 91.

91   Chattopadhyay, *Inner Recesses, Outer Spaces*, p. 224.

92   Thompson, *A Letter From India*, p. 6 (Dedication page).

people and a disease in subject races,[93] India and its nationalist stir earned Thompson's appreciation. India, he wrote, 'longs to be brought in, to the full stream of the world's life'.[94] He admired Gandhi, but criticised his attempt to play a lone hand at the Round Table Conference, in isolation from men of proven integrity and patriotism. His early sympathy for Gandhi gave way to stern judgments. His relation with Jawaharlal were cordial.[95] Tagore, with whom he exchanged ideas on a wide variety of issues, was his guru. He regretted that Great Britain had done so little to understand him, the Congress goals, and Indian thought and literature.[96]

Quaker Interventions

The Quakers agreed that one should be friends with the world and regard the whole human family as one, and that one who distinguishes between the votaries of various religions opens the way for discord and irreligion.[97] After the war of 1914-18, the Quakers did astonishingly good work over vast areas in Poland, Russia, and elsewhere. They did it quietly without fuss or drama. Starting with Michael Coates, Marjorie Sykes, a Cambridge graduate born and brought up in a coal mining area in South Yorkshire, Horace Alexander, and Agatha Harrison were three of Gandhi's most distinguished Quaker followers.[98] As one of the leading lights of the India Conciliation Group which was set up in 1931 at Gandhi's behest,[99] Alexander had visited India in the spring of 1928. He met Tagore. Sabarmati ashram was strikingly ascetic in contrast to the joyous asceticism at Shantiniketan, but Alexander enjoyed seeing so many children accompanying Gandhi on his daily walk. Gandhi, he wrote, is essentially a Quaker, or rather:

---

93   Parry, *Delusions and Discoveries*, p. 136.

94   Thompson, *Enlist India for Freedom!*, p. 14.

95   Uma Das Gupta (ed.), *A Difficult Friendship: Letters of Edward Thompson to Rabindranath Tagore 1913-1940* (Delhi, 2003), p. 6.

96   Ibid., p. 8

97   Pyarelal, *Mahatma Gandhi*, vol. 1, p. 359.

98   To Nan darling, 9 Apr. 1943, Sahgal (ed.), *Before Freedom*, p. 368.

99   For the role of the Indian Conciliation Group, Chakravarty, *The Raj Syndrome*, pp. 174-83.

The kind of man my ideal Quaker would be: a man full of practical sense, intensely alive to present evils, to injustice and cruelty, spending himself in the effort to overthrow them, wise and tolerant, sympathetic and affectionate, wonderfully modest; but above all deeply religious, sure of himself insofar as he is sure of divine guidance, seeking not his own will but the will of God, to whose voice he is ever attentive.[100]

In September 1931, Alexander and the Friends of India, buoyed by the election of a Labour government, tried promoting Gandhi's mission in London. Although Krishna Menon, head of the India League, showed impatience with the 'missionaries of goodwill', he acknowledged their role in disseminating Gandhi's message. At a time when the Conservatives were becoming more and more belligerent, Alexander and Agatha Harrison lowered the impact of the anti-Congress rhetoric. For this, they invited the viceroy's rebuke, who thought that they were 'completely sold to Gandhi'.[101] The fact is that the Quakers were men and women of principles who endeavoured to build bridges between the coloniser and the colonised.

A prominent YMCA worker who came to India as an assistant to Beryl Power, a member of the Royal Commission on Labour (1929-31), Agatha Harrison, attracted notice as Andrews' secretary during the Round Table Conference. With her contacts growing, she interviewed Patel in Nasik jail in mid-March 1934, and thereafter accompanied Gandhi to the devastated areas in North Bihar. In Delhi, Ansari hosted her.[102]

On her return to London, she corresponded with him in order to broaden the base of the Indian Conciliation Group.[103] And Scotland Yard furnished information of her passport (no. 148152, issued in London on 30 August 1938) and her address: 2 Cranbourne Court, Albert Bridge,

---

100   Geoffrey Carnall, *Gandhi's Interpreter*, p. 80.

101   Ibid., p. 197.

102   IOR.L/PJ/12/444.

103   To Ansari, 25 Mar. 1935, Hasan (ed.), *Muslims and the Congress*, pp. 254-5.

Battersea, and S.W. 11.[104] In 1942, she wanted the 'reservoir of help and experience to be tapped'.[105]

After the Second World War, Agatha Harrison pleaded with Zetland, the secretary of state, for Dominion status and a Constituent assembly.[106] Cripps relied upon her counsel and contacts with Congress leaders.[107] During the period of extreme tension in Bengal in March 1947, she visited north Calcutta's jute mills where Muslim workers had been attacked, and dedicated herself to communal peace. In this way, she lessened the bitter impact of the colonial presence, and communicated the import of Gandhi's message to a receptive audience.

Reginald Arthur Reynolds, educated at a Quaker school, came from an eminently respectable Somerset family in Surrey. Under the influence of Horace Alexander and other Quakers, he spent time at Sabarmati towards the end of the summer of 1929. He carried Gandhi's historic letter to the viceroy on 2 March 1930 announcing civil disobedience and returned home in June 1930 to promote pro-Congress sentiments under the aegis of the Friends of India Society, which he launched with Laurence Housman. A critic of British imperialism and a conscientious objector, the Sea Customs Act of 1878 was applied to prohibit the circulation of his book, *The White-Sahibs in India*.[108]

I conclude with an anecdote. On the prowl for a gift, Irene Gilbert came upon a little statue of Gandhi in solid silver. 'Will you have the kindness to sell this to me?' she asked the shopkeeper. 'Why do you, a foreign woman, wish the likeness of Gandhiji?' 'Because I also,' she replied, 'have been to his ashram.' 'Then take it and welcome,' was the answer. 'I can accept no money for any likeness of his.'

One can add many more names to the list of Gandhi's admirers, such as the American missionary, Frederick Fisher, who sought light, shed fear and anger, and embraced love, compassion and humanity.

---

104   Extract from New Scotland Yard Report no. 157, 27 Dec. 1938, IOR. L/PJ/12/444.

105   2 Dec. 1943, IOR. R/3/1/309.

106   Moore, *Churchill, Cripps, and India*, p. 5.

107   Clarke, *The Cripps Version*, p. 409.

108   Secy of State to Viceroy, 18 Mar. 1930, IOR.L/PJ/12/411.

However, the mere mention of names would merely lend variety to my account and not necessarily add to what drew them to form part of the charmed circle that Gandhi so assiduously cultivated.

The persons mentioned above, mostly British, belonged to different backgrounds, but they were personally devoted to a peacemaker who would make the world a better and a safer place to live in. Moreover, they desired to bridge the gulf between the East and West, on the one hand, and between India and Great Britain, on the other. A British traveller summed up this sentiment: '... East and West should meet. In fact, they are meeting right now in this woman, in whom the best of Indian and English culture is so remarkably blended.'[109] Individuals like Polak and Andrews loved their country and its Christian traditions, but they wanted Great Britain to be judged not by racism or its colonial project but by the rich and enlightened heritage embodied in the life and mission of Jesus Christ. Reaffirming his faith in the universal significance of 'the meek and lowly Christ', Andrews felt motivated by what he had done by his Christian faith.[110] Although hot-headed evangelists described him as 'a heretic of the most dangerous kind', he was bent upon correcting his country's distorted and one-sided image. Before his death on 5 April 1940, he whispered a message to a friend, thanking those who had been near him at the end: Tagore, in spirit, Gandhi, and 'above all ... the Metropolitan, whose Christian faith has marvellously sustained me'.[111]

As discussed earlier, Gandhi's personal sentiments were most strongly and explicitly spoken for some of his British associates. At the same time, he used them to be en rapport with officials in Whitehall. He knew their limitations vis-à-vis the more dominant political currents in the Labour and Conservative parties, and, at the same time, drew strength from them. He wanted them to stay in London and explain his demands to the British public. He advised Andrews, then in London, to work amongst the religious circles.

---

109   Dorothy Clarke Wilson, *Fly with me to India* (Nashville, Tennese, n.d.), pp. 34-35.

110   Daniel O'Connor, *A Clear Star: C.F. Andrews and India 1904-1914*, p. 191.

111   Tinker, *The Ordeal of Love*, p. 305.

Andrews performed his role admirably, discussing the Government of India Bill with the BBC and explaining Gandhi's position to Ramsay MacDonald, Lloyd George, Jan Smuts, and Samuel Hoare. He himself wrote to *The Times* just before he sailed for India that he'd 'seek to preserve a generous atmosphere and a non-violent and cooperative mentality' for discussing the Bill.[112]

Inside India: Halide Edip

As Gandhi stationed himself at the doorstep of Jamia's main entrance, of which there is no trace now, his expressive features kindled at the sight of the throng of children standing nearby. He recounted the days when Jamia was founded, not at its present site but in Aligarh from where it moved to Karol Bagh, Delhi, in 1925. He remembered old friends, Ajmal Khan and Mohamed Ali, both of whom were dead. To the common observer, who could understand nothing of his feelings, Gandhi's presence was a major and memorable event, for there would have been no Jamia without him, and no funding without his persistent appeals to the rich. He repeated all his arguments, over and over again, until they paid up. Much mutual affection flowed between the two.

Gandhi knew Halide Edip rather well. If ever there was a lady born and set apart from the rest by her courage, learning, and creativity, it was this very Turkish author-revolutionary. Gandhi respected her a great deal for her national pride, her intellect and heart, and the glow of her exquisite spirit. This he mentioned at Jamia as chairperson of Edip's extension lectures on 19 January 1935. 'May Begum Saheba's coming in our midst result in binding Hindus and Muslims in an indissoluble bond!', he said.

Halide Edip proved to be Gandhi's best known interpreter in the non-Western world. She'd studied the world at street corners, and at other posts equally well adapted for observation, reflection, and analysis. Having escaped the grime and sordidness of Mustafa Kamal Pasha's regime, with which she and her husband were identified, she visited India in January-February 1935 but wrote her travelogue sitting in Istanbul.

---

112   Ibid., p. 275.

In her fascinating account, Edip described the implications of a swift, mechanised industry on the 'primate masses', and explained how, within Gandhi's development paradigm, villages were to be organic units and not passive slaves of the nation. Her description was in the context of Gandhi's accent on an ordered rather than a mechanised rural life and a productive and self-supporting population living within its means and adhering to moral and spiritual mores. Gandhi's countenance glowed, as he discussed with composure and singular energy, his theory on reinvigorating Hinduism. His approach reminded Edip of the economic and moral revival of Turkish society in the thirteenth century by the mystic-economic orders called the 'Ahiler' in Anatolia. She had a handle on Gandhi's mental picture, soft, gentle, and clear in outline and purpose.[113]

Endowed with heroism during the Allied occupation of Constantinople (later Istanbul), the world looked wild and hostile to Edip, her life lonesome and dreary, and her future a shapeless gloom. However, crossing the threshold to India, hope, warmth, and joy came in her life. Meeting Gandhi was a blissful moment. She met a man who conceived of justice as a balancing of the social scales. She met a man who evolved a firm system of belief and a fair standard of behaviour to obtain self-government and a modus operandi to replace revolution. Edip approvingly quoted T.A.K. Sherwani:

> Satyagraha will take the place of revolutions in the future. It is essential for India even when she is independent. For in such an event the people will have to face dictatorships, which can be very bad. There is no other weapon for a people suffering from tyranny in modern times. Any ordinary revolution can always be suppressed with gas bombs and machine-guns. But, when millions refuse to pay taxes, and large enough numbers of the administrative machine refuse to co-operate, it instantly paralyses a government, no matter how strong it may be. Specially for a country of three hundred million if a few millions are cured from all fear and willing

---

113   Halide Edip, *Conflict of East and West in Turkey* (Delhi, 1935), p. 247; Edip, *Turkey Faces West: A Turkish View of Recent Changes and their Origin* (New York, 1930), p. 218.

to face death, the most tyrannical government will be helpless. The question is to instil this into the minds of all peoples, and to create the organizations necessary to start it.[114]

'Hindu Indians' should support Gandhi and serve him, for he alone could eradicate the superstitions and the degenerative elements in their religion. Likewise, Edip advised 'Moslem Indians' to accept that Gandhi's synthesis reflected, in effect, the everlasting principles of Islam.[115]

Gandhi's relevance as an interlocutor between the different cultural inheritances is, by all accounts, one of the compelling themes; the other is the blending of faiths, and tolerance of and sympathy with them. It is possible, Gandhi conceded, for the best Englishmen and the best Indians to never to separate till they have evolved a formula acceptable to both.[116] Incontrovertibly, without disentangling the different strands in the texture of his thinking, it is possible to follow Gandhi adapting himself in a spirit that was neither too Western nor too traditional.

India had evolved within the ambit of a broader compass, and its past as well as its destiny was ineluctably connected with South East Asia, Central Asia, and West Asia. This created opportunities for interaction, for comparison, and mutual assessment of civilisations, as never before, and technology overcoming the traditional constraints on global understanding. Of course, Gandhi warned of intense friction increasing owing to the disintegration of much that constitutes cultures, and fancied a genuine and sustained dialogue to preserve some sense of priority and scale in what took place.

Edip and others noted Gandhi's quirky habits and unorthodox views, and contested his health experiments. When, for example, smallpox raged in Sabarmati, Gandhi maintained that 'no provable virtue of vaccination will therefore move us'.[117] An incident in South

---

114   Edip, *Inside India*, p. 176.

115   Edip, *Turkey Faces West*, p. 218.

116   Gandhi, *My Experiments with Truth*, p. 504; Andrews, *Mahatma Gandhi's Ideas*, p. 13.

117   To Ansari, 3 Mar. 1930, Hasan (ed.), *Muslims and the Congress*, p. 118.

Africa made him describe hospitals as 'the instrument of the Devil'.[118] In 1924, however, he agreed to an operation for appendicitis. 'Why,' a friend asked, 'did he not use soul force as the remedy for body ills?'[119]

Every now and again the Mahatma's personal life raised a few awkward and probing questions. Allowing that many, many years earlier, in early and reckless youth, he had committed a wrong act, or that the inevitable force of circumstances had made him a less than caring husband and indulgent father should not have foreshadowed his many good deeds. At the same time, it wasn't easy for overseas visitors to close their eyes to the unpleasant and cheerless circumstances of Kasturba's life as she became 'the spirit of Indian wifehood'. In Gandhi's presence, she appeared voiceless and long-suffering.[120]

As regards parenthood, he described himself as one who exacted complete obedience. He was free to distrust his children and give erroneous judgements, but he didn't want them to do the same.[121] This lent credence to the view that he suppressed Harilal, Manilal, Ramdas, and Devdas, overlooked their wishes at any time, and treated them as of no account. The eldest boy wanted to go to a proper boys' school, but Gandhi seemed to think that bookish knowledge obscured, if indeed, it didn't destroy, the capacity to perceive the inner vision. He was a strict disciplinarian who wouldn't take no for an answer, and yet Harilal, the eldest, took courage in both hands to protest: 'You have never encouraged us in any way; you have spoken to us not in

---

118   After being set free from the Aga Khan Palace, a homeopath was sent for Gandhi, now convalescing in Juhu. Gandhi had no faith in homeopathy, but agreed to consult one as a tribute to the memory of Das and Motilal. They desired this form of medication to be given a trial.

119   Ayurvedic, Unani, and homeopathic systems of treatment were acceptable to him, although they too didn't escape criticism for the lack of 'the spirit of humility and research'. When Gandhi's grand niece underwent an appendectomy, he sadly wrote to his naturopath friends: 'My pride has had to fall ... I hope and pray that won't expose me any further.' Subsequently, he became stubborn: 'My faith in the nature cure is interesting. It is the only thing for the masses. But it has its limitations.' Jones, *Tumult in India*, p. 81.

120   Arun Gandhi, *Kasturba: A Life* (Delhi, 2000), p. 50.

121   To Amrit Kaur, 24 Jan. 1940, *CWMG* (1 Dec. 1939- 5 Apr. 1940), p. 138.

love but always in anger.'[122] Gandhi chided him for throwing away his whole life in a moment by one false step. He saw in him all his faults magnified and merits minimised: 'my virtues, generosity for instance, have been enlarged in him into defects'. A strong, uncaring, and unsympathetic statement from a father! Devdas compensated him for the dissatisfaction he felt from his three other sons.[123]

Harilal's conversion to Islam on 14 May 1936 was the last straw. Whether this implied a denial of God and religion is conjectural; Islam and Christianity routinely allowed proselytisation. For someone who believed that 'conversion is a matter between man and his Maker who alone knows His creatures' hearts,'[124] Gandhi exaggerated his 'hurt'. As it transpired, Harilal embraced Islam as a mere charade and re-entered the Hindu fold on 12 November.

Unlike those who defended inter-caste and inter-community matrimonial alliances in order to break down caste and communitarian barriers, Gandhi objected to Vijaya Lakshmi marrying Syed Hossain, a young journalist in Allahabad, who took charge of the *Independent* for a while.[125] Therefore, even though his relationship with Manilal was on an even keel, he berated his 'love affair' with a Muslim girl in South Africa. Ramdas worked with the peasants in Bardoli and was imprisoned during Civil Disobedience. He blamed his father for not giving him any formal Western education.

Did Gandhi suffer from a sense of self-delusion in regard to his relations with the opposite sex? Endowed with the liveliest sensibility to feminine influence, his life of self-discipline and self-development, and, as he aptly called it, self-abandon, enabled him to weld together in his own person the masculine and feminine qualities into a single whole, free from tension.[126] In many ways he had a strong feminine trait: a sense of compassion and nurturing of others. His strategy for winning freedom was more feminine than masculine too. It was a

122   Chandulal Bhagubhai Dalal, *Harilal Gandhi: A Life*, p. xxviii.
123   Desai (ed.), *Day-to-Day with Gandhi*, vol. 1, pp. 101-2.
124   Ibid., p. 105.
125   Vijaya Lakshmi, *The Scope of Happiness*, p. 64.
126   Horace Alexander, *Consider India: An essay in values* (New York, 1961), p. 58.

political triumph, where the strength of the weak, their confidence, their capacity for self-sacrifice and their inner will—all feminine qualities—were used to combat colonial rule.[127] He deliberately surrounded himself with women to prove that his mastery over 'lust' wasn't achieved by avoiding them.[128] Every evening for his prayer meeting, he'd lean on the shoulders of two girls, 'a means of showing affection and identifying women as partners and helpers'.[129]

During the Home Rule Movement and Rowlatt Satyagraha, the spirit of reaction and revolutionary discontent became intense. Sarojini Naidu was one of those who bore the hardships with stoicism and humour. She had entered the political fray in 1919 as one of the 600 signatories of the Satyagraha pledge, and was thereafter in the thick of it all. Once seen, she couldn't be forgotten because of her powerful oratory skills. She didn't prepare speeches. To speak was as easy for her as it was for a fish to swim. She talked of things with Gandhi that she would never have thought of discussing with any other man. There was something very beautiful in their relationship; so closely and constantly were they linked together. She was, admittedly, struck by Gandhi's single-mindedness, consistency, his good faith and large-heartedness.

Whenever Gandhi embarked on a fast, she'd worry. She was by his side on 20 September 1932. Her daughter Padmaja thought of 'a catharsis' cleansing of 'the accumulated corruption' of centuries.'[130] On 2 March 1943, Gandhi ended one of his many fasts. A relieved Sarojini Naidu referred to the problem and paradox of 'the marvellous little Mickey Mouse who nibbled his way back to life from the lightly spread and knotted nets of death'. She told 'Papi', her daughter, of his 'horrid scrubby little chin growth which made him look like a gnome and he had himself shaved and trimmed to "look nice" because he thought I was being rude about his appearance.'[131]

---

127   Baig, *Portraits of an Era*, p. 72.

128   Fischer, *The Life of Mahatma Gandhi*, p. 440.

129   Baig, op. cit., p. 72.

130   Rajmohan Gandhi, *Mohandas*, p. 373.

131   To Leilamani Naidu, 3 March 1943, in Paranjape (ed.), *Sarojini Naidu: Selected Letters*, p. 309

During the Quit India movement, there was thunder in the air. Sarojini Naidu sniffed that thunder and anticipated mass arrest to take place. She prepared herself in her Bombay house for eventual arrest. The bell rang at 4 a.m. The police came in. Her hunch proved right. She and others were led into prison on 8 August 1942. For Beverley Nichols, a political analyst, it was 'more interesting to consider her merely as a cultured, charming woman, swept into gaol as the result of her convictions.'[132] Sarojini Naidu found prison life to be monotonous. The rooms were pleasant, the food was good, and the British were most polite but they were utterly isolated. For three weeks they had not a scrap of news. All the papers were banned, and there was no radio; even their families had no idea where they had been taken.

Now and then, of course, there were brighter moments; one of them occurred when C. Rajagopalachari, himself an ex-President of Congress, came to visit Gandhi. The last time C.R. had seen him, Gandhi had been reading the poem 'Hound of Heaven', and Sarojini Naidu had been sitting by him trying to explain what it all meant. 'Well,' said C.R. 'have you finished that dog poem yet?'

Perhaps the most dramatic thing Sarojini Naidu told Nichols was about Gandhi's famous fast of February 1943. A number of unsavoury things have been said about that fast; it was suggested that the state of the Mahatma's health chart varied according to the political situation, that when the Viceroy looked like yielding, Gandhi grew rapidly worse, and when the Viceroy appeared adamant, Gandhi took a marked turn for the better. According to Nichols, 'our contempt for this form of political masochism does not justify us in assuming that it was a fake.'

Sarojini Naidu, at least, had a very different story to tell. She said that towards the end of the seventh day, Gandhi, to all appearances died. 'He had been sinking rapidly since the morning; they were gathered round his bedside, fearing the worst. As the dusk deepened the worst seemed to happen; his breathing ceased, his pulse faltered and stopped. It was as though a light had gone out of the world,' she said. How he came back, by what miracle the frail, wizened body reasserted itself, she couldn't explain; she was too moved by the memory of it. All she could suggest

---

132   Nichols, *Verdict on India*, p. 152.

was that it was a supreme effort of will. Did she follow Gandhi's rules in diet? She cried out: 'Good heavens, all that grass and goats milk? Never, never, never!'[133] 'Ah! You must be Mrs Naidu! Who else dare be so irreverent? Come and share my meal!' Gandhi is reported to have said to Sarojini Naidu.

They met in London on 8 August 1914. Gandhi had gone there to organise an ambulance corps during World War I. 'And so, laughingly', recalled Sarojini Naidu on the occasion of Gandhi's 78th birthday, 'we began a friendship that has lasted, grown and developed through all these many years.' Sarojini Naidu was the only one who could joke with Gandhi on *brahmacharya* and chastity. Once when an article suggested ways of avoiding the temptation of females, the writer advised, among other things, the wearing of dark glasses. As Rajagopalachari always wore them, Naidu made all kinds of naughty remarks about him in which both Gandhi and CR himself would join. CR's views were as staunch as Gandhi's, but both put up with her merciless teasing.[134]

'*True as the peach to its ripening taste/Is destiny to her hour*'. Like the poet's deep and unwavering faith in the future, Sarojini Naidu foresaw and foretold the day of freedom. She saw the flag of freedom on the rampart of the Red Fort, but she also witnessed the death and dislocation of men, women, and children at the time of Partition. Before long, a massive tragedy—the assassination of the 'Father of the Nation'—overtook the festivities. For Sarojini Naidu, who did more than most to bring out the light and colour in his life, the most poignant of all was the last picture of his walking to his prayers at the sunset hour, translated in a tragic instant of martyrdom from mortality to immortality.[135] When finally, Gandhi succumbed to bullet wounds, Sarojini Naidu wrote:

The most epic event of modern times ended quickly. The pent-up emotion of the people burst in a storm of sorrow as a long slow procession moved towards Gandhi in a mournful pilgrimage of farewell, clinging to the hands that had toiled so incessantly, bowing

---

133   Sengupta, *Sarojini Naidu*, p. 344.

134   Vijaya Lakshmi, *The Scope of Happiness*, p. 67.

135   Sengupta, op. cit., p. 345.

over the feet that had journeyed so continuously in the service of his country. In the midst of all this poignant scene of many-voiced and myriad-hearted grief, he stood, untroubled, in all his transcendent simplicity, the embodied symbol of the Indian Nation—its living sacrifice and sacrament in one.

They might take the Mahatma to the utmost ends of the earth, but his destination remains unchanged in the hearts of his people who are both the heirs and stewards of his matchless dreams and his matchless deeds.

And, her broadcast to a shocked nation ended with the stirring words,

My father, do not rest. Do not allow us to rest. Keep us to our pledge. Give us the strength to fulfil our promise, your heirs, your descendants, your stewards, the guardians of your dreams, the fulfillers of India's destiny. You, whose life was so powerful, make it so powerful in your death, far from mortality you have passed mortality by a supreme martyrdom in the cause most dear to you.

The Nightingale's own voice was stilled on 2 March 1949. Sarojini Naidu was the Governor of Uttar Pradesh. 'I am a Governess', she used to say. As in life, she would have faced death with a light heart and a song on lips and smile on face. The 'Nightingale of India' saw herself as an individual whose experiences, opinions, and inner feelings had a right to be heard, and were certainly worth hearing. She was one of the most remarkable women of any age, anywhere, writes Tara Ali Baig, a family friend. 'Never have I met a more extraordinary woman', spoke out the British writer Somerset Maugham after meeting her at a dinner organised by Baig.'[136]

Gandhi led and guided another redoubtable lady, Rajkumari Amrit Kaur. She belonged to the Kapurthala state. Charming and intelligent with a clear perception of life, character, and individuality, he never failed to inquire after her well-being. She and Mirabehn

---

136   Baig, *Portraits of an Era*, p. 36.

would kiss his hands; he'd stroke their cheeks. However, after his 'lust dream' in 1936, he retreated into six weeks' silence and refrained from putting his hand on women's shoulders. Yet the small talk, whispers, and innuendos continued over the *brahmacharya* test with Manubehn, his grandniece. It was rumoured that some objected to Gandhi's experimenting in *brahmacharya*: the problem was tidied over when he agreed not to allow any one of his family members to sleep on his bed. Apparently, in one of his Gujarati letters to Gandhi in Shrirampur, K.G. Mashruwala, editor of *Harijan*, objected to leaning upon girls while walking, or allowing them to use the same bed with him which 'sprang from a residuum of sensuality which lay unburnt in the depth of Gandhi's being.'[137] Thakkar Baba disagreed, pointing out that it would seem churlish to detract from the achievements of such a busy and remarkable holy man.

But this verdict didn't however prevent the cynics from adding fodder to the stories of Gandhi's 'sexual experiments'. He did, of course, clarify that he was the same celibate that he had been in 1906, and that his experiment had made him a confirmed *brahmachari*. 'The link between you and me,' he told Birla, 'is your faith that my life is pure, spotless and wholly dedicated to the performance of dharma ...What my well-wishers have to decide is whether I take Manu in my lap as a Simon Pure father or as a degenerate one.'[138] Then, when Horace Alexander reminded him of his motto ('moderation in all things'), he agreed to put a stop to the experiment.[139] Friends nonetheless continued to voice their disquiet. R.P. Parasuram, a loyal and devoted stenographer, resigned on New Year's Day 1947; Nirmal Kumar Bose did so on 19 March 1947.[140] 'Personally,' wrote Bose, 'I have accepted the genuineness of your experiment and the explanation that you have given me, although the character of the actual experiment still

---

137   K.G. Mashruwala to Bose, 22 Mar. 1940, N.K. Bose papers (269 C).

138   Gandhi to Birla, 15 Feb. 1947, in Birla (ed.), *Bapu: A Unique Association*, vol. 4, pp. 440, 456; Gandhi to J.B. Kripalani, 23 Feb. 1947, *CWMG* (21 Feb. 1947-24 May 1947), pp. 13-14.

139   Note by Bose, 16 Aug. 1953, vol. 2, N.K. Bose papers (269 C); Carnall, *Gandhi's Interpreter*, p. 208.

140   Bose, *My Days with Gandhi*, pp. 76, 119.

remains unknown. But then one can flout opinion if it comes in the way of one's practice of truth.'[141]

Letters and writings of this period were either destroyed or mysteriously disappeared from Sabarmati. Parasuram destroyed them, 'except one or two'. He regretted deserting Gandhi at a time when his services were required. Mashruwala, who objected to Gandhi allowing Manubehn to sleep in his bed, dismissed 'the whole episode as a painful dream' and urged Bose not to 'publish anything about this anywhere and in my language.'[142] Innuendos notwithstanding, Manubehn was the companion, or whatever is the fittest phrase, of the grand old man. Her presence revived his drooping spirits, particularly when she spoke and made passing occurrences vivid by accompanying descriptions. She had taken charge, and although there were others as well, the public speedily expressed their decided preference for this arrangement.

In politics, A.J. P. Taylor, the British historian, once wrote that there can only be one or two answers: 'Yes or No, For or Against.' Gandhi didn't doubt what had happened or which side was in the right. He knew, to paraphrase Taylor's comment, that the steady men of solid principle and minds are the ones who achieve effective success.

To sum up, Gandhi, in spite of his misgivings about the West, engaged in the process of conceptualised pluralism to balance the West with the Eastern social and cultural milieu. Nehru and Azad made a special effort to recognise 'Western' perspectives and approaches in the concrete world of nation-building. Tagore tried balancing the affirmation of separate identities and a sense of the universal human community, and, using his extraordinary imagination and breadth of vision, he sought to identify areas of East-West cooperation. These divergent approaches produced what might be called a cultural renaissance that became an essential foundation for a strong secular democracy and, even more, a necessary part of a multi-religious society.

---

141 Bose to Gandhi, 3 Jan. 1947, N.K. Bose papers (269 C).

142 Parasuram to Bose, 7 Mar. 1948; Bose to Mashruwala, 23 Mar. 1950; Mashruwala to Bose, 24 Mar. 1950; Bose to Mashruwala, 31 Mar. 1951, N.K. Bose papers (269 C).

In the next chapter, I explore the convergence of Gandhi's views on untouchability with the great current of the time: attainment of swaraj. Others have, of course, examined the ambiguity and uncertainty of Dalit politics in a society resistant to caste mobility or to any fundamental change in the caste structure.[143]

---

143   Oliver Mendelsohn and Marika Vicziany, *The Untouchables: Subordination, Poverty and the State in Modern India* (Cambridge, 2000), p. 103.

8
Of Paupers and Princes

What is there in Gandhism which is not to be found in orthodox Hinduism?
There is caste in Hinduism, there is caste in Gandhism.
Hinduism believes in the law of hereditary profession, so does Gandhism.
Hinduism enjoins cow-worship. So does Gandhism ... All that Gandhism
has done is to find a philosophic justification to Hinduism and its
dogmas.

-Ambedkar, *What Congress and Gandhi Have*
Done to the Untouchables, p. 307.

Removal of untouchability means love for and service of the whole world
and thus merges into ahimsa. Removal of untouchability spells the breaking
down of barriers between man and man, and between the various orders of
beings. We find such barriers erected everywhere in the world, but here we
have been mainly concerned with the untouchability which has received
religious sanction in India and reduced lakhs and crores of human beings to
a state bordering on slavery.

-Gandhi to Narandas, 9 September 1930, *CWMG* (July-Dec. 1930) p. 134

Through this book I have endeavoured to connect and discuss
Gandhi's 'big moments' through the lens of his relations with many
people of diverse backgrounds, women and men – 'significant others'—
who were around him and in different kinds of relations with him along
these events. I have explored such relations from the early days of his
experimentation with Satyagraha in South Africa. This approach brings
a kind of life into the time and events, which helps to get a sense of
Gandhi. It throws light on emotions that drove events, or that were at
their background, and helps to better understand, as I aim to do, what
affected and shaped Gandhi's politics and the role these relations played
in his politics. But since I examine the development of his ideas, the
secret of their appeal and his politics by foregrounding, or bringing
more light into his relations with many significant other people, my
story goes beyond Gandhi.

The twentieth century was blessed in having Gandhi, the New Teacher, and 'the needed servant of humanity'. Halide Edip was going to visit Gandhi for the first time in January 1935 to understand him. He was, after all, 'so important a happening in twentieth-century history'.[1] The same year, Mrs Joan Cruickshank met Gandhi. He radiated charm and a certain calm dignity which was compelling. Besides the attractive quality of his low voice, his eyes beamed with kindness and goodwill.[2] Cruickshank knew, of course, that he had only just emerged from an ordeal. This requires explanation.

They were called *achhut*s or untouchables until Gandhi found for them a new and generic term, *Harijan*, indicating their proximity to God.[3] The disabilities to which they were subject aroused in Gandhi poignant sympathies. His life-long passion was to eradicate untouchability, but not the caste hierarchies and the pan-India *Varna*. He regarded the caste system as synonymous with Hinduism, which he described as essentially inclusive and ever-growing and ever responsive, but he wanted to purge it of a terrible blight. The claim was not only bold, but accompanied by an equally strong commitment to it. With his moral scruples and his belief in the dignity of men and women, for which he adduced irrefutable evidence in the *Gita*, he stressed not only the ugly and inhuman aspects of untouchability but suggested an outright revision of the existing way of thinking.[4] In this sense, he didn't live with his ideology alone, but pushed it and worked with it as the basis of his actions.[5]

---

1   Edip, *Inside India*, p. 34.

2   Mary Thatcher, *Respected Memsahibs: An Anthology* (Scotland, 2009), pp. 221-22.

3   The Statutory Commission Report (1930) described them as 'Depressed Classes', who comprised some 20 per cent of the total population of British India, or some 30 per cent of the Hindu population. *Report of the Indian Statutory Commission: Survey*, vol. 1 (Calcutta, 1930), p. 37.

4   'The Hindu mind', he wrote, 'has therefore to be educated to regard intrinsically as equals the lowest, the fallen and the downtrodden and to give them a helping hand so as to make them level with the rest.' He also said: 'So long as untouchability disfigures Hinduism, so long do I hold the attainment of Swaraj to be an utter impossibility.' To Gregg, 29 May 1927, Reddy, *Mahatma Gandhi: Letters to Americans*, p. 69.

5   Ashis Nandy, *Traditions, Tyranny and Utopias: Essays in the Politics of Awareness* (Delhi, 1992), p. 6.

The eradication of untouchability had figured in the Congress agenda at the end of 1916,[6] but Gandhi was the one to introduce a new plank in September 1920,[7] and announce at the Second Round Table Conference on 13 November 1931, that he'd prefer the demise of Hinduism to the survival of untouchability.

Sustained criticism of and movements against caste oppression are manifest in the histories of Hindu devotionalism from Tukaram in the early seventeenth century to Kabir (d. 1518).[8] Gandhi's mission of low-caste upliftment is seen as merely an update of the sayings of the Ramanandi gurus and other devotional preceptors in the eighteenth and nineteenth centuries. This was, in effect: abjure sin, adopt ascetic purity, humbly submit to the preceptor, and be admitted on sufferance to mystical communion.[9]

However, the Satyashodak movement under Mahatma Jotirao Phule was a startling new departure from older social and cultural forms and an instrument of radical social reforms. Exemplary, as he is portrayed in most narratives, he impacted on an emerging intelligentsia among the Mahars.[10] In Madras and Bombay Presidencies, non-Brahmanism

---

6   Estimates of untouchables vary, but the figure is estimated to be as high as 60 million. By excluding the aboriginals, the Simon Commission Report brought it down to 43.6 million, which is approximately 28.5 per cent of the total Hindu population.

7   'It is easy enough for the *Panchama* friends to see,' he observed when later propagating this resolution (*Young India*, 27 Oct. 1920):
     'The Hindus must realise that if they wish to offer successful non-co-operation against the government they must make common cause with the *Panchamas,* even as they have made with the Mussulmans.
     Non-co-operation, when it is free from violence, is essentially a movement of intensive self-purification.'

8   Milind Wakankar, *Subalternity and Religion: The Prehistory of Dalit Empowerment in South Asia* (London, 2010); Utham Bhoite, 'Pre-Ambedkar Untouchable Liberation Movement in Maharashtra', in N.K. Wagle (ed.), *Writers, Editors and Reformers: Social and Political transformations of Maharashtra, 1830-1930* (Delhi, 1991).

9   Susan Bayly, *Caste, Society and Politics in India from the Eighteenth Century to the Modern Age* (Cambridge, 1999), p. 250.

10   Rosalind O'Hanlon, *Caste, Conflict, and Ideology: Mahatma Jotirao Phule and Low Caste Protest in Nineteenth-Century Western India* (Delhi, 2002 paperback), p. 304.

emerged as a political force uniting activists from a mixed array of social/caste groups.[11] In Madras, the Justice Party spearheaded the non-Brahmin movement. In Travancore, Sri Narayana Guru's unitarian doctrine of 'one caste, one religion and one God for man' appealed to his own Ezhava community.

There was however no deep or broad commitment of mainstream opinion to the liberation of the Dalits until Gandhi invested the inseparability of the self and the other, the philosophical mainstay of the Bhakti movement, with a new form of radical militancy.[12] Moreover, he transformed the notion of historical guilt into a concrete model of action for the present.[13]

He therefore considered the eradication of untouchability to be a powerful factor in the process of attaining swaraj. This however required sustained efforts; Gandhian workers attended to some of the special problems of the Dalits and tribes in, for example, the old *girasia* chiefdoms of the southern Gujarat hinterland,[14] and inaugurated Satyagraha within the boundaries of an Indian state to demonstrate the Dalit right to proceed along a certain road, from the use of which they had previously been debarred by caste Hindus. They were attracted to the fight because it introduced a new conception: Hinduism without a social hierarchy.

However, the path of reform was strewn with numerous difficulties. One of them was this: after setting up his ashram, Gandhi faced a dilemma: should he admit a Dhed, who traditionally deal with animal carcasses and hides, or concur with Kasturba's strong objections? Kasturba could be overruled but not the helpers, including Gandhi's own sister, Raliatbehn, who ultimately deserted him.[15] Another problem erupted when Kasturba objected to cleaning his formerly untouchable law clerk's chamber pot. There was, then, the adverse reaction to a

---

11   Susan Bayly, op. cit., pp. 238-40.

12   Mendelsohn and Vicziany, *The Untouchables*, p. 96.

13   D.R. Nagaraj, *The Flaming Feet and Other Essays: The Dalit Movement in India* (Delhi, 2010), p. 77.

14   Susan Bayly, op. cit., pp. 247-48.

15   Lelyveld, *Great Soul*, p. 150.

resolution of the Gujarat Vidyapith.[16] Gandhi shared his predicament with Kallenbach.[17]

Gandhi decided to give an altogether different thrust to his drive. The path that best suited him in South Africa had been the well-worn track of law courts, and it worked. In India however he impregnated the issue not with 'modernity' or modernisation but with human sensibilities, and established, by adopting a wider perspective and a deeper insight, that rank, dignity, and station had all proved illusory and that human reverence, equality, and justice alone would bring happiness to the world. He did that to keep Hinduism in its old place. With a ready tact, the result of an ever-active and wholesome sensibility, he supported temple entry at Vaikam in Travancore in 1921 and March 1925 and at two Maharashtra temples in 1929-30. At both places, he described untouchability as a 'horrible and terrible' stain on the faith, an 'evil', and an 'insult to religion and humanity'. He didn't think that much 'supreme philosophical truth' was involved in being acquainted with the simple truth that no human being should be regarded as untouchable by reason of his birth.[18] He spoke of purifying the collective conscience as a means of achieving a grouping not only of those who desired immediate change of one kind or another in the existing caste equation but also of those susceptible to appeals of high moral content.

Gandhi backed these appeals and exhortations by his fast of 1932, his tour to Assam, south Bihar, and Orissa on behalf of Harijan Sevak Sangh (Servants of Untouchables Society), which he founded in 1932, and his columns in *Harijan* which appeared from 11 February 1933 onwards. At Puri, the holy city of Lord Jagannath, he walked through the crowded street to emphasise the spiritual nature of the Dalit movement,[19] and opened a temple to all Hindus, including the Dalits, on 15 May, at Balianta.[20] In UP, many temples were thrown open for a

---

16   The resolution was to the effect that no school which excluded Antyajas (the lowest caste among Hindus) would be recognised.

17   Lelyveld, *Great Soul*, p. 150.

18   *Young India*, 5 Feb. 1925, *CWMG* (Jan. 16 1925-April 30, 1925), p. 67.

19   Tendulkar, *Mahatma*, vol. 3, p. 269.

20   Ibid., p. 273.

time, but many others remained closed, and the Brahmins in some of them worked hard at night to cleanse and purify the temples after the departure of the last Dalit worshipper.[21] Clearly, in-built prejudices of generations couldn't be eradicated in a month or two.

Who could, then, challenge Gandhi's moral authority in pushing through the temple entry bills five years later in both the Madras legislature and the Central Legislative Assembly? In 1939, Bishop V.S. Azariah, the first native Indian bishop of an Anglican diocese, credited him with having revolutionised the attitude of thinking men and women towards untouchability.[22]

Against this background, Gandhi's stout defence of the *Varna* system appears to be paradoxical. How could he stand for the destruction of the existing political structures to secure freedom and, at the same time, seek to maintain intact the caste system which permits the domination of one class by another on a hereditary basis? Gandhi agreed that the soul of Hinduism needed air; a wide sweep and frequent change. He however saw no apparent paradox in his own position. In his understanding, the caste system was a living institution;[23] an organic, unifying, and inclusive system that could divest itself of hierarchical ideologies. As regards the division of people into four and more water-tight compartments, they were fundamental, natural, and essential for the continuity of hereditary occupation, order, structure, human relationships, and for saving religion and culture from disintegration. Any rupture in their mutual interdependence would, inevitably, cause a major cataclysm within the macrocosm no less than the microcosm of Hinduism.

From this time on, Gandhi set out to right the ills without disturbing the relationship between caste Hindus and the untouchables. This could be done with the aid of the *Gita*, *ahimsa*, limiting the anti-untouchability operation to 'reforming Hinduism', and defending an indivisible Hinduism. In fact, he gave an astutely cultural and civilisational twist to what was palpably a political issue. He suggested improvement

---

21   FR (UP), Sept. 1932, Home Pol. File no 18/12, 1932.

22   Susan Billington Harper, *In the Shadow of the Mahatma*, p. 315.

23   *CWMG* (21 Feb. 1947-May 24, 1947), p. 303.

rather than digging up a system that had such deep roots and, as a self-governing social unit, performed legislative, executive, judicial, and other quasi-governmental functions. With the four stages *(ashramas)* in life—the student, the householder, the member of a community wider than one's family, and renouncer—useful and capable of world-wide application, he almost automatically assumed for himself the role of an arbiter of class-and caste-based disputes.

The question was whether or not he could debate the religious and cultural fault lines with Ambedkar. It was imperative that he did so. A breakup with the Dalit leader would have wrecked his and other people's reformist initiatives and, what is more, weakened the political and moral arguments against recognising Muslims as a separate and distinct community.[24] If they were entitled to preferential treatment, how could the Dalits be left out?

The conversations with Ambedkar were easy because Gandhi respected his intellectual rigour, commitment, integrity, and accomplishments at Columbia in New York, the London School of Economics, and the Bombay legislative council. They however disagreed with each other on fundamentals. Firstly, Gandhi fostered the cultural and moral autonomy, self-respect, and pride of various groups to cleanse society and change the social outlook of the upper castes,[25]and he was, therefore, sensitive to tradition, context, and culture. Ambedkar, by contrast, was not tied to context and tradition,[26] not regarding them to be the essential prerequisites for Dalit liberation. While elaborating his own theory of caste, he shaped new identities to emancipate the Dalits, and endow them with a separate, prestigious individuality deriving

---

24 Gandhi's biographer, Judith Brown, has written: 'The political implications of separate electorates were very important to him. Compounding separate electorates for Muslims, a similar concession to untouchables would shatter the united polity for which he had worked so long, and would cast Congress in the role of sectarian religious party rather than representative of an Indian nation. But he didn't want to publicize this dimension of the problem for he felt it would only exacerbate communal conflict.' Brown, *Gandhi: Prisoner of Hope*, p. 265.

25 Parekh, *Gandhi's Political Philosophy*, p. 211.

26 Valerian Rodrigues, 'Reading Texts and Tradition: The Ambedkar-Gandhi Debate', *EPW*, 8 Jan. 2011.

from the special status of Buddhism.[27] In this way, he became one of the only two social leaders in Maharashtra who resorted to conversion as a form of protest against the iniquities of caste society, the other being Pandita Ramabai Saraswati.

Conversion deeply disturbed Gandhi, but, interestingly enough, not Tagore. The poet's logic was that the Harijans' conversion to Sikhism or Buddhism will not necessarily mean neglecting or abandoning Hindu culture.[28]

Babasaheb wanted the ideology of Hinduism to be discarded in its entirety to undermine the traditional social order rather than idealise the caste system, eliminate the line of 'least social discord' and a 'voluntary change of heart', and uphold the principles of 'Liberty, Equality, and Fraternity'.[29]Without demonstrating any interest in preserving the traditional social equilibrium, he wanted to establish, once and for all, the irreversible principle of equality and social justice. Convinced that the philosophical framework of Hinduism embodying *avidya* and hierarchies would bring no redemption, he asked the Southborough Committee, on 27 January 1919, to recognise Dalits as distinct in various constitutional arrangements. Nearly a decade a later, he enjoined the Simon Commission to do the same.[30]

> We claim we must be treated as a distinct minority, separate from the Hindu community. There is really no link between the Hindus

---

27   Jaffrelot, *India's Silent Revolution*, p. 23.

28   Tagore to Mahadev Desai, 4 Jan. 1937, Alam and Chakravarty (eds), *The Essential Tagore*, p. 114.

29   'The religion which regards the recognition of man's self-respect as sin is not a religion but a sickness. The religion which allows one to touch [an] animal but not a man is not religion but madness. The religion which says that one class may not acquire wealth, may not take up arms, is not a religion but a mockery of man's life. The religion which teaches that the unlearned should remain unlearned, that the poor should remain poor is not a religion but a punishment.'

Collected *Works of B.R. Ambedkar* (Bombay, 1979), vol. 1, p. 93.

30   The Congress and other parties boycotted the Statutory Commission in Dec. 1927 because of its 'all-white' composition.

and the Depressed Classes. Therefore we must be regarded as a distinct and separate community. We deserve far greater political protection than any other minority in India because of our educational backwardness and economical and social barriers.[31]

By this time, Gandhi was pitted against two formidable adversaries: Ambedkar and Jinnah. As it transpired, both disputed his claim to represent them and demanded separate electorates, though for very different reasons. Both raised the cry of the tyranny of numbers. Jinnah's Fourteen Points, which challenged the provisions of the Nehru Report, demanded protection of Muslim majorities in the NWFP, Punjab, and Bengal; Ambedkar, too, demanded for Dalits, after so many generations of unemployment, penury, abjectness, and servility, power-sharing at a time when political authority was only just beginning to pass from the British into the hands of those wielding economic, social, and religious sway.[32] Political power was the only means by which Dalits and Muslims could bolster their position.[33]

It wasn't worth pursuing democracy, said Ambedkar, as an ideal in all circumstances and in all climes. Jinnah, too, interpreted democracy as majority rule, and insisted on safeguards for Muslims. Like Ambedkar, he feared that swaraj implied the tyranny of the 'majority'.[34] Ambedkar gave precedence to Dalit loyalty; he wasn't 'a part of the whole. I am a

---

31   Eleanor Zelliot, *From Untouchable to Dalit: Essays on the Ambedkar Movement* (New Delhi, 1996), pp. 150-78, and Ravinder Kumar, 'Gandhi, Ambedkar and the Poona Pact, 1932', in Jim Masselos (ed.), *Struggling and Ruling: The Indian National Congress, 1885-1985* (Delhi, 1985).

32   Sukhadeo Thorat and Narender Kumar (eds), *B.R. Ambedkar: Perspectives on Social Exclusion and Inclusive Policies* (Delhi, 2008), p. 134.

33   B.R. Ambedkar, *Thoughts on Pakistan* (Bombay, 1941), p. 59.

34   'This whole question of minority representation is really the crux of the whole situation, and if the majority community desire that all minorities should associate with them in having or in claiming a constitution which will give India what they call Dominion Status, or what we prefer to call Government by the people, for the people and in the name of the people, then I am afraid that the majority community must see to it that all fears of the minorities are set at rest.' Thorat and Kumar (eds.), *op. cit.*, p. 142.

part apart.'[35] Jinnah's notion of an exclusive and differentiated *qaum* ran along similar lines. While Gandhi identified a borrowing of symbols and ideas, a frequently shared vocabulary, and an interweaving of motifs within a common landscape, Jinnah advanced the 'two-nation' theory. Ambedkar agreed that Islam and Hinduism were mutually exclusive and at their core and centre irreconcilable. He surmised: 'There seems to be an inherent antagonism between the two which centuries have not been able to dissolve.'[36]

The convergence of ideas and interests are remarkably similar. Both held the belief that Gandhi's principal aim was to dissolve the Dalit-Muslim identity into the larger notion of the collective Hindu self. Ambedkar made it abundantly clear that even the worst of enemies wouldn't suspect Jinnah of being a tool in its hands. Both questioned the 'mad plan' of *mass contact*, which generated exasperation, bitterness, and hostility,[37] and underlined the gross misconduct of the Congress ministries.

Jawaharlal took cognizance of their bitter campaign and invited one of them—Jinnah—for talks on 4 November. Given their long-standing distrust, they were hardly in a position to break the ice. The two took to accusing each other of irresponsible conduct. 'Jinnah is completely and deliberately ranging himself on the side of reaction,' Jawaharlal stated publicly.[38] Jinnah, in fact, took the position of plenipotentiary on behalf of the Muslims by challenging the conception of an *Indian* nation; Ambedkar did the same on 1 September 1943.[39]

Jinnah hankered after a *Muslim* share of the cake; Ambedkar insisted on the Dalit portion. While joining Jinnah's call to celebrate the resignation of the Congress ministries,[40] the Dalit leader asserted that if

---

35   Ramashray Roy, *Gandhi and Ambedkar*, pp. 79-80.

36   Ambedkar, *Thoughts on Pakistan*, p. 332.

37   Ibid., p. 345.

38   23 Dec. 1939, *SWJN*, vol. 10, p. 416.

39   'The nation does not exist, it is to be created, and I think it will be admitted that the suppression of a distinct and separate community is not the method of creating a nation.'

40   Hasan (ed.), *TF*, 1939 (pt 2), pp. 1826, 1830.

the Qaid proved 5 out of 100 cases of alleged oppression, he'd prove 100 out of 100 cases before an impartial tribunal. Jawaharlal made known, sadly, that some of his statements beat that of Jinnah in distortion and exaggeration.[41] It is needless to say that their fundamental contention remained unproved and questionable. Consequently, they were vitiated from the very outset.

The Epic Fast

It is averred that the Communal Award, if accepted, would have turned Hindu society upside down. This is a highly doubtful proposition. Indeed, had Gandhi accepted the award, he would have lowered the communal temperature and also to a certain degree empowered the Dalits. Fittingly, Ambedkar maintained that power emanated from elections, and their outcome depended on numbers. This being the case, Dalits were more likely to derive full advantage with separate electorates. He therefore discarded Gandhi's assumptions as unwarranted, arguing that separate electorates would cancel total dependence on the sweet will of caste Hindus in matters affecting his constituency's destiny.

'God was never nearer to me than during the fast,' Gandhi disclosed to Horace Alexander.[42] He wanted, among other things, an atmosphere of trust between the depressed classes and the so-called caste Hindus, arouse the conscience of upper caste Hindus, and sensitise them to their wrongs vis-a-vis the Dalits. At the same time, he had no intention of polarising caste sentiments, for his notion of stability in the social arrangements in Hindu society, which had fallen in place over the centuries and needed to be defended, militated against this project. For one, he ruled out violence as a recipe for disaster.

This stance appears to be consistent with what he said in the context of the government's repression in 1919. He allied himself with the weak to make them feel strong and capable of defying the physical might. He wanted them to regain self-confidence and know that the remedy lay

---

41   To Krishna Menon, 21 Dec. 1939, SWJN, vol. 10, p. 414.

42   For some of Alexander's impressions, see Alexander, Gandhi Through Western Eyes, pp. 52, 87, 91, 116, 120, 161, 172, 197.

with them to redress the wrong.[43] Ambedkar, pushed into a corner by Gandhi's fast, dismissed as hollow the suggestion of generosity radiating from some of his statements.[44] He however sensed that Gandhi's martyrdom would trigger upper caste reprisals. Under the circumstances, he had no choice but to yield. He was swimming against the enormous tide of human passion generated by Gandhi's fast. Sudhir Chandra, the historian, adds: 'Gandhi's life saved, caste Hindus returned to their somnolence, not heeding his pathetic exhortation—if the spirit of the Yervada Pact wasn't adhered to.'[45] Meanwhile, newspapers highlighted, in long quotations, the responsibility of caste Hindus to end all social and religious disabilities for untouchables and editorial homilies about the lesson that had emerged for India from the confrontation.[46]

In December 1932, the Bombay government reported that 'orthodox Hindus' were lining up against the anti-untouchability campaign. Therefore, 'the new line of activity doesn't so far appear to be increasing the influence of the Congress or providing a stimulus to its waning activities.'[47] If this assessment is correct, it is fair to assume that Gandhi wouldn't have wanted to stiffen upper caste opposition to the eradication of untouchability or make his position vulnerable. Even the Guruvayur temple in Malabar refused to permit entry to untouchables, although almost everyone knew that Gandhi seriously intended to go on a fast unto death for that purpose. Rajaji's visit to Conjeeveram resulted in a

---

43   12 May 1929, Iyer (ed.), *The Essential Writings of Mahatma Gandhi*, p. 47. 'The newness in their situation was that, rather than dying out during their newly acquired freedom, their persecution became more and more pronounced.' M. K. Gandhi, *Delhi Diary: Prayer Speeches from 10.9.47 to 30.1. 48* (Ahmedabad, 1948), pp. 201-2.

44   'If a man cannot be convinced by argument that he has done wrong, he is not likely to be converted by his friend starting a fast … Gautam Buddha tried fasting as a means of enlightenment and miserably failed', Hasan (ed.), 11 Mar. 1939, *TF*, 1939 (pt 1), p. 665.

45   Sudhir Chandra, 'Gandhi's Twin Fasts and the Possibility of Non-violence', *EPW*, 4 June 2011. Notice Henry Polak's exaggerated view that 'Gandhi has given untouchability a smashing blow, from which it can never recover.' Alexander, *Gandhi Through Western Eyes*, p. 88.

46   Milton Israel, *Communications and Power: Propaganda and the press in the Indian nationalist struggle, 1920-1947*, p. 177.

47   FR (Bombay), Dec. 1932, Home Pol. file no. 18/15, 1932.

rebuff over the use of a public tank. Already, murmurs were heard in certain quarters about Gandhi's leadership, and the efficacy of his goals. He conceded, on 17 September 1934, that his method and approach was different from that of others, and that he would have been untrue to himself had he not withdrawn the civil resistance struggle in order to embark upon the fast against separate electorates.[48]

In short, Gandhi has lost rather than gained in present-day re-evaluations. His arguments against separate electorates for the Dalits weakened his concern for them.[49] Critics argue that by calling them Harijans and preaching intangible reform of Hindu society, he succeeded in keeping them within the Hindu fold. Untouchability persists and the Harijans are still brutalised by, mostly the upper castes. At times, the OBCs (Other Backward Castes) also join in the fun. The rural-based projects, which were expected to aid their progress, have been irretrievably damaged by an elitist conception of planning, heavy industrialisation, technology, and environmental degradation. Today, the growing unrest in large parts of Orissa, Andhra Pradesh, and Bihar is due to insufficient land reforms. Academically, the spinning wheel remains central to an understanding of nation formation, visual political rhetoric, and the role of symbolism in political cultures,[50] but it has, for all practical purposes, faded from the popular visual imagery of Gandhi and moved to the periphery of the political spectrum.

Nonetheless, Gandhi's modus operandi contributed to the awakening in the justness of his cause. Considerable activity against untouchability followed in many districts.[51] In Nagpur and Akola, caste Hindus visited depressed quarters, swept the streets, and bathed the children.[52] In Delhi, local temples were thrown open.[53] No single argument but the combined moral, religious, and political arguments worked at

---

48   Tendulkar, *Mahatma*, vol., 3, p. 297.

49   V. Geetha, 'Periyar, Women an Ethic of Citizenship', in Mary John (ed.), *Women's Studies in India*, p. 135.

50   Brown, *Gandhi's Spinning Wheel*, p. 116.

51   FR (Madras), Dec. 1932, Home Pol., file no. 18/15, 1932.

52   FR (Central Provinces & Berar), ibid.

53   FR (Delhi), ibid.

different times to bring about a change of heart. After Independence, political parties have attended to both Gandhi and Ambedkar without necessarily pitching their perspectives diametrically in opposition to each other. Attempts are, in fact, underway to recast their relationship as a dialogic exchange between the two idioms of non-European cosmopolitanism: *non-violence* as hybridised Hindu life-practice, and *democratic* development as a non-hierarchical Buddhist orientation to life. Therefore, NGOs, voluntary organisations, peace and social bodies count both Gandhi and Ambedkar as progenitors whose ideas inspired them.[54] This being the case, it may be useful to keep the dialogue open in order to achieve 'a synthesis of Ambedkar and Gandhi'.

I may recount, in concluding this section, that Gandhi, despite having frittered away some of the gains of the popular ferment, enjoyed undisputed power and authority in his party. Even though Muslims nursed a grudge against him, and Ansari whined that he hadn't done enough to restore communal amity,[55] he kindled in men and women high hopes of a new battle and a new victory. As a man of his time who asked the deepest questions, even though he couldn't answer them, he became a man for all times and all places.[56] Some officials, too, appreciated the values he stood for. H.A.N. Barlow reported from Lucknow: 'There is no doubt in my mind that he is a great man however much I may disagree with him.'[57]

On 19 May 1934, Gandhi dedicated his walking tour through Orissa to the eradication of untouchability. He and M.R. Masani, the young socialist, set out around 5 a.m. and walked for about four miles to the next village, the stop of the day. Just before sunset, they started walking again through the twilight and camped in another village, not too distant, about four miles away.[58] Describing an incident in one of the villages, Mirabehn observed:

---

54   L.I. Rudolph and S.H. Rudolph, *Postmodern Gandhi and Other Essays: Gandhi in the World and at Home* (Chicago, 2006), p. 34; David Hardiman, *Gandhi and His Times and Ours*, Nagaraj, *The Flaming Feet and Other Essays*, p. 80.

55   Ansari to Gandhi, n.d., Ansari collection, The Nehru Memorial Museum & Library (NMML).

56   Brown, *Gandhi: Prisoner of Hope*, p. 394.

57   11 Oct. 1931, Barlow papers.

58   Masani, *Bliss was it in that Dawn*, p. 56.

The evening march is in progress. All along the way, lines of eager villagers are standing, waiting across the road for Gandhiji's arrival. Here is an extra big crowd and they have spread across the road. A dear old woman, with white hair and her eyes dimmed with age, suddenly rushes hither and thither and amongst the people. 'Where is he? Where is he? I must see him.' In her agitation she is about to miss him, when Gandhiji, noticing her distress, stops and calls her. 'Well, well,' says Gandhiji laughingly, and putting his hand under her chin. 'Can you now see my face properly?' Her joy knew no bounds, and twining her arm around his neck, she lays her head on his breast and is lost in bliss. He gently disengages her arms, she passes back into the crowd as one in a dream, but the light remains with her, illuminating her aged face.[59]

Gandhi's statement on 17 September 1934, which was more in the nature of a political manifesto, followed by his retirement from Congress affairs, didn't signal his defeat. On 28 October, the last day of the Congress session in Bombay, 'the entire audience of 80,000 stood up to a man to show their respect to the great leader'. When the session concluded, he made it clear that, 'no one will think that the *khaddar* clause and the labour franchise do not come into operation. They do.'[60] As 'a penance for the negligence', he introduced amendments to the Congress constitution. They made the intention of the great leader very clear. Rajendra Prasad, the president, accordingly set out the Congress goal:

The method is crystal clear. It is active dynamic non-violent mass action. We may fail once, we may fail twice, but we are bound to succeed some day. Many have lost their lives and all. Many more have sacrificed themselves in their struggle for freedom. Let us not be deterred by the difficulties which confront us nor diverted from our straight course by fear or favour. Our weapons are unique and the world is watching the progress of great experiment with interest and high expectation.[61]

---

59   Tendulkar, *Mahatma*, vol. 3, p 272.

60   Ibid., p. 304, and for the khaddar clause, p. 300.

61   Ibid., p. 302.

The Princes' Remedy

'Whatever may be said to the contrary,' Gandhi wrote in mid-December 1939, 'I must continue to claim to be a friend, a well wisher of the princes.'[62] Elsewhere, he referred to the policy advocated by some towards the states: 'I have given many an anxious hour to the question, but I have not been able to alter my view.'[63] But the quick turn of events, which the socialists and communists backed, led to a proactive drive.

'Just as we were about to go up the hills,' a disappointed H.A.N. Barlow informed his parents in England, 'Gandhi has chosen to interfere in one of our states: Talcher, where the Raja was on weak ground and his subjects had much to complain of. He has wired to the viceroy, and stirred up a hornet's nest ...'[64] A decade or so earlier, Gandhi had been reluctant to interfere in any of the 700 princely houses which covered nearly a third of the Indian territory and almost two-fifths of the population within their borders. Among them seventy-three of their princes received eleven gun salutes. Hyderabad, the largest state, had an area of 82,698 sq. m. and a population of 13.5 million. It had a Muslim ruler. Kashmir had a Dogra ruler; the state covered 84,238 sq. m. Speaking generally, the princes were potentates of the old Oriental type—lazy, luxurious, reactionary, and veritable exploiters.[65] The government, in league with the feudal and conservative elements, bolstered their prestige and used their troops to quell revolts against them. This is why 'Princely India', a distinction which was as superficial as any other category invented by the colonial ethnographers, had remained largely insulated from the political turmoil that had gripped the other regions.

Gandhi believed in reformation and modification in consonance with the true spirit of democracy. He hoped the changes taking place in

---

62   *Harijan*, 16 Dec. 1939, *CWMG* (1 Dec. 1939-15 Apr. 1940), p. 24.

63   Tendulkar, *Mahatma*, vol. 3, p. 297.

64   23 Apr. 1939, Barlow papers.

65   For the princely states and the thorny issue of their integration, Ian Copland, *The Princes of India in the Endgame of Empire, 1917-1947* (Cambridge, 1999); Robin Jeffrey (ed.), *People, Princes and Paramount Power: Society and Politics in the Indian Princely States* (New Delhi, 1978); Barbara N. Ramusack, *The Princes of India in the Twilight of Empire: Dissolution of a Patron-Client System, 1914-1939* (New York, 1978).

British India would impact the princely states. Curiously, he was more concerned with India's dismemberment than the prince's autocracy. If, for certain purposes and in certain contexts, he supported democracy, he didn't commit himself to popular or representative government in the princely states. In line with aspects of traditional thought, which turn to inner virtue rather than institutional restraints as the guarantor of public morality, he engaged with the personal debauchery of princes, where it existed, rather than with their failure to grant political liberty.

The Congress didn't get embroiled with the local vagaries of the states, with Gandhi defending its limited capacity to intervene.[66] Although he put in train the Vaikom Satyagraha of 1924-5 against the ban on the lower castes using the roads near Vaikom temple, he didn't, despite demands from various quarters, stir up a hornet's nest. He watched over this as a perfect piece of statesmanship: 'that part of India which is described as British has no more power to shape the policy of the states than it has [say] that of Afghanistan or Ceylon'. In all probability, he felt that foreign autocracy was more reprehensible than its indigenous counterpart.

In Mysore, the nationalist zealots tried in vain to develop some form of tie-up with the Karnataka Provincial Congress in Bombay Presidency to which Mysore was formally attached.[67] In reality, neither Gandhi nor the Congress could insulate the princely states from the political currents elsewhere. The All-India States People's Conference was formed in 1927, and even though C. Y. Chintamani and Ram Chandra Rao, former chief minister of Mysore, kept it dormant, words like Satyagraha, *ahimsa*, and khadi were placed firmly in their vocabulary.[68] Jawaharlal declared the states to be anachronistic and not deserving to exist.[69] Gandhi envisaged, as in Aundh, a place for states with princes

---

66   Gandhi, *The Indian states problem*, p. 92.

67   James Manor, 'Gandhian Politics and the Challenge to Princely Authority in Mysore, 1936-47', in D.A. Low (ed.), *Congress and the Raj: Facets of the Indian Struggle, 1917-1947* (New Delhi, 1977), p. 411.

68   Robin Jeffrey, 'A Sanctified Label—"Congress", in Travancore Politics, 1938-48', ibid., p. 446.

69   Gopal (ed.), *SWJN*, vol. 9, pp. 418-19.

as constitutional trustees.[70] In Travancore, however, he wanted the state Congress to concentrate not so much on the dethronement of the dewan as on getting the reins of power into its hands.

Spurred into action by the expectation of a federation which would include delegates from the states, the Congress changed its course around 1936, a year after the Act of 1935 came into effect. In 1938, it set up a committee of the princes on certain conditions. The reason was simple enough: as long as they were autocratic, their nominees could be counted upon to support a conservative standpoint in the federal legislature. Faced with a combination of such delegates and other elements, the Congress could expect to be in a minority. But, by devoting greater attention to the freedom movement in the princely states, it hoped to soften or neutralise, if not capture, the prince's representatives. In the event, the princes couldn't make up their minds to join the federation, and a federal legislature didn't meet. N.G. Gore summed up the strategy:

> Once the rulers decided to join the Federation, the Imperialist-Federal axis will be still more strengthened. To counter its influence we must forge a parallel axis, the Congress-State people. And as that axis already exists the only question is that of cementing and reinforcing it. We can do so if instead of fixing our gaze on Delhi and wasting our time on calculations as to the possible outcome of Gandhi-Linlithgow confabulations, we prepare to strike at the root, viz., the Act of 1935.

Even though Gandhi justified non-intervention,[71] he couldn't close his eyes to the awakening in the states. While claiming to be their friend ('their service has been an heirloom in my family for the past three generations'), he had to back the people's urges to the extent of commenting on repression in Travancore, reviewing the reforms in Aundh, and guiding the Jaipur Praja Mandal (Jaipur People's Society). Moreover, as 1938 ended, the occurrence in Rajkot led to the change of

---

70   *Harijan*, 18 Feb. 1939, Gandhi, *The Indian states problem*, p. 168.

71   Ibid., p. 79.

heart, vis-à-vis the people's struggle. In consequence, the post-Haripura struggle began with Gandhi succinctly placing his engagement:

> The policy of non-intervention by the Congress was ... a perfect piece of statesmanship when the people of the States were not awakened. That policy would be cowardice when there is all-around awakening among the people of the States and a determination to go through a long course of suffering for the vindication of their just rights.[72]

As the year passed into history, India stood on the threshold of 1939: 'the movement for freedom gathers pace, and the whole of India looks with sympathy and understanding on this great struggle in the States,' announced Jawaharlal at the All-India States' Peoples' Conference in February 1939.[73] As is clear by now, some of the princely states developed complex 'national' feelings and a political nationalism of the kind in most parts of 'British India'. They tended to express their aspirations through the Kisan Sabhas and other bodies, whose character was certainly affected and partly transformed by them. They energised many sections of the population in Travancore, Rajkot, Jaipur, Hyderabad, and certain states of Orissa. In state after state it was the same story of 'fiendish cruelty exercised by the State myrmidons under the shadow of the police supplied by the Paramount Power'. Talcher and Dhenkanal led the way to repression. Sneering at the doctrine of 'kicks and kisses', Gandhi wanted ministers to assume moral responsibility towards the people. He felt they were morally bound to take note of the gross misrule.[74] This was an instance, if ever one was needed, of a leader responding to and adapting his strategy to the changing political landscape. When some people resented his stand on the arrest of Jamnalal Bajaj, Gandhi replied: 'There has been a gradual evolution in my environment and I react to it as a satyagrahi.'[75]

---

72 *Harijan*, 14 Jan. 1939, Gandhi, *The Indian states problem*, p. 133.

73 Nehru, *The Unity of India*, p. 27.

74 *Harijan*, 3 Dec. 1938, *CWMG*, vol. 68, p. 153.

75 *Times of India*, 25 Jan. 1939, ibid., p. 327.

Rajkot had for Gandhi a personal touch about it. He had lived in the city for nearly 13 years (till 1988), and his father had served as dewan from 1875 to 1881. Kasturba was brought up in Rajkot though born in Porbandar, and Jamnalal Bajaj, close friend and financier, belonged there. Once Kasturba heard of Maniben's arrest, she rushed to Rajkot: Gandhi hoped that posterity would recognise her role.[76] They were reacting to a cold blooded breach of a solemn covenant between the Rajkot ruler and his subjects. All hell broke loose once Gandhi embarked on a fast on 3 March 1939 to bring about a change of Thakore Saheb's heart. He defended his stand by pointing out that, 'my words and deeds are dictated by prevailing conditions'. He described 'every Indian Prince [as] a Hitler in his own state'.[77]

Suddenly, Rajkot, the hub of Kathiawar, became the hub of the world. Gandhi met the viceroy and pressed every point in connection with an agreement which he thought he had the least chance of success.[78] When asked if he'd gained anything, he responded with, 'the letter killeth; the spirit gives life'. He conceded that a false step taken by him during the fast had thwarted the brilliant result he had expected to achieve.[79] The fact is that, on 25 April 1939, his efforts to settle the constitution of the Reforms Committeee failed, and that Durbar Shri Virawala had outwitted him. 'I have left Rajkot empty handed', he conceded, 'with my body shattered and hope cremated.' At the same time, the Rajkot Satyagraha boosted nationalist activity in Kathiawar (called Saurashtra after Independence).[80]

After Rajkot, the wheel turned full circle. Now, Gandhi wrote more and more about the changing situation in Travancore, about the thousands of refugees in Talcher, Orissa, for which he relied on the reports of Harekrushna Mahtab and Thakkar Baba, about violence in Ramdurg and Jaipur prisoners, and other princely states. It would

---

76   *Harijan*, 11 Mar. 1939, *CWMG*, vol. 68, p. 153.

77   Ibid., 14 Jan. 1939, ibid., p. 115.

78   Linlithgow to Hallet, n.d., *TF*, 1939 (pt 1), p. 673.

79   *Harijan*, 11 Mar. 1939, Gandhi, *Indian States' Problem*, p. 228.

80   John Wood, in Robin Jeffrey (ed.), *People, Princes and Paramount Power*, p. 269.

appear that until his involvement in Jaipur, Gandhi had very little idea of the enormity of oppression and exploitation there and elsewhere. He didn't therefore take the risk of disturbing the apple cart. However, once he became conscious of the bitter realities in the Kathiawar region, as also in other princely states, he took up the cudgel on their behalf.

As for Jaipur, Gandhi made clear that his party wouldn't let the people 'die of mental and moral starvation'. Even though the Praja Mandal was banned, Gandhi announced that the states' people 'cannot be in chains and what is called British India becomes free.'[81] Similarly, he spoke against repression in Travancore, but advised the freedom fighters not to let the seeds of disunity to grow.

If, for certain purposes and in certain contexts, Gandhi supported democracy, he did so without any commitment to popular government. In 1938, he spoke of constructive service without outlining any ambitious political objective.[82] Jawaharlal and his leftist colleagues nonetheless welcomed this as a field of action.[83]

Rajkot was a success story. Nevertheless, Willingdon, who presided over the Indian summer of British rule, refused to climb down. Linlithgow, governor-general from 1936 to 1943, fared no better. 'With his unwieldy frame, triple chin and ponderous dignity', commented a young Indian civil servant, Linlithgow, known to his friends as 'Hopie', personified an expiring imperialism which had outlived whatever purpose it might have had in the past.[84]

Ignoring the man who was imposing in stature but aloof in bearing, Gandhi moved from strength to strength. As in 1920, he mobilised supporters to nip in the bud the subversive tendencies. 'Authoritarianism has at last secured', Independent India commented, 'pseudo-democratic sanction.'[85] Bose became unacceptable owing to his defiant stance

---

81   *Harijan*, 4 Feb. 1939, op. cit., p. 203.

82   Gandhi, *The Indian states problem*, p. 93.

83   Gopal, *Jawaharlal Nehru: A Biography*, vol. 1, pp. 254-5.

84   K.P.S. Menon, *Many Worlds: An Autobiography* (London, 1965), p. 263.

85   *Independent India*, 19 Mar. 1939, Hasan (ed.), *TF,* 1939 (pt 2), p. 1265.

towards Gandhi.[86] His mighty fall on 29 April 1939 brought relief to the Gandhians, but not to an outraged Bengal. Sentiments ran high and Bose 'has become not only the hero of the new drama but the martyr as well.'[87]

The Tripuri Congress established, beyond doubt, Gandhi's political hegemony. In reality however there was one other serious challenge to his ethical or idealistic imperatives in political life. It emanated not from a *maulvi* or a theologian but from a barrister trained at Lincoln's Inn. The outcomes were markedly different: Ambedkar agreed to be co-opted by the Indian Union, whereas Mohammad Ali Jinnah resolutely refused to turn back and chose, instead, to join the trek to Pakistan.

86   Taya Zinkin, *Reporting India* (London, 1962), p. 217.

87   Amrendra Nath to Roy, 19 Aug. 1939, Hasan (ed.), *TF,* 1939 (pt 2), p. 1712.

Section III

Gandhi with Jinnah, c. 1943

9
Gandhi, Islam and the Nation

You see, Sir, that in this enlightened age I am bold enough to confess, that we are generally men of untaught feelings; that instead of casting away all our old prejudices, we cherish them to a very considerable degree, and, to take more shame to ourselves, we cherish them because they are prejudices; and the longer they have lasted, and the more generally they have prevailed, the more we cherish them. We are afraid to put men to live and trade each on his own private stock of reason; because we suspect that this stock in each man is small, and that the individuals would do better to avail themselves of the general bank and capital of nations and of ages. Many of our men of speculation, instead of exploding general prejudices, employ their sagacity to discover the latent wisdom which prevails in them. If they find what they seek, and they seldom fail, they think it more wise to continue the prejudice, with the reason involved, than to cast away the coat of prejudice, and to leave nothing but the naked reason; because prejudice, with its reason, has a motive to give action to that reason, and an affection which will give it permanence.

- Edmund Burke, *Reflections on the Revolution in France.*

As one who does not see the world through the prism of faith and commitment, I approach identity, history, belief, culture and social mores from a secularised, if not 'secular' position, and underline that Muslim identity should not be reduced to a mere rationalisation of normative Islamic discourse. I had argued in *Legacy of a Divided Nation: India's Muslims Since Independence* (1997) that being a Muslim is just one of several competing identities for any individual; that there has never been a homogeneous 'Muslim India', whether in doctrine, custom, language or political loyalty; and that to make the most of their potential, Muslims should hold firmly to the idea of a society committed to social justice and freedom.

Tracing the roots of communal (I don't use it in a pejorative sense) consciousness is a legitimate exercise, but it is equally important not to lose sight of the significant variations in its articulation, mode of expression, and manifestation. Besides, we'll do well to take note of the vital differences in the consciousness of the *ashraf* (high born) and the *ajlaf* (low born), a fact conveniently ignored by the proponents of the two-nation theory. These categories (notice the recent demand of Dalit Muslims for reservations) illustrate the great social and cultural divide that could not be bridged by the likes of Altaf Husain Hali, Mohammad Iqbal, and Jinnah.

In my more recent book *Moderate or Militant: Images of India's Muslims* (2008), I offer a bird's eye view of the many different traditions within the broad sweep of Islam across the length and breadth of South Asia: from pan-Islamism to Socialism, from an appeal to nationalism to an equally rousing call for Unitarian Islam, and from sectarianism to Sufism. Here you have a picture of the many Islams. But those who thought in communitarian terms or political representation did not understand the people of whom they wrote, and, for this reason, they falsified them with trappings of make-believe. They misled the poor Muslims into believing that they had been the 'rulers', and that the resurgence of Islam would answer their dilemmas and predicaments.

In this chapter, I analyse Gandhi's engagement with and developing attitudes towards 'Muslim Nationalism', Islam, various Muslims leaders, politicians and intellectuals (going back to his days in South Africa). I also discuss their character, sources of influences and intellectual background.

As I have already suggested with regard to the general approach of the book, this makes history far more vivid. More importantly, it helps to better understand Gandhi's limited (or specific) understanding of Islam, and how his approach (during the Khilafat) later 'led him to a dead end'. It also forms a new vantage point for my discussion on Gandhi and religion more broadly; and Gandhi's own prejudices about Hindus and Muslims. These discussions ultimately make up the core of the narrative.

When he was forty years old, the son of Abdullah and a merchant for decades announced his prophethood and preached the exclusive worship of a single, transcendent God. He sermonised on justice and equality in a tribal society, discouraged slavery, raised women's status, and recognised differences only on the basis of piety and

God-fearing.[1] Mohammad Ali, the Khilafat leader, broadcast that Islam alone bases itself on a great religious principle, obedience to the will of God.[2] With *umma* or brotherhood as 'a single hand, like a compact whose bricks support each other', Mohammad, the Prophet, left no room for distinctions of birth, ranks, and hierarchies.

The diffusion of the message continued with greater or less speed. Colonies of Muslim merchants existed at trading depots on the shores of the Indian Ocean. Islam spread from Zayla (a port situated opposite Aden) in the twelfth century; in sub-Saharan West Africa, almost two centuries earlier.[3] Muslims arrived in South Africa from 1658 onward as a coincidence of geography, colonisation, slavery, and the geopolitics of mercantile commerce. As early as 1725, holy men, mostly convicts, provided the core of the Cape's early ulama and also much of the genetic stock until the twentieth century. In the late-nineteenth century, Mirza Abu Taleb Khan met a number of Muslims who had hired lodgings in 'the house of worthy Mussulmans'.[4] Cape Town had its own share of mosques and religious publications. Separated by geography, doctrine, class, history, and language from the Natal, Indian Muslims, until well into the twentieth century, spoke Creole, Dutch, or Afrikaans.

The introduction of Islam to Natal came through the migration of indentured labourers from India during the 1880s, with a second, larger, movement following from the 1870s onwards. Between 1860 and 1868, and again from 1874 to 1911, some 176,000 Indians of all faiths were brought to Natal. Approximately 7 to 10 per cent of the

---

1   'O ye folk, verily we have created you of male and female ... Verily the most honourable of you in the sight of God is the most pious of you,' says the Quran.

2   H.G. Alexander, *The Indian Ferment: A Traveller's Tale* (London, n.d.), p. 207.

3   Based on *Encyclopaedia of Islam*, new edn, vol. 4, pp. 172-73; Nehemia Levtzion and Randall L. Pouwels (eds), *The History of Islam in Africa* (Ohio, 2000); Brent Singleton, '"That Ye May Know Each Other": Late Victorian Interactions between British and West African Muslims', *Journal of Minority Affairs*, vol. 29, no. 3, Sept. 2009.

4   Mirza Abu Taleb, *Westward Bound: Travels of Mirza Abu Taleb*, trans. Charles Stewart, Mushirul Hasan (ed.), *Exploring the West: Three Travel Narratives* (Delhi, 2009), p. 27.

first shipment was Muslim; then 80 to 90 per cent of the second, but smaller, shipments (termed Passenger Indians, because they paid their fares) were Muslim. They spoke Urdu, Gujarati, Tamil, Sindhi, and English, and their congregations were based on powerful mosque committees dominated by merchants. Of them, most were labourers, but a powerful stratum of commercial elite also developed in northern Natal and the Transvaal. Abdullah Haji Adam and two others managed Dada Abdullah & Company. Abu Bakr Amod Jhaveri, the first passenger merchant to reach Natal, owned a company in Durban; after his death, it was renamed Tayob Haji Khan Abdullah & Co. There were others too, notably Ahmad Mohammad Cachalia, chairperson of the British India Association, and Haji Mahomed Haji Dada, all firmly linked from the Natal coast to the interior of the colony and into Transvaal.[5]

Let us now see, very briefly, how the old maritime trade between southern Arabia and south India brought into being the oldest Muslim communities. With the first stage of incursion beginning in north India towards the year 1000, Islam spread to Malaya (now Malaysia) and the islands of Sumatra, Java, and Borneo. Following Mahmud Ghazni's saga of his plundering Somnath temple, in great part apocryphal,[6] the Turks, the Afghans, and the Lodis retained their hegemony until Zahiruddin Mohammad Babur captured Delhi in 1526 and his grandson Jalaluddin Mohammad Akbar (1556-1605) built an enormous imperial apparatus. The empire was however brought to its knees by military adventurism, by the deepening agrarian crisis, by Aurangzeb's religious policy, and by the intense competition between the old and new elites to share the economic surplus.[7] As a consequence of a new age of soldiers and machines,

---

5   Robert Ross, *A Concise History of South Africa* (Cambridge, 1999), p. 46; Robert C.H. Shell, 'Islam in Southern Africa', in Levtzion and Pouwels (eds), *The History of Islam in Africa*, pp. 339, 340; James Kritzeck and William H. Lewis (eds), *Islam in Africa* (New York, 1968); Mervyn Hiskett, *The Course of Islam in Africa* (Edinburgh, 1994); Maureen Swan, *Gandhi: The South African Experience* (Johannesburg, 1985), p. 8.

6   Romila Thapar, *Somanatha: The Many Voices of a History* (Delhi, 2004).

7   Andrea Hintze, *The Mughal Empire and Its Decline: An Interpretation of the Sources of Social Power* (Ashgate, 1997), p. 271.

the EIC inherited the mantle from Bahadur Shah Zafar, the last Mughal *padshah* (emperor). The event in its entirety disturbed the social equilibrium, without undermining the resilience of cultural and linguistic identities. Adequately equipped, through its own light, Islam penetrated the hearts of men.

'There is no compulsion in religion: the right way is indeed clearly distinct from error,' says the Quran. It built, accordingly, the foundation for the principle of tolerance.[8] It considered the force of arms to be powerless when matched against the force of love or the soul. The Sufis integrated specific Hindu doctrines but also sometimes, if not always, contested the existing orthodoxies. They pleaded that conflicting phenomena be blended even when the balance in inter-community relationships turned awry.[9] Faqirs and yogis lived almost the same kind of life, illustrating one aspect of the pluralist inheritance, a capital accumulated over centuries, devolving downwards to become part of everyday culture.[10]

The converts to Islam often carried with them Hindu/Buddhist practices into their new faith. Apart from being divided into endogamous sections, their panchayats exercised much the same powers as did the Hindu castes. Some didn't allow widow remarriage, refrained from eating beef, worshipped Hindu deities, as in Mewat,

---

8   'Abuse not those whom they call upon besides Allah, lest, exceeding the limits, they abuse Allah through ignorance. Thus to every people have We made their deeds fairseeming; then to their Lord is their return so He will inform them of what they did.' Regardless of what others thought, Gandhi contended that Islam spread rapidly because of its simplicity and its virtue of regarding all as equals.

9   Muzaffar Alam, *The Languages of Political Islam India: 1200-1800* (Delhi, 2004), p. 110.

10   This despite the zealots who pressed their own respective versions of Islam and Hinduism, or for that matter, the colonial notion of India's enduring Hindu-Muslim division, and of 'history' as a validation for one's actions in the present. Metcalf, *Ideologies of the Raj*, p. 155. On the interaction between different traditions, Susan Bayly, *Saints, Goddesses and Kings: Muslims and Christians in South Indian Society, 1700-1900* (Cambridge, 1989). Arguably, Tipu Sultan's assertion of his identity as an Islamic ruler took place against the background of, and in harmony with, south India's syncretism. Kate Brittlebank, *Tipu Sultan's Search for Legitimacy: Islam and Kingship in a Hindu Domain* (Delhi, 1995), p. 154.

and took a dip in the sacred Ganges on designated dates.[11] *Pirs* had Hindu disciples, Hindu yogis had Muslim *chelas*. Rishis in Kashmir drew heavily from the Buddhist-Brahmanical traditions, including vegetarianism. At Girot in Punjab, Hindus and Muslims alike venerated the tombs of two ascetics, Jamali Sultan and Diyal Bhawan.[12] In medieval Maharashtra, Hindu-Muslim symbiotic relations are found in the sphere of law. Besides, some of the poet-saints were canonised as great saints by Hindus on account of their contributions to the Bhakti traditions. While staying within the framework of the monotheistic concepts, they accommodated gods of the Hindu pantheon as they conformed to their conception of God as devoid of definable attributes, indistinct, and being a single entity.[13]

The *Hir-Ranjha* narrative was part of a vernacular literary tradition participated in by poets of all religions. Such texts were employed for a discourse on piety that wasn't, at the levels of either production or consumption, limited to Muslims alone.[14] Observing Muharram was a shared tradition, both in urban and rural areas. Urdu poetry became not only a symbolic escape from various forms of orthodoxies and rigidities, but it also constitutes a much cherished cultural and inspirational space for the layout of twentieth-century Urdu progressive literature.[15]

The French philologist and historian, Joseph Ernest Renan, described a nation as a living soul; a spiritual principle. Two things constituted this soul. One was the past, the other the present: one is the common possession of a rich heritage of memories; the other the actual consent, the desire to live together, the will to preserve worthily the undivided inheritance. This intricate process was at times and in certain places tense and conflict-ridden; yet, epistemological pluralism offered

---

11   Sir Edward Blunt, *Social Service in India*, p. 57.

12   Valerian Rodrigues (ed.), *The Essential Writings of Ambedkar*, pp. 462-3.

13   N.K. Wagle, 'Hindu-Muslim Interactions in Medieval Maharashtra', in Günther-Dietz Sontheimer and Hermann Kulke (eds), *Hinduism Reconsidered* (Delhi, 2001), p. 145.

14   Farina Mir, *The Social Space of Language: Vernacular Culture in British Colonial Punjab* (Delhi, 2010), pp. 180, 181.

15   Syed Akbar Hyder, 'Ghalib and His Interlocutors', in Bhagavan (ed.), *Heterotopias*, p. 101.

the key to diverse social groups and classes to remain committed to common rules and, above all, to mutual tolerance and mental respect as the binding value-based consensus. In each case, the *watan* or the *bhoomi* emerged refreshed 'as one would rise out of a hot bath with a warm glow'.

A variety of images are associated with Gandhi, but there is one which so few can dispute: his love for the *Gita* and his great pride in being a staunch *sanathani* Hindu. This pride couldn't possibly leave him, not even when an assassin's bullet killed him almost instantaneously. Spontaneously, the cry of *'He Ram'* went out not once, not twice, but three times.[16] This is not in the least surprising, for there was never any ambiguity in Gandhi's grasp of the existential content of the Vedas, 'a boundless ocean teeming with priceless gems'. He strove, with his abiding faith in *atman* and in its immortality, for *moksha*, the central principle of Hinduism.[17] He brought up to date a missionary friend by telling him to watch his life: how he lived, ate, sat, spoke, and behaved in general.[18] The Hindu world is like a sea. All refuse that finds its way into its bosom gets purified.[19] It looks upon all without distinctions.

Gandhi considered all religions equally good, for they teach the very same truth, and point to the very same goal: the spiritual regeneration of man. The method of worship was important to him, but the spiritual force of a religion counted more and its power to uplift the soul and to transform the man. 'Our temple is in our ashram,' Gandhi cited from Kabir, 'nay it is in our hearts. A temple constructed of a few stones has no meaning. Only a temple raised in our hearts is useful.'[20] The Quran and the Upanishads had enunciated the same idea—one should respond to evil with good. Human beings have the faculty of reasoned choice, and it is up to them to determine which way to go. The outcome of right conduct and right living will then be happiness. Here, too, Gandhi's

16   20 May 1905, *CWMG* (Oct. 1903-June 1905), p. 431.

17   *Navjivan*, 6 Feb. 1921, *CWMG*, (Aug. 21-14 Dec. 1921), p. 328.

18   Pyarelal, *Mahatma Gandhi*, vol. 1, p. 329.

19   *Navjivan*, 6 Feb. 1921, *CWMG* (Nov. 1920-Apr. 1921), p. 328.

20   Nanda, *In Gandhi's Footsteps*, p. 130.

much-loved Vaishnava mantra and the following Quran verse put into
words an identical message:

> Only men possessed of minds remember; who fulfil God's covenant ...
> patient men, desirous of the Face of their Lord,
> who perform the prayer, and expend of that
> We have provided them, secretly and in public
> and who avert evil with good.

A tree has many branches, each distinct from the other but each has
the same source.[21] An individual is, in fact, virtuous without having
to shave his head, without donning saffron robes, or covering himself
with ash. Behind their disputes is the failure to recognise that all faiths
embody sufficient inspiration for their adherents. The Quran says in
so many words that God sends messengers for all peoples, and they
are their prophets, and they should compete with one another in good
works (5:48 and 11:118). It exhorts all monotheists to work together
for the common good (3:64). Fine points differ, in the same way as
each faith derives the flavour of the soil from which it springs.[22] Now, if
religions were like different leaves on the same tree with differences in
shades and forms, it was necessary to seek Him in the heart to recreate
both Karim and Rama. If Allah dwelt only in a mosque, to whom does
the country beyond belong?[23] When viewed in this light, Islam and
Hinduism appear to be different from each other, but Gandhi also saw
their beliefs as the products of a Ram or Rahim.

Who said the Vedas and the Quran were false? They were false
to thoughtless individuals. Within all these bodies there was but one
and no second. Man or woman, they assume but Thy form. Kabir was
no other than a child of Allah-Rama and He is at once his own Guru
and *Pir.* 'Say: O disbelievers, I serve not that which you serve, nor do

---

21   Bhikhu Parekh, *Colonialism, Tradition and Reform: An Analysis of Gandhi's
        Political Discourse* (Delhi, 1989), p. 76.

22   Patel and Sykes, *Gandhi*, p. 69.

23   See also *Harijan*, 6 April 1940, in Mushirul Hasan (ed.), *India's Partition:
        Process, Strategy and Mobilization*, pp. 69-71.

you serve Him Whom I serve. For you is your recompense and for me my recompense.' Or, 'Do not argue with the People of the Book unless it is with something that is better, except with such of them who do wrong. And say: We believe in what has been revealed to us and revealed to you. Our God and your God are one, and to him we surrender' (29:46).

Imaging Islam

In the Middle Ages also we had received gifts from Muslim sources ... We should have no hesitation in admitting freely that this message [of purity and liberation] was inspired by contact with Islam. The best of men always accept the best of teaching, whenever and wherever it may be found, in religion, moral culture, or in the lives of individuals. But the Middle Ages are past, and we have stepped into a New Age. And now the best of men, Mahatma Gandhi, has come to us with this best of gifts from the West.

-Tagore, 'Mahatma Gandhi', *Boundless Sky*
(Calcutta, 1964), pp. 330-31.

Gandhi read from the Quran and commended it to his readers of *Indian Opinion*. He came down hard on Islam's denigration by Swami Shankerananda, a Punjabi Brahman turned sanyasi and a successor of Swami Parmananda who hastened the disintegration of the Natal Indian Patriotic Union.[24] Whenever he came across coarse intolerance or religious bigotry, he reacted sharply rather than remaining a detached onlooker. It was a denial of God to revile one religion, to break the heads of innocent men, and to desecrate temples or mosques.[25]

From the time it first appeared, writes Albert Hourani, the religion of Islam was a problem for Christian Europe. Those who believed in it were the enemy on the frontier.[26] European writers in general laboured both in the choice and in the treatment of themes

---

24   Swan, *Gandhi: The South African Experience*, p. 199; 30 Aug. 1909, *CWMG*, vol. 7, p. 376.

25   Gandhi, *The Way to Communal Harmony* (Ahmedabad, 1963), p. 42.

26   Albert Hourani, *Islam in European Thought* (Cambridge, 1991), p. 7.

in the shadow of their predecessors. What had been said about Islam before so dominated their approach as to preclude a complete reassessment.[27] A number of British writers construed Islam as an emblem of repellent otherness, and some of the late-nineteenth century reformers built their images on Islam's fundamental incompatibility with Hinduism.[28] Christian missionaries confronted Muslim scholars. A major confrontation took place at Agra in 1854 between Karl Pfander, a German missionary, and Shaikh Rahmatullah Kairanawi. Similarly, William Muir, a British official, wrote *Life of Muhammad*, a source of many disagreements.[29] It led Syed Ahmad Khan to research and refute William Muir's thesis.

The world outside their limited frame didn't exist for the late-nineteenth century reformers or publicists. If it did, it had to be crossed out or be a subject of derision. They were chiefly interested in substantiating the theory that Islam progressed almost entirely by force, and that it led to the degradation of Hindus.[30]

The production of a sense of Hindu communalism, a process through which some of these stereotypes tend to form a routinised discourse, stressed the need for a Hindu reaction. In the 1920s, Vinayak Damodar Savarkar, author of *Hindutva: Who is a Hindu* (1923), codified the ideology of Hindu nationalism as a response to the perception of a new level of Muslim militancy and developed the mechanisms of a Hindu nationalist through the stigmatisation and emulation of 'threatening Others'. Using different logic but arriving at more or less the same conclusion, Abul Ala Maududi and Savarkar viewed their respective communities as 'special' so that they could be kept separate from the other. The leader of the Jamaat-i Islami delineated Muslim nationality that were bound together by a commitment to follow the

27   Norman Daniel, *Islam and the West* (Edinburgh, 1960), p. 317.

28   Mushirul Hasan, 'The Myth of Unity: Colonial and National Narratives', in David Ludden (ed.), *Contesting the Nation: Religion, Community, and the Politics of Democracy in India* (Philadelphia, 1999).

29   Avril A. Powell, *Muslims and Missionaries in Pre-Mutiny India* (London, 1993), Chapter 7.

30   See the collection of essays on this theme in Mushirul Hasan (ed.), *Islam in South Asia: Theory and Practice*, vol. 1 (Delhi, 2008).

will of Allah, while Savarkar formulated a reified image of Hinduism, Hindu culture, and Hindu civilisation, and, in the process, stigmatised Islam and Christianity. The creation of a Hindu nationalist activity was his pet project.[31]

Scholars focus on the impact of Jainism on Gandhi and his affinity to the ideal of Christendom[32] without taking into account his debt to and intellectual engagements with Islam. He had a different approach to matters considered Islamic, rebuffed the polemical frame in which Islamic studies were enclosed, and unravelled a common intellectual heritage permeating the social and cultural spaces. He desired to study Islam as a historical reality and bring Muslims to the fullness of truth through *ahimsa* and truth. In the following section, I therefore attempt to recover this theme to establish his aversion to the xenophobic approach and his disapproval of the easy categorisation of the 'good' and 'bad' variant of Islam. I also try and underline the eclectic nature of his belief structure in acknowledging the Islamic code to embody acceptance of the habits, viewpoints, and faiths of others.[33]

It was Id, the festival following a month of fasting. Gandhi was in Yeravda Jail, sharing to the full the festive spirit of Mr Ali (full name is not known), a friend from Rangoon, and other Muslim prisoners. Throughout the day, he exchanged greetings with co-prisoners that he could see across the barbed wire fence and exuberantly blessed Ali. In the evening, he appeared to be even more anxious than Ali to catch a glimpse of the crescent moon during the few minutes it was visible hanging, as it were, in mid-air just above the trees, peeping over the high stone wall of the inner prison. His joy knew no bounds when he

---

31   Gyanendra Pandey, 'Which of us are Hindus?' in G. Pandey (ed.), *Hindus and others: The question of identity in India today* (Delhi, 1993), p. 244; Christophe Jaffrelot, *The Hindu Nationalist Movement and Indian Politics* (London, 1996), p. 78.

32   Message to the Americans, 3 Aug. 1942, Reddy, *Mahatma Gandhi: Letters to Americans*, pp. 332-33; Winslow and Elwin, *The Dawn of Indian Freedom*, pp. 44, 45.

33   The Quran proclaimed, 'and certainly we raised in every nation a messenger saying: Serve Allah and shun the devil,' and 'we sent no messenger but with the language of his people, so that he might explain to them clearly.'

eventually sighted it. The warmth of life seeped through his veins. Eager for a clearer view of the digit of the moon, he actually over-stepped the boundary of the barbed wire fence. He immediately and excitedly called Ali from his cell. They and others thronged together in the open compound watching the frail beauty of the crescent moon for a few minutes before seeing it vanish behind the trees. Indulal Yagnik, who shared the prison with Gandhi, had this to say:

> I had watched at close quarters Mr. Gandhi's heroic efforts at Hindu-Mohammedan rapprochement on the political stage. I had also vivid memories of his personal fraternisation with all classes of Mohammedans, from big political leaders and priests down to the meanest of them. Still his enthusiastic celebration of the Muslim *Id* festival, his exuberant greetings to his Muslim fellow prisoners, and above all his abundant joy at the sight of the crescent moon brought home to me, as nothing else had done before, his romantic conception of Hindu-Muslim unity. For it revealed to me how he, by making a clean sweep of excrescences like idolatry and ceremonies, had developed a new ideal of Hindu religion which could be easily reconciled to the best in Mohammedanism, so that the votaries of both religions could fraternise with one another on the occasions of their religious festivals.[34]

Gandhi's convictions were the true expression of his nature. They reflected the impact of the composite traditions of the pre-colonial state of Gujarat.

The Mughal state largely rested on the principle of universal transcendence, allowing for the interplay of wider identity structures provided by kin, clan, ethnicity, or religion. When political influences were not at work, Hindus and Muslims lived side by side, each respecting the prejudices of the other, and each following his faith without fear or hindrance. Besides the Prophet's normative model, the *Sunna* confirmed the acceptance of pluralism in Islam. On the strength of the Quranic verse, the Prophet entered into a covenant with the

---

34   Yagnik, *Gandhi As I Knew Him*, p. 306.

Jews in Medina.[35] This served as a historical precedent for Hindus and Muslims to cooperate in mutual support. Isardas, a contemporary of Aurangzeb, is reported to have made light of differences among religions and sects. A minor riot occurred in Delhi in 1711 and in Ahmedabad, the hub of Islamic culture in medieval India, but by and large these were sporadic incidents.[36]

Islam was introduced in western India by Arab and Persian merchants in coastal towns like Broach and Cambay. Later, a mercantile community developed in Surat.[37] Here and elsewhere in Gujarat, Hinduism, Jainism, and Islam all contributed to the kind of religious environment that Arnold Toynbee described as a 'cultural composite', a fertile seedbed that encouraged new social and spiritual conceptions to germinate and take root.[38] The Hindus brought with them Vaishnavism, the Jains their asceticism and veneration of saints, and the Muslims their monotheism and mysticism. Readers may dispute that the religious world of the Hindus and Jains would have been influenced by Sufi influence, though historians have, in recent years, documented the profound changes that came about, whether from within or from without. The multiple motifs from many streams of thought manifested themselves in the ecumenical outlook; consequently, Persian and Urdu motifs and ideas were incorporated into Jain poetry and Muslim images and language found a place in Jain music generally and in interaction

---

35 'We have created you into nations and tribes so that ye may get to know each other and compete with each other in good deeds' ('The Jews ... are a community along with the believers. To the Jews their religion and to the Muslims theirs').

36 Syed Ali Nadeem Rezavi, 'The Dynamics of Composite Culture: Evolution of an Urban Social Identity in Mughal India' (paper presented at the Indian History Congress, Dec. 2011), p. 143.

37 Ghulam A. Nadri, 'Muslims of Early Modern Gujarat: A Study of Inter-Community Relationships' (paper presented at the Indian History Congress, Dec. 2011).

38 On religious pluralism embedded in the daily religious practice and beliefs of both Muslims and Hindus, Carolyn Heitmeyer, 'Religion as Practice, Religion as Identity: Sufi Dargahs in Contemporary Gujarat', *South Asia*, vol. 34, no. 3, Dec. 2011.

in literary as well as social contexts.[39] Devotional music opened the way for an appreciation of mutual values.[40] Brahmans and Baniyas observed the Islamic legal system; indeed they approached the court of the *qazi* or invoked the *sharia*.[41] Equally, the mercantile communities, notably the Jain and Vaishnava Banias, resolved conflicts of interests through compromise. In an otherwise feudal society, public life and business dealings were governed by the *kajiyanu mon kaalu* norm, that is, 'conflict is always inauspicious'.[42]

Sind is still farther to the west and also on the border of the desert. Here, the Hindus sang songs that were difficult to distinguish from those of the Sufi mystics. They appreciated Islamic mysticism and its absorbing central truth of the unity and majesty of God.[43] Eclectic beliefs were, indeed, embedded into the social and cultural lives of the Lohanas and other Hindu trading castes, while marriage rules, commensality, social precepts, and moral codes bound the Hindus, Parsis, the Memons, Khojas, and Bohras.[44] A number of Hindu customs survived the Khoja adoption of Islam; their *jamaat* was nothing but a caste meeting of the various Hindu castes.[45] The *ginan*, sacred songs of the Ismaili Khojas, mirror aspects of Hinduism. A survey of names given to God illustrates their debt to the bhakti of the *sants*. There are other borrowings from mystical Hinduism in the *ginan*.[46] Bernard Lewis declared the Nizari

---

39   M. Whitney Kelting, *Singing to the Jinas: Jain Laywomen, Mandal Singing, and the Negotiations of Jain Devotion* (Oxford, 2001), p. 84.

40   Mohammad Mujeeb, *The Indian Muslims* (London, 1967), p. 236.

41   Rezavi, op. cit., p. 144.

42   Achyut Yagnik, 'The Pathology of Gujarat', *Seminar*, 513, May 2002.

43   Andrews, *Mahatma Gandhi's Ideas*, p. vii.

44   Harish Damodaran, *India's New Capitalists: Caste, Business, and Industry in a Modern Nation* (Delhi, 2008), p. 10.

45   The Khojas had spread out of Sind to Kutch and Kathiawar, and thence, from the late nineteenth century, down to Bombay town and island, as well as to across to Zanizibar, Muscat and other overseas centres of trade, J.C. Masselos, 'The Khojas of Bombay: The Defining of Formal Membership Criteria During the Nineteenth Century', in Imtiaz Ahmad (ed.), *Caste and Social Stratification among Muslims in India* (Delhi, 1978).

46   Francoise Mallison, 'Hinduism as seen by the Nizari Ismaili Missionaries of Western India: The Evidence of the Ginan', Sontheimer and Kulke (eds), *Hinduism Reconsidered*, p.197.

Ismailis in South Asia as 'Hindus under a light Muslim veneer'. Many others recognise an intricate weaving of Hindu and Muslim ideas that created a religious and cultural synthesis.[47]

The Gandhis had many Muslim friends, dating from the time when Muslim soldiers died guarding the house of one of their ancestors.[48] In school, Mohandas celebrated festivals with fellow students.[49] He would have learnt Persian, but the Sanskrit teacher curbed his desire by reminding him of his Vaishnavite ancestry. In Porbandar, Sheikh Mehtab drew him into eating goat's flesh, and entering a brothel. Other Muslim friends and acquaintances lived in Rajkot. Gandhi mentioned 'Latib' (Latif) and 'Usmanbhai' and others, who bade farewell to him in Rajkot and at railway stations up to Bombay.[50] This circle widened in South Africa. Prelates and priests of almost every denomination and degree were among his friends.

Early in 1893, Sheth Abdul Karim Jhaveri, a Memon and a partner of Abdullah & Co., hired Gandhi to assist in a lawsuit against a Transvaal merchant. Abdul Kadir, who managed the Durban branch of M.C. Camrooden & Co., chaired the Natal India Congress. Gandhi enjoyed talking to them and Abdul Ghani, H.O. Ally, Haji Saheb, and Imam Sheikh Ahmad. In Durban, he signed the sale deed for Hazrat Soofie Saheb, a migrant from Kalyan in Bombay to South Africa in 1895. The Sufi had set up hospices on the northern banks of Umgeni River. Gandhi handled the legal points in the land transaction.[51] Natal's cosmopolitan and uprooted population offered expanding markets for a wide range of missionary firms, including scores of Christian missions, the Arya Samaj, and Ghulam Mohammad 'Sufi' Sahib. The Sufi was however only one player in the large market in which he had to compete with rival firms promoting other versions of Islam, including the spread of the Aga Khan's message from Bombay.[52]

---

47   Ali S. Asani, *Ecstasy and Enlightenment: The Ismaili Devotional Literature in South Asia* (London, 2002), pp. 6-7.

48   Ibid., p. 7.

49   Andrews, *Mahatma Gandhi's Ideas*, p. 208.

50   Rajmohan Gandhi, *The Good Boatman*, p. 51.

51   http://www.raza.co.za/personalities_soofie_saheb.html

52   Nile Green, *Bombay Islam: The Religious Economy of the West Indian Ocean, 1850-1915* (Delhi, 2011), p. 210.

There is little information on Gandhi's links with the Arya Samajists, but the few contacts he had may help to explain his veneration for Khwaja Bakhtiar Kaki's shrine in Mehrauli, outside Delhi. When rioters desecrated this holy site during the Partition riots leading to the postponement of the annual fair (*urs*), he ensured its restoration and the festival's revival. For this he sought the help of the Jamiyat al-ulama leader, Maulana Hifzur Rahman. He visited the *mazaar*, hands folded, face smiling. Begum Anis Kidwai said to her friend, 'A living saint has come to meet a dead one!'[53] This did not mean that Hindu-Muslim tension melted away, but Gandhi generated a certain camaraderie, in a period after the bonding ideology of nationalism had fractured. He was at his very best.

Gandhi lived largely in a mixed community where racial, religious, ethnic, or caste divisions weren't perceptible. Consequently, he encouraged Muslims to live in Tolstoy Farm, the first major endeavour at community living, and made friends with Cachalia, whose bravery, sincerity of purpose, and spirit of sacrifice he extolled.[54] Contact with Abdullah Sheth acquainted him with a practical knowledge of Islam. He bought Sale's translation of the Quran, held it to be the word of God, and recognised justice to be transcendent in the Islamic tradition.[55] As his knowledge and insight increased not only into the outward facts of Islamic tradition but into the inward life of the servants of Allah, he became more and more aware of the godliness of his Muslim friends. While arguing his client's case, he quoted chapter and verse from the Quran.[56]

Gandhi worked closely with the Hamidia Islamic Society in Johannesburg, and with H.O. Ally, the prime mover in organising his mass meeting in September 1906,[57] and Abdul Gani, president of the British Indian Association in Transvaal. He told his audience that what was possible for his other associates—Valliammai, Nagappan,

---

53   Kidwai, *In Freedom's Shade*, p. 32.

54   Desai (ed.), *Day-to-Day with Gandhi*, vol. 2, p. 58.

55   Gandhi, *My Experiment with Truth*, pp. 106, 137.

56   Walter Wragg, the Supreme Court Judge, wondered whether he knew the intricacies of Muslim law.

57   Swan, *Gandhi: The South African Experience*, pp. 120-1.

Narayanaswami, and Ahmed Mohamed—were possible for each one of them. In April 1907, he corresponded with Mushir Hosain Kidwai, who had links with the international Red Crescent Society in the Transvaal, to ascertain his opinion on Hejaz Railway.[58] The *taluqdar* of Gadia (in Barabanki district) was beholden to him for this.[59] He went on to form an Islamic Society in London in 1916.[60] In London, Gandhi made the acquaintance of Ameer Ali, who organised the Red Crescent Society during the Balkan War, and Major Hussain Ali Bilgrami of Hyderabad, a member of the Council of India in London until November 1909. He gave Gandhi 30 letters of introduction.[61] In May 1947, Gandhi recalled that he had found evidence of pan-Islamism during his student days.[62]

In South Africa, Gandhi believed that, in view of the acculturation between Islam and the followers of other religions, the future held out hopes of the diversity of values enriching the human heritage as a whole. When that happens, each community will show tolerance towards the other's scale of values. The Prophet pronounced: 'Actions will be judged according to intentions. No man is a true believer unless he desires for his brother that which he desires for himself.' According to this precept and the philosophy of *advaita*,[63] to which Gandhi subscribed, he brought to light, at the outset, the significance of Islam in giving brightness and a sense of well-being to an embattled world. What makes some of these remarks invaluable even to this day is the width of information, constituted simply by the knowledge Gandhi had accumulated from books and friends.

In India, Gandhi learnt from Azad, an indefatigable, conscientious, and meticulous scholar, and C.F. Andrews, who studied Islam at the feet of E.G. Browne, a champion of Egyptian independence and a critic of

---

58   *Indian Opinion*, 11 May 1907, *CWMG* (1904-1907), p. 443. He was the founder of the Islamic Information Bureau in London.

59   Ibid., 22 June 1907, *CWMG* (June-Dec, 1907), p. 11.

60   Note by Hose, 1916, IOR. L/PJ/12/752.

61   Gandhi to Kallenbach, 17 July 1909, Gandhi-Kallenbach papers.

62   Rajmohan Gandhi, *The Good Boatman*, p. 61.

63   Narayan Desai, *My Life is My Message*, vol.2, p. 289.

French encroachments in North Africa, specifically in Morocco. He and the historian T.W. Arnold disputed the widespread Christian stereotype of violence as the only reason for the spread of Islam, and established that the building blocks for a tolerant version of Islam were actually available in the Muslim tradition itself.[64]

In Simla, an island of European settlement, Andrews uncovered the 'inner spirit' of Islam with the help of Maulvi Shams-ud-Din, an Urdu teacher with a deeply religious bent of mind.[65] Back in St. Stephen's College, his interest was stimulated by his colleagues and by the old city's literati, notably Maulvi Zakaullah, the historian, Maulvi Nazir Ahmad, the novelist, and Hakim Ajmal Khan. He saw Islamic matters from the Islamic point of view, and chanced upon deeper parallels in Muslim and Christian theology and the congruence of their basic tenets.[66] He saw the best in one another, for that was an essential feature of love,[67] and expected other interlocutors to develop an equally expanded humanism in approaching Christianity and understanding Christian ways.[68]

---

64   Daniel O'Connor, *The Testimony of C.F. Andrews* (Madras, 1974), p. 13; Arnold spoke at the Muhammadan Educational Conference in 1890 on the 'peaceful' spread of Islam in China and Java. Sayyid Ahmad to S. Muhammad Ali Hasan, 20 Nov. 1890, Mushtaq Husain (ed.), *Makatib*, p. 345; K. Watt, 'Thomas Walker Arnold and the Re-evaluation of Islam, 1864-1930,' *MAS*, 36, 1, 2002. p. 19.

65   'He was a very old man and in Simla he used to wear boots with patties as he was not used to the cold. When he went to teach an officer to whom I recommended him as a Munshi, this officer used to make him undo his patties and take off his boots. The officer was quite young and the Munshi was quite old ... Altogether I was quite disgusted with what I saw and it made me very unhappy.' Daniel O'Connor, *Gospel, Raj and Swaraj: The Missionary Years of C.F. Andrews, 1904-14* (Frankfurt, 1990), p. 32; Marjorie Sykes (ed.), *C.F. Andrews: Representative Writings* (Delhi, 1973), p. 32; Tinker, 'Between Old Delhi and New Delhi: C.F. Andrews and St. Stephen's in an Era of Transition', R.E. Frykenberg (ed.), *Delhi Through the Ages: Essays in Urban History, Culture, and Society* (Delhi, 1986), p. 359.

66   MSS.EUR. D 1113/109, C.F. Andrews Collection, Oriental and India Office Collection, British Library (BL).

67   O'Connor, *The Testimony of C.F. Andrews*, p. 121.

68   For example, Ziauddin Ahmad Barni, *Azmat-i Rafta* (Karachi, 1961), pp. 168-9.

The time and consideration Gandhi extended to traditional and Western-educated Muslims indicated his desire to learn and interpret the Quran. His respectful responses weren't a matter of political pragmatism, but extended far beyond to a philosophical understanding of the supreme deity.[69] In a while, he began citing from the Quran on justice to all, on personal and political morality, and on its distinct contribution to fostering the brotherhood of man for those within its fold.[70] He used the *Surah Fatiha* in his daily prayer service, his accent on the opening of the self to God, his giving weight to help and guidance in keeping on the straight path, and according prominence to resisting the temptations of the devil. In its discard of rigid rites, rituals, and chain of religious command,[71] Islam served as a cleansing medium and Divine Unity as one of its greatest blessings.

Gandhi made known that Hindus and Muslims were sons of the same soil, and pointed to their common ancestry.[72] Throughout his career he broadcast their old habits of accommodation, religious open-mindedness, and cultural acceptance as a well-established convention. He underlined that Muslims were required to accept the right of non-Muslims to profess their own faith; they couldn't consider themselves as the sole possessors and upholders of truth. He didn't deny the doctrinal divergences between Islam and Hinduism, but attempted to bring together the everyday life of Hindus and Muslims. Emancipation implied unlocking the shackles of the past and creating a social order worthy of human dignity,[73] and swaraj or *azadi* meant celebrating the unity of sentiment in ancient songs and traditions and translating the expectations of *all* Indians into a reality.

The principle underlying *sarvodaya* stemmed from the conception of human brotherhood, in which every man is equal in the eyes of Allah. Horace Alexander, who closely studied Gandhi's religious beliefs, felt

---

69   *Young India*, 21 Aug. 1924, *CWMG* (Aug. 1924-Jan. 1925), p. 19.

70   Iyer (ed.), *The Essential Writings of Mahatma Gandhi*, p. 152.

71   C.F. Andrews, *Mahatma Gandhi: His Life and Ideas* (Bombay, rpt, 2005), p. 201.

72   Parel (ed.), *'Hind Swaraj' and Other Writings*, p. 53.

73   Ibid., pp.103-6.

that the conception of *sarvodaya* in the most fundamental human and religious sense came through Gandhi, and it would seem that he derived it primarily from Islam.[74] He stressed concisely and clearly on Islam's distinctive contribution to the unadulterated belief in the oneness of God, on the brotherhood of believers, and on Sufism ushering in a broad-based spiritual frame of mind. With typical inspiration, and in his shining style, he stressed that the common ecstasy of the Divine in the human soul had inspired them and their counterparts among *sants* and sadhus,[75] and that congregational prayers established human unity through common worship[76] conducted in Sabarmati and Wardha, as also in public places, to which all were invited.

Lastly, Gandhi portrayed Islam as a religion of peace in the same sense as Christianity, Buddhism, and Hinduism, and established that neither the strict conditions for jihad could be fulfilled nor the charge of conversion by force be substantiated against Muslims as a body. Even after years of heated debates and polemical controversies, he didn't find a single passage to condone forced conversion; 'real conversion proceeded from the heart and a heart conversion was impossible without an intelligent grasp of one's own faith and of that recommended by adoption.'[77] Islam spread by the prayerful love of an unbroken line of saints and faqirs.[78]

---

74   Alexander, *Consider India*, p. 42.

75   'Hari is made to dwell in the East, Allah in the West. But seek Him in your heart. You will find there both Karim and Rama. If God is only in the mosque, to whom does the country outside belong? Rama is supposed to be in the pilgrim places and in His images. But they have found Him in neither yet. Who said that the Vedas and the book [the Quran] are false? They are so to those who do not think. Within all bodies there is but One and no second. Man or woman, they take but Thy form. Kabir is but a child of Allah-Rama and He is his Guru and Pir alike.' This proved the hollowness of the theory of 'inborn enmity.'

76   Pyarelal, *Mahatma Gandhi*, vol. 1, p. 69.

77   Speech at prayer meeting, 10 Jan. 1947, *CWMG* (21 Oct. 1946- 20 Feb. 1947), p. 338.

78   'The Prophet's whole life is a repudiation of compulsion in religion. No Mussalman has to my knowledge ever approved of compulsion. Islam would cease to be a world religion if it were to rely upon force for its propagation. Secondly, historically speaking, the charge of conversion by force cannot be proved against its followers as a body. And whenever attempts have been made to convert by force responsible Mussalmans have repudiated such conversions.' *Young India*, 29 Aug. 1921.

Norman Daniel points out that Christians should view Mohammad as a holy figure; to see him, that is, as Muslims did. Without that, they must cut themselves off from comprehending Islam, and cut themselves off from Muslims.[79] Agreeing with Shibli Nomani, Aligarh's scholar-historian who protested that the moral portrait presented by Western historians pictured all manner of evils, Gandhi dwelt on the Prophet's sublime ethical deeds, the stirrings of pity, self-sacrifice, and heroism. After studying Washington Irving, Thomas Carlyle, who accepted Mohammad as a Prophet, Ameer Ali and Shibli Nomani, who defended Islam and the Prophet from 'Orientalism', he acknowledged that Mohammad sought to establish order and harmony within a standard of justice, and dealt with the problems of the day with uprightness, balance, and fairness. He described the sayings of the Prophet, compiled by Abdullah Suhrawardy, as treasures of mankind, not merely Islam. In sum, Gandhi had an opinion about the Prophet which is clearly formulated and favourable.

Islam earned a place for itself through Mohammad's self-effacement, his intense devotion to the believers (*ahl-i iman*), his intrepidity, his fearlessness, and his absolute trust in God.[80] He equated *hijrat* [Prophet's journey from Mecca to Medina] with the Non-Cooperation movement.[81] The duty of Non-Cooperation with unjust men and kings is enjoined in Islam as well as other religions. Gandhi asked: 'How can a Truth-seeker like me help respecting one whose mind was constantly fixed on God, who ever walked in God's fear and who had boundless compassion for mankind?'[82] This picture is easily recognisable to a believer.

The first four *Khulafa* (Caliphs) had the riches of the world at their feet, but they lived simply and were devoted to the poor. Umar ibn-al-Khattab, the second Khalifa, wouldn't brook the idea of his lieutenants in distant provinces wearing anything other than coarse fabric, and got

---

79 Daniel, *Islam and the West*, p. 336.

80 *Young India*, 11 Sept. 1924, *CWMG* (Aug. 1924-Jan. 1925), p. 127.

81 4 Aug. 1920, Iyer (ed), *The Essential Writings of Mahatma Gandhi*, p. 336.

82 Speech in Poona, 23 June 1934, ibid., p. 99.

those who wore muslin or velvet to discard them in favour of khadi.[83] Gandhi wanted the Congress ministers to emulate him. He believed that Ali ibn-i Abu Talib, cousin and son-in-law of the Prophet, was an exemplar for all satyagrahis.[84]

As regards the great conception of suffering injury without retaliation, Gandhi invoked repeatedly Imam Husain's spirit of rejection and sacrifice for truth.[85] He wanted people to ponder over the life of the 72 martyrs of Karbala, who embodied the deepest pathos and whose heroic endurance, silently borne, profoundly moves the human heart. 'Ashura,' the tenth day of the month of Muharram, sums up the Shia spiritual consciousness: the dichotomous world view in which the corrupted powerful sit atop the deprived and the tormented, and their ethos of sacrifice, courage, and tolerable pain. Powerful rituals aren't enactments of the past, but reminders of the present. They are events staged in the historical present, in time that is no time.[86]

The greatest lesson of Karbala, a city on the banks of the River Euphrates, was that self-sacrifice should be admired for its own sake, as right should in itself be prized as a trophy. As one who believed that a man of God is never afraid to die or lose his possessions for the sake of his self-respect or religion, Gandhi valued Imam Husain's stand, which was that violence is avoidable once right becomes manifest. This was similar to *tapascharya*, the Hindu belief in the power of suffering to transform consciousness. The 'irresistible might of meekness', as Milton called it, appealed most to Gandhi and he found it exemplified in Islam.[87]

---

83   Speech at Jamiyat al-ulama conference, Karachi, 1 Apr. 1931, *CWMG* (Dec.1930-Apr. 1931), p. 382.

84   According to Gandhi, if Ali hadn't restrained his anger when his adversary spat on him in the course of combat, Islam wouldn't have maintained its unbroken passage of progress up to the present time.

85   20 Nov. 1921, 3 Apr. 1924, Iyer (ed.), *The Essential Writings of Mahatma Gandhi*, pp. 223, 232.

86   Richard Norton, 'Musa al-Sadr', in Ali Rahnema (ed.), *Pioneers of Islamic Revival* (London, 2005), p. 191; Toby M. Howarth, *The Twelver Shia as a Muslim Minority in India* (London, 2005); Diane D'Souza, 'Gendered Ritual and the Shaping of Shi'ah Identity', in Kelly Pemberton and Michael Nijhawan (eds), *Shared Idioms, Sacred Symbols, and the Articulation of Identities in South Asia* (London, 2009).

87   Andrews, *Mahatma Gandhi's Ideas*, pp. 63, 64.

Renan, the German philosopher, said that the minutiae of the acts of the martyrs, even if for the most part false, unroll a dreadful picture which was nevertheless a reality. The true nature of the terrible struggle has often been misconceived but its seriousness has not been exaggerated.[88] Gandhi felt the same way. From the perspective of comparative studies of mystic consciousness, there might be said to be agreement with Gandhi's discernment that to suffer for faith is a general human ideal not restricted to any single religious tradition.[89]

The sage from Sabarmati set before his people, young, Hindu and Muslim alike, an example of the power of suffering to overcome the hardest heart. In his own way, he looked up to the Prophet, whose tenets are compatible with *ahimsa*.[90]

'A Saint in Action'

Gandhi's comfort zone expanded or shrank in exact proportion to the awakening or failing of those around him. 'We can kill him with our moral faults,' Mirabehn remarked, 'or serve him into a ripe old age by awakening to his word.'[91] Through different lenses and from widely differing points of view, leading scholars, theologians, and publicists spelt out why Gandhi came across to them as an admixture of rugged strength and enthusiasm, untiring in effort and rich in accomplishment. As their assessments are still very much with us, I briefly recall some of the ways in which they viewed him.

In South Africa, the indentured held their head high owing to Gandhi's presence in their midst. Respect and veneration went hand-in-hand. Wives, daughters and sisters abandoned the purdah in his presence. The ulama invited him to the mosques to explain *tauhid* or the

---

88   Georges Sorel, *Reflections on Violence* (Cambridge, 1999), p. 183.

89   McDonough, *Gandhi's Responses to Islam*, p. 46.

90   *Navajivan*, 2 Nov. 1924. This is what Halide Edip wrote about Hazrat Ali in her memoirs: 'The Western mind's conception of Christ's achievement of success in the highest spiritual domain, obtained at the cost of suffering, shame, and a humiliating death, has its counterpart in the mind of the Moslem in the personality of Ali.'

91   Quoted in D. S Sharma, *Studies in the Renaissance of Hinduism* (Benares, 1944), p. 558.

affirmation of divine unity as a principle of liberation; he was summoned by non-religious platforms for inter-faith dialogue and reconciliation.[92] Gandhi conveyed to Maganlal, Gandhi's 'hand, feet and eyes':

> My enthusiasm is such that I may have to meet death in South Africa at the hands of my own countrymen. If that happens, you should rejoice. It will unite the Hindus and the Mussalmans. In this struggle a twofold inner struggle is going on. One of them is to bring the Hindus and the Muslims together. The enemies of the community are constantly making efforts against such a unity. In such a great endeavour, someone will have to sacrifice his life. If I make that sacrifice, I shall regard myself, as well as you, my colleagues, fortunate.[93]

Enlightened Muslim opinion affirmed the validity of Gandhi's line of reasoning on certain matters. Azad praised his actions in South Africa in 1913: 'fire burns in the hearts of all Indians' because of him. *Al-Hilal* carried his photograph on its front page,[94] introducing him as the turbaned man who sought Muslim goodwill, exerted himself to accomplish inter-community amity, toiled to unite hearts and minds,[95] and performed penance and eventually paid for it with his life.[96]

Gandhi and Azad accorded saliency to the idea of *watan* or *matrabhoomi* in their topical allusions and penetrating elucidation. To them, *watan* wasn't an abstract concept, imagined or invented, but a hospitable home for cultures and religions. Hence they saw the confluence or *sangam* taking place in language, art, literature, manners

---

92   *Indian Opinion*, 22 Feb. 1908, *CWMG*.

93   Letter to Maganlal Gandhi, *CWMG*, vol. 9.

94   Ian Henderson Douglas, *Abul Kalam Azad: An Intellectual and Religious Biography* (Delhi, 1988), pp. 145-46.

95   *CWMG* (Aug. 1918-July 1919), p. 297.

96   Gandhi, *My Experiments with Truth*, pp. 325, 442. On another occasion he told a Khilafat meeting that his desire to meet 'good' Muslim leaders was satisfied after meeting the Ali Brothers. His circle of friends widened after he had met Ansari and Abdul Bari. Speech on Khilafat, Bombay, 9 May 1919, *CWMG* (1 May-28 Sept. 1919), p. 295; *Young India*, 24 Nov. 1921.

and customs. These two patriots whose life encompassed the cross-currents in the twentieth century, became part of an 'indivisible unity', that is Indian nationality.[97] They drew upon the richness of Hinduism and Islam as well as the self-critical, rational, and practical Indo-Muslim thought. They sought guidance, boldness, inner peace, and endurance from the sacred texts.

Gandhi once wrote that 'bluster is no religion, nor is vast learning stored in capacious brains. The seat of religion is in the heart'. Maulvi Abdul Bari agreed. He belonged to Firangi Mahal, a theological seminary located in a narrow alley of Lucknow's old city.[98] It was pleasant to be in the hub and focus of the pan-Islamic movement: to be in contact and companionship with Gandhi and the Ali brothers whose names were household words; to be part of the bustle and buzz of the Khilafat conferences; and, not least, to meet and entertain constituents who listened with bated breath to his sermon. Abdul Bari advanced ideas without diluting them with a stream of interpretations, and followed closely Gandhi's view that, 'the last Great War has shown ... the Satanic nature of the civilization that dominates Europe today. Every canon of public morality has been broken by the victors in the name of virtue.' In panegyric, he found the theoretical justification necessary to block his adversaries who went to bizarre lengths to ridicule the growing Hindu-Muslim assemblage. He established religious sanction against cow-slaughter,[99] confirmed spinning and Satyagraha to be compatible with Islam,[100] and idolised Gandhi, the person who mattered most in such a situation:

Please excuse me. I know you want to help, because our cause is just and because we are children of the same soil, and not because you want any *quid pro quo*. But do we not owe a duty to ourselves? Islam will fall to pieces if it ever takes and never gives. It must be faithful above all. The nobility of our creed [he used the expression

---

97   Hasan (ed.), *India's Partition*, p. 66.

98   Francis Robinson, *Separatism Among Indian Muslims*, pp. 287-9.

99   Qureshi, *Pan-Islam in British Indian Politics*, p. 104.

100   Ibid., pp. 103-4; Brown, *Gandhi's Rise to Power*, pp. 195-6.

khandani] requires us to be strictly just to our neighbours. Here it is a question of taking service. The Hindus will judge our faith, and rightly, by our conduct towards them. That is why I say: if we take from you, we must give to you.

Hakim Ajmal Khan, the commanding figure of the 'Delhi Renaissance', applied not only Islamic ideas to daily life but valued living in the *national* tradition.[101] He lived in the old city in a house which his distinguished ancestors had built in Ballimaran, a street associated with Ghalib. In all he did, including *Hikmat* (the Yunani system of medicine), a family vocation for generations, he demonstrated mental and moral integrity, the pride of Delhi's intellectuals, Syed Ahmad Khan and Ghalib included. Personally, he set aside a certain percentage of his own earnings as a physician to meet his personal needs. This may explain why, without any rhetorical embellishment, he recorded Gandhi's spirit of sincere humility, his strengthening the sense of civic solidarity, and his bringing the prestige of religious faith to bear in directing the people's smouldering discontent into a powerful anti-colonial struggle.

Dr M. A. Ansari lived in Daryaganj, for long the British cantonment. He appraised Gandhi's life at its full value at the League's session in 1918. A surgeon of repute, he rose to prominence during the Rowlatt Satyagraha. His estimation was firm, decided, and it rested upon principles that were clearly conceived, and his loyalty to Gandhi remained unshaken. Gandhi reciprocated warmly to him, his 'infallible guide' on Hindu-Muslim matters. As a sick man in May 1933, he said, 'I should love to die with my head in Ansari's lap' to which Ansari's response was, 'I won't let him die at all.'[102]

---

101   Andrews had already, by degrees, made his contribution acceptable by tracing the rekindling of thought to Syed Ahmad Khan, who bequeathed his legacy and financially kept Jamia afloat. He identified himself fully with its weal and woe, because he recognised the power of education in forming character and opinion. He didn't want free enquiry to be checked and the child to be met with dogma or with stony silence.

102   Sarojini Naidu to Padmaja and Leilamani Naidu, in Paranjape (ed.), *Sarojini Naidu: Selected Letters*, p. 289.

Towards Mazharul Haque, the lawyer from Patna, Gandhi exuded warmth and affection. They were together in England and returned to Bombay on the same ship in 1891. They got together in Bombay at the Muslim League session; Mazharul Haque chaired. The change of heart he experienced led him to give up alcohol, grow a beard, and live in a *kuccha* house near the Ganga at Digha Ghat. He built Sadaqat Ashram, a hermitage at Digha outside Patna. During Non-Cooperation, his wife, Badruddin Tyabji's niece, presented Gandhi with her choicest four bangles made of pearls and rubies. Gandhi was happy to know the Tyabjis.[103]

Perched on the dizzy pinnacles of triumph in South Africa, Gandhi was introduced to the Ali brothers in 1915: 'it was a question of love at first sight between us'.[104] He assumed that they'd be valuable to him both as a means through which to cement a communal concordat, and also because they were a splendid example of that mingling of Hindu and Muslim cultures in the Indo-Gangetic belt.[105] At the home of Sushil Kumar Rudra, principal of St. Stephen's College, he discussed with them his philosophy of non-violence, the divine light itself that left no room for cowardice or weakness and had to be accepted as the most natural and the most necessary condition of national existence.

The people must nurse a real grievance and approach it with pure hands, for the tool of *Satyagraha* is *ahimsa*, i.e., self-suffering (without inflicting suffering on the opponent), to vindicate an absolutely just cause.[106]

Elsewhere, he'd say that only *ahimsa* will endure, and that Islam and Christianity will survive only to the degree to which their followers imbibe non-violence.[107] The Ali brothers, who were convinced by these

---

103   *CWMG* (Dec. 1921-Mar. 1922), p. 54.

104   Robinson, *Separatism Among Indian Muslims,* pp. 297-8.

105   Brown, *Gandhi's Rise to Power,* p. 152.

106   *Harijan,* 9 July 1938, M.K. Gandhi, *The Indian states problem,* p. 80.

107   Tendulkar, *Abdul Ghaffar Khan,* pp. 257-8; Rajmohan Gandhi, *The Good Boatman* ch. 1.

arguments, pronounced non-violence to be an Islamic obligation.[108] In May 1920, they reiterated that violence wouldn't be allowed to continue alongside non-violence.[109] In those great and glorious days, non-violence proved infectious. Under its spell there was a mass awakening such as had not been seen before. Halide Edip justifiably thought that Gandhi's fondness for Muslims was due to personal contacts, and to sympathy with the Islamic principles of bringing the Truth about God nearer the lives of the masses.[110]

On one occasion, Sarojini Naidu and Asaf Ali debated the comparative merit of Mohamed Ali and Jinnah. Writes Asaf Ali: 'My zealous advocacy on behalf of Mohamed Ali evoked Sarojini's retort, now proved true: "My Mohamed Ali will go further than your Mohamed Ali!"' Mohamed Ali graduated from Aligarh College, went to England in September 1898, and matriculated from Lincoln College, Oxford, in 1902. Here, he studied with John Simon, who headed, in later years, the all-white Statutory Commission.[111] In Paris,

---

108   *Harijan*, 10 Feb. 1940, *CWMG* (1 Dec. 1939-15 Apr. 1940), p. 178. On Shaukat Ali, *Navajivan*, 21 Nov. 1920, *CWMG* (Nov. 1920-Apr. 1921), pp. 10-11. 'Shaukatali's speech has not disturbed me because I think I see what he means. I admit that all [non-cooperating] Mohammedans do not look at non-cooperation from my angle. But there has been a distinct understanding with them that violence would never be allowed to go on side-by-side with non-violence. And even if the Mohammedan brothers accept non-violent non-cooperation in a spirit of hatred, it is possible to bring good out of even such non-cooperation, since it will save the country from bloodshed. Whatever the attitude at the back, some good at least is bound to come out of a good act. If a man observes truth or self-restraint simply out of fear of public exposure, he does at least some good to society and himself by his factual observance. That is the glory and grandeur of a good deed.' Desai (ed.), *Day-to-Day with Gandhi*, vol. 2, p. 162.

109   Brown, op. cit., p. 331.

110   Edip, *Inside India*, p. 171. The reference to Asaf Ali is in G.N.S Raghavan (ed.), *M. Asaf Ali's Memoirs: The Emergence of Modern India* (Delhi, 1994), pp. 102-03.

111   There is considerable historical literature on Mohamed Ali. In particular, Francis Robinson, Gail Minault, Peter Hardy, and M. Naeem Qureshi have examined his role at great length. See my essay in *Islam, Communities and the Nation: Muslim Identities in South Asia and Beyond* (Delhi, 1998), and the three edited volumes of his speeches and correspondence in *Mohamed Ali in Indian Politics: Select Writings*.

this oracle of the generation of young pan-Islamists missed Gandhi's advice. After the Prophet, he obeyed his command.[112] Full of talk and gossip, he learnt to spin. Yarn cones, he said, were the bullets with which India would win swaraj.[113] He protested when Gandhi desired abdication during the early days of Non-Cooperation.[114] He was so 'impelled by the love I bear towards Mahatmaji to pray to God that he might illumine his soul with the true light of Islam'. As his chief, Gandhi alone led India, Muslims, as well as Hindus.[115] C.Y.Chintamani, editor and Liberal leader, noticed Gandhi's enormous influence over Mohamed Ali.[116]

The change in appearance, if not in outlook, was visible in elder brother Shaukat Ali, although he embodied much less romance and idealism. Once, this Aligarh-educated graduate used to be fashionably dressed, but under Gandhi's influence he donned a loose, long green coat of peculiar cut, his shaggy beard symbolising his grievance against Europe and Christendom.[117] 'I have been a thorough Englishman,' he said. 'I wore a dress suit and was a good bat at cricket; but never again. I am now all Indian.'[118] Gandhi hoped that on seeing the success of non-violence, he'd recognise its excellence.[119] Shaukat Ali however turned the idea inside out. No one could curb his violent temper and unprovoked outbursts when it came to discussing non-violence and other related matters.[120]

---

112 Mohamed Ali to Shaukat Ali, 15 May 1920, Mohamed Ali to Swami Shraddhanand, 26 Mar. 1924, Mohamed Ali papers, Jamia Millia Islamia (JMI).

113 *CWMG* (1 Dec. 1939-15 Apr. 1940), p. 62.

114 *Harijan*, 6 Jan. 1940, ibid. p. 71.

115 *Comrade*, 9 Jan. 1925, 16 Oct. 1925.

116 To Srinivasa Sastri, 6 Oct. 1924, T.N. Jagadisan (ed.), *Letters of The Right Honourable V. S. Srinivasa Sastri* (Delhi, 1963), pp. 139-40.

117 Mohamed Ali, *My Life: A Fragment*, Mushirul Hasan (ed.) (Delhi, 1999), p. 88, Mohamed Ali to F.S.A. Slocock, 29 Jan. 1917, Hasan (ed.), *Mohamed Ali in Indian Politics* (New Delhi), vol. 2, pp. 13-14, and A.M.Dariabadi, *Insha-i Majid* (Calcutta, 1991), p. 479.

118 Brockway, *The Indian Crisis*, p. 121.

119 Sept. 1920, Desai (ed.), *Day-to Day with Gandhi*, vol. 2, pp. 237-38.

120 19 May 1920, ibid., p. 162.

Like Mazharul Haque, Khan Abdul Ghaffar Khan and his brother Dr. Khan Saheb were drawn close to Gandhi by their pure and ascetic life.[121] The latter was married to an Englishwoman, who wore European clothes and lived in British style in Peshawar cantonment. However, once he decided to throw himself heart and soul into the Gandhian campaigns, he took to *khaddar*. As for Ghaffar Khan, scores of legends quickly crystallised around him, and his fetters, grinding prison labour, and solitary cells were aptly drawn into the construction of an indivisible nationalist struggle. His connection with Gandhi was an out of the ordinary blend of ideological divergences with personal regard and fondness. Whenever a question of great pith and moment arose in Gandhi's life, he'd instinctively say to himself, 'this is the decision of one who has surrendered himself to God, and God never guideth ill'. Also, because he referred problems to God and always conformed to His commands, his standard measure was to surrender to God.[122]

Some Muslims found, in their different ways, a true contentment of mind and heart in Gandhi's *ibadat khana*. Rehana Tyabji, daughter of Abbas Tyabji, the 'jewel of Gujarat', sang *bhajans* as well as recited the Quran.[123] Gandhi told her jestingly, 'you convert the ashram inmates to Islam. I shall convert you to Hinduism.' In June 1926, Zakir Husain, Abid Husain, and Mohammad Mujeeb, three academic liberals, discussed the Jamia Millia project. Mujeeb, fresh from Berlin, felt out of place in an atmosphere of deliberately cultivated poverty and spoke of an 'almost oppressive consensus' on the 'essentials' of life and health: no smoking, no tea, no tasty food, no colourful clothes. A smoker, he shared this weakness with many people who had accomplished great things. He asked if this signified weakness, a moral fault, or whether Sevagram pointed to the path which the world must follow if it had to save itself from destruction or moral collapse?[124]

---

121   Tendulkar, *Abdul Ghaffar Khan*, p. 175.

122   Quoted in J.H. Holmes, *My Gandhi*, p. 57.

123   Aparna Basu, *Abbas Tyabji* (Delhi, 2007). For an appreciation of Abbas Tyabji's role, see Gandhi to Abbas Tyabji, 14 Nov. 1930, *CWMG*, (July-Dec. 1930), p. 305.

124   Mohammad Mujeeb, 'Gandhi and the Muslim Masses', in *Islamic Influence on Indian Society* (Meerut, 1965), Hasan (ed.), *Negotiating Diversities*, vol. 5, p. 74.

No such questions assailed the Khan brothers, who were remarkable for their perspicacity and interest in the ethical side of every question. Gandhi's friendship with them was 'a gift of God'.[125] Being with them was to love them more. He found them nice, simple and yet so penetrative.[126] In September 1934, they shared the simple fare at Wardha, which became the site of the Gandhi-Cripps conclave on 19 December 1939. The tiny hut was a study in asceticism: 'a little bamboo furniture about, a few books in a packing case on its side, false teeth in a box, some papers, a bed on the floor on which he was sitting, and several rush mats.'[127]

On 4 December, Ghaffar Khan returned to Wardha with his twelve-year old son and fourteen-year-old daughter. Often, he read the Quran at the evening prayer and joined in reading Tulsidas' *Ramayana*. He loved the tune and listened intently. 'The music of that *bhajan* fills my soul,' he once proclaimed. He served the sick and, what is more, helped Gandhi wash his feet. Once, Badshah Khan came along with his two sons. At the midday meal, one of them asked, 'isn't it your birthday today?' 'Yes, it is. Why?' 'Well you see, I thought ... there might be something special to eat—cake and chicken pilau perhaps. But there is simply plain boiled pumpkin, just as usual!' Gandhi chuckled, and made the children laugh. Afterwards, he took the Frontier Gandhi aside and suggested that, 'we ought to get something they would really enjoy; some meat or something. 'No, no, they were only joking; we always eat gladly whatever our host provides.' The children agreed. The affectionate parental-like tie; a young boy or girl turning for advice and the Bapu, in turn, showering his affection and blessing!

Gandhi asked K.G. Saiyidain, an educationist trained at the University of Leeds in England: 'Are you quite comfortable [in Sevagram]?' He said 'Yes'. Having noticed some reservation in his tone, he inquired: 'But you seem to hesitate in saying so. What it is?' He said, 'Yes I have some small inconveniences. I get no tea in the morning or in

---

125 Tendulkar, *Abdul Ghaffar Khan*, p. 171.

126 Bapu to Mirabehn, 7 Sept. 1934, M.K. Gandhi, *Bapu's Letters to Mira 1924-1928* (Allahabad 1948), p. 270.

127 Clarke, *The Cripps Version*, p. 135.

the afternoon.' Gandhi grinned with a twinkle in his eye, and directed Aryanakayam to arrange tea for the guest.[128]

He expected Muslim friends and associates of these men to respond, believing as they did in an alternate path of salvation, in a manner worthy of their traditions but without disavowing their values. Indeed, he wanted them to be sufficiently brave to trust, and all would be well.[129] Ultimately, he hoped that a confluence of the national interests of all the communities would govern the relationship among the communities.

Gandhi-Nama: In Praise of the Mahatma

Gandhi gathered around him a circle of young men who absorbed his ideas. They came to him along various paths. Abdul Majid Daryabadi declared Islam and Satyagraha to be almost interchangeable terms. He was a good writer following Mohamed Ali's trail all his life. That was not the best course for him, but he moved, as did his benefactor Mohamed Ali, from a Western rationalist position to an Islamist perspective. Instead of engaging with the recovery of an enlightened outlook, they became more and more attached to doctrinal Islam. Their liberal sources of inspiration, for which contemporary Turkey offered a good example, dried up.

The writings and speeches of Abdur Rahman Siddiqui, Choudhry Khaliquzzaman, T.A.K. Sherwani, Shuaib Qureshi, and Rafi Ahmed Kidwai are determined by the same sentiment and are, consequently, in the main, a formulation in literary language of the judgement expressed in political manifestos and resolutions.

Hasrat Mohani had a retiring and meditative personality, but his poems, including those reverential of Tilak, are infused with a single central impulse that carries them to their single conclusion: *azadi*. He set himself up from the outset as an anti-romantic, but retained in himself all the romantic virtues. Swayed by earnest moral thoughts and by an ardent mysticism, he venerated Lord Krishna as well as the Sufis. All things considered, his poetry pulsates with the spirit of patriotism from the heart. Despite turning down some of Gandhi's formulas and ruffled

---

128   Shukla (ed.), *Reminiscences of Gandhiji*, pp. 87-91.

129   McDonough, *Gandhi's Responses to Islam*, p. 53.

by his proposal that every Congressman should spin,[130] he revered him. So did his wife, a devoted companion for better or for worse through years of vicissitudes and successes, sorrows and aspirations, clouds and sunlight. She went to jail and wrote her prison diary in Urdu.

Hasrat matured into an accomplished Urdu poet before earning fame as a fiery journalist. His free spirits didn't however find a happy place in any organised movement. His whimsical humour worked against his reputation; in later years, his whimsical world became a place of imaginative personal refuge. He joined Congress in 1904, launched *Urdu-e-Mualla* four years later, and was gaoled for anti-British activities. He wrote: 'The toil of poetry goes side by side with the jail's grinding mill; O what a queer thing is Hasrat's mind?' He knew Gandhi when he first landed in Bombay.[131] At the Amritsar Congress in 1919, he wanted something quicker and speedier than the boycott of purely British goods. Gandhi however opposed his idea.[132] Another showdown with him occurred in December 1921, when Hasrat demanded complete Independence. Gandhi put his foot down and gave cogent reasons for not agreeing to a boycott. Nonetheless, he was neither ill-tempered nor unkind to him, nor did he feel less warmth of heart than always. He spoke highly of his patriotic fervour but turned down his entreaty.[133] Ardent in humanitarian feeling and political ardour, Hasrat didn't give up his doggedness to rid India of the British but wondered, 'the practice of tyranny, how long will it last? The patriot spirit, how long it would remain asleep'. He resigned from the Congress in 1925.

In the 1940s, Hasrat was ferried on a cycle carrier to various whistle-stop meetings to galvanize support for the raging anti-colonial pressure groups. This was also the time of the first modern trade unions in UP, and their workers regarded him as a man who, as their leader championed

---

130   Jawaharlal to Gandhi, 15 Sept. 1924, Iyengar and Zackariah (eds.), *Together They Fought*, p. 15.

131   *CWMG* (21 Dec.- Mar. 1922), p. 165.

132   Andrews (ed.), *Mahatma Gandhi: His Own Story*, pp. 316-17.

133   At the AICC meeting, Hasrat insisted on deleting those phrases in the resolution that excluded the possibility of resorting to violence. He also demanded, against Gandhi's wishes, complete Independence. His amendments were rejected, but as many as 52 members supported them. *CWMG* (Aug. 1924-Jan. 1925), pp. 339-54; Qureshi, *Pan-Islam in British Indian Politics*, pp. 307-8.

their interests. Having chaired the first meeting of the newly-formed Communist Party of India in 1925, he waited all his life for the promised revolution to come his way. The promised dawn of freedom didn't however elude him. He made several significant interventions in the Constituent Assembly debates which were largely idealistic and unrealistic.[134]

Zafar Ali Khan was an Aligarh graduate and a contemporary of Hasrat.[135] In his day he was well known for his prose and verse, and his popular poems ran through scores of editions. He inherited the mantle of the daily *Zamindar* from his father. Incapable of economy of expression, his pen, more often than not dipped in vitriol, celebrated Gandhi. His declamatory lines leave his poems the merit of action, and above all that of poetry.[136]

> *Gandhi ne aaj jung ka ailaan kar diya*
> *Ba-til se haq ko dast-o-garibaan kar diya*
> Gandhi has declared war today,
> And made Truth try conclusions with Falsehood
> *Parwardeegar ne ke woh hai manzuilat shanaas*
> *Gandhi ko bhi yeh martaba pehhchaan kar diya*
> God who knows the worth of people,
> Has given this high position to Gandhi after due thought?

'Action is the end of thought. All thought which does not look towards action is an abortion and a treachery. If then we are the servants of thought we must be the servants of action,' wrote Romain Rolland.[137] Akbar Ilahabadi, who died the year Non-Cooperation gathered momentum, mirrored the wounded sensibility against colonialism

---

134   Mohammad Arshad (ed.), *Adabiyat: Mohammad Atiq Siddiqi ke Adabi Mazameen* (Delhi, 2010), for a series of informative essays on Hasrat Mohani.

135   Zafar Ali Khan (1873-1956) graduated from the M.A.O. College, Aligarh, in 1895; Hasrat Mohani, alias Fazlul Hasan (1877-1951), went to Aligarh and graduated in 1903, the year he launched the Urdu paper, *Urdu-e-Mualla*, which was published intermittently until the 1930s; Shaukat Ali (1873-1938) joined Aligarh College in 1888; Mohamed Ali (1878-1931) graduated from Aligarh and attended Lincoln College, Oxford, from 1898 to 1902.

136   Sadiq, *Twentieth Century Urdu Literature*, p. 87.

137   Nehru, *Glimpses of World History*, p. 953.

and gave birth to a new idealism attached to romanticism. Stirred by Gandhi's evocative powers, he stressed the amalgam of truth and falsehood within him, and sang paeans of praise in verbal quibbles, satire, irony, proverbs, and humour. *Gandhi-Nama*, a collection of verses on Gandhi, manifests his inventive power, imagination, fluency, and acute observation:

> The Revolution has come, there a new world and a new commotion;
> It is all over with *Shahnama*, it is now time for *Gandhi-Nama*.

10
Engaging the 'Traditional' and the 'Modern'

'To resume the story of the Non-co-operation Movement,—whilst the powerful Khilafat agitation set up by the Ali brothers was in full progress, I had full discussions with the late Maulana Abdul Bari and others, especially as to the extent to which a Musalman could observe the rule of non-violence. In the end all agreed that Islam did not forbid non-violence as a policy, and further, that so long as they were pledged to that policy they were bound faithfully to carry it out.'
-C.F. Andrews (ed.), *Mahatma Gandhi: His Own Story*, p. 328.

'You of course come to see me every day. For a long time now I have been feeling that nationalist Muslims are perhaps a prey to fear. They come to me every day and talk a good deal but the impression I get is that they exaggerate somewhat. If we indulge in exaggeration it will do no good anyone—be he Hindu or Muslim. If we think that we alone are right and suppress others in the belief that we are great and that therefore there is no harm in coercing others, we shall fall; we shall be deceiving ourselves. But if we are truthful we shall show fearlessness, discretion and earnestness in our conduct. If we are in error we should duly admit it. We shall not fall thereby, we shall only rise higher.'
-M.K. Gandhi, 18 December, 1947, Letter to a Muslim,
CWMG (11 Nov. 1947-30 Jan. 1948), p. 254.

Two individuals shaped Indian politics in the 1920s. One was of course Gandhi, the other Mohamed Ali, whose autobiography mesh some of the major strands of Muslim/Islamic thinking on the most germane cultural and political issues. He wrote no commentary on religious texts, no ethical works or homiletic pamphlets, but cultivated an interest in the canonical foundation of the Khilafat and the attributes of the Islamic state, on one hand, and the Western challenge to Islam as a total ideology, on the other. Quite apart from the mental and spiritual results of certain events after the death of Syed Ahmad in 1898, *My Life: A Fragment* sets out all the storms, rages and pains of his life. In its unification of public and personal problems, his autobiography deals mainly with the impact of British rule on well bred Muslims and their worries in a colonial system.

Mohamed Ali's father died young. He was born in Rampur, a princely state in Rohilkhand. For Abadi Bano Begum, her three sons (Mohamed, Shaukat, and Zulfiqar) were the entire world to her, with the moon and the stars thrown in for good measure. Her resources were inadequate and the opposition to Western education was stiff, but she expected education to open the door to the world for the boys. She sent Mohamed Ali to Aligarh in 1890 to study Persian classics, history, Urdu, and religion, and attend lectures by Shibli Nomani, the Arabic professor. However, the latter's knowledge and understanding didn't broaden his horizon or make him aware of his heritage. Like many other students studying overseas in those days, he found himself immersed in a Western culture, struggling to retain his faith, freedom and autonomy. He however eventually discovered himself in Oxford and a sense of moral purpose. Imbued with a deep historical consciousness, he began thinking of his future.

Engaged in the grim task of eking out a living, a teaching career eluded him; as a student he had been an agitator and the pro-establishment syndicate refused to employ him in the Aligarh College. His British friends led him along false alleyways. He served the Gaekwad of Baroda and, although the occasion for his resignation in 1910 was court intrigues, his time was running out. A post in the princely state could hardly satisfy his insatiable appetite for action, activity, and high drama, and yet no other avenue to fame and fortune was open to him in those days. Unremitting in his pursuit, journalism was just up Mohamed Ali's street. All he sought were distinction and celebrity status. He struck gold. 'Allah be praised!' said he with a sigh of relief. *Comrade* appeared on 14 January 1911. Besides offering free play to his wit and mockery, its contents were intimately harmonious with the spirit of the time: an anti-government and pan-Islamic wave. Increasingly, the paper drifted towards an Islamic option. Informed by a unique synthesis of Islamic belief and Western philosophy, *Comrade* and the Urdu daily, *Hamdard*, discovered an Islam that could argue with the West on its own terms. Judged by the inspiration animating the contributors, 8500 copies were sold out. Mohamed Ali enjoyed with proper gusto the personal success it brought, but sometimes the necessity of maintaining it directed his talents to trivial ends. Of extraordinary readiness and fluency of speech, he possessed oratorical skills, and as people listened to him, they couldn't but regret that he wasn't afforded the opportunity of displaying his talent in a wider sphere.

What Mohamed Ali spoke and wrote appealed equally to the humble and the great, and penetrated to all minds in terms of religious feelings. They beckoned new paths by introducing modes of Muslim consciousness at once simple and clear. Once *Comrade* and *Hamdard* moved from Calcutta to Delhi, the new capital, the office in Kucha-i Chelan in the meandering by-lane in the old city became a political salon and offered the perfect setting for Delhi's 'Bloomsbury group'. Once writers gathered around some of the leading figures at Delhi College, but now they rallied around Mohamed Ali, the star performer and an iconic figure. Those were exciting times, with poets flaunting their patriotism and their readiness to court imprisonment. Two examples from Hasrat Mohani and Zafar Ali Khan, both contemporaries of the Ali brothers at Aligarh, will suffice.

In vain you frighten me of tyrannical imprisonment;
My devoted spirit would feel free there all the more. [Hasrat Mohani.]
I am interested neither in the conch nor the call to prayer
If I love anything it is India. [Zafar Ali Khan.]

The Ali brothers were like two laughing schoolboys, generous and full of good fun.[1] They were interesting and were, of course, gaining influence. Mohamed Ali, the younger of the two, was a noticeably stocky and powerfully built man with a somewhat glowering expression. He radiated an air of boyishness; he was dreamy, romantic, melancholic, and very Indian. He identified himself with pan-Islamism and tied his community's fate to Turkey as one of the great powers in Europe. His unrestricted pursuits, his example, and precepts exercised the widest influence; he scanned India for the likeliest possibility of trouble: Aligarh, Kanpur,[2] Lucknow, and Delhi. His writing was vehement and

---

1   Brockway, *The Indian Crisis*, p. 120.

2   Robinson, *Separatism Among Indian Muslims*, pp. 212-16, for the Anglo-Muslim conflagration in 1913 sparked by the demolition of a portion of the Kanpur mosque.

combative, occasionally rancorous and hostile, and he frequently found himself at the centre of fierce controversies. Used to his intransigence and certainly less awed by his pan-Islamic dreams, the government promptly imprisoned him on 15 May 1915 for publishing 'The Choice of the Turks'. From now on, the Ali brothers were to raise a cry against the terror of imprisonment in prisons.

First interned at Mehrauli, on the outskirts of Delhi, the Ali brothers were transferred to Lansdowne and, finally to Chhindwara where they arrived wearing 'grey astrakhan caps with large Turkish half moons in the front, also Khuddam-i Kaaba badges'. Mohamed Ali didn't care whether he was under the jurisdiction of one deputy-commissioner or another.[3] Designating themselves as Khuddam-i Kaaba (Servants of Kaaba), he related to the British with alienation and condescension, anxiety and hostility. Jawaharlal remembered them in his statement at the trial by K.N. Knox, district magistrate of Allahabad:

> I shall go to jail again most willingly and joyfully. Jail has indeed become a haven for us, a holy place of pilgrimage since our saintly and beloved leader was sentenced. Big-bodied, great-hearted Shaukat Ali, bravest of the brave, and his gallant brother are there and so are our thousands of co-workers.[4]

Thousands sought their release. Gandhi added to the clamour of voices that filled the air. Talking to Indulal Yagnik, he unfolded a vision of the good things that might be wrought by securing their release. He wanted to go with them to Bihar to unite the Hindus and Muslims. With the thought of also persuading the Muslims to avoid cow-slaughter,[5] he could hardly afford not to be at hand when the Khilafat issue surfaced. A characteristic Gandhian gesture, it succeeded. He wanted to strengthen Mohamed Ali's hand. 'It is our duty,' he once wrote, 'to strengthen by our fasting those who hold the same ideals but are likely to weaken under pressure.'[6]

---

3   Home Dept.,f.no. 1920, UPSA.

4   Statement at Trial, *The Leader*, 19 May 1922, *SWJN*, vol. 1, p. 257.

5   Yagnik, *Gandhi As I Knew Him*, p. 60.

6   Fischer, *The Life of Mahatma Gandhi*, p. 221.

In South Africa, the *Gita* determined Gandhi's life's character and rhythm. Whenever he experienced disappointment, he stumbled on a verse here and there, which brought a smile to his face in the midst of tragedies. The *Gita*, after all, contributed to the efflorescence of humanism, dented religious dogmatism, broke down prejudice, and allowed the human personality to grow and adapt itself to new circumstances. Put in plain words, this accounts for Gandhi's appeal to the common sense and the critical faculty against the formidable structures of orthodoxies.

Similarly, the Quran suffused Mohamed Ali's feelings and way of thinking; it spiritually gratified him as *tauhid* grew upon him as a personal reality, man in the dignity of his 'service' as vicegerent of God, and himself as part of this great strength. After years of ignorance, he realised that the Quran offered a complete scheme of life, a perfect code of conduct and a comprehensive social policy.[7] In Chhindwara, Islam revealed itself to him. This is glaringly obvious from the manner in which he exalted Islam, the abiding source of his pride and the most potent stimulant of his own individualism. Earlier, he conceptualised Hindus and Muslims as distinctive communities, and dreamt of a 'United Faiths of India'. At that time his project had very few takers.

The knowledge that one is a chosen vessel in history can do strange things to a man. To Mohamed Ali, it offered the excuse for extravagant self-indulgence. He saw himself a reformer with democratic ideals of free opinion, free speech, free assembly, and government, and as a reformer of the heart and not the head. His patriotism was intense, even aggressive, but his ideas developed on the ruins of a romantic and undisciplined fancy, a 'Muslim world' combining the exalted pan-Islamic sentiments of the late-nineteenth century roving reformer Jamaluddin Afghani, and the sonorous melodies of Altaf Husain Hali, the Panipat-born poet-author. In a little while, he girded up his loins to act as the supreme helmsman steering the Khilafat ship in an uncertain direction. The sources nurturing his thinking weren't intellectual; he collected evidence uncritically, laced them with puerile anecdotes, and interpreted Islamic history from the lofty height of orthodox classicism.

---

7   Ali, *My Life: A Fragment*, p.71.

Some of his inferences were exciting, but he was essentially a lazy thinker putting new wine into old bottles.

While serving one of his prison jail terms, Mohamed Ali put together a series of invitations to probe and penetrate the subtleties of his mind. *My Life: A Fragment* focuses closely on the internal dynamics of the early twentieth century as seen through the eyes of its protagonist who imperceptibly matured as he witnessed the forces that impacted their lives. This single book of Mohamed Ali still preserves, in its vigorous and picturesque passages, some strength in the intensity with which he represents his times. His thoughts were however shorn of originality by the constant tension of a public figure absorbed by the theoretical application of ideas to the changing global landscape. While approaching politics through experience, he sought to locate in politics examples or analogies to underline a moral already drawn.

It plainly follows that we are looking at an idealist who hankered after an ideal 'Muslim society' steeped in the high traditions of the Prophet and the four orthodox Khalifs. Few serious analysts deny that he is antiquated in certain respects. Even those sympathetic to him concede that there was little factual basis for the hope that pan-Islamism would emerge and destroy the ugly features of nationalism. Mohamed Ali sailed in deep waters; waters deeper than he could fathom.

In a voice filled with emotion, he frequently recited from Iqbal's *Asrar-i Khudi* (Secrets of Self) and *Rumuz-i Bekhudi* (Secrets of Selflessness), repeating the same verse over and over again, hypnotically casting a spell over his listeners, explaining its nuances, every now and again crying copiously over something that struck him as particularly apt in their circumstance, and causing his audience to weep too.[8] Incidentally, Iqbal continued to be a favourite poet of the Aligarh and Jamia students. Their most favoured verses were drawn from *Khizr-i Rah, Tulu-i Islam, Payam-i Mashriq*, and *Bang-i Dara*. Gandhi asked Iqbal to head Jamia, but he declined.[9] He came to the campus in 1933 and 1935 only to move his audience to tears with his poem on the Cordova mosque.

---

8   Ali, *My Life: A Fragment*, p. 71.

9   Before 27 Nov.1920, for Gandhi's letter, *CWMG* (Nov. 1920–Apr. 1921), p. 35; McDonough, *Gandhi's Responses to Islam*, pp. 59–61.

Mohamed Ali's impetuous flights of imagination and robust optimism attracted friends and followers, but they also knew that he could wield an acid pen and work systematically to demolish them, sometimes with sarcasm and not infrequently with petulance. As he once wrote, he had 'an inherent and almost ineradicable tendency towards diffusion and a fatal attraction for tangents'. This applied to Shaukat Ali too, a rebel who in almost every act articulated the most forceful aspects of pan-Islamism.[10] For sheer perversity of character, honours must go to him as also for the indisputable eccentricity of his ideas.

It is indeed difficult to say whether the Ali brothers were more the object of wonder or of scandal, of regard or of disapproval. Both showed exemplary courage when their consciences called upon them to do so, but their urges seemed almost completely fulfilled by their transnational obsessions which were fundamentally inconsistent. Zafar Ali Khan, a contemporary of theirs at Aligarh and editor of *Zamindar* (Lahore), said it all:

Dono ne mil ke daali hai Islamion me phook
Hai sulha aashti se Ali bhaion ko zid
Unka qalam laghw naveesi me be-misaal
Unki zabaan baseehdagoi me munfirad
Both have caused a split in the Muslim camp,
The Ali brothers have ever been at war with peace and amity.
The pen of this one has no equal in writing nonsense,
And the tongue of the other in talking gibberish.

It is said of George Bernard Shaw that his feet were as frequently off the ground as on it, but his mind was equally confident in direction when airborne as when pedestrian. This holds true of Mohamed Ali. Prone to shocking susceptibilities and coming close to airing awkward

---

10 This is what Gandhi thought of him: 'I tell you that there is not a better soldier living in our ranks in British India than Shaukat Ali. When the time for the drawing of the sword comes, if it ever comes, you will find him drawing that sword and you will find me retiring to the jungles of Hindustan.' Desai (ed.), *Day-to-Day with Gandhi*, vol. 2, p. 193.

and ungainly views, he limited himself to giving further certitude and strength to his pan-Islamic visualisations. We know the reasons for his way of thinking: but he didn't realise the distinction, which nowadays appears so obvious to us, between nationalistic aspirations and the utopias Jamaluddin Afghani created, because he didn't move in circles that had a satisfactory idea of the chasm between ideals and reality. Therefore his dramatic approach was often singularly ineffectual. While an intriguing debate took place on the wisdom and feasibility of the Khilafat institution itself and most wished to reduce its dependency on the people, Mohamed Ali engaged in pointless projects and forlorn hopes. In October 1923 and February 1924, he and Shaukat joined Ubaidullah Sindhi, a Sikh convert to Islam from the Deoband seminary, to unite the oppressed nations of Asia against England.[11] This was after Mustafa Kemal Pasha had bundled out the Khalifa from Istanbul.

Mohamed Ali was not one to bury the hatchet, to let bygones be bygones, and to sort out differences with opponents. As such, he wanted to strip away the veil of hypocrisy and unconscious self-deception that concealed the ugly realities of power politics. It was however his fundamental puritan earnestness that brought him into conflict with Gandhi. When they first came together, he treated Gandhi with respect, esteem, and a little irony, then with a stronger attachment, and in the end with disdain and cynicism. He precipitated angry comments by suggesting, in 1924, that the creed of even a fallen and degraded Muslim is entitled to a higher place than that of any other non-Muslim, irrespective of his high character even if the person in question were Mahatma Gandhi himself.[12] Much hullabaloo followed this emotional outburst, which Peter Hardy, the historian, regards as 'substitutes for clear objectives and clear vision.'[13] Gandhi was sufficiently large-hearted to point out that Mohamed Ali had proved the purity of his heart and his faith in his own religion and that he merely compared two sets of

---

11   IOR. L/PJ/12/241.

12   Rajmohan Gandhi, *Understanding the Muslim Mind* (Delhi, 2000), pp. 109-10.

13   Peter Hardy, *The Muslims of British India* (Cambridge, 1972), p. 211.

religious principles and gave his opinion on which one was superior.[14] In point of fact, Gandhi's hurt can be understood by the fact that, in 1927 and 1936, he mentioned Mohamed Ali's crude remarks about him.[15] Andrews was justified in rejecting Mohamed Ali's stance.[16]

Gandhi's friendly relations with Mohamed Ali were periodically punctuated with disagreements, which flowed and ebbed like the tides as the years passed. Notwithstanding loyal protestations, their paths began to diverge and the fine ideals of the Khilafat and Non-Cooperation movements were swamped by petty squabbles. Gandhi's strong expressions of goodwill were slowly dissipated, and his principles and standards, which had become virtually sacrosanct, were held up to sceptical scrutiny, and his entire conception of Hindu-Muslim *bhai bhai* was rudely shaken.

Two issues stand out. Gandhi denied that Islam had been established with the help of the sword: its foundation, he stated, had been laid by the Sufis and by men of learning through their saintliness.[17] He however saw the sword too much in evidence during the Moplah and Kohat riots: 'it must be sheathed if Islam is to be what it means—peace'.[18] He called Muslims a 'bully' and Hindus as 'docile to the point of cowardice'. 'Hindus must cease to fear the Musalman bully, and the Musalmans should consider it beneath their dignity to bully their Hindu brothers,' he wrote.[19] The mild Hindu was usually used as a term of reproach, but Gandhi took it as a term of honour. In a majority of quarrels, the latter came out second best. Where there were cowards, according to Gandhi, there will always be bullies. He appealed to Muslims to forbear because, being bullies, they could fight well and protect themselves. On the contrary, he advised Hindus to

---

14   Sheila McDonough, 'The Muslims of South Asia (1857-1947)', in Jacques Waardenburg (ed.), *Muslim Perceptions of Other Religions: A Historical Survey* (New York, 1999), pp. 254-5.

15   Mohamed Ali said that although he respected Gandhi, he held that the faith of a Muslim who believes in the Quran is greater than Gandhi's faith.

16   Tendulkar, *Mahatma*, vol. 4, p. 98.

17   Rekha Trivedi (ed.), *Gandhi Speaks on Non-Cooperation in UP*, p. 211.

18   Tendulkar, *Abdul Ghaffar Khan*, p. 49.

19   Gandhi, *The Way to Communal Harmony*, pp. 16, 17.

fight back because 'quarrels must break out so long as Hindus continue to be seized with fear. Bullies are always to be found when there are cowards. The Hindus must understand that no one can afford them protection if they can go on hugging fear.' This is curious advice from the proponent of non-violence.[20] What is particularly strange is that Gandhi treated Hindus and Muslims as an undifferentiated whole; a world intact and bound by common solidarities. He concludes on an equally disturbing note: 'It will take some time before the average Hindu ceases to be a coward and the average Musalman ceases to be a bully.'[21]

Gandhi, of course, modified his earlier remark that 'Islam was born in an atmosphere of violence'. But this did not help to remove the shadow of doubts. With the storm created by *Rangila Rasul* (The Playboy Prophet) and other expressions of anti-Muslim/Islam sentiments, Muslim publicists read Gandhi's statement with a fair degree of scepticism. Mohamed Ali seized the opportunity to proclaim that any of those whom Gandhi called cowards were first rate bullies and vice versa. Many cowards among Hindus engaged in considerable bullying and many bullies among Muslims turned on their heels the moment they were pitted against persons superior in strength. If so, there was neither merit in this contention nor in portraying Muslims as 'comparatively quarrelsome'. However, men of strong minds, great force of character, and a hard-textured sensibilities are very capable of committing errors of this kind. Discretion, notes Rajmohan Gandhi, grandson and biographer of Gandhi, was even difficult for a Mahatma.[22] It would appear that Gandhi was convinced that Muslims were using jihad as an instrument for universalising Islam. Here, again, he failed to notice scores of scholars and theologians who interpreted jihad in terms of salvation of the soul and found violence, whether in Turkey or Iran, an expression of disenchantment over exclusion, underdevelopment, and discrimination.

---

20 Mohibbul Hasan, 'Mahatma Gandhi and the Indian Muslims', S.C. Biswas (ed.), *Gandhi Theory and Practice: Social Impact and Contemporary Relevance* (Simla, 1969), p. 138.

21 *Young India*, 11 May 1921, 18 Sept. 1924, *The Way to Communal Harmony*, pp. 16, 17.

22 Rajmohan Gandhi, *Understanding the Muslim Mind*, p. 111.

Gandhi discovered that 'we have no data as yet for distributing blame', and implored everyone to avoid the language of anger and hatred.[23] If so, there was no need to serve out a most exalted homily to the so-called Hindu cowards or to advise them to fight back, even if Gandhi believed that inter-community strife would break out so long as Hindus continued to be seized by fear. For that matter, he had no reason to expect 'the Hindu' to develop sufficient strength of will to withstand brute force and, if necessary, die in the act. In so politically charged a climate, the 'bully'/'coward' categorisation made it even more difficult for moderate, pluralist discourses to find a voice.

All things considered, Gandhi's ideas remained hovering above, like Plato's utopia: besides articulating the fight against communalism in the language of a governess, he believed that riots could be ended as easily as they had begun. He saw the growing violence in black and white, good and evil, and overlooked complex social and cultural issues. He conceded that sectarian violence couldn't be curbed by posturing and platitudes, but he also declared that the Hindu-Muslim problem had passed out of human hands, and been conveyed into the hands of God alone.[24]

Behind this deluge of hand-wringing and despondency, Gandhi kept a distance from 'unity conferences' which tended to whitewash the existence of a deep divide. He remained away from the All-Parties meetings between February and June 1928, for which his healthy irreverence for constitutional issues was also a factor, but endorsed the verdict against separate electorates and reservation of seats: 'the finishing kick to communalism'.[25] Hardly had the ink dried when he hailed the Nehru Report as 'the most brilliant victory achieved at Lucknow'.[26] Mohamed Ali, who stood for complete Independence, thundered that Gandhi had admitted the bondage of servitude. Shaukat

---

23 Statement to the Press on communal problem, 6 Apr. 1931, *CWMG* (Dec. 1930-Apr. 1931), p. 395.

24 *Young India*, 13 Jan. 1927, p. 13.

25 Jawaharlal on the results of the All Parties Conference, *SWJN*, vol. 3, p. 61.

26 Gandhi to Motilal, 3 Mar. 1928, Motilal Papers, NMML; Kumar and Sharma (eds), *SWMN*, vol. 6, pp. 242-43.

Ali dubbed his associate, Ansari, a 'useless limb' who, he alleged, was controlled by Hindu leaders, adding: 'It is so easy to play the generous liberal minded patriot at the expense of one's own people'.[27] Ansari dismissed his allegation as sour grapes. The Ali brothers preferred to scapegoat Gandhi or the Congress Muslims for making peace over the issue of complete Independence, i.e., agreeing to dominion status in the Nehru Report.

When it came to discussing the imminent dangers of mixing religion with politics, Gandhi juggled with words, which were by and large too abstract to be understood by laypersons. Mohamed Ali charged him for hunting with both the hare and the hounds.[28] Throughout, he put pen to paper with his usual prodigality and sermonised on how Gandhi had given a free hand to the 'Lala-Malaviya gang' to pursue the goal of 'Hindu Rashtra', and that he was unprepared to condemn Hindu fanatics. With Gandhi fighting for the supremacy of Hinduism, he expected Jawaharlal's colleagues to leave him in the lurch in a crisis, and eventually send him to the gallows.[29] The flow of his rhetoric continued unchecked and unchanged, declaring every effort in resolving inter-community disputes as being inimical, biased, and downright ill-conceived. He intended to upset Gandhi with his outburst and succeeded; the bitterness remained. More generally, while Gandhi claimed to head a pan-Indian, if not a typically 'secular' brand of polity, Mohamed Ali was consumed by instantly recognisable communitarian interests. Mohamed Ali was, in particular, obsessed with one major theme which infused most of his articles: preserving and fostering his community's *separate political personality.*

Gandhi contended that he hadn't changed in the least from the Khilafat days, and that he was still prepared to lay down his life for permanent peace.[30] In *Young India*, he commented:

---

27   Kumar and Sharma (eds.), *SWMN*, vol. 6, pp. 238-39; Shaukat Ali to Ansari, 6 Sept. 1928, *SWMN*, vol. 6, p. 245.

28   Quoted in I.H. Qureshi, *Ulema in Politics: A Study Relating to the Political Activities of the Ulema in the South-Asian Subcontinent from 1556 to 1947* (Karachi, 1974); Gandhi to Mohamed Ali, 21 July 1924, Mohamed Ali papers.

29   Nehru, *An Autobiography*, p. 120.

30   Pyarelal, *The Epic Fast*, p. 81.

I know that I have not the Ali Brothers with me. Maulana Shaukat
Ali will no longer have me in his pocket. Do not think, I do not
miss him. I hold no difference between him and blood brother. His
resistance therefore can be short-lived. If truth is in me, the brothers
must capitulate. They cannot keep out of the battle.[31]

Owing to his litany of complaints and distrust of Gandhi's associates,
Mohamed Ali reacted with his customary scepticism.[32] After returning
from Baghdad on 1 December 1928, he made his peace with the All-
India Muslim Conference, an organisation comprising in the main
cranks and opportunists. Jawaharlal felt hurt that he did so. In London,
his outbursts captured media attention but in his 'Last Statement', he
took recourse to harsh judgements and a mocking tone. Reginald Arthur
Reynolds thought that there were 'many nationalist Mohammedans of
more worth than Mohamed Ali as a representative'.[33]

Benthall, president of the Bengal Chamber of Commerce in
India, took him to Oxford where he stayed for a weekend with A.D.
Lindsay, Master of Balliol College. The students had heard Gandhi
just a fortnight earlier. He imprinted an image of him [Gandhi] on
Badruddin Tyabji's mind which persisted, and undoubtedly influenced
him greatly in the years to come.[34] By contrast, Mohamed Ali talked
cricket and made the students laugh without putting across the case
for the Muslims to a youthful but intelligent audience who were to
provide a fair number of the nation's political leaders in later years.[35]
There was in his voice a tinge of conflict, failure, and disappointment.
He spoke like a man who had come to the end of his journey, within
sighting distance of death. On 26 November 1928, he reached Baghdad
with the intention of going to Palestine but the British government
denied him permission. He, therefore, sailed from Basra for Bombay
a year later. He died in London, the imperial city that had hosted

---

31   *Bombay Chronicle*, 5 Apr. 1930, Jayakar papers (354).

32   Gandhi to Motilal, 12 Aug. 1928, Motilal papers (G-1).

33   Extract from Scotland Yard, 15 Oct. 1930, L/PJ/12/411, BL.

34   Badruddin Tyabji, *Memoirs of an Egoist*, vol. 1 (Delhi, 1988), p. 35.

35   N.d., Benthall papers.

him once before as a student, and was buried in the Al-Aqsa mosque in Jerusalem.

As a patriot, Mohamed Ali stuck to his anti-colonial moorings. 'For me,' he pointed out in a letter to Shaukat Ali which the intelligence department intercepted, 'all politics is Islamic and Indian. We detest their imperialism and are determined to free Islam and India from their imperialist shackles ... We openly preach to Muslims and Indian masses to love freedom and hate bondage and never to rest until freedom is won. We have to take the fullest advantage of our numbers—our teeming millions—and that can't be done if we conspire secretly.'[36]

He also defended the demand for self-determination at the First Round Table Conference.[37] However, his co-participants noticed, as others had done previously, that he neither recognised diversity nor the plurality of values. He admitted of only two divisions, Hindu and Muslim, and not nationalist and reactionary or non-cooperating and cooperating.[38] He had a choice between, what R.W. Emerson called, 'soft' and 'turbulent' dreams, but he proved to be a dreamer of dreams that far too frequently ran to seed or were stultified in action through futile compromise and the evasion of precise issues on occasions when proven facts had to be faced. Like any dreamer, he couldn't contend with the frictions of reality.[39] He disparaged learning and the intellectual life, and urged doing. He wanted to do more and more until he ran out of steam.

Public opinion itself is a kind of weathercock which is turned by any change in the wind, but which in itself has little influence in changing the direction of the wind.[40] Mohamed Ali pursued what the wiseacres of his time called a mad chimera but it cannot be denied that without him the pan-Islamic movement would never have taken off

---

36   Mohamed Ali to Shaukat Ali, 5 July 1928, IOR, L/PJ/12/374.

37   Mohamed Ali to Irwin, 11 Sept. 1930, ibid.

38   Ansari to Mazharul Haque, 7 Sept. 1929, Hasan (ed.), *Muslims and the Congress*, pp. 86-7; Mujeeb, *The Indian Muslims*, p. 539.

39   I owe this thought, expression, and insight into the Utopian Socialists to Robert L. Heilbroner, *The Worldly Philosophers: The Lives, Times, and Ideas of the Great Economic Thinkers* (New York, 1972), p. 121.

40   FR (NWFP), Mar. 1932, Home Pol., File no. 18/5, 32.

the ground. Shaukat Ali, too, orchestrated his brother's criticism of the Nehru Report, and pointed out, in his evidence before the enquiry into the Bombay riots in February 1929, that the Congress turned its back on the resolutions of the Madras Congress in 1927, and that Ansari and others had betrayed their community.

There was, nonetheless, an easing of tension in early 1930, but Sapru, taking advantage of the favourable political climate, convened a conference in Bombay in May 1930. With the Congress involved in Civil Disobedience and the Muslim leaders speculating on getting better terms from the government, this Liberal party initiative failed, lending credence to Shaukat Ali's wild charge that 'nationalist' opinion was arrayed against the Muslims. In March 1932, he told the Peshawaris to strengthen Islam first and foremost, expressly against the Hindus, and work the reforms. In 1937, he continually referred to a possible civil war. He said he would make a Spain of India and so on and so forth.[41] Above and beyond, he brought disrepute to himself by splurging the Khilafat funds on an extravagant standard of living to the point of recklessness. Reduced to modest circumstances and then to virtual penury, he then approached the government for a pension. This was a mighty fall. He curried favour with Jinnah, acting as his mouthpiece.[42] For his part, Abbas Tyabji, Gandhi's lieutenant in Bombay, thought that the Ali brothers weren't the type he had faith in,[43] and Lucknow's Urdu newspaper, *Hamdam*, castigated Shaukat Ali for his *volte-face*.

> He who was yesterday trying to dig the foundations of Englishmen in India is today their best friend and is trying his utmost to injure national movements. The fact is that Muslims are a very grateful people. When a man who has always subsisted on public subscriptions is invited to lunch by Viceroys and Governors, it isn't strange that he should abandon his past beliefs and rub his forehead

---

41   Jawaharlal to Gandhi, 13 July 1937, Iyengar and Zackariah (eds), *Together They Fought*, p. 305.

42   Chatterjee (ed.), *TF*, 1938, (pt 1), p. 286.

43   Brown, *Gandhi's Rise to Power*, p. 276.

on the threshold of government. Government's favours have benefited M. Shaukat Ali in many ways. Why should he not then serve it instead of serving the community for which he had always to suffer imprisonment? Personal interests are supreme.[44]

For all his failings, Mohamed Ali had a warmer side and, on the credit side, accomplished much to compensate for his enthusiastic gaffes. Gandhi couldn't help admiring what he saw as his heroism, his independent thinking, and courage. He was truly the stuff of which heroes are made. It was almost a marvel how a cycle of estrangement was ever so often followed by this burst of affection. Gandhi retained an unfailing loyalty to the Ali brothers. He hoped that, if truth was in him, they'd give in and their misunderstandings would be allayed.[45] Love that couldn't stand the strain of differences is like 'a sounding brass and tinkling cymbal'.[46] Gandhi went a step further to mollify him: 'the only non-violent solution I know is for Hindus to let minorities take what they liked. I wouldn't hesitate to let minorities govern the country'.[47] Even so, grim and worn out, the diabetes-afflicted Mohamed Ali became irresponsive to Gandhi's overflow of cordial sentiments but mercifully didn't get angry. He didn't lash back; instead he grinned.

The Ali brothers had every right to disagree with Gandhi without suspecting his motives. They should have known that his 'Kingdom of God on earth' was to be, if politically translated, one of equal opportunities, justice, freedom of worship, speech, and the press. His state was to be based on Truth and non-violence with prosperous, happy, and self-contained village communities. The more the Truth develops in all its implications, the greater will be the opportunity of detecting any element of error that it may contain: and, conversely, if no

44   2 Feb. 1932, UPNNR.

45   Gandhi to Motilal, 12 Aug.1929, Motilal Papers (G1); *Young India*, 3 Apr. 1930, *CWMG*, vol. 43, p. 126. To Horace Alexander, 23 Dec. 1930, in Alexander, *Gandhi through Western Eyes*, p. 194.

46   *Young India*, 19 Feb. 1931, *CWMG* (Dec. 1930-Apr. 1931), p. 203.

47   Note on the Press, UP of Agra and Oudh, for the week ending 31 May 1930.

error appears, the more completely does it establish itself as truth in its entirety and nothing other than the truth.[48]

Partners in Freedom

The urge to strike the straight road and to tread it is inherent in human nature, observed Azad.[49] The 'Congress Muslims' was a title that would have gratified that collectivity because it is faithful to their actual intent and to the consciousness they had of themselves. Of course, no one would place all of them on exactly the same plane of political or intellectual attainments, but they had valuable things to say about religion, politics, and education. Gandhi spoke of their commanding presence: 'Each has his own dharma, and each had to follow it implicitly, come what might.'[50] They were 'clear-eyed and courageous fellow-travellers' living up to their ideal of plurality in thought and action and, what is more, sharing Gandhi's craving for truth.[51] I engage in recovering the forgotten, weigh their experiences, value them, and open new ways of understanding their cherished goals. Perhaps I have cavalierly dismissed some of them with a line or two or not mentioned them at all; others of lesser importance may merit several pages. Readers may describe this as an arbitrary re-arrangement of the Hall of Fame, but my selection is bound to be somewhat random and subjective.

So long as the Gandhi charisma worked and his will prevailed, individual Muslims turned vegetarian, spun yarn, wore hand-woven cloth, and welcomed small-scale industries. After a short time, however, the voice of the revivalists rang louder than it had ever in the recent decades; their militancy is prima facie evidence that Gandhi's message hadn't gone down well with them. The Barelwi ulama were, in particular,

---

48 This was close to the ideas of the British sociologist Leonard Hobhouse (1864-1929). Sidorsky (ed.), *The Liberal Tradition in European Thought*, p. 99.

49 Kenneth Cragg, *The Pen and the Faith: Eight Modern Muslim Writers and the Qur'an* (Delhi, 1988 edn), p. 26.

50 Speech at Ghatkopar, 15 June 1921, *CWMG* (Mar. 22-May 1924), p. 291.

51 To Hakim Ajmal Khan, 12 Mar. 1922. 'I have been drawn so close to you, chiefly because I know that you believe in Hindu-Muslim unity in the full sense of the term.'

up in arms. The Ahl-i Hadith debated the legitimacy of an alliance with Gandhi. The Jamiyat al-ulama had no such doubts but insisted on defending what they judged to be minority rights. Now Gandhi set aside the theological niceties and, instead, threw his weight behind the moral arguments, which he used in the case of Dalits. However, judging from what transpired, the political classes disapproved of Gandhi's tone and tenor in negotiated minority rights. On 26 September 1932, Tagore reminded Gandhi 'to make a desperate effort to win over the Mahommedans to our common cause'.[52]

One of the most familiar views in old Delhi is of Ansari Road, with Daryaganj in the foreground, outlined against the background of Ring Road. It is in every way appropriate that Ansari, Delhi's most prominent citizen and a leading Congress Muslim, be associated with the locality. Certainly there have been few more distinguished figures, notably Ajmal Khan, but Ansari's extended career as a politician speaks for itself and his hold on the everyday life in his clinic as a doctor.

In the welter of remedies and actions, his voice was moderate. However, his finessed judgement opened up a way for reinterpretation of a certain 'nationalistic' perspective. With Gandhi expecting him to pilot a Hindu-Muslim pact as Congress president, a position he was elected to in August 1927, his agenda was towards emancipation. He assailed the swarajists, advocated direct action, implored others who still desired to go to the councils to confess that they were co-operators, sink their differences, and form a people's party. With the warring factions bent on destroying one another, he paid special attention to the communal malaise.[53]

The Madras Congress was Ansari's finest hour. Enthusiasm overflowed as hundreds of huts were built in a new and temporary town with an enormous hall, rapidly erected of bamboo and leaves. A new railway line and station were built for the 7000 delegates. Volunteers controlled them; the medical service attended to their health.[54] Gandhi

---

52   To Gandhi, 30 Sept. 1932, Krishna Dutta and Andrew Robinson (eds), *Selected Letters of Rabindranath Tagore* (Cambridge, 1997), p. 417.

53   Pyarelal, *Mahatma Gandhi*, vol. 1, p. xvi.

54   Brockway, *The Indian Crisis*, pp. 115-16.

entered the pandal greeted by sustained cheers. The debate commenced following Ansari's presidential address. Gandhi didn't say much to inspire confidence in the speaker.

Once the printed version of the statement appeared, Gandhi advised Ansari to keep his thoughts to himself, tear his statement to pieces, accept the election with grace, dignity, and thankfulness, and announce that he didn't have his own policy. He advised him: 'You owe it to the country as a Mussalman and a staunch nationalist to vindicate the religion of the Prophet and the honour of the country by giving all the talents you have for securing a domestic peace honourable to all parties.' Ansari was, when all is said and done, sent packing with an admonition to unlearn his entire perspective. He was told: 'if you wish to place them before a few friends gathered together in a drawing-room enjoying hookah, you may certainly enliven the company with your views. But beyond the four walls of such a drawing-room, your views may not travel.'[55] Ansari replied briefly and dryly to this patronising tone.

The Gandhi-Ansari rift came out into the open after 14-16 February 1930. The CWC meetings on these days were expected to formulate plans for defying British authority. Ansari couldn't attend, but warned Gandhi against getting carried away by the exuberance over Independence Day on 26 January: 'it is one thing to join a procession, but it is quite another to face hardships and to withstand repression when time comes for real action.'[56] With conditions being quite the reverse of what they were a decade earlier, he pleaded with Gandhi to retrace his steps, concentrate on restoring communal fellowship, 'the one and only basic thing' in the Congress agenda, and reappraise Congress policies in view of the fact that Gandhi's way of achieving unity had already proved ineffective.[57] His letter, for all its exaggerations, contained a deeply felt and sincere indictment of a leader he revered. Gandhi recognised the 'problem of problems', but approached it differently. Not only did he

55   Gandhi to Ansari, 10 Aug. 1927, *CWMG* (June-Sept. 1927), p. 305; Gandhi to Ansari, 26 Aug. 1927, Hasan (ed.), *Muslims and the Congress*, pp. 21-2.

56   Ansari to Gandhi, 10 Feb. 1930, Hasan (ed.), *Muslims and the Congress*, p. 93.

57   Ansari to Gandhi, 13 Feb. 1930, ibid. pp. 94-101.

seek Independence through a redressal of the age-old ill-treatment which touched the masses, but he called for adjustments *after* and not before the transfer of power.[58] In plain words, the time had now come for the intellectuals to abandon their detachment and to arouse in the people the patriotic spirit. Usually courteous in bearing and chivalrous in state of mind, he believed that Ansari and his friends had mistaken his movement's aim and purpose and that they were posturing for the wrong reasons.

Gandhi's reply dismayed Sherwani, Syed Mahmud and Choudhry Khaliquzzaman.[59] Like Ansari, they had expected Gandhi to do more than he had done to foster the cause of Hindu-Muslim amity: they too were dissatisfied and always felt unjustly treated. However, although frustrated, they shared Ansari's belief that, eventually, the Congress needed them as much as they needed the Congress. A crestfallen Ansari made known: 'my heart is with you my brain is not, in spite of all the bias in your favour'.[60]

The little group of quasi-intellectuals was at once branded as idealistic and cynical, courageous and fragile. Its members spoke with individual voices, expressing opinions and convictions at variance with one another, but their emotional, political, and intellectual responses derived from a feeling of being outside party circles. Consequently, they cultivated the image of a lonely, misunderstood, and thwarted group. Khaliquzzaman, to whom the faults of the Congress were more apparent than its merits, made the break.[61] For most however, leaving

---

58   Gandhi to Ansari, 16 Feb. 1930, *CWMG* (Oct. 1929-Sept. 1930), pp. 510-11.

59   Ibid., to Ansari, 16 Feb. 1930, pp. 161-2; Ibid., 3 Mar. 1930, ibid., p. 113; Ibid, 1930, ibid., pp. 106-7.

60   Ansari to Gandhi, n.d, Ansari collection.

61   Attia Hosain probably alludes to Khaliquzzaman, known to be a slippery character: 'And then one day he and his family had stealthily crossed the Eastern border. But his delusions of political grandeur had come to nothing. Others were already entrenched in positions of power; his genius for political scheming proved unsuccessful among those born and bred in the regions where he tried to become a leader. He was not even made an ambassador like most of his erstwhile colleagues. He had to content himself with living on the profits of the vast property he has claimed as compensation for the alleged wealth he had left behind.' Attia Hosain, *Sunlight on a Broken Column*, p. 295.

the Congress would have been close to political harakiri.[62] Thus, Ansari's heart wasn't in civil disobedience, and yet he stayed in the thick of things. He played host to the CWC meeting at Dar-us-Salam, but warned Gandhi to avoid making wrong calculations.[63] He went to jail with many of his colleagues, but they remained in the Congress as reluctant partners.

In November-December 1941, the issue of freedom to speak resurfaced with Satyamurti, a respected Congress leader who had worked closely with Ansari, B.C. Roy, and Bhulabhai Desai in the Swarajya party. Owing to the rapidly worsening international situation, he suggested that civil disobedience be restricted to select satyagrahis, the parliamentary front should be revived, and the Congress should be allowed to function as an opposition in the central legislature, and popular governments be formed in the provinces.[64] He referred to Gandhi's actions in the past and the freedom of dissent the Congress socialists enjoyed.

However, Gandhi didn't want the Congress to participate in parliamentary activity. While Satyamurti wanted 'unconditional freedom', Gandhi advocated silence,[65] and later reminded him of his duties.[66]

Patel and Azad didn't take too kindly to Satyamurti's defiance. The strong current of hostility in their exchanges reinforced the impression, which had gained ground after the treatment meted out to Ansari and his friends, that exchanging ideas freely had ceased to be a cherished Congress policy. Their letters, autobiographies, and memoirs speak about the illusions, the constraints, the doubts and the disappointment with Gandhi.

---

62   Ansari to T.A.K. Sherwani, 6 Jan. 1930, Hasan (ed.), *Muslims and the Congress*, p. 90.

63   Ansari to Gandhi, 10 Feb. 1930, 13 Feb. 1930, ibid., pp. 93, 94-101.

64   Satyamurti to Gandhi, 27 Aug. 1941, Ramanathan (ed.), *The Satyamurti Letters*, vol. 2, pp. 316-17.

65   Gandhi to Satyamurti, 1 Sept. 1941, ibid., p. 319.

66   Gandhi to Satyamurti, 30 Oct. 1941, ibid., p. 323.

Like the morning sun in the luminosity of his intelligence.
Like the candle in the mehfil *which gives light to all but be aloof*
from all
MISLE KHURSHID-I SEHAR FIKR KI TABANI ME
SHAMA-I MEHFIL KI TARAH SAB SE JUDA, SAB KE RAFIQ

'Calcutta is an upstart town with no depth of sentiment in her face and in her manners,' wrote Tagore.[67] When he was over forty (b. 1861), the capital of British India, also a major centre of the Bengal Renaissance, boasted a galaxy of talent. A visitor in 1913 would quite probably have learned of a certain Mohiuddin Ahmad by picking up a copy of *Al-Hilal*, an Urdu newspaper published in a Bengali-speaking region with a vast countrywide readership. The learned reader, and there were scores of them in those days, would have been struck by the dignity and erudition that went with the title: Maulana.

Abul Kalam's early writings in *Al-Hilal* and *Al-Balagh* are ultra-conservative. He championed pan-Islamism; this commitment was reinforced after visiting some parts of the Arab world. The closure of the Khilafat era brought him close to the nationalist struggle. He brought with him a unique blend of charisma, energy, and good sense. The steadiness of his behaviour, the constancy of his views, and the scholarship he produced made him a familiar figure in wide circles. As years rolled on, he personified a synthesis of the Persian, Arabic, and Indian cultures, and helped to re-orient thinking on the strength of the combination of traditional training and exposure to the modern world. It was a refreshing and stimulating know-how, for the realm of Indian Muslim thought had been hitherto elitist or dominated by the *ashraf*. He took a stand on most issues and left nothing in a state of indecision. He voiced his beliefs honestly, without trickery and without reservation as they emerged from questioning and conviction. He claimed:

There is hardly a single conviction in me which has not had to bear the sting of doubt, or a single belief which has not faced the test of

---

67   Rabindranath Tagore, *My Life in my Words,* Selected and edited by Uma Das Gupta, p. 9.

denial. I have gulped in poison mixed with every draught applied to
my lips, and have administered to myself Elixir coming forth from
every quarter.[68]

Prison was Azad's home and it taught him to triumph over it. Jawaharlal
found him, during their 18 months of close companionship in
Ahmednagar Fort, to be dignified and restrained.[69] His own seclusion
enabled him to arrange his thoughts and evolve his political creed
undisturbed by external influences, but he failed to understand why
Azad, having cast his net wide and revealed a breadth of view and
patient learning, wrote so little. The explanation is simple enough: both
as an intensely reserved man and a careful and deliberate writer, Azad
kept his public and his private lives apart.

One of his essays on Sarmad, the martyr, adumbrates an outlook
marked by a comprehensive, Muslim religious humanism, very much
in the line of the humanism embodied in the classical Persian Sufi
poetical traditions. In his reflection on Sarmad's faith, the young Azad
unambiguously opted for a kind of religious outlook that was to mark
the decades of his public career. Advocating composite nationalism,
as against territorial separatism, had its firm roots in an outlook and
an option within the wider Indo-Muslim tradition. This option Azad
chose before his later party-political affiliation.[70]

The *Masla-i Khilafat wa Jaziratul Arab* had been a *tour de force*,
albeit a small one. It pulsates with the spirit of impassioned pan-
Islamism. Azad didn't create the ingredients that went into its making,
but synthesised them and gave the resulting pan-Islamism a specific
political-ideological aspect. *Tarjuman al-Quran*, which he began
writing in 1916 but only partially completed in Meerut District Jail on
20 July 1930, made an éclat. By this time, he had found a new political
vocation, away from the pieties of pan-Islamism and from the pull of

---

68   Abul Kalam Azad, *Basic Concepts of the Quran*, trans. by Syed Abdul Latif
      (Hyderabad, 1958), Mushirul Hasan (ed.), *Islam in South Asia: The Realm of
      the Traditional*, vol. 3 (Delhi, 2008), p. 148.

69   To Nan darling, 9 Apr. 1943, Sahgal (ed.), *Before Freedom*, p. 319.

70   Christopher Shackle (ed.), *Urdu and Muslim South Asia: Studies in Honour of
      Ralph Russell* (Delhi, 1991), p. 114; Douglas, *Abul Kalam Azad*, pp. 286-90.

the old Khilafat cause. He came to the Congress eager to work for the pluralist idea.

Ghubar-i Khatir (1946) offered a point of mediation between the past and the present; a thread of spiritual continuity. The descriptive passages are often diffused, but they are frequently written in a grand manner and rise to epic heights. No doubt some sections of the book are tendentious, but they expound ideas quite honestly and legitimately—ideas which have to be reckoned with as the ideas of the Egyptian reformer Shaikh Mohammad Abduh, the roving pan-Islamist, Jamaluddin Afghani, and his bête noire Syed Ahmad Khan. The essays published in various collections have a special character: reminiscence tinged with elusive pathos and veined with literary allusion. More often than not, they conceal a little and not reveal the self so that the reader is left to penetrate beneath the surface of the text. Still, their learning brings pleasure to the reader. The lectures have won and will retain a place in Urdu literature, undisturbed by changing fashions and enthusiasm, for they are firmly rooted in knowledge and humanity.

Then, to top it off, the central theme of Azad's *India Wins Freedom* is decolonisation of a people bustling with excitement and expectation. Its principle is derived not from the religious form of legitimation but from the specificity of India's own distinctive social history and secular nationhood.[71] These writings, to which Azad devoted so much time and effort, must stand on their merit and be studied in the forms in which he presented them. The Urdu-speaking intelligentsia was hungry for new ideas after Syed Ahmad's death in 1898; it benefited from Azad's natural power of writing and considerable self-taught erudition. In monologues he demonstrates the protean quality of his mind. Herein, he presents a wide variety of opinions and convictions other than his own. This is only an example of his many-sidedness.

Gandhi pontificated that 'the more we advance in true knowledge, the better we shall understand that we need not be at war with those

---

71   Aijaz Ahmad, 'Azad's Careers: Roads Taken and Not Taken', Mushirul Hasan (ed.), *Islam and Indian Nationalism: Reflections on Abul Kalam Azad* (Delhi, 2001). p. 127.

whose religion we may not follow'.[72] A couple of pathetic misadventures may well have marred Azad's public career. For example, he endorsed the fatwa which called upon the faithful to migrate (hijrat) from the land of war (*dar al-harb*) to the land of Islam (*dar al-Islam*).[73] It was a silly thing to do. More problematic still is when he threw all caution to the winds in order to become *Imam-ul Hind*, India's Chief Theologian. Clearly, Azad gladly ventured his life on these foolhardy enterprises, but who shall say his motive was objectionable? The ulama, who were what they were and couldn't change, opposed him as he didn't belong to any of the established schools, and whose interpretation of the shariat was anathema to them. In such circumstances, no *alim* of upright character could lay claim to being the most learned of his peers.

Both the incidents reveal a tiny chink in Azad's armour. Like new-built ships upon the launch ways, he pressed on towards his destiny. On one occasion he led the pan-Islamic crusade, for which the government accused him of exciting disaffections.[74] However, when Mustafa Kemal Pasha wrecked the Khilafat boat, he took up a challenge which only he could undertake: forging a dialectical and harmonious relationship between various religions. Remarkable for his perspicuity and his ethical approach to every question, he embodied, unlike Mohamed Ali who revolted against this ideal, the blending if not the fusion of cultures. He strove for cultural harmony to construct a world true to reality and to bequeath a legacy of reasoning and tolerance in the fullest sense of that noble word.

Balanced by a strong sense of irony and a sceptical and analytical intelligence, Azad's mystical evaluation of life incorporated Mohammad, albeit as the instrument of final revelations, in the entire fraternity of prophethood.[75] This lay behind the logical, elegant, and valid principle of 'oneness of religion' (*wahdat-i din*) expounded in *Tarjuman al-Quran*. The *Surat al-Fatiha* sums it all up. Here a person sings the praise of his Lord, but the Lord he praises is not the Lord of any particular race, community

72   Parel (ed.), 'Hind Swaraj' and Other Writings, p. 54.

73   Qureshi, Pan-Islam in British Indian Politics, pp. 195-221.

74   Note by Biggane, 29 Nov. 1920, Home Dept., file no. 1, 1920, UPSA.

75   Cragg, The Pen and the Faith, p. 27.

or religion. He is Lord of all, *Rabbul-Aalamin*, the source of sustenance and mercy for all mankind. Azad uses the Commentary on the *Fatiha* to discuss Providence, Mercy, and Justice, the three attributes of God. Throughout, he emphasises three principles: (a) that all religions are in their own sphere perfectly true, (b) that all teachers sent by God are true, and (c) that Islam is nothing more than a confirmation of the true faith taught by previous religions. Without a doubt, while lesser men found conflicts in life, he traversed innumerable valleys to preserve the unity behind all that diversity. He exerted intuitively to reduce to bare bones the entangled demands of organised political bodies.[76]

It wasn't easy, in that period of twentieth-century history, to cite texts or historical precedents to propagate Islamic humanism and the composite ideals that went with it. Syed Ahmad tried, but his college project led him to redefine his preference. He worked towards an Anglo-Muslim rapprochement in politics and a Christian-Islam dialogue to discover points of convergence. The Deobandi ulama wanted a political alliance with the Congress and with Hindu groups, but they weren't inclined to broach the larger issue of composite nationality and plural nationhood. The exertions of its Principal, Husain Ahmad Madani, were subordinated to the survival of Islam and the practice of *sharia*.

While avoiding the intricate theological arguments, Azad based his conclusions on the evolution of Islam in different social and cultural settings. He dwelt at length on the Treaty of Hudaibiya between the Prophet and the Jews of Medina, in CE 622, to justify a Hindu-Muslim alliance, and employed the concept of *ahsan* (gratitude) in the *Sura-i Mumtahina* to buttress the cause of Hindu-Muslim cooperation. He didn't mean that Hindus and Muslims would cease to be different, but he did propose, as W.C. Smith did in the context of Christians and Muslims, that intellectually their understandings must converge, even if morally they choose to respond differently.[77] Once more, he pointed out: 'if Islam has bound Mahommedans to protect the Arabian Peninsula, I tell you, my friends, that it has also bound them to secure India's deliverance from the British slavery.'

---

76   *SWJN*, vol. 11, p. 612.

77   W.C. Smith, *Questions of Religious Truth* (New York, 1967), p. 61.

One may question Azad's reference point—his invocation of Islam and, in particular, episodes from its history—but he did so simply because religious/Islamic idioms and codes made sense to his constituency. Besides, Azad was not the first to use the Islamic imagery to harness anti-colonial sentiments. The difference between him and others was that some of his predecessors used Islam to invent a corporate Muslim identity,[78] whereas he fought for a pluralist layout for the communities to live together harmoniously.

Azad doubted and cared little whether there was such a thing as a homogenous community. He gave, on the other hand, a cry born of frustration and despair, but it left unanswered two basic questions: why were religious groups fired by a spontaneous hatred of one another? Why did religious passions come to the fore, relegating the heterogeneity of the society into the background. He would have had to penetrate far enough into the historical processes to answer these questions.

In *India Wins Freedom*, Azad appears to be weary with a jilted idealism. This arose out of his belief that the Congress' acceptance of the coalition offer would have, for all practical purposes, taken the wind out of the League's sails. His optimism was based on Jinnah's plea for a united front, which, in turn, is supposed to have led the Congress to agree to a coalition after the election. Others shared his optimism. Sardar Singh Caveeshar, president of the Punjab Congress in 1932-33, asked pertinently: 'When we have accepted separate electorates, how can we close the eyes to the Moslem League demand to be represented in the ministries, especially when Congress has not been able to win any respectable number of Moslems on its own side?' Azad and Caveeshar should however have known that Jawaharlal, who is held responsible for scuttling the Congress-League coalition, had no reason to share the ministerial berths after his party's electoral triumph. Additionally, he had

---

78   There are a great many theories devoted to a discussion of what Muslim identity is and what are its essential features. It is possible that I have not mentioned Farzana Shaikh's theory as attentively as I should have. Nonetheless, I have explored, here and elsewhere, her main arguments sufficiently well to locate them in the current discourses on Muslim identity politics. *Community and Consensus in Islam* affords its readers the luxury of revisiting a theme that will remain central to our concerns for a very long time.

no reason to either build up Jinnah's power, an impression Cripps gathered in his conversation in December 1939,[79] or forfeit Congress' claim of being the sole embodiment of nationalism.[80] Finally, he was morally committed to the Congress Muslims and couldn't let them down.[81]

Azad's theory is, in effect, doubtful in its fundamental and secondary assumptions. In fact, all such explanations that are based on individual actions or the lack of them are intrinsically speculative. In this specific case, for all its intellectual elegance, Azad seemed confused, bewildered, and indecisive by the breakdown of the national consensus after the Quit India movement. According to Asaf Ali, the Delhi lawyer, 'with Gandhi pulling towards Heaven and Jawaharlal trying to bring down from Heaven an ideal world, Maulana is unsure what to do with the reins of the chariot. This is a tragedy.'[82]

At the CWC meeting on 2 June 1947 (when the Mountbatten plan received ratification) and at the AICC meeting on 16 September 1947 he sat silent and impassive, resembling, with his pointed beard, Cardinal Richelieu.[83] In *India Wins Freedom*, he claimed to have opposed Partition but, according to J.B. Kripalani, he didn't do so in places where his opinion would have mattered, that is, the CWC and the AICC.[84] Ram Manohar Lohia, the socialist leader who resisted the two-nation idea, offers the following version of the CWC meet:

> Maulana Azad sat in a chair throughout the two days of this meeting in a corner of the very small room which packed us all, puffed away at his endless cigarettes, and spoke not a word. He may have been pained. But it is silly of him to try to make out as though he were the only one opposed to partition. Not only did he keep unbrokenly silent at this meeting, he also continued in office as a minister of partitioned India for an entire decade and more.

---

79   Moore, *Churchill, Cripps, and India*, p. 13.

80   E.W.R. Lumley, *The Transfer of Power in India* (London, 1954), p. 21.

81   Birdwood, *A Continent Experiments*, p. 18.

82   22 June 1943, Raghavan (ed.), *M. Asaf Ali's Memoirs*.

83   Campbell-Johnson, *Mission with Mountbatten*, p. 194.

84   Kripalani, *Gandhi: His Life and Thought*, p. 289.

I may concede and even understand that he was unhappy at the partition and tried to oppose it in his own way ... But this was an opposition that did not object to the service of the thing opposed, a strange combination of opposition and service in a conscience which was greatly wise or equally elastic. It might be interesting to explore Maulana Azad's conscience, for I sometimes suspect that wisdom and elasticity go together.[85]

Azad's travails are embodied in a lip-tied individual in an hostile environment in which he felt ever more marginalised. Probably, with his shrinking constituency, he felt bitter and helpless. On the other hand, very few enlightened souls ever attained the same commanding position in the freedom struggle as Azad. Shorish Kashmiri, the Urdu writer, summed up their fate:

Those who got the worse of it ... were the honest, sincere Nationalist Muslims who, in the eyes of Hindus, were Muslims, and vice versa. All their sacrifices were reduced to ashes. Their personal integrity and loyalty were derided. Their morale had been shattered like a disintegrating shooting star; their lives had lost meaning. Like the crumbling pillars of a mosque they could neither be saved nor used. India, for whose independence they had kept fighting the British, had refused to offer them refuge. So much so, that for doing just that they invited the wrath of their own community. They were like that distant sound which rises in the desert and then descends and disappears into the sand dunes ... For them the special day of independence was unusual, spent in the seclusion of the four walls of their homes. The League had made them untouchables to their fellow-Indians; they were reduced to the state of political harijans in India.[86]

---

85   Rammanohar Lohia, *Guilty Men of India's Partition*, p. 21.

86   Shorish Kashmiri, 'Boo-i-gul Naala-i, Dil-Dood-i Chiragh-i Mehfil,' in Mushirul Hasan (ed.), *India Partitioned: The Other Face of Freedom* (Delhi, 1995), vol. 2, p. 155.

The entire life was spent on idol-worship, O Momin!
At the fag end, how on earth can you become a Muslim!
UMAR SARI TO KATI ISHQ-E-BUTAN ME MOMIN
AKHRI WAQT ME KYA KHAAQ MUSSALMAN HONGE.

-MOMIN

Gandhi and Azad were two individuals very widely separated in their backgrounds and careers, and yet they harnessed their respective energies as companions, compatriots, and colleagues, raised human beings to a high moral level, and sought remedies for what they feared would be a universal disorder in the making. They shared the conviction that power achieved through self-rule resides in the people and is entrusted to their chosen representatives. Both were deeply religious, one inspired by the *Gita* and the other by the Quran. Both questioned orthodoxies of one kind or another and cited religious texts to justify Hindu-Muslim amity. Both held religion as the regulator of morality and of law to stem the tide of social anarchy and moral decay. Both regarded religion as one of the forces conditioning social processes and allowed the permeation of politics by religion and the imposition of a new value system. Both respected each other for their convictions and moral uprightness, and counteracted the formal religious mechanisms, which acted as an impediment to individual growth and the collective happiness of humanity. The God of the Quran is also the God of the *Gita*, and all human beings, no matter what their designation, are children of the same God. Iqbal and Kitchlew (Saifuddin) as names were common to Hindus and Muslims. Those whom God has created as one, man will never be able to divide.[87] Both rebelled against the idea that they represented two cultures and doctrines. In addition, as one analyses their careers, or, rather, their many careers, one notices not continuity but unceasing shifts,[88] and these shifts begin early in the cases of both Azad and Gandhi.

Gandhi respected Azad for his learning and calm, quiet evocative style. He respected him also for drawing nourishment from the common

---

87   *Harijan*, 6 Apr. 1940.

88   Aijaz Ahmad, 'Azad's Careers: Roads Taken and not Taken', in Hasan (ed.), *Islam and Indian Nationalism*, pp. 124-7.

treasure of critical wisdom in Islam, for being a less partisan figure, for being relatively free from the ideological insularity of the Deobandi ulama, and, in short, for bequeathing a synthesis of intellectual magnanimity. He came within reach of representing the 'modern' and embodied in his position and person perhaps the foremost symbol of Gandhi's aspiration to be a nationalist. In reality, he freed himself from minorityism to a more inclusive political conception. His thoughts took a definite bent in strengthening Gandhi's ideal of pluralist democracy.

Azad, in turn, had nothing but praise for Gandhi: 'a true heart beats in Mahatma Gandhi's breast, and his heart contains a perch of the nest of truth; the change [non-cooperation], he thought out was in reality the same which the Quran prescribed thirteen centuries ago'.[89] He fell in line when Gandhi launched a limited Satyagraha on 18 September 1940. In April 1940, he placed proposals to overcome the constitutional deadlock and, at the same time, contested the League's claims. The conference declared India to be an indivisible whole and as such the common homeland of all citizens, irrespective of race or religion.[90] As Congress president, he negotiated with Stafford Cripps and the UP Viceroy, Wavell, and again, after the War, with the cabinet mission. He was moderate and friendly. Cripps complimented him for sticking to his guns.[91] After meeting Azad on 26 April, he expected the Congress to negotiate on the basis of a federal three-tier approach. Little wonder then that he lauded Azad as forthcoming and helpful, though he doubted his ability to carry the CWC with him. Azad's precarious position was patent: 'He didn't want me to say anything to Gandhi or Jawaharlal about this as he said it would make it more difficult for him to put it across to his Working Committee.'[92] Like the other Congress Muslims, Azad, a beleagured individual merely barked but couldn't bite.

---

89   17 Oct. 1920, Home Dept, File no. 1920, UPSA.

90   Humayun Kabir, *Muslim Politics, 1906-42* (Calcutta, 1944).

91   Wavell to J. Colville, 8-9 July 1946, and Note by Wavell, 19 Aug. 1946, *TP*, vol. 8, pp. 23, 103. Azad, in turn, found him to be courteous, tactful, and resourceful.

92   Clarke, *The Cripps Version*, p. 419.

Various accounts confirm the impression of a quiet, serious, sharp-faced man, not to be trifled with, but without shyness or arrogance. His status and not his skills became the focal point of Gandhi's clash with Jinnah, who maintained that politically no one but a Leaguer could speak for the community. Azad's following, which was at any rate not large, not even comparable to that of Mohamed Ali, eroded and he couldn't convert, despite several openings, his assets into becoming a popular and charismatic statesman. Gandhi clarified that the Maulana represented a strong point of view,[93] but the fact is that his opinions virtually disappeared from the documentary record after July 1946.[94] During the high-level negotiations, he was politely ignored.[95] For him, in his writing as in his life, the way to truth was through living and not, as Thoreau agreed, 'through the having lived'.

The Gandhi-Azad differences began with the War. The former didn't want India to take part in the War in any circumstance, whereas Azad felt that Indians had the right to take to the sword if they had no choice, and violence was a matter of policy and not creed. He was sensitive to the minorities being troubled by their future,[96] but Gandhi saw no inherent dichotomy between the majority and the minority, and he didn't want the latter to fear the former.[97] Yes, he said, the depressed classes were weak and deserved protection but not the religious minorities. In such formulations Gandhi left no room for any manoeuvre. Beside, he overlooked the fact that Syed Ahmad had spoken of representation

93   Diary, 27 Feb. 1940, Benthall papers.

94   Editor's Conclusions, Douglas, *Abul Kalam Azad*, p. 304.

95   Campbell-Johnson, *Mission with Mountbatten*, p. 254. On the Gandhi-Azad differences over the Quit India movement and over the conduct of negotiation with the Cabinet mission, see V.N. Datta, *Maulana Azad*, pp. 168, 174, 175, 176. For Gandhi's response to Azad's proposal for alleviating Muslim fears, *see* Jenkins to Abell, 28 Aug. 1945, reporting on an intercepted letter from Gandhi to Azad. *TP*, vol. 6, p. 76. Azad's own version of his differences with Jawaharlal is revealing. For its refutation, Gopal, *Jawaharlal Nehru*, vol. 1, p. 227, and S.R. Mehrotra, 'The Congress and the Partition of India', in C.H. Philips and M.D. Wainwright (eds), *The Partition of India: Policies and Perspectives, 1935-1947* (London, 1970), pp. 178-9.

96   Azad, *India Wins Freedom*, p. 139.

97   Gandhi, *The Way to Communal Harmony*, pp. 123, 140, 223.

for the Muslim minority, that the League had pressed the same idea, and that the government perpetuated this exclusive category in its constitutional provisions. So did the Congress in the Lucknow pact. Matters might well have rested there, for Gandhi merely reiterated the Nehru Report, which had questioned the minority/majority categories. Matters didn't however rest there. Gandhi added that unity wouldn't precede but succeed freedom. Like the Wars of the Roses in England, in India, too, he expected order out of the existing chaos.[98] That however simply couldn't happen.

Azad found anger and despair clouding the vision of two men he held in high esteem: Bapu and Jawaharlal. They were both hypnotised by Mountbatten into accepting his offer.[99] Imagine the frustrations of a man so deeply entrenched in the composite culture which he had done so much to raise to new levels! Azad asked: 'Is there—can there be—amongst us anyone whose heart has not been wounded at the sight of the misery that surrounds us?' Now virtually an exiled intellectual, he lamented: 'If the hand of the Muslim is awash with the blood of his victim, so is the Hindu's hand red, and that of the Sikhs. No sanctuary, no relief is to be found. What a dangerous sickness is upon us!'[100]

Differences eventually attracted only a small portion of Gandhi's attention, but the situation we have here, to which we must pay some attention, is one in which enlightened Muslim opinion disagreed with Gandhi on certain issues. This may still be misleading as a way of expressing the difference. The generalisation may not also suffice, but it serves to indicate the different fates the people suffered in different political situations. The feeling was strong that the Congress Muslims didn't receive their due and that their own party, to which they had been loyal for so long, doubted their ability to deliver in the face of Jinnah's juggernaut.

True, Azad couldn't match Jinnah's relentless drive and energy. Nonetheless, they envisaged a federal arrangement of safeguarding

---

98   Ibid., pp. 139, 198.

99   Azad, *India Wins Freedom*, pp. 208, 226.

100   Goplakrishna Gandhi (ed.), *Gandhi is Gone.*, p. 73.

minority rights through adult franchise. Even if their scheme found little favour with the League, they showed the way for the future, i.e., in the making of a federal constitution. Their greatest setback however was that Gandhi failed to convince a large number of Muslims that swaraj would not curtail their religious rights and civil liberties. When Jinnah promised to them a paradise on earth, even the UP and Bihari Muslims were swept off their feet. Later, of course, they realised, much to their dismay and disgust that Pakistan yielded rich rewards to the Punjabi and Sindhi Muslims but ruin and disaster to them.

'The tragedy is that the world worships words instead of meanings', Azad had once written. This applies to Gandhi who let go of his most consistent *Muslim* followers. Whenever they protested against his overtures to the League, he'd either brush them aside or persuade them to to quieten down.[101] Therefore, they saw no chance for him, as long as he was hunting with the hounds and running with the Muslim League hare. Asaf Ali summed up their feelings:

> Both the Congress and League are, I fear, drifting into the mood of piqued children. What we need are not obdurate and logic-chopping politicians, but large-hearted statesmen. Now Gandhi is a great man but is too great for India and has therefore brought India to grief. Jawaharlal Nehru has a large heart, I think, and big dreams, but he has come a cropper at this crisis because he has surrendered to mass hysteria.[102]

---

101   Gandhi to Khwaja, 2 Dec. 1944, Khwaja papers.
102   7 Dec. 1943, Raghavan (ed.), *M.Asaf Ali's Memoirs.*

11
Gaye, Gita, Ganga, *Gayatri*, and Gandhi[1]

To me it has been a matter of great sorrow and regret that for the last many years the Hindus and Muslims in Northern India, in which I also include Bihar, have been drifting apart and that there has been a deliberate attempt on the part of each to disown and repudiate those cultural affinities and common tastes which had been the uniting bond between the two during the Moghul period. In this respect I certainly hold the Hindus much more responsible as the attack on their side on common culture has been persistent and has led to most unfortunate consequences.

-Sapru to Syed Mahmud, 4 June 1942, Dutta and Cleghorn (eds), *A Nationalist Muslim and Indian Politics*, p. 228.

'To me, Hindus and Muslims are one, possessing a common heritage, belonging to a common Motherland, fighting common battles,' he said. 'We are intermingled, living together side by side. Surely, you can't divide up each little plot of land and say this is Hindu India and that is Muslim India? To me that sounds like a graveyard!'

'I don't say that we have to divide the country up.' Bashir spoke in a hard metallic voice, as if dispensing judgement. 'I only say that there is justification of what some Muslims have started saying ... In a democracy we shall always be under the Hindus. We cannot tolerate that. We belong to the race of conquerors.'

-Zeenuth Futehally, *Zohra*, p. 204.

Shah Jahan, the Mughal emperor, built the Jama Masjid in Shahjahanabad, his capital. A congregation at this grand mosque could look out towards a world generously planted with Muslims like them, stretching all the way from the Himalayan peaks to the Andaman and Nicobar Islands. On 14-15 August 1947 were created borders and boundaries. Although a porous entity, even the fuzzy frontiers, which the Radcliffe Award brought about, ensured that the *muezzin*'s call for *namaz* stopped at the Wagah border.

---

1   Khwaja Hasan Nizami added 'Gandhi' to what he described as the four essentials of Hinduism.

Why Partition? Was it not the outcome of the elemental clash of two worlds on Indian soil; a clash that was bound to come back after the British hold slackened? How did matters go so terribly wrong that the Punjabi poet-writer, Amrita Pritam, had to bring into play Haji Waris Shah, the composer of the epic love ballad of the legendary Punjabi lovers 'Heer-Ranjha', to restore freedom from strife to her land? What happened to the popular culture, the more expressive of the experienced reality than the culture of the ruling classes or the intellectual elite which usually stems from books and from scientific, religious, or cultural texts?[2]

However much we may celebrate, the nationalist movement had very little to deliver in the way of *immediate* satisfaction to whichever group made up the coalition: tribal, religious, ethnic, and political. It could only dispense the symbolic satisfactions of Independence, ideology, and identity, and otherwise promise a pie in the sky. Sadly, Gandhi created next to nothing as strong a bond of unity as he would have himself liked. He also did not generate an integrating faith in nationalism much stronger than any distribution of scarce favours can ever hope to be, as it can remain above considerations of scarcity and conflicting demands.[3] All that he offered were promises of a better future, rich or poor, as much as a generation or more away, bought at the price of sacrifice then made. In this context, all that his party offered was freedom before the distribution of the spoils amongst the rich and powerful groups.

In other words, Independence would follow rather than precede a clear understanding of state formation and its ideology. The League however controverted the argument with the remark that the stronger party thought that it could defeat the weaker one if a conflict arose between the two after the withdrawal of the 'third party', the British.

---

2   Popular culture is composed of the stories, the tales, the proverbs, the axioms, the songs, the legends, the jokes and the anecdotes that people invent, that they produce and consume, that they exchange in their daily life, that become part of their talk and nightly gatherings, orally passed down from one generation to another, preserved in the individual and collective memory. *The Nawal El Saadawi Reader* (London, 1998), pp. 178, 179.

3   Peter H. Merkl, *Modern Comparative Politics* (New York, 1970), p. 281.

It was therefore up to the weaker party to retain the third party until they became sufficiently strong to resist the future belligerence of the stronger party.[4]

In or about 1932, Mohammad Rafiq Khavar published *Gandhi-Nama*. Reminiscent of Marlowe's *Faustus*, the poem is pervaded by a gentle atmosphere of honest worth and love. It is touching in that the poet zestfully uses Biblical images and representations to paint lively and fresh pictures of Gandhi; it is, indeed, 'the highest tribute paid in an imaginative form to Gandhi's genius'.[5] But similar combinations of general and specific verses from other quarters reveal considerable fluidity and an inherent vagueness and ambiguity. While most writers retained their adulatory tone, Manto does no more than to make an oblique and ironic allusion to him in 'Swaraj ke Liye'.[6]

In 1939, Gandhi claimed, just as he had done on many previous occasions, to be the friend and guide of the Muslims.[7] But he knew well enough that they had no heart in the Congress enterprise.[8] A number of families across the country—the Tyabjis in Western Bombay and Poona, the Kidwai's in Barabanki district, and the Sherwani's in Allahabad—still stood by Gandhi, but the 'Directory of Gandhian Constructive Workers' listed only four Muslims.[9] An aggrieved Gandhi conceded, in April 1947, that he didn't command the same influence as he used to.[10] Sadness and poignancy marked his lines.

---

4   Syed Mahmud to Jawaharlal, 5 Feb. 1942, Datta and Cleghorn (eds), *A Nationalist Muslim and Indian Politics*, p. 222.

5   Sadiq, *Twentieth Century Urdu Literature*, p. 184. He edited a literary journal but found his métier in verse translations, including *Hir* by Waris Shah and *Risala* by Shah Bhitai.

6   Indra Nath Chaudhuri, 'A Note on Some Myths About Manto', Alok Bhalla (ed.), *Life and Works of Saadat Hasan Manto* (Delhi, rpt, 2004), p. 216.

7   *Harijan*, 28 Jan. 1939, *CWMG* (15 Oct. 1938-Feb. 28 1939), p. 323.

8   Mahadev Desai to Birla, 16 July 1942, in Birla (ed.), *Bapu: A Unique Association*, vol. 1, p. 318.

9   K. Balasubramanian (ed.), *Directory of Gandhian Constructive Workers* (Delhi, 1996).

10   Discussion at Hindustan Talim Sangh, 22 Apr. 1947, *CWMG* (21 Feb. 1947-24 May 1947), p. 331.

Civil Disobedience and Quit India movements didn't in any way resemble the enchanting pictures of Non-Cooperation days. For one, the disenchantment followed the Chauri Chaura incident, when Gandhi, having exhausted all he had on his programme, was left with no arrows in his quiver.[11] Opinion-makers passed disparaging remarks on his mystic and ascetic bent of mind. 'It is against our scriptures to keep the knees bare,' Abdul Bari wrote.[12] A small matter but blown out of proportion by a man who had once hosted Gandhi in Lucknow, endorsed Satyagraha, and eschewed cow-slaughter during Baqr Id. Now, Gandhi's gentle images of love were replaced by the images of a Hindu nationalist.[13]

He and the Ali brothers had appreciated Gandhi's attachment to the cow and, as a reciprocal gesture of goodwill, given up cow-slaughter during Baqr Id. However, once the Khilafat bubble burst, they found the resources to vindicate the change in their new way of thinking. They were able to pattern their behaviour and control their choices and select their goals in accordance with the Quran and *Hadith*, day after day, year in, and year out.

Once, Mohamed Ali went into raptures: 'it is Gandhi, Gandhi, Gandhi that has got to be dinned into the people's ear, given that he means Hindu-Muslim unity, non-cooperation, *Swadharma* and *Swaraj*.'[14] He took to weaving and wearing khadi and becoming an evangelist for the *charkha*. 'We laid the foundation of our slavery by selling off the spinning wheel,' he preached. 'If you want to do away with slavery, take up the wheel again.'[15] He used to say that there was no freedom without *charkhas* in every cottage and a loom in every village. They were, in fact, instruments of war, and the cones of yarn turned out by them were their ammunition.

The faith of those early days couldn't however be sustained. Once spinning and the *charkha* became identified with Hindu deities,[16] the

---

11   Abdul Bari, quoted in Robinson, *The 'Ulama of Farangi Mahall and Islamic Culture in South Asia*, p. 157.

12   Lelyveld, *Great Soul*, p. 164.

13   *Navajivan*, 10 July 1927, *CWMG* (June-Sept. 1927), p. 2.

14   Afzal Iqbal, *Life and Times of Mohamed Ali* (Delhi, 1978), p. 308.

15   Lelyveld, *Great Soul*, p. 161.

16   Ibid., pp. 110-13.

Ali brothers declared that such deification had no place in Islam. Just as they couldn't visualise a divine political order conceptualised, narrated, and historically grounded in *Ramarajya*, they couldn't either picture Gandhi as Ram fighting Ravana, with the spinning wheel and the spindle (rather than the bow and arrow) as his weapons.

Marmaduke Pickthall, a novelist and editor of *Bombay Chronicle*, followed Gandhi as enthusiastically as any other leader, and styled him as 'the greatest leader of the East', 'the great commander', and 'Mahatmaji'. He delighted at the opportunity of sharing a platform with him, always dressed on such occasions in *khaddar* and a Gandhi cap.[17] By the late-1930s, however, he succumbed to the view that collaboration with the British would benefit Muslims rather than 'sedition' in the company of the Hindu-dominated Congress.

When Gandhi embarked on a south India temple-entry tour in mid-January 1937, he asked Kanu, his grand nephew, to have Tulsidas's *Ramayana* read everywhere, and once in a while at public places. This wasn't an uncommon occurrence, but on this occasion Muslims disapproved. They also objected to the singing of Ramdhun. In Masimpur village and at a prayer meeting in Noakhali, the audience walked out.[18]

In Mohamed Ali's fan club were some Urdu poets, bright and brilliant, who were fulsome in their praise of Gandhi. But Hasrat Mohani and Zafar Ali Khan, the two leading poets, became the precursors of gloom. As they gradually revived from the chill torpor of life, their verses signified the drubbing that Gandhi's image received from his erstwhile admirers. They scoffed at his non-violent means,[19] and, in the case of Zafar Ali Khan, editor of *Zamindar* (Lahore), suggested in 1938 that there would be no Hindu-Muslim compromise until the former admitted the existence of a Muslim nation.[20] Gandhi's swaraj, he said, aimed at installing a Hindu theocracy.

---

17   Israel, *Communications and Power*, p. 231.

18   Mujeeb, 'Gandhi and the Muslim Masses', op. cit., p. 141.

19   Let acclamation sound, and keep on spinning all you will/But mark my word: When all is done, the Sahibs will be here still.

20   *Hindustan Times*, 30 Apr. 1938, *TF,* 1938 (pt 2), p. 248.

Bharat me balain do hi hain ek Savarkar ek Gandhi hai
Ek jhoot ka chalta chakkar hai ek makr ki uththi andhi hai
In India there are two evils, one Savarkar and the other Gandhi.
One is the whirlwind of lies and the other the rising dust storm
of deceit.

Likewise, Hasrat became a vocal critic of Gandhi when he justified the conduct of the Moplah, in August 1923, by applying to them the rules of war, according to which those who helped the enemies became enemies themselves, holding that the Moplahs deserved punishment for acting as informers. During the debate over the Nehru Report, Hasrat raised the spectre of living under the double domination of Hindu majority and British suzerainty, and lashed Gandhi mercilessly with harsh words:

Gandhi ki tarah baith ke kyon kaatege charkha
Lenin ki tarah denge na duniya ko hila hum?
Why spend time on the spinning wheel like Gandhi
Shouldn't we rather shake the world like Lenin?

Finally, a class of 'new religious intellectuals' and activists emerged. Maulana Abul Ala Maududi belonged to this class. Between 1918 and 1919, he wrote essays praising Gandhi and Malaviya, worked for the pro-Congress weekly *Taj* in Jabalpur, joined the Khilafat movement, and promoted pro-Congress sentiments. However, from 1937 to 1941, he developed misgivings over the *shuddhi* movement. Gradually, he harangued Gandhi, as did Khwaja Hasan Nizami, for his 'Hindu' point of view. On *shuddhi*, he and Nizami held similar views.

The Jamaat-i Islami, founded on 26 August 1941, argued that the Congress party's secular pretensions were conveniently obfuscating its promise of Hindu rule. Its founder lost faith in Hindu-Muslim unity, arguing that Islam is totally self-sufficient and is different from, incompatible with, and superior to any other religion. Therefore, one must maintain a barrier between Islam and the non-Muslim world. He criticised the Western intellectual colonisation, the corollary of political and military conquest, but pooh-poohed nationalism and all forms of popular Islam. His *Tarjuman al Quran* was 'radical communalism as it articulated Muslim interests and sought to protect their rights, and demanded the severance of all cultural and hence social and political ties with Hindus in their interests of purifying Islam'.[21] At the time of Partition, Maududi lived in a small religious community in East Punjab which he called *Dar al-Islam*.

Religion in Politics

In Europe, religion was for the masses, in the main, a method of coping with the increasingly bleak and inhuman oppressive society of middle-class liberalism: in Marx's phrase, it was the 'heart of a heartless world, as it is the spirit of spiritless conditions ... the *opium* of the people'. In the case of the middle-classes, E.J. Hobsbawm explains religion as a powerful moral prop; a justification of social existence against the contempt and hatred of traditional society, and an engine of expansion.[22] It was the same with the Ganapati festival in Maharashtra or the Durga cult in Bengal.

In the writings of some middle-class intellectuals, India was symbolised by an image of a suffering woman called Bharat Mata, a semi-divine figure being adorned with a crown with flowing black tresses wearing a carefully draped sari. She inspired patriotism, inviting her followers to free themselves from the shackles of imperialism.[23] Muslims couldn't however venerate Bharat Mata or pray at the Kali temples. Their place in the social firmament was an emotional and cultural issue, and as it touched on the new identity the *bhadralok* wished to create, part Bengali and part British, it also had political ramifications.

From the early days, Gandhi drew attention to cow-protection as an economic necessity and its sanctity in Hindu religion. In the 1940s,

21   Seyyed Vali Reza Nasr, 'Mawdudi and the Jama'at-i Islami: The Origins, Theory and Practice of Islamic Revivalism', Rahnema (ed.), *Pioneers of Islamic Revival*, p. 103.

22   E.J. Hobsbawm, *The Age of Revolution 1789-1848* (Delhi, 1992, paperback), p. 278.

23   R.K. Laxman, *The Common Man At Large* (Delhi, 1994), p. vi.

Ramarajya made Gandhi ultimately not simply a Hindu but also an indirect spokesman for upper caste interests.[24] Along with Bharat Mata and cow-protection, *Ramarajya* constituted essential elements in a Hindu concept and couldn't be discarded without damage to the valid core. In this way, his 'externals' impeded the expression of the universal in his beliefs and personality.[25] Obaidullah Sindhi, who spent many years in exile, returned to India in 1939 having forsaken Islamic universalism to support nationalism. He however had no love lost for Gandhi, who had 'kept the nation backward' through his stubborn insistence on winning Indian Independence with a spinning wheel and handloom.[26]

From other quarters too, Gandhi invited ridicule for elevating spinning to a form of worship, and for idealising life where medicine and surgery could be done away with.[27] Very few educated Bengalis were eager to undertake village work. Andrews concluded that Gandhi's asceticism was alien to their pride of intellect. Hostile to his austere ideals of rustic simplicity, they had faith in the richness and pre-eminence of urban culture.[28]

Similarly, simplicity made no impression on the theologians, who regarded abstinence or self-denial as a form of ingratitude to Allah, unless there were obvious and compelling reasons for it. His asceticism and some of the consequences that followed from it in his policy and public acts didn't go down well with them. They opposed his dress, diet, and tone of moral dryness. While they understood why he had to dress like the masses, they couldn't explain his diet in the same way. The poor man, after all, ate dry bread or cooked or uncooked cereals, not fruit and milk. The charkha could hardly save his interest, a point Akbar Ilahabadi made eloquently:

---

24   Gail Omvedt, *Understanding Caste: From Buddha to Ambedkar and Beyond* (Delhi, 2011), pp. 5-6.

25   Mujeeb, 'Gandhi and the Muslim Masses', op. cit., p. 75.

26   Ayesha Jalal, *Partisans of Allah: Jihad in South Asia*, p. 222.

27   1 Nov. 1921, Iyer (ed.), *The Essential Writings of Mahatma Gandhi*, p. 31.

28   Ray, *Social Conflict and Political Unrest in Bengal*, pp. 246-47.

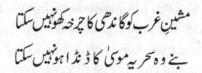

Gandhi's spinning wheel cannot dislodge the Western machines,
Devoid of any magic, it cannot become the rod of Moses.

The ulama and the religious-minded took the words of the Quran literally (not to 'throw yourselves into death with your own hands'). In other words, just as the Quran describes killing the innocent as sinful, so does it not allow one to kill oneself. Besides, they asserted: first, it is easier to sacrifice one's life than to live under difficult conditions and work for their eradication; second, they blamed Gandhi, just as Ambedkar did, for such a dreadful fast in September 1932 in order to achieve a 'minor' point while major issues concerning the Muslims were unsolved.

Smallpox raged in Sabarmati. The inmates were 'anti-vaccinationists from religious motive', using strong permanganate solution and warm baths followed by a wet sheet pack and liquid diet. Andrews wasn't impressed; his vows had proved incapable of being fulfilled for all. Besides, Christ had opposed such mortgaging of the future with his declaration 'Sufficient unto the day'. 'Life is always a growth into something new and unexpected and original,' he told Gandhi: a vow was a form of 'self-mutilation'.[29] Gandhi's 'spectacular austerities' failed to leave an impression on the Muslims either, for Prophet proclaimed, 'God has not sent down a disease without sending down a remedy for it'.

True, Gandhi spoke of *Indian* civilisation not of *Hindu* civilisation, and that he didn't substitute the category of 'Indian civilisation' with 'Hindu culture or civilisation'. These subtle distinctions however made little sense to an ordinary Muslim or Hindu.[30] Similarly, when referring to the land of Karma, he pleaded for preserving Indian values. There is however no getting away from his thinking being heavily spiced with

29   Tinker, *The Ordeal of Love*, p. 149.

30   Sabyasachi Bhattacharya, *Talking Back: The Idea of Civilization in the Indian Nationalist Discourse* (Delhi, 2011), p. 49.

Hindu symbolism; he had no reason to change his world-view only to soothe communitarian or sectarian passions.

Nirad Chaudhuri refers to an interesting encounter in a public tank at Kishorganj, in early 1921. Among the crowd in the water was an old Brahmin washing his sacred thread and muttering his mantras. A small group near him discussed the new movement, and Nirad Chaudhuri joined in. Suddenly, the wizened old individual looked at him out of a pair of gleaming eyes and exclaimed explosively in a voice that was piercing in its exultation and raucous in its fanaticism, 'He's come to re-establish Hinduism'. Gandhi would have shuddered at this reference to him, but then 'it did not lie in his power, once he had cut his teaching adrift to go among the multitudes, to prevent its discriminatory exploitation by the atavistic horde'.[31]

On these lines, I introduce certain impressions of individuals known for their ecumenical outlook. Mahmuduzzafar and his wife Rasheed Jahan wrote short-stories; they created a furore by contributing to *Angare*, an anthology. The earthly Rasheed Jahan, in particular, simply shattered all the ivory idols of Ismat Chughtai to pieces. Life, stark and naked, stood before her.[32] They were close to Jawaharlal, the husband serving as his secretary. An intelligence report described them as 'one of the most dangerous Communists Nehru had gathered round him in the AICC to retain contact with foreign communist organisations'.[33]

On 15 October 1937, they represented Gandhi as hostile at heart to Muslims, putting them in disadvantageous positions by opposing their legitimate claims, as in the debate about a single national language, in which he didn't want to take any account of Urdu. The two caricatured him as a Hindu bigot, anchored in his backward piety, and allied with the upper Hindu bourgeoisie and applying himself to maintaining their pact of alliance with England, reading nothing, not even the new Constitution. They claimed that, with the exception of Ghaffar Khan, all of 'Muslim India' were against him, though the Hindu masses were still

---

31   Nirad Chaudhuri, *The Autobiography of an Unknown Indian*, p. 517.

32   Ismat Chughtai, *A Life in Words: Memoirs*. p. xviiii.

33   R.M. Maxwell to R.J. Peel, 21 Jan. 1938, f.no. 41/A, 1938, PC Joshi Archives, Jawaharlal Nehru University, New Delhi.

with him. After listening to these impressions, Romain Rolland made the following comment:

> It is most curious, and rather worrying, that these elite Indians who are, in a sense, Nehru's right arm, give evidence of a sharp distaste for Gandhi. Mahmud at least is president, and watches his word. But his wife speaks without restraint, and he does nothing to correct her.[34]

Mohammad Mujeeb was educated in Oxford and Germany. He belonged to a *taluqdari* family that had done rather well as lawyers and teachers. A quintessential liberal, he posited that Gandhi's moral universe was derived essentially from Hinduism, and that his sense of what was morally right and morally wrong was strong. The moral came before the intellectual; the intellectual served merely as a tool to implement the moral. The moral wasn't separate from the intellectual, a thought process that could have averted some serious failures of Gandhi's political career. Several of his proposals couldn't be put into practice owing to the high moral significance he attached to them. For instance, the production of hand-woven cloth did not blossom into a successful cottage industry.

Asaf Ali, a lawyer in Delhi, was confronted with all possible conundrums whenever Gandhi followed the logic of his faith.[35] This may have been one of the reasons, though by no means the only one, why more and more educated Muslims, who were otherwise liberal and enlightened, distanced themselves from him. This trend had the tragic aspect with which it has been periodically credited.

Among the different theological schools, the Barelwis lambasted the Deobandi ulama, their arch rivals, for their marriage of convenience with a Hindu bania whose pretensions stood exposed in 1922 and 1930-31 when he struck deals with the British.[36] There was a time

---

34   F. no. 20/A 1937, ibid.

35   Asaf Ali to Satyamurti, 9 June 1942, Ramanathan (ed.), *The Satyamurti Letters*, vol. 2, p. 366.

36   Usha Sanyal, *Devotional Islam and Politics in British India: Ahmad Riza Khan Barelwi and his Movement, 1870-1920* (Delhi, 1996), pp. 293-4.

when the Deobandis agreed that the Mahatma incarnated virtue, love, and honour. However, their enthusiasm waned over time. Those who joined the League bandwagon didn't mince words to describe him as a mischievous meddler in Islamic affairs, and found his views on conversion, on inter-community dining, and purdah as unwarranted intrusion.[37] They resented, moreover, coupling the name of Rama with Rahim, name of God; similarly, of Krishna with Allah. 'Even if I am killed,' Gandhi affirmed, 'I shall not give up repeating the names of Rama and Rahim, which means to me the same God. With these names on my lips I shall die cheerfully.'[38]

Converting the Converted

The enlargement of areas of conflict and disagreement cannot be ascribed to any single precipitating cause. In the 1940s however the *spirit* behind the divergences produced uncompromising and emotionally revivalist forces to make adjustment and accommodation difficult.

Conversion experiences may come about in different circumstances, in different ways, and with different outcomes. The converts, for their part, entered into the fold of Islam through various means and for a variety of reasons. Some accepted it after study; others under the influence of Tablighi Jamaat, founded by Maulvi Mohammad Ilyas in Delhi.

Whatever the reason, conversion inflamed religious passions. This was brought to light by two cases of youths in Bombay: Dhanjibhai Nauroji in 1839 and of Shripat Sheshadari in 1843.[39] The issue of safeguarding identity and community rights remained alive in the decades to come. When Henry Whitehead, Gandhi's host in Madras in February 1916, heard his guest at a missionary conference, he announced: 'He represents in rather an extreme form the modern reaction against

---

37   Pyarelal, *Mahatma Gandhi*, vol. 1, p. 64. There were, of course, notable exceptions, and they have taken credit for their sacrifices during the 1930-31 Civil Disobedience and the 1942 Quit India movements. He appealed to Muslim women to discard purdah as an outmoded custom.

38   *Harijan*, 20 Apr. 1947, Gandhi, *The Way to Communal Harmony*, p. 83.

39   Jesse S. Palsetia, 'Parsi and Hindu Traditional and Non-traditional Responses to Christian Conversions in Bombay, 1839-45', *Journal of the American Academy of Religion*, Sept. 2006, vol. 74, no. 3, pp. 615-42.

Western influences and Western civilisation, and naturally he is opposed to all proselytising on the part of the missionary.'[40]

Tabligh and *shuddhi* societies weren't new to north India. The former existed well before Tablighi Jamaat secured a stronghold in Delhi and its outlying region of Mewat, in the mid-1920s. Similarly, the Arya Samaj gave impetus to *shuddhi*. Gandhi dealt with them at great length and wanted *shuddhi* and *tabligh* to be conducted honestly and by men of proven character. When however he agreed to the return of the Malkanas, who were still called 'Adhh-barya—half Muslim, half Hindu'—to the Hindu fold, his critics denounced him.[41]

Gandhi recalled his Rajkot days when 'the Preacher near the High School corner still stands vividly before me haranguing the school boys and belittling Hinduism.'[42] From that day onwards, he went up against the Christian missionary ardour that prevailed in the complex skein of attitudes, expressed disgust at their zeal to convert the poor, and resisted their habitually typecasting the adherents of other faiths for not letting rational disputations take place. If Jawaharlal pointed out that the gospel of Jesus was a tool of imperialism, capitalism, political domination, and social injustice, Gandhi objected to proselytisation. He disliked undermining the faith of others. [43]

In early November 1936, Gandhi discussed conversion and the role of missionaries with Andrews and Dr. John Mott, an evangelist. His sole aim was to eliminate untouchability, which he described as a question of life and death for Hinduism. For someone who had no reason to cut himself off from his *sanathani* roots, this conviction had stayed with him. In fact, he wanted this ancient religion to be a living faith and exist alongside other religions. The wheat will be purer when the chaff is removed. If, on the other hand, Hinduism had to learn from any other religion, he had to fight the curse of

---

40   Harper, *In the Shadow of the Mahatma*, p. 294.

41   Mohibbul Hasan, 'Mahatma Gandhi and the Indian Muslims', in Biswas (ed.), *Gandhi Theory and Practice*, p. 141.

42   To Dr. Taylor, 16 Feb. 1925, IOR, Hugh Robert Scott papers.

43   29 Mar. 1929, Iyer (ed.), *The Essential Writings of Mahatma Gandhi*, p. 153.

untouchability. Christian, Muslim, and Sikh bodies angered him; his grouse was that they weaned ignorant people away from the religion of their forefathers. They engaged in such activities not because the untouchables were, for example, suddenly awakened by spiritual hunger, as some suggested, but because the missionaries exploited their hunger and backwardness and offered visions of 'liberation'. 'It is one thing to preach one's religion to whomsoever may chose to adopt it, another to entice masses,' Gandhi told an American missionary in December 1939.[44]

Gandhi resisted conversion without quite putting it down,[45] but he didn't accept the change of religion, forced or voluntary, at any cost or under any circumstance. Therefore, he felt repelled by Harijan youth abandoning Hinduism at the Depressed Class Conference on 13 October 1935, or the Mahars getting converted on 31 May 1936. Religion wasn't like a house of cards or a cloak to be changed at will. A year later, he attributed Harilal's conversion to Islam to his 'pecuniary ambition'. It was a bitter pill to swallow.[46]

Gandhi increased in both frequency and bitterness his criticisms of conversions; these frequently drew on the reports of Thakkar Baba, secretary of the Harijan Sevak Sangh.[47] When Bishop J.W. Pickett claimed that 4.5 million Dalits had become Christians, he argued that the 'real miracle' lay not in such claims, but in over 2000 temples in Travancore state being opened recently to Harijans on the basis of internal reform.[48] He was, consequently, hell bent on directing his movements against conversion. He told a missionary that, 'your duty is done with the ulterior motive of proselytizing.'[49] India didn't

---

44   *Harijan*, 30 Dec. 1939, *CWMG* (1 Dec. 1939-15 Apr. 1940), p. 53.

45   Sudhir Chandra, 'Denial of Plurality: Thinking of Conversion through Gandhi', in Jamal Malik and Helmut Reifeld (eds), *Religious Pluralism in South Asia and Europe* (Delhi, 2005), p. 213.

46   *Harijan*, 20 Apr. 1940, *CWMG*, vol. 71, p. 429.

47   Harper, *In the Shadow of the Mahatma*, p. 316.

48   Hardiman, *Gandhi in His time and Ours*, p. 181.

49   Note to Dr. Thornton, 23 Feb. 1931, *CWMG* (Dec. 1930-Apr. 1931), p. 223.

require a 'converting spirit'.[50] Gandhi was rarely as blunt, as he was on t his occasion.

If all religions were merely different roads converging to the same point, how does conversion militate against the dharmic order, or, alternatively, how did Gandhi square his thesis with the claim that religions have no irreconcilable differences? Moreover, conversion had a long-standing career, starting with the coming of the Ghaznavides, pursued with vigour by the Sufis under the early Turkish Sultans, and continuing under the British. How, then, did Gandhi expect to put an end to this long-standing practice? The fact is that some of his views on conversion resulted in a curious marriage between him and the Hindu nationalists, who in all other instances deprecated him for making concessions to Muslims but nonetheless heralded him as the voice of reason when he opposed proselytism.[51] Moreover, smaller groups, such as the Ahmadiyas in Punjab, remained aloof from him because they were not given the assurance to conduct missionary activity and conversion. Just as the British earned Ahmadi sympathy by allowing the movement to engage in missionary activity, the Congress lost it by not following their example.[52]

All said and done, Gandhi disillusioned the Christians. Without being short of Christian enthusiasts like S.K. Datta, an invitee to the Delhi Unity Conference in 1924, B.L. Rallia Ram, and Rajkumari Amrit Kaur, a key figure in the All-India Women's Conference,[53] they apprehended that freedom wouldn't bring full freedom for them, and that electoral and

---

50   Ibid., 14 Dec. 1927. The industrialist made known that, 'we [also] find that those Hindus were converted to Islam two hundred years ago are now as bigoted Muslims as those originally hailing from Arabia or Iran'. Birla to Gandhi, 11 June 1924, Birla (ed.), *In the Shadow of the Mahatma: A Personal Memoir*, p. 4.

51   Gauri Vishwanathan, 'Literacy and Conversion in the Discourse of Hindu Nationalism', in A.D. Needham and R.S. Rajan (eds), *The Crisis of Secularism in India* (Durham, 2007), p. 334

52   Yohanan Friedmann, *Prophecy Continuous: Aspects of Ahmadi Religious Thought and its Medieval Background* (Berekeley and Los Angeles, 1989), p. 38.

53   John C.B. Webster, *A Social History of Christianity: North West India since 1800* (Delhi, 2007), pp. 243-53.

legislative battles for political advantage would exacerbate old conflicts and chip away at the greater national good.[54] History, however, proved Azariah and his followers, who advocated this line, to be wrong.

Language and Politics

Language and thought are inextricably interwoven, and interact with each other. Words have a history and association, which, for those who used them, contribute an important part of the meaning. Urdu wasn't spoken by Muslims alone. Nawal Kishore Press, a truly remarkable institution in Lucknow, defied the ongoing dichotomisation of Hindi and Urdu, with its multifaceted translation activities—from Sanskrit into Urdu, from Hindu into Urdu and vice versa—constituting one of the last sustained efforts at propagating the values of a shared and composite culture.[55] Unlike UP where Hindi received official recognition in 1900,[56] Urdu was the language of commerce, lower government and journalism in Punjab, and the undisputed centre of Urdu publishing, and by extension of Urdu reading.[57] On the basis of language alone, there was no identifiable 'Muslim', 'Sikh', or 'Hindu' identity that could be abstracted from the particular circumstances of individual events or specific societies.[58]

Nonetheless, despite being popular in urban areas and spoken by the Kayasths and Kashmiri Pandits, Urdu passed through difficult times. Petty jealousies and a distorted perspective guided its opponents.

---

54 Harper, *In the Shadow of the Mahatma*, p. 345.

55 Ulrike Stark, *An Empire of Books: The Naval Kishore Press and the Diffusion of the Printed Word in Colonial India* (Delhi, 2008), p. 444.

56 The UP government, headed by a man who was obsessively anti-Muslim, set the ball rolling with the Hindi Resolution in Apr. 1900. With the equal recognition accorded to Hindi, Anthony MacDonnell turned Urdu into a minority language, stifled creativity and its spread, and heightened cultural anxieties in the *qasbas* of Awadh and its Urdu-speaking inhabitants. Jobs and employment were only secondary to this larger concern, which so few publicists understood in the early twentieth century. Robinson, *Separatism Among Indian Muslims*, pp. 43-4, 135-40.

57 Markus Daechsel, *The Politics of Self-Expression: The Urdu Middle-Class Milieu in mid-twentieth century India and Pakistan* (London, 2006), p. 13.

58 C.A. Bayly, 'The Pre-history of "Communalism"? Religious Conflict in India, 1700-1860', *MAS*, 19, 2, 1985, p. 202.

Urdu, with its script and the large number of Arabic and Persian words, belonged to the other world, whereas Hindi, along with the cow, symbolised Hindu identity. In other words, Hindi's emergence as a major rival to Urdu was driven by a number of factors, including a newly-formed Hindu consciousness, however well-camouflaged, that eventually led to a 'Hindu public sphere' by the inter-war period. This consciousness was insular, exclusive, and anti-syncretic.

Urdu became a soft target for expressing finer cultural and religious sensibilities.[59] One of its greatest poets, Ghalib, wrote a long poem on Banaras which expressed sentiments of piety and devotion. An Aligarh graduate, Abdur Rahman Bijnori, mentioned two sacred (*muqaddas*) books—the *Diwan-i Ghalib* and the *Rig Veda*. The Gujarati-speaking Gandhi wouldn't have known all this. In a way, he sought to bridge the stylistic difference between Hindi and Urdu by making Hindustani the lingua franca. He spoke in Hindustani at the Prarthana Mandir (Prayer Hall) at Visva Bharati in 1920, and wanted it to be a compulsory subject.[60] Five years later, Hindustani became the official language for Congress proceedings. Endorsing this decision, Gandhi expected a perfect and happy blend of Hindi and Urdu to occur.[61] The Nehru Report (15 August 1928), too, recommended Hindustani, written both in the Nagri and Persian scripts, with English concurrently in use. Probably, that decision led Gandhi to suggest that he didn't mind Devanagri and Urdu being optionally used. The surviving script would be the one whose users had greater vitality.[62]

'Languages fade away or are forced into oblivion,' remarked Qurratulain Hyder in her celebrated novel *Aag ka Darya*.[63] Cracks

---

59   Vasudha Dalmia, *The Nationalization of Hindu Traditions: Bharatendu Harischandra and Nineteenth-Century Banaras* (Delhi, 1997); Christopher R. King, *One Language, Two Scripts: The Hindi Movement in Nineteenth Century North India* (Bombay, 1994); Tariq Rahman, *From Hindi to Urdu: A Social and Political History* (Delhi, 2011).

60   Desai (ed.), *Day- to-Day with Gandhi*, vol. 2, p. 236.

61   *Harijan*, 29 Oct. 1938, *CWMG* (Oct. 15, 1938-Feb. 28, 1939), p. 25.

62   Gandhi to Jairamdas Doulatram, 9 Sept. 1928, Jairamdas Doulatram papers, NAI.

63   Quarratulain Hyder, *River of Fire* (New York, 2003), p. 426.

appeared in Gandhi's way of thinking once he tended to identify Hindustani with Hindi; he even propagated the Devanagri script to the exclusion of the Persian script. At the Hindi Sahitya Sammelan in 1935, of which he was a member since 1918, if not earlier, he, having vouchsafed for the Devanagri script and included Urdu in Hindi, felt that the movement for 'universalising' had a sound basis. Two years elapsed before he advocated the Devanagri script on the plea that it was akin to the provincial scripts of the languages descended from Sanskrit,[64] more scientific, phonetically sounder, and more adaptable than either the Urdu or the Roman scripts.[65] The Urdu-speaking population wasn't however prepared to give up the Persian-Arabic script. This led to bitter controversies in which Maulvi Abdul Haq played a major part. The Maulvi, a leading scholar and linguist, left for Pakistan leaving Urdu's future in jeopardy.

As for the Congress, it did little to evolve Hindustani; most of its prominent leaders vouched for Sanskritised Hindi. This, stated a resolution of the All India Progressive Writers' Conference in December 1938, made the Urdu-speaking population nervous and insecure.[66] As for Gandhi, the more vocal elements accused him of inconsistency, despite appealing to educated Hindus and Muslims to show greater tolerance towards each other.[67] Towards the end of his life, he talked once more of Hindustani as India's inter-provincial language,[68] but the die was cast. Partition had sealed the fate of Urdu in the country of its birth.

Eventually however the juxtaposition of language with political interests made Gandhi's task difficult, because his arguments didn't impress Urdu speakers, Hindu, Muslim and Sikhs alike. Their fears were, moreover, reinforced by the Hindi Sahitya Sammelan, led by

---

64 To Jawaharlal, 3 Aug. 1937, Iyengar and Zackariah (eds), *Together They Fought*, p. 309.

65 Jyotindra Das Gupta, *Language Conflict and National Development* (Berkeley, 1970), p. 119. Mohibbul Hasan, 'Mahatma Gandhi and the Indian Muslims', op. cit., p. 143.

66 Chatterjee (ed.), *TF*, 1938 (pt 1), p. 383

67 Tendulkar, *Mahatma*, vol. 4, p. 84.

68 Gandhi, *The Way to Communal Harmony*, p. 384.

Purshottamdas Tandon in UP.[69] Having declared in 1941 that Hindi and Urdu were two different entities, the Sammelan refused to accommodate Urdu within the scope of its conception of Hindi. Gandhi quit the Sammelan to establish Hindustani Prachar Sabha for disseminating Hindustani. This was a case of too little, too late. Moreover, he gave the Urdu and Hindi-speakers the impression that the use of two scripts was only a temporary measure and that eventually a single script would be acceptable to all.

Language and religion are unrelated but Hindi became identified with Hindu solidarity long before it secured the official language status. On the other hand, Urdu earned a bad name because some of the votaries of Pakistan spoke it. Both in UP and Punjab, partisans of the two languages assiduously worked to mark distinctions between communities in such a way that they exacerbated antagonisms.[70] Simultaneously, Hindustani made a quiet and unceremonious exit from the normative emotional universe of the new Hindi and Urdu speakers of north India and Pakistan who have, nonetheless, continued to speak that language without identifying with it.[71]

The 'Communal' Imbroglio: Summing Up

In early January 1946, a poor Muslim in Daspara village consented to receive Gandhi, but later excused himself on the ground that his gesture would enrage fellow Muslims.[72] On the road to Atakora, Gandhi wanted to meet the little boys and girls in a school, but the *maulvi* wouldn't let him. In vain, he tried to beckon to them. On 27 October 1946, he painfully acknowledged that some Muslims looked upon him as an enemy, and that they had advised him that his place was more in Bihar, where they were in point of numbers much greater sufferers, than the

---

69   Gandhi entered into a controversy with him on the Hindi-Hindustani issue. See Ramachandra Guha, *India after Gandhi*, p. 119.

70   Farina Mir, *The Social Space of Language*, p. 23.

71   Salil Misra, 'Transition from the Syncretic to the Plural: The World of Hindi and Urdu', in Malik and Reifeld (eds), *Religious Pluralism in South Asia and Europe*, pp. 297.

72   Ibid., p. 141.

Noakhali Muslims.[73] 'Why do you want to go to Noakhali?', they asked. 'You did not go to Bombay, Ahmedabad or Chapra? Was it because in other places it was the Muslim who was the effective sufferer, whereas in Noakhali the Hindus suffered?'[74] When Gandhi visited Srirampur on 20 November 1946, a predominantly Muslim area with only a sprinkling of houses that were burnt down, only one Muslim, Amtussalaam,[75] his adopted daughter, attended his meeting. In Noakhali, his Muslim opponents dirtied the roads and boycotted meetings.[76] At a prayer meeting in Bhatialpur on 14 January 1947, only a handful turned up. Women didn't come out of their rooms. Gandhi recounted the days when, in the company of the Ali brothers, he'd speak to them without purdah.[77] Clearly, he was left to plough his lonely furrow.

Everything depended upon one's purity in thought, word, and deed. What, then, explains the Muslim rage? Gandhi had, after all, done his best, first, last, always, to prevent the Hindu-Muslim edifice from falling to pieces. He repeated ad nauseum Iqbal's message that Hindus and Muslims had long lived together under the shadow of the Himalayas and had drunk the waters of the Ganga and Jamuna.[78] Few could doubt his enormous services to the masses of all the communities. Whether a Hindu, Muslim, Sikh, or a Christian, he infused in them the spirit to fight for a just cause. However, despite all this, the pathways to division kept widening only to reach breaking point. The Christians disapproved of his stand on conversion; the Sikhs did not think of him as their friend; the RSS brigade addressed him as 'Mahmud Gandhi'; some others said that his reading of the Quran defiled a temple. To this, he simply said, 'How can it be a sin to chant God's name in Arabic?'

---

73   Press report, 27 Oct. 1946, M.K. Gandhi, *Hindu-Muslim Unity* (Bombay, 1965), (ed.) Anand T. Hingorani, p. 135.

74   Pyarelal, *Mahatma Gandhi*, vol. 1, bk 2, p. 6.

75   See Narayan Desai, *My Life is My Message: Svarpan (1940-1948)*, vol. 4, pp. 265-7.

76   Ibid., p. 132.

77   *The Hindu*, 17 Jan. 1947, *CWMG* (21 Oct. 1946-20 Feb. 1947), p. 356.

78   *Harijan*, 16 Mar. 1947, *CWMG*, p. 480.

Gandhi despaired with 'anger-heart-searching' questions: 'Where could I have missed my way? There must be something terribly lacking in my *ahimsa* and faith which is responsible for this.'[79] He cannot, of course, be held responsible for Partition, but he and the Congress weren't at their very best in analysing the unease of religious minorities.[80] They dismissed their anxieties rather clumsily without realising their obligation towards them or anticipating the long-term consequences of their indifference. The Nehru Report was a serious enterprise; so was the programme outlined in the Karachi resolutions (1931). Not much was however done to translate them into practice. Thus, Randive called for soul-searching and an end to viewing communal identities as sacrosanct. He added:

Years of isolation from the Muslim masses have invested the Congress with a peculiar Hindu atmosphere. Congress celebrations partake of the nature of Hindu festivals. Political speeches savour of Hindu ideology. Congress members in legislatures and municipalities do not make any special effort to serve the Muslim community. Congress Committees neglect the Muslims in their districts and taluks and approach only the majority community. Unless every Congressman makes a conscious effort to get rid of these shortcomings, unless the annual session gives a mandate to every Congressman to live up to his national convictions, no swing in favour of the Congress is possible. The impending struggle as well as the war situation demands an immediate change in these directions. Imperialism hopes to secure the necessary man-power for war with the aid of Muslim communalists. Sir Sikandar Hyat Khan with his rank anti-nationalism has already become the recruiting agent of the British Government. The game can be defeated only if the Congress shows sufficient vision and courage to save the minority masses from slaughter and the nation from the calamitous disaster.[81]

---

79   Gandhi to Chhotubhai, 3 Jan. 1947, *CWMG*, p. 302; Manubehn, *Last Glimpses of Bapu* (Agra, 1962), p. 81.

80   Bose, *My Days with Gandhi*, p. 217.

81   Mushirul Hasan (ed.), *TF,* 1939 (pt 2), p. 1764.

Gandhi approached these issues from the standpoint of the early attainment of swaraj. Fair enough. He couldn't subordinate the Hindu-Muslim disputes to the larger goals. At the same time, the dust of internal strife often blurred his vision and he'd settle for outward unity on some working formula. Within weeks he'd however discover that the half-baked ideas aired in Congress bodies weren't, as a rule, sufficiently effective to thwart conflict-ridden leanings and inclinations. Rather than seizing the bull by the horns, he dissipated his energies in phraseological discussion on the doctrine of non-violence.

The enormous overlap in personnel, assumptions, and symbols between Indian nationalism and Hindu communalism created many Saharas in Gandhi's search for communal peace. His own party had a conservative orientation; its truculence had to be factored in. Still, as Sapru warned, 'the thing has got to be faced and must be faced and the sooner it is faced the better.'[82] They had to plod away regardless of stiff opposition. Undoubtedly, the want of clear ideals and objectives aided the growth of communalism.[83]

Gandhi's interest was always more in the realities of the human situation and how to amend it through Truth, Satyagraha, and *Ahimsa* rather than in abstract philosophical and even theological argumentation.

Gandhi assumed that part of the solution lay in the hands of Mohamed Ali in the 1920s, Ansari in the 1930s, and Azad and Ghaffar Khan in the 1940s. He brought them to the forefront only as a counterweight to the League. Thus he played with the idea that Ansari should join the Second Round Table Conference to countersign the blank political cheque which he seemed ready to offer the Muslim leaders. Later, he abandoned the idea, but the Congress Muslims grumbled that he appeared to be running after Jinnah and cajoling him through praise.[84] Abdul Majid Khwaja remonstrated with a touch of self-righteousness and self-pity:

---

82 Sapru to Syed Mahmud, 23 June 1942, Datta and Cleghorn (eds), *A Nationalist Muslim and Indian Politics*, p. 233. Sumit Sarkar, 'Indian Nationalism and the Politics of Hindutva', in Ludden (ed.), *Contesting the Nation*, pp. 271-3.

83 Nehru, *An Autobiography*, p. 137.

84 *Himmat*, Note on the Press, UP of Agra and Oudh, for the week ending 5 Sept. 1931.

It means that you are prepared to surrender the Congress
Muslims who have fought the battles of the country side by side
with you to those Mussalmans who have done nothing except
for themselves, their seats, their posts, their salaries and their
lunches and dinners at the Government Houses .... So far they
[Congress Muslims] have fought against the Government and
against the self-seekers of their own community .... If now they
are thrown overboard by the Congress or by you, they must
clear out of the field altogether or must henceforth fight against
the Congress.[85]

Gandhi, of course, denied using the Congress Muslims as bargaining
chips. Instead, he subscribed to any solution evolved by them, as long as
it didn't commit him to a breach of any fundamental conviction.[86]

The Congress Muslims were, nonetheless, stunned and secluded,
surrounded by barbed wire. With their leader and guide feeling
restricted, their own escape route stood blocked. They felt the light going
out of their lives. This feeling weighed heavily on their minds. Some, if
not all of them, felt that their own record of complete application of
their own ideas was less stellar.

Syed Mahmud and his political mentors were poles apart. Like
Azad and Ansari, he didn't like being treated cavalierly. When this
became known, Jawaharlal, whose contemporary he was, reproached
him for changing his approach to the political and communal
questions.[87] Again, he disregarded his point of view on the Urdu/
Hindustani question and on minority affairs.[88] Mahmud had voiced
his fears without following the members of the old guard like dumb,
driven cattle. Then, in 1942, Mahmud's relatively mild disapproval of
the Congress ministries annoyed Jawaharlal. 'My ways of dealing with
it [Hindu-Muslim problem] are different .... I am tired of this pottering

---

85   Khwaja to Gandhi, 12 Mar. 1931, A.M. Khwaja papers, NMML.

86   Gandhi to Jairamdas Doulatram, 9 Sept. 1928, Jairamdas Doulatram papers.

87   Jawaharlal to Syed Mahmud, 12 Oct. 1940, Datta and Cleghorn (eds),
       A Nationalist Muslim and Indian Politics, pp. 201-2.

88   5 Oct. 1936, ibid., p. 159.

about and trying to please reactionaries and fools of those who belong to the upper strata.'[89]

Clearly, the role of the intellectuals-politicians was the most difficult and the most endangered. They were concentrated in one place so the remaining groups were, or appeared to be, peripheral. At no time were they sufficiently resourceful to influence major policy decisions. The All-India Nationalist Muslim Party, the party founded in 1929, comprised isolated men who differed considerably in philosophy and tactics, and the charge levelled against them was that, in adapting themselves to their situation, they increasingly concentrated on constitutional niceties and less and less on poverty, illiteracy, and social backwardness. In addition to their other constraints, the Congress Muslims faced another predicament: for example, the *Bombay Chronicle*, edited by Syed Abdullah Brelvi, the only Muslim editor of a major national English language paper, was categorised as 'socialist' by the Congress right, 'Islamic' by defensive Hindus and anti-communalist and 'undependable' by all who measured loyalty in terms of absolute acceptance of their position.[90] In 1936, Jawaharlal censured them in his autobiography, an otherwise succinct exposition, and virtually wrote them off from the pages of history.

The same year, Gandhi's differences with the dominant Muslim leadership surfaced in public more sharply than ever before. 'I should even now refuse to go to heaven without Mussalmans,' he said to Syed Mahmud who critiqued his line on the communal question.[91] He also called, in subsequent years, the Partition proposal an untruth and refused to compromise with it. At the same time he said that if the 8 crore Muslims desired separation, he couldn't prevent it. He reiterated on 19 April 1942 what he had said on 4 May 1940. This was followed by the disclaimer on 1 June 1942. Pyarelal heard him muse audibly, 'let posterity know what agony this old soul went through thinking of it [Partition]. *Let it not be said that Gandhi was party to India's*

---

89   Jawaharlal to Syed Mahmud, 7 Feb. 1942, ibid., pp. 225-6.

90   Israel, *Communications and Power*, p. 245.

91   Gandhi to Syed Mahmud, 2 Oct. 1936, Datta and Cleghorn (eds), *A Nationalist Muslim and Indian Politics*, p. 155.

vivisection.[92] By that time, his sense of impotence had increased, along with the others who too floundered in darkness. The old work, if it was continued, was more often than not continued elsewhere. By this time, also, Gandhi had concluded that the Congress Muslims were perhaps a prey to fear and tended to exaggerate somewhat.[93] He was right.

Once, Gandhi asked: 'Was it not up to those Muslims who thought that he was going the wrong way to correct Jinnah?' Some of their leaders tried, for a good reason, cultivating Jinnah only to discover that he acted like a dictator at various conferences.[94] Ansari reposed little faith in a nationalist at heart, turned into a communalist by the exigencies of the time.[95] Mohammad Yunus, the Bihar leader, summed up Jinnah's state of mind: 'Alas! ... Either you follow Jinnah or you get out of the Muslim League.'[96] (Sir) Sultan Ahmad described Jinnah as 'the greatest enemy of Islam and the Mussalmans of India'.[97] That was cruelly and unkindly assessed. As the political cartoons of the period suggest, the proliferation of such narratives allowed Jinnah's contemporaries to locate him in images of power and simulatenously hint at defeat in the not-too-distant future, or simply subject him to ridicule.[98]

As will be clear by now, Gandhi, notwithstanding his elevated precepts and persistent denials, tended to negotiate with pan-Islamists and with the men of religion. But his inclination to do so hardly released him from his troubles. Indeed, they were seen for what they were: the concessions of a great leader now unsure of himself. In 1921, he called on Syed Shah Badruddin, Phulwari Sharif's *sajjada-nashin*, with

---

92   Pyarelal, *Mahatma Gandhi*, vol. 2, p. 211.

93   Letter to a Muslim, 18 Dec. 1947, *CWMG* (Nov. 11, 1947-Jan. 30, 1948), p. 254.

94   To Ansari, 3 Mar. 1930, Mushirul Hasan (ed.), *Muslims and the Congress* p. 113.

95   To Akka, Sarojini Naidu, 26 June 1927, ibid., p. 20.

96   Pyarelal, *Mahatma Gandhi*, vol. 2, p. 262.

97   Sultan Ahmad to Syed Mahmud, 7 Oct. 1941, Datta and Cleghorn (eds), *A Nationalist Muslim and Indian Politics*, p. 211.

98   Sukeshi Kamra, *Bearing Witness: Partition, Independence, End of Raj* (Calgary, Alberta, 2002), p. 62.

Azad and Mazharul Haque.[99] The problem lay not with the observance of such courtesies but what others made of them. Thus, on the eve of the transfer of power, Gandhi wooed the Jamaat-i Islami leader, Maududi.[100] He attended Amin Ahsan Islahi's lecture in April 1947, during the Jamaat's regional convention in Patna. Besides the tumult this generated, Maududi hit back by encouraging Muslims to choose Pakistan over the 'Indian Republic'.

Why did Gandhi favour the Ali brothers, who were essentially backward-looking, refusing to recognise, let alone accept, Turkey entering 'modern' times? As for keeping Azad under some sort of check, Gandhi replied that he desired to remain a backbencher.[101] Gandhi may have been right, but Azad's presidential address at Ramgarh in 1940 belied Ambedkar's assertion, which appeared a year later in *Thoughts on Pakistan*, that 'Islam can never allow a true Muslim to adopt India as his motherland ...' Whereas Ambedkar ruled out 'socialisation of ways, modes, and outlooks' between the followers of Islam and Hinduism, Azad disallowed his contention without, of course, denying the sources of discontent and antagonism. Ambedkar's tone tended to be polemical; Azad had a judicious refrain. What's more, he left a great idea behind him, combining high sense of duty with wide human sympathies. After Independence, he sought to transform the standpoints of Muslims regarding the inherently secular nature of the state and the critical role of constitutionalism, human rights, and citizenship in mediating the tension between Islam, the state, and society. He provided strength to learned bodies which he founded, as minister of education.

Gandhi knew the direction taken by the theologians by their thinking about society and about the place of Islam in the world, and, as a deeply religious man, he felt comfortable with their way of thinking. He assumed that he had to engage with them. But, then, he engaged mainly with the 'traditional', because he assumed, on the

99   Hasan Nizami, *Gandhi-Nama*, p. 55.

100 Seyyed Vali Reza Nasr, *The Vanguard of the Islamic Revolution: The Jama'at-i Islami of Pakistan* (Berkeley, 1994), p. 115.

101 Datta, *Maulana Azad*, p. 222.

strength of the contemporary discourses in India and Europe, that
the liberal, rationalist, and modernist, counter-narratives in Islam,
were weak and not deserving of much political support. Moreover,
while returning again and again to the theme of composite culture
and Hindu-Muslim unity, he showed limited awareness of the depth
and scale of Muslim integration with local cultures and traditions.
Hence he could not much understand why Ansari, Azad, and Syed
Mahmud stood for the unity of a cultural and civlisational ethos
in the same sense in which Arab nationalism united the Arabic-
speaking people, Muslims, Christians, and Jews. He respected them
and honoured them, but turned a blind eye to their point of view
on two issues which were on everybody's lips—minority rights and
Muslim identity.

Gandhi attached much less importance to the Muslim populace, who
needed adequate assurances from a leader of his stature. Their problem
could be best addressed through mass contact.[102] Therefore, Minoo
Masani, the socialist, wanted parties to identify with minority needs
and aspirations.[103] There was no ostensible reason why Gandhi couldn't
do so. In the 1937 elections, Congress contested 58 of the Muslim seats
showing 'a highly deplorable vacillation and lack of self-confidence; the
field was left entirely open to communal and reactionary individuals and
organisations.[104] Again, in the same elections, the Congress secured as
propitious a mandate as any party could have expected, and Jawaharlal
noticed the middle-class awakening among the Muslims.[105] Instead
of using their enthusiasm to lay a solid foundation for the future, and
creating conditions for eradicating the scourge of communalism from
the body politic, Gandhi opposed Muslim enrolment on the ground that
the two communities hadn't yet learnt to trust each other. This was an
error of judgement. He should not have frittered away the good times;

---

102   *The Congress Socialist*, 28 May 1938, P.N. Chopra (ed.), *TF, 1938* (pt 2), pp.
       260-1.

103   Ibid., 14 May 1938, p. 256.

104   Quoted in Thompson, *Enlist India for Freedom!*, p. 60.

105   To Gandhi, 13 July 1937, Iyengar and Zackariah (eds), *Together They Fought*,
       p. 304.

instead, reaching out to the Muslims with the intensity and vigour it demanded would have worked well for the nationalist consensus that was sought to be achieved. Political time and tide wait for no one, and that tide was not caught.

Acharya Narendra Deva advised Jawaharlal in 1937, the year the Congress ministries were installed, to be restrained in approaching Muslim audiences in towns, and, instead of abusing the League leaders, draw attention to the economic aspects of the national struggle.[106] Gandhi realised, belatedly, that this is what should have been done. He also realised that the Congress message bypassed the villages,[107] and, in the context of Hyderabad's Hindu-Muslim riots, he wanted Jawaharlal to concentrate on the rural areas where communal clashes were less frequent.[108] After Partition, he spoke of communal fellowship in the villages. How and why the same approach wasn't followed and pursued later is a theme of perpetual charm and interest. After all, Gandhi had been told that there was no truth in the popular myth that the 70 million of Muslims were solidly against Congress and dominion status.[109]

Gandhi's profound sense of political morality wasn't in doubt, but part of his problem was his belief that only his sense of patriotism was consistent with purification, the good of humanity, and the freedom of all nationalities under colonial rule, and that only he provided the cure for those whose sickness looked increasingly terminal. With political animus heavy in the atmosphere, this stance was scarcely conducive to an amicable settlement with political adversaries. In fact, Jinnah charged that Gandhi often tried to get out of awkward corners by falling back upon his inner voice of silence.[110]

Experience shows that the framing of a future, in some indeterminate way, could, when it is done in a certain way, be ineffective. This happens

---

106   H.D. Sharma (ed.), *Selected Works of Acharya Narendra Deva*, vol. 1, p. 108.

107   Gandhi to Jawaharlal, 30 July 1937, Iyengar and Zackariah (eds), *Together They Fought*, p. 307.

108   Gandhi to Jawaharlal, 10 Aug. 1940, K.N. Panikkar (ed.),*TF, 1940* (pt 2), p. 1351.

109   Thompson, *Enlist India for Freedom!*, p. 60.

110   8 Oct. 1938, P.N. Chopra (ed.), *TF*, 1938 (pt 1), p. 288.

when the anticipation of the future takes the form of those assumptions that enclose with them all the strongest inclinations of a party, or of a group; inclinations that rest on mistaken beliefs and unsubstantiated theories. The truth of this will be shown through numerous examples in the following chapter.

12
'Heads I Win, Tails I also Win'

For good or evil, the present direction of Indian political thought lies largely in the hands of two great adversaries, Gandhi and Jinnah: determined, domineering men, impatient of opposition, clever in their various ways, but completely obsessed with conflicting ideals which they are pursuing with an almost appalling relentlessness ... Both want power for themselves and are contemptuous of power exercised by a third party; but each is mortally afraid of isolation by the other ... Whether Gandhi or Jinnah will come out on top in the ensuing fight for political ascendancy depends on circumstances which cannot at present be foreseen.

-G. Ahmed, 1 Aug. 1941, IOR.L/PJ/12/644.

The complex nature of the Indian national movement makes rather necessary a variety of approaches and methods of study. Likewise, attacking the two-nation theory also requires a variety of methods and various sound standpoints to uncover its roots rather than relying on or celebrating only one standardised method. Already, the latter approach has led to a degeneration of real sociological knowledge into lifeless scholastics. In other words, as ethnic and sectarian violence overwhelms Pakistan, it is worth re-visiting the discrepancy between various components of Muslim nationalism in a more rounded fashion.

Among the numerous monographs on nationalism, two biographies constitute in themselves a separate cluster; the general resemblance of their subject matter associates one with the other, and reveals the piquant contrast of the personalities concerned. In the same vein, some social scientists tend to emphasise the 'opposite poles' of 'Hindu' and 'Muslim' thought in the histories of nationalisms. They describe one as fluid and complex, the other rigid and barren.[1]

---

1   Jones, *Tumult in India*, p. 113.

As we renew, and we must, our discussion about the meanings of Partition and its direction, we might also revisit the approaches of Gandhi and Jinnah as history makers and try to capture their sense of historicality.[2] Our story rotates around them because of their use of ideas and associations to link up with the political actuality and everyday existence. The reader will recognise this claim, even if the notion is getting a bit old. 'Politics,' Jinnah had said sharply and hurriedly, 'means power and not relying on the basis of gentlemen politicians negotiating a fair and equitable agreement.'[3] Even if his views are at irregular intervals masked, depending upon the mapping of his own position, he considered the living and conspicuous representation of world-views differing in their intrinsic essence and in their highest aim. This will bring us to comparing him with Gandhi and to their 'unexpected' solutions.

Preaching in a banyan grove to listeners of all persuasions, Gautam Buddha had proclaimed that the illusion of separateness was the only heresy. Now that the fog of nationalist myth-making has been thick and coats the Partition histories in a dark cloak of inevitability,[4] we must objectively study the responses of those who accepted the idea of Pakistan as feasible, began to see Pakistan as they did: as a possibility, very close to them, palpable and real.

Undeniably, the crowds came out with banners reading 'Pakistan Zindabad', but they deluded themselves, hiding divisions and warring aspirations in the drapery of false solidarity. Rather, the data goes against the suggestion that Pakistan was just round the corner and inevitable. The data also puts to rest the notion that the Hindus and Muslims constituted two separate and antagonistic communities, and refutes linking the relatively brief history of conflicts with the long and almost uninterrupted history of cultural fusion and harmonious

---

2   Apart from some journalistic interventions, notably by Jaswant Singh, an activist of the Bharatiya Janata Party, a number of monographs focus on Jinnah's political career until the 1930s. Ian Bryant Wells, *Ambassador of Hindu-Muslim Unity: Jinnah's Early Politics* (Delhi, 2005).

3   Wells, op. cit., p. 244.

4   Yasmin Khan, *The Great Partition: The Making of India and Pakistan* (Delhi, 2007), p. 206.

existence. On the other hand, the two-nation theory adds little to one's ability to think in new ways. In addition, by representing heterogeneous entities in a unified manner, it obstructs creative imagination and makes it harder to separate religion from the 'secular' domains that hold them together.

Why Pakistan?

Shamim Karhani, the Urdu poet, questioned:

> Do we live in an unconsecrated land?
> The pillars of our faith, do they rest on polluted soil?
> Is the ground of Ajmer profane?
> By the soul of Waris [Ali Shah] is the earth of Dewa unsanctified?
> Are the mausoleums of Imams [in Lucknow] on unblessed ground?

The poet concludes:

> Forbear for God's sake from shouting Pakistan,
> Forbear from insulting thy forefathers;
> Forbear from cutting a heart in two;
> The nation will die, and the English will rule.

I shall, in addition to these verses, register the views of an educationist-reformer, a professional historian, and a poet-philosopher. All valued harmony above all else, opposed violent events that sometimes accompanied fragmentation, espoused stability as a baseline for survival, and urged their community to build up a store of domain-specific knowledge. Accordingly, it makes sense to first of all turn to Syed Ahmad and ask him if he'd allow Hindustan to become the site of one of the most cataclysmic events in twentieth-century history.

Historiography in Pakistan has, of course, propagated the myth that Syed Ahmad and Muslim nationalism, for better or for worse, are intertwined. The fact is that he had no truck with the two-nation theory. Apart from the deep furrows that ran through 'Muslim identity', members of Syed Ahmad's class eagerly traced their genealogy to north India's Urdu-speaking elites and pointed out, often animatedly, that their difference with the Kashmiri Pandits, Kayasths, and other service communities were superficial, those of contact were deep and permanent. Islam and Hinduism throve cheek-by-jowl.

Mirabehn, a neutral observer, lived in a region where the two communities had dwelt together for centuries and where the Muslim peasants were, if anything, better off than their Hindu counterparts.[5] This is an incontestable truth. That Muslim shopkeepers joined a Hindu procession in Punjab's non-colony tract is also an incontestable truth. In fact, the Ranjhas (a tribe living along the Chenab), whose members were related to the Jats and Rajputs, blamed the newspapers for spreading hatred. 'A true word and it would be a good thing if they could all be stopped for a year,' someone suggested. 'Forever,' a voice from the rear came, as if the Unseen itself had spoken.[6] The men in conversation unwittingly introduced and broadened the concept of relevance. If the ties weren't as close as they described, ideas and associations wouldn't have appeared relevant to them.

Evidently, we are looking at a distinct type of culture whose intellectual foundations were qualitatively different. If however we seek to understand the changes in thinking that attended the change from 'composite' to 'separate' living, we must recognise the shifts to be neither uniform nor related to religious beliefs.

Shafaat Ahmad Khan, a historian of medieval India at Allahabad University, was a notable exponent of composite culture before he switched his loyalties to the League, a trend which became commonplace, later when another historian from St. Stephen's College, I.H. Qureshi, joined the trek to Pakistan. In 1938, the year after the founding of the Indian History Congress, Shafaat Ahmad's introduction underlined 'the resurgence of national spirit, the epic progress of the Indian Renaissance, the liberation of reason in science and conscience in religion.'[7] He referred to the early Congress leaders as 'men of vision and imagination ... inspired by lofty patriotism'. In all of this, there is no vision whatsoever of a Muslim nation.

---

5   Mirabehn, *The Spirit's Pilgrimage*, p. 262.

6   Darling, *Wisdom and Waste in the Punjab Village*, pp. 8-9.

7   *Proceedings of the Indian History Congress*, Allahabad, 1938, p. iii.

No one in his or her right mind would question Iqbal's intellectual abilities. He called his land of birth a garden inhabited by a *qaum* (nation), with the two circles of Islam and *watan* (country) intersecting and at several places coalescing into a coherent whole. Portraying the *watan* as a sacred entity requiring devotion, allegiance, and sacrifice, he loved it in a poetic, mystical way, and wrote of the fair dreams of adventure and love which stirred the generation: the somewhat mysterious and indeterminate people's migration, and the romance of their coming and settling in a land of plenty (*Ai aab rud Ganga woh din hain yaad tujh ko, utra tere kinare jab karawan humara*). *Watan* isn't today's national homeland, but the place and time of the poet's fulfilled desire; the 'home ground' of love and youth.[8] Nostalgia filled him with the memory of this lost paradise. Hafiz of Shiraz (Iran) used the same motif in the lines: 'Desire for your street won't leave my mind/the stranger's bewildered heart is always in his homeland.'

Iqbal had faith in the *qaum* being moulded into a nation whose principal axis was Islam. He gave a new image of what it might be, and spoke of autonomous states being formed, obviously not all Muslim, based on the unity of languages, race, history, religion, and identity of common interests. There is no denying his pronounced Islamic vision, but one must quickly discount much of what he aired in his presidential address of 1930 to the League. Its importance is not the quality of content, which was at best pedantic, but the fact that it has one at all, in contrast to other opinion-makers like the Aga Khan and Fazl-i Husain, thinking of a confederation within the Union. While demanding a consolidated Muslim state he referred to 'a duty towards India, where we are destined to live and die'. In early 1935, while declining to chair Halide Edip's Jamia lecture, he suggested a national pact for future cooperation.[9] This didn't jeopardize the integrity of his earlier perspective. While exploring many plausible angles of possible interpretations, there is no hint of a 'Muslim nation' and no

---

8   Javed Majeed reads it differently. *See* 'Geographies of Subjectivity, Pan-Islam and Muslim Separatism: Muhammad Iqbal and Selfhood', in Shruti Kapila (ed.), *An Intellectual History for India* (Cambridge, 2010), p. 140.

9   Iqbal to Ansari, 1 Jan. 1935, Hasan (ed.), *Muslims and the Congress*, p. 233.

evidence, in his exchanges with Husain Ahmad Madani, to construct a two-nation theory. In fact, he suggests that, 'precisely the invisible relations between the two, tied to popular prejudices and not to liberal categories like representation, contract, and interest, make a genuine and productive coexistence possible.'[10] He was laid to rest before the League meeting in March 1940.

Even so, Iqbal buttressed Jinnah's claims. He promoted, without making a fully-fledged commitment to a clearly formulated option or worked within an open-ended context of a spectrum of possibilities,[11] a new sense of awakening by emphasising Islam's monotheism, its glorious past, and its social dynamism. Much of his latter-day poetry was about 'religious'/Islamic matters, but he enriched also an understanding of the value of Islamic history, and thus prepared whosoever wanted to follow him, to dispense with the old ways and be wary of the new ideologies. To those who failed to think too deeply, and they were the greatest number of a hundred to one, his rhetorical invocations struck a chord. It was they who threw their heart and soul into the Pakistan movement without a murmur.

Iqbal turned down the fiction of a secular, homogenising nationalism which assumes the existence of a 'universal amalgamation' of communities. This is implied in poetry, in allegory, in the use of emblems, and in the structure of language. The combination of forces hardly warranted such a conclusion, and yet he inspired a new sense of dignity and importance in upper India's urban bureaucratic and liberal Muslim intelligentsia living in colonial subjection and in competition with their Hindu counterparts. *Zarb-i Kaleem* and *Bal-i Jibrail* (Gabriel's Wing) stimulated Maulana Abul Hasan Ali of Nadwat al-ulama in Lucknow. He read Iqbal after 1935 and agreed with his project of the reconstruction of Islam. Exceptions apart, he believed in a unified and homogenised Islam which had no room for multiple interpretations. He disagreed that multiple Islams is an existential reality in Iqbal's

---

10   Faisal Devji, 'Muhammad Iqbal and the Crisis of Representation in British
       India', in Bhagavan (ed.), *Heterotopias*, p. 140.

11   Javed Majeed, *Muhammad Iqbal: Islam, Aesthetics and Postcolonialism*
       (London, 2009), p. 81.

text,[12] and that sections among his brethren forged their own dialectical relationship with the others.

Why did Pakistanis make so much of Iqbal? Aziz Ahmad, the historian from Toronto, replied, 'because he made us feel good'. Like many off-the-cuff remarks, this stated a truth of a kind less commonly and less openly found in academic writings.[13] No wonder, outward observances, such as trimming the beard and moustache to the traditional length and shape, assumed significance. For every sound of *Jai-Ram Siya-Ram*, the cry of *Allah-o-Akbar* rented the air. In normal times voices of piety rent the air; now open declarations of war were commonplace. Riding out of one of the villages in Lyallpur in 1946, Malcolm Darling heard cries of '*Pakistan zindabad!* (Long live Pakistan!)'[14] 'Without neighbourliness,' he commented, 'there can be no comfort in village life.' The two-nation creed had turned the village from a theory into a bloody fact.[15]

Rehmat Ali, a Cambridge student, had no claim to fame and no part in the making of Pakistan. Skilled in the verbal arts but incapable of generating an original idea, he may have produced a wave of imitation in certain regions but its effect was similar to a stone thrown into a sea. This was a time when the formation of Pakistan was still a matter of Joes and jibes. As *normality* ruled, there wasn't anything inevitable or pre-planned about the way it unfolded.[16] The *real* threat came not from religious passions running high but from the communists wiping out all 'aristocracies'.[17] True, the clouds of religious animus darkened the horizon, but very few, in fact, spoke of Islam as an arbiter of Muslim destiny. Clement Attlee, the British prime minister, conceded: 'You might have got a united settlement at the beginning of the 1930s.'[18]

---

12   Ibid.

13   Russell, *Pursuit of Urdu Literature*, p. 186.

14   Malcolm Darling, *At Freedom's Door* (London, 1949), p. 84.

15   Ibid., pp. 302–3.

16   Khan, *The Great Partition*, p. 206.

17   Winslow and Elwin, *The Dawn of Indian Freedom*, p. 27.

18   Narendra Singh Sarila, *The Shadow of the Great Game: The Untold Story of India's Partition* (Delhi, 2005), p. 199.

'Those whom God has made one, man will never be able to divide,' said Gandhi.[19] An American journalist, after talking to Jinnah for an hour, didn't notice 'Islamic discontent' either in his carefully couched legalisms or in his elegantly dressed person.[20]

The League was itself a pack of sycophants hunting after titles and offices, with its managers inviting henchmen to provide speeches fitted to the idiosyncrasies of particular lieutenant-governors or the known proclivities of local audiences. That is why it won only 4.4 per cent of the Muslim vote in 1937. The pendulum however swung from one end to the other within a decade and a faded dream turned into a reality. Without playing the blame game and shifting the responsibility to either the British or the Congress, Jinnah mastered more constraints and thus had a greater prospect of making the Pakistan idea work. As the wife of one of his secretaries (until he left Jinnah in 1940) noted:

> To countless Muslims he represented the power of past glory and the possibility of future glory, because of his fearless advocacy of their cause, and an assurance that, whatever their own fears and shortcomings, he would somehow create a better world for them.[21]

That said; let us pause for a while for a synoptic view of how this happened.

Muslim Nationalism 1937-47

In his play *You can never tell* (1898), Bernard Shaw heralded the new age through Mrs Clandon. One can say the same about Syed Ahmad Khan but not about Jinnah's arrogant and heartless determination to achieve Pakistan. Similarly, Iqbal's whimsical world of a Muslim haven in India was a place of imaginative personal rufuge. Some of his poems pass into the realm of fantasy and betray his great emotional immaturity. I suspect that he lacked both Syed's intellectual strength as a critic of contemporary Muslim inhibitions, and Azad's verve and buoyancy of spirit.

---

19   *Harijan*, 6 Apr. 1940, *CWMG* (Dec. 1, 1939-April 15, 1940), p. 390.

20   Ibid., p. 116.

21   Baig, *Portraits of an Era*, p. 66.

Nakarda gunahon ki bhi hasrat ki mile dad
Ya rab agar in karda gunahon ki saza hai
If we are to be punished for the sins we have committed,
At least we should be praised for not yearning for the sins we have
not committed.

When Churchill succumbed to the need to revive the Cripps offer in June 1945, Jinnah had already etched the writing of Pakistan so deep upon the Muslim consciousness that he could defeat any proposal unsuited to his interests.[22] When the British appointed the Cabinet Mission (arrived in Delhi on 24 March 1946), its plan granted maximum autonomy to the regional units and allowed for a federal government at the centre with limited powers. This was the nearest to what Jinnah could hope to secure. Eventually however the mission returned home without breaking the impasse.

An American journalist surmised: 'To put it simply, his [Jinnah's] is not a discursive mind. It clings to the conclusion, refusing the intellectual responsibility for exploring the hows and whys.'[23] In March 1940, he showed no inclination to closely define the situation,[24] and kept the problem elements 'in mind' while letting the rest of one's thoughts stay loose enough for other sources to emerge. This avoided him getting tangled up in interminable discussions. On 1 August 1942, Linlithgow feared that, 'all we should get would be something pretty woolly and general'.[25]

Even on the eve of the transfer of power, Jinnah hadn't the first inkling about any single piece of the mechanics necessary to divide a country and an army, and bring a new State into being.[26] On balance, the Partition he preached became 'a Muslim Land of Cockaigne, a repository for every dream, a salve for every disappointment. The

22   Moore, *Churchill, Cripps, and India*, p. vii.

23   Jones, *Tumult in India*, p. 115.

24   'The Situation in India', Diary 4 Mar. 1940, Benthall papers.

25   L/P&J/8/686.

26   Lionel Carter (ed.), *Mountbatten's Report on the Last Viceroyalty, 22 March-15 August 1947* (Delhi, 2003), pp. 66-7.

mystique of the two nations was enthroned, and Mohammad Ali Jinnah was the Anti-Mahatma.'[27]

Wishes, desires, or interests aren't constant and vary in their intensity and power of stimulation. Their distribution varies from person to person and within the same person from man to man. In sociological analysis, only when these and many other problems are solved may these 'variables' be used as real variables and correlated with overt actions and interpreted as functions of the 'wish-desire-interest-variables.' From this perspective, I wish to examine which of the wishes, desires, interests, and the like were stronger when, where, and why.

The Valley

The picture was a bit hazy in Kashmir, a Muslim-majority state ruled by a Dogra ruler; its political forces were divided, as in Punjab. When it came to its future, a strong body of opinion was ambivalent.[28] However, the sympathies of Shaikh Mohammad Abdullah rested on an understanding with the Congress in Delhi. A powerful orator, Abdullah thundered at a social order historically doomed and an economic system resting on inequity, injustice, and exploitation. Without being a firebrand revolutionary, he worked the system as a consummate behind-the-scenes insider who influenced everyday events through connections and friendships. He embraced the mission of reaching out to the hundreds and thousands of people who wanted to be liberated from the clutches of rulers and secure a dignified place under the sun. In 1939, Jawaharlal informed Gandhi that his movement was 'more national in outlook', and that the agitation in Kashmir had an all-India significance and affected the Congress' handling of the Hindu-Muslim question.[29] At Shaikh Abdullah's invitation, Jawaharlal, accompanied by Khan Abdul Ghaffar Khan,

---

27   Ashe, *Gandhi*, p. 344.

28   On Kashmir's accession, D.N. Panigrahi, *Jammu and Kashmir: The Cold War and the West.*

29   To Gandhi, 24 Nov. 1929, Iyengar and Zackariah (eds), *Together They Fought*, p. 383.

visited the valley in 1940 amidst displays of public enthusiasm by National Conference supporters.[30]

Kashmiriyat, which is nowadays grossly misunderstood, seemed appropriately compatible with the principle of 'Unity in Diversity'. It was a political rather than a religious statement reflecting the regional fears and aspirations of Muslims and Kashmiri Pandits alike. It connected well with the regional and linguistic manifestations of nationalism elsewhere. Unlike Jawaharlal, who searched for enduring and transcendental truths, Abdullah was a mass preacher and public teacher busy preparing the masses for their redemption through a social-economic orientation. This was the idea behind the *Naya Kashmiri* plan, or the New Kashmir Manifesto of September 1944, an expression of a fiercely egalitarian world-view.

Opinions vary widely on a final evaluation of Abdullah's role in Kashmir politics, but there is no doubt that he was admired by those who knew him as a warm and generous individual, guided by high principles and the desire to do the right things. There were some, to be sure, who thought he was petty and vindictive. Like most public figures, he was riven by contradictions and ambivalences. He lived and spoke spontaneously and saw words as the agent of instant change. He wasn't quite aware of the inexorable influence of time and historical development. He exaggerated and indulged in myth-making, like the fantasy of *azadi*. He heightened expectations which he himself was in no position to fulfil; hence the great fall and the charge of betrayal. The price a politician pays is, quite literally, out of sight, out of mind. Yes, Abdullah, prime minister of Jammu & Kashmir (1947-53), had gone into near total eclipse. Once people heard him everywhere, which is the key to his phenomenal influence during his lifetime. He made his mark through his oratory skills and incredible energy. With his death however his reputation declined rapidly. Today, policemen guard his shrine in Srinagar. Nobody turns the pages of the *Atish-i Chinar* (Flames of the Chinar), Abdullah's autobiography. The flame is extinguished, probably for good.

30	For a critical analysis of Shaikh Abdullah and the National Conference, Chitralekha Zutshi, *Languages of Belonging: Islam, Regional Identity, and the Making of Kashmir* (New York, 2004).

The Land of Five Rivers

During the war years, the British deliberately built up Jinnah's prestige in order to operate the war machine with maximum efficiency.[31] His real strength however lay in the provinces, where one by one he stepped into the existing power vacuum by destroying the existing combinations and alignments. This was by no means an easy task in Punjab where the landowning class was spineless, internally divided, and subservient even to the British deputy-commissioner. Besides, the Punjab Unionist Party had won the 1937 elections with a resounding 90 out of 175 seats, the Congress bagged 29 seats, the League only two. This enabled Sikandar Hyat Khan to cobble together a coalition, in October 1937, of a multi-religious character. Even though Fazl-i Husain had achieved the same, this arrangement came into being under very different circumstances.

As a first step, therefore, what Jinnah said was this: 'In the Punjab you Muslims are surrounded by enemies waiting to destroy your culture, your religion and your economic progress. You must defend yourself if you wish to avoid annihilation.' This form of rhetoric, in which all that mattered was that India consisted of Muslims and their enemies, reversed an established trend of communal fellowship. Once this was achieved, Jinnah strengthened his bargaining power vis-à-vis his adversaries. After the Sikandar-Jinnah Pact, he alerted the political classes to the League's presence without questioning the continuance of the Unionist Party in either name or effect. At this stage, a British army officer from Punjab quite effectively summed up the situational:

> The pact was fully accepted by the Council of the League and the situation was such that, so far as the internal affairs of the Punjab were concerned, Muslim Assembly members were Unionists while, in matters of an all-India interest such as general questions of Muslim culture and education and economic welfare. This was a perfectly

---

31   Anita Inder Singh, *The Origins of the Partition of India 1936-1947* (Delhi, 1987), pp. 238, 241-42. The provincial scene is best surveyed by Ayesha Jalal, *The Sole Spokesman: Jinnah, the Muslim League and the Demand for Pakistan* (Cambridge, 1985).

rational situation under which dual loyalties could concurrently be respected.[32]

Summarising what has already been written up, let's remember Sikandar Hyat Khan meeting Gandhi in July 1939. We need reminding because their getting together produced the Punjab leader's proposal postulating the virtual abandonment of the Partition scheme.[33] However, the 'Lahore Resolution' triggered certain changes, including the expulsion of the Punjab premier, the virtual repudiation of the Jinnah-Sikandar Pact, the break up of the Unionist coalition, and the consequent regrouping of forces. In April 1943, Jinnah regretted that Punjab hadn't yet played the part it ought to have done. Remember, he said, Punjab was the cornerstone of Pakistan. It was clear that, 'in a situation full of doubts and difficulties', Pakistan couldn't be forced on Punjab from outside. It could only be achieved on the expressed desire of its people.[34]

The contest for sovereignty entered a new phase with visible effects not only in the formal and informal arenas of provincial politics but well beyond.[35] The interplay between religious consciousness and the political world suggests that provincial autonomy on a widened franchise found even the apparently impregnable Unionists casting around for a new popular justification for their rule. This pushed Sikandar Hyat Khan into a closer association with Jinnah, though they also fell out because of the dependence of one on the colonial system and the resolve of the other to replace it.

Jinnah, on the other hand, transcended such tensions and directed 'Muslim politics' towards symbolic goals. He offered concessions to

---

32   Birdwood, *A Continent Experiments*, p. 123.

33   For Punjab, David Page, *Prelude to Partition: The Indian Muslim and the Imperial System of Control 1920-1932* (Delhi, 1982); David Gilmartin, *Empire and Islam: Punjab and the Making of Pakistan* (Berkeley, 1988); Ian Talbot, *Provincial Politics and the Pakistan Movement: The Growth of the Muslim League in North-West and North-East India 1937-47* (Karachi, 1988); Neeti Nair, *Changing Homelands: Hindu Politics and the Partition of India* (Delhi, 2011).

34   Birdwood, op. cit., p. 128.

35   Ayesha Jalal, *Self and Sovereignty: Individual and Community in South Asian Islam Since 1850* (Delhi, 2001), pp. 318-19.

the Punjab Unionists and encouraged the Punjab Muslim Students' Federation, whose members came mostly from the urban centres of central and eastern Punjab, to adopt the Pakistan demand as early as 1937. 'I wanted to pull them [Muslims] up step by step,' he said, 'and before making them run I wanted to be sure they are capable of standing on their own legs.'[36] Besides, he forged what approximated to a marriage of convenience between the professional classes of the Hindu-dominated areas and the landlords of the future Pakistan regions.[37] Thus, the League's electoral success in 1946 justified a new cultural redefinition of the state. As Peter Hardy pointed out: 'the enfranchised Muslims had recorded their conviction that the things which they did not share with their non-Muslim neighbours were more important than the things which they did share, and that this conviction required political expression in the partition of the sub-continent.'[38]

Jinnah's pronouncements exploited the image of Hindu hegemony and the extinction of Islam. *Azadi* meant the loss of land and the establishment of Hindu raj. 'Azadi' 'is *barbadi*—destruction, and Pakistan is *qabaristan*—a graveyard.'[39] Hindus, Muslims, and Sikhs, thus, began to eye one another critically. After the Unionist Party disintegrated, the last hope of a multi-party and multi-religious coalition,[40] millions were sucked into the vortex of all-India politics; Punjabis ceased to be Punjabis and became Muslims, Hindus, and Sikhs. The Akalis demanded a 'Khalistan' as a buffer between Pakistan and Hindustan. Prominent Hindus seriously considered a partitioned India over a united country.[41]

On the popular level, a specific approach to cultural and political empowerment, based on Islamic symbols and the flow and effusion

---

36   Khalid Bin Sayeed, *Politics in Pakistan: The Nature and Direction of Change* (New York, 1980), p. 10.

37   Ian Talbot, *Pakistan: A Modern History* (New Delhi, 1999), p. 5.

38   Peter Hardy, *The Muslims of British India*, p. 252.

39   Darling, *At Freedom's Door*, p. 51.

40   Memorandum by E.M. Jenkins, 4 Aug. 1947, Carter (ed.), *Mountbatten's Report on the Last Viceroyalty*, p. 365.

41   Neeti Nair, *Changing Homelands*, p. 176.

of the religious rhetoric, led to a movement variously described as separatism and political Islam. *Pirs* and *sajjada-nashins*, all tied to the landowning class, exploited these sentiments. The pro-Pakistan ulama in UP and Bihar weren't far behind, except that they didn't have the same degree of leverage either through ownership of land or a nexus with the imperial establishment. Most made a living out of religious endowments, seminaries, or *maktabs* and madrasas. Most led the *namaz* in the local masjid or imparted lessons on how Islamic teachings, norms, and institutions are both necessary and sufficient for a just society. Their rhetoric bordered on the xenophobic. Their sheaves of Fatwa were characterised by a deep distrust of a stereotypical 'Gandhi' who seemed determined to undermine and even destroy their identity. They blamed virtually all the Indian Muslim problems and shortcoming on the Congress.

Bengal

In Bengal, another Muslim-majority province, Fazlul Huq, the Krishak Praja Party's undisputed chief, headed a loose coalition of urban and rural interests. The same maxim that one cannot create something from nothing also applied to the provincial realm. Now, Jinnah felt that both the leaders were operating in the dark, with no idea of what they were doing or where they were going. There were only two options: to implement the Lahore Resolution or to rubbish it. Protracted equivocation wasn't possible, he said, with cynical thoughtlessness. The League couldn't hop from one compromise to another; it disgraced him personally. Fazlul Huq had to fall in line and his desire to achieve an autonomous and united Bengal, which was at any rate ill-fated, had to fall through the trap door of history.[42] Besides, 'the competing savageries' on 16 October had already decided Bengal's destiny.[43] Partition was the considered choice of large and powerful sections of the Hindu politicians. 'When push came to shove', Joya Chatterjee writes, '*bhadralok* Hindus preferred to carve out Bengal rather than to accept the indignity of being ruled by the Hindus.[44]

---

42   Wolpert, *Jinnah of Pakistan*, pp. 192-5, 216-17.

43   Amit Kumar Gupta, *Crises and Creativities: Middle-Class Bhadralok in Bengal c. 1939-52*, p. 223.

44   Joya Chatterjee, *Bengal Divided*, p. 266.

UP

In 1928, the fear of being overwhelmed by the masses had driven the Ali brothers to throw out the Nehru Report. The same concern gripped the next generation of publicists once the Act of 1935 consummated the process of devolving power and the UP ministry enacted a nerve-racking piece of legislation for the rajas, nawabs, and *taluqdars*. Acharya Narendra Deva recalled how the League in the UP Assembly supported every measure for the amelioration of mill and factory workers, but not the legislation in favour of the peasantry on the verge of starvation.[45] With the position of clients endangered, its leaders joined hands with the landowning class, Hindu and Muslim alike, to thwart agrarian reforms. Little by little, the Nawab of Chattari and other smaller zamindars in Aligarh district read the writing on the wall and switched allegiances.[46] The Awadh *taluqdars* and their counterparts in Western UP were the prototype of the anti-liberal, antagonistic to the extension of franchise and to the peasantry's participation in public affairs. While they favoured strong governmental powers to avoid anarchy in the countryside, they were in no position to influence their patrons and benefactors. After their defeat in the 1936 elections, they kept crying hoarse but weren't heard. They were attacked by the Kisan Sabhas, which generated unprecedented consciousness on the inequities of the landed system.

The needs that found political expression weren't the community needs as a whole but those of a class consisting of big and small landlords, lawyers, doctors, and government servants.[47] The Muslim League's principal goal was, thus, to motivate people to assert their Islamic identity so that the bourgeoisie-landlord combination could disguise their own ulterior motives. Islam became a convenient tool in their hands and Jinnah desired preventing radical changes or democratisation not because of the Hindu majority but because the radicals would put an end to semi-feudal privileges.[48]

---

45   Sharma (ed.), *Selected Works of Acharya Narendra Deva*, vol. 1, p. 132.

46   *Leader*, 10 Nov. 1939, *TF, 1939* (pt 2), p. 1265, p. 1815.

47   M. Mujeeb, 'The Partition of India in Retrospect', in Philips and Wainwright (eds), *The Partition of India*, p. 410.

48   Jawaharlal to Syed Mahmud, 2 Feb. 1942, Datta and Cleghorn (eds), *A Nationalist Muslim and Indian Politics*, p. 219.

To begin with, Jinnah and the *ashraf* took the wind out of the Congress sails by publicising the sufferance of UP and Bihar Muslims. They made public their hurt over their exclusion from the ministries, and peddled all manner of theories to raise the spectre of the Congress playing dirty with them. Their complaints, which Maulana Munshi Sajjad, Naib Amir-i Shariat, summed up were: Muslim children were made to sing *Bande Mataram*; Hindi was exalted and Hindi chauvinists attacked Urdu, the heart and soul of UP Muslim culture; ministers were excluded Muslims from local bodies and services; and the law and order machinery failed to save Muslim lives in riots.[49]

In the second stage, i.e. after the Lahore resolution, Jinnah painted *all* the Congress leaders with the same brush: anti-Muslim and anti-Islam. They were either white or black, without any intermediate shades. Jawaharlal became, in consequence, the target, his impatience and self-importance coming in the way of an amicable settlement. His bellicosity was 'a serious disqualification for a person invested with the task of negotiation in a spirit of compromise,'[50] and he linked his comments in 1940 with some 'of the more outrageous and metonymic constructions' within which Jinnah's adversaries positioned him.[51] Jawaharlal's belligerence may have come in the way of a dialogue with Jinnah or he may have put the cart before the horse, but their ideological incompatibility was such that they failed to discover a common meeting ground.

On the road to Pakistan, however Jinnah refrained from disturbing the apple-cart in UP and Bihar, where the cream of the Muslim intelligentsia repeated the *Pakistan zindabad* slogan with monotonous regularity and

---

49   Hasan (ed.), *India's Partition*.

50   B.B. Misra, *The Indian Political Parties: An Historical Analysis of Political Behaviour up to 1947* (Delhi, 1976), p. 429. Two extracts reflect Jawaharlal's attitude. In Nov. 1939 he observed exasperatedly: 'Certain remarks of Bapu in a recent statement seem to be unfortunate. Jinnah has ... nothing to talk to us about except because of Provincial and Central Governments. This we cannot do till a satisfactory declaration is made by the British Government. If, however, we say to him that we are going to do nothing in the nature of aggressive action till he agrees to it, he knows that he is in a dominant position and can play the tune.' A month later, he wondered: 'If Jinnah claims to represent the Muslims why is he afraid of an election by adult franchise for the Constituent Assembly on separate electorates?'

51   Kamra, *Bearing Witness*, p. 52.

where the stakes were higher because of their, comparatively, strong position in the professions and government. He actually assumed a position like Gandhi as far as the Muslims were concerned: 'a sword of Islam resting on a secular scabbard'.[52] He tamed the students, teachers, and academic liberals by the reality that he was now immensely popular and they weren't.[53] Once upon a time his solution for the Hindu-Muslim problem was: 'You destroy your orthodox priestly class and we'll destroy our mullahs and there will be communal peace'.[54] The same mullahs, whom he despised, became the instruments for getting on with the particular job at hand. With their imaginary construction of self, they upheld doctrinal probity, scoffed at composite inheritances, and turned the 'Muslim nation' into their cherished ideal. Ashraf Ali Thanwi and Shabbir Ahmad Usmani were his prized trophies from Deoband. In addition, silent support came from other individuals and institutions.

Even if the UP Muslims didn't see themselves as benefactors of a bountiful providence, their eyes were nevertheless set on the road to material progress. Naive and short-sighted, they saw themselves as the makers of a Muslim destiny. Paradoxically however, Jinnah paid no attention to them or their future. Too bound up in the current of those exciting times to view the problem coolly and clearly, he simply said, 'give us Pakistan, and we will take care of that problem when we come to it'.[55] By ignoring UP and Bihari Muslims, he almost killed the goose that had laid the golden egg.

NWFP

In between various developments, from the capitulation of the Muslim-majority provinces to the release of Shah Nawaz, P.K. Sehgal, and G.S. Dhillon, the three officers in the Indian National Army with their image

---

52   R.W. Sorenson, *My Impression of India* (London, 1946), p.109.

53   The Aligarh students were radically inclined in the 1920s and 1930s, but had now no qualms about turning their backs on Azad and Husain Ahmad Madani, the Deoband *alim* who argued that the Partition would weaken Islam in the Muslim-minority provinces.

54   Shiva Rao, 'The Terrible Price of Opportunism', *Hindustan Times*, 20 June 1969.

55   Chagla, *Roses in December*, p. 80.

as proud patriots, produced much excitement. Similarly, the Naval mutiny in Bombay on 19 February 1946 showed the way to life and honour. Other groups too saw themselves as fighting the forces of evil, but the Congress failed to harness their sentiments.[56] This was partly because it was continually placed under a ban: its top leaders were either in jail during those five years or the party machinery was out of gear.[57] Some were tired, unenthusiastic, and pulling in opposite directions. Besides, 30 per cent of the adult population in a narrow electorate hadn't registered, and the candidates contesting the elections to the general and urban constituencies were very often weak and ineffective.[58]

In the NWFP, the League had been so weak that the local unit didn't even mention 'Pakistan' in the 1943 by-election campaign.[59] By the spring of 1945, the region was the sole Muslim province without a League ministry. However, the tide reversed once the Congress accepted Partition and Jawaharlal agreed, much to the dismay of Badshah Khan and the Khudai Khidmatgars, to a referendum. In July 1947, Maududi encouraged the Muslims of the NWFP to turn out the Congress ministry and to vote for Pakistan.[60] With the Congress denying the option of Pakhtunistan, the Khudai Khidmatgars were thrown to the wolves. Gandhi urged them to make Pakistan really *pak* (pure).

The enfranchised voted in 1946, for the first time, not for a person but for Partition. In some places, Jinnah's many claims appealed to his followers for whom the force of Islam was judged to extend beyond the sphere of religion to touch vital matters of temporal existence, including the conditions of modern nationhood.[61] Here, more than anywhere else, the appeal to *azadi* was perverted through its adulteration with rhetoric that portrayed another religious community as the barrier

---

56   Gopalkrishna Gandhi (ed.), *Gandhi is Gone.*, p. 87.

57   Gopal, *Jawaharlal Nehru*, vol. 1, p. 305; Jawaharlal to Azad, 31 Oct. 1945, *SWJN*, vol. 14, p. 115, complaining of lack of Congress organisation and 'small cliques controlling Congress committees'.

58   Introduction, Hasan (ed.), *India's Partition*, pp. 40-1.

59   Mukulika Banerjee, *The Pathan Unarmed*, p. 177.

60   Nasr, *The Vanguard of the Islamic Revolution*, p. 115.

61   Farzana Shaikh, *Making Sense of Pakistan* (London, 2009), p. 2.

to this freedom. It eventually proved to be a dangerous game and one over which Jinnah and the League ultimately lost control.[62]The League's arsenal were formed of landowners of Sind and Punjab, the Awadh *taluqdars*, the zamindars of Bihar, and the Aligarh students.[63] As a rule, the city Muslims rallied around the green flag with a crescent.[64]

All in all, Jinnah juggled the existing political and social arrangements to produce new and politically useful configurations. What of the non-Muslim minorities claim to be a nation? 'There is no comparison,' Jinnah retorted. The eye of a statesman was needed to view the scene with added clarity and perspective. It involved, among other things, collision with an organisation already present in the political process, reinterpreting a problematic phenomenon like 'Muslim nationalism' which Iqbal did for him, and breaking through mental barriers created by regional, class, and sectarian loyalties. They were either frozen or weakened for the time being by the rising tide of a religion-based nationalism, but they carried, as is evident from Pakistan's histories since 1971, seeds of separation and division. Iqbal may have captured the public's fancy, as much of the theorising in the 1940s did, but the poet, claiming to speak a different language hardly broached the complex aspects of identities, ideologies, and nation-building. It is easy to build castles in the air but enormously difficult to create a nation out of diverse and contradictory interests. In the specific instance of Pakistan, it became, for the reasons mentioned above, far more difficult to create a consensual model that would rest on democracy, federalism, and linguistic reorganisation of the state.

Between Scylla and Charybdis

Ajnabi khaak ne dhundla diye qadmon ke suragh
The alien dust has bedimmed the footprint

-Faiz Ahmad Faiz

---

62   Omar Noman, *Pakistan: A Political and Economic History Since 1947* (London, 1988), p. 6.

63   Mushirul Hasan (ed.), *Knowledge, Power & Politics: Educational Institutions in India* (Delhi, 1998), pp. 204-5.

64   Jawaharlal to Krishna Menon, n.d., *SWJN*, vol. 14, p. 97.

Educated in a local madrasa (1887) and Christian Missionary High School (1891), Mohammad Ali Jinnah, son of Jinnahbhai Poonja (d. 17 April 1902), followed his sister Fatima to Bombay. As a student in London, he imbibed aspects of upper class life, struck friendships, earned his teacher's testimonials, and picked up a law degree before returning home in May 1896. He established a new student organization 'to build up such staunch traditions of cooperation and fellowship, that the young association might eventually grow into a perfect minature and model of the federated India of the future, the India of their dreams'. Gokhale, the guest on the occasion, set before the students at Caxton Hall 'those sublime lessons of patriotism and self-sacrifice which he alone sings singularly ... was competent to teach with grace and authority and grace.' In next to no time, he built an enviable standing under Naoroji's patronage, with whom he worked as personal secretary at the 1906 Congress. Pherozeshah Mehta made him prominent in the Bombay Presidency Association and sent him to London as one of his representatives. The best was yet to come: as a prelude to a thriving vocation, his unimpeachable integrity became his major asset. Later, P.K. Telang, Chimanlal Setalvad and Kanji Dwarkadas mentioned him for the faithfulness of his public service, and the rigid consistency with which he adhered to its principles.[65] He was, moreover, endowed with a high order of debating power, and his relationship with Ruttie Petit, whom he married in 1918, indicates a warm-hearted and caring nature.

Jinnah had few doctrinal affinities with either the Shia or Sunni orthodoxies. Once he told friends that a sect among the Muslims (to which he belonged) believed in the ten *avatars* and had much in common with Hindus in their inheritance laws and social customs. Language requires that we shift between unstructured thoughts and an ordered system; Jinnah spoke no Urdu and therefore the two Urdu poets, Mir and Ghalib, stood outside his cultural zone. He couldn't acclimatise himself to the other currents in north India: the Turco-Italian War in 1911, the Kanpur mosque incident in 1913, or the Aligarh Muslim University project, the three major issues that breached Anglo-Muslim

---

65   Dwarkadas, *India's Fight for Freedom*, pp. 60-7.

relations in early twentieth century. Matters didn't rest there. He had no time for religious observances, and no great regard for the *maulvis* and theologians who had begun to throng the League sessions from 1918 onward. If, as the Muslim proverb says, every evil finds its Moses, so does every blessing find its devil. The devil that stalked was the fury of the mullahs, and Jinnah spoke with unreserved candour against them.

Hindus and Parsis were Jinnah's natural allies, and he dealt with them professionally. He married ('plucked the Blue Flower of his desire', in the words of Sarojini Naidu) the daughter of Dinshaw Petit, a Parsi. He didn't carry the can for a policy the pan-Islamists orchestrated, which he believed was even more ingeniously doomed to failure. He recognised only power as a force in politics; tradition, pan-Islamism, and aristocracy were outworn things for him. While the ever-vitalising ideas embodied in Islam inspired Iqbal and Maududi, the Jamaat-i Islami leader, Jinnah, much like the poet Ghalib, yearned for a paradise on earth without awaiting the doomsday to descend. No one thought of him as a visionary or a dreamer with a single line of thought. No one commented on his ability to navigate the rough current of 'Muslim politics'.

Their background and larger social concerns rendered Gandhi's affinity with Jinnah acceptable and striking. As fellow Gujaratis, they had many mutual concerns and every reason to act in unison. Indeed, for a while, each person respected the other for the work he had done. For example, Jinnah made mention of Gandhi's activism in South Africa on 14 January and on 21-23 October 1915. Gandhi responded with his usual warmth.[66] They discussed war recruitment in June 1918.[67]

Jinnah fêted Gandhi on Gokhale's sixth death anniversary on 19 February 1921. Gandhi, in turn, described him as the 'learned Muslim gentleman',[68] and the rising hope of the Congress.[69] His friendly note to Fatima, Jinnah's loyal and dutiful sister, said it all.

66	Yagnik, *Gandhi As I Knew Him*, pp. 5-6.
67	4 July 1918, Desai (ed.), *Day-to Day with Gandhi*, vol. 1, p. 169.
68	21 Oct. 1916, *CWMG* (July 16-Nov. 30, 1916), p. 304.
69	*CWMG* (Jan. 1915-Oct. 1917), p. 212.

Please remember me to Mr. Jinnah and do coax him to learn Hindustani or Gujarati. If I were you, I should begin to talk to him in Gujarati or Hindustani. There is not much danger of your forgetting your English or your misunderstanding each other. Is there? Will you do it? Yes, I would ask this even for the love you bear me.[70]

Both worked their way through the existing organisations, with Jinnah masterminding the Lucknow pact. This merited clamorous applause.

Emboldened to resign his imperial council seat, Jinnah berated the government for trampling upon the principles for which it avowedly fought the war. This is how he responded to the Rowlatt Act. With this premise, he established a base from which others could advance, renew and refresh the sources of both inter-community amity and composite culture, and support Gandhi's amendments to a major resolution on reforms at the Amritsar Congress in December 1919.

However, in the process, Jinnah's initial warmth for Gandhi was much less pronounced. The arrogant quip at Nagpur scarcely augured well for the future. Remarkably, Jinnah presented a reasoned argument on separating religion from politics and looked for those Congressmen who could disentangle themselves from the tight pledges in which their leader seemed to have them bound. He asked to pause and cry halt before it was too late. Without opposing Non-Cooperation as such, he objected to the resolution as neither logical nor fit to being put into execution. Gandhi however refused to budge.

Still, Jinnah hoped to return to the Congress fold, just as the extremists had done at Lucknow four years ago. He hadn't forgotten his strong criticism of the Jallianwala Bagh massacre and, later, the all-white Simon Commission.[71] He also drew comfort from the happy days with Motilal in the central legislative assembly. Intellectually, they were on the same track; they also shared each other's cultural affinities. In their adoration of Europe, they gave England a special place, seeing in that country the standard-bearer of European civilisation.

---

70   Desai (ed.), *Day-to-Day with Gandhi*, vol. 2, p. 141. This is an extract from an undated letter.

71   Wolpert, *Jinnah of Pakistan*, p. 90.

Motilal had the felicitous ability to create an atmosphere in which every participant did his best to contribute to the common undertaking. He triumphed over all the difficulties of his position by his tact and good temper and masterly adroitness. Jinnah was alien to the wheeling-dealing tactics of various factions and therefore displayed an occasional wildness of judgement. As a member of the Assembly, he towered head and shoulders above many of his colleagues, and there was no second. Kanji Dwarkadas, a disciple of Annie Besant, records a conversation at Jinnah's house. Motilal and R.D. Tata were present. Jinnah kept the table roaring with laughter by recalling certain incidents in the Assembly. One of them occurred before the final voting on a particular bill. Tata rushed to his suite of rooms at the Cecil Hotel, complaining that an assembly member had asked for a substantial consideration to vote in favour, and threatened that if he didn't get it, he'd vote against it. He belonged to Motilal's party. Jinnah at that late hour immediately sent for the member staying in the same hotel and told him, 'R.D. Tata has complained to me that you have demanded ten thousand rupees for your vote. You'll not get that money. You go to hell and now you get out of this room.' Crestfallen, the member withdrew rapidly and the next day he voted for the Bill. 'Ruttie, Motilal and I enjoyed this story,' Dwarkadas wrote, 'as R.D. Tata confirmed that what Jinnah had said was true and Motilal already knew all about it.'[72]

A liberal with cross-party appeal is what Jinnah was. 'Meet this young man, old lions must learn from young cubs,' were the words with which Sarojini Naidu introduced him to the Berlin-educated K.A. Hamied in November 1927. When the two came together, the young man suggested that Jinnah should devote time to *Muslim* education. Jinnah replied: 'Young man, you think I am a leader of the Muslims. I'm not. I'm a national leader of India. I can't work for the Muslims alone.'[73] Able, cultured, and upright, he spoke 'not as a Mussalman but as an Indian'.[74] No wonder then that Motilal told Sarojini Naidu, 'it's your

---

72   Dwarkadas, op. cit., pp. 276-77

73   K.A. Hamied, *An Autobiography: A Life to Remember* (Bombay, 1972), p. 64.

74   Dwarkadas, op. cit., pp. 62-6; M.C. Chagla, *Roses in December*. p. 79.

business now to bring Jinnah back'[75] (from the All-Parties Conference leading to the publication of the Nehru Report). She couldn't, but as India's 'Sir John Simon', Jinnah took a wider view of politics. He 'is an Indian (though a moderate one) first and Moslem afterwards'.[76] This was Fenner Brockway writing in 1927.

Aware that conditional appeasement of those in authority was always a better course than confrontation, Jinnah held out an olive branch on 20 March 1927 by foregoing separate electorates if the Bengali and Punjabi Muslims earned seats in the legislative councils in proportion to their population, and if the Muslims secured one-third seats in the legislative assembly. The other two conditions were to separate Sind from Bombay Presidency and introduce reforms in the NWFP. However, the Mahasabha and the Sikh League thrust aside the 'Delhi Proposals', pointing the finger at Gandhi for his failures not just of recent months but, with convenient selectivity, for those of the past few years.[77] The Mahasabha, having used national unity as a cover to masquerade its illiberal designs, jettisoned the prospect of an amicable settlement.[78] Generosity is not only good morals, wrote the younger Nehru in 1929, it was often good politics and sound expediency. The Mahasabha, with its quasi-fascist ideology, constantly sought formulas to assuage its Hindutva conscience.

The path which brought Jinnah to the Calcutta Convention on 28 December 1928 had twisted and turned unexpectedly.[79] The contrast between the Congress and the League hit him between his eyes, and thrust him out into a different world. His chief amendments to the Nehru Report were unwanted by a majority. After four hours' debate, the Congress Subjects Committee adopted Gandhi's compromise

---

75   Shiva Rao, op. cit.

76   Brockway, *The Indian Crisis*, p. 121.

77   Mushirul Hasan, 'The Communal Divide: A Study of the Delhi Proposals', Mushirul Hasan (ed.), *Communal and Pan-Islamic Trends in Colonial India* (Delhi, 1985), pp. 287-90.

78   Ansari to Gandhi, 13 Feb. 1930, Mushirul Hasan (ed.), *Muslims and the Congress*, p. 96.

79   Over 1,200 delegates discussed the Nehru Report to resolve the issue of dominion status versus *purna* swaraj.

resolution. It declared that, if the British Government did not by the end of the year accept the Dominion Status Constitution in its entirety, the Congress would organise a Non-Cooperation movement that would include non-payment of taxes.

The Congress wirepuller's were frustrated in their effort to push through the Nehru Report; equally, a defeated, dejected, and crest-fallen Jinnah sailed into years of disappointment and near-despair, and marched on alone without the comradeship of certain people who had meant so much to him elsewhere. Anxious but not disconsolate, he stood aside for a while. Faced with the blockade of suspicion and being too much of an individualist to fit comfortably into any party except his own, he explored the ordinary routes to attaining power. Nonetheless, he could draw comfort from the Muslim parties closing their ranks behind his 'Fourteen Points'.

The spirit of haggling was not calculated to make negotiations fruitful, and yet Gandhi travelled from Ahmedabad in the Gujarat Mail to Bombay. He met Jinnah on 11 August 1929 at Mani Bhawan, the home of Revashankar Jagjivan at Gamdevi. However, the noises produced by K.D. Malaviya, Lajpat Rai, B.S. Moonje, M.R. Jayakar and N.C. Kelkar multiplied claims at every stage of negotiations without realising that no degree of safeguards would make the Muslims a majority community. In this way, they jettisoned the prospect of a meaningful dialogue.[80] On 1 May 1939, the 'Responsivists' urged Gandhi not to accede to Jinnah's demands which were 'incompatible with nationalism.'[81]

Notwithstanding their stance, Jinnah reached an accord with Ansari on substituting joint electorates for separate electorates after a specified period. His standpoint cleared the way for a joint front against Samuel Hoare's White Paper presented to Parliament in March 1933.[82] The clock kept ticking until early January 1935, when Jinnah accepted

---

80   Lajpat Rai to Motilal, n.d., AICC Papers (108/Supplementary); Moonje to Malaviya, 31 July 1928, Jayakar to Gandhi, Jayakar papers (437).

81   *Times of India*, 7 May 1930, Jayakar papers (354).

82   Jinnah to Chagla, 5 Aug. 1929, M.C. Chagla papers, NMML. Wolpert, *Jinnah of Pakistan*, pp. 135-6.

Ansari's invitation to the Congress parliamentary board.[83] He agreed to joint electorates without any change in the number of seats allocated to the Muslims under the Communal Award.[84] Moreover, he hoped to wean the Congress away from its dependence on the Mahasabha and made his offer thus:

> I have nothing in common with the Aga Khan. He is a British agent. I am devoted to my old policy and programme. . . . If the Congress can support the Muslims on the question of the Communal Award, I would be able to get all the Muslim members except 7 or 8. . . . As things stand, the practical way would be for just a few leaders of political thought to combine for the purpose of preparing a formula which both the communities might accept. The Congress I admit would have to change its attitude in some respects, but looking to the great interests at stake Congress leaders should not flinch. I think the future is with the Congress Party and not with me or the Aga Khan.[85]

In the assembly, Jinnah had secured the backing for three resolutions, the first acquiescing in the Award pending a settlement by the communities themselves; the second criticising the provincial part of the Act of 1935 but not condemning it outright; and the third, denouncing the federal part as 'fundamentally bad and totally unacceptable' and demanding full responsible government in a federated British India. This alliance brought about the rejection of the budget and forced the governor-general to 'certify' it. Everything turned out to be perfect.

Discussions began on 23 January and continued until the end of February 1935.[86] The two parties agreed to, (a) the franchise being adjusted to reflect the proportion of population of the various

---

83   He was re-elected that October to represent Bombay city Muslims in the central assembly.

84   Syed Abdullah Brelvi to Ansari, 2 Jan.1935, Jinnah to Ansari, 3 Jan. 1935, Hasan (ed.), *Muslims and the Congress*, pp. 233, 235.

85   Quoted in Mujahid, 'Jinnah and the Congress Party', op. cit., p. 229.

86   The following discussion is based on Notes on Conversation held between Jinnah and Prasad on 13-14 Feb. 1935, AICC papers, NMML.

communities in the electoral rolls for the province as well as the centre; (b) no overlapping of electorates or constituencies; (c) the Sikhs in Punjab would choose the number of constituencies for the seats allotted to them in the award. Thereafter, the Hindus would fix such constituencies for the number allotted to them. The remaining constituencies would go to the Muslims, excluding the seats given to Europeans, Anglo-Indians, Indian Christians, and special constituencies; (d) in Bengal, if any seats were obtained from Europeans they would be split between the two communities in proportion to their population. However, seats reserved for Muslims would remain, excluding those given to Europeans, Anglo-Indians, Indian Christians, and special constituencies; (e) in other provinces and in the central legislature, reserved seats for Muslims would be the same as in the award; (f) joint electorates would replace separate electorates in the provinces and at the centre.[87]

Gandhi responded positively,[88] fearing, nonetheless, that the Sikh leaders would back out if the concessions offered to the Punjabi Muslims went beyond the Nehru Report.[89] Birla however hoped to bring into play his monies to persuade the 'Hindu masses' to make use of them.[90] Ultimately, he failed, and, after a while, the Mahasabha and the Sikhs refused to give Gandhi a carte blanche over the reservation of seats. At the end of the day, they balked at Jinnah's Fourteen Points, 'the Magna Carta of Muslim India'.[91] A disappointed Birla cried out: 'How is it that Moonje, Jagatnarainlal can be better Hindus than Vallabhbhai, Rajendra Babu and others?'[92] Gandhi piously expected the storm to pass and the fratricidal strife to end, but the atmosphere proved to be too foggy for

---

87   I have discussed these talks in detail in my book *M.A. Ansari: Gandhi's Infallible Guide* (Delhi, 1987), pp. 258-62.

88   Gandhi to Rajendra Prasad, 7 Feb. 1935, Valmiki Choudhary (ed.), *Dr. Rajendra Prasad: Correspondence and Select Documents*, vol. 1 (Delhi, 1984), p. 6; Gandhi to Rajendra Prasad, 28 Feb. 1935, *CWMG*, vol. 60, p. 266.

89   Rajmohan Gandhi, *The Good Boatman*, p. 134.

90   Birla to Mahadev Desai, 21 Feb. 1935, *Bapu: A Unique Association*, vol. 3, p. 38.

91   They were placed before the Muslim League session in March 1929. For Draft Resolution, *see* Jayakar Papers (354).

92   Birla to Mahadev Desai, 28 Feb. 1935, *Bapu: A Unique Association*, vol. 2, p. 38.

him to see clearly. This debilitating sense of defeatism soon permeated the Congress too.

As for Jinnah, he exuded a kind of military vigour and frigid aloofness. He was conscious of superiority of birth, of wealth, or some other adventitious aid, and his letters to close friends exude a kind of stern, almost formal, correctness. His previous instincts were to wait before committing himself to any agreement, but with Hindu-Muslim-Sikh relations worsening, he felt that time spent on coining phrases and making inconsequential gestures was time taken off from more crucial things. Prone to ups and downs, he could either make peace with Gandhi or fight on in the hope of sharing the spoils with the Congress. From now on he took time to build up a record of experiences and narratives to justify distrust of the federal objective which would necessarily result in majority rule under the guise of a parliamentary government. He went to extremes. Paradoxically, he became indifferent to all his old loves; the love of the moment monopolised his attention. He scoffed at the attempts to legitimise the Congress as the sole spokesman. Having spoken against mixing religion with politics, he stood out against modernity or enlightenment.

Jealous of his importance, which appealed to his vanity as it placed him on a level with Gandhi, Jinnah's image kept changing in government circles. He was strongly anti-British, according to Reading, the viceroy, though sensible and subtle.[93] After meeting him on 4 March 1940, Benthall left in an ambivalent mood.[94] Linlithgow was struck by his stubbornness, extreme haughtiness, and indifference to the feelings of others. Wavell called him 'vain, shallow and ambitious', and one who opposed rapprochement with the Congress.[95] Major Alexander Greenwood, ADC to General Auchinleck, found him 'voluble, rude and arrogant.'[96] After the 4 May meeting at which Gandhi agreed to demit power either to the League or to the Congress to run the entire country, Mountbatten took note of his rigid, haughty, and disdainful frame of

---

93   Qureshi, *Pan-Islam in British Indian Politics*, p. 300.

94   Discussion at 7 Aurangzeb Road, 4 Mar. 1940, Benthall papers.

95   Wolpert, *Jinnah of Pakistan*, p. 225.

96   Alexander Greenwood, *Field-Marshal Auchinleck* (Durham, 1990), p. 251.

mind. This is how he poured his heart and strength into Pakistan.[97] Some of these views were, admittedly modified during the war years when the government had to come to terms with Jinnah as the 'sole spokesman'. For example, Linlithgow's predicament, which he shared with the secretary of state, was his own as well as his successor's.

> I am certain that matters have reached a point at which it will be necessary to pay increasing attention to the Muslims and to their importance as a community; and that it is desirable that we should in Parliament and elsewhere endeavour to bring out our sense of their significance, and our anxiety to give the weight properly attached to their views. And here and elsewhere in the Indian political field, even if we regard that sensitiveness as unjustified or exaggerated, it constitutes a political point which you will, I am sure, agree with me in thinking well worth watching.[98]

Gandhi versus Jinnah

Politics in the hands of Gandhi and Jinnah became a competition in extravaganza.[99] The seeds of contrast were laid in the similar soil from which they grew, and yet they could have worked together sufficiently well until the late-1930s. My reasoning is based on the early years of their association, though there is no determining where Jinnah stopped and Gandhi and his associates began.

First, what set them so much apart? They were strikingly different in their style and demeanour: one wore Saville Row suits, the other a mere dhoti; one habitually spoke English, the other Gujarati and Hindi. Tara Ali Baig had the image of Jinnah, grey and thin as a sword, his elegant white streaked hair crowning his lean, sharp ascetic face. He wore a monocle at times and was superbly dressed in the British manner of those days.[100] One lived on the periphery; the ashram in Sabarmati or Wardha, the other in splendid isolation. One endeared himself to the

---

97   Carter (ed.), *Mountbatten's Report on the Last Viceroyalty*, p. 65.

98   Linlithgow to Zetland, 28 Nov. 1939, IOR. L/PJ/8/691.

99   Rodrigues (ed.), *The Essential Writings of Ambedkar*, p. 129.

100   Baig, *Portraits of an Era*, p. 66.

masses and led them from the front; the other feared political Jacobinism and had an equal distaste for the multitude. Setting himself apart from a generation of statesmen, elitism was alien to Gandhi's nature and anathema to his political culture. It was not so with Jinnah. Indeed, there was as much difference between him and the masses as between Saville Row and Bond Street and the villages with its mud huts.[101] The difference in persona reflected contrasting postures and world views. The contrast was however not so striking until Jinnah became the 'sole spokesman' of the two-nation theory.

The leader's claim to fame in South Asia rested as much on political integrity as personal and family sacrifices. On this score, Gandhi spent as many as 2089 days in Indian and 249 days in South African prisons (starting with his incarceration in September 1903 in the grim precincts of Johannesburg gaol, virtually at the centre of the wealthiest goldfields in the world). Indeed, the march against injustice had been broken up, and Gandhi and Kasturba were cast into prison at Bloemfontein. 'The gaol life for me,' Gandhi wrote to Kallenbach, 'is the best'.[102] Jinnah walked in and out of courts but never walked into a prison cell.

Gandhi ceaselessly drew attention to the plight of those toiling millions who didn't even get a square meal a day and had to scratch along with a piece of stale bread and pinch of salt. This concern manifested itself in different ways, including the 1931 Resolution of the Karachi Congress, which widened the definition of political freedom to encompass an end to exploitation and economic freedom for the starving millions. Gandhi desired and secured unrestricted access to them. He covered a distance of 12,500 miles during the 9 months of his 'Harijan tour'. In the summer of 1934, alone, he covered 750 miles by train/car and met at least 150,000 people.[103] He walked through the towns and villages of Orissa covering 40 miles in just 5 days. During the last years, he set out on foot covering 49 villages in Noakhali district and 7 in Tipperah in east Bengal. In all, this amounted to a total of 116

101   Nehru, *An Autobiography*, p. 68.

102   Gandhi to Kallenbach, 3 July 1909, Gandhi-Kallenbach papers.

103   Tendulkar, *Mahatma*, vol. 3, p. 272.

miles![104] Week after week, the bare-footed pilgrim emerged from his hut with his bamboo stick in hand to exhort the masses to become masters of their own destiny.[105] To friend John Haynes Holmes, he wrote: "'Do or die" was the motto given in 1942. It is the motto, having given it then, I must endeavour to live it myself.'[106]

Jawaharlal was cast in much the same mould. During a frenetic 130 days tour in 1937, he covered over 50,000 miles by rail, train, motor car, and plane, and spoke at a dozen meetings and to upwards of 1,00,000 people a day. He addressed something like 10 million people in all. No previous president had strained himself to that degree and done so much to awaken the masses.[107]

Jinnah showed no interest in the regeneration of hundreds of millions of fellow countrymen. With little or no idea of exploitation and deprivation, his experiences began and ended with law books. Typically, he had no pretension of either articulating a Gandhi-like conception of politics or reflecting on the disharmony between ideals. To him, the primary focus of power lay in the political system, and in pursuit of this he encountered the Congress's intransigence. In effect, his narrative was that his own cause was just, but diabolical forces were arrayed against the Fourteen Points, his political manifesto. Without admitting to either weaknesses or discrepancies in his own arguments, he underlined the wide divergence of opinion and outlook',[108] adding

---

104   From 7 Nov. 1946, a month after a brutal assault on the Hindus in Noakhali, to 2 Mar. 1947. Pyarelal, *Mahatma Gandhi*, vol. 1, p. 201.

105   Ibid., p. 150.

106   Gandhi to Holmes, 5 Feb. 1947, *CWMG* (21 Oct. 1946-20 Feb. 1947), p. 431.

107   D.A. Low, *Britain and Indian Nationalism: The Imprint of Ambiguity 1929-1942* (Cambridge, 1977), p. 260; Prasad, *Autobiography*, p. 434.

108   'Ours is a case of division and carving out two independent sovereign States by way of settlement between two major nations, Hindus and Muslims, and not of severance or secession from any existing union, which is *non est* in India. The right of self-determination, which we claim, postulates that we are a nation, and as such it would be the self-determination of the Muslims, and they alone are entitled to exercise that right.'Jinnah to Gandhi, 21 Sept. 1944, *Gandhi-Jinnah Talks: Text of Correspondence and Other Related Matters* (New Delhi, July-Oct. 1944), p. 21.

that Gandhi had no locus standi unless he engaged with him as a Hindu for Hindus.[109] In the end, the two didn't speak freely, didn't talk to each other as equals, and didn't interact as people who trusted each other. The expression of failure overcame the expression of anxiety.

Their difference in outlook centred on conceptions of religion and civic life as well. Gandhi was wedded to a community's self-realisation within a pluralist society, as community existence had significance only in such a set up. He reminded those, to whom the images of common inheritance made sense, of the nobility of mind and spirit in their traditions, and points of contacts and convergences. Jinnah was uncomfortable with diversity, though he himself lived in a highly diverse social and cultural milieu. The substance, he contended, without being overly familiar with his history, was that his Muslim brethren lived in virtual isolation as a distinct entity, and this was the principal factor in everyday life and not their imaginary intermingling with the other communities. He dismissed the fact that the Muslim social life, so to speak, was honeycombed with Hindu customs. The mingling of devotees took place at the dargah of *Pir* Imam Shah and Nur Mohammad Shah at Pirana, about 16 miles from Ahmedabad.[110] Hindu and Muslim Rajputs observed purdah in the tract between the Beas and the Sutlej;[111] and the Meos in Mewat took to exogamy after conversion and disallowed cousin marriage.[112] The maternal uncle of the historian K.M. Ashraf, a Meo, placed two flowers before Mahadev's image.[113] Pushed to its

109   Patel and Sykes, *Gandhi*, p. 148.

110   It is said that these two personages embody a dual Hindu/Muslim identity, on the one hand as avatars of Indra and Vishnu respectively and, on the other, as imam-like Sufi *syeds/pirs* directly descended from the first Imam, Ali ibn-i Abi Talib. Zawahir Moir and Dominique-Sila Khan, 'New Light on the Satpanthi Imamshahis of Pirana', *South Asia: Journal of South Asian Studies*, no. 2, vol. 33, Aug. 2010.

111   Imtiaz Ahmad and Helmut Reifeld (eds), *Lived Islam in South Asia: Adaptation, Accomodation and Conflict* (Delhi, 2004).

112   Mujeeb, *Islamic Influence in Indian Society*, p. 75; On the Meos, see Shail Mayaram, *Resisting Regimes: Myth, Memory and the Shaping of a Muslim Identity* (Delhi, 1997). This was regardless of the sharia permitting such a marriage which had been the rule and not an exception among the generality of Muslims.

113   Horst Krüger (ed.), *Kunwar Mohammad Ashraf*, pp. 395-6.

conclusion, Jinnah's theory leads to the belief that men live mainly in, and react principally to, a political environment, having virtually no prospect of being in contact with the real world.

In theoretical matters, Jinnah possessed no particular competence. His speeches were divested of a discriminating and cultural intelligence; his letters attended to details without being animated by a warm demonstrative zeal. Like Franklin Roosevelt, he was a 'juggler' who would do whatever it took to secure his Pakistan, even if it meant an unholy alliance with the Muslim orthodox elements. Without being bound down by any political shibboleth, he threw his full weight behind the government during the war years, took advantage of the Congress exiting the ministries in September 1939, and prevented it from recovering the ground lost during the war. It is not as if he didn't cherish freedom or that he didn't want the end of British rule. He did, but his instinctive distrust of collective action led him to advocate a safe, secure, and stable environment. He was uncomfortable with *Inquilab* or revolution; the very mention of it sent shock waves among his allies in the politically conservative establishment. For these and many other reasons, he scoffed at the talk of *dal-bhat*,[114] chastised Gandhi for the political hysteria in the *purna swaraj* resolution,[115] and blamed Jawaharlal's unbridled radicalism to the inexperienced youth, the ignorant, and the illiterate.[116] He warned that a federal or even a confederal form of government would not be acceptable to Muslims, since the experience showed that a central government always gathered strength at the expense of the federating units. Stanley Wolpert, the historian, cites Sarojini Naidu, who spoke of Jinnah as of Lucifer, a fallen angel, one who had once promised to be 'a great leader of Indian freedom, but had instead, cast himself out of the Congress heaven.'

Jinnah blamed Gandhi and Jawaharlal for their arrogance and haughtiness. His criticism was hardly tenable. Gandhi, for one, reacted to Jinnah's wild over-statements with calmness. Generally speaking, he reasoned with him, suavely, endlessly. On 8 May 1943, he invited Jinnah

---

114   S.S. Pirzada, *Foundations of Pakistan: 1924-1947*, vol. 2, p. 303.

115   Wolpert, *Jinnah of Pakistan*, p. 113.

116   Noman, *Pakistan*, p. 23.

for talks but the government withheld his letter.[117] Prepared to rectify his own mistakes,[118] he elicited his opinion on whether or not they could agree to differ on the question of two nations. The only real test of nationhood arose out of common political subjection. If this were to end by common effort, Gandhi asserted, India would politically be a free nation.[119] He contended, moreover, that the land of Amir Khusro, Kabir, and Guru Nanak, to whom he made a reference in Johannesburg in 1905, had to unite on the strength of a common destiny,[120] and good sense, self-interest, and religion would counter a tidal wave of religious fanaticism and forbid the obvious suicide which Partition would mean. He hyperbolised, but in essence his exchanges reflected both a commitment to a political agreement and a profound spiritual and cultural attachment to Hindu-Muslim unity.

Jawaharlal was conscious of his own strength and reputation, and therefore brushed aside dissent. Moreover, he thought too much about his party, laying claims such as, 'there is more statesmanship in the Congress ... than there is in most of the big cabinets in Europe put together.'[121] What is more, he refused to treat Jinnah as an equal or as a representative of a powerful party, and his father, with whom he shared this opinion, described Jinnah as conceited at a time when he, the most recent ambassador of Hindu-Muslim unity, was doing all the right things.[122] Jawaharlal turned him down when he sent out conciliatory signals. At a time when a coalition ministry in UP and Bombay may have been a prudent course to take, though not necessarily the best one, Jawaharlal made Jinnah appear as an evil force ready to wreck the Congress ship with the help of his reactionary and feudal allies. This

---

117   IOR. L/PJ/8/517.

118   'Euclid's line is one without breadth, but no one has been able to draw it and never will,' he said shortly after the outbreak of religious strife in 1946. 'All the same it is only by keeping the ideal line in mind that we have made progress in geometry.'

119   Gandhi to Jinnah, 15 Sept. 1944, *Gandhi-Jinnah Talks*: p. 13.

120   Gandhi, *My Experiments with Truth*, p. 39.

121   Jawaharlal to Syed Mahmud, Datta and Cleghorn (ed.), *A Nationalist Muslim and Indian Politics*, p. 188.

122   Motilal to Jawawharlal,16 Feb. 1919, *SWMN*, vol. 2, p. 5.

was a patently false line of argument; it may well have driven Jinnah into the enemy's camp. The League, he said in April 1943, was now the voice of the people, the authority of the *millat*, and the Congress had to bow before it.

The Gandhi-Jinnah rift extended to the Congress Muslims, who painted Jinnah in the lurid colours of 'betrayal', 'sell out', and 'renegade'. Asserting his sole right to nominate Muslims to the new council, he insisted on their exclusion from the Simla conference on 14 July 1945 and the interim government.[123] *As* Tej put it, 'virtually he wanted the viceroy to bolster up the Muslim League by coercing the dissentients among the Muslims to join the League if they were anxious to enter the government'. The viceroy overlooked his claim.[124] This was not all. The Muslim Conference in Kashmir, an adjunct of the Muslim League, tried to break up the procession in honour of Azad and Jawaharlal. The students of Aligarh Muslim University mocked Azad at the railway station when he was travelling from Simla to Calcutta. Over and above Azad and other Congress Muslims, the League workers portrayed Badshah Khan as a Hindu stooge. It was said that he had replaced his turban with a Gandhi cap, the crescent and star with the *charkha*, and that the wily Gandhi had captivated the simple-minded Pathan.[125] Gandhi laughed out loud at these assertions while steadfastly maintaining that his dharma didn't allow him to be disloyal to his fellow nationalists.

Notwithstanding their vulnerability to attacks from both Hindu and Muslim communalists, the rules of propriety wouldn't permit Gandhi to forsake the Congress Muslims' prudent and balanced rationalisation of social relations, free from past or contemporary animus. He wouldn't sacrifice them to pacify Jinnah. After all, Bombay had a Congress ministry in place with the greatest proportion of Muslims, and 1 million

---

123   The Simla Conference in June 1945, like the one a year earlier, failed because Jinnah regarded the presence of Azad and Ghaffar Khan as a gratuitous and deliberate provocation.

124   Sapru to Jayakar, 20 July 1945, Hooja (ed.), *Crusader for Self-Rule*, p. 450.

125   Banerjee, *The Pathan Unarmed*, pp. 176, 177.

Muslims had voted against the League in 1937.[126] Jinnah was, of course, asked to give way on the question, and in exchange to secure his other points. However, while Gandhi asked for bread, Jinnah sent him a stone. Finally, there were hopes of the Congress appointing a 'nationalist' Muslim only if the League conceded its right to do so. However, Jinnah, who had the knack of embarrassing the Congress, refused to commit. With the status of the Congress Muslims in contention, the unresolved question was just how far Gandhi could resist the tidal flow of events towards Partition.[127]

The RSS-Mahasabha combine added to the cacophony of voices by introducing the Hindutva discourse that ran contrary to the Congress ideals. Until the late-1920s, they were not a major political force, though they had gained sufficient leverage as the defender of the Hindu faith against aggressive Muslim designs. Soon, they rapidly took advantage of the Congress's weakness and its uncertain stand on certain issues. Thus Sapru, acting as an honest broker, convened the All Parties Conference in July 1930, but the Mahasabha stayed away, saying that, 'it is sinful to let the poison of communalism infect Swaraj in its very conception'. It was typical of this line of stubborn and unthinking recalcitrance cultivated by the Mahasabha.

Sapru was, similarly, unhappy with Moonje's and Jayakar's obduracy at the First Round Table Conference. On the Communal Award, too, Malaviya, M.S. Aney, Chintamani parted company with Gandhi to create a broad-based Hindu front. All the Congress committees in Bengal echoed their sentiments.[128] The theoretician Vinayak Damodar Savarkar pressured the Congress not to yield to the League's demands; Jayakar and Gokul Chand Narang from Punjab feared that Jinnah would have the whip hand in the negotiations and might force a compromise upon the Congress.[129] The Unity Conference in Allahabad in November

126   Wavell to A. Clow, 7 Oct. 1946, ibid., p. 675.

127   Campbell-Johnson, *Mission with Mountbatten*, p. 85.

128   Chatterjee, *Bengal Divided*, pp. 44-49.

129   Jayakar to Ganpaat Rai, 22 Apr. 1938, Jayakar Papers (355), p. 242; Birla to Mahadevbhai, 14 July 1942, Birla (ed.), *Bapu: A Unique Association*, vol. 1, p. 317.

1932 went for a six.[130] On the eve of the Gandhi-Jinnah meeting on 9 September 1944, Savarkar, Jayakar, and Moonje scoffed at the CR proposals. Savarkar wanted unity against the 'pseudonationalistic [sic] Congressite'.[131]

Ignoring their stern warnings, Gandhi trudged his way in the sun on 18 successive days on Mount Pleasant Road in Malabar Hill, Bombay. He did so as the servant and friend not only of the Muslims but the entire world. However, he knew what to expect: 'the two mountains have met and not even a ridiculous mouse has emerged'.[132]

What went wrong? Well, the talks broke down owing to the differences over the nature and scope of Pakistan, and on the order in which they placed the events necessary to Independence. Gandhi wanted Independence first, as he had mentioned to Ansari in 1930, with some kind of self-determination for Muslims to be granted by a provisional government which should be predominantly Hindu. Jinnah wanted Pakistan first and Independence afterwards. He overlooked Gandhi's entreaties, and, as in the case of the Hindu Mahasabha, said 'No' to the CR formula, which Gandhi had agreed to with a precondition.[133] 'I'm a Moslem, not an Indian,' he stated to an American journalist in 1947-8; 'the Muslims are a nation'. Sapru alone sounded a note of optimism: 'The darkest night,' he tried to console Gandhi, 'is followed by the morning and I very strongly hope that the morning for which we have been waiting may soon come.'[134]

In any form of competitive politics, an individual leader, whatever his or her standing, can hardly be a free agent. Given the antagonistic spirit in which Jinnah re-invented himself, he had no option but to raise the spectre of 'Hindu raj', and also keep the partisan fires of community interest burning by showing the faults of the past very plainly, and even

---

130   Jayakar papers (355).

131   Savarkar to Jayakar, 5 Aug. 1944, Jayakar papers.

132   Wolpert, *Jinnah of Pakistan*, p. 236.

133   Ibid., pp. 263-4, 274-5; Wavell to Amery, 3 Oct. 1944, IOR. L/PJ/8/55; Medha M. Kudaisya, *The Life and Times of G.D. Birla*, p. 232.

134   Sapru to Gandhi, 14, 25 Oct. 1944, Hooja (ed.), *Crusader for Self-Rule*, pp. 408, 411.

more than those of the future.[135] Once he said that both the British and Congress had held pistols to his head. 'Today we also have forged a pistol and are in a position to use it ... This day we bid goodbye to constitutional methods.' Judging, as this belief does, on the basis of the contemporary religious and Islamist rhetoric, his fears may appear to have been valid in regard to some issues, but not generally.

Invariably, Jinnah stressed one side and forgot the other. He, therefore, had a tendency to be biased and myopic in coming to terms with historical and contemporary issues. Situations, mishaps, circumstances, and popular passions move beyond control, as they tend to become in political negotiations, but unlike Azad who modified or adapted himself to the changing times, Jinnah's theory was essentially practical. In the process, he roused the crude nature of religious emotions without attacking prejudice and destroying false impressions, and laid the seeds of transforming the higher and nobler idea of common nationality into an Islamic theocracy. Dissenters invited his wrath: it seemed as if there was no tolerance for any proposal that deviated by a hair's breadth from what had been agreed to by the Muslim League high command.

It is not as if Jinnah didn't possess at least a part of this truth. He did. How great this part is remains to be discovered. On the face of things, he glossed over the cultural and civilisational unities with bland phrases, thinly disguised clichés, and discarded all ideals other than those that served his political goals. His two-nation theory itself merely blocked the path to a united subcontinent and led to the great schism between him and Gandhi. Moreover, Jinnah lost control, step by step, over the savage fury of the Jamaat-i Islami, National Guards, and the Khaksars. So did Gandhi. If the National Guards wrote *Pakistan Zindabad* on the walls, the RSS wiped it out and wrote *Akhand Bharat*. If the RSS and the Arya Samaj converted 200,000 Muslims to Hinduism in East Punjab, the National Guards made adequate preparations for a conflagration in Punjab. In early 1945, Birla had summed up the state of affairs: 'Muslims are abusing Hindus and Bapu the most. Hindu Sabha is abusing the Congress and the League. The Congress sees no good in

---

135   Campbell-Johnson, *Mission with Mountbatten*, p. 44.

its opponents. In its own camps too there are wheels within the wheel...
I wonder where all this will lead to.'[136]

These elements generated the coercive pressure to block, forestall,
delay, hinder, or frustrate any negotiation or settlement. Even if the
great majority of them were passive (the absence of a voice in the
council chamber or the negotiation table), their sentiments influenced
the reasonings of their representatives. As one who had built up his
position to the point where he claimed to look after Muslim welfare,
Jinnah *had* to, first of all, pitch his demands higher and higher, and then
to bolster his bargaining position with implicit threats and promises.
Without this, he would have been swept aside by his opponents.[137]
Similarly, Gandhi couldn't discount the growing pressure from below
not to yield to Jinnah. In the end, thought Sapru, 'the real factor is the
political cussedness of some leaders'.[138]

The very last time Gandhi met Jinnah was at 7 Aurangzeb Road on
6 May 1947. They had a 'very pleasant' meeting, discussing the joint
statement on non-violence. At the end of it, Gandhi folded his hands,
palms joined in traditional Indian greeting, in front of Jinnah. Possibly,
both lost the sense of what they were dealing with or talking about.
Jinnah seemed more the official than the man, watching his bête noire
carefully for signs of wavering, of weakening. He found none. A few
months later Gandhi told one of the British governors: 'Man is veritably
clay in the hands of the great Potter.'

---

136   Birla (ed.), *Bapu: A Unique Association*, vol. 4, p. 368.

137   On July 1946, the Muslim League Council withdrew its acceptance of the
       Cabinet Mission plan. Direct Action Day was celebrated on 16 August.

138   Sapru to Rushbrook Williams, 28 Nov. 1946, Hooja (ed.), *Crusader for Self-
       Rule*, p. 473.

13
'The World is a Playground Before Me'

Bazeecha-i Itfaal hai Duniya Mere aage

-Ghalib

پوچھتا ہوں '' آپ گاندھی کو پکڑتے کیوں نہیں؟''

کہتے ہیں '' آپس میں تم لوگ لڑتے کیوں نہیں؟''

"Why don't you imprison Gandhi?", I ask,
They say, "Why don't you quarrel among yourselves?"

-Akbar Ilahabadi

Most books, essays, articles, and speeches that constitute the ideological writings of Partition/Pakistan are straightforward polemics. Indian nationalists laid stress on the government's 'divide and rule' policy. This view found favour with several British historians.[1] If we turn to Pakistani historians drawing sustenance from, and basing their arguments on, the two-nation idea and, flowing from it, we find the inevitability of division on religious lines. In that country, for a long time scholarship was much less informed or balanced and patriotic history much more blatantly taught. In the 1950 and 1960s, historical writing and teaching was haphazard. There was a common purpose—to vindicate the two-nation theory—but without a sense of proportion, and small regard for impartiality. Much of the propaganda effort is, consequently, devoted to reaffirming this unacceptable proposition.

Besides the 'muddling through' British and Congress tactics, Pakistan's birth is sometimes attributed to the psychological difference between Gandhi, fully cognizant of his limitations, and Jinnah, whose

---

[1] According to Edward Thompson, 'from Warren Hastings's time onwards, men made no bones of the pleasure the Hindu-Muslim conflict gave them; even such men as Monstuart Elphinstone and Malcolm and Metcalfe admitted its value to the British'. Thompson, *Enlist India for Freedom!*, p. 50.

ambiguities were a deliberate smokescreen, under cover of which he wanted to get clean away from the critical points under discussion. Much is made of Jinnah's mélange of obduracy, dialectical skill, and deliberate [and] dogged negation of anything less than a sovereign Pakistan.[2] Some other writers notice his appetite growing with what it fed on, and his demand for an 800 mile corridor to join West and East Pakistan illustrated his irredentist tactics.[3] This interpretation has a very substantial plausibility.

The picture is extremely complex rather than simple or clear cut. On the positive side, careful research brings to light four key motifs: first, the causes leading to the 'The Great Divide'; second, the breakdown of Gandhi-Jinnah talks, to which we have made a reference in the previous chapter; third, dislocation and disruptions of millions; and lastly, 'a day of freedom ... but a freedom slashed and streaked with blood. A day choked by smoke and fire'.[4] These are just a few of the pieces in the puzzle. Gandhi often tried to get out of awkward corners by relying upon his not even being a four-anna Congress member.[5] But from Jinnah's perspective, Gandhi had no scruples or any standard or principle in his methods. He insisted on a separate Muslim nationality enjoying the sole right to decide in the areas he chose to describe as Muslim-majority provinces.[6]

No society exists or can exist in complete harmony. Literary works, particularly those of a realist dispensation, have emerged as an alternate archive of the time, concentrating on rupture and genocide, as also on 'the procedures of nationhood, history, and particular forms of sociality'.[7] With single-mindedness, writers bring together the narratives

---

2   Anita Inder Singh, *The Origins of the Partition of India*, p. 251.

3   Campbell-Johnson, *Mission with Mountbatten*, p. 98.

4   Kidwai, *In Freedom's Shade*, p. 5; Tai Yong Tan and Gyanesh Kudaisya, *The Aftermath of Partition in South Asia* (London, 2000).

5   Chatterjee (ed.), *TF, 1938* (pt 1), p. 288.

6   Mirabehn, *The Spirit's Pilgrimage*, p. 262; Wolpert, *Jinnah of Pakistan*, pp. 231-6.

7   Mushirul Hasan (ed.), *India Partitioned: The Other Face of Freedom*, vols 1-2; Bashabi Fraser (ed.), *Bengal Partition Stories: An Unclosed Chapter* (London, 2006); Pandey, *Remembering Partition*, p. 1.

of immigration, exile, and refuge, and turn to the political and civic faultlines that still run through our lives.[8] Many short stories also attest to the disintegration of *mohallas*, which acted as a buffer between warring groups.[9] Many invoke memories of, say Subhashini, an Arya Samajist, which suggests a commitment to a cause but turns out to be the story of a fanatic. For these writers, whose numbers are growing by the day, the Partition was not only a major theme but an obsession.

Memoirs and autobiographies are also useful narratives of trauma and pain. Suresh Kamra has provided useful insights into the editorial cartoons of the leading nationalist dailies. The battle lines are clearly drawn; the League press promotes a reading of Partiton and its violence as the persecution of Muslims, the final hardship in the battle to win a homeland.[10] As for the 'nationalist' press, Jinnah is singled out for blame and held responsible for violence.[11]

Violence is widely depicted in the cartoon and, obviously, extensively reported in the newspapers. The 1940s was, after all, definitely grotesque in its brutality and medieval in its aggression. Between 200,000 and 360,000 died, and 10 to 12 million crossed the boundaries between India and Pakistan. Refugees clambered on to the tops of railway carriages only to be brutally attacked and slaughtered. The few gentile passengers, by contrast, kept strolling nonchalantly to and fro on the platform, with their hands clasped behind them, and only when the police arrived did they leisurely climb on to the train. Kamal broke down when the train crossed the border and he saw, for the last time, the grinning, jovial face of a Sikh soldier standing alert with his gun under a telegraph pole. Suddenly, the other country began leaving the gun-toting Sikh soldiers behind, not a single traveller disembarking

---

8   Ritu Menon and K. Bhasin, *Borders & Boundaries: Women in India's Partition* (Delhi, 1998); Urvashi Butalia, *The Other Side of Silence: Voices from the Partition of India* (Delhi, 1998); Anjali Gera Roy and Nandi Bhatia, *Partitioned Lives: Narratives of Home, Displacement, and Resettlement* (Delhi, 2008), p. xxv; Suvir Kaul (ed.), *The Partitions of Memory: The Afterlife of the Division of India* (New Delhi, 2001), p. 25.

9   Kamra, *Bearing Witness*, p. 125.

10   Ibid., p. 100.

11   Ibid., p. 77.

from a train pulling into Lahore station. A little later the driver jumped down on the platform, raving hysterically: the only person on board left alive. Over a 1000 Muslims had boarded that train. All of them, men, women, and children had been slaughtered.[12]

If the months preceding the transfer of power were a gloomy period in Delhi's social life, they were a black one in the country as a whole. In Delhi, as in other places, 'the pristine tricolours that had proudly fluttered atop every house and shop, in every lane and street, were spattered with blood ...'.[13] Innocent citizens were driven out; their property burnt; goods looted from Muslim shops were displayed in front of Shri Ram, the industrialist owner of Delhi Cloth Mills (DCM).[14] Shaukatullah Ansari and wife Zohra, Gandhi's Urdu tutor, were thrown out of Dar-us-Salam, the late Dr. Ansari's home. The fountain therein, next to which Gandhi had his briefing sessions before his talks with Irwin, the viceroy, had dried up. Zohra lived in a hotel for fear of attack from Hindus and Sikhs. Paul Brass, the political scientist, points out:

> The deliberate use of violence was a principal mechanism in changing the terms of partition by forcing the displacement of peoples in such a way as to carry the implications of partition itself to its logical conclusion, namely, the concentration of all peoples defined in categorical terms as belonging to particular religious groups on opposite sides of the partition line.[15]

Stories of arson, pillage, rape, and carnage did the rounds, as the city walls smouldered by day and blazed by night. Mixed *mohallas* were

---

12   Garga, *From Raj to Swaraj*, p. 125. Ishtiaq Ahmed, *The Punjab: Bloodied, Partitioned and Cleansed* (Delhi, 2011).

13   Kidwai, *In Freedom's Shade*, p. 7; Badruddin Tyabji, *Memoirs of an Egoist*, and essays/extracts in Hasan (ed.), *India Partitioned*, vol. 2; Tan and Kudaisya, *The Aftermath of Partition in South Asia*, pp. 196-98; Pandey, *Remembering Partition*, pp. 122-31.

14   Vinay Bharat Ram, *From the Brink of Bankruptcy: The DCM Story* (Delhi, 2011), p. 53.

15   Paul R. Brass, 'The Partition of India and Retributive Genocide in the Punjab, 1946-47: Means, Methods, and Purposes', *Journal of Genocide Research*, 2000, 5 (1), p. 82.

set ablaze. Stabbing and looting spread from the narrow streets of Daryaganj and Bara Hindu Rao to the broad boulevards of Lutyens' New Delhi.[16] A massacre in Bengali market took place, with Sikhs going on a rampage. Jawaharlal actually ran after miscreants in Connaught Place.[17] Those who survived congregated in their thousands at the railway station or at Purana Qila and Humayun's Tomb. Brave men and women hoped, like Byron, to rescue those in peril. In October 1947, there were 60,000 of them in Purana Qila, down from the 80,000 that had crossed in September.[18]

'Today we saw for ourselves something of the stupendous scale of the Punjab upheaval,' reported Campbell-Johnson, referring to the nearly half-a-million refugees. Impelled by some deeper instinct, they pushed forward obsessed only with the objective beyond the boundary.[19] The beating of distant drums at night meant that Muslims were on the move; Hindu and Sikh families would take turns to mount guard on the roof. Elsewhere, their brethren attacked isolated villages at night slaughtering people. Sikhs, who were central in the violence,[20] reacted with unbridled fury.[21] Master Tara Singh, their leader, told Paul Brass long ago, 'We took the decision to turn the Muslims out'. By this, he meant the decision to violently attack the Muslim population in East Punjab to force them to migrate west so that the Sikhs in West Punjab could migrate east to replace them and seize their lands and property in exchange for what they would lose in the west. The states of Patiala, Faridkot, and Nabha provided arms and safe haven for marauding bands roaming about the eastern Punjab districts.[22]

One morning, George Maconachie Brander, Amritsar's district magistrate, saw an enormous fire in the Muslim quarter. Huge masses of

---

16   Carnall, *Gandhi's Interpreter*, p. 213.

17   Vinay Bharat Ram, op. cit., p. 53.

18   Kidwai, *In Freedom's Shade*, p. 38.

19   Campbell-Johnson, *Mission with Mountbatten*, p. 201.

20   Tan and Kudaisya, *The Aftermath of Partition in South Asia* on Sikhs, pp. 111-121, for 'Sikh politics' and the implications of Partition.

21   Brass, op. cit., p. 99.

22   Ibid., pp. 77, 78.

smoke darkened the sky and the smoke glowed red from the flames. The next morning a loud explosion, followed by an uproar of human cries startled him. He saw several hundred Indians running around screaming. With blood everywhere, he stumbled on bodies being carried away. Some persons lobbed a Mills grenade at Muslims seated in a circle in the shade discussing a case. All the forty-two Muslims died on the spot.[23]

Think of Hakiman or Hakko. Her last will was that she'd receive the shroud she had finished weaving only a day before her death. She was the first one to be buried in a *khaddar ka kafan,* a patriot unto death! Forty-five years later, Khwaja Ahmad Abbas went to Panipat to pay homage to his ancestors and grandmother Hakko. By this time all the Muslims (with the exception of his immediate family) had left for Pakistan. The writer saw the graveyard ploughed over. If only they had spared one grave, that of Hakko, who had given her all to the Mahatma, and woven her own *kafan* on her handloom. After all, she had been the first in whose image Abbas had seen the face of Mother India![24]

Riots in northern and western Punjab heralded the catastrophe that embraced Bengal. Disturbances in Calcutta commenced early in the morning in the Manicktola area and gradually spread to adjacent Hindu and Muslim areas. Unscrupulous elements recruited the *goondas* and let them loose to plunder, persecute, and murder. It was a kind of Greek drama where men go willy-nilly to their fate, and in which they all unwillingly cooperate to bring about their own destruction.[25] Thousands lost their homes and hearths. Myriads of flowers, yellow and orange marigolds and pink rose petals, lay scattered on the ground, stale, scentless, trampled.[26]

The distance between the propaganda and the action, between the party and its release on the people, had become too short. By the 1940s, the 'explosive fusion of communal with nationalist and class modes of

---

23   Typescript of talk, n.d., G.M. Brander papers, MSS EUR F. 409, IOR.

24   Khwaja Ahmad Abbas, 'The Mahatma and the Older Weaver Woman', Hasan (ed.), *Negotiating Diversities*, p. 49.

25   Heilbroner, *The Worldly Philosophers*, p. 154.

26   Kusum Nair, *Blossoms in the Dust: The Human Element in Indian Development* (London, 1961), p. xx.

consciousness' culminated in overtly communal riots. They manifest a conjunction between the elite and popular communalism.[27] Thanks to an intricate series of manoeuvres in 1946, Jinnah, who was becoming more and more truculent and self-assertive, let loose the elemental forces of savagery. As an instance of 'heroic violence oriented towards a remote goal',[28] some of his actions stirred the baser violent sentiments. Paul Brass' thesis is valid: violence was the genesis and catastrophic result of 'Direct Action Day' on 16 August 1946 and the consequent 'Calcutta Killing'.[29] The exact figure of dead isn't known, but 5000 plus 15,000 injured wouldn't be an over-estimate. The rational miscalculations of H.S. Suhrawardy, the Bengal premier, didn't for a moment break the historical continuum of violence.[30] Wavell noted on 5 November 1946: 'Suhrawardy, looking as much of a gangster as ever, described to me the measures he proposed for stricter enforcement of law and order.'[31] In the ensuing power struggle in East Bengal, he lost the battle to Khwaja Nazimuddin, the Leaguer. He even toyed with the idea of a united Bengal.[32]

Finding Faith in the Fury

Manto had a natural and powerful talent for story-telling, reflecting 'the single-minded dedication with which men had killed men, about the remorse felt by some of them, the tears shed by murderers who couldn't understand why they still had some human feelings'. He is also good at reflecting the agony and ambivalences of the people caught up in the cross-fire of communal antagonisms, including those for whom the quest for Pakistan had been more in the nature of a Utopia, without the hope or the prospect of ever achieving it.[33] Bringing to the fore the

---

27   Suranjan Das, *Communal Riots in Bengal 1905-1947* (Delhi, 1991), pp. 208, 213.

28   Edward A. Shils, in Sorel, *Reflections on Violence*, p. 20.

29   Gupta, *Crisis and Creativities*, p. 213.

30   Notes by Wavell, 31 Dec. 1946, *TF*, vol. 9, p. 16.

31   Ibid.

32   Record of interview between K.S.Roy and F. Burrows, *TF*, vol. 10, p. 6.

33   Abdul Rahman Siddiqi, *Smoke Without Fire: Portraits of Pre-Partition Delhi* (Delhi, 2011), p. 262.

destructive human impulses, he dedicated a story to the man who, 'in the course of narrating his bloody exploits, conceded: 'when I killed an old woman only then did I feel that I had committed murder'.

Manto neither allowed any room for over-romanticisation nor posed as a reporter and chronicler of the communal case or its judge and propagator.[34] If anything, he wants us to understand that maps don't bestow virtue, that sharply defined religious enclaves don't ensure the sanctity of moral practices within them, and that the separation of communities from each other doesn't legitimise their cultures.[35] His works have won a permanent place, and a significant one, in Urdu literature. He wrote over 250 stories and scores of plays and essays, the first collection appearing in 1940. Some were well received, but most were overlooked or condemned for their obsession with sex and the seamy side of life.

Manto, of course, couldn't quite comprehend the savage and barbaric instincts of fellow men, the dreadful sense of agony, and a presentiment that it couldn't cease or be diminished! Why did this happen? He gave many answers, each more painful than the other. Tremors of his iconoclastic impatience can be felt in his stories, which also reveal a synthesis of intellectual magnanimity and the emotional impulse and comic and earthy side of human beings. Without being simple transcripts of personal experience, they are creative artefacts that mirror the contradictions, travails, anxieties, and concerns of an age. Manto had insisted that the literati must 'present life as it is, not as it was, not as it will be, not as it ought to be', and that 'literature is not a sickness, but rather a response to sickness. It is also not a medicine. It informs of its health and sickness.' He concludes his poised and reflective sketch of 'Jinnah Sahib' in the following note:

> Mohammad Hanif Azad is alive in the Pakistan that his Quaid-i-Azam gifted to him, a country which is trying to survive in a harsh world under the leadership of his talented pupil, Liaquat Ali Khan.

---

34   Shamim Hanfi, 'Qurratulain Hyder and the Partition Narrative', Rakhshanda Jalil (ed.), *Qurratulain Hyder & the River of Fire* (Delhi, 2011), p. 144.

35   Bhalla (ed.), *Life and Works of Saadat Hasan Manto*, p. 33.

On this piece of free land, he sits on a broken cot outside the office of Punjab Art Pictures, close to a betel leaf seller, and waits for his sahib and prays for the day when he'd receive his salary on time. He is even prepared to become a bit of a Hindu, just as the Quaid-i-Azam had advised, provided there is an opportunity.

Manto as a novelist, a moral prophet, an atheist: these moving forces impelled him towards the creation of the new prose style in the aphoristic sketches in *Siyah Hashiye* or *Black Margins*. Divided up into short notes jotted down from day to day during the ravages of the Partition violence and littered with images of suffering, destruction, and the resultant dislocations, they reveal a dramatic power of description, intense representations of violence, and vividness of observation. With his artistic conscience, Manto spoke with his innermost voice and with the voices of all his known selves. After all, he boldly developed a new form through a deliberate process, in gradual stages. The language is entirely spontaneous, has the slips, the abbreviations, but unlike the grave and virtuous figure of Qurratulain Hyder, Manto's story is clear, almost invariably limpid, and easy to comprehend, lively and impulsive.

Manto's stories generate a measure of antagonism with his reader: a relation that might be likened to certain kinds of confrontations in the art world. He invites them to appreciate human reality, because he had built out of the moans and the cries of anguish a powerful discourse which has filled even his harshest of critics with awe. The questions he asks are too often felt to have been either swept under the carpet or evasively answered. As he put it, 'I am not seditious. I do not want to stir up people's ideas and feelings. If I take off the blouse of culture and society, then it is naked. I do not try to put clothes back on, because that is not my job.' He is disdainful of the refined and elegant world which the creative writers erected in and around their tavern, because he brought to bear on the Partition literature that most devastating of all weapons, ridicule. His detractors, of whom he always had many, didn't take too kindly to his literary adventures and attacked him for desecrating the dead, and robbing them of their possession to build a collection. Twice he was prosecuted: first in the early 1940s and then in 1948 but the judge acquitted him with the remark: 'If I had rejected your appeal, you would have gone around saying that you had been done in by a bearded maulvi.' Ismat Chughtai, another outstanding fiction writer, travelled with Manto to attend the trial and produced a 'hilarious account.'[36]

Manto was smart enough to distinguish between patriotic hope and personal and family benefits; so, he abandoned India in search of a better life. At the same time, it was infinitely painful for him to leave and to view memory and migration through the prism of a pervasive yet challenging nostalgia, prompted by a series of endings, many of which remain enigmatic.[37] Giving up Bombay meant more than change in residence; it meant leaving a city which had taken him 'to its generous bosom.'[38] It meant learning a new language of an Islamic state and thinking and experiencing within and through it. As with Josh Malihabadi, who went to Karachi in 1956 for different reasons, his adjustment was enormously difficult. Exile was intellectually catastrophic. Josh, the poet of revolution, a non-conformist and a relentless crusader for social justice, human dignity, and equality, died in misery in a land which was never going to be his own. Karachi, the city he chose to live in, had yet to find out the means of hosting a man of his talent and creativity.

Consequently, Manto and Josh, the two bright jewels in the Urdu crown, who were an intrinsic part of an Indo-Islamic civilisation, which they had done so much to raise to new levels, felt lost and frustrated. Manto virtually drank himself to death when he was forty-three. 'No one,' Pascal once said, 'dies so poor that he doesn't leave something behind'. Manto published his own epitaph on 18 August 1954, a year before he died: 'Here lies Saadat Hasan Manto. With him lie buried all the arts and mysteries of short story writing.'

The unbridled energy released on the eve of the transfer of power flouted the ideals of all faiths; it also makes us blush. Cyrill Radcliffe turned India into two slices of a single loaf of bread.[39] Before reaching

---

36   Chughtai, *A Life in Words: Memoirs.* p. xv.

37   Dennis Walder, *Postcolonial Nostalgias,* p. 101.

38   Khalid Hasan, 'Saadat Hasan Manto: Not of Blessed Memory', *Annual of Urdu Studies,* vol. 4, 1984, pp. 88-89.

39   Manto, *Black Margins,* p. 275.

Delhi on 8 July 1947, he hadn't been to the subcontinent, and had no knowledge of its complex affairs. Five weeks later, working on maps with a long ruler, he completed his task of geometrically slicing into three parts a nation of 330 million. The colonialists did the same to the African continent, savagely dividing land and territories. In India, those five weeks disrupted the lives of millions. Radcliffe's labours led to the division of Punjab, the land of five rivers. It was a cruel act.[40]

The new readers quickly developed a genuine thirst for modern fiction written in their own everyday language and reflecting the reality of their everyday lives, even when that was presented in a less than flattering light. They wanted to know about the long convoys of suffering on the march, of the thousands who fell by the wayside, women torn from children, and men hacked to pieces in front of their women.

For example, *Jarein* (Roots) by Ismat Chughtai and *Tadposaiyan* (Shadowlines) by the Lyallpur-born Surinder Prakash unfold the disaster of Partition, the struggles of the *muhajirin* in Pakistan, the pangs of exile and, above all, the human bond that survives it all. In three of her novels (*Mere bhi Sanamkhane*, *Safina-i-Gham-i Dil*, and *Aag ka Darya*), Qurratulain Hyder, the great star, depicts the erosion of certain ideas and values associated with living together and with a certain conception of life. In *Aag ka Darya*, she projects Partition in the perspective of a cultural life of 2500 years in a manner as if this event is not just the story of a particular country or class but a part of human history.[41] A careful researcher will appreciate the labour she invested, and the punctilious loyalty with which she discharged her obligation as a writer.

Gandhi's Intervention

'For thousands of us, all over the world', remarked Krishna Hutheesing in 1943, 'and especially for us in India, there can be no rest or peace till freedom is won, whatever the cost may be.'[42] Gandhi had shown

---

40   K.S. Duggal, *Folk Romances of Punjab* (Delhi, 1979), p. 10.

41   Mehmood Ayaaz, quoted in Shamim Hanfi, 'Qurratulain Hyder and the Partition Narrative', Jalil (ed.), *Qurratulain Hyder & the River of Fire*, p. 150.

42   Hutheesing, *With No Regrets*, p. 156.

his mettle during 'Quit India' by proving that he alone fired the shots. In early 1942, he was at the centre of the political stage. Without holding office, he virtually controlled Congress policies. During the Cripps mission, he undeniably cast a very long shadow with his 'post-dated cheque argument'. He is seen to be almost celebrating, an uncharacteristic trait, with the remark: 'How nice it would have been if he hadn't come with that dismal mission.'[43] Churchillian conservatism crushed the mission, but the culprits were 'Englishmen who differed from him'.[44] They were held responsible for disorder and accused of treachery to their own principles.

The recurrence of disappointments might well have weakened the energy of a strong man, but Gandhi did not lose his buoyancy. Meeting him on 31 March 1946, Cripps found Gandhi to be physically very fit. He added: 'I am really very fond of the old man though he is no child at negotiations! He's got an unassailable position in the country and knows it ....' On another occasion, he offered Cripps hot water and honey. In the first twenty days of June 1947, he gave 137 interviews, and as many as twenty-four to a single person. He called on the viceroy five times, exchanged notes with diplomats, four provincial premiers, and interacted with Jinnah twice. On top of all this, he delivered twenty-six speeches.

When Gandhi joined a political deputation, Edwin Montagu, the secretary of state for India, exclaimed, 'how you, a social reformer, found your way into this crowd?' Gandhi responded that serving mankind necessitated participation in politics. The entire gamut of man's activities constitutes an indivisible whole.[45] He attached, no doubt with good reason, the greatest value to his political activity not in a restricted but wider sense. Politics 'encircles us today like the coil of a snake from which one cannot get out, no matter how much one tries'.[46]

43	The high hopes raised by the Cripps proposals were dashed into smithereens. Initially, he and Jawaharlal struck a friendship of sorts, but they soon fell apart. Cripps saw Gandhi's hand behind every move to thwart a settlement. Clarke, *The Cripps Version*, p. 323.

44	Moore, *Churchill, Cripps, and India*, p. 133.

45	*Harijan*, 24 Dec. 1938, CWMG (Oct. 13 1938-Feb. 28 1939), p. 201.

46	12 May 1920, Iyer (ed.), *The Essential Writings of Mahatma Gandhi*, p. 45; CWMG (Feb.-June 1920), p. 406.

He wrestled with the snake from his South Africa days; his job was like walking on the edge of a sword. Indeed, throughout this book, we have noticed him prodding, pushing, cajoling, and reminding people that Truth and non-violence were as old as the hills. Although years of high hope were sometimes shattered, he'd still speak on the corrosive forces of poverty, hunger, and violence. With the torch of his thought in hand, he'd admonish the future rulers to be like the pipal tree, to serve people and bear their thorns. On top of all this, he'd proclaim that his message and methods were indeed in their essentials for the whole world. As a non-violent revolutionary, he aspired after a new order of things. He wasn't one to be led astray through dependence for strength upon others; he destroyed letters that praised his work.[47] He didn't crave for power, not for Heaven, or for freedom from rebirth. Love and pity for mankind governed his actions and not heaven and self-perfection.[48]

To Gandhi, civility meant an inborn greatness and desire to do the opponent good.[49] As early as 1931, he told party men that the very act of voluntary surrender would clothe them with a power they had not dreamt of earlier.[50] His party however paid no heed to exhortations on piety, self-sacrifice, and self-abnegation. He was palpably shocked by their deviant behaviour. It almost seemed as if change could neither be conceived nor entertained; as the strategies for coping with the political environment were becoming untenable. Therefore, Gandhi proposed, before the rot set in further, that the Congress be dissolved and a Lok Sevak Sangh created on the lines of the All-India Spinner's Association, All-India Village Industries Association, Hindustani Talim Sangh, Harijan Sevak Sangh, and Go-Seva Sangh. He wanted to extend the right to vote to eighteen-year-olds, but to deny this to those over fifty. Was this a romantic reflection or building a kind of Gandhian castle in the sky? It was probably both. It surprised some that Gandhi visualised

---

47   Gandhi, *My Experiments with Truth*, pp. 504-5.

48   Ibid., p. 172.

49   Andrews (ed.), *Mahatma Gandhi: His Own Story*, p. 279.

50   Speech at a public meeting, Delhi, 7 Mar. 1931, *CWMG* (Dec. 1930-Apr. 1931), p. 271.

creating a vast following any time he pleased, with a magician's wand as it were, and that he should be so imaginative as to dream of the day when he'd be turned out and stoned by his nearest followers.[51]

Large-scale organisations necessarily encourage leaders to act only for aggrandisement and become prey to the enervation and corruption that is produced by the exercise of power and opportunities for advantage.[52] Without awareness of this thesis or conceiving of Edmund Burke's concept of the imponderable consensual bond that holds a society together, Gandhi was aware of the elites' power-arrogating tendencies, and their scramble for loaves and fishes for gaining leverage for themselves, their families, caste, or religion. Their wits were singularly sharpened by their voracious appetites; in them the hunt for fat jobs developed the cunning of Apaches.[53]

No wonder, then, that such men challenged Gandhi's authority, particularly after he endorsed Mountbatten's 3 June 1947 plan which envisaged Partition. His principal virtue had been to know when conditions were ripe for growth and action, but at this juncture the high command found that very quality lacking in him, and found his ideas unacceptable. They placed him on a pedestal, listened to him respectfully, but bypassed him on serious policy matters.[54] On Partition, he was told to retire to the Himalayas.

The Congress had already taken a tacit decision on Partition. J.B. Kripalani, general secretary, was most emphatic in repudiating the view that Partition was an illusion. According to him, the choice was whether there should be just one or many divisions. He thought that Gandhi's policies were unacceptable.[55] Closely related to this influence, indeed an expression of it, was the insistence of Pant, former chief minister of UP, that Partition had become unavoidable after the forces of hatred were

---

51   Yagnik, *Gandhi As I Knew Him*, p. 10.

52   Sorel, *Reflections on Violence*, p. 18.

53   Ibid., p. 151.

54   Speech at Prayer Meeting, 10 Sept. 1947, *CWMG* (Aug. 1- Nov. 10, 1947), p. 167.

55   Kripalani, *Gandhi: His Life and Thought*, p. 686; Tendulkar, *Mahatma*, vol. 8, p. 19.

unleashed in Punjab, Bihar, and Bengal.[56] Morarji Desai, another right-winger, this time from Gandhi's Gujarat, stated: When you get gangrene in your leg, 'you have to cut it off. If you allow it to remain the whole body gives in'.[57] Patel, of course, wanted to eliminate Jinnah's nuisance value, or, as Jawaharlal expressed it privately, to cut off the head to get rid of the headache.[58] To him, Partition alone could break the impasse; he foreclosed all other options.[59] He reminded those Muslims who raised the Pakistan cry that the sword will be answered by the sword.[60]

As we look back over the last seven decades, all of us become conscious of the malaise or discomfort which oppresses the thoughtful study of post-Partition politics. Referring to the direction in which the wind was blowing, Kamaladevi, a prominent satyagrahi during Civil Disobedience and founder of the All-India Women's Conference, pronounced: 'True, we swore we didn't accept the two-nation theory, nevertheless we acted on that palpable fallacy.'[61] The Congress had by now perhaps become alive to the danger of Hindu public opinion tilting in favour of the Mahasabha in Bengal and Punjab, where the League's hostility made the religious minorities feel insecure. In its anxiety to meet their point of view, the Congress ran the risk of seeming to encourage communalism.[62]

As early as 1917, Gandhi had said that fellow Indians had lost the robust faith of their forefathers in the absolute efficacy of *Satya*, *Ahimsa*, and *Brahmacharya*. Nearly four decades later, he encountered exaggeration and falsity in his dealings.[63] As a result, old friendships snapped. Those whose careers he had nurtured had moved on in life and were no longer committed to truth and *ahimsa*, by which their

---

56   Interview between Mountbatten and Pant, 3 May 1947, in Brown, *Prisoner of Hope*, pp. 380-1.

57   Brian Lapping, *End of Empire* (London, 1989), p. 108.

58   Campbell-Johnson, *Mission with Mountbatten*, p. 98.

59   Sucheta Mahajan, *Independence and Partition: The Erosion of Colonial Power in India* (Delhi, 2000), pp. 358-59

60   Acharya Kripalani, *My Times: An Autobiography* (Delhi, 2004), p. 634.

61   Chattopadhyay, *Inner Recesses, Outer Spaces*, p. 303.

62   Misra, *The Indian Political Parties*, p. 538.

63   *Harijan*, 1 Dec. 1946, CWMG (21 Oct.-20 Feb. 1947), p. 138; Pyarelal, *Mahatma Gandhi*, p. 36.

mentor had sworn for six decades.[64] Party men had once abandoned bright careers and plunged into the nationalist struggle; now, they didn't adhere to his line of action. Although Jawaharlal wanted him to be accessible,[65] his voice ceased to have its once magical effect.[66] Charmed friends changed into dangerous enemies. Prayer meetings didn't receive the same resonance as before; attendance dwindled appreciably on 10 January.[67] With the Congress disintegrating, Gandhi cried in the wilderness. Pyarelal noticed the sorrowful expression on his face.[68]

Gandhi was unhappy with Jawaharlal and Patel, and, in a moment of utter disgust, gave to Mountbatten a clean chit on 2 June, saying that he was left with no choice after the Hindu and Muslim disagreements.[69] He called Jawaharlal as 'Our King', adding that there was no reason to be impressed by everything he did or didn't do.[70] Lastly, he was hurt by the running argument between him and Jinnah and the stridency of Urdu newspapers.[71] Their animus crossed the bounds of reason. They peddled conspiracy theories and little else and wanted the Congress Muslims to join their cause. They pursued some of the latter. When they didn't come, Altaf Hussain, editor of *Dawn*, used offensive language for Azad and Ghaffar Khan.[72] Such men related to the Congress Muslims in general with alienation, arrogance, anxiety, and hostility. Muslims boycotted the funeral of Syed Mahmud's mother-in-law in March 1940; that very year, League workers attempted to disrupt his daughter's wedding.[73]

---

64   From the Hindi, *CWMG* (21 Feb.-24 May 1947), p. 187.

65   *SWJN*, vol. 1, New Series, p. 111.

66   Shriman Narayan, *Memoirs: Windows on Gandhi and Nehru*, p. 71. Tendulkar, *Mahatma*, vol. 8, p. 245; *CWMG* (25 May 1947-31 July 1947), p. 118.

67   Bose, *My Days with Gandhi*, p. 250; Narayan, *Memoirs*, p. 69.

68   Pyarelal, *Mahatma Gandhi*, vol. 2, p. 686; Manubehn, *Last Glimpses of Bapu*, p. 2.

69   Ibid.

70   Campbell-Johnson, *Mission with Mountbatten*, p. 110.

71   Raghuvendra Tanwar, *Reporting the Partition of Punjab 1947: Press, Public and other options* (Delhi, 2006).

72   Siddiqi, *Smoke Without Fire*, pp 247-8.

73   Datta and Cleghorn (eds), *A Nationalist Muslim and Indian Politics*, p. xviii.

Let us recount that, with the Communal Award exacerbating conflicts and the Act of 1935 opening a wider arena for communitarian claims, Gandhi's rift with the League was over entitlements; it was also over his *Weltanschauung*. What hurt him was that he had lost the battle of mind and heart for no fault of his. The popular wisdom was that Muslims, having thrown off the shackles of Hindu domination, were undergoing a great transformation to secure their rightful place at the centre of the South Asian stage. Success appeared to be round the corner; the fact is that the publicists figured out that the formidable Gandhi-Jawaharlal combination stood between their present misfortune and usual condition of success, and that once their influence on the Muslims was rooted out, they would regain their glory.

Previous disputes were easily settled, as in December 1916 or in Bengal's 'Das Pact', and some form of consensus existed in Punjab with a Sikh, Muslim, and Hindu combination in the Unionist Party. In several other regions, the Congress fared well during the Muslim mass contact campaigns in March-June 1937. In 1938, Shafaat Ahmad, the historian at Allahabad, testified to the breadth, depth, and statesmanship of the Congress leaders.[74] In the mid-1940s, Gandhi, regardless, reached a point in his discussions with Jinnah where these possibilities were virtually ruled out. With his own authority in the Congress weakened, contemporaries began to doubt his ability to deliver.

No one should invade another's civil rights and worldly goods on pretence of religion, wrote John Locke, the seventeenth-century British philosopher. Those who did so should consider 'how pernicious a seed of discord and war, how powerful a provocation to endless hatreds, rapines, and slaughters they thereby furnish unto mankind'.[75]

Digargoon hai jahan taron ki gardish tez hai saqi!
Dil-i har zarrah main ghogha-i rastakhez hai saqi.
O Saqi! The whole world is in turmoil, the stars are in a whirl
The heart of each particle is filled with the din of doom.

---

74   *Proceedings of the Indian History Congress*, Allahabad, 1938, p. iii.

75   Sidorsky (ed.), *Liberal Tradition in European Thought*, p. 51.

"'All right Rosie," her father (Rev. Bannerjee) said morosely. "Turn the British out. Then see what happens to all of you ultranationalists. The moment they leave, your beloved Hindus and Muslims will be at one another's throat. There will be a horrible civil war. Bloodbath. You just wait and see. Then you will remember what this ignorant old parson had told you." His voice choked.'[76] How prophetic!

The Pangs of Separation

AYYAM-I JUDAI KE SITAM DEKH JAFA DEKH

O THE DAYS OF SEPARATION! THEIR AFFLICTIONS! THEIR CRUELTIES!

Throughout this dark and troubled period which Manto painted with his broad brush, no one wanted to upset the stable constellation of social, economic, and political structures evolving around a successful paradigm. Gandhi was exceptional: in the face of indifference or outright hostility to his ideas, he experimented with the non-violent techniques to bring about reconciliation, for which he had worked in South Africa and earned the esteem of, among others, Naoroji. He spoke in his low and soft voice against war, violence, and hatred to clear the debris of death and destruction. 'Violence like water, when it has an outlet,' Gandhi wrote in another context, 'rushes forward furiously with an overwhelming force.'[77] It did. Darkness prevailed, but he still looked forward to the light at the end of the tunnel. 'When will God take me out of this darkness into His Light?'[78] Violence surrounded in a number of places, but in spite of the ups and downs, and in the teeth of energetic opposition from both religious and political rivals, Gandhi expected the men and women he had trained in non-violence for an unbroken period of thirty-two years[79] to survive this catastrophe. They didn't. The very people, who had paid lip-service to Satyagraha and non-violence, let him down. His hopes lay in tatters.

During the night as I heard what should have been the soothing sound of gentle life giving rain, my mind went out to the thousands

---

76   Hyder, *Fireflies in the Mist: A Novel*, p. 165.

77   *Harijan*, 21 Jan. 1939, *CWMG*.

78   Pyarelal, *Mahatma Gandhi*, vol. 1, p. 470.

79   Fischer, *The Life of Mahatma Gandhi*, p. 486.

of refugees lying about in the open camps in Delhi. I was sleeping
snugly in a veranda protecting me on all sides. But for the cruel
hand of man against his brother, these thousands of men, women,
and children would not be shelterless and in many cases foodless. In
some places they could not but be in knee-deep water ... Was this
the first fruit of freedom, just a month old baby? These thoughts
have haunted me throughout these last twenty hours. My silence has
been a blessing. It has made me enquire within. Have the citizens of
Delhi gone mad? Have they no humanity left in them? Has love of
the country and its freedom no appeal for them?[80]

Lothian had predicted in 1937 that Gandhi was held in the highest
regard and people were in awe of him because of his saintly image. Still,
he did not expect them to submit tamely to him.[81] In more ways than
one, the pro-Partition lobby in the Congress did just that in the mid-
1940s. Initially it looked to the past for guidance and decided on 'unity'
as the goal. But the motive for seeking national unity was to bring large
areas of the ruling class under the control and stave off challenges from
the hoi polloi. However, once the League exerted its power, constraining
choices to its followers to the point where even fine-tuning became
inconceivable, opinion and thoughts were gradually modified. As
indicated earlier in our discussion, this happened on the grounds that
life would get tough sooner rather than later.

The business community had been silent until they viewed Partition
as disruptive of the social order, which it was. Hindu nationalism may
have lost its hold over them, but deference to the Hindutva ideology
animated a substantial number of traders, merchants and industrialists.
Rather than looking to the imagined past for guidance, as the
'nationalists' did, they contemplated the future. Their links with the
Congress and their self-image of being the custodians of social order
impacted on their intervention in the Partition debates.

Ramkrishna Dalmia claimed to be the first of the top industrialists
to publicly endorse the Partition outline. Homi Mody joined him. Birla

80   *Delhi Diary: Prayer Speeches from 10.9.47 to 30.1.48* (Ahmedabad, 1948).

81   Birla to Mahadev Desai, 30 July 1937, in Birla (ed.), *Bapu: A Unique
      Association*, vol. 3, p. 37.

had, of course, been influenced by its inevitability in 1942 and saw the correlation between 'Muslim separatism' and political fragmentation. Lala Shri Ram, the Delhi industrialist, agreed to Partition.[82] Businessmen, with whom Gandhi, Patel, and Morarji Desai had close links, had already agreed to 'vivisection'.

Good could emerge from mistakes, but not when the major political parties were hopelessly divided. While the Communist Party reinvented the idea of self-determination,[83] the socialists were mixed up with the caste and linguistic politics of the Hindi-Hindu heartland. Moreover, even though they were composed principally of those whose interests were in accordance with the aspirations of the poor, a considerable number of rich men, zamindars, and urbanised intellectuals made up the socialist leadership. Parting company with the Congress reinforced their divisions.

The activism of the RSS, the Hindu Mahasabha, the National Guards, and other quasi-fascist Muslim organisations, such as the Khaksars, offered no respite to Gandhi. Even so, he refused to lower his ideals on the grounds that imperfections prevailed all around. Having described life as an inspiration and not an aspiration,[84] he coped with the perilous state. During the Second World War, Bertrand Russell observed that men needed a clear faith and well-grounded hope, and, as the outcome of these, the calm courage which takes no account of hardships along the way. Continuing his own ascent to the goal which clearly beckoned—to share the pain and give the people a strong voice of his own—Gandhi impulsively wanted to either succeed or perish.[85] He therefore brought to the fore some of his hidden reservoir of strength, optimism, joy, and

---

82   Claude Markovits, 'Businessmen and the Partition of India', in D. Tripathi (ed.), *Business and Politics in India: A Historical Perspective* (Delhi, 1991), pp. 295, 300; Alan Ross, *The Emissary: G.D. Birla, Gandhi and Independence* (London, 1986), p. 163; Kudaisya, *The Life and Times of G.D. Birla*, pp. 233-34; Mahajan, *Independence and Partition*, pp. 358-39.

83   Sunanda Sanyal and Soumya Basu, *The Sickle and the Crescent: Communists, Muslim League and India's Partition* (Kolkata, 2011).

84   Pyarelal, *Mahatma Gandhi*, vol. 2, p. 587.

85   Bose, *My Days with Gandhi*, p. 84; Manubehn, *Last Glimpses of Bapu*, p. 2; Gandhi to Birla, 26 Nov. 1946, in Birla (ed.), *In the Shadow of the Mahatma*, p. 288.

peace.[86] An excellent example of this was his visit to Calcutta in the autumn of 1947, less than three weeks after Independence, and his fast in September to put an end to the Hindu-Muslim conflagration. In the past, Rajaji had pleaded with him not to take such a risky step but on this occasion he refused to wrangle: 'The only sane man today is Gandhi,' he said.[87]

Gandhi stayed in a tumbledown house near one of the scenes of a gruesome Hindu-Muslim riot, the kind Manto described in some of his short stories. Here, millions lived in slums. He summoned leading businessmen to ask them to rebuild Calcutta. When they came, they found him sitting on a low wooden platform, spinning, and wearing only a loincloth. A small girl sat nearby, apparently learning to spin or perhaps ministering to his needs. Twenty minutes later, a mob of young Hindus broke in. Gandhi didn't stop spinning. One of the young men then aimed a blow at his head with a lathi. The little girl sitting beside him caught the blow on her arm. Gandhi continued spinning. No one else in the crowd then had the courage to strike him again. They merely pulled the window frames out of the walls, smashed doors, and reduced the scanty furniture to matchwood. Rioting ceased from the moment the girl saved Gandhi. Embarrassed, they cleared their throats and uttered not a word of ill-will towards the Muslims, pretending that nothing had really happened. Here was a modern-day Jesus bringing some sense to his people! As the fasting was on and drop by drop strength ebbed out of the frail little man on the fasting bed, it caused a deep churning in the hearts of all concerned.[88] Much regret and remorse followed. Peace and friendship became the order of the day. At 9.15 p.m., a relieved Gandhi broke his fast. Rajaji declared that he had been a 'successful one-man Boundary Force in Bengal'.[89]

In Noakhali, the social unrest triggered by Hindu and Muslim zealots burst out of control. Gandhi, nonetheless, demonstrated that they could

---

86   Pyarelal, *Mahatma Gandhi*, vol. 2, p. 685.

87   Rajmohan Gandhi, *The Rajaji Story, 1937-1972* (Bombay, 1984), p. 153.

88   Pyarelal to Birla, 6 Sept. 1947, Birla (ed.), *Bapu: A Unique Association*, vol. 4, pp. 146-4.

89   Rajmohan Gandhi, *The Rajaji Story*, p. 149.

improve their understanding of each other and work as equals. Without this, they'd be torn asunder by mutual strife and remain engrossed in barbarity.[90] Unlike the previous top-down efforts, this time Gandhi reached out to the common people. In retrospect, his efforts didn't have much of a chance not because it was bandied about on a grand scale but because it embarrassed the British authorities.

In Noakhali

> Husain ibn-i Ali Karbala ko jaate hain
> Magar ye log abhi tak gharon ke undar hain
> Husain Ibn-i Ali proceeds to Karbala
> But people still are inside their homes!
> –Sheharyar

Sadhus and saints routinely tread the paths through jungles and deserts. The believers walk to a mosque or the graveyard and perform *tawaaf* around the Kaaba, an obligatory religious duty. The wandering Sufis and *qalandar*s traverse deserts and forests to seek communion with the ultimate reality. The Shias walk in the Muharram procession to the local Karbala, the burial site for *tazia*s, to mourn Husain's martyrdom. Gandhi, in an out of the ordinary manner, universalised the local and regional practices of diverse religions. Once he marched at the head of a straggling column on the dusty, undulating road from Standerton to Greylingstad in South Africa. Now, he walked barefoot with a lathi in hand.

It is dangerous to be good, mentioned George Bernard Shaw. From August to December 1946, Gandhi, now seventy-nine years old, undertook life's most complicated and difficult mission. Imagine him, weighing 106.5 lbs, walking from village to village under the blazing sun. There was a Biblical appeal around this walk. His six-week stay in Srirampur exemplified teachings from the *Gita*, the Bible, and the Quran on personal courage, goodness, and piety.[91] He was determined to stay until the Hindus and Muslims became well-disposed towards

---

90   *Harijan*, 1 Dec. 1946, *CWMG* (21 Dec. 1946-20 Feb. 1947), p. 139.

91   Pyarelal, *Mahatma Gandhi*, vol. 1, bk 2, pp. 38-44.

each other. He bade good-bye to Delhi, to Sevagram, to Uruli, and undertook the 'do-or-die mission' to put his non-violence to test.[92]

At the crack of dawn he visited Muslim peasants and, with Sushila Nayar's help, saw the sick being treated. He had undertaken such a lone sojourn previously, but this one on 21 November 1946 had an exceptional quality: 'Calm of purpose, serene and unmoved, doing his job and not caring overmuch for the result of his action.'[93] Even so, he admitted to Nirmal Kumar Bose, a companion, that suffering and evil overwhelmed him. Whenever that happened in those grim and tragic days, Gandhi would stew in his own juice.[94]

Attackers besieged 200 or more villages in Noakhali, a heavily jute-growing district with a predominantly Muslim population, and Tippera. Violence affected Ranigunj, Lakhimpur, Begumgunj, and Senbag *thanas*, and the former Chandpur and Faridgunj *thanas*. An 'indescribable darkness' seized Gandhi's soul when he set out for these areas with the end of (William) Blake's 'golden string' to unravel.[95] He referred to the hazardous tasks ahead of him. He said he was putting himself more and more in God's hand.[96] When asked how long he expected to stay, he replied he had set no time limit. Islam hadn't forgotten Karbala, a tragedy that had occurred so long ago. How could he forget his Karbala that was Bihar?[97] Non-violence was essentially an instrument of redress. If an imperfect man like him could practice it, everyone in Noakhali could follow suit. 'The way to truth is paved with skeletons over which we dare to walk,' an anguished Gandhi wrote to Mirabehn.[98]

The sky was overcast. It was dark: it hadn't been darker before. With darkness providing the cover, the perpetrators of violence retreated quietly to prepare themselves for the assault the following morning.

---

92   Gandhi to Birla, 26 Nov. 1946, Birla, *In the Shadow of the Mahatma*, p. 288.

93   Nehru, *An Autobiography*, p. 74.

94   Bose, *My Days with Gandhi*, p. 84; Manubehn, *Last Glimpses of Bapu*, p. 284.

95   Pyarelal, *Mahatma Gandhi*, vol. 1, p. 8.

96   Ibid.,p. 431.

97   Ibid., p. 263.

98   Gandhi to Mirabehn, 6 Feb. 1947, *CWMG* (21 Oct. 1946-20 Feb. 1947), p. 626.

That is when Gandhi's village-to-village tour, his voyage of faith, got underway. The road along which he walked carried him by the side of a school, where Muslim boys (with a population of two million; there were only forty girls in the one and only high school for girls in the district) sat in the sun reciting the Quran. Gandhi stopped and listened. He felt like telling them what he had once said to the Italian educationist, Maria Montessori, 'if we want to achieve true peace in the world and if we really want to fight against war, we should start from the children'.

Leaning upon a lathi that had stood him in good stead during his political expeditions, he wanted to soothe violent tempers through his personal endurance rather than formalistic ideologies. He appealed to the gathered crowd to shun hatred, to distinguish between the evil thing and the evildoer, to think frankly about their future,[99] to magnify their own faults a thousandfold, and to close their eyes to the faults of neighbours.[100] He expected elders to interpret and adapt contemporary ideologies to the changing circumstances. 'Beloved Pilgrim,' an emotionally-charged Sarojini Naidu wrote, 'setting out on your pilgrimage of love and hope, 'Go with God', in the beautiful Spanish phrase. I have no fear for you—only faith in your mission.'[101]

Gandhi's mission continued until riots flared up in the capital in January 1948. The general situation was terrible, but there were good and bad things happening. The good thing was that one of the most upright figures of an age, when noble figures were rare, trudged the muddy paths to throw off the shackles of constraints and rescue the beleaguered. A contemporary observer assessed his success and failure:

> I feel that Gandhi during the weeks at Delhi, which culminated in his death, was the saint and a martyr at his best and at his worst. His attempt to rehabilitate the Muslims in Delhi was both courageous and Christian in spirit, but, in the face of the vast

---

99   Ashis Nandy, *Traditions, Tyranny, and Utopias*, p. 160; Ronald J. Terchek, *Gandhi Struggling for Autonomy*, p. 230.

100   19 Oct. 1947, *Delhi Diary*, p. 98.

101   Sarojini Naidu to Gandhi, 26 Dec. 1946, in Paranjape (ed.), *Sarojini Naidu: Selected Letters*, p. 316.

numbers of Hindus who had fled in panic from Punjab, it was
futile and utterly impractical. He was swimming dead against the
enormous tide of human passion—whereas throughout most of
his career he had already been swimming with the tide. He was,
I think, partly misled by his success in Noakhali, Calcutta and
Bihar and didn't properly grasp the huge magnitude of the Punjab
movement of population and the implications of its being a two-
way movement.[102]

Christian missionaries deciphered Gandhi's Christ-like qualities, and
were comfortable with his representation as 'the patient sufferer for the
cause of Righteousness and Mercy, a truer representative of the Crucified
Saviour.'[103] Nonetheless, it must be realised, and realised particularly for
the full understanding of nationalism, that his fame and glory rested on
his crusade against the enemy which, according to his belief, violated
the moral principles of the Indian community and against blind hatred
and diabolical fanaticism.[104]

On 30 December 1946, Jawaharlal visited Srirampur 'like a meteor-
burst across the overcast skies'. For a brief while, he lifted the gloom and
filled all hearts with the cheering glow of his presence. He was there to
persuade Gandhi to be in Delhi. Gandhi didn't agree.[105] A Christian
hymn, translated by Rajkumari Amrit Kaur, was her parting gift to him.
It could well have been a short poem he sent from the prison cell to the
children of the ashram, shortly after his arrest in May 1922:

> Ordinary birds cannot fly without wings. With wings, of course, all
> can fly. But if you, without wings, will learn how to fly, then all your
> troubles will indeed be at an end. And I will teach you.
> See, I have no wings, yet I come flying to you every day in thought.
> Look, here is little Vimala, here is Hari and here also Dharmakumar.

---

102   13 Feb. 1949, Malcolm Darling papers.

103   Harper, *In the Shadow of the Mahatma*, p. 293.

104   Madho Prasad, *A Gandhian Patriarch*, p. 287. For a moving description, *see*
       Rajmohan Gandhi, *Mohandas*, pp. 565-72.

105   I have based this paragraph on Pyarelal, *Mahatma Gandhi*, vol. 1, p. 487.

And you also can come flying to me in thought. Send me a letter signed by all, and those who do not know how to sign may make a cross.[106]

If you don't already know it, this is Gandhi's *Sulh-i Kul*. Tragically, he predicted the catastrophe in 1947, but his solution was inadequate just when it was most needed.

Abdicating Responsibility

'We are on the eve of great events here,' the viceroy's aide informed his mother on 1 June 1947, 'and I am up to my eyes in planning the last-minute details of planning the publicity for Mountbatten's momentous announcement on the transfer of power which is due to be made on Tuesday.' Gladstone had advised Northbrook, after appointing him viceroy in 1872, that, 'when we go, if we are ever to go, we may leave a good name and a clean bill of health behind us'.[107] He retired, in April 1876, being hostile to both the frontier and fiscal policies of Lord Salisbury, the secretary of state. Coincidentally, almost exactly a century later, Cripps expected a settlement to precede the British withdrawal; otherwise, he anticipated chaos and bloodshed to occur.[108] Mountbatten didn't do that.[109] While the British Empire pretended to stand immovably upright, its majestic posture invited ridicule. The empire had good reasons to bow its head, almost in apology. Kenneth McRae, superintendent of police in the NWFP, confirms this view: 'We went out to India with high ideals. We went out to look after the people, and we left the country in utter chaos.'[110] Therefore, 'we have had a most terrible time in this part of the world, of which there is no precedent in any history of the world. The killings and atrocities are almost without example and quite unimaginable.'[111] P. D. Martyn,

---

106   Brockway, *The Indian Crisis*, p. 112.

107   David Gilmour, *The Ruling Caste*, p. 230.

108   Clarke, *The Cripps Version*, p. 413.

109   Campbell-Johnson, *Mission with Mountbatten*, p. 178.

110   Kenneth McRae papers, IOR. MSS EUR (Photo) 467.

111   Rashid to G.M. Brander, 4 Dec. 1947, IOR.MSS EUR F.409.

district magistrate in Bengal, sensed that the British were drifting, as the war dragged on, and coming to the end of the road. He said so to Wavell in Calcutta.[112]

When violence escalated, Mountbatten thought that it was inevitable. Others contested this assertion,[113] pointing to the passive role of the Punjab Boundary Force, which was created in July under Major-General Rees and remained in the barracks while trainloads of refugees were being butchered. Mountbatten's lame excuse was that the deployment of British troops would have incurred the odium of both sides. If so, how does one explain General Claude Auchinleck's refusal to send a British brigade to police Delhi? He was the commander-in-chief. Other officials feared attacks, and lived on the very margins of the empire. 'We have lost,' Wavell conceded: 'we are simply running on the momentum of our previous prestige.'[114] A belated admission of the failure of all the King's horses and all the King's men!

True, rumours fanned hatred, but the slaughter could have been averted or minimised with less haste and greater care. Penderel Moon, the civil servant, felt that the Punjab holocaust could have been avoided had the administration acted sufficiently promptly on the spot. Hodson, another civil servant, made similar assertions.[115] Lately, an author defends Mountbatten on the grounds that he couldn't have acted against the wishes of Whitehall, the British services, and Jawaharlal's government, all insisting on the withdrawal of troops at the earliest.[116] Martial law in Punjab was ruled out on the grounds that the situation had deteriorated too far and too fast beyond the point where things could be brought back into control. It had to be accepted that the 30-odd million people in an area of 100,000 square miles were being

---

112   'Memoirs', P.D. Martyn papers, CSAS, Cambridge,

113   Sudhir Ghosh, 31 Oct. 1946, *TF*, vol. 9, p. 26.

114   Penderel Moon (ed.), *Wavell: The Viceroy's Journal* (London, 1973), p. 402.

115   H.V. Hodson, *The Great Divide: Britain-India-Pakistan* (Karachi, 1997 edn), pp. 402-07; Allen (ed.), *Plain Tales from the Raj*, p. 246; Penderel Moon, *Divide and Quit: An Eye-witness Account of the Partition of India* (New Delhi, 1998), p. 27.

116   Alex von Tunzelmann, *Indian Summer: The Secret History of the End of an Empire* (New York, 2007), p. 219.

dragged into an entirely new way of life. They were entirely bewildered and quite simply terrified by the gathering pace of events.[117] According to the Punjab governor, he wasn't dealing with a situation in which troops could act decisively: 'Cloak and dagger' activities were difficult to control.[118] In Bengal, the army's role after the Great Killing was not worth writing home about.[119]

Mountbatten should have stuck to Atlee's timetable of June 1948 and used the government agencies to facilitate migration across the borders. In this way, commented Gerald R. Savage, an official in the Central Intelligence Department in Lahore, much of bloodshed could have been avoided.[120] Preponing the event added to the already growing panic and uncertainties in everyone's mind.

A 'Sapper Subaltern' with the 2nd Indian Airborne Division had a different concern: 'Was Partition really necessary? Wouldn't Wavell, Auchinleck, and Mountbatten have more time to make the military and security arrangements?'[121] Auchinleck tried convincing Mountbatten that half-measures and appeasement of the Sikhs (the ban on carrying a *kirpan* was withdrawn) was fraught with the gravest danger for the future.[122] This was not to be. While the apologists of the Raj celebrated Britain's swift exit and a slapdash Partition, Mountbatten had blood on his hands. As for his subordinates, very few of them had their hearts in the task of maintaining law and order. Civil chaos wasn't without its allure.[123] Cold, cynical, and brutally insensitive, they sought the safety of bungalows and cantonments, drank beer, played cricket, listened to music, went hunting in the safety of the jungle, and read Kipling. Edward Blunt, who served

---

117   'Melons and Dust', Gerald R. Savage papers.

118   Memorandum by E.M. Jenkins, 4 Aug. 1947, Carter (ed.), *Mountbatten's Report on the Last Viceroyalty*, p. 379.

119   'Memoirs', P.D. Martyn papers, CSAS, Cambridge.

120   Gerald R. Sewage Papers, IOR. MSS EUR (Photo) 436, Misc.

121   Brigadier DA. Barker-Wyatt CBE, 'Partition of India 1947: The Memoirs and Experiences of a Sapper Subaltern with 2nd Indian Airborne Division', IOR. MSS (Photo) EUR. 425.

122   To Dickie, 13 Sept. 1947, Greenwood, *Field-Marshal Auchinleck*, p. 277.

123   Andrews, *A Lamp for India*, p. 237.

in UP from 1901-36, suggested that shooting and pig-sticking weren't merely forms of sport; they were often works of agricultural improvement.[124]

Nearly 12 million people moved across borders. Regardless of their plight, Mountbatten hosted a reception, on 28 July 1947, for over fifty ruling princes and a 100 states' representatives. One of Punjab's former governors bemoaned that, 'worst of all is the way we have left our friends and faithful servants to their fate. It is a shameful abandonment and the most disgraceful episode in our history.'[125] While Mountbatten hurried to enjoy the benefits of royalty, others recalled the glorious days gone by, and revelled in their achievements.[126] They couldn't imagine the dismantling of the imperial structures or the removal of the emblem and the portraits. In 1941, Linlithgow shared the belief with others that British rule would last another thirty years.[127] Churchill, the prime minister, appointed Field Marshall Lord Wavell to keep India quiet until the war was over, but the popular disquiet, of which the Quit India was a manifestation, ensured the disappearance of British cantonments with Lancers and Gurkhas guarding them, special burial with gravestones honouring the fallen in Kipling's *Thin Red Line of Heroes*, and silver trophies polished daily by *abdars* in the Officers' Mess. Iris Portal, whose husband commanded the governor's bodyguard in Bombay for five years, made it clear that 'you must never take land away from people. People's land has a mystique. You can go and probably order them about for a bit ...' but 'you must then go away and die in Cheltenham'.[128] Characteristically, Josh Malihabadi said it all:

You merchants, now your welfare lies in this alone,
That you should bow your necks before time's decree.
A story will be written by time on a new theme,

---

124   Edward Blunt, *The I.C.S.: The Indian Civil Service* (London, 1937).

125   Rashid to G.M. Brander, 4 Dec. 1947, IOR.MSS EUR F.409.

126   V. G. Kiernan, *European Empires from Conquest to Collapse, 1815-1960* (New York, 1982), pp. 228-9.

127   Moore, *Churchill, Cripps, and India*, p. 158.

128   Allen (ed.), *Plain Tales from the Raj*, p. 263.

Whose headline will require the redness of your blood?
Time's commandment cannot change direction
Death may be diverted, but this commandment may not be
　　turned aside.[129]

The ordinary citizens were, for all intents and purposes, left to flounder. The golden phase of life passed away. The glow of inner happiness disappeared, like a drop of dew in the sun.[130] 'When would Gandhi Baba be returning to Noakhali?' 'Well, well, he will come sometime,' replied Satish Chandra Das Gupta, Gandhi's follower. 'But when?' persisted the Muslim inquirer, and then added with a sigh: 'if *he* were here, he at least would have cared for us. Who else is there to feel for our woes?'[131] This would have given Gandhi a rare sense of public acceptance, but, alas, such feelings were short-lived. Elsewhere, the government had lost the will to control disorder and violence. This was a terribly dangerous state of affairs, not only for the present, but for the future and from the widest point of view, not merely the local.

Bhangi Colony stands on the verge of the wasteland encircling Delhi, and was once set against a round of barren boulders and dusty earth. Just a fortnight before the day of Independence, Campbell-Johnson carried the following impression after meeting Gandhi:

> The sense of awe among the acolytes exceeded anything I had witnessed since attending an audience of Pope Pius XI; and as for the charm and magnetism of Gandhiji himself, the only similar experience I could recall was a long talk with Lloyd George in 1936. The contrasts in pomp and circumstance, between the Vatican and the Bhangi Colony, the Mahatma and the Wizard from Wales, are sufficiently obvious to be misleading. The points of religious and political comparison are perhaps the deeper reality.[132]

129　Shobna Nijhawan (ed.), *Nationalism in the Vernacular*, p. 202.

130　Popati Hiranandani, *The Pages of My Life: Autobiography and Selected Stories*, trans. from Sindhi by Jyoti Panjwani (Oxford, 2010), p. 83.

131　Pyarelal, *Mahatma Gandhi*, vol. 2, p. 57.

132　Campbell-Johnson, *Mission with Mountbatten*, pp. 146-47.

As a final note, Bapu had reasons to feel disillusioned, except that he followed his own hunches, however much they conflicted with the opinions of others, for example, nurturing Jawaharlal as his political heir. Having already explored this relationship, a quite unique one, we examine, in the next chapter, how Gandhi's legacy worked with Jawaharlal during his mammoth task of nation-building.

Section IV

Gandhi collecting money for the Harijan Fund on his way to Poona, June 15, 1944

14
Let colour fill the flowers,
Let the breeze of early spring blow

The flowers were blooming in the garden; some had only just blossomed. The people who had gathered that evening were delighted by the perfume of the flowers and by their beautiful form. Their enjoyment was accompanied by a rare but most welcome meeting with Gandhi at this reception in Delhi. In the words of Lady Violet Haig, the host and wife of G.A. Haig, home secretary and later home member, it was 'a rather notable picture, the power of that little man over sixty years old, one of the most famous figures in the world today'.[1] This image of the man didn't change over time. George E. Jones, an American journalist and a long-standing follower, was pleasantly surprised by his robust appearance and twinkling eyes behind steel-rimmed glasses which gave the seventy-eight year old a genial expression;[2] a smile of broad benevolence with which he made it a point to gladden the entire world. Mountbatten's senior aide came away from a meeting with Gandhi on 27 September 1947, not with the impression of a very old man but of one who lives with 'the intensity of youth and retains the boyish sense of fun which tragedy and the passing of time cannot wither'.[3]

It is difficult to imagine how many pleasant incidents continually came to pass in that secluded part of the garden, and what the guests thought of them. I recount some of them: those incidents, apparently so trifling, had become a part of everyone's memory.

What is there in this book that we do not already know? In the spirit of this question, it must be said that, notwithstanding what

---

1   Lady Violet Haig, in IOR, G.A. Haig papers.

2   Jones, *Tumult in India*, p. 74.

3   Campbell-Johnson, *Mission with Mountbatten*, p. 208.

Jawaharlal told Martin Luther King Jr., Gandhi's influence down to the present moment, and into all future times, has spread over posterity like a shadow that keeps growing in the sun. This has to be ascribed to many factors; to his being, for example, the prototype of an optimist and his ability to separate true knowledge from evil and falsehood, and ascribe to knowledge and truth the power of a panacea. Unless we value and strictly judge this fact, we will not understand his frontal attack on contemporary moral and intellectual assumptions.

Gandhi is entitled to our admiration for resuscitating the Congress, the principal political force behind the fight for Independence. He created a large following across the board, and mobilised the rich and the poor, the urban and the rural: 'now the peasants rolled in and, in its new garb, it [Congress] began to assume the look of a vast agrarian organization with a strong sprinkling of the middle classes'.[4]

The other reason why he is entitled to our affection is his passion for unsettling traditional dividing lines and dichotomies and engaging in conflict management within a system that permitted opposing points of view to coexist fairly.[5] This makes him relevant in this day and age, when the advantages of non-violent means over the use of force are manifest. Non-violent campaigns are better able to withstand government repression and have even turned it to their benefit.[6] A recent study concludes by addressing the Palestinians: 'you and generations of Palestinians have suffered greatly and over the decades have risked all in the continuing struggle for justice. New struggles for freedom lie ahead. If guided by Gandhian principles, they can wield a higher power and have greater hope of success'.[7]

---

4   Jawaharlal, *The Discovery of India*, p. 360.

5   For a discussion on how a conception of citizenship rooted in Gandhian ideas, which entrenched in India's political culture forms of dissent that did not generally threaten the existence of the state, allowed governments to tolerate social antagonisms and let conflicts to exist within the state, rather than enforcing an artificial institutional consensus, see Ornit Shani, 'Gandhi, Citizenship and the Resilience of Indian Nationhood', *Citizenship Studies*, vol. 15, nos. 6-7, Oct. 2011, pp. 660-662.

6   David Cortright, *Gandhi and Beyond: Nonviolence for a New Political Age* (London, 2010), pp. 224-25.

7   Ibid., p. 240.

Admittedly, Gandhi's moral and spiritual ideas were diffused and disparate. For this, the political classes castigated him for calling off Non-Cooperation to prevent it from lapsing entirely into spasms of violence, and for signing the truce with Irwin on 5 March 1931. More generally, they doubted his 'stiff' and 'unbending' stand on non-violence.[8] In the process, they forgot that Gandhi was hardly a pacifist in the usual, fully-fledged meaning of the word but someone who maintained that the evils of capitulation outweighed the evils of war. The British taunted him later for drawing a dividing line of 'big' and 'little' bridges which could be destroyed without violating the non-violent creed.

Gandhi, however, recorded that 'the risk of riots has to be run. Non-violence will be born out of such risks, if at all it is to form a part of national life.'[9] He felt in the innermost recesses of his heart that the world was sick unto death of blood-spilling, but that it was, after all, seeing a way out. He wanted Elwin's countrymen to know:

I love them as I love my own countrymen. I have never done anything towards them in hatred or malice and God-willing I shall never do anything in that manner in future. I am acting no differently towards them now from what I have done under similar circumstances towards my kith and kin.[10]

Three aspects of Gandhi's goals are quintessentially *modern*: first and foremost, the anti-colonial struggle itself; second, reconciling modern and traditional imageries and symbols to self-regulate national life;[11] third, inculcating a 'traditional' society with certain 'modern' values. 'Everyone is his own ruler,' he said.

---

8   'His stress on *ahimsa* was marred by his even greater emphasis on suffering and endurance which, since he exemplified it in his own 'fasts unto death', points to a strong sado-masochistic streak in his character.' Burton Stein, *A History of India* (New York, 2010), pp. 290-1.

9   *Harijan*, 9 March 1940, CWMG (1 Dec. 1939-15 Apr. 1940), p. 298.

10   To Verrier Elwin, n.d., IOR, Elwin papers (D 950-22).

11   Occasionally he used the images of Rama fighting the demon Ravana to the Muslim image of God opposing Satan (*shaitaan*). McDonough, *Gandhi's Responses to Islam*, p. 26.

The Left, however, erred in castigating him as illiberal or anti-secular. Similarly, the League construed *Ramarajya* as 'Hindu raj' and not a raj of full realisation and self-expression of a regime beneficial to all. Its leaders did this despite Gandhi's explanation that his Rama was another name for *Khuda* or God, and that he wanted *Khuda* Raj, the same as the Kingdom of God on Earth. He compared the rule of the four *Khulafa* after the Prophet to *Ramarajya*.[12]

In truth, *Ramarajya* was meant to achieve the ultimate good not for oneself but for all. It couldn't be converted into a tool for self-aggrandisement or Hindu raj. What also remained blurred was the search for 'national unity', on the one hand, and the use of transcendent Hindu symbols to accomplish Hindu 'unity'.

The Congress was not a 'Hindu' body as such, but its composition could be mistakenly construed as 'Hindu'. So that terms like 'Hindu mind' and 'Hindu aspirations' gained currency among its opponents. The only difference some people saw between the Congress and the Mahasabha is that the latter was crude in its utterance and brutal in its actions while the Congress tended to be politic and polite.[13]

Gandhi took time to shake off the dust accumulating around the reformers, recommended an open-ended interpretation, and eschewed engagement with olden times for the future.[14] It's not as if past memories cease to haunt peoples and nations.[15] Spain and Croatia still remember Turkish rule with a sense of irony and bitterness; the Turks, in turn,

---

12   Pyarelal, *Mahatma Gandhi*, vol. 1, p. 549.

13   Ambedkar, *Thoughts on Pakistan*, p. 42.

14   He said: 'If we go on remembering old scores, we would feel that unity is impossible, but at any cost we ought to forget the past. History teaches us that these things have happened the world over, and that the world has forgotten them, because public memory is always short and forgiving. This is another instance of love by a compelling mental effort. Hinduism is so liberal and broad-minded that, I think, it can achieve this consummation.' 3 March 1918, Desai (ed.), *Day-to-Day with Gandhi*, vol. 1, p. 56.

15   J.S. Grewal, *Muslim Rule in India: The Assessments of British Historians* (New Delhi, 1970); Partha Chatterjee, 'History and the Nationalization of Hinduism', in Vasudha Dalmia and H. von Stietencron (eds), *Representing Hinduism: The Construction of Religious Traditions and National Identity* (New Delhi, 1995), for the debates, including the communal bias fostered by the colonial historians.

deride the Allied powers for occupying their land. In India, nationalism drew upon and recast some patterns of social relations, and sentiments, doctrines, and also embodied memories of pre- and colonial rule.[16] Bankimchandra Chatterjee and Dayanand Saraswati looked back at forced conversion and temple destruction to shout at Muslims and Islam.

Gandhi, for his part, didn't like their kind of scolding. Instead, he tried to raise the standing of Muslims and Christians in the eyes of Hindus, recognised political and religious diversities, and borrowed ideas from Buddhist, Jain, Muslim, and Christian thinkers.[17] He kept the requirements in balance, a goal that meshed well with his own style and ideals. Also, unlike the Bengal *bhadralok*, who disliked the Muslim peasantry with which it had some contact as the exploiting class, Gandhi downplayed injuries to his co-religionists which the medieval Sultans perpetrated, and emphasised, instead, the sufferings of Muslims at each other's hands (Shia-Sunni and Ahl-i Hadith versus Ahmadiyas) as well as from outsiders like Nadir Shah and Ahmad Shah Abdali. He appreciated the fine qualities of Islam, and delivered a long panegyric so gushing that it would make a present-day writer blush.

Gandhi's thoughts rested on an unusually broad philosophical foundation.[18] He breached his generation's moral complacency, and conceived of an inclusive cultural and civilisational entity. He quickened a *national* consciousness, which so few among his contemporaries did, and wanted it to be the hope of all the exploited races, whether in Asia, Africa or in any part of the world.[19] He therefore devoted himself to reorganising village life and improving its economic condition.[20]

True, many didn't learn much from his conception of the public good and his understanding of the morals and ethics shaping his world, and they, consequently, forsook kindness, charity, and truth.

---

16   C.A. Bayly, *Origins of Nationality in South Asia* in *The C.A. Bayly Omnibus*, p. 1.

17   Sabyasachi Bhattacharya (ed.), *The Mahatma and the Poet: Letters and Debates between Gandhi and Tagore 1915-1941* (Delhi, 4th imp., 2008), p. 37.

18   Parekh, *Gandhi's Political Philosophy*, p. 195.

19   Gandhi, *The Way to Communal Harmony*, p. 408.

20   Ibid., p. 406.

What is more, they broke his heart by spreading hatred, greed, and terror. Such disappointments apart, Gandhi built up his life of political zeal and moral scruple upon his conscience. Having found the Truth he imparted it to others.[21] As a result, he was the best not only of his generation but the leader of mankind for centuries. While George Washington stood at the forefront of a nation and wrote American history, he stood at the forefront of the human race writing the chapter of a *new* history.[22] By spurning material progress at the cost of moral values, he took a line in direct opposition to the two dominant ideologies of the twentieth century, capitalism and communism.[23]

The last few months of Gandhi's life were the crown and climax of his career. Despite Partition, he expected India to survive the 'death dance'. He looked down on the idea of a theocratic state, and upheld equal rights for the minorities and cultural democracy.[24] Holmes told him before leaving India, 'you were never as great as in these dark hours'.[25]

Any person has the right to differ from Gandhi.[26] To share with the reader what one believes to be true is a privilege and moral obligation in history. Without imposing a moral judgement, the best way is to separate the genuine and the spurious in Gandhi's larger heritage, and to base one's conclusion on a patient study of the facts. If he is presumed to articulate the essence of his philosophy, it is well worth exploring his mind to gauge the good or bad substance of the causes he espoused. Gandhi, however noble, wasn't prepared to do this himself, if only from a sense of propriety.[27]

The history of twentieth-century India began with Gandhi. All that went before him were sporadic eruptions.[28] It would however be wrong,

---

21   L/PJ/12/297, IOR, BL. Holmes, *My Gandhi*, p. 177.

22   IOR.L/PJ/12/297.

23   B. R. Nanda, *Mahatma Gandhi: A Pictorial Biography* (Delhi, 1958), p. 52.

24   Gandhi, *The Way to Communal Harmony*, pp. 394-396.

25   Fischer, *The Life of Mahatma Gandhi*, p. 492.

26   A.K. Azad, *Speeches of Maulana Azad, 1947-1955* (Delhi, 1956), p. 320.

27   Andrews (ed.), *Mahatma Gandhi: His Own Story*, p. 332.

28   Kamaladevi, quoted in Jasleen Dhamija, *Kamaladevi Chattopadhyay* (Delhi, 2007), p. 21.

as he himself said to Saraladevi Chowdharani, a close disciple, to elevate him to sainthood or place him up on some shelf among the gods.[29] One is, of course, taken back to his prophet-like or Christ-like qualities, but he refused to be considered worthy of that honour.[30] A humble seeker after Truth must not take anything for a gospel of truth, even if it comes from a Mahatma.

With this state of mind, we find Gandhi to be comfortable among ourselves, where he always loved to be, and not out of the reach of ordinary mortals. As for the verdict of history, it cannot be anticipated by those who make it.[31]

Ho chukin Ghalib balain sab tamam

ALL THE CALAMITIES ARE OVER GHALIB

In England, Gandhi came across Francis Bacon's quotation: "To think that an handful of people can, with the greatest courage and policy in the world, embrace too large extent of dominion, it may hold for a time, but it will fail suddenly."[32] Europe's hegemony over Asia and Africa, which was uncontested at the beginning of the twentieth century, weakened at the end of the First World War. Great Britain emerged from it torn, wounded, and bankrupt. Between 1945 and 1960, no less than forty countries with a population of 800 million, over a quarter of the world's inhabitants, revolted against colonialism. Never before had so revolutionary a reversal occurred with such rapidity![33]

The Labour government in Whitehall and the pressures from Roosevelt in Washington precipitated the downfall. Long ago, John Strachey, the civil servant, had expounded the thesis that India did

---

29   4 Dec. 1920, CWMG (Nov. 1920-Apr. 1921), p. 69.

30   'I do not consider myself worthy to be mentioned in the same breath with the race of prophets. I am a humble seeker after truth, impatient to realize myself, to attain *moksha* [spiritual deliverance] in this very existence. ...
I have no desire for the perishable kingdom of earth. I am striving for the kingdom of Heaven, which is *moksha*.' 3 Apr. 1924, Iyer (ed.), *The Essential Writings of Mahatma Gandhi*, p. 32.

31   Fischer, *The Life of Mahatma Gandhi*, p. 492.

32   Ashe, *Gandhi*, p. 47.

33   Geoffrey Barraclough, *An Introduction to Contemporary History* (London, 1964), p. 153.

not possess any sort of physical, political, social or religious unity.[34] He was wide off the mark. India is a myth and an idea, a dream, and a vision, and yet very real and present and pervasive, Jawaharlal stated. Unity survived in language and literature, in revenue manuals, legal codes, census reports, and ethnographic literature. What was indistinct to some at the time appeared in full glow after Independence. Holmes reassured Gandhi: 'Of course, you have been sad, well-nigh overborne, by the tragedies of recent months, but you must never feel that this involves any breakdown of your life work.'[35]

The story of sacred rivers is the story of a civilisation, of the ascent and descent of empires, of imposing and proud cities, of the adventure of man and the quest of the mind which has so engaged thinkers, of the richness and fulfilment of life as well as its denial and renunciation, of ups and downs, of growth and decay, of life and death. The sacred rivers are, in short, emblems of unity. The same motif, incidentally, describes Gandhi's martyrdom.

> The Ganga and the Yamuna have been throughout the ages the classic rivers that have taken into their bosom the ashes of the many millions of men and women who sought the final absolution in the united waters; but never in the history of India have the Ganga and the Yamuna received the ashes of so glorious a human being whose life and death are an imperishable example for us to revere and emulate.[36]

Late in 1947, Gandhi assented, grudgingly, to the title 'Mahatma'. A young and sophisticated Indian prince asked a British author: 'Tell me what he is really like.' The author came back with the answer: 'That is too difficult a question. What would you say if I asked you to describe Christ?'[37]

That year, on 19 October, the chill in the air had delayed Gandhi's prayer meeting beyond the usual time: 6.30 p.m. As always, a truly

---

34   John Strachey, *India: Its Administration and Progress* (London, 1911), p. 5.

35   Fischer, op. cit., p. 492.

36   Sarojini Naidu, in Sengupta, *Sarojini Naidu*, p. 331.

37   Rosita Forbes, *Princely India* (Delhi, 2009, rpt), p. 39.

powerful ritual fused the ethos and the people's worldview, evoking a broad range of moods and motivations, on the one hand, and metaphysical conceptions, on the other. As the sound of a *bhajan* rented the air with Maganlal's favourite song—the poet expressing disappointment at not seeing God face to face—the night of waiting seemed like ages. Maganlal's God was the realisation of the dream of swaraj, i.e. the Kingdom of God. As the *bhajan* wafted to him, or was more remotely heard, Gandhi sat silently with a gentle pleasure gleaming over his face, brighter now, and now a little dimmer. He announced that as the days were getting shorter the prayer meetings from Monday would be held half an hour earlier. He was conscious of this admirably arranged life in progress every day. He gazed mournfully around him, as if missing something precious, and missing it the more acutely, for he knew exactly what it was. Maganlal was no more; his death had left a deep void in Gandhi's life.

'Action is my domain,' Gandhi had said in March 1946. This is a precise statement. It says, and with some truth, that 'the world, doesn't hunger for *shastras*. What it craves, and will always crave, is sincere action.'[38] He didn't fear death: in fact, when his brother died he shared his feelings with Kallenbach. 'It is because we fear death so much for ourselves that we shed tears over the death of others.' He added:

> How could one who knows the body to be perishable & the soul to be imperishable mourn over the separation of body from soul? But there is condition attached to a real belief in this beautiful and consoling doctrine. He who believes in it must not pamper the body to master him. And to grieve over the death of others is to accept a state almost of perpetual grief. For this connection between the body & soul is itself grievous.[39]

In quoting this passage I do not imply that Gandhi had any premonitions of what was coming. My point rather is that his countenance conveyed

---

38 *Harijan*, 3 March 1946, Iyer (ed.), *The Essential Writings of Mahatma Gandhi*, p. 42.

39 Gandhi to Kallenbach, n.d., Steve Linde papers.

the deepest sorrow that is consistent with resignation.[40] This people observed at the 19 October prayer meeting. He spoke freely, in short sentences. Despite the hostile climate around him, he was prepared to die for Truth and *ahimsa* in order to give a much-needed sense of their value in politics. There is no evidence to cloud belief in his single-mindedness. 'There is art in dying also. As it is, all die, but one has to learn by practice how to die a beautiful death,' he wrote in October 1946.[41] Once, he quoted Prophet Mohammad: 'Be in the world like a traveller, or like a passer on, and reckon yourself as of the dead.' With escalating, death seemed like 'a glorious deliverance'. On 30 January, he sent for his letters: 'I must reply to them today, for tomorrow I may never be.'[42] It was 5.00 p.m. Would he live or die? He would be a true Mahatma if he were to die by an assassin's bullet.[43]

Abul Hasan Ali Nadwi headed the Nadwat al-ulama, Lucknow's famous seminary. In January 1948, he performed Haj, an obligatory duty for every believer. When he reached home on the 30th, friends and followers greeted him at Charbagh railway station. Just when he was exchanging pleasantries, a bomb exploded at a prayer meeting in New Delhi. The Firangi Mahalis were dumbfounded by the news; the elderly remembered Abdul Bari hosting Gandhi in 1920. Not too far from Chowk/Nakhas, the physical location of Firangi Mahal, the stately Mahmudabad House in Qaiser Bagh wore a deserted appearance, as if Muharram had seized its pious inmates. Remember, this is where the Congress-League entente was signed in December 1916. Remember, too, that the Nehrus caught their first glimpse of Gandhi at Mahmudabad House, the home of an earnest nationalist. It is often the case in history that people who saved others weren't able to save themselves. This happened to Gandhi.[44] The sun was shining, as it

---

40   See Mirabehn, in *Bapu's Letters to Mira 1924-1948*, p. 366.

41   Gandhi to Harihar Sharma, 21 Oct. 1946, *CWMG* (21 Oct. 1946-20 Feb. 1947), p. 6.

42   Tendulkar, *Mahatma*, vol. 8, p. 287.

43   Manubehn, *Last Glimpses of Bapu*, p. 252; Pyarelal, *Mahatma Gandhi*, vol. 1, p. 562; Tendulkar, *Mahatma*, vol. 8, p. 345.

44   Gandhi, *Speeches and Writings*, p. xiii.

were, on him but melted into a gloom as soon as he was gone. *Allah-o-Akbar, Allah-o-Akbar*, the muezzin called for prayers from Shah Najaf, the mausoleum named after Ali Ibn-i Abu Talib the Prophet's gallant, fearless, and learned cousin and son-in-law. *La-ilaha-illalah*, the prayer leader announced from Mehrauli, Delhi. Qutubbidin Bakhtiyar Kaki, a venerable Sufi in the line of Chishti saints, endeared themselves to Hindus and Muslims alike. Gandhi saved his shrine during the Partition riots.[45]

The cobbler on the main street of Daryaganj mourned Gandhi's death. Sitting in a dark corner with his tool box and broken sandals spread before him, he was saying almost as if to himself: 'Gandhiji is dead. Murdered, they say. Who would murder a good man, a saint?'[46] Vijaya Lakshmi Pandit remembered reading a poem with her brother when they hadn't met Gandhi. It told of a time when the world thought the sun was dying, and there would be darkness on earth forever. Then, from a shadowed corner, an earthen lamp said, 'Light me, and I will do the best I can.'[47]

Kamaladevi, who fought for Hindu Women's Right to Divorce and to prevent polygamous marriages, was a high priestess in the temple of freedom. She felt alone in a vast empty void, with not one she could hold on to, nothing she could look up to. The Mahatma died even as he had lived, adhering to his principles no matter what the cost.[48] She watched the millions gather in deathly silence, too stunned, bewildered and dumb. Occasionally, she'd hear *Mahatma Gandhi Amar Raho* (Long Live Mahatma Gandhi), but the shriek would vanish into the fading light. There was no answering voice, not even an echo. A million throats were frozen amidst an eerie, weird, and unreal scene.[49] Bob Dylan could sing that:

> There was a man named Mahatma Gandhi
> He would not bow down, he would not fight

---

45   Gandhi, *The Way to Communal Harmony*, p. 74.

46   Anita Desai, *Clear Light of Day* (Delhi, 1980), p. 93.

47   R.H. Andrews, *A Lamp for India*, p. 4.

48   Chattopadhyay, *Inner Recesses, Outer Spaces*, p. 309.

49   Kamaladevi, in Hasan (ed.), *India Partitioned*, vol.2, pp. 210-12, 278.

He knew the deal was down and dirty
And nothing wrong could make it right away
But he knew his duty and the price he had to pay
Just another holy man who tried to be a friend
My God, they killed him.[50]

Yes, a glory had departed and the sun that had warmed and brightened the lives of people had set. An American writer introduced another thought: 'Prophets like him [Gandhi] must end as martyrs. It is inevitable.'[51] Yes, of course. Martyrs live forever (*zinda-i javed*) in the Sunni, Islamic tradition; immortality is Allah's reward for their lifelong service to humanity.

'The only thing that matters,' Jawaharlal wrote many years earlier but is aptly fit for Gandhi, 'is the cause that one works for, and if one could be sure that the best service to it is to die for it, then death would seem simpler.'[52] His generation had reasons to rejoice the triumph of the ideals that had spurred Gandhi to action and kept them buoyed through stormy weather. The memory of the old days of their unbroken companionship lingered; no charm could be more sweet and tender than the joyous convert of comrades which old times recall, and it is this charm that hallowed Jawaharlal and his colleagues.

Who was this extraordinary man? He was the man who more than anyone else helped to supersede the Raj. He was the one who received in death homage beyond the dreams of any viceroy. He died one evening; the cremation took place the following morning.

The viceroy's leading aide had his last *darshan* of him along the imperial avenue. Without a long-heralded state funeral, he saw people flock within the hour and by the hundred thousand for one last glimpse. Who, in the face of this overwhelming tribute, could honestly assert that Gandhi had no genuine following?[53] The Good Boatman's death 'printed on millions of minds in India and elsewhere, the reminder

---

50   L.I. and S.H. Rudolph, *Postmodern Gandhi and Other Essays*, p. 33.

51   Chattopadhyay, *Inner Recesses, Outer Spaces*, p. 313.

52   5 May 1933, Iyengar and Zackariah (eds), *Together They Fought*, p. 182.

53   Campbell-Johnson, *Mission with Mountbatten*, p. 278.

that justice and reconciliation are goals worth dying for.[54] The 'Sole Spokesman' wouldn't have known what this was all about.

Part of Gandhi's ashes were committed to the Hooghly at the bend of the river between Serampore and Barrackpore. The committal was to be from a barge anchored in the middle of the river. Then, at the critical moment, the police launch hooted for silence but pandemonium broke out instead. Every launch and steamer on the river hooted. Benthall, an eyewitness, concluded:

> The strange thing wasn't that all this was unseemly but as if Gandhi was going to his last rest with a sort of unpremeditated Last Post which seemed thoroughly appropriate to the occasion and even more impressive than a continuation of silence which would have no beginning and no end.[55]

We have another vivid description of what happened. It is so moving that I reproduce it in full.

> The news of Mahatma Gandhi's death came through the other evening. Everything stopped. It was as though all the clocks in India stood still in time and everything stopped with them. Thought even, seemed numbed. Taxis, horse-drawn vehicles, rickshaws, went home. Shops and cinemas closed. People gathered in small groups and spoke in hushed tones. A friend came in and cried like a child. Others came to hear our radio; they sat listening with tears running down their faces. A servant came and asked me 'Is this the end of us all?' We all prayed, Hindu, Muslim and Christian alike that the assassin might not prove to be a Muslim or a refugee. When Jawaharlal announced over the radio that later evening that he was a Hindu from central India, a breath of relief went over the entire country.
>
> The next day was a day apart—stopped in time we thought about the simple little dauntless man who had been for so long

---

54   Rajmohan Gandhi, 'Looking for the Dust', p. 37.

55   Diary, p. 117, Benthall papers.

India's voice and heart. Told the people to gather at the time of the funeral and pray, if possible beside open water, if there was no water in parks and open spaces. I took a friend to help with the language and drove out to tell as many outlying villages as I could so that they might not miss out from the ceremonial of common grief.

Men were working in the fields, in the lime quarries, in all the daily occupations of caste and village. Wherever a group of men worked together we told them the news. They too stood stunned. Then: 'We will stop work and go home,' they said simply, 'and at the time appointed, we will gather together and pray.' It wrung our hearts to share the loss with them; where would they go leaderless, the poor men of India?

We prayed then together, all religions, all nationalities in this land. Parsis prayed in the fire temples, Christians in the churches, Muslims in the mosques, vast multitudes grief stricken beside the rivers and open spaces. In Allahabad, they said that even the birds prayed, that a flock of starlings hovered over the funeral there. We prayed together, the people of India, prayed remembering the years of the Mahatma's work for the oppressed, his long fasts in the cause of unity, his years in jail for the objects he believed in, his march to the sea to right a wrong, his still longer journey in his old age, barefooted, to bring peace back to devastated villages. Hatred didn't frighten him; danger he could brush aside; death he could welcome when it came, as a friend.

When they no longer ask: 'Is he Hindu? Is he Muslim? Is he Christian, Parsi or Sikh? Is he North, South, East or West?' When they ask only, 'is he a citizen of a united India?' then only will they have walked in Mahatma Gandhi's footsteps and carried out his plan.[56]

The CWC singled out Birla House as a national memorial, but Jawaharlal didn't approve of a capitalist's home. Similarly, Patel couldn't conceive of a more objectionable way of perpetuating Gandhi's memory or of

---

56　　　Hicks Collection.

bequeathing to the nation and to posterity a reminder of that great and grim calamity.[57]

Ab Dua-i neem shab mein kis ko yaad aenge hum

IN WHOSE MIDNIGHT PRAYER WILL I DWELL NOW?

A leading Congressman from Madras raised two important questions in 1940. These were: Is Gandhiji to be adored and worshipped like a lifeless tree or stone or is his dynamic message to be put into force on an organised basis?[58] Harivansh Rai Bachchan, the Hindi poet, cites a large chunk from Brij Narain Chakbast, the Urdu poet from Lucknow, and his generous tribute to Gokhale and says that much of it now seems equally apt for Gandhi. Progressive Urdu poets put in writing how Gandhi filled the country with something of his own spirit, bold and daring, and developed an ethos in which they made sacrifices. They pictured him living in a world of truth and harmony and not discord and violence. The masses thought of him with respect and gratitude. His willingness to put his experience at their disposal never failed, and some of them remembered how, after his visit to Champaran, he would proceed to his discourse with utmost care and gravity. In whatever form we'd like to see it, Gandhi has endured in many circles and in different forms; even amongst the environmentalists. In the forefront of the popular discourses, which blame the model of development for the environmental crisis, and many Gandhians have been involved with people's movement of various kinds since the mid-1970s.[59]

Gandhi had, indeed, set in motion 'a great wave of purification … [to] wash off the accumulated toxin of centuries in the old body of Sanathan Dharma.'[60] In the Poona Pact, he neither doubted the justice of the arrangements, nor about the general nature of the attempted settlement. Today, the constitutional guarantees to the Dalits mirror

---

57   Patel to Jawaharlal, 13 May 1948, in Durga Das (ed.), *Sardar Patel's Correspondence, 1945-50*, (Ahmedabad, 1973), vol. 6, pp. 71-73.

58   V. Sadananda to Nirmal Kumar Bose, 3 July 1940, N.K. Bose papers.

59   Sumi Krishna, 'The Environmental Discourse in India: New Directions in Development', in T.V. Sathyamurthy (ed.), *Class Formation and Political Transformation in Post-Colonial India* (Delhi, 1996).

60   Ibid., p. 111.

his agenda, they are wide and deep. Sure enough, their lives are still beset with difficulties and hardships and embittered by inhuman caste practices, but their status has improved considerably over time. Sure enough, untouchability exists in the rural hinterland, but Gandhi's crusade is a powerful weapon to combat the scourge. With Dalit consciousness scaling new heights, the seeds Gandhi had sown are bound to fructify in the future.

We may be sure that Gandhi saw women not as objects of reform and humanitarianism, but as self-conscious arbiters of their own destiny.[61] He showed to many of them a picture of a new life through action-oriented policies.[62] He could have, so to speak, done more, but went ahead of most in a society where the education of sons was a prime consideration and the woman's place considered to be at home. He changed not only their status but encouraged them, without disturbing patriarchy, to contribute as equals in the fight for swaraj. Swimming in the waters of tradition was good, but to sink in them was suicidal. As an illustration of what I mean I will quote a passage by Kamaladevi in Halide Edip's *Inside India*:

When Mahatma Gandhi decided to break the Salt Law by which the poor man's salt was taxed, it seemed the most natural thing for us to follow his path and plunge into the movement. Particularly for us women it was our golden morn of glory. In one instant age-old walls seemed to crumble under some magic touch, chains of tradition broke, veils of old usages were torn and women came out of their century-old seclusion into the wide glare of the battlefield as radiant soldiers in the cause of freedom. It was a great revelation for all of us who were at the time working amidst the women, and chafing at their slowness. This rise of women to heroic heights I put down as the most striking feature of the Civil Disobedience movement and my happiest association in it.[63]

---

61   Madhu Kishwar, 'Gandhi on Women', *EPW*, Oct. 1985, p. 1698.

62   Chattopadhyay, *Inner Recesses, Outer Spaces*, p. 47.

63   Edip, *Inside India*, pp. 268-9.

No wonder then that Gandhi's movements produced an extraordinary mix of talented and imaginative women.

Little by little the course of events swept them along with the tide and they were carried away. Sarojini Naidu, who combined her widely-acclaimed poetry with wisdom, was one of them. Her conversations and warmth were irresistible,[64] but she also commented on the government's woeful and even wilful ignorance of conditions, opinions, and aspirations about India.[65] She didn't expect justice from those who were as a race so blind and drunk with the arrogance of power.[66] In 1925, she was pitchforked into the Congress presidency. Aldous Huxley, the English writer, was present in Kanpur when she spoke. What he saw he described, including Sarojini Naidu consoling the nation in agony. This is what she said: 'I, who have rocked the cradle—I who have sung soft lullabies—I, the emblem of Mother India, am now to kindle the flame of libety ... In electing me chief among you, through a period fraught with grave issues and fateful decisions, you have reverted to an old tradition and restored to Indian women the classic epoch of our country's history.'

The next year, Sarojini Naidu told the women at the Prayag Mahila Samiti, an organisation concerned with women's education and political participation, that they were the custodians of the destiny of race and must exercise their rights. Sometime during the year, Gandhi vowed 'not to accept any public engagement', and not to leave the Sabarmati Ashram in Ahmedabad. Sarojini Naidu addressed one of her letters to him in July 1926, 'From the Wandering Singer to The Spinner-Stay-At-Home, Greetings'.

Honours and distinctions were already showered upon Sarojini Naidu. In 1928, she visited the United States of America and kept Gandhi informed of the freedom fighters in that country. In 1929, she presided over the East Africa Congress in Mombasa, and delivered lectures all over South East Africa. In January 1932, she attended the

---

64   Tyabji, *Memoirs of an Egoist*, p. 35.

65   Sarojini Naidu to Gandhi, 17 July 1919, in Paranjape (ed.), *Sarojini Naidu: Selected Letters*, p. 142.

66   Ibid., p. 147. The following references are based on Sengupta, op. cit., pp. 177-78; Nehru (ed.), *A Bunch of Old Letters*, p. 25; Chagla, *Roses in December*, p. 89.

Round Table Conference as a representative of Indian womanhood; the Congress Working Committee permitted her to go to London as such. V.S. Srinivas Sastri, a loyalist, wondered how she was included in the Indian delegation. She replied: 'I came here because my leader Mahatma Gandhi was not quite sure of the wisdom of the East and insisted on his being supported by the immemorial wisdom of the women of the East!'

Durgabai Deshmukh was another extraordinary woman of those times, untiring in her efforts to address the plight of the *devadasis*, 'servants of the gods', who were virtually temple prostitutes. She attended the Kakinada session of the Congress in 1923, where she received her political inspiration from Gandhi.

> Who can supply the impetus for greater understanding and magnanimity more than the women's organisations? ... They are out to use their great faith in recently acquired civic powers, to change the whole scheme of life, re-moulding it nearer to the heart's desire. Let India merit their serious thought and support![67]

This is Rameshwari Nehru, editor of the Hindi magazine *Stri Darpan* (Mirror of Womanhood). She looked up to Gandhi as 'the personification of the spirit of the ancient Hindu Dharma'.[68] A young woman, she had made up her mind about the great isues of life and the way in which she should direct her own life. Without being lured into accepting office, she joined the Harijan Sevak Sangh in October 1932, worked for the eradication of untouchability, and promoted truth-force and moral striving. In 1935, she toured Travancore in support of temple entry. The Royal Proclamation followed, and all temples were thrown open to Dalits. A miracle in a state where even the shadow of a Harijan was considered to pollute a caste Hindu! In 1928, at the age of nineteen, crusader, activist and rebel, Aruna Ganguli defied convention to marry a Muslim lawyer, Asaf Ali, participated in the Salt Satyagraha

---

[67]   Rameshwari Nehru, *"Gandhi is My Star": Speeches and Writings* (Patna, 1950), p. 201.

[68]   Ibid., p. 89, Sushila Nayar and Kamla Mankekar (eds), *Women Pioneers in India's Renaissance* (Delhi, 2002).

and, in the early 1930s, worked with the Women's League affiliated to the All Indian Women's Conference. During the Quit India campaign, she went underground to stand out as a fighter.[69] Similarly, Mridula Sarabhai, daughter of the industrialist Ambalal Sarabhai, and her three aunts, Anasuya, Nirmala, and Indumati, spent several years in jail during the 1930s and 1940s. She, Subhadra Dutt (later Joshi), and Anis Kidwai displayed unsurpassed courage in rehabilitating refugees and in rescuing abducted women.[70] The Little Man worked his magic on them. Anis Kidwai came to Gandhi to drown her grief—her husband had been murdered in Mussoorie in October 1947—in the hope that she might stumble on some clue to the future. Gandhi motivated her not to become appendages to anyone but an individual moving forward with dynamic urges. He sent her to Sushila Nayar to work in the Purana Qila camp.[71]

Since then, Anis Kidwai nurtured an appreciation of Gandhi's 'high ideals, his simple life, his sweet words—and the way he had been made the target of his opponents' ire and sarcasm.'[72]

The glowing candle of intellect,
The stars that illumine the mind,
The passion that burns in the heart—
All these lamps have borrowed their light from thy *mehfil*.

---

69   Nehru, 'When Freedom Beckoned', in Verinder Grover and Ranjana Arora (eds), *Aruna Asaf Ali: Her Contribution to Political, Economic and Social Development* (Delhi, 1994).

70   Aparna Basu, *Mridula Sarabhai: Rebel with a Cause* (Delhi, 1996); Mushirul Hasan, *From Pluralism to Separatism: Qasbas in Colonial Awadh*, p. 67.

71   Kidwai, *In Freedom's Shade*, pp. 20-21.

72   Ibid., p. 22.

15
'Bapu is Finished'—Is He?[1]

You with bloodshot eyes and bloody hands
Night is short-lived.
The detention room lasts not forever
Nor yet the links of chain
-Mahmoud Darwish, *The Music of Human Flesh*.

Blood, toil, tears, and sweat were present still but paradoxically Gandhi's assassination, instead of polarising Hindu-Muslim sentiments hastened the collapse of the Mahasabha and led to the banning of the RSS. Public revulsion against them came out strongly. Angry demonstrations were followed by the stoning of Syama Prasad Mookerjee's house in Calcutta. In the 1952 elections, the Jan Sangh and the Ram Rajya Parishad failed to convince the electorate of their worn-out communal concepts and religious prejudice. Instead, a great many people stood up to promote Gandhi's powerful message against reviling one another's religion. JP and Vinoba Bhave's Shanti Sena contended with violence in Bihar.[2] The integration of some 565 odd princely states was less of a headache, though collectively they comprised a major slice of the pre-1947 Indian body politic: two-fifth of the area and one-third of the erstwhile Indian empire, excluding Burma. At the beginning of the nineteenth century, Hyderabad State was as large as Turkey, Italy or Great Britain, and almost equal in size to Kashmir, Gwalior and Indore combined. Its erratic Nizam, Mir Osman Ali Khan, presided over a kingdom whose income and expenditure in 1947 rivalled Belgium's and exceeded that of twenty member states of the United Nations. He naively believed that he could stay out of the Union and proclaimed independence. However, the Police Action in September 1948 shattered

---

1   This is the heading of a chapter in E.S. Jones, *Mahatma Gandhi*, p. 191.

2   Hardiman, *Gandhi in his Time and Ours*, pp. 191-95.

his dreams. The misguided Razakars were disbanded, their leader fleeing to Pakistan.

In Hyderabad, the path from feudalism to democracy was arduous and those who enjoyed privileges in the past were reluctant to join in the march of time. Yet the Nizam, already unpopular with the vast majority of the people, capitulated. After the Police Action, popular opinion in Hyderabad inclined to a coalition between state Congress and the Socialists.

The Communists led an armed struggle in the Telengana region of Hyderabad State. At its height, over three million people in 3,000 villages spread over several districts in Telengana fell under its influence. The second Congress of the Communist Party of India, held at Calcutta in February 1948, had already concluded the conditions for armed revolution were ripe in India following Ranadive's thesis of insurrection to seize power. P.C. Joshi was replaced by Ranadive, a new militant leader, influenced by R.P. Dutt's interventions, criticized the bourgeois leadership. He wasn't, however, the only one to ask: Freedom from what and for whom?

For anyone looking down on the world of the 1950s and comparing it with the world of 1915 or 1920, nothing will probably be more striking than the transformed leadership. True, the kind of India which Gandhi visualised as the Utopian fulfilment of swaraj was by no means the India which the Congress party had in view. Nonetheless the political classes, undeterred by the forebodings of a tired postcolonial bureaucracy, reconciled the ambiguities of the inclusive ideology within a single differentiated political structure and appropriated its meanings in the body of the same discourse. The constituent assembly meeting in New Delhi at midnight on 14 August 1947 put in place a federal and democratic constitution, concurred with the pluralist principles which Gandhi had enunciated, held in contempt the language of *pratishodh* and *pratikaar,* all synonyms for revenge, retribution, and retaliation, and maintained an equidistance of the state from all religions.[3] Its definition of secularism neither conflicted with

---

3   Christophe Jaffrelot, *Religion, Caste and Politics in North India* (Delhi, 2010).

an individual's beliefs nor threatened religious identities. Historically speaking, the constitution expressed the nationalistic ideal of 'Unity in Diversity'.

Long ago, Iqbal had speculated that 'the process of becoming a nation is a kind of travail and in the case of Hindu India involves a complete overhauling of her social structure'. He doubted whether the gamble of elections, retinues of party leaders, and hollow pageants of parliaments will suit the peasants for whom a money-economy of modern democracy is absolutely incomprehensible. Nation-building, then and now, has not involved the overhauling of social structures as such, whereas adult suffrage and democratic institutions, the significance of which was of little consequence to Iqbal and his pro-landlord oriented politics, has brought some relief to the masses.

A total of 36 million voted in 1937, an average of 27.6 per cent of the population. In the first general election in 1952, 170 million men and women lined up at the polling booths. There were a total of 18,300 candidates, 224,000 polling booths, and 3,293 constituencies. Indians had at last spoken their mind in no uncertain terms. Gandhi's dream of placing the peasant and the 750,000 villages on the map was beginning to become a reality. This great experiment should not be judged either by the tough-and-ready operation of its machinery or the comparative ignorance of the electorate. It is as an educational process in the business of learning democracy that we should regard the 1952 election.[4] The cynics were to discover, the golden key of democracy opened new doors to progress and prosperity: 'in front of us the road still stretches long and hard but steadily we move forward to a new life in which the fruits of freedom and democracy will be available to each one of India's large family'. Everything about Indian democracy that appears familiar or inexplicable in terms of modern democracies, must not be flung into the basket of Indian exceptionalism.[5]

---

4   Lord Birdwood, *A Continent Decides* (London, 1953), p. 111.

5   V.L. Pandit, *The Evolution of India* (London, 1958), p. 46; Niraja Gopal Jayal (ed.), *Democracy in India* (Delhi, 2001); Ramchandra Guha, *India After Gandhi*.

The Congress chose a pair of bullocks as its symbol. The Socialists, who resigned from the UP Assembly and the Congress on 31 March 1948, mocked the choice: what use were a couple of bullocks yoked together without a driver? How would they know where to go? They might even want to wander in different directions!

Unable to deal fully with all these aspects, I have restricted myself to a passing reference to Jawaharlal, three months short of his fifty-eighth birthday. Attired in an *achkan*, with a crimson rose tucked in his buttonhole, churidar pyjama, and a Gandhi cap, all in spotless white *khaddar*, he persuaded the nation to accept that what its citizens desired was attainable, and that he, through his visualisation, was the man to achieve their goals. Independence was his most elevated moment, as also the darkest, when he saw the concept of secularism and its rising edifice in tatters. He fought desperately, as his dreams were all woven around India's glowing future.[6] The legend had grown that he'd make a good prime minister in normal times but fail in a crisis; at the end of the day, he gave a certain direction and thrust to the nation-building goals and reassured the nation, reeling under the bloodbath of Partition, that anarchy wouldn't be allowed a free run.

Was he an aristocrat? 'No,' said Ram Manohar Lohia, his most trenchant socialist critic in parliament. 'I can prove that the prime minister's grandfather was a *chaprasi* in the Mughal court.' Jawaharlal retorted: 'I am glad the Hon'ble Member has at last accepted what I have been trying to tell him for so many years—that I am a man of the people!'[7] That he was.

One morning Horace Alexander came to meet Gandhi. When Jawaharlal dropped by, he withdrew across the room to let the two discuss Delhi's nightmare. Then, to Alexander's astonishment, the two laughed. When the prime minister emerged from the room a few minutes later, Alexander realised the enormity of the task ahead of him.[8] All agreed that he would confront the turmoil of communalism.

---

6 Chattopadhyay, *Inner Recesses, Outer Spaces*, pp. 313.

7 B.K. Nehru, *Nice Guys Finish Second*, p. 65.

8 Horace Alexander, 'Mahatma Gandhi: What Manner of Man?' Benthall papers, box 2.

The hero's victory, commented Toynbee after meeting with Jawaharlal, is not his alone; it is a common victory for mankind.[9]

From 1947 to 1950, Benthall met Jawaharlal sometimes in the company of others, and occasionally alone. Once they met in Calcutta. The prime minister sat at a desk that had on it a large inkpot, some pens and pencils, and the weighty volume of Thacker's *Indian Directory*. The discussion proceeded, but after a while some Marwaris wanted the army to go into East Pakistan to rescue beleaguered Hindus. Jawaharlal listened before he lost his temper, picked up the directory, raised it to the full length of his arms above his head, and brought it smashing down on the desk. He repeated this action three or four times, leaving the inkpot, pens, etc., scattered on the floor. He lambasted the Marwaris of deliberately planning a massacre of Muslims, though he reminded them Jainism forbade its adherents from taking up arms or even crushing a mosquito. He continued with extraordinary eloquence until the Marwaris slunk out of the room.[10]

In Delhi, Jawaharlal intervened wherever justice was delayed or denied on account of the draconian evacuee property laws which deprived Muslims from getting back their properties, and owing to the unauthorised occupation of *waqf* properties and mosques. He denied the existence of conflict potential and assumed that they were constructed to disturb the ideal world of harmonious living. His mission, to which he was committed, was to change the provincial outlook and adhere to liberal and democratic principles. People who talked of Hindu culture, he said, rejected the assimilating and absorbing nature of an ancient and glorious culture and showed a narrow, barren, and limited outlook on life. He expected them to keep the windows and doors of their minds open and to let all the winds from the four corners of the earth blow in to refresh their minds. This they never did.

---

9   Arnold J. Toynbee, *Acquaintances*, p. 300.

10   Benthall added that no Hindus were massacred in East Bengal at that time, though hundreds of thousands were driven out to take refuge in West Bengal. Nehru was of course right in refusing to send the army across the new frontier, and his violent reactions to such a suggestion were characteristic of the man.

'Except as regards books,' JP referring to Jawaharlal's arrest, 'he does not take advantage of the latitude shown to him [by the British].'[11] Indeed, his books show not only a 'beauty of soul, nobility of ideal, and egocentrism', but the changes in attitudes to science and religion. They deal with the concomitants and consequences of colonial rule, and almost all of them are written within a wider framework of the changes accompanying it. One is proud of *The Discovery of India*, not for its intrinsic merits, which are great, but for the humane and sympathetic spirit towards the sufferings of the colonised people that permeates it. Nehru's autobiography scrutinised both self and events. There was something moving about the narration of India's hopes and aspirations. They drew readers to Jawaharlal as a duck to water.[12]

Sections of the Muslim intelligentsia distinguished between the political integration that Jawaharlal envisioned, and assimilation, Hindutva's pet project. They were prepared for political integration but not cultural absorption. Madani, the Deoband head, regarded the 'nations' based on ethnicity, language, and territory, whereas he identified and classified 'communities' by ties of faith. Indian Muslims therefore formed an *Indian* nation together with the Hindus, even as they remained part of an invisible, global *umma*.[13] Madani's message was 'to act with fortitude and endurance, perseverance and high mindedness, endurance, to be assiduously engaged in strengthening Islam is our and your religious duty.' Unlike Maududi and some Barelwi ulama,

---

11   JP to Roger N. Baldwin, 11 June 1930, Bimal Prasad (ed.), *Jayaprakash Narayan: Selected Works*, vol. 1, p. 50.

12   In his foreword to the second Hebrew edition, published in 1957, Jawaharlal recalled: 'This book was written when we in India were in the middle of our struggle for freedom. That struggle was long drawn out and it brought many experiences of joy and sorrow, of hope and despair. But the despair didn't last long because of the inspiration that came to us from our leader, Mahatma Gandhi, and the deep delight of working for a cause that took us out of our little shells.... All of us are older now and our days of youth are long past. Yet, even now, when we face the troubles and torments that encompasses, something of that old memory of our leader gives us strength.'

13   Muhammad Qasim Zaman, *The Ulama in Contemporary Islam: Custodians of Change* (Princeton and Oxford, 2002), pp. 32-37; Y. Friedmann, 'The Attitude of the *Jam'iyyati-i 'Ulama-i Hind* to the Indian National Movement and the establishment of Pakistan', Hasan (ed.), *Inventing Boundaries*, p. 173.

he insisted on the flexibility of Islam in adjusting to different social configurations and in interacting with non-Muslims. On the strength of their arguments, he favoured a united, secular nation-state.[14]

'We must demonstrate to the Mussalmans that their interests are quite safe in the hands of the Congress ... Within the Congress itself they must be made to feel that they are not strangers and that it is as much their organisation as it is that of the Hindus.' These words of wisdom came from Acharya Narendra Deva while the Congress ministries were in power in December 1937.[15] After Independence, family after family gravitated towards Jawaharlal.[16] They needed not so much their own leaders who were fishing in muddy waters, but the prime minister.[17] In season and out of season, through good and evil repute, inside the ministerial camp and out of the House, Rafi Ahmad Kidwai a minister, was chiefly concerned to safeguard his prime minister's position vis-à-vis right-wing conservatives. Without batting an eyelid, he confessed, 'the last thirty years' association has so developed me that all you say assumes the form of my ideology'.[18] He was even prepared to be the prime minister for six months, but added, 'I will do so well in the job that people may not want Nehru back'. A friend cautioned that the fear of displacement might prevent Jawaharlal from taking leave. Rafi answered back: 'Exactly! I want him to think twice before he relinquishes office.'[19] Beneath Rafi's ebullient, man of the world façade, there ran a sentimental streak.

Tagore likened Jawaharlal to the *rituraj*; to the spirit of spring which is the spirit of eternal youth. Vinoba Bhave said of him, 'After

---

14   Zaman, op. cit.

15   Sharma (ed.), *Selected Works of Acharya Narendra Deva*, vol. 1, p. 109.

16   The Kidwais of Barabanki district in UP; Abdul Majid Khwaja's clan in Aligarh; the descendants of Altaf Husain Hali, led by Khwaja Ahmad Abbas; the Tyabjis of Bombay among whom were some high-profile individuals like the Islamic jurist A.A.A. Fyzee; the descendants of Sir Wazir Hasan of Lucknow (the Zaheer brothers); and Syed Mahmud.

17   Tyabji, *Memoirs of an Egoist*, p. 177.

18   Rafi to Jawaharlal, 17 July 1951, *SWJN*, 2nd series, vol. 14, p. 438.

19   A.P. Jain, *Rafi Ahmed Kidwai: A Memoir of his Life and Times* (London, 1965), p. 5.

Gandhi, his is the one name that stands for India—is India'.[20] Like Krishna who lured the *gopis* (milkmaids) with his flute, Jawaharlal tried to lure the people with the magic of his name.[21] He embodied an idea which moved India on the path of change and progress. An oasis in the desert of illiteracy, superstition, intolerance, and ignorance, he identified the Indian tradition as characterised primarily by the synthesis of multiple streams. Progressive writers and poets, who admired his approach and reactions to ordinary incidents of everyday life, hoped to raise the people's understanding of his contribution so that they wouldn't fritter away their energies in conflicts. The terrible times under the British were an aberration; the better days under Jawaharlal would from now on be the norm. They saw before them an era of happiness and contentment such as their countrymen were deprived of for generations.

However, as the years of bitter strife continued, developmental strategies fell short of promises. Jawaharlal, their architect, became a modern Hamlet, always on the horns of a dilemma that he couldn't boldly overcome. On some other issues he acted precipately without thinking through the problem.[22] JP accused him of building socialism with the help of capitalism; B.T. Ranadive, the Communist leader, of 'compromise, collaboration and national betrayal'. E.M.S. Namboodiripad, Jawaharlal's follower until 1931, rejected the model of bourgeoisie democracy at the very time when the bourgeoisie system had landed itself into a deep crisis. Averse to the privileged, the prime minister could have abolished privy purses which the princes enjoyed but he seem to have followed Gandhi, who had written in December 1939 that 'my picture of free India has a definite place for them [princes]'.[23]

While dreaming and seeing visions of the future, the prime minister knew that many hopes had been dashed and ideals tarnished. For this, he blamed the bureaucracy and the party which was simply

---

20   Frank Moraes, *Jawaharlal Nehru: A Biography* (New York, 1956), p. 491.

21   Ibid., p. 491.

22   Badr-ud-Din Tyabji, in Royle, *Last Days of the Raj*, p. 276.

23   *Harijan*, 16 Dec.1939, *CWMG* (1 Dec. 1939-15 Apr. 1940), p. 24.

fading away before his eyes. The civil service, mostly drawn from the upper castes, used the system to consolidate and enlarge their gains. After Independence, the civil servants got busy, using their family background and contrived Oxbridge accent to milch the not-so fattening Indian cow. Jawaharlal had a weakness for free India's gold-diggers; he didn't want to know that they would not only close avenues of empowerment for the disadvantaged but also retard the country's progress.

On the social/legal front, Jawaharlal could have enforced a uniform civil code but he held back in order to avoid hurting Muslim susceptibilities. This was a feeble response, a soft approach to urgent social issues. One couldn't introduce a degree of enlightenment in one community and leave the others in darkness. The prime minister had to narrow rather than widen the areas of darkness.

Sadly, the liberal Muslim voices were weak. Zakir Husain and his Jamia colleagues defended the status quo. They could have taken a stand, but developed cold feet. They had set their eyes on what eventually came their way, high offices in government. On the other hand, the Muslim orthodoxies possessed, ever after losing the battle, so to speak, the resources to stifle dissent. Their authoritarian structures were intact, and they were, as always, censuring and condemning dissenters. The vocal members of the Jamiyat al-ulama members were reined in through patronage, including nominated seats in the Rajya Sabha or memberships of commissions, the rank and file, mostly impoverished and illiterate, received a free hand to stew in its own juice.

Much pent-up fear and anger boiled over in relation to failures and shortcomings in other spheres as well. The prime minister bowed his head in shame when an old peasant complained of official neglect. That he did, explained why so many relied on him, why they noticed a running thread in his diverse interests and an awareness of the continuity between the past, the present, and future hopes. Why they drew encouragement from his references to the weight of the past, the greatness of the civilisation he had inherited, not as a burden to be carried but as a reference point for judging the moral worth and wisdom of his decisions. He was one of those of whom Keats wrote:

... to whom the miseries of the world
Are misery, and will not let them rest.

Jawaharlal's life became a long succession of tests. External observers reminded him of his ideals, but right-wing elements in the party thwarted his radical notions. A major obvious pressure for ideological conformity came from the home minister, Vallabhbhai Patel, who bustled with aggressive self-assurance owing to the integration of the princely states into the union.

He differed on the Kashmir issue, and made several objectionable remarks in his speech at Lucknow,[24] which were, in fact, 'that of a Congressman who was prepared to envisage members of the Mahasabha and the RSS being admitted to the Congress fold and of a Hindu who felt justified in specifying standards of conduct not only for India's Muslim minority but also for Pakistan.'[25] He suspected Muslim loyalty, encouraged their exodus to Pakistan, and when it came to resettling thousands of Meos who had returned to their homeland, he restricted not only their entry but also ensured that they were kept out of already Muslim pockets.[26]

To such beleaguered groups, Jawaharlal alone offered a glimmer of hope. Once he said to a colleague in a little while after Independence, 'there are only two things left for us now, to go under or overcome our difficulties.'[27] This notwithstanding, he began with a sense of optimism.[28]

---

24   Kidwai, *In Freedom's Shade*, p. 29.

25   B. D. Graham, *Hindu Nationalism and Indian Politics: The Origins and Development of the Bharatiya Jana Sangh* (Cambridge, 1990), p. 10.

26   Patel to Satyamurti, 23 May 1942, Ramanathan (ed.), *The Satyamurti Letters*, p. 361; Patel to K.C. Neogy, 27 Feb. 1948, in Das (ed.), *Sardar Patel's Correspondence*, vol. 6, p. 254, for the Meos. Gopal, *Jawaharlal Nehru*, vol. 2, pp. 155-56; Tyabji, *Memoirs of an Egoist*, p. 178.

27   K.A. Abbas, *The Second Year* (Delhi, 1949), p. 22-25; Peter Manuel, 'Music, the Media and Communal Relations in North India', in Ludden (ed.), *Contesting the Nation*, pp. 127-8. Tunzelmann, *Indian Summer*, p. 235.

28   Patel's death on 15 December 1950, followed by Purshottamdas Tandon's resignation from the Congress presidency, gave respite, but not sufficient to translate his plans into proactive action. Intra-party factionalism and indiscipline compounded Jawaharlal's difficulties.

The arts, music and the dance, even the cinema, provided a more reliable index to the state of the nation than the economists' statistics or the politician's platitudes. Hindustani music and many of the most popular and widespread folk music genres continued to be enjoyed and patronised by members of all religions. The poems of Kabir, synthesising Hindu and Muslim devotion, remain paradigmatic and still-cherished symbols of pluralism. The doors of the Sufi shrines were wide open for the devotees to chant *Allah-o-Akbar, Allah-o-Akbar*. The beacon light lay in many spheres; for example, in the side lanes of creativity.[29] Indian People's Theatre Association (IPTA), a culturally avant-garde theatre group, impacted cinema by producing realist films. Among its leading lights was Zohra Segal of Prithvi Theatre. Two of her Urdu plays—*Dhani Bankey* and *Naukrani ki Talash*, which also starred Shaukat Azmi, became quite famous.[30] In 1953, Bimal Roy's *Do Bigha Zamin* (Two Acres of Land) reflected its imprint at thematic and formal levels.[31] Others signify not only the joy and expectancy of a boisterous, buoyant era but opened the doors of the stage and illumined life. They held street-theatre performances at the gates of Bombay mills, played in *chawls* with skits improvised on the problems of the *chawl*-dwellers, and performed in restaurants.[32] The Bengal IPTA enacted Tagore's *Muktadhara* in Delhi, and a ballet under Uday Shankar's guidance.[33] Habib Tanvir directed Begum Qudsia Zaidi's production. In Delhi's Sapru House, Ustad Bade Ghulam Ali Khan, the great classical singer, held a concert.[34] Elsewhere, poets and writers welcomed the removal of blinders and chains on eyes and hearts without giving up their ceaseless search for that 'Promised Dawn'. They fostered a sense of togetherness in the pursuit of a greater good.

29　　　Chattopadhyay, *Inner Recesses, Outer Spaces*, p. 385.

30　　　Kiran Segal, *Zohra Segal: 'Fatty'* (Delhi, 2012).

31　　　Gupta, *Crisis and Creativities*, p. 207. Jeannine Woods, *Visions of Empire and Other Imaginings: Cinema, Ireland and India 1910-1962* (Bern, 2011), pp. 140-41; Gyan Prakash, *Bombay Fables* (Delhi, 2010), pp. 132-33.

32　　　Vasudha Dalmia, *Poetics, Plays, and Performances: The Politics of Modern Indian Theatre* (Delhi, 2006), p. 253.

33　　　Gupta, *Crisis and Creativities*, p. 208.

34　　　Hyder, *River of Fire*, p. 416.

Stories of survival, triumph, and optimism circulated. Soft winds blew across Roshan Ara Bagh and Bela Road in Delhi. Roses bloomed in the bungalows of the old Civil Lines and New Delhi.[35] With Partition came 4.75 million refugees in India—of these, 495,391 came to Delhi. They accepted their fate with astonishing fortitude, setting up booths not with any apparent sense of despair, but with an animation obviously born of new hope. In Faridabad, twenty minutes out of Delhi, one could discern evidence of those tragic days of 1947, and yet the night glare of the new factories lit up the skyline, and out of the unhappiness of millions emerged the will and opportunity to make a fresh start.[36] Individual fortunes varied and fluctuated: the sense of 'homelessness' and 'nationlessness' seized the Sindhi writer Popati Hiranandani, but in the course of time she and her family were nicely settled.[37] This however wasn't the experience of another family living in the slums of Karachi and Lahore. There was no justice for them in *God's Own Land*.[38]

Dust of the Caravan

Manto is elegiac, melancholic, and inconsolable in the catastrophic collapse of his dream world; the vista before Jawaharlal seemed to have been too glorious to be true. Creative writers tread the same path[39], then and later. The communities that had survived random attacks and the general devastation of riots, now found themselves swimming in calmer waters and exploring the potential for a more liberated life. 'The stories of riots are over. The stories of life had begun, because

---

35   Ibid.

36   Birdwood, *A Continent Decides*, p. 71; V.N. Datta, 'Panjabi Refugees and the Urban Development of Greater Delhi', in Hasan (ed.), *Inventing Boundaries*, pp. 266-284.

37   Hiranandani, *The Pages of My Life*, pp. 83, 84.

38   Shaukat Siddiqi, *God's Own Land (Khuda ki Basti)*, trans. David J. Mathews (Delhi, 1993).

39   The existing literature on the subject is too vast for me to cite, though the stories translated and edited by Alok Bhalla are very useful. Increasingly, our attention is being drawn to the literary writings in Bengali and to scores of autobiographies and memoirs of those who were a witness to the Partition of their province.

the stories of life never end,' wrote Rahi Masoom Reza, author of *Aadha Gaon*.[40] For another Hindi writer, Krishna Sobti, it was the time to rehabilitate and not the time to count the miseries or losses. The great gain, according to her, was to secure the citizenship of a free nation.[41]

It is not as if there were no traces of the catastrophe. There were, but everything that had to be done to restore order was being done, quietly, effectively and promptly. In a sense there was only one *Weltanschauung* of major significance which the poet and writer shared; a number of other views, including the Marxian, were narrow, in the main negative, and ill-considered critiques.

> Tonight a sneeringly hot breeze is blowing,
> Tonight on this footpath there will be no sleep
> Come let us arise, you and I, and you too, and you
> A window in this wall will surely find an opening.[42]
>
> -Kaifi Azmi

Aptly, I conclude not with the tale of blood and tears but with birth and regeneration. Qurratulain Hyder, writing in her inimitable style, depicted the spirit animating the people: 'Jamia Nagar, Nizamuddin Aulia, Lodhi tombs. Everything will be left behind. Life shall continue. The falling off of one man does not make any difference. These were different people now, they had been travelling on a separate road....'[43] 'Instead of dirt and poison', remarked the British poet Mathew Arnold, 'we have rather chosen to fill our hives with honey and wax; thus furnishing mankind with the two noblest of things, which are sweetness and light.'

What if Gandhi was alive today? Perhaps, he would have reiterated what Jawaharlal had written in one of his reflective moods:

---

40   Sudhir Chandra, 'The Harvest of Fear: A Retrospective Critique of Hindu-Muslim Relations in Two Hindi Novels', in T. V. Sathyamurthy (ed.), *Region, Religion, Caste, Gender and Culture in Contemporary India* (Delhi, 1995), p. 199.

41   Hiranandani, *The Pages of My Life*, p. 17.

42   Kaifi Azmi, *Selected Poems*, trans. Pavan K. Varma (Delhi, 2000), p. 3.

43   Hyder, *River of Fire*, p. 418.

I have given you the barest outline; this is not history; they are just fleeting glimpses of our long past. If history interests you, if you feel some of the fascination of history, you will find your way to many books which will help you to unravel the threads of past ages. But reading books alone will not help. If you would know the past you must look upon it with sympathy and with understanding. To understand a person who lived long ago, you will have to understand his environment, the conditions under which he lived, the ideas that filled his mind. It is absurd for us to judge of past people as if they lived now and thought as we do. There is no one to defend slavery today, and yet the great Plato held that slavery was essential. Within recent times scores of thousands of lives were given in an effort to retain slavery in the United States. We cannot judge the past from the standards of the present. Everyone will willingly admit this. But everyone will not admit the equally absurd habit of judging the present by the standards of the past. The various religions have especially helped in petrifying old beliefs and faiths and customs, which may have had some use in the age and country of their birth, but which are singularly unsuitable in our present age.

If, then, you look upon past history with the eye of sympathy, the dry bones will fill up with flesh and blood, and you will see a mighty procession of living men and women and children in every age and every clime, different from us and yet very like us, with much the same human virtues and human failings. History is not a magic show, but there is plenty of magic in it for those who have eyes to see.[44]

The general picture is that the quiet and apparently less eventful periods lay between and after the cataclysmic events of Partition. Personally, I would add that the guiding principle of Gandhi's life, of believing the truth as it appears to us at any given time in any particular situation,[45] inspired Jawaharlal, among the profusely conflicting views, to offer this and many such thoughtful descriptions. They come from truthful

---

44   Jawaharlal, *Glimpses of World History*, pp. 950-1.

45   On this point, *see* Raghavan N. Iyer, *The Moral and Political Thought of Mahatma Gandhi* (Delhi, 2000), p. 169.

and loving men and women, and embodied the spirit of Satyagraha. Their message:

> *Phoolon ki agar havas hai khaaron ko na dekh*
> *Ishrat ki hai dhun to sogwaron ko na dekh*
> *Tameer hayat hai pesh nazar*
> *Mur kar bhi mite hue nazaaron ko na dekh*
> Art thou a lover of flowers, look not at the thorns
> Dost thou want to enjoy thyself, look not at the mourners.
> If thou art intent upon the creation of life, look not back at the
> smouldering graves!
>
> —Josh Malihabadi

Catherine Clement, the French writer, once wrote that 'you cannot divide the two, it is both together—India and Nehru.' A substantial body of people give Jawaharlal the credit of initiating a series of protracted discussions on an extraordinary range of subjects, though they are also uneasy about the distance between reality and hope. Their concerns and fears are justified, and yet, India is not a paralysed or sinking ship. India lives on, as it has done for centuries. Today, Jawaharlal's idea of tolerance and inclusiveness beckons, as it must do, always and forever. We will see many seasons go by, following each other into oblivion. We will watch many moons wax and wane and the pageant of the stars move along inexorably and majestically. The detractors will be busy finding fault, but they will still remain the great men that they were.

Generalisations sound like the definition of an elephant in the fable, in which five blind men describe the proportion of the creature traced by each with his finger. Without venturing into any form of serious comparison,[46] I suggest that any summing cannot dispense with neighbouring Pakistan where a new nation struggled to set its house in order.

---

46   Mushirul Hasan, 'India and Pakistan. Why the Difference?', Mushirul Hasan and Nariaki Nakazato (eds), *The Unfinished Agenda: Nation-Building in South Asia* (Delhi, 2001); Ayesha Jalal, *Democracy and Authoritarianism in South Asia* (Cambridge, 1995).

Jinnah sought to make amends in his oft-quoted speech to the Constituent Assembly on 11 August 1947. It was a noble gesture towards religious minorities, but the genie was out of the bottle. Too much blood was needlessly shed for a nation that would be divided once again in 1971 and is still struggling today against its internal enemies. To Jinnah, Ghalib would have said,

Ki mere qatl ke baad us ne jafa se toba
Haye us zood pashemaan ka pashemaan hona
After my murder, she swore off cruelty/tyranny,
Alas – the repentance of that quick temper!

From today's vantage point, it is arguable that seldom in history did so few err so monumentally in using religion for the purpose of creating a nation. Like the Zionists in Israel, another trouble spot on the world map, Pakistan's ruling elite have exploited Islam as a code word for more subtle propaganda, the reinforcement of stereotypes, the stimulation of fears, and the quieting of disturbing doubts. Some sections of the elite, who help the army to remain in power, also suffer from, what Erich Fromm called 'group narcissism', the myth of the collective superiority of a nation or a community. This seemed to have compensated for feelings of Pakistan not having lived up to the grand vision of its founder.

Viewed from this perspective, Pakistan had a troubled existence from the very start. Farzana Shaikh alludes to its weak foundations.[47] Abdul Rahman Siddiqi, who migrated from Delhi to Karachi, remarks in a recent book: 'The curtain suddenly rose to unfold a tableau of dumbfounded players turned to stone. It had nothing of the gloss and glitter of the dream we had dreamt of, the vision, we had projected on our mental screens of a wonderland with flowers blossoming and birds singing.'[48] The League politicians dressed the Pakistan idea 'in glittering phrases to allure and attract the ignorant masses and this diverted them from the real issue of bread and freedom.'[49] In other

47   Farzana Shaikh, *Making Sense of Pakistan*, p. 209.
48   Siddiqi, *Smoke Without Fire*, p. 263.
49   Sharma (ed.), *Selected Works of Acharya Narendra Deva*, vol. 2, p. 182.

words, the golden age of Pakistan has faded fast, as golden ages do, the Pakistan sky is darkening with the approach of the great storm of fundamentalism.

The ideological betrayal has been assailed by many a poet. Syed Zamir Jafery's (b. 1917) poem *Iqbāl aur Hum* (Iqbal and We) brings the gap between our ideal and our practice into sharp focus:

اقبال کا پیام اخوت کا ترجماں

ملت کو دیکھئے کہ ہے آپس میں ہم نبرد

داعی وہ فقر کا تھا پیمبر خودی کا تھا

تن پر ہمارے قرض کی پوشاکِ لاجورد

کہتا تھا شالا مار میں کل ایک برگِ زرد

"بلبل چہ گفت، گل چہ شنید وصبا چہ کرد''

Iqbal gave us the message of unity,

But the nation is beset with internal strife.

That prophet of self-reliance took pride in poverty,

But we are proud of colorful garments of borrowed luxury.

Yesterday in the Shalamar Gardens, a dry leaf said:

The nightingale said one thing, while the rose understood another and the

Zephyr acted in a totally different manner.

The same conflict between the ideal and the reality inspires Mirza Mahmud Sarhadi to burst out in satire:

ہم نے اقبال کا کہا مانا

اورفاقوں کے ہاتھوں مرتے رہے

جھکنے والوں نے رفعتیں پائیں

ہم خودی کو بلند کرتے رہے

Our commitment to the ideals of Iqbal has brought us

to the brink of death through starvation.

Those who could stoop low acquired the heights of progress while
we struggled hard to preserve our *khudī*.[50]

Meanwhile, as Jawaharlal travelled seeing South Asia's moving drama,
he felt excited and inspired. What struck him was the tremendous
drama, of 'India moving as if by the dictates of some predestined fate
and destiny towards its goal.'[51]

The lamp flickered, the night was at an end; in no time, the gust of
the morning breeze would extinguish it forever. But—

Kar-i duniya kaise tamam na kard
No one has ended the work of the world.[52]

50   Christina Oesterheld and Peter Zoller, *Of Clowns and Gods, Brahmans and
      Babus* (Delhi, 1999), pp. 68-9.
51   Hasan (ed.), *Nehru's India*, p. 183.
52   Kidwai, *In Freedom's Shade*, p. 313.

Select Chronology

1856   Awadh is annexed and Wajid Ali Shah banished to Calcutta. Lord Canning takes over as Governor-General.
The (Hindu) Widow Remarriage Act passed.

1857   The 19th Bengal Native Infantry mutiny at Berampur (Berhampore); it is later disbanded at Barrackpur.
Rebellion breaks out at Meerut, with sepoys marching to Delhi; revolts at Jhansi and Allahabad.
British forces storm and enter Delhi; Captain Hodson captures Bahadur Shah II.

1858   Trial of Bahadur Shah II; later (October) he is sent to Calcutta and transported (December) to Rangoon. Queen Victoria's proclamation at Allahabad Durbar transfers authority from the Company to the Crown.
Lord Canning takes over as first Viceroy *and* Governor-General.

1859   Dalhousie's Doctrine of Lapse is countermanded. Nana Saheb, with his family, seeks asylum in Nepal.
The Company's English troops, protesting against their summary transfer to the Crown, mutiny.

1868   The Viceroy formally opens the railway line joining Delhi to Ambala.

1872   Lord Mayo assassinated at Port Blair in the Andamans.

1875   The Theosophical Society is founded by Madame Blavatsky.
Dayanand Saraswati founds the Arya Samaj at Bombay.

1876   The age-limit of competitors for the ICS examinations is lowered.

1877   Proclamation of the Queen's new title made at a Durbar held in Delhi.

1878   Vernacular Press Act passed.

1882   Ripon repeals Vernacular Press Act, 1878.

1883   C.P. Ilbert's Criminal Procedure Amendment Bill introduced amidst acute controversy.

Surendranath Banerjea sentenced to imprisonment for gross libel.
First session of the National Conference held at Calcutta.

1884	Ilbert Bill amended and finally passed.
1885	Inauguration of Bombay Presidency Association. Bengal Tenancy Act passed.

First session of the Indian National Congress convenes at Bombay.

1894	The Earl of Elgin takes office as Viceroy and Governor-General.
1896	Severe famine throughout India.
1897	Outbreak of plague in Bombay presidency.
1898	Death of Syed Ahmad Khan.
1899	Lord Curzon takes over as Viceroy and Governor-General.
1905	Partition of Bengal effected, leading to widespread public agitation in and outside the province.

Lord Minto takes over as Viceroy and Governor-General.

1906	Minto receives Muslim deputation headed by Aga Khan. The All-India Muslim League founded at Dacca.
1907	Lala Lajpat Rai and S. Ajit Singh deported. Ordinance restricting the right to hold public meetings promulgated. The Council of India Act becomes law.
1908	Tilak sentenced to six years' transportation.

Criminal Law (Amendment) Act passed.
Young Turk Revolution in Turkey.

1909	Indian Councils Act passed.
1910	Aurobindo Ghosh retires to Pondicherry.

Seditious Meetings Act renewed.

1912	Delhi is proclaimed a province.

Abul Kalam Azad publishes the Urdu paper *Al-Hilal*.

1913	Indian Criminal Law Amendment Act passed.

The Ghadr Party founded at San Francisco.

1914	Tilak released from internment in Mandalay; Gandhi concludes agreement with General Smuts regarding Indians in South Africa; Annie Besant publishes *New India*.
1914-18	First World War.
1915	Gandhi arrives in India.

Gokhale dies; Annie Besant announces the formation of her Home Rule League.

1917 Gandhi tried for his role in the Champaran satyagraha.
Annie Besant interned by the Madras government.
Rowlatt (Sedition) Committee appointed.
The October Revolution in Russia.

1918 Rowlatt (Sedition) Committee report submitted; Montagu—Chelmsford report on constitutional reform, published.
President Wilson's Fourteen Points.

1919 Gandhi takes over *Young India* and *Navajivan;* introduction of the Rowlatt Bills is marked by an all-India *hartal.* Dr Satyapal and Dr Saifuddin Kitchlew deported; trouble breaks out at Amritsar; General Dyer imposes curfew, followed by the Jallianwala Bagh massacre at Amritsar.
The Hunter Committee of Inquiry into the Punjab massacres begins work.
Government of India Act, 1919 (also Montagu–Chelmsford Reforms) becomes law.
Treaty of Versailles; League of Nations formed; founding of the Third (Communist) International.

1920 First meeting held of the All-India Trade Union Congress. Aligarh Muslim University is established and the Central Advisory Board of Education constituted.
Death of Tilak.

1921 Scheme of reforms under the Government of India Act, 1919, comes into operation.
Moplah Rebellion in Malabar.

1922 The Chauri Chaura incident, leading to Gandhi's suspension of the Non-cooperation Movement.
Rabindranath Tagore establishes Visvabharati University at Shantiniketan.

1925 Death of C.R. Das.
The All-India Congress Committee permits the Swaraj Party to work in the legislatures.

1928 Simon Commission's arrival in Bombay marked by an all-India *hartal.*
All-Parties Conference considers the Nehru Report.

1929 All-Parties Conference adjourned *sine die.*
Thirty-one members of the Communist Party arrested in connection with the Meerut conspiracy case.

Under Jinnah's leadership, the All-Parties Muslim Conference formulates its 'fourteen points'.

Bhagat Singh drops bombs into the Legislative Assembly. Irwin announces Dominion Status as the political goal of British policy in India.

1929-33 The Great Depression.

1930 The Congress adopts Civil Disobedience resolution. Gandhi begins his Salt Satyagraha with the Dandi March. Chittagong armoury raid.

Simon Commission report published.

First Round Table Conference inaugurated in London.

1931 Gandhi-Irwin Pact concluded (March); Gandhi sails for England (August) to attend the Second Round Table Conference (September-November); returns to Bombay (December).

1932 Whitehall announces the Communal Award; Poona Pact regarding scheduled caste representation is signed.

Third Round Table Conference (November-December) held.

1933 British government's White Paper on constitutional reforms published.

Gandhi starts the weekly *Harijan;* he is arrested and later (8 May) released.

Civil disobedience temporarily suspended (May); is restarted (August); Gandhi arrested (1 August) and released (23 August).

1934 Congress policy on the Communal Award leads to the birth of the Nationalist Party.

Jinnah returns from London to head the Muslim League.

1935 Rahmat Ali publishes a leaflet on the formation of Pakistan.

The Government of India Act, 1935, receives royal assent.

1936 The Congress, Muslim League, and other political parties campaign for elections to the provincial legislatures and to the Central Legislative Assembly under the Act of 1935.

1937 The Congress permits its members to accept office under the Act of 1935.

The All-India National Education Conference under Gandhi's leadership formulates a new education policy.

1938 V.D. Savarkar elected president of the All-India Hindu Mahasabha.

Pirpur Committee submits report.

1939   Gandhi comments adversely on the election of Subhas Chandra Bose as
         Congress President; the latter resigns. India inducted into the Second World
         War by the British; Linlithgow declares Dominion status as the ultimate
         goal of British policy. Congress ministries resign office in the provinces;
         Jinnah declares 22 December as a Day of Deliverance for Muslims.

1939-45 Second World War.

1940   Lahore Session of Muslim League adopts the Pakistan resolution.
         Linlithgow announces a new constitutional (August) offer which the
         Congress rejects but the Muslim League welcomes.
         The Congress starts (17 October) and later suspends (17 December)
         individual Civil Disobedience.

1941   The Congress absolves Gandhi of responsibility to lead a Satyagraha
         movement.
         Germany invades Russia; the proclamation of the Atlantic Charter
         (British Prime Minister Churchill affirms it did *not* apply to India);
         Japan attacks the USA.

1942   Cripps fails to break the political deadlock; the Congress and League
         reject his proposals.
         The Congress passes (9 August) the Quit India resolution; its leaders
         are arrested.

1943   Subhas Chandra Bose leaves (February) for Germany, arrives in
         Singapore (July), proclaims (October) the Provisional Government of
         Free India.
         The Karachi session of the Muslim League adopts the slogan 'Divide
         and Quit'.

1944   INA forces engage the British in Burma (March), hoist the national flag
         on Indian soil, capture (May) a British post which soon (September)
         changes hands.
         Allied invasion of France (D-Day: 6 June).

1945   Landslide victory for the Labour Party in the British general elections
         (June).
         Wavell's Simla conference fails to break the political deadlock. Atom
         bombs dropped on Hiroshima and Nagasaki to end the Second World
         War; Labour Government comes to power in Britain, UNO formed.

1946   British parliamentary delegation in India; Wavell announces
         Whitehall's intention of setting up a politically representative Executive
         Council at the centre.

Large-scale mutiny of Indian naval rating in Bombay.

Three-member British Cabinet Mission arrives (March) and, after consultations, issues its proposals (May).

Elections to Constituent Assembly completed.

The Muslim League repudiates (29 July) the Cabinet Mission Plan, and after Nehru is invited to form an interim government (6 August) proclaims 'Direct Action Day' (16 August) which is followed by the 'Great Calcutta killing'.

The Interim Government is sworn in (2 September); it is joined by the League (13 October).

Nehru, Baldev Singh, Jinnah, Liaquat Ali Khan, and Wavell visit (3-6 December) London to break the political impasse.

The Constituent Assembly convenes (9 December).

1947　　The Muslim League declares that the Cabinet Mission Plan has failed and the Constituent Assembly is illegal. Attlee announces the end (June 1948) of British rule; Mountbatten is sworn in (March) as the last Viceroy and Governor-General; he presents (3 June) his plan for Partition and announces (9 June) the transfer of power (14-15 August) to the separate Dominions of India and Pakistan.

Indian Independence Bill introduced (4 July) in Parliament; it is passed (15-16 July) and receives (18 July) royal assent. Pakistan's Constituent Assembly meets (11 August) and elects Jinnah as President; he is sworn in as Governor-General; Pakistan is born (14 August); with Mountbatten sworn in as Governor-General, India attains Independence (15 August).

Acknowlegements

It has taken me more than five years to complete writing this book. During this period I have incurred many debts to academic institutions and to colleagues and friends. I cannot give due recognition to all, but I must begin by mentioning the Maison Science de l'Homme for hosting visits to Paris for three consecutive years. Jean-Luc Racine, Christophe Jaffrelot and France Bhattacharya invited us to their homes and offices and shared their thoughts. In London, I have over the years enjoyed the friendship and hospitality of my school friend Farrukh Jamal, a Chartered Accountant, his charming wife Naheed, and Irfan Mustafa, a civil servant with much promise. I would like to thank them for everything they have done for me.

I thank Bhikhu Parekh, Chris Bayly, and Sunil Khilnani for endorsing *Faith and Freedom: Gandhi in History*. Sincere thanks to Professor Muchkund Dubey, who offered me a Visiting Professorship at the Centre for Social Development to write my book on Gandhi. I have pleasant memories of my brief association with that institution. Professor Suranjan Das, Professor Suparna Gooptu, and Ornit Shani read the first draft of this book. I am grateful to each one of them. In Calcutta, Hari Vasudevan has been a source of critical guidance and support.

Coming to my other friends, I must mention Rakhshanda Jalil, Javed Laiq, Bharati Bhargava, Saeed Naqvi, Aruna Naqvi, Syed Shahid Mahdi and his wife, Maqbool, Arif and Sarwat Ali, for their kind encouragement. I miss Abid Hussain Sahib's kindness, generosity and gentle manners. I also thank Sanjay Garg for the Urdu translations of the verses of Akbar Ilahabadi.

I owe a great deal to my brother Mujeebul Hasan, who lives in the United States. He has been an avid reader, perhaps the only one, of my writings. My sister, Salma, and her children Nazli, Sameena and Samir, have given me a lot of affection and love. Thank you, all of you! I hope I have been able to reciprocate some of that.

Adil Tyabji read through the final draft of the book, but all the hard work has been done by Nandita Jaishankar and Shaurya Shaukat Sircar. They have shown great patience, and have been extremely cooperative over all the details that had to be addressed.

I have published a few books with Niyogi Books, a relatively • new publishing house, and enjoyed the experience. I have found Mr Bikash Niyogi willing to support scholarship without expecting immediate rewards. My sincere thanks for this.

For comments, corrections, and assistance of many kinds, I am obliged to Babli Parveen. She has been very supportive in running my office at the National Archives of India

Finally, so much of my life has been centred round Zoya. She continues to inspire by example. She has stood by me all these years, and made light of the many strenuous experiences in my career. Many times, I was beset by doubts about the relevance of writing yet another book, but she generously shared her own rich research experience and her time. Without her companionship, I would not have written this book. What is more, she helped me keep my feet on the ground.

I dedicate this book to Sir Christopher A. Bayly, a long-standing friend. I can still recall my association with him as a Ph.D. student. A scholar of eminence, he has inspired me and many others the world over.

Bibliography

Private Papers
AICC Papers.
Andrews Papers (B 264).
A.P. Hume Papers, Centre for South Asian Studies (CSAS), Cambridge.
A.R. Chamney Papers.
Barlow Papers, CSAS.
Benthall Papers, CSAS.
C.F. Andrews Collection, Oriental and India Office Collection, British Library.
Gandhi-Kallenbach Papers, National Archives of India (NAI), New Delhi.
Gandhi, S.N. Papers (21331), (21250), NAI.
G.A. Haig Papers, CSAS.
Gerald R. Savage Papers, India Office Records (IOR).
G.M. Brander Papers, IOR.
Hicks Collection, p. 3, CSAS, Cambridge.
Home Department folio no. 1920, UPSA.
Hugh Robert Scott Papers, IOR.
Irene Bose Papers, box 2, CSAS.
Kenneth McRae Papers, IOR.
L. Brander Papers (F-4111), IOR.
L.N. Brown Papers, IOR.
Malcolm Darling Papers, IOR.
M.C. Chagla Papers, The Nehru Memorial Museum & Library (NMML).
Motilal Papers, NMML.
Nirmal Kumar Bose Papers, NAI.
Noel Carrington papers, IOR.
P.D. Martyn Papers, CSAS.
Purshotamdas Thakurdas Papers.
Steve Linde Papers, Jerusalem.

Public & Judicial Department, IOR, British Library
L/PJ/8/584
L/PJ/8/600

L/PJ/8/618A
L/PJ/8/630
L/PJ/8/686
L/PJ/8/688
LP/J/12/13
L/PJ/12/241
L/PJ/12/292
L/PJ/12/293
L/PJ/12/297
L/PJ/12/313
L/PJ/12/374
L/PJ/12/411, BL
L/PJ/12/444
L/PJ/12/499
L/P&J/8, 686
R/3/1/309
R.R/3/1/318

MSS EUR D 1113/109
MSS EUR (Photo) 436
MSS EUR (Photo) 467
'Brigadier DA. Barker-Wyatt CBE, 'Partition of India 1947: The Memoirs and Experiences of a Sapper Subaltern with 2nd Indian Airborne Division', IOR. MSS (Photo) EUR 425.

Printed Documents
Gandhi-Jinnah Talks: Text of Correspondence and Other Related Matters (Hindustan Times, New Delhi, July-October 1944).
Himmat, Note on the Press, UP of Agra and Oudh, for the week ending 5 Sept. 1931.
Press report, 27 Oct. 1946, M.K. Gandhi, Hindu - Muslim Unity (Bombay, 1965), (ed.) Anand T. Hingorani.
Proceedings of the Indian History Congress, Allahabad, 1938, p. iii.
Report of the Indian Statutory Commission: Survey, vol. 1 (Calcutta, 1930).

National Archives of India
Home Political Records, Miscellaneous Files.

Uttar Pradesh State Archives, Lucknow
Collectorate Record on Hardoi and Sultanpur.

Report on Native Newspapers
Files from various 'provinces' of British India

Speeches, Correspondence and Diaries

Alam, Fakrul and Radha Chakravarty (eds), *The Essential Tagore* (Visva Bharati, 2011).

Amrendra Nath to Roy, 19 Aug. 1939, Mushirul Hasan (ed.), *Towards Freedom*, 1939 (pt 2).

Ansari to Gandhi, 10 Feb. 1930, Mushirul Hasan (ed.), *Muslims and the Congress.*

Ansari to Gandhi, 13 Feb. 1930, ibid.

Azad, A.K. *Speeches of Maulana Azad, 1947-1955* (Delhi, 1956).

Birla, G.D. (ed.), *Bapu: A Unique Association* (Delhi, 1977), vols 1-4.

Birla to Gandhi, 11 June 1924, Birla (ed.), *In the Shadow of the Mahatma: A Personal Memoir* (Bombay, 1968).

Blunt, W.S. *India Under Ripon: A Private Diary* (London, 1909).

Carter, Lionel (ed.), *Mountbatten's Report on the Last Viceroyalty, 22 Mar.-15 Aug. 1947* (Delhi, 2003).

Choudhary, Valmiki (ed.), *Dr. Rajendra Prasad: Correspondence and Select Documents*, vol. 1 (Delhi, 1984).

Das, Durga (ed.), *Sardar Patel's Correspondence, 1945-50*, vol. 6 (Ahmedabad, 1973).

Datta, V.N. & Cleghorn, B.E. (eds), *A Nationalist Muslim and Indian Politics: Being the Selected Correspondence of the late Dr. Syed Mahmud* (Delhi, 1974).

Desai, Mahadev. *Day-to-Day with Gandhi: Secretary's Diary*, in 2 vols, (ed.) Narhari D. Parikh (Varanasi, 1968).

Gandhi, M.K. *Bapu's Letters to Mira 1924-1948* (Allahabad, 1948).

————. *Delhi Diary: Prayer Speeches from 10.9.47 to 30.1.48* (Ahmedabad, 1948).

————. *Speeches and Writings*, with an introduction by C.F. Andrews (Madras, n.d.).

————. *The Collected Works of Mahatma Gandhi* (Delhi: Publications Division) (*CWMG*).

Gandhi to Ansari, 10 Aug. 1927, *CWMG*, vol. 34.

————, 26 Aug. 1927, Hasan (ed.), *Muslims and the Congress*.

————, 16 Feb. 1930, *CWMG*, vol. 42.

————, 18 Mar. 1934, Hasan (ed.), *Muslims and the Congress*.

Gandhi to Birla, 9 Apr. 1925, in G.D. Birla (ed.), *In the Shadow of the Mahatma*.

————, 26 Nov. 1946, ibid.

Gandhi to Janramdas Doulatram, 9 Sept. 1928, Jairamdas Doulatram papers, NAI.

Gandhi to J.B. Kripalani, *CWMG*.

Gandhi to Khwaja, 2 Dec. 1944, Khwaja Papers.

Gandhi to Thakkar, 2 Nov. 1938, *CWMG*, vol. 74.

Gandhi to: Abbas Tyabji; Chhotubhai; Harihar Sharma; Holmes; Mirabehn; and Narandas, *CWMG*.

Gopal, S (ed.), *Selected Works of Jawaharlal Nehru (SWJN)* (Delhi: Jawaharlal Nehru Memorial Fund).

Hasan, Mushirul (ed.), *Muslims and the Congress: Select Correspondence of Dr. M.A. Ansari, 1912 - 1935* (Delhi, 1985).

_____ (ed.), *Nehru's India: Select Speeches* (Delhi, 2007).

_____ (ed.), *Mohamed Ali in Indian Politics*, 3 vols. (Delhi).

Khwaja to Gandhi, 12 Mar. 1931, A.M. Khwaja Papers, NMML.

Mehrotra, S.R. & Edward C. Moulton (eds), *Selected Writings of Allan Octavian Hume*, vol. 1 (1829-1867) (Delhi, 2004).

Message to the Americans, 3 Aug. 1942, in E.S. Reddy, *Mahatma Gandhi: Letters to Americans* (Mumbai, 1998).

Panikkar, K.M. & A. Pershad (eds), *The Voice of Freedom: Selected Speeches of Motilal Nehru* (Delhi, 1961).

Paranjape, Makarand (ed.) *Sarojini Naidu: Selected Letters, 1890s to 1940s* (Delhi, 1996).

Ramanathan, K.V. (ed.), *The Satyamurti Letters: The Indian Freedom Struggle Through the Eyes of a Parliamentarian* (Delhi, 2008), vol. 2.

R.M. Maxwell to R.J. Peel, 21 Jan. 1938, f.no. 41/A, 1938, PC Joshi Archives, Jawaharlal Nehru University, New Delhi

Sahgal, Nayantara (ed.), *Before Freedom: Nehru's Letters to His Sister 1909-1947* (Delhi, 2000).

Sharma, Hari Deo (ed.), *Selected Works of Acharya Narendra Deva*, vol. 1 (Delhi, 1998).

To Amrit Kaur, 24 Jan. 1940, *CWMG* (1 Dec. 1939-5 Apr. 1940).

To Edward Thompson, 27 Oct.1937, Uma Das Gupta (ed.), *A Difficult Friendship*.

Transcripts of reports of D.M. Darbhanga to Chief Secretary of Bihar and Commissioner of Tirhut Division, IOR. R.N. Lines papers, MSS Eur. F. 346/2.

Published Books & Articles

Abbas, K.A. 'The Mahatma and the Older Weaver Woman', in Hasan (ed.), *Islam in South Asia: Negotiating Diversities*, vol. 5.

_____. *The Second Year* (Delhi, 1949).

Aberigh-Mackay, George R. *Twenty-One Days in India, or, the Tour of Sir Ali Baba, K.C.B.; and the Teapot Series* (London, 1910).

Ahmad, Aijaz. 'Azad's Careers: Roads Taken and Not Taken', in Mushirul Hasan (ed.), *Islam and Indian Nationalism: Reflections on Abul Kalam Azad* (Delhi, 2001).

Ahmad, Imtiaz and Helmut Reifeld (eds), *Lived Islam in South Asia: Adaptation, Accommodation and Conflict* (Delhi, 2004).

Ahmed, Ishtiaq. *The Punjab: Bloodied, Partitioned and Cleansed* (Delhi, 2011).

Alam, Muzaffar. *The Languages of Political Islam in India: 1200-1800* (Delhi, 2004).

Alexander, Horace. *Consider India: An essay in values* (New York, 1961).

_____. *Gandhi Through Western Eyes* (Philadelphia, 1984).

_____. *The Indian Ferment: A Traveller's Tale* (London, n.d.).

Ali, Mohamed. *My Life: A Fragment*, (ed.) Mushirul Hasan (Delhi, 1999).

Allen, Charles (ed.), *Plain Tales from the Raj* (London, 1975).

Altabach, Philip G. in *Daedalus*, Winter 1968.

Ambedkar, B.R. *Thoughts on Pakistan* (Bombay, 1941).

_____. *What Congress and Gandhi Have Done to the Untouchables* (Bombay, 1945).

Amin, Shahid. 'Gandhi as Mahatma: Gorakhpur District, Eastern UP, 1921-22', in *Subaltern Studies III*, (ed.) Ranajit Guha (New Delhi, 1984).

_____. *Event, Metaphor, Memory: Chauri Chaura 1922-1992* (New Delhi, 1995).

Andrews, C.F. (ed.), *Mahatma Gandhi: His Own Story* (London, 1930).

_____. *Mahatma Gandhi's Ideas: Including Selections from his Writings* (London, 1929).

_____. *Mahatma Gandhi: His Life and Ideas* (Bombay, rpt, 2005).

Andrews, Robery Hardy. *A Lamp for India: The Story of Madame Pandit* (London, 1967).

Arnold, David. *Colonizing the Body: State Medicine and Epidemic Disease in Nineteenth-Century India* (California, 1993).

Arshad, Mohammad (ed.), *Adabiyat: Mohammad Atiq Siddiqi ke Adabi Mazameen* (Delhi, 2010), for a series of informative essays on Hasrat Mohani.

Asani, Ali S. *Ecstasy and Enlightenment: The Ismaili Devotional Literature in South Asia* (London, 2002).

Ashe, Geoffrey. *Gandhi* (New York, 1968).

Ayde, Shivaji Rao. *Message of Ashiana* (Calcutta, 1962).

Azad, Abul Kalam. *Basic Concepts of the Quran*, trans. by Syed Abdul Latif (Hyderabad, 1958), Mushirul Hasan (ed.), *Islam in South Asia*, vol. 3.

_____. *India Wins Freedom* (rev. edn Delhi, 1988).

Azmi, Kaifi. *Selected Poems*, trans. Pavan K. Varma (Delhi, 2000).

Bagchi, Amiya Kumar. *The Political Economy of Underdevelopment* (Cambridge, 1982).

Baig, M.R.A. *In Different Saddles* (Delhi, 1967).

Baig, Tara Ali. *Portraits of an Era* (Delhi, 1989).

Baker, D.E.U. *Changing Political Leadership in an Indian Province: The Central Provinces and Berar 1919-1939* (New Delhi, 1979).

Balasubramanian, K (ed.), *Directory of Gandhian Constructive Workers* (Delhi, 1996).

Banerjea, Surendranath. *A Nation in Making: Being the Reminiscences of Fifty Years of Public Life* (Calcutta, 1925, rpt, 1963).

Banerjee, Mukulika. *The Pathan Unarmed: Opposition & Memory in the North West Frontier* (Oxford, 2000).

Bannerman, G. E. 'The "Nabob of the North": Sir Lawrence Dundas as government contractor', *Historical Research*, vol. 83, no. 219, Feb. 2010.

Barni, Ziauddin Ahmad. *Azmat-i Rafta* (Karachi, 1961).

Barraclough, Geoffrey. *An Introduction to Contemporary History* (London, 1964).

Basu, Aparna. *Abbas Tyabji* (Delhi, 2007).

_____. *Mridula Sarabhai: Rebel with a Cause* (Delhi, 1996).

Bayly, C.A. 'The Pre-history of "Communalism"? Religious Conflict in India, 1700-1860', *Modern Asian Studies (MAS)*, 19, 2, 1985.

_____. *Origins of Nationality in South Asia: Patriotism and Ethical Government in the Making of Modern India*, in *The C.A. Bayly Omnibus* (Delhi, 2009).

_____. *The Local Roots of Indian Politics: Allahabad, 1880-1920*, in *The C.A. Bayly Omnibus* (Delhi, 2009).

Bayly, C.A. in Sugata Bose (ed.), *South Asia and World Capitalism*.

Bayly, Susan. *Caste, Society and Politics in India from the Eighteenth Century to the Modern Age* (Cambridge, 1999).

_____. *Saints, Goddesses and Kings: Muslims and Christians in South Indian Society, 1700-1900* (Cambridge, 1989).

Beames, John. *Memoirs of a Bengal Civilian* (London, 1961).

Bhalla, Alok (ed.), *Life and Works of Saadat Hasan Manto* (Delhi, rpt, 2004).

Bhattacharya, Sabyasachi (ed.), *The Mahatma and the Poet: Letters and Debates between Gandhi and Tagore 1915-1941* (Delhi, 4th imp., 2008).

_____. *Rabindranath Tagore: An Interpretation* (Delhi, 2011).

_____. *Talking Back: The Idea of Civilization in the Indian Nationalist Discourse* (Delhi, 2011).

Bhoite, Utham. 'Pre-Ambedkar Untouchable Movement in Maharashtra', in N.K. Wagle (ed.), *Writers, Editors and Reformers: Social and Political transformations of Maharashtra, 1830-1930* (Delhi, 1991).

Bilgrami, Akeel. 'Value, Enchantment, and the Mentality of Democracy: Some Distant Perspectives from Gandhi', *Economic and Political Weekly (EPW)*, 10 Dec. 2009.

Biradar, G.A. *Mahatma Gandhi's Campaign Against Untouchability in Karnataka* (Mysore, 2011).

Birdwood, Lord. *A Continent Decides* (London, 1953).

Birdwood, Lt.-Colonel The Hon. C.B. *A Continent Experiments* (London, 1945).

Blunt, Edward. *The I.C.S.: The Indian Civil Service* (London, 1937).

_____. *Social Service in India: An Introduction to some social and economic problems of the Indian people.*

Bose, Nirmal Kumar. *My Days with Gandhi* (Calcutta, 1974).

Bose, S.K. *Tej Bahadur Sapru* (Delhi, 1978).

Bowen, H.V., Margarette Lincoln, and Nigel Rigby (eds), *The Worlds of the East India Company* (Suffolk, 2002).

Brailsford, H.N. *Rebel India* (London, 1931).

Brass, Paul R. 'The Partition of India and Retributive Genocide in the Punjab, 1946-47: Means, Methods, and Purposes', *Journal of Genocide Research*, 2000, 5 (1).

Brittain, Verra. *Envoy Extraordinary: A Study of Vijaya Lakshmi Pandit and her contribution to Modern India* (London, 1943).

Brittlebank, Kate. *Tipu Sultan's Search for Legitimacy: Islam and Kingship in a Hindu Domain* (Delhi, 1995).

Brockway, A. Fenner. *The Indian Crisis* (London, 1930).

Brown, Judith M. *Gandhi: Prisoner of Hope* (Cambridge, 1991).

_____. *Gandhi's Rise to Power: Indian Politics 1915-1922* (Cambridge, 1972).

_____. *Gandhi and Civil Disobedience: The Mahatma in Indian Politics 1928-34* (Cambridge, 1977).

Brown, Rebecca M. *Gandhi's Spinning Wheel and the Making of India* (London, 2010).

Burke, Edmund. *Reflections on the Revolution in France.*

Butalia, Urvashi. *The Other Side of Silence: Voices from the Partition of India* (Delhi, 1998).

Campbell-Johnson, Alan. *Mission with Mountbatten* (London, 1951).

Carnall, Geoffrey. *Gandhi's Interpreter: A Life of Horace Alexander* (Edinburgh, 2010).

Chagla, M.C. *Roses in December* (Delhi, 1973).

Chakrabarty, Bidyut. *Local Politics and Indian Nationalism, Midnapur, 1919-1944* (Delhi, 1997).

Chakravarty, Suhash. *The Raj Syndrome: A Study in Imperial Perceptions* (London, 1980).

_____. *V.K. Krishna Menon and the India League, 1925-47,* vol. 2 (Delhi, 1997).

Chandra, Sudhir, *Continuing Dilemmas: Understanding Social Consciousness* (Delhi, 2002).

_____ (ed.), *Social Transformation and Creative Imagination* (Delhi, 1984).

_____. 'Changing Images of Caste and Politics', *Seminar* (450), Feb. 1997.

_____. 'Denial of Plurality: Thinking of Conversion through Gandhi', in Jamal Malik and Helmut Reifeld (eds), *Religious Pluralism in South Asia and Europe* (Delhi, 2005).

_____. 'Gandhi's Twin Fasts and the Possibility of Non-violence', *EPW*, 4 June 2011.

_____. 'The Harvest of Fear: A Retrospective Critique of Hindu-Muslim Relations in Two Hindi Novels', in T. V. Sathyamurthy (ed.), *Region, Religion, Caste, Gender and Culture in Contemporary India* (Delhi, 1995).

Chatterjee, Basudev (ed.), *Towards Freedom* (*TF*), 1938 (pt 1).

Chatterjee, Joya. *Bengal Divided: Hindu communalism and partition, 1932-1947* (Cambridge, 1994).

Chatterjee, Partha. *Nationalist Thought and the Colonial World: A Derivative Discourse* (Delhi, 1986).

_____. 'History and the Nationalization of Hinduism', in Vasudha Dalmia and H. von Stietencron (eds), *Representing Hinduism: The Construction of Religious Traditions and National Identity* (New Delhi, 1995).

Chattopadhyay, Kamaladevi. *Inner Recesses, Outer Spaces: Memoirs* (New Delhi, 1986).

Chattopadhyay, Sarat Chandra. 'The Current Hindu-Muslim problem' in Joya Chatterjee's *Bengal Divided*.

Chaturvedi, Benarsidas and Marjorie Sykes. *Charles Freer Andrews: A Narrative* (London, 1949).

Chaudhuri, Indra Nath. 'A Note on Some Myths About Manto', in Bhalla (ed.), *Life and Works of Saadat Hasan Manto*.

Chaudhuri, Nirad C. *The Autobiography of an Unknown Indian* (Hyderabad, 1994).

_____. *Thy Hand Great Anarch! India 1921-1952* (Delhi, 1987).

Chughtai, Ismat. *A Life in Words: Memoirs*. Translated from Urdu by M. Asaduddin (Delhi, 2012).

Churchill, Randolph S. *Winston S. Churchill: Youth 1874-1900* (Cambridge, 1966).

Clarke, Peter. *The Cripps Version: The Life of Sir Stafford Cripps 1889-1952* (London, 2002).

Cohn, Bernard S. *Colonialism and its Forms of Knowledge: The British in India* (Princeton, N.J., 1996).

Collingham, E.M. *Imperial Bodies: The Physical Experience of the Raj, c. 1800-1947* (London, 2001).

Copland, Ian. *The Princes of India in the Endgame of Empire, 1917-1947* (Cambridge, 1999).

Cortright, David. *Gandhi and Beyond: Nonviolence for a New Political Age* (London, 2010).

Cotton, Henry J.S. *Indian & Home Memories* (London, 1911).

_____. *New India or India in Transition* (London, 1907).

Cragg, Kenneth. *The Pen and the Faith: Eight Modern Muslim Writers and the Qur'an* (Delhi, 1988 edn).

D'Souza, Diane. 'Gendered Ritual and the Shaping of Shi'ah Identity', in Kelly Pemberton and Michael Nijhawan (eds), *Shared Idioms, Sacred Symbols, and the Articulation of Identities in South Asia* (London, 2009).

Daechsel, Markus. *The Politics of Self-Expression: The Urdu Middle-Class Milieu in mid-twentieth century India and Pakistan* (London, 2006).

Dalal, Chandulal Bhagubhai. *Harilal Gandhi: A Life* (Delhi, 2007).

Dalmayar, Fred. 'Gandhi and Islam: A Heart-and-Mind Unity?' in V.R. Mehta and Thomas Pantham (eds), *Political Ideas in Modern India: Thematic Explorations* (Delhi, 2005).

Dalmia, Vasudha. *Poetics, Plays, and Performances: The Politics of Modern Indian Theatre* (Delhi, 2006).

_____. *The Nationalization of Hindu Traditions: Bharatendu Harischandra and Nineteenth-Century Banaras* (Delhi, 1997).

Dalton, D. *Mahatma Gandhi: Nonviolent Power in Action* (New York, 1993).

Damodaran, Harish. *India's New Capitalists: Caste, Business, and Industry in a Modern Nation* (Delhi, 2008).

Daniel, Norman. *Islam and the West* (Edinburgh, 1960).

Dariabadi, A.M. *Insha-i Majid* (Calcutta, 1991).

Darling, Malcolm. *At Freedom's Door* (London, 1949).

_____. *Wisdom and Waste in the Punjab village* (Oxford, 1934).

Das Gupta, Jyotindra. *Language Conflict and National Development* (Berkeley, 1970).

Das Gupta, Uma (ed.), *A Difficult Friendship: Letters of Edward Thompson and Rabindranath Tagore 1913-1940* (Delhi, 2003).

Das, Sisir Kumar (ed.), *The English Writings of Rabindranath Tagore* (New Delhi, 1996).

Das, Suranjan. *Communal Riots in Bengal 1905-1947* (Delhi, 1991).

Datta, K. K. *History of the Freedom Movement in Bihar*, vol. 1 (Patna, 1958).

Datta, V.N. *Maulana Azad* (Delhi, 1990).

_____. 'Panjabi Refugees and the Urban Development of Greater Delhi', in Hasan (ed.), *Inventing Boundaries.*

Desai, Anita. *Clear Light of Day* (Delhi, 1980).

Desai, Meghnad. *The Rediscovery of India* (Delhi, 2009).

Desai, Narayan. *My Life is My Message: Satyagraha (1915-1930)*, vol. 2 (Delhi, 2009).

_____. *My Life is My Message: Svarpan (1940-1948)*, vol. 4 (Delhi, 2009).

Desai, Sanjiv P. (ed.), *Calendar of the 'Quit India' Movement in the Bombay Presidency* (Bombay, 1985).

De Souza (ed.), Peter R. *Contemporary India: Transitions* (Delhi, 2000).

Devji, Faisal. 'Muhammad Iqbal and the Crisis of Representation in British India', in Bhagavan (ed.), *Heterotopias: Nationalism and the Possibility of History in South Asia* (Delhi, 2010).

Dhamija, Jasleen. *Kamaladevi Chattopadhyay* (Delhi, 2007).

Digby, William. *Prosperous British India: A Revelation from Official Records* (New Delhi, 1969, rpt).

Dirks, N.B. (ed.), *Castes of Mind: Colonialism and the Making of Modern India* (Delhi, 2002).

_____. *Colonialism and Culture* (Michigan: Ann Arbor, 1992).

Douglas, Ian Henderson. *Abdul Kalam Azad: An Intellectual and Religious Biography* (Delhi, 1988).

Douglas, James. *Round about Bombay* (Bombay, 1886).

Dove, Marguerite Rose. *Forfeited Future: The Conflict over Congress Ministries in British India, 1933-1937* (Delhi, 1987).

Drieberg, Trevor. *Indira Gandhi: A profile in courage* (New Delhi, 1972).

Duggal, K.S. *Folk Romances of Punjab* (Delhi, 1979).

Dutta, Krishna and Andrew Robinson (eds), *Selected Letters of Rabindranath Tagore* (Cambridge, 1997).

Dwarkadas, Kanji. *India's Fight for Freedom, 1913-1937: An Eyewitness Story* (Bombay, 1965).

Eden, Emily. *Up the Country: Letters from India* (London, 1983).

Edip, Halide, *East Faces West: Impressions of a Turkish Writer in India*, (ed.) Mushirul Hasan (Delhi, 2009).

_____. *Conflict of East and West in Turkey* (Delhi, 1935).

_____. *Inside India*, intro. and ed. Mushirul Hasan (Delhi, 2000).

_____. *Turkey Faces West: A Turkish View of Recent Changes and their Origin* (New York, 1930).

Elkins, Caroline. *Imperial Reckoning: The Untold Story of Britain's Gulag in Kenya* (New York, 2005).

Erikson, Erik H. *Gandhi's Truth: On the Origins of Militant Nonviolence* (New York, 1969).

Fagg, Henry. *A Study of Gandhi's Basic Education* (Delhi, 3rd imp., 2008).

Fischer, Louis. *The Life of Mahatma Gandhi* (New York, 1983 edn).

Forbes, Rosita. *Princely India* (Delhi, 2009, rpt).

Fraser, Andrew H. L. *Among Indian Rajahs and Ryots: A Civil Servant's Recollections & Impressions of Thirty-Seven Years of Work & Sport in the Central Provinces & Bengal* (London, 2006).

Fraser, Bashabi (ed.), *Bengal Partition Stories: An Unclosed Chapter* (London, 2006).

Friedmann, Yohanan. *Prophecy Continuous: Aspects of Ahmadi Religious Thought and its Medieval Background* (Berekeley and Los Angeles, 1989).

_____. 'The Attitude of the *Jam'iyyati-i 'Ulama-i Hind* to the Indian National Movement and the establishment of Pakistan', in Hasan (ed.), *Inventing Boundaries*.

Fuller, J.F.C. *India in Revolt* (London, 1931).

Futehally, Zeenuth. *Zohra* (Delhi, 2004).

Galanter, Marc. *Law and Society in Modern India* (Delhi, 1994, 2nd imp.).

Gandhi, Arun. *Kasturba: A Life* (Delhi, 2000).

Gandhi, Gopalkrishna (ed.), *Gandhi is Gone. Who will Guide us now?* (Delhi, 2007).

Gandhi, M.K. *An Autobiography or the Story of My Experiment with Truth*, trans. from the original in Gujarati by Mahadev Desai (Ahmedabad, 1927).

_____. *The Gospel of Selfless Action: or The Gita according to Gandhi*, trans. Mahadev Desai (Ahmedabad, 2007, rpt).

_____. *The Indian states problem* (Ahmedabad, 1911).

_____. *The Way to Communal Harmony* (Ahmedabad, 1963).

Gandhi, Manubehn. *Last Glimpses of Bapu* (Agra, 1962).

Gandhi, Rajmohan. 'Looking for the Dust', *EPW*, 3 Dec. 2011.

_____. *Mohandas: A True Story of a Man, his People and an Empire* (Delhi, 2006).

_____. *The Good Boatman: Portrait of Gandhi* (Delhi, 1995).

_____. *The Rajaji Story, 1937-1972* (Bombay, 1984).

_____. *Understanding the Muslim Mind* (Delhi, 2000).

Ganguli, Debjani and John Docker (eds), *Rethinking Gandhi and Nonviolent Relationality: Global Perspectives* (Delhi, 2009).

Garga, B.D. *From Raj to Swaraj: The Non-fiction Film in India* (Delhi, 2007).

Geetha, V. 'Periyar, Women and an Ethic of Citizenship', in Mary John (ed.), *Women's Studies in India* (Delhi, 2008).

Gilmartin, David. *Empire and Islam: Punjab and the Making of Pakistan* (Berkeley, 1988).

Gilmour, David. *The Ruling Caste: Imperial Lives in the Victorian Raj* (New York, 2005).

Gonsalves, Peter. *Clothing for Liberation: A Communication Analysis of Gandhi's Swadeshi Revolution* (Delhi, 2010).

Gooptu, Suparna (ed.), *On Gandhi* (Calcutta, 2012).

Gopal, S. *Jawaharlal Nehru: A Biography*, vol. 1 (Delhi, 1986).

_____. *Radhakrishnan: A Biography* (Delhi, 1989).

Graham, B. D. *Hindu Nationalism and Indian Politics: The Origins and Development of the Bharatiya Jana Sangh* (Cambridge, 1990).

Green, Nile. *Bombay Islam: The Religious Economy of the West Indian Ocean, 1850-1915* (Delhi, 2011).

Greenwood, Alexander. *Field-Marshal Auchinleck* (Durham, 1990).

Gregg, Richard B. *The Power of Non-Violence* (Ahmedabad, 1938).

Grewal, J.S. *Muslim Rule in India: The Assessments of British Historians* (New Delhi, 1970).

Grover, Verinder and Ranjana Arora (eds), *Aruna Asaf Ali: Her Contribution to Political, Economic and Social Development* (Delhi, 1994).

Guha, Ramachandra. *India after Gandhi*.

_____. *Savaging the Civilized: Verrier Elwin, His Tribals, and India* (Delhi, 1999).

Gupta, Amit Kumar. *Crisis and Creativities: Middle-Class Bhadralok in Bengal c. 1939-52* (Delhi, 2009).

Guthrie, Anne. *Madame Ambassador: The Life of Vijaya Lakshmi Pandit* (New York, 1962).

Haithcox, J.P. *Communism and Nationalism in India: M.N. Roy and Comintern Policy, 1920-1939* (Princeton, N.J., 1971).

Hamied, K.A. *An Autobiography: A Life to Remember* (Bombay, 1972).

Hanfi, Shamim. 'Qurratulain Hyder and the Partition Narrative', in Rakhshanda Jalil (ed.), *Qurratulain Hyder & the River of Fire.*

Hardiman, David. 'The Quit India Movement in Gujarat', in Gyanendra Pandey (ed.), *The Indian Nation in 1942.*

_____. *Gandhi and His Times and Ours.*

Hardy, Peter. *The Muslims of British India* (Cambridge, 1972).

Harper, Susan Billington. *In the Shadow of the Mahatma: Bishop V.S. Azariah and the Travails of Christianity in British India* (Michigan, 2000).

Hasan, Khalid. 'Saadat Hasan Manto: Not of Blessed Memory', *Annual of Urdu Studies*, vol. 4, 1984.

Hasan, Mohibbul. 'Mahatma Gandhi and the Indian Muslims', in S.C. Biswas (ed.), *Gandhi Theory and Practice: Social Impact and Contemporary Relevance* (Simla, 1969).

Hasan, Mushirul. *A Nationalist Conscience: M.A. Ansari, the Congress and the Raj* (Delhi, 1989).

_____. *From Pluralism to Separatism: Qasbas in Colonial Awadh.*

_____. *India's Partition: Process, Strategy and Mobilization* (Delhi, 1993).

_____. *India Partitioned: The Other Face of Freedom*, in 2 vols (Delhi, 1995).

_____. *Inventing Boundaries: Gender, Politics and the Partition of India* (Delhi, 2000).

_____ (ed.), *Islam in South Asia*, vols 1, 3-5. *Theory and Practice*, vol. 1 (Delhi, 2008); *The Realm of the Traditional*, vol. 3 (Delhi, 2008); *The Realm of the Secular*, vol. 4 (Delhi, 2009); *Negotiating Diversities*, vol. 5 (Delhi, 2010).

_____. *Islam, Communities and the Nation: Muslim Identities in South Asia and Beyond* (Delhi, 1998).

_____ (ed.), *Knowledge, Power & Politics: Educational Institutions in India* (Delhi, 1998).

_____. *Legacy of a Divided Nation: India's Muslims since Independence* (Delhi, 1997).

_____. *M.A. Ansari: Gandhi's Infallible Guide* (Delhi, 1987).

_____. *Moderate or Militant: Images of India's Muslims* (Delhi, 2008).

_____ and Rakhshanda Jalil, *Partners in Freedom: Jamia Millia Islamia* (Delhi, 2006).

_____. *Wit and Humour in Colonial North India* (Delhi, 2007).

_____ (ed.), *Towards Freedom* (TF), 1939 (pt 1).

_____. 'India and Pakistan. Why the Difference?', in Hasan and Nariaki Nakazato (eds), *The Unfinished Agenda: Nation-Building in South Asia* (Delhi, 2001).

_____. 'The Communal Divide: A Study of the Delhi Proposals', in Hasan (ed.), *Communal and Pan-Islamic Trends in Colonial India* (Delhi, 1985).

_____. 'The Myth of Unity: Colonial and National Narratives', in Ludden (ed.), *Contesting the Nation: Religion, Community, and the Politics of Democracy in India* (Philadelphia, 1999).

Hauser, Walter. 'Changing Images of Caste and Politics', *Seminar* 450, Feb. 1997.

_____. 'Swami Sahajanand and the Politics of Social Reform, 1907-1950', *Indian Historical Review*, vol. 18, nos. 1 - 2, July 1991 and January 1992.

Heilbroner, Robert L. *The Worldly Philosophers: The Lives, Times, and Ideas of the Great Economic Thinkers* (New York, 1972).

Heitmeyer, Carolyn. 'Religion as Practice, Religion as Identity: Sufi Dargahs in Contemporary Gujarat', *South Asia*, vol. 34, no. 3, Dec. 2011.

Herman, Arthur. *Gandhi & Churchill: The Epic Rivalry that Destroyed an Empire and Forged Our Age* (London, 2008).

Hintze, Andrea. *The Mughal Empire and Its Decline: An Interpretation of the Sources of Social Power* (Ashgate, 1997).

Hiranandani, Popati. *The Pages of My Life: Autobiography and Selected Stories*, trans. from Sindhi by Jyoti Panjwani (Oxford, 2010).

Hirschmann, Edwin. *Robert Knight: Reforming Editor in Victorian India* (Delhi, 2008).

_____. *White Mutiny: The Ilbert Bill Crisis in India and the Genesis of the Indian National Congress* (Delhi, 1980).

Hiskett, Mervyn. *The Course of Islam in Africa* (Edinburgh, 1994).

Hobsbawm, E.J. *The Age of Revolution 1789-1848* (Delhi, 1992, paperback).

Hodson, H.V. *The Great Divide: Britain-India-Pakistan* (Karachi, 1997 edn).

Holmes, John Haynes. *My Gandhi* (London, 1954).

Hooja, Rima (ed.), *Crusader for Self-Rule: Tej Bahadur Sapru & the Indian National Movement* (Delhi, 1999).

Hosain, Attia. *Sunlight on a Broken Column* (New Delhi, 2009).

Hourani, Albert. *Islam in European Thought* (Cambridge, 1991).

Howarth, Toby M. *The Twelver Shia as a Muslim Minority in India* (London, 2005).

Hubel, Teresa. *Whose India?: The Independence Struggle in British and Indian Fiction and History* (Leicester, 1996).

Hunt, James D. *Gandhi in London* (Delhi, 1978).

Hunter, W.W. *The India of the Queen and Other Essays* (London, 1903).

Husain, Mushtaq (ed.), *Makatib*.

Hutheesing, Krishna Nehru. *We Nehrus* (Bombay, 1967).

_____. *With No Regrets* (London, 1944).

_____. 'My Brother—Then and Now', Zakaria (ed.), *A Study of Nehru*.

Hyder, Qurratulain. *Fireflies in the Mist: A Novel* (Delhi, 1994).

_____. *River of Fire* (New York, 2003).

_____. *The Sound of Falling Leaves* (Delhi, 1994).

Hyder, Syed Akbar. 'Ghalib and His Interlocutors', in Bhagavan (ed.), *Heterotopias*.

Ikeda, Daisaku. *A New Humanism: The University Addresses of Daisaku Ikeda* (London, 2010).

Iqbal, Afzal. *Life and Times of Mohamed Ali* (Delhi, 1978).

Israel, Milton. *Communications and Power: Propaganda and the press in the Indian nationalist struggle, 1920-1947* (Cambridge, 1994).

Iyengar, Uma (ed.), *The Oxford India Nehru* (New Delhi, 2007).

Iyengar, Uma and Lalitha Zackariah (eds), *Together They Fought: Gandhi-Nehru Correspondence 1921-1948* (Delhi, 2011).

Iyer, Raghavan N. *The Moral and Political Thought of Mahatma Gandhi* (Delhi, 2000).

_____ (ed.), *The Essential Writings of Mahatma Gandhi* (Delhi, 1996).

Jaffrelot, Christophe. *India's Silent Revolution: The Rise of the Low Castes in North India* (Delhi, 2003).

_____. *Religion, Caste and Politics in North India* (Delhi, 2010).

_____. *The Hindu Nationalist Movement and Indian Politics* (London, 1996).

Jagadisan, T.N (ed.), *Letters of The Right Honourable V. S. Srinivasa Sastri* (Delhi, 1963).

Jain, A.P. *Rafi Ahmed Kidwai: A Memoir of his Life and Times* (London, 1965).

Jalal, Ayesha. *Democracy and Authoritarianism in South Asia* (Cambridge, 1995).

_____. *Partisans of Allah: Jihad in South Asia.*

_____. *Self and Sovereignty: Individual and Community in South Asian Islam Since 1850* (Delhi, 2001).

_____. *The Sole Spokesman: Jinnah, the Muslim League and the Demand for Pakistan* (Cambridge, 1985).

Jalil, Rakhshanda (ed.), *Qurratulain Hyder & the River of Fire* (Delhi, 2011).

Jayakar, M.R. *The Story of My Life*, vol. 1 (Bombay, 1958) & vol. 2 (Bombay, 1959).

Jayal, Niraja Gopal (ed.), *Democracy in India* (Delhi, 2001).

Jeffrey, Robin (ed.), *People, Princes and Paramount Power: Society and Politics in the Indian Princely States* (Delhi, 1978).

_____. 'A Sanctified Label—"Congress" in Travancore Politics, 1938-48', in Low (ed.), *Congress and the Raj.*

Jones, E. Stanley. *Mahatma Gandhi: An Interpretation* (London, 1948).

Jones, George E. *Tumult in India* (New York, 1948).

Kabir, Humayun. *Muslim Politics, 1906-42* (Calcutta, 1944).

Kaif, Saraswat Saran. *Chakbast* (Delhi, 1986).

Kakar, Sudhir. *Mira and the Mahatma* (Delhi, 2004).

Kamra, Sukeshi. *Bearing Witness: Partition, Independence, End of the Raj* (Calgary, Alberta, 2002).

Kapur, Sudarshan. *Raising Up a Prophet: The African-American Encounter with Gandhi* (Boston, 1992).

Kashmiri, Shorish. '*Boo-i gul Naala-i Dil Dood-i Chiragh-i Mehfil*', in Hasan (ed.), *India Partitioned*.

Kaul, Suvir (ed.), *The Partitions of Memory: The Afterlife of the Division of India* (New Delhi, 2001).

Kazmi, Ali Ahmad. *Sajjad Zaheer: Ek Tarikh ek Tehrik* (Allahabad, 2006).

Kelting, M. Whitney. *Singing to the Jinas: Jain Laywomen Mandal Singing and the Negotiations of Jain Devotion* (Oxford, 2001).

Khaliquzzaman, Choudhry. *Pathway to Pakistan* (Lahore, 1961).

Khan, Yasmin. *The Great Partition: The Making of India and Pakistan* (Delhi, 2007).

Kidwai, Anis. *In Freedom's Shade* trans. by Ayesha Kidwai (Delhi, 2011).

Kidwai, M.H. *Swaraj and How to obtain it* (Lucknow, 1924).

Kidwai, Sadiq-ur-Rahman. 'Poet who Laughed in Pain: Akbar Ilahabadi', in Hasan (ed.), *Islam in South Asia*, vol. 4 (Delhi, 2008).

Kiernan, V. G. *European Empires from Conquest to Collapse, 1815-1960* (New York, 1982).

Kincaid, Dennis. *British Social Life in India, 1608-1937* (London, 1938).

King, Christopher R. *One Language, Two Scripts: The Hindi Movement in Nineteenth Century North India* (Bombay, 1994).

Kishwar, Madhu. 'Gandhi on Women', *EPW*, Oct. 1985.

Kolsky, Elizabeth. *Colonial Justice in British India: White Violence and the Rule of Law* (Cambridge, 2011).

Kripalani, J.B. *Gandhi: His Life and Thought* (Delhi, 1970).

_____. *My Times: An Autobiography* (Delhi, 2004).

Krishna, Sumi. 'The Environmental Discourse in India: New Directions in Development', in T.V. Sathyamurthy (ed.), *Class Formation and Political Transformation in Post-Colonial India* (Delhi, 1996).

Kritzeck, James and William H. Lewis (eds), *Islam in Africa* (New York, 1968).

Krüger, Horst (ed.), *Kunwar Mohammad Ashraf: An Indian Scholar and Revolutionary, 1903-62* (Delhi, 1969).

Kudaisya, Medha M. *The Life and Times of G.D.Birla* (Delhi, 2003).

Kumar, Dharma and Meghnad Desai (eds), *The Cambridge Economic History of India*: vol. 2, c. 1757-c. 1970.

Kumar, Ravinder (ed.), *Essays on Gandhian Politics: The Rowlatt Satyagraha of 1919* (Oxford, 1971).

_____. 'Gandhi, Ambedkar and the Poona Pact, 1932', in Jim Masselos (ed.), *Struggling and Ruling*.

_____ and Hari Dev Sharma (eds), *Selected Works of Motilal Nehru* (*SWMN*), vol. 1.

Lambert-Hurley, Siobhan. *Atiya's Journeys: A Muslim Woman from Colonial Bombay to Edwardian India* (Delhi, 2010).

Lapping, Brian. *End of Empire* (London, 1989).

Laxman, R.K. *The Common Man At Large* (Delhi, 1994).

Lelyveld, Joseph. *Great Soul: Mahatma Gandhi and His Struggle with India* (New York, 2011).

Levtzion, Nehemia and Randall L. Pouwels (eds), *The History of Islam in Africa* (Ohio, 2000).

Lohia, Rammanohar. *Guilty Men of India's Partition* (Delhi, 2000).

Low, D.A. *Britain and Indian Nationalism: The Imprint of Ambiguity 1929-1942* (Cambridge, 1977).

_____ (ed.), *Congress and the Raj: Facets of the Indian Struggle, 1917-1947* (New Delhi, 1977).

_____ (ed.), *The Indian National Congress: Centenary Hindsights* (Delhi, 1988).

Lumley, E.W.R. *The Transfer of Power in India* (London, 1954).

Lyon, Jean. *Just Half a World Away: My Search for the New India* (London, 1955).

Macnicol, Nicol. *C.F. Andrews: Friend of India* (London, 1944).

Mahadevan, T.K. *Gandhi My Refrain: Controversial Essays: 1950-1972* (Bombay, 1973).

Mahajan, Sucheta. *Independence and Partition: The Erosion of Colonial Power in India* (Delhi, 2000).

Majeed, Javed. *Muhammad Iqbal: Islam, Aesthetics and Postcolonialism* (London, 2009).

_____. 'Geographies of Subjectivity. Pan-Islam and Muslim Separatism: Muhammad Iqbal and Selfhood', in Shruti Kapila (ed.), *An Intellectual History for India* (Cambridge, 2010).

Malhotra, Inder. *Indira Gandhi: A Personal and Political Biography* (London, 1989).

Mallison, Francoise. 'Hinduism as seen by the Nizari Ismaili Missionaries of Western India: The Evidence of the Ginan', in Günther-Dietz Sontheimer and Hermann Kulke (eds), *Hinduism Reconsidered* (Delhi, 2001).

Mann, Rajwanti. *Social Radicalism in Urdu Literature: A Study of Gender Issues and Problems, 1930-1960* (Delhi, 2011)

Manor, James. 'Gandhian Politics and the Challenge to Princely Authority in Mysore, 1936 - 47', in D.A. Low (ed.), *Congress and the Raj*.

Manto, Saadat Hasan. *Black Margins*, (ed.) Muhammad Umar Memon (Delhi, 2001).

_____. *Naked Voices: Stories and Sketches*, trans. from the Urdu by Rakhshanda Jalil (Roli Books, 2008).

_____. 'Not of Blessed Memory', *Annual of Urdu Studies*, vol. 4, 1984.

_____. *Mottled Dawn: Fifty Sketches and Stories of Partition* (New Delhi, 1997).

Manuel, Peter. 'Music, the Media and Communal Relations in North India', in Ludden (ed.), *Contesting the Nation*.

Markovits, Claude. *Indian Business and Nationalist Politics 1931-1939: The Indigenous Capitalist Class and the Rise of the Congress Party* (Cambridge, 1985).

_____. 'Businessmen and the Partition of India', in D. Tripathi (ed.), *Business and Politics in India: A Historical Perspective* (Delhi, 1991).

Marshall, P.J. 'British Society and the East India Company', *MAS*, 31, 1, 1997.

Martin, Briton Jr. *New India, 1885: British Official Policy and the Emergence of the Indian National Congress* (Bombay, 1970).

Masani, Minoo. *Bliss was it in that Dawn: A political memoir upto Independence* (Bombay, 1977).

Masani, R.P. *Dadabhai Naoroji: The Grand Old Man of India* (London, 1939).

Masselos, J.C. 'The Khojas of Bombay: The Defining of Formal Membership Criteria During the Nineteenth Century', in Imtiaz Ahmad (ed.), *Caste and Social Stratification among Muslims in India* (Delhi, 1978).

_____ (ed.), *Struggling and Ruling: The Indian National Congress, 1885-1985* (Delhi, 1985).

_____. *The City in Action: Bombay Struggles for Power* (Delhi, 2007).

Mathai, M.P. and John Moolakkattu (eds), *Exploring Hind Swaraj* (Delhi, 2009).

Matthews, Roderick. *The Flaws in the Jewel: Challenging the Myths of British India* (Delhi, 2010).

Mayaram, Shail. *Resisting Regimes: Myth, Memory and the Shaping of a Muslim Identity* (Delhi, 1997).

McDonough, Sheila. *Gandhi's Responses to Islam* (Delhi, 1994).

_____. 'The Muslims of South Asia (1857-1947)', Jacques Waardenburg (ed.), *Muslim Perceptions of Other Religions: A Historical Survey* (New York, 1999).

McGuire, John. 'The World Economy, the Colonial State, and the Establishment of the Indian National Congress', in Mike Shepperdson and Colin Simmons (eds), *The Indian National Congress and the Political Economy of India, 1885-1985* (Aldershot, n.d.).

Mehrotra, A.K. (ed.), *The Last Bungalow: Writings on Allahabad* (Delhi, 2007).

Mehrotra, S.R. *The Emergence of the Indian National Congress* (Delhi, 1971).

_____. 'The Early Congress' in B.R. Nanda (ed.), *Essays in Modern Indian History* (New Delhi, 1980).

_____. 'The Congress and the Partition of India', in C.H. Philips and M.D. Wainwright (eds), *The Partition of India: Policies and Perspectives, 1935-1947* (London, 1970).

Memmi, Albert. *The Colonizer and the Colonized* (Boston, 1957).

Mendelsohn, Oliver and Marika Vicziany. *The Untouchables: Subordination, Poverty and the State in Modern India* (Cambridge, 2000).

Menon, K.P.S. *Many Worlds: An Autobiography* (London, 1965).

Menon, Ritu and K. Bhasin. *Borders & Boundaries: Women in India's Partition* (Delhi, 1998).

Merkl, Peter H. *Modern Comparative Politics* (New York, 1970).

Metcalf, T.R. *Ideologies of the Raj*, III. 4 (Cambridge, 1998).

Middleton, John (ed.), *Black Africa: Its People and their Cultures Today* (London, 1970).

Mir, Farina. *The Social Space of Language: Vernacular Culture in British Colonial Punjab* (Delhi, 2010).

Mirabehn. *The Spirit's Pilgrimage* (London, 1960).

Misra, B.B. (ed.), *Select Documents on Mahatma Gandhi's Movement in Champaran 1917-18* (Bihar, 1963).

_____. *The Indian Political Parties: An Historical Analysis of Political Behaviour up to 1947* (Delhi, 1976).

Misra, Salil. 'Transition from the Syncretic to the Plural: The World of Hindi and Urdu', in Malik and Reifeld (eds), *Religious Pluralism in South Asia and Europe*.

Mitra, Chandan. 'Images of the Congress: U.P. and Bihar in the Late Thirties and Early Forties', in Low (ed.), *The Indian National Congress*.

Moir, Zawahir and Dominique-Sila Khan, 'New Light on the Satpanthi Imamshahis of Pirana', *South Asia: Journal of South Asian Studies*, no. 2, vol. 33, Aug. 2010.

Moon, Penderel. *Divide and Quit: An Eye-witness Account of the Partition of India* (New Delhi, 1998).

_____ (ed.), *Wavell: The Viceroy's Journal* (London, 1973).

Moore, R.J. *Churchill, Cripps, and India, 1939-1945* (Oxford, 1979).

Moraes, Frank. *Jawaharlal Nehru: A Biography* (New York, 1956).

Moulton, Edward C. 'The Early Congress and the British Radical Connection', in Low (ed.), *The Indian National Congress*.

Mujeeb, Mohammad. *Islamic Influences on Indian Society* (Meerut, 1965).

_____. 'Gandhi and the Muslim Masses', in *Islamic Influence on Indian Society*.

_____. *The Indian Muslims* (London, 1967).

_____. 'The Partition of India in Retrospect', in Philips and Wainwright (eds), *The Partition of India*.

Mukherjee, Meenakshi. *An Indian For All Seasons: The Many Lives of R.C. Dutt* (Delhi, 2009).

Nadri, Ghulam A. 'Muslims of Early Modern Gujarat: A Study of Inter-Community Relationships' (paper presented at the Indian History Congress, Dec. 2011).

Nadwi , A.H.A. *Karawan-i Zindagi* (Lucknow, 1983).

Nagaraj, D.R. *The Flaming Feet and Other Essays: The Dalit Movement in India* (Delhi, 2010).

Nair, Kusum. *Blossoms in the Dust: The Human Element in Indian Development* (London, 1961).

Nair, Neeti. *Changing Homelands: Hindu Politics and the Partition of India* (Delhi, 2011).

Nanda, B. R. *In Gandhi's Footsteps: The Life and Times of Jamnalal Bajaj* (New York, 1990).

————. *Mahatma Gandhi: A Pictorial Biography* (Delhi, 1958).

————. *Gandhi: Pan-Islamism, Imperialism and Nationalism in India* (Bombay, 1989).

———— (ed.), *Selected Works of Govind Ballabh Pant* (Delhi, 1997), vol. 8.

Nandy, Ashis. 'Obituary of a Culture', *Seminar* (Delhi), May 2002.

————. *Traditions, Tyranny and Utopias: Essays in the Politics of Awareness* (Delhi, 1992).

Naravane, V.S. *Sarojini Naidu: An Introduction to her life, Work and Poetry* (New Delhi, 1996).

Narayan, Badri. *Woman Heroes and Dalit Assertion in North India: Culture, Identity and Politics* (Delhi 2006).

Narayan, Shriman. *Memoirs: Windows on Gandhi and Nehru* (Bombay, 1971).

Nasr, Seyyed Vali Reza. *The Vanguard of the Islamic Revolution: The Jama'at-i Islami of Pakistan* (Berkeley, 1994).

————. 'Mawdudi and the Jama'at-i Islami: The Origins, Theory and Practice of Islamic Revivalism', Rahnema (ed.), *Pioneers of Islamic Revival.*

Nayar, Sushila and Kamla Mankekar (eds), *Women Pioneers in India's Renaissance* (Delhi, 2002).

Nehru, B.K. *Nice Guys Finish Second* (Delhi, 1997).

Nehru, Jawaharlal (ed.), *A Bunch of Old Letters: Being mostly written to Jawaharlal Nehru and some written by him* (Delhi, 1988).

————. *An Autobiography* (London, 1936).

————. *Glimpses of World History* (Allahabad, 1939).

————. *The Discovery of India* (Delhi, 1985).

————. *The Unity of India: Collected Writings, 1937-1940* (London, 1928, 3rd imp., 1948).

Nehru, Rameshwari. *"Gandhi is My Star": Speeches and Writings* (Patna, 1950).

Nichols, Beverley. *Verdict on India* (London, 1944).

Nietzsche, Friedrich. *The Birth of Tragedy and the Case of Wagner*, trans. with commentary by Walter Kaufman (New York, 1967).

Nijhawan, Shobna (ed.), *Nationalism in the Vernacular: Hindi, Urdu, and the Literature of Indian Freedom* (Delhi, 2010).

Nizami, Hasan. *Gandhi-Nama* (Delhi, 1922).

Nizami, Khwaja Hasan Sani. *Khwaja Hasan Nizami* (Delhi, 1987).

Noman, Omar. *Pakistan: A Political and Economic History Since 1947* (London, 1988).

Norton, Richard. 'Musa al-Sadr', in Rahnema (ed.), *Pioneers of Islamic Revival.*

O'Connor, Daniel. *A Clear Star: C.F. Andrews and India 1904-1914* (Delhi, 2005).

_____. *Gospel, Raj and Swaraj: The Missionary Years of C.F. Andrews 1904-14* (Frankfurt, 1990)

_____. *The Testimony of C.F. Andrews* (Madras, 1974).

Oesterheld, Christina and Peter Zoller, *Of Clowns and Gods, Brahmans and Babus* (Delhi, 1999).

O'Hanlon, Rosalind. *Caste, Conflict, and Ideology: Mahatma Jotirao Phule and Low Caste Protest in Nineteenth-Century Western India* (Delhi, 1902, paperback).

Okri, Ben. *The Famished Road* (New York, 1991).

Omvedt, Gail. *Understanding Caste: From Buddha to Ambedkar and Beyond* (Delhi, 2011).

Page, David. *Prelude to Partition: The Indian Muslim and the Imperial System of Control 1920-1932* (Delhi, 1982).

Pal, Bipin Chandra. *Swadeshi and Swaraj (The Rise of New Patriotism)* (Calcutta, 1954).

Palsetia, Jesse S. 'Parsi and Hindu Traditional and Non-traditional Responses to Christian Conversions in Bombay, 1839-45', *Journal of the American Academy of Religion*, Sept. 2006, vol. 74, no. 3.

Pande, B.N. (ed.), *A Centenary History of the Indian National Congress, 1935-1947*, vol. 3 (Delhi, n.d.).

Pandey, Gyanendra. *The Ascendancy of the Congress in Uttar Pradesh: Class, Community and Nation in Northern India, 1920-1940* (Delhi, 2002).

_____. *The Hindu Nationalist Movement and Indian Politics* (London, 1996), p 78.

_____ (ed.), *The Indian Nation in 1942* (Calcutta, 1988).

_____. *Remembering Partition: Violence, Nationalism and History in India* (New York, 2001).

_____. 'Which of us are Hindus?', in G. Pandey (ed.), *Hindus and others: The question of identity in India today* (Delhi, 1993).

Pandit, Vijaya Lakshmi. *The Evolution of India* (London, 1958).

_____. *The Scope of Happiness: A Personal Memoir* (New Delhi, 1979).

Panigrahi, D.N. *Jammu and Kashmir: The Cold War and the West* (Delhi, 2009).

Parekh, Bhikhu. 'Making Sense of Gujarat', *Seminar* (Delhi), May 2002.

_____. *Colonialism, Tradition and Reform: An Analysis of Gandhi's Political Discourse* (Delhi, 1989).

_____. *Gandhi's Political Philosophy: A Critical Examination* (London, 1989).

Parel, Anthony J. (ed.), *Gandhi: 'Hind Swaraj' and Other Writings* (Delhi, 1997).

Parry, Benita. *Delusions and Discoveries: India in the British Imagination, 1880-1930* (London, rpt, 1998).

Patel, Dinyar. 'Like the Countless Leaves of One Tree', 'Gandhi and the Parsis', the 'Prince of Wales Riots', and the 'Rights of Minorities'(unpublished paper).

Patel, Jehangir P and Marjorie Sykes, *Gandhi: His Gift of the Fight* (Goa, 1986 edn).

Pati, Biswamoy (ed.), *Bal Gangadhar Tilak: Popular Readings* (Delhi, 2010).

Patterson, Steven. *The Cult of Imperial Honor in British India* (London, 2009).

Philips, C.H. and M.D. Wainwright (eds), *The Partition of India: Policies and Perspectives, 1935-1947* (London, 1970).

Pirzada, S.S. *Foundations of Pakistan: 1924-1947*, vol. 2.

Polak, Millie Graham. *Mr. Gandhi: The Man* (Bombay, 1949).

Polak, H.S.L. and M.G. 'Mohandas Karamchand Gandhi', in L.F. Rushbrook Williams (ed.), *Great Men of India* (Colombo, n.d.).

Pouchepadass, Jacques. *Champaran and Gandhi: Planters, Peasants and Gandhian Politics* (Delhi, 1999).

Powell, Avril A. *Muslims and Missionaries in Pre-Mutiny India* (London, 1993).

Powicke, F.M. *Modern Historians and the Study of History* (Watford, 1955).

Prakash, Gyan. *Bombay Fables* (Delhi, 2010).

Prasad, Bimal (ed.), *Jayaprakash Narayan: Selected Works*, vol. 1 (1929-1935) & vol. 2 (1936-1939) (Delhi, 2000).

Prasad, Madho. *A Gandhian Patriarch: A political and spiritual biography of Kaka Kalekar* (Delhi, 1965).

Prasad, Rajendra. *Autobiography* (Bombay, 1957).

Pyarelal, *Mahatma Gandhi: The Last Phase*, vol. 1 (Ahmedabad, 1956).

_____. *Mahatma Gandhi: The Last Phase*, vol. 2 (Ahmedabad, 1956).

_____. *The Epic Fast* (Ahmedabad, 1932).

Qureshi, I.H. *Ulema in Politics: A Study Relating to the Political Activities of the Ulema in the South-Asian Subcontinent from 1556 to 1947* (Karachi, 1974).

Qureshi, M. Naeem. *Pan-Islam in British Indian Politics: A Study of the Khilafat Movement 1918-1924* (Leiden, 1999).

Radhakrishnan, S. *The Bhagavadgita* (London, 1943).

Raghavan, G.N.S (ed.), *M. Asaf Ali's Memoirs: The Emergence of Modern India* (Delhi, 1994).

Rahman, Tariq. *From Hindi to Urdu: A Social and Political History* (Delhi, 2011).

Rahnema, Ali (ed.), *Pioneers of Islamic Revival* (London, 2005).

Rai, Alok. 'Introduction', in Premchand, *Ranghbhumi. The Arena of Life*, trans. Christopher King (Oxford, 2010).

Rajagopalachari, C. in Ved Mehta, *Mahatma Gandhi and His Apostles* (New York, 1976).

Ram, Vinay Bharat. *From the Brink of Bankruptcy: The DCM Story* (Delhi, 2011).

Ramagundam, Rahul. *Gandhi's Khadi: A History of Contention and Conciliation* (Hyderabad, 2008).

Ramakrishnan, E.V. *Locating Indian Literature: Texts, Traditions, Translations* (Delhi, 2011).

Ramusack, Barbara N. *The Princes of India in the Twilight of Empire: Dissolution of a Patron-Client System, 1914-1939* (New York, 1978).

Rao, Shiva, 'The Terrible Price of Opportunism', *Hindustan Times*, 20 June 1969.

Ray, Baren (ed.), *Gandhi's Campaign Against Untouchability, 1933-34: An Account from the Raj's Secret Official Records* (Delhi, 1996).

Ray, Rajat Kanta. *Social Conflict and Political Unrest in Bengal, 1875-1927* (New Delhi, 1984).

Ray, Sibnarayan (ed.), *Selected Works of M.N. Roy, 1932-1936*, vol. 4 (Delhi, 2000, paperback).

Reid, Escott. *Radical Mandarin: The Memoirs of Escott Reid* (London, 1989).

Reddy, E.S. *Mahatma Gandhi: Letters to Americans* (Mumbai, 1998).

Revel, Louis. *The Fragrance of India: Landmarks for the world of tomorrow* (Bombay, 1946).

Rezavi, Syed Ali Nadeem. 'The Dynamics of Composite Culture: Evolution of an Urban Social Identity in Mughal India' (paper presented at the Indian History Congress, Dec. 2011).

Robinson, Francis. *Separatism Among Indian Muslims: The Politics of the United Provinces' Muslims, 1860-1923* (Cambridge, 1974).

_____. *The 'Ulama of Farangi Mahall and Islamic Culture in South Asia* (Delhi, 2001).

Rodrigues, Valerian. 'Reading Texts and Tradition: The Ambedkar-Gandhi Debate', *EPW*, 8 Jan. 2011.

_____ (ed.), *The Essential Writings of Ambedkar*.

Ross, Alan. *The Emissary: G.D. Birla, Gandhi and Independence* (London, 1986).

Ross, Robert. *A Concise History of South Africa* (Cambridge, 1999).

Rousselet, Louis. *India and its Native Princes: Travels in Central India and in the presidencies of Bombay and Bengal* (London, 1882).

Roy, Anjali Gera and Nandi Bhatia. *Partitioned Lives: Narratives of Home, Displacement, and Resettlement* (Delhi, 2008).

Roy, M.N. *India's Message* (Calcutta, 1950).

Roy, Ramashray. *Gandhi and Ambedkar: A Study in Contrast* (Delhi, 2006).

Royle, Trevor. *The Last Days of the Raj* (London, 1997).

Rudolph, L.I. and S.H. *Postmodern Gandhi and Other Essays: Gandhi in the World and at Home* (Chicago, 2006).

Russell, Bertrand. *The Autobiography of Bertrand Russell* (London, 1968).

Russell, Ralph (ed.), *Hidden in the Lute: An Anthology of Two Centuries of Urdu Literature* (Delhi, 1995).

_____. *Pursuit of Urdu Literature: A Select History* (Delhi, 1992).

Saadawi, Nawal El. *The Nawal El Saadawi Reader* (London, 1998).

Saberwal, Satish. *Spirals of Contention: Why India was Partitioned in 1947* (Delhi, 2008).

Sadiq, Muhammad. *Twentieth Century Urdu Literature* (Karachi, 1983).

Sahgal, Nayantara. *Jawaharlal Nehru: Civilizing a Savage World* (Delhi, 2010).

_____. 'Life with Uncle', in Rafiq Zakaria (ed.), *A Study of Nehru* (Delhi, 1959).

_____. *Prison and Chocolate Cake* (London, 1954).

Salim, Hameeda. *Shorish-i Dauran: Yaden* (New Delhi, 1995).

Sanyal, Sunanda and Soumya Basu. *The Sickle and the Crescent: Communists, Muslim League and India's Partition* (Kolkata, 2011).

Sanyal, Usha. *Devotional Islam and Politics in British India: Ahmad Riza Khan Barelwi and his Movement, 1870-1920* (Delhi, 1996).

Sarila, Narendra Singh. *The Shadow of the Great Game: The Untold Story of India's Partition* (Delhi, 2005).

Sarkar, Sumit. 'Indian Nationalism and the Politics of Hindutva', in Ludden (ed.), *Contesting the Nation*.

Sayeed, Khalid Bin. *Politics in Pakistan: The Nature and Direction of Change* (New York, 1980).

Scarfe, Allan and Wendy. *J.P.: His Biography* (Delhi, 1977).

Seal, Anil. *The Emergence of Indian Nationalism: Competition and Collaboration in the Later Nineteenth Century* (Cambridge, 1971).

Segal, Kiran. *Zohra Segal 'Fatty'* (Delhi, 2012).

Sen, Sudipta. *Distant Sovereignty: National Imperialism and the Origins of British India* (London, 2002).

Sender, Henny. *The Kashmiri Pandits: A Study of Cultural Choice in North India* (Delhi, 1998).

Sengupta, Padmini. *Sarojini Naidu: A Biography* (Bombay, 1966).

Shackle, Christopher (ed.), *Urdu and Muslim South Asia: Studies in Honour of Ralph Russell* (Delhi, 1991).

Shaikh, Farzana *Making Sense of Pakistan* (London, 2009).

Shani, Ornit. 'Gandhi, Citizenship and the Resilience of Indian Nationhood', *Citizenship Studies*, vol. 15, nos. 6-7, Oct. 2011.

Sharma, D. S. *Studies in the Renaissance of Hinduism* (Benares, 1944).

Shell, Robert C.H. 'Islam in Southern Africa', in Levtzion and Pouwels (eds), *The History of Islam in Africa*.

Sheth, D.L. 'Caste and the Secularisation Process in India', in Peter R. De Souza (ed.), *Contemporary India: Transitions* (Delhi, 2000).

Shukla, Chandrashanker (ed.), *Reminiscences of Gandhiji by forty-eight contributors* (Bombay, 1951).

Siddiqi, Abdul Rahman. *Smoke Without Fire: Portraits of Pre-Partition Delhi* (Delhi, 2011).

Siddiqi, Atiq (ed.). *Begum Hasrat Mohani aur unke khutut* (Delhi, 1981).

Siddiqi, Shaukat. *God's Own Land* (*Khuda ki Basti*), trans. David J. Mathews (Delhi, 1993).

Sidorsky, David (ed.), *The Liberal Tradition in European Thought* (New York, 1970).

Singh, Anita Inder. *The Origins of the Partition of India 1936-1947* (Delhi, 1987).

Singleton, Brent. "'That Ye May Know Each Other": Late Victorian Interactions between British and West African Muslims', *Journal of Minority Affairs*, vol. 29, no. 3, Sept. 2009.

Sitaramayya, B. Pattabhi. *The History of the Indian National Congress 1885-1935* (Madras, 1935).

Skaria, Ajay. 'The Strange Violence of Satyagraha: Gandhi, *Ithihaas*, and History', in Bhagavan (ed.), *Heterotopias*.

Smith, W.C. *Questions of Religious Truth* (New York, 1967).

Sorel, Georges. *Reflections on Violence* (Cambridge, 1999).

Sorenson, R.W. *My Impression of India* (London, 1946).

Speirs, Malcom. *The Wasikadars of Awadh: A History of certain Nineteenth Century Families of Lucknow* (Delhi, 2008).

Spiller, R. E. (ed.), *Selected Essays, Lectures, and Poems of Ralph Waldo Emerson* (New York, 1965).

Srinivas, M.N. (ed.), *Caste: Its Twentieth Century Avatar* (Delhi, 1997).

Stark, Ulrike. *An Empire of Books: The Naval Kishore Press and the Diffusion of the Printed Word in Colonial India* (Delhi, 2008).

Stephens, Ian. *Monsoon Morning* (London, 1966).

Stein, Burton. *A History of India* (New York, 2010).

Stein, Maurice and Arthur Vidich (eds), *Sociology on Trial* (Englewood Cliffs, N.J., 1965).

Strachey, John. *India: Its Administration and Progress* (London, 1911).

_____. *The End of Empire* (New York, 1964).

Studdert-Kennedy, Gerald. *Providence and the Raj: Imperial Mission and Missionary Imperialism* (New Delhi, 1988).

Swan, Maureen. *Gandhi: The South African Experience* (Johannesburg, 1985).

Sykes, Marjorie (ed.), *C.F. Andrews: Representative Writings* (Delhi, 1973).

Tagore, Rabindranath. *Boundless Sky* (Calcutta, 1964).

_____. *My Life in My Words*. Selected and edited by Uma Das Gupta (Delhi, 2006).

Talbot, Ian. *Pakistan: A Modern History* (New Delhi, 1999).

_____. *Provincial Politics and the Pakistan Movement: The Growth of the Muslim League in North-West and North-East India 1937-47* (Karachi, 1988).

Taleb, Mirza Abu. *Westward Bound: Travels of Mirza Abu Taleb*, trans. Charles Stewart, in Hasan (ed.) *Exploring the West: Three Travel Narratives* (Delhi, 2009).

Tan, Tai Yong and Gyanesh Kudaisya. *The Aftermath of Partition in South Asia* (London, 2000).

Tanwar, Raghuvendra. *Reporting the Partition of Punjab 1947: Press, Public and other options* (Delhi, 2006).

Tendulkar, D.G. *Abdul Ghaffar Khan: faith is a battle* (Bombay, 1967).

_____. *Mahatma: Life of Mohandas Karamchand Gandhi* (New Delhi: Publications Division, Govt. of India), vol. 3, 4, 6 & 8.

Terchek, Ronald J. *Gandhi Struggling for Autonomy* (New Delhi, 2000).

Thapar, Romila. *Somanatha: The Many Voices of a History* (Delhi, 2004).

Thatcher, Mary. *Respected Memsahibs: An Anthology* (Scotland, 2009).

Thompson, Edward. *A Farewell to India* (London, 1931, 2nd imp.).

_____. *A Letter From India* (London, n.d.).

_____. *Enlist India for Freedom!* (London, 1942).

_____. *The Other Side of the Medal* (London, 1925).

Thompson, Mark. *Gandhi and his Ashrams* (Bombay, 1993).

Thorat, Sukhadeo and Narender Kumar (eds), *B.R. Ambedkar: Perspectives on Social Exclusion and Inclusive Policies* (Delhi, 2008).

Tinker, Hugh. *The Ordeal of Love: C.F. Andrews and India* (Delhi, 1979).

_____. 'Between Old Delhi and New Delhi: C.F. Andrews and St. Stephen's in an Era of Transition', R.E. Frykenberg (ed.), *Delhi Through the Ages: Essays in Urban History, Culture, and Society* (Delhi, 1986).

Toynbee, Arnold J. *Acquaintances* (Oxford, 1967).

Trivedi, Madhu. *The Emergence of the Hindustani Tradition* (Delhi, 2012).

_____. *The Making of the Awadh Culture* (Delhi, 2010).

Trivedi, Rekha (ed.), *Gandhi Speaks on Non-Cooperation in UP* (Lucknow, 1998).

Trumbull, Robert. *As I see India* (London, 1957).

Tunzelmann, Alex von. *Indian Summer: The Secret History of the End of an Empire* (New York, 2007).

Tyabji, Badruddin. *Memoirs of an Egoist*, vol. 1 (Delhi, 1988).

Vatsyayan, Kapila. 'Education through the Arts: Values and Skills' (First Kamaladevi Chattopadhyay Lecture), Centre for Cultural Resources and Training, 29 May 2009.

Vernède, R.E. *An Ignorant in India* (London, 1911).

Vernède, R.V. (ed.), *British Life in India: An Anthology of Humorous and Other Writings perpetrated by the British in India, 1750-1947 with some latitude for works completed after Independence* (Delhi, 1995).

Vishwanathan, Gauri. 'Literacy and Conversion in the Discourse of Hindu Nationalism', in A.D. Needham and R.S. Rajan (eds), *The Crisis of Secularism in India* (Durham, 2007).

Wagle, N.K. 'Hindu-Muslim Interactions in Medieval Maharashtra', in Sontheimer and Kulke (eds), *Hinduism Reconsidered*.

Wakankar, Milind. *Subalternity and Religion: The Prehistory of Dalit Empowerment in South Asia* (London, 2010).

Walder, Dennis. *Postcolonial Nostalgias: Writing, Representation, and Memory* (London, 2011).

Washbrook, D.A. *The Emergence of Provincial Politics: The Madras Presidency 1870-1920* (Cambridge, 1976).

Watt, K. 'Thomas Walker Arnold and the Re-evaluation of Islam, 1864-1930,' *MAS*, 36, 1, 2002.

Weber, Thomas. *On the Salt March: The Historiography of Gandhi's March to Dandi* (Delhi, 1997).

_____. 'Gandhi Moves: Intentional Communities and Friendship', in Ganguli and Docker (eds), *Rethinking Gandhi and Nonviolent Relationality*.

Webster, John C.B. *A Social History of Christianity: North West India since 1800* (Delhi, 2007).

Wedderburn, William. *Allan Octavian Hume: Father of the Indian National Congress, 1829-1912* (London, 1913).

Wells, Ian Bryant. *Ambassador of Hindu-Muslim Unity: Jinnah's Early Politics* (Delhi, 2005).

Wilson, Dorothy Clarke. *Fly with me to India* (Nashville, Tennessee, n.d.).

Wilson, John. *The Parsi Religion* (Bombay, 1843).

Winslow, Jack C. and Verrier Elwin. *Gandhi: The Dawn of Indian Freedom* (London, 1931).

Wolpert, Stanley A. *Jinnah of Pakistan* (New York, 1984).

_____. *Tilak and Gokhale: Revolution and Reform in the Making of Modern India* (California, 1962).

Woods, Jeannine. *Visions of Empire and Other Imaginings: Cinema, Ireland and India 1910-1962* (Bern, 2011).

Yadav, Bhupendra. 'Tilak: Communalist or Political Pragmatist', in Biswamoy Pati (ed.), *Bal Gangadhar Tilak*.

Yagnik, Achyut. 'The Pathology of Gujarat', *Seminar*, 513, May 2002.

Yagnik, I.K. *Gandhi As I Knew Him* (Lucknow, 1943).

Zaidi, Zahida. *Glimpses of Urdu Literature: Select Writings* (Delhi, 2010).

Zakaria, Rafiq (ed.), *A Study of Nehru* (Delhi, 1959).

Zaman, Muhammad Qasim. *The Ulama in Contemporary Islam: Custodians of Change* (Princeton and Oxford, 2002).

Zelliot, Eleanor. *From Untouchable to Dalit: Essays on the Ambedkar Movement* (New Delhi, 1996).

Zinkin, Taya. *Reporting India* (London, 1962).

Zulfiqar, Ghulam Husain. *Mohandas Karamchand Gandhi: Lisaul Asr ki Nazar Me* (Lahore, 1994).

Zutshi, Chitralekha. *Languages of Belonging: Islam, Regional Identity, and the Making of Kashmir* (New York, 2004).

Index

Other titles by Mushirul Hasan with Niyogi Books

Proceedings of the Indian National Congress Vol. 1 (1885-1889)

Sarojini Naidu: Her Way with Words

Wit and Wisdom: Pickings from the Parsee Punch

Partners in Freedom: Jamia Millia Islamia

Mutiny Memoirs by Col. A.R.D Mackenzie

Avadh Punch: Wit and Humour in Colonial North India